ASPEN PUBLISHERS

M000293854

The EMTALA Answer Book

2013 Edition

Jeffrey C. Moffat

Wolters Kluwer

Law & Business

This publication is designed to provide accurate and authoritative information in regard to the subject matter covered. It is sold with the understanding that the publisher and the author(s) are not engaged in rendering legal, accounting, or other professional services. If legal advice or other professional assistance is required, the services of a competent professional should be sought.

—From a *Declaration of Principles* jointly adopted by
a Committee of the American Bar Association and
a Committee of Publishers and Associations

Published by Wolters Kluwer Law & Business in New York.

Wolters Kluwer Law & Business serves customers worldwide with CCH, Aspen Publishers and Kluwer Law International products.

Printed in the United States of America

1 2 3 4 5 6 7 8 9 0

ISBN: 978-1-4548-1035-3

ISSN: 1544-2772

Certified Chain of Custody
Product Line Contains At Least
20% Certified Forest Content
www.sfiprogram.org
SFI-00756

ASPEN PUBLISHERS

The EMTALA Answer Book
2013 Edition

by Jeffrey C. Moffat

The EMTALA Answer Book provides an authoritative, easy-to-access guide for addressing the thorny issues surrounding COBRA for emergency department physicians, emergency nurse managers, emergency administrators, and risk managers, helping them to understand the implications of their decisions vis-à-vis this law. The potentially problematic aspects of medical screening, treatment, transfer, and other EMTALA responsibilities of hospitals are explored from the medical perspective, and practical suggestions for compliance are provided.

Highlights of the 2013 Edition

The changes to the 2013 Edition include:

- Discussion of the 2012 Department of Health and Human Services pronouncement regarding application of EMTALA

- A summary of the latest civil penalties for EMTALA violations

- Updated and new court cases interpreting EMTALA

- Reorganization of the chapters and questions for a more intuitive search process

10/12

For questions concerning this shipment, billing, or other customer service matters, call our Customer Service Department at 1-800-234-1660.

For toll-free ordering, please call 1-800-638-8437.

About Wolters Kluwer Law & Business

Wolters Kluwer Law & Business is a leading global provider of intelligent information and digital solutions for legal and business professionals in key specialty areas, and respected educational resources for professors and law students. Wolters Kluwer Law & Business connects legal and business professionals as well as those in the education market with timely, specialized authoritative content and information-enabled solutions to support success through productivity, accuracy and mobility.

Serving customers worldwide, Wolters Kluwer Law & Business products include those under the Aspen Publishers, CCH, Kluwer Law International, Loislaw, Best Case, ftwilliam.com and MediRegs family of products.

CCH products have been a trusted resource since 1913, and are highly regarded resources for legal, securities, antitrust and trade regulation, government contracting, banking, pension, payroll, employment and labor, and healthcare reimbursement and compliance professionals.

Aspen Publishers products provide essential information to attorneys, business professionals and law students. Written by preeminent authorities, the product line offers analytical and practical information in a range of specialty practice areas from securities law and intellectual property to mergers and acquisitions and pension/benefits. Aspen's trusted legal education resources provide professors and students with high-quality, up-to-date and effective resources for successful instruction and study in all areas of the law.

Kluwer Law International products provide the global business community with reliable international legal information in English. Legal practitioners, corporate counsel and business executives around the world rely on Kluwer Law journals, looseleafs, books, and electronic products for comprehensive information in many areas of international legal practice.

Loislaw is a comprehensive online legal research product providing legal content to law firm practitioners of various specializations. Loislaw provides attorneys with the ability to quickly and efficiently find the necessary legal information they need, when and where they need it, by facilitating access to primary law as well as state-specific law, records, forms and treatises.

Best Case Solutions is the leading bankruptcy software product to the bankruptcy industry. It provides software and workflow tools to flawlessly streamline petition preparation and the electronic filing process, while timely incorporating ever-changing court requirements.

ftwilliam.com offers employee benefits professionals the highest quality plan documents (retirement, welfare and non-qualified) and government forms (5500/PBGC, 1099 and IRS) software at highly competitive prices.

MediRegs products provide integrated health care compliance content and software solutions for professionals in healthcare, higher education and life sciences, including professionals in accounting, law and consulting.

Wolters Kluwer Law & Business, a division of Wolters Kluwer, is headquartered in New York. Wolters Kluwer is a market-leading global information services company focused on professionals.

WOLTERS KLUWER LAW & BUSINESS
SUPPLEMENT NOTICE

This product is updated on a periodic basis with supplements to reflect important changes in the subject matter. If you have purchased this product directly from Wolters Kluwer Law & Business, we have already recorded your subscription for the update service.

If, however, you purchased this product from a bookstore and wish to receive future updates and revised or related volumes billed separately with a 30-day examination review, please contact our Customer Service Department at 1-800-234-1660 or send your name, company name (if applicable), address, and the title of the product to:

Wolters Kluwer Law & Business
Distribution Center
7201 McKinney Circle
Frederick, MD 21704

Important Contact Information

- To order any title, go to *www.aspenpublishers.com* or call 1-800-638-8437.

- To reinstate your manual update service, call 1-800-638-8437.

- To contact Customer Service, e-mail *customer.service@wolterskluwer.com*, call 1-800-234-1660, fax 1-800-901-9075, or mail correspondence to: Order Department—Aspen Publishers, Wolters Kluwer Law & Business, PO Box 990, Frederick, MD 21705.

- To review your account history or pay an invoice online, visit *www.aspenpublishers.com/payinvoices*.

Preface

The EMTALA Answer Book provides an authoritative, easy-to-access guide to aid emergency department physicians, emergency nurse managers, emergency administrators, and risk managers in addressing the complex issues surrounding COBRA, helping these hospital personnel understand the implications of their decisions as they relate to this law. The potentially problematic aspects of medical screening, treatment, transfer, and other EMTALA responsibilities of hospitals are explored from the medical perspective, and practical suggestions for compliance are provided.

Format. The question-and-answer format, as well as case examples and appendixes, help clarify for the reader the important issues in this complex area. The format enables the reader to focus quickly on particular problems arising in complying with EMTALA.

List of Questions. The detailed List of Questions that follows the Table of Contents helps the reader locate areas of immediate interest. A series of subheadings groups and organizes the questions by topic within each chapter.

Appendixes. Appendixes place at the reader's fingertips various documents, including statutes, regulations, checklists, and other useful material, to further clarify EMTALA issues.

Index. A detailed topical index is provided at the back of this book. All references in the index are to question numbers.

This volume contains the most timely and authoritative answers necessary for navigating your way through EMTALA requirements.

Jeffrey C. Moffat
September 2012

About the Author

   Jeffrey C. Moffat practices law full time in Pasadena, California. Mr. Moffat received his J.D. from the J. Reuben Clark Law School. In 1981, he joined the law firm of Bonne, Bridges, Mueller, O'Keefe & Nichols, where his practice was exclusively devoted to representing physicians in civil actions. He was elected a shareholder in 1987. In 1995, he began serving as the firm's Administrative Shareholder. From 1999 to 2005, he directed the firm as the Chief Operating Officer. In 2006, Mr. Moffat left Bonne, Bridges to form The Captive Counsel Law Group, Inc.

   Mr. Moffat maintains a nationwide practice in which he advises physicians in matters of risk management, professional liability, professional liability insurance, and compliance with the increasingly complex federal and state regulation of medicine.

   Mr. Moffat is co-author with Dr. Herb Wigder of *Standards of Care in Emergency Medicine* (Wolters Kluwer Law & Business).

   Mr. Moffat gratefully acknowledges the substantial contributions of Tab Artis, Esq. and Sydney Wright to the 2013 Edition.

To Barbara—the wellspring of everything good in my life for 35 years

Contents

Contents

List of Questions

Chapter 1 EMTALA Overview and Post-Enactment History

Chapter 2 Comes to the Emergency Department

Locations

Chapter 3 Medical Screening Examination

Finding an Emergency

Misdiagnosis

Patient Consent and Payment

Chapter 4 Treatment Required to Stabilize

Stabilizing Treatment

The Pregnant Patient

Limits on Stabilization

Chapter 5 Transfers

EMTALA Transfers

Requirements for Transfer

Receiving Hospitals

Transportation Between Hospitals

Chapter 6 Hospital Compliance with EMTALA

Chapter 7   EMTALA Enforcement

Chapter 8 EMTALA and On-Call Physicians

Hospital Duties

Chapter 9 EMTALA and Managed Care

Chapter 10 EMTALA and Psychiatry

Chapter 11 Role of Quality Improvement Organizations

Chapter 12 EMTALA Preemption

Chapter 1

EMTALA Overview and Post-Enactment History

Under common law tort principles, there is no duty to aid another. Thus, without an affirmative duty imposed by statute, neither a hospital nor the physicians who staff its emergency department are required to examine or treat patients seeking emergent medical care. If hospitals and physicians have no legal duty to provide care, patients who are refused examination and treatment have no legal remedy against those who refused to aid them.

Despite this lack of legal constraint, hospital emergency departments have a long tradition of providing care to all, even those unable to pay. However, some believed that the quickly escalating medical costs in the 1980s threatened the practice of providing emergent care to those without the ability to pay. This impression was fostered by several highly publicized incidents where hospital emergency departments refused to provide indigent individuals the same treatment they provided to paying patients. Such indigent patients were referred to other facilities, often county hospitals.[1] For details regarding the events and debate surrounding the enactment of the Emergency Medical Treatment and Active Labor Act (EMTALA), see **Appendix H**.

In response to these concerns, the U.S. Congress adopted the EMTALA. It was enacted as part of the Comprehensive Omnibus Budget Reconciliation Act of 1986.[2] Although usually referred to by its acronym, EMTALA, the statute is sometimes referred to as the "Anti-Dumping Act."

---

[1] *See* H.R. Rep. No. 241(I), 99th Cong., 1st Sess., 27 (1986); reprinted in 1986 U.S. Code Cong. & Admin. News 42, 579, 605. *See also* Note, Preventing Patient Dumping, 61 N.Y.U.L. Rev. 1186, 1187-88 and nn.11-12 (1986).

[2] Pub. L. No. 99-272, § 9121, 100 Stat. 82, 164-67 (1986); codified at 42 U.S.C.A. § 1395dd. The complete text of EMTALA is reproduced in **Appendix A**.

Q 1:1   Statutory Requirements: What are the fundamental requirements of EMTALA?

The text of the EMTALA statute is short. On first reading, the requirements appear deceptively simple. However, both the language of EMTALA and unforeseen details related to its implementation have added complexity to the seemingly simple idea underlying EMTALA.

EMTALA has three fundamental requirements, each contained in a separate subsection.

Under Section 1395dd(a),[3] the hospital must "provide for an appropriate medical screening examination within the capability of the hospital emergency department" to "any individual" who "comes to the emergency department" and requests examination or treatment. The purpose of this screening examination is to "determine whether or not an emergency medical condition . . . exists."[4]

If the hospital determines that the individual has an emergency medical condition, Section 1395dd(b)[5] requires one of two courses of action. The hospital may provide "such further medical examination and such treatment as may be required to stabilize the medical condition."[6] Or the hospital may transfer the patient "to another medical facility in accordance with subsection (c)" of the Act.

Section 1395dd(c)[7] states that "an individual at a hospital" who has an emergency medical condition "which has not been stabilized"[8] may not be transferred unless one of three conditions[9] is met and the transfer is appropriate.[10] First, a transfer may occur when the patient requests the transfer in writing after he or she is informed of the hospital's obligations under EMTALA and the risk of transfer. Second, a physician may certify in writing that "based on the information available at the time of transfer, the medical benefits reasonably expected from the provision of appropriate medical treatment at another medial facility outweigh the increased risks" of the transfer. The written certification must include a summary of the risks and benefits that the physician weighed. Third, if not physically present, a physician may consult with a

---

[3] 42 U.S.C. § 1395dd(a).

[4] An emergency medical condition is defined by the Act to mean any condition manifesting itself by acute symptoms such that the absence of immediate medical attention could result in serious jeopardy, serious impairment to bodily functions, serious dysfunction of any bodily organ, or, with respect to a pregnant woman who is having contractions, inadequate time to transfer prior to delivery or a transfer that may pose a threat to the health of the woman or the unborn child. 42 U.S.C. § 1395dd(e)(1).

[5] 42 U.S.C. § 1395dd(b).

[6] "To stabilize" is defined as providing such "medical treatment of the condition as may be necessary to assure, within reasonable medical probability, that no material deterioration of the condition is likely to result from or occur during the transfer . . . ." 42 U.S.C. § 1395dd(e)(3)(A).

[7] 42 U.S.C. § 1395dd(c).

[8] "Stabilized" means that "no material deterioration" of the emergency medical condition "is likely, within reasonable medical probability, to result from or occur during the transfer" of the patient.

[9] 42 U.S.C. § 1395dd(c)(1)(A)(i)-(iii).

[10] 42 U.S.C. § 1395dd(c)(1)(B).

qualified medial person who is physically present within the emergency department and then orally certify the transfer. The person who is physically present prepares the written certification that the physician subsequently countersigns.

An appropriate transfer under Section 1395dd(c)[11] is one in which the transferring hospital provides medical treatment, within its capacity, that minimizes risks to the patient's health and the receiving facility has agreed to accept the transfer and has qualified personnel to provide appropriate care. In addition, the transfer must be "effected through qualified personnel and transportation equipment . . . ." All of the patient's medical records must be sent to the receiving hospital.

Enforcement of EMTALA is provided by administrative sanctions[12] imposed by the Department of Health and Human Services (HHS) as well as civil lawsuits brought by individual patients who suffered personal harm as a result of the hospital's violation of the Act.[13]

Q 1:2   Constitutionality: Are EMTALA's requirements constitutional?

EMTALA's requirements, which force hospitals and physicians to provide a service even when there is no compensation, are constitutional because EMTALA is part of Medicare's "voluntary" requirements. The authority supporting the statute is the taxing and spending clause of the Constitution. In essence, Congress has the right to demand certain services from vendors receiving federal tax dollars. In the EMTALA statute, obligations are tied to hospitals' participation in Medicare. If a hospital wants to relieve itself of EMTALA obligations, it can choose to drop out of the Medicare program.

Cautions: The courts have ruled that EMTALA does not affect an unconstitutional public taking of a physician's services without just compensation. Forcing a citizen to provide services without compensation is a form of indentured servitude that is not allowed by U.S. laws. EMTALA gets around this prohibition by incorporating EMTALA within the rules of Medicare. By accepting Medicare payments, the hospital indirectly "volunteers" to accept all the terms of Medicare, one of which is EMTALA. The hospital has contracted in writing to comply with EMTALA in exchange for payment. The physician provider voluntarily applies for privileges in a Medicare hospital, thereby agreeing to comply with those rules.

In *Burditt v. United States Department of Health and Human Services,*[14] Burditt tried to claim that EMTALA violated his constitutional rights by a public taking of his services without just compensation in contravention of the Fifth Amendment to the Constitution. The court in *Burditt* ruled that EMTALA imposed no responsibility directly on physicians, but unambiguously required

---

[11] 42 U.S.C. § 1395dd(c)(2).

[12] 42 U.S.C. § 1395dd(d)(1).

[13] 42 U.S.C. § 1395dd(d)(2).

[14] 934 F.2d 1362 (5th Cir. 1991).

hospitals to meet its requirements, and a physician was free to negotiate with the hospital regarding his or her responsibility to facilitate the hospital's compliance with EMTALA. A hospital voluntarily participates in the Medicare program and, therefore, its EMTALA requirements. Physicians also voluntarily accept responsibilities under EMTALA by participating in Medicare.[15] As such, the court left open the possibility of a Fifth Amendment violation if physicians were directly obligated under EMTALA.[16]

Once a hospital establishes a call system, physicians are required to comply with it or resign their medical staff privileges.

The Eastern District of North Carolina addressed the constitutionality of EMTALA in *Jones v. Wake County Hospital System.*[17] Philip Jones went to the emergency department of Wake Medical Center with a complaint of pain and weakness stemming from burns suffered two days earlier. Dr. Solovieff, the emergency physician, examined him. Dr. Solovieff ordered blood tests and consulted with Dr. Nolan, another physician in the emergency department, concerning the possibility of infection. Both decided that Jones could be safely discharged.

The next day Jones returned to the emergency department with severe pain, paralysis, and disorientation. Shortly afterward, Jones suffered septic shock, respiratory arrest, and renal failure. He died the next day from cardiac arrest caused by sepsis. Vastine Jones, administratrix of Philip Jones's estate, filed an EMTALA suit, alleging that Jones had received unfavorable treatment by the defendants because of his race and socioeconomic status. Among other arguments, the defense claimed that EMTALA was unconstitutional because hospitals are essentially forced to comply with EMTALA, given that Medicare funding is essential to the operation of so many hospitals.

The court in *Jones* reasoned that the defendants' argument would prevent Congress from imposing any conditions at all on hospitals that receive Medicare funding because any Medicare condition imposed by Congress would by its nature be coercive. The court added, "While it is undeniable that there are many hospitals who benefit greatly from Medicare payments, those hospitals remain free to disassociate themselves from the Medicare program if they find the requirements of [EMTALA] too onerous."[18]

The defense in *Jones* also argued that the EMTALA requirements were unconstitutionally vague. The court admitted that while several of the terms set out in the text of EMTALA do not lend themselves to a fixed and precise definition, it is not difficult to discern the duties EMTALA imposes on hospitals. The court found that EMTALA is not impermissibly vague for due process purposes.

---

[15] *Burditt*, 934 F.2d 1362, 1376.

[16] E. McHugh, *The New EMTALA Regulations and the On-Call Physician*, J. Health L., 37(1):61-84 (77) (Winter 2004).

[17] 786 F. Supp. 538 (E.D.N.C. 1991).

[18] *Jones*, 786 F. Supp. 538, 546.

Finally, the defense argued that EMTALA violates the Tenth Amendment by usurping the traditional powers of the states. The court rejected this argument, reminding the defense that EMTALA explicitly states that it does not preempt any state laws or requirements except those that directly conflict with its provisions. Moreover, even the broad interpretation courts have given EMTALA does not seriously encroach on state medical malpractice law. Although there is some overlap between EMTALA and state malpractice law, the overlap is not extensive.

Nevertheless, EMTALA's constitutionality remains suspect because of its coercive effect. The Supreme Court has historically recognized a difference between conditions attached to spending grants that simply induce and those that coerce, finding coercion violates the spending power.[19] Just like other spending power limitations, the coercion test is interpreted broadly. The general view is that recipients of federal funds are free to accept the funds with the strings attached or reject them and act without restriction—no coercion is involved. The choice, however, between accepting Medicare funding with EMTALA restrictions attached or losing Medicare funding is hardly a choice at all. The economic reality is that hospitals depend on Medicare funding for survival, and this distinguishes Medicare/EMTALA compliance from other spending power cases where the loss of federal funds has a minimal impact on the recipient.[20]

Q 1:3   Post-Enactment History: What has happened to the scope of EMTALA since its enactment?

The scope of EMTALA has been greatly expanded beyond Congress's original limited intentions to halt the discrimination of emergency medical care for the indigent. The regulatory expansion of EMTALA has been described as occurring in seven phases since its passage in 1986.[21]

The first phase was incorporated into the binding regulations published in 1994, which applied the law's basic screening and stabilization requirements to patients anywhere on hospital property (including ambulances owned and operated by the hospital). It also obligated hospitals to report inappropriate transfers.[22]

The second phase occurred in 1998 when the Health Care Financing Administration (HCFA), now the Centers for Medicare & Medicaid Services (CMS), published interpretive guidelines for surveyors. These guidelines stated the agency's position that EMTALA obligations include (1) distinct responsibilities for on-call physicians, (2) an obligation to provide screening and treatment of patients with psychiatric emergencies, (3) approaching the medical screening

---

[19] Steward Mach. Co. v. Davis, 301 U.S. 548, 590 (1937).

[20] Andrew McClurg, *Your Money or Your Life: Interpreting the Federal Act Against Patient Dumping*, 24 Wake Forest L. Rev. 173, 232-233 (1989).

[21] Robert Wanerman, *The EMTALA Paradox*, 40 Ann. Emerg. Med., 5, 464-469 (Nov. 2002).

[22] 42 C.F.R. §§ 489.20 and 489.24.

examination as a dynamic process, and (4) a distinction between patients who are stable, stable for transfer, or stable for discharge.[23]

The third phase was the November 1999 publication of a Special Advisory Bulletin authored jointly by HCFA and the OIG. The Special Advisory Bulletin provided specific guidelines on the handling of patients who require authorization for care from their managed care insurance companies. Although EMTALA was enacted to address discrimination of emergency care for the indigent, CMS specifically stipulates that EMTALA governs the emergency care for all patients including those with managed care insurance.[24]

The fourth phase occurred through the Medicare Outpatient Prospective Payment System (OPPS) regulations in 2000. CMS codified its informal interpretation of EMTALA, expanding it to include inpatient areas, hospital buildings that are within 250 yards of the hospital's main campus, and off-campus facilities that are considered part of the hospital for Medicare cost reimbursement purposes. CMS also required off-site locations to follow EMTALA rules concerning signage and patient care standards established by EMTALA.[25]

The fifth phase of EMTALA expansion occurred when the OIG published a set of regulatory clarifications and technical corrections on April 17, 2002. Among other things, these regulatory clarifications state that OIG may consider, for purposes of determining an administrative penalty for EMTALA violations, "any other instances" of such conduct. The previous language had permitted OIG to consider only the hospital's "prior history of offenses." This widened the OIG's authority, permitting it to consider subsequent as well as previous violations, and to consider incidents that had not been found to be violations by a court or by an administrative law judge.[26]

The sixth phase of EMTALA was presented in the *Federal Register* on September 9, 2003, as the "final rules."[27] The final rules represented a significant attempt by CMS to clarify and limit the application of EMTALA after years of expansion. The final rules dealt with the issues of:

- Prior authorization;
- Clarification of the term "comes to the emergency department" by coining the new term "dedicated emergency department";
- Allowing an exception to EMTALA for non-emergency services in the dedicated emergency department;
- Defining EMTALA applications for non-dedicated emergency department presentations on a hospital's campus;

---

[23] Health Care Financing Administration, State Operations Manual, App. V (Rev. 2, May 1998).

[24] Office of Inspector General and Health Care Financing Administration. Special Advisory Bulletin on the Patient Anti-Dumping Statute, 64 Fed. Reg. 61,353 (Nov. 10, 1999).

[25] 67 Fed. Reg. 31,404, 31,476-478 (May 9, 2002).

[26] 67 Fed. Reg. 11,928 (Mar. 18, 2002); 42 C.F.R. § 1003.106(a)(4)(iii).

[27] 68 Fed. Reg. 53,250 (Sept. 9, 2003).

- Limiting EMTALA's governance to emergency patients rather than inpatients or scheduled outpatients;
- Applicability to off-campus hospital departments;
- Clarifying a hospital's on-call requirements; and
- Applicability to hospital-owned ambulances, especially in areas of community-wide disaster protocols and bioterrorism emergencies.

The seventh phase started in December 2003 when President George W. Bush signed the Medicare Prescription Drug, Improvement, and Modernization Act of 2003 (MMA).[28] This law required the Secretary of HHS to establish the EMTALA Technical Advisory Group (EMTALA TAG) to:

1. review EMTALA regulations;
2. provide advice and recommendations to CMS concerning these regulations and their effect on hospitals and physicians;
3. solicit public comments regarding the implementation of the regulations; and
4. disseminate information on application of the regulations to hospitals, physicians, and the public.

Q 1:4 TAG Recommendations: What recommendations did TAG make and were there changes as a result of its charter?

Over the course of its 30-month charter, which ended on September 30, 2007, the TAG was able to introduce significant recommendations, many of which have been adopted by CMS.

As itemized in its final report,[29] most of the TAG's discussion and recommendations focused on the following questions:

- What constitutes appropriate and adequate emergency on-call services by a hospital in a given community and what should be required of individual physicians?
- When do a hospital's EMTALA obligations end?
- Do specialty hospitals or hospitals with specialized capabilities have different EMTALA obligations than other hospitals?
- What are the duties of transferring and receiving hospitals?
- Is EMTALA enforcement fair and consistent across the country?
- Should behavioral health issues be treated differently from other health conditions under EMTALA?
- Does EMTALA hinder communication among health care providers?

---

[28] Medicare Prescription Drug, Improvement, and Modernization Act of 2003 (MMA), Pub. L. No. 108-173, § 945.

[29] *See* http://www.cms.gov/Regulations-and-Guidance/Legislation/EMTALA/downloads/EMTALA_Final_Report_Summary.pdf.

The TAG made the following significant recommendations:

1. *False Labor:* Regulations were revised to permit, in accordance with state law and hospital bylaws, a qualified non-physician clinician to certify that a woman is experiencing false labor.

2. *Specialty Hospitals:* Specialty hospitals are not required to have their own dedicated emergency department but are otherwise bound by the same responsibilities under EMTALA as other full-service hospitals. For example, specialty hospitals are required to maintain a call list and to accept an appropriate transfer if they have the ability to treat the individual.

3. *Private Physician Communications:* A treating physician or qualified medical person is not precluded from contacting the patient's physician to discuss the patient's medical history and care relevant to the medical treatment and screening.

4. *Specialized Capability:* The presence of a specialty physician on the call roster is not, by itself, sufficient to be considered a specialized capability. At the time of the transfer, the receiving hospital should also have available the necessary equipment, space, staff, and so on to accommodate the patient transfer.

5. *On-call Response Time:* Response time should be defined in a range of minutes, should refer to the initial response by the physician, and may occur by phone (or other means). Hospitals should develop policies and procedures to address the response time and appropriate exemptions.

6. *Selective Call:* When a physician is not on the call roster, he or she may still take call for his or her own patients and is not obligated to provide call coverage when in the hospital seeing private patients. A physician on call must see patients without regard for any patient's ability to pay.

7. *State of Emergency:* HHS should pursue statutory and regulatory changes, as well as changes to the Interpretive Guidelines (State Operations Manual) addressing waiving EMTALA obligations in states of emergency as declared by a federal, state, county, or city government.

8. *End of EMTALA Obligations:* HHS should amend the Interpretive Guidelines with respect to follow-up care to clarify that once a patient has been stabilized, the hospital and physician have no further follow-up care obligation under EMTALA.

9. *Mode of Transfer:* A hospital may not refuse to accept an individual protected under EMTALA on the grounds that it (the receiving hospital) does not approve the method of transfer arranged by the attending physician at the sending hospital.

10. *On-call Physician to the Emergency Department:* The treating physician ultimately determines whether the on-call physician should come to the emergency department. The treating physician may use a variety of methods to communicate with the on-call physician. A potential violation occurs only if the treating physician requests that the on-call

physician come to the emergency department and the on-call physician refuses to do so.

11. *Psychiatric Screening:* For the purpose of screening psychiatric patients, a hospital may utilize contracted agencies or services to assist with the psychiatric medical screening examination (MSE) if they are properly credentialed.

12. *On-call Coverage:* Hospitals should annually evaluate their on-call coverage requirements as well as back-up plans when they lack capacity and/or capability.

13. *EMTALA Web site:* HHS should develop a more comprehensive, prominent, and user-friendly CMS EMTALA Web site.

14. *State Survey Education:* HHS should institute annual EMTALA surveyor education sessions.

15. *Appeals Process:* HHS should establish an appeals process for hospitals/providers before making a termination decision.

16. *Levels of Sanctions:* HHS should establish intermediate sanctions for less serious EMTALA violations such as technical violations for signage, log books, and so on.

17. *Data Collection:* HHS should establish a method for consistent data collection of all EMTALA violations and central evaluation of the information, in a format determined by CMS to improve consistency of enforcement across the regions, and that can serve as a resource for providers.

18. *State Surveyors:* HHS should establish a system to improve consistency in regional office EMTALA interpretations and enforcement, monitor effectiveness of surveyor education, and demonstrate surveyor competencies.

19. *In-patient Emergencies:* EMTALA should not apply when a patient develops an emergency medical condition after being admitted to a hospital.

20. *Psychiatric Patients:* HHS should remove the current separate guidance on psychiatric emergency conditions so that the remaining rules apply equally to emergency conditions of either psychiatric or medical origin. In addition, HHS should generate unique examples to define psychiatric emergency conditions more specifically.

21. *Stabilization:* An emergency condition (such as abdominal pain) does not need to be resolved to be considered stabilized if it is determined that further evaluation can be performed in an outpatient setting.

The TAG's efforts in reaching consensus on a significant number of vital issues concerning EMTALA are admirable. CMS has adopted a number of the TAG's recommendations. It is the belief of this author that the adoption of the TAG's recommendations will be significant in clarifying EMTALA's application in emergency care for the nation.

The EMTALA TAG issued its Final Report to the Secretary of the United States Department of Health and Human Services on April 2, 2008. On May 29, 2009, CMS issued a revised State Operations Manual that incorporated many major changes proposed by the TAG. On October 1, 2008, 42 C.F.R. § 489.24 was revised to reflect these changes.

Chapter 2

Comes to the Emergency Department

In the case of a hospital that has a hospital emergency department, if any individual (whether or not eligible for benefits under this subchapter) comes to the emergency department and a request is made on the individual's behalf for examination or treatment for a medical condition . . . .

42 U.S.C. § 1395dd(a)

Stated simply, subsection (a) of EMTALA[1] requires that if an individual comes to the emergency department requesting care, the hospital must provide an appropriate screening examination to determine whether the individual suffers from an emergency medical condition. If the individual is found to have an emergency medical condition, subsection (b) requires the hospital, within its capability, to provide the medical treatment necessary to stabilize the patient.[2] Subsection (c) prohibits transfer of patients who are not stabilized unless specific requirements are met.[3]

In the years following enactment of EMTALA and prior to promulgation of the final regulations in 2003, EMTALA's seemingly simple but largely undefined statutory language was widely litigated. Most of the contests arose from disputes relating to subsection (a) and particularly to the statutory language "any

---

[1] 42 U.S.C. § 1395dd(a).

[2] 42 U.S.C. § 1395dd(b).

[3] 42 U.S.C. § 1395dd(c).

individual . . . comes to the emergency department and a request is made on the individual's behalf for examination or treatment . . . ."

Every word and phrase seemed open to interpretation. Does a hospital need to have an emergency department? Who constitutes an "individual"? How does one interpret "comes to"? What constitutes a "request"? How is the government going to measure the extent of the hospital's "capability"? What is an "appropriate" screening examination? The 2003 final regulations resolved many of these issues.[4] The regulations define "emergency department," "come to an emergency department," and "request." The regulations set the scope of EMTALA's application to individuals on hospital property but outside the confines of the emergency department. The regulations specify the circumstances under which the hospital's obligations under EMTALA end after the patient leaves the emergency department.

There are now answers to many of the questions regarding when, where, and to whom EMTALA applies. This chapter answers questions dealing with the application of EMTALA to locations, to persons, and to specific issues that can arise when a person "comes to the emergency department."

Locations

Q 2:1   Hospitals: Which hospitals must comply with EMTALA?

EMTALA applies to any hospital that (1) participates in the federal Medicare health insurance program and (2) operates a "dedicated emergency department."[5] Critical access hospitals, physician-owned specialty hospitals, and hospitals without formal or licensed emergency departments can all fall into this category.[6]

As a section of the Social Security Act (SSA), EMTALA incorporates the SSA's definition of "hospital."[7] Under this definition:

> (e) . . . The term "hospital" . . . means an institution which—
>
> (1) is primarily engaged in providing, by or under the supervision of physicians, to inpatients (A) diagnostic services and therapeutic services for medical diagnosis, treatment, and care of injured, disabled, or sick persons, or (B) rehabilitation services for the rehabilitation of injured, disabled, or sick persons . . . . [8]

A "participating hospital" is one that has entered into a "provider agreement" under the Medicare program. Through these agreements, a hospital accepts

---

[4] The full text of the current EMTALA regulations is reproduced in **Appendix B**.

[5] 42 U.S.C. § 1395dd(e)(2); 42 C.F.R. § 489.24(b).

[6] 42 U.S.C. § 1395dd(e)(5); 71 Fed. Reg. 47,870, 48,097 (2006).

[7] *See* Jackson v. East Bay Hosp., 246 F.3d 1248, 1260 (9th Cir. 2001).

[8] 2 U.S.C. § 1395x.

payment from the Department of Health and Human Services (HHS), CMS for services provided to Medicare beneficiaries.

The Code of Federal Regulations states:

> Participating hospital means (1) a hospital or (2) a critical access hospital as defined in section 181(mm)(1) of the Act that has entered into a Medicare provider agreement under section 1866 of the Act.[9]

The State Operations Manual states:

> The term "hospital" is defined in § 489.24(b) as including critical access hospitals as defined in § 1861(mm)(1) of the Act. Therefore, a critical access hospital that operates a dedicated emergency department (as that term is defined below) is subject to the requirements of EMTALA.[10]

Cautions: By accepting Medicare payment, hospitals "voluntarily" agree to abide by EMTALA's dictates. The lack of a formal emergency department does not release the hospital from EMTALA requirements. This "agreement" covers almost all hospitals in the United States because virtually every hospital in the United States has entered into a Medicare provider agreement with the federal government. Hospitals that do not accept Medicare funds, such as some Veterans Administration hospitals, Indian reservation hospitals operated by the U.S. Public Health Service,[11] and a few private hospitals (generally psychiatric hospitals), do not have to comply with EMTALA.

In *Williams v. United States*,[12] the Fourth Circuit ruled that a U.S. Public Health Service hospital on a Cherokee Reservation did not violate EMTALA when it refused emergency care to a person because he was a non-Indian. Berlie White developed respiratory distress and went to the emergency department of Cherokee Indian Hospital. Hospital staffers refused to treat White or refill his oxygen tank because he was not Indian. They referred White to Swain County Hospital in Bryson City, about ten miles away. When White arrived there he was in extreme respiratory distress, and he died the following day. White's estate, administrated by Sarah Williams, sued the United States under the Federal Tort Claims Act, claiming that the United States violated EMTALA.

Hospitals operating under the Indian Health Care Improvement Act are prohibited, with certain exceptions, from treating non-Indians. The Fourth Circuit found that, because the Federal Tort Claims Act does not waive the United States' sovereign immunity for a permissible exercise of discretionary judgment, the hospital's decision to refuse care to a non-Indian was not

---

[9] 42 C.F.R. § 489.24(b).

[10] U.S. Dep't HHS, Centers for Medicare & Medicaid Servs. (CMS), State Operations Manual, App. V, Emergency Medical Treatment and Labor Act (EMTALA) Interpretive Guidelines, Part II, Tag A-2400/C-2400 (revised 5/29/2009).

[11] *See* Williams v. United States, 242 F.3d 169 (4th Cir. 2001).

[12] *Williams*, 242 F.3d 169; 13 Emergency Dep't Law, no. 2, 30 (Mar. 2001).

actionable. EMTALA notwithstanding, the Cherokee Indian hospital had discretion to treat or not treat non-Indians.

On June 15, 2011, the U.S. District Court for the District of Puerto Rico dismissed with prejudice an EMTALA claim that was brought against Mennonite General Hospital (Mennonite Hospital) by the relatives of Juan Bautista Aponte-Díaz, the decedent.[13]

The decedent received treatment at Orocovis Centro de Diagnóstico y Tratamiento (Orocovis CDT), a diagnostic treatment center as defined under Puerto Rico law, and Plaintiffs contended that the facility failed to perform appropriate medical screening and discharged him without stabilization of his medical condition, in violation of EMTALA. In support of their claim against Mennonite Hospital, Plaintiffs asserted that Orocovis CDT was a "dedicated emergency department," part of Mennonite Hospital. In its motion to dismiss, Mennonite Hospital contended that Orocovis CDT was not part of its hospital and thus not subject to EMTALA.

In reaching its conclusion, the district court examined, among other things, the contract for professional services between the Department of Health of Puerto Rico and Mennonite Hospital, whereby Mennonite Hospital was engaged by the Department of Health to provide medical services at the Orocovis CDT emergency room through a sublease arrangement. The district court found that the language of the contract demonstrated that although the emergency room is an integral part of Orocovis CDT operated in conjunction with the hospital, it is not an independent facility belonging to Mennonite Hospital. The district court also looked at the facility licenses and certificates of need, which supported its factual findings.

After conducting an extensive review of the facts, the district court then considered the following question of law decided in the First Circuit Court's decision in *Rodriguez v. American International Insurance, Puerto Rico*[14]:

> [W]hether a CDT, defined by Puerto Rico law as "an independent facility [or one operated in conjunction with a hospital] which provides community services for the diagnosis and treatment of ambulatory patients under the professional supervision of persons licensed to practice medicine, surgery or dentistry in Puerto Rico," 24 P.R. Laws Ann. § 331a(A)(4), qualifies as "a hospital that has a hospital emergency department" under EMTALA, 42 U.S.C. § 1395dd(a).

The district court agreed with the First Circuit, determining that a CDT, which is a facility type unique to Puerto Rico, does not qualify as a hospital with an emergency department for purposes of EMTALA. The district court noted that CDTs offer only outpatient services, and Puerto Rico law "clearly distinguishes

---

[13] Aponte-Colon v. Mennonite Gen. Hosp., Inc., No. 10-1434CCC (D.P.R. June 15, 2011).

[14] 402 F.3d 45 (1st Cir. 2005).

between hospitals and diagnostic and treatment centers." Accordingly, Mennonite Hospital's motion to dismiss as to the EMTALA claim was granted.[15]

Critical access hospitals (CAHs) that operate dedicated emergency departments must also comply with EMTALA. A facility may be designated a CAH if it meets certain criteria, including:

- located more than a 35-mile drive from any other hospital
- maintains Conditions of Participation (CoPs), including the requirement to make available 24-hour emergency care services 7 days per week.

In the State Operations Manual released in 2008, there are now separate Tag numbers for regular hospitals with an "A" prefix and for critical access hospitals with a "C" prefix.[16]

Q 2:2   "Comes to": What does "comes to the emergency department" mean?

There are four ways by which a patient can fulfill the "comes to" requirement of EMTALA:

1. The patient presents to a hospital's dedicated emergency department and requests care for a medical condition;
2. The patient is outside the dedicated emergency department but on hospital property within 250 yards of the main building and presents with an emergency medical condition;
3. The patient is in a hospital-owned and operated ambulance for purposes of examination or treatment of a medical condition even if the ambulance is not on hospital property; or
4. The patient is in a nonhospital-owned ambulance that has arrived on hospital property for examination and treatment of a medical condition at the hospital's dedicated emergency department.

The Code of Federal Regulations states:

> Comes to the emergency department means, with respect to an individual who is not a patient (as defined in this section), the individual—
>
> (1) Has presented at a hospital's dedicated emergency department, as defined in this section, and requests examination or treatment for a medical condition, or has such a request made on his or her behalf. In the absence of such a request by or on behalf of the individual, a request on behalf of the individual will be considered to exist if a prudent layperson observer would believe, based on the

---

[15] This case summary was written by Keith A. Mauriello, Partner, and Jessica T. Grozine, Associate, in the Healthcare Practice Group at Arnall Golden Gregory LLP, Atlanta, Georgia. It should not be construed as legal advice or opinion on specific matters.

[16] Thomas E. Hamilton, *Revised State Operations Manual Appendix V—EMTALA*, CMS S&C Memorandum to State Survey Agency Directors, No. 08-15 (Mar. 21, 2008).

individual's appearance or behavior, that the individual needs examination or treatment for a medical condition;

(2) Has presented on hospital property, as defined in this section, other than the dedicated emergency department, and requests examination or treatment for what may be an emergency medical condition, or has such a request made on his or her behalf. In the absence of such a request by or on behalf of the individual, a request on behalf of the individual will be considered to exist if a prudent layperson observer would believe, based on the individual's appearance or behavior, that the individual needs emergency examination or treatment;

(3) Is in a ground or air ambulance owned and operated by the hospital for purposes of examination and treatment for a medical condition at a hospital's dedicated emergency department, even if the ambulance is not on hospital grounds. However, an individual in an ambulance owned and operated by the hospital is not considered to have "come to the hospital's emergency department" if—

   (i) The ambulance is operated under communitywide emergency medical service (EMS) protocols that direct it to transport the individual to a hospital other than the hospital that owns the ambulance; for example, to the closest appropriate facility. In this case, the individual is considered to have come to the emergency department of the hospital to which the individual is transported, at the time the individual is brought onto hospital property;

   (ii) The ambulance is operated at the direction of a physician who is not employed or otherwise affiliated with the hospital that owns the ambulance; or

(4) Is in a ground or air nonhospital-owned ambulance on hospital property for presentation for examination and treatment for a medical condition at a hospital's dedicated emergency department. However, an individual in a nonhospital-owned ambulance off hospital property is not considered to have come to the hospital's emergency department, even if a member of the ambulance staff contacts the hospital by telephone or telemetry communications and informs the hospital that they want to transport the individual to the hospital for examination and treatment.[17] The hospital may direct the ambulance to another facility if it is in "diversionary status," that is, it does not have the staff or facilities to accept any additional emergency patients. If, however, the ambulance staff disregards the hospital's diversion instructions and transports the individual onto hospital property, the individual is considered to have come to the emergency department.[18]

Cautions: The EMTALA statute states that ". . . if any individual (whether or not eligible for benefits under this subchapter) *comes to the emergency*

---

[17] Whether a hospital that is not in diversionary status may divert a nonhospital-owned ambulance before it reaches the hospital campus remains a controversial issue. See Q 2:14 of this chapter.

[18] 42 C.F.R. § 489.24(b).

department and a request is made on the individual's behalf for examination or treatment for a medical condition,"[19] then EMTALA is activated. A plain reading of this wording would lead one to assume that a patient needs to physically arrive at the emergency department. However, due to court rulings and federal administrative decisions, the term "comes to" has been expanded to include anywhere on hospital property within 250 yards of the main hospital building, off-campus hospital facilities that offer acute care, and hospital-owned ambulances.

EMTALA's reach out of the emergency department proper began with cases in which appropriate care was denied in other areas of the hospital. In *McIntyre v. Schick, Virginia Beach General Hospital*,[20] the court ruled that physical appearance in the emergency department is unnecessary for an EMTALA violation. Theresa McIntyre came to Virginia Beach General Hospital for obstetric care without going to the emergency department. She had labor contractions, persistent sinusoidal fetal heart patterns, and lack of fetal beat-to-beat variability. She did not have insurance and was discharged after 11 hours of waiting without being formally admitted or examined by a physician. She returned to the hospital the next day with persistent contractions and this time examination by a physician revealed fetal distress. The physician transferred McIntyre to Norfolk General Hospital, where her baby boy died after a Caesarean section. A suit was filed for violation of EMTALA. The hospital argued that EMTALA did not apply because the patient never physically came to the emergency department. However, the court ruled that EMTALA did apply, stating that the "anti-dumping statute is not based upon the door of the hospital through which a patient enters, but rather upon the notion of proper medical care for those persons suffering medical emergencies, whenever such emergencies occur at a participating hospital."[21]

On March 31, 2011, the U.S. District Court for the Eastern District of Pennsylvania granted summary judgment in favor of the Cleveland Clinic (the Clinic) for claims relating to an affiliated hospital's alleged violation of EMTALA's screening requirement.[22] Specifically, the district court found that the Clinic could not be held directly liable since Plaintiff Byrne never physically entered the emergency department of the Clinic, located in Cleveland, Ohio. Rather, all medical care that the Plaintiff received was provided on the premises of Chester County Hospital (Chester Hospital), located in West Chester, Pennsylvania.

According to the complaint, the Plaintiff went to Chester Hospital's emergency room complaining of severe chest pain and shortness of breath. He was allegedly seen by a nurse 20 minutes after his arrival but not seen by a physician until hours later. He ultimately underwent a catheterization procedure at Chester Hospital. The Plaintiff sued Chester Hospital and the Clinic asserting,

---

[19] 42 U.S.C. § 1395dd(a).

[20] 795 F. Supp. 777 (E.D. Va. 1992).

[21] *McIntyre*, 795 F. Supp. 777, 780.

[22] Byrne v. Cleveland Clinic, No. 2:09-cv-00889-GP (E.D. Pa. Mar. 31, 2011).

among other things, violations of the EMTALA screening and stabilization requirements and claiming that Chester Hospital was an agent/representative for the Clinic that should be held vicariously liable. The district court, in an earlier decision, dismissed the EMTALA stabilization claim but permitted the screening claim to proceed.

The district court rejected the Plaintiff's claim that the Clinic could be held vicariously liable for the screening violation due to its affiliation with Chester Hospital. The Plaintiff argued that an affiliation agreement between Chester Hospital and the Clinic created an agency relationship under which liability could be imputed. The district court disagreed, stating that the evidence presented, including Web site pages (with one page describing a cooperative arrangement for information sharing purposes) and apparent hospital marketing materials identifying and describing an "affiliation relationship," showed an affiliation that is merely associative in nature and was insufficient in demonstrating a link to support vicarious liability. The district court also referenced evidence indicating that the affiliation was limited to Chester Hospital's cardiac surgery program and did not extend to the emergency department. The district court held that even presuming that the Clinic qualified as a "participating hospital" and was a "hospital" for purposes of EMTALA, it could not be held directly liable for the alleged screening violation because the Plaintiff never went to, or received any medical care at, the Clinic.

Overall, the district court found that "[b]ecause there is no indicia of a principal-agent relationship in Mr. Byrne's exhibits, nor an evidentiary basis to find that the Clinic could be held liable for the Hospital's rendering care to Mr. Byrne, there is no sufficient evidence upon which a reasonable jury could conclude that the Clinic could be held vicariously liable for Mr. Byrne's screening claim." Accordingly, summary judgment was granted in favor of the Clinic.[23]

The new definition of "comes to the emergency department" raises compliance questions in the absence of an explicit request for emergency medical care. Previously, an individual who comes to the emergency department needed to make a specific request for an examination. Now, if an individual presents to the dedicated emergency department but does not "request" treatment, the hospital's EMTALA obligations are nonetheless triggered if a prudent layperson observer would believe, based on the situation at hand, that the individual needs treatment for a perceived emergency condition.[24] Also, if that individual presents elsewhere on the hospital campus, the question is solely whether a prudent layperson observer would believe that the individual needs emergency care.

The problem with the "prudent layperson observer" standard is that what a "prudent layperson" considers an emergent condition is vague and not defined.

---

[23] This case summary was written by Keith A. Mauriello, Partner, and Jessica T. Grozine, Associate, in the Healthcare Practice Group at Arnall Golden Gregory LLP, Atlanta, Georgia. It should not be construed as legal advice or opinion on specific matters.

[24] 42 C.F.R. § 489.24(b)(1).

Everyone would agree that a person who has passed out has an emergency condition, but what if the person merely feels a sudden rush of dizziness? Dizziness could be a benign condition but also could signify an impending stroke or cardiac dysrhythmia. In the preamble to the final rule, CMS stated that it would review "all actual relevant facts and circumstances to ensure that the regulations are applied appropriately."[25] Essentially, hospitals need to train all personnel who have any contact whatsoever with the public (essentially everyone) and establish appropriate policies and procedures that err on the side of caution to help ensure compliance with EMTALA.

Q 2:3 Dedicated Emergency Department: What is the definition of "dedicated emergency department"?

As stated in the opening line of EMTALA, the Act's primary obligations apply to *"hospital[s] that [have] a hospital emergency department."*[26] The Code of Federal Regulations specifies that a "hospital with an emergency department" is defined as a hospital with a "dedicated emergency department," a term with distinct legal implications.[27] Ultimately, a "dedicated emergency department" refers to a far greater range of facilities than those formally designated as emergency departments. Congress did not intend to limit the scope of EMTALA to hospitals with formal emergency departments because if it did, "a facility could easily circumvent its responsibilities . . . by simply renaming the department . . . or by using an approach other than departmentalization in providing hospital services. This would clearly contravene the underlying principle of the statute.[28]

The Code of Federal Regulations definitively states:

> Dedicated emergency department means any department or facility of the hospital, regardless of whether it is located on or off the main hospital campus that meets at least one of the following requirements:
>
> (1) It is licensed by the State in which it is located under applicable State law as an emergency room or emergency department;
>
> (2) It is held out to the public (by name, posted signs, advertising, or other means) as a place that provides care for emergency medical conditions on an urgent basis without requiring a previously scheduled appointment; or
>
> (3) During the calendar year immediately preceding the calendar year in which a determination under this section is being made, based on a representative sample of patient visits that occurred during that calendar year, it provides at least one-third of all of its outpatient visits for the treatment of emergency medical conditions on an

---

[25] 68 Fed. Reg. 53,222, 53,237 (2003).

[26] 42 U.S.C. § 1395dd(a).

[27] 42 C.F.R. § 489.24(b).

[28] 59 Fed. Reg. 32,806, 32,101 (1994). *See* 42 C.F.R. § 489.24(c)(3).

urgent basis without requiring a previously scheduled appointment.[29]

Any hospital that offers, for example, an urgent care center, psychiatric intake, a labor and delivery department, or an ambulatory care clinic and meets one of the three requirements for classification as a dedicated emergency department must comply with EMTALA's obligations. Even a Medicare-participant hospital without a formal emergency department, such as a specialty hospital or one that may have closed its formal emergency department, must comply with EMTALA if other departments are "held out" to the public as appropriate places to come for the treatment of emergency medical conditions on an urgent, non-appointment basis. EMTALA applies to most psychiatric hospitals that are accredited by the Joint Commission and have an emergency department that takes reasonable care in determining whether an emergency exists, renders lifesaving first aid, and makes appropriate referrals to the nearest organizations capable of providing needed services.

The first requirement in the definition of a dedicated emergency department—the state licensing requirement—is fairly straightforward. A handful of states license emergency departments separately from hospitals as a whole, and CMS defers to state law in these cases. Accordingly, the first requirement accounts for some hospitals with formal emergency departments.

However, for states that do not license their emergency departments, CMS created the second, "held out," requirement. This problematic requirement treats hospital departments (e.g., labor and delivery, psychiatry) and non-hospital facilities as dedicated emergency departments if they are "held out" to the public as places that provide care for emergency medical conditions on an urgent, non-appointment basis. But how does one truly assess whether a facility is held out to the public for purposes of treating emergency medical conditions? If a hospital does not want a department to be under the governance of EMTALA, should it then make sure with signage, advertisement, and so forth that the public be aware that certain departments are not areas that treat emergency medical conditions? What if the department holds itself out as a department that treats only urgent conditions but not "emergency medical conditions?"

CMS did not mandate in the final rule that a facility's signage use the term "emergency" or a well-recognized synonym to help identify how the facility is held out to the public. At present, if hospital signage or advertising presents the department as a care center where patients may arrive without a scheduled appointment for emergency medical care, then the hospital must make sure that the department is administered as a "dedicated emergency department" under EMTALA.

The third requirement, or "one-third rule," based on whether a third of a representative sample of outpatient visits were for non-scheduled emergency care, presents further problems because it relies on a retrospective review of

---

[29] 42 C.F.R. § 489.24(b).

selected patient records to determine whether a hospital department meets the test. Non-scheduled visits to a department may vary significantly from year to year. A department may meet the one-third definition one year, but, because of census variations, the present year has only 20 percent non-scheduled emergency visits. Is the department then free of EMTALA requirements for the next year? Can this application vary from year to year? Do hospitals have to reassess their department's non-scheduled emergency visits yearly to determine whether it needs to abide by EMTALA's rules? If a hospital wishes a certain department to be free of EMTALA requirements, can it manipulate the department so that it never meets the one-third rule?

The CMS Interpretive Guidelines instruct the state surveyor "to select a representative sample of patient visits that occurred the previous calendar year in the area of the hospital to be evaluated for status as a dedicated emergency department."[30] The guideline instructs the surveyor to select 20 to 50 charts of patients with presenting complaints or diagnoses associated with an emergency medical condition. Is this the same "emergency medical condition" as defined in the Act? Since the surveyor will select only cases of patients with likely emergency medical conditions, the representative sample will be skewed. A department that may have only a 10 percent overall unscheduled patient visit census may still meet the one-third rule if more than 33 percent of the selected sample of patients with emergency conditions present without appointments. As a result, for certain hospital departments on the threshold, it may be difficult to authoritatively determine whether they qualify as a dedicated emergency department.

Cautions: Any hospital department (whether on- or off-campus) that meets the definition of a "dedicated emergency department" must comply with all EMTALA's clinical and administrative requirements. The EMTALA clinical requirements involve a medical screening examination, stabilizing treatment, and transfer restrictions, as discussed in later chapters. In addition, these departments must also now act like a formal emergency department and provide the following administrative requirements:

1. Adopt a compliance policy to ensure compliance with EMTALA;

2. Adopt a policy setting forth which medical personnel are qualified to perform the medical screening examination;

3. Maintain a list of on-call physicians, and adopt policies guiding procedures to follow if the on-call physician is legitimately unavailable;

4. Post signs informing the public of the hospital's EMTALA obligations;

5. Maintain a central log of all individuals who come to the emergency department; and

---

[30] U.S. Dep't HHS, CMS, State Operations Manual, App. V, Emergency Medical Treatment and Labor Act (EMTALA) Interpretive Guidelines, Part II, Tag A-2405/C-2405 (revised 5/29/2009).

   6. Keep records of persons transferred to or from the hospital for at least
      five years from the date of transfer.

In the end, hospitals must independently conduct a close evaluation of each
of their departments to see whether any department meets the definition of a
"dedicated emergency department." Examples of departments that may meet
the definition are urgent care centers, ambulatory care centers, family medicine
centers, obstetric evaluation departments, and psychiatric outpatient
departments.

Q 2:4 Off-Campus Emergency Departments: Does EMTALA apply to off-campus or freestanding emergency departments?

CMS defines a "dedicated emergency department" as any department or
facility meeting one of three criteria, "regardless of whether it is located on or off
the main hospital campus."[31] On January 11, 2008, CMS released a memorandum addressing the mounting interest in "freestanding" emergency
departments.[32] CMS concluded that EMTALA applies to off-campus facilities
that (1) meet one of the three requirements for "dedicated emergency department" and (2) are owned and operated by a Medicare-participating hospital.
Should a hospital with an off-site emergency department undergo investigation
for an EMTALA violation, however, its conduct will be judged according to the
capabilities and capacities of the hospital's main campus, not just the off-
campus emergency department.[33]

> **Cautions:** To fall under EMTALA, an urgent care center needs to be owned
> and operated by the hospital under the same Medicare provider number and
> meet one of the three criteria to meet the definition for "dedicated emergency
> department": (1) is licensed by the state as an emergency department; (2)
> holds itself out to the public as providing care for emergency medical
> conditions; or (3) during the preceding calendar year, provided at least
> one-third of its outpatient visits for the treatment of emergency medical
> conditions.[34]

CMS has yet to discuss the distinction between "emergency care" and
"urgent care." It is therefore unclear whether an urgent care center that has
less than one-third non-scheduled patients with emergency conditions, yet
holds itself out as a place that treats only "urgent" conditions but not
"emergency medical" conditions, is exempt from EMTALA responsibilities.
This issue needs to be clarified by CMS. At present, it can only be said that if
an urgent care center operates independently of the hospital or does not meet

---

[31] 42 C.F.R. § 489.24(b).

[32] Thomas E. Hamilton, *Requirements for Provider-based Off-campus Emergency Departments and
Hospitals that Specialize in the Provision of Emergency Services,* CMS S&C Memorandum to State Survey
Agency Directors, No. 08-08 (Jan. 11, 2008).

[33] Thomas E. Hamilton, *Requirements for Provider-based Off-campus Emergency Departments and
Hospitals that Specialize in the Provision of Emergency Services,* CMS S&C Memorandum to State Survey
Agency Directors, No. 08-08 (Jan. 11, 2008).

[34] 68 Fed. Reg. 53,222, 53,234 (2003).

any of the three criteria for a dedicated emergency department, then EMTALA does not apply.

The CMS memorandum also addressed growing interest in proposed "emergency services hospitals," essentially emergency departments operating independently of parent Medicare-participating hospitals. CMS noted that the statutory definition of hospital under Section 1861(e) of the Social Security Act requires that the provider be primarily engaged in inpatient services.[35] CMS therefore expressed doubt that a freestanding emergency services facility could qualify as a Medicare-participating hospital on its own. Because EMTALA applies only to hospitals that accept Medicare payments, some emergency services hospitals could theoretically be exempt from responsibilities under the Act. However, it bears noting that virtually every hospital in the United States chooses to enter into Medicare provider agreements with the federal government.

Interestingly, during debates on the bill that became EMTALA, Representative Michael Bilirakis (R-Fla.) specifically mentioned "freestanding emergency centers" in his discussion on the House floor.[36] To date, other than cases involving Puerto Rico's unique "Centros de Diagnostico y Tratamiento" (CDTs), there have been no published EMTALA cases involving freestanding emergency centers or remote sites that were not hospital owned and operated.

Still, CDTs serve as useful test subjects for the potential application of EMTALA to freestanding emergency services facilities. A "CDT" is defined as an independent facility or one operated in conjunction with a hospital that provides community services for the diagnosis and treatment of ambulatory patients under the professional supervision of persons licensed to practice medicine, surgery, or dentistry in Puerto Rico. In the case of *Rodriguez v. American International Insurance Co.*,[37] a district court held that the Corozal CDT, which hosted a 24-hour emergency room, was governed by the rules of EMTALA. Rather than follow the literal wording of EMTALA, the court focused on "the end result" in its ruling. It reasoned that EMTALA should be extended to cover the Corozal CDT because the services it rendered—namely, 24-hour outpatient treatment without appointments—are the types of services that EMTALA was designed to cover.

The First Circuit reversed, cautioning that "[f]ederal courts are not free to ignore the letter of the law in favor of the 'spirit' of the law."[38] The court emphasized that "EMTALA does not apply to all health care facilities; it applies only to participating hospitals with emergency departments."[39] The Corozal CDT failed to qualify as a hospital because it was engaged entirely in outpatient,

---

[35] Thomas E. Hamilton, *Requirements for Provider-based Off-campus Emergency Departments and Hospitals that Specialize in the Provision of Emergency Services,* CMS S&C Memorandum to State Survey Agency Directors, No. 08-08 (Jan. 11, 2008).

[36] 131 Cong. Rec. H9503 (daily ed. Oct. 31, 1985) (statement of Representative Michael Bilirakis/R. Fla.).

[37] 263 F. Supp. 2d 297 (D.P.R. 2003), *rev'd by* 402 F.3d 45, 49 (1st Cir. 2005).

[38] *Rodriguez,* 402 F.3d 45, 49.

[39] *Rodriguez,* 402 F.3d 45, 48.

rather than inpatient, care. Moreover, it was not licensed as a hospital under Puerto Rican law. For these reasons, the First Circuit held that the Corozal CDT was not bound by the requirements of EMTALA. The plaintiff's claims against the defendant CDT were dismissed with prejudice.

By this reasoning, a privately owned urgent care center or hospital off-campus facility that is not part of a participating hospital's Outpatient Prospective Payment System (OPPS) reimbursement under Medicare would not be subject to EMTALA's dictates, because it is not an independent hospital nor is it receiving Medicare funds. However, because CMS retains the right to make case-by-case determinations as to which areas are covered by OPPS EMTALA requirements, any facilities that appear to be part of the hospital are at the mercy of this ad hoc determination. Facilities in this gray space could include primary care clinics that do not normally provide emergency services yet meet one of the three criteria for "dedicated emergency department."

The potential for confusion is evident. These clinics, if considered dedicated emergency departments, would have to avoid taking any insurance or payment information until an appropriate screening examination is in progress. They would need to have the same EMTALA policies for medical screening examinations, stabilization, making appropriate transfers, clarifying performance of the screening examination, waiting room signage, and so on. Any transfer from an off-campus urgent care site to the main hospital would require a medically appropriate transfer but would not necessarily require EMTALA certification since the transfer is within the same system. Transfers to a facility other than the home hospital would require the EMTALA transfer certification.

Fortunately, if it is fairly obvious that a certain off-campus department does not provide emergency services, the requirements are less complex. In that case, a hospital need only draft and adopt written policies and procedures for the off-campus department that provide for the appraisal of emergencies and transfers when appropriate.[40]

Q 2:5   Part-Time Emergency Departments: What if the emergency department is open only part-time?

EMTALA applies to part-time emergency departments, but the hospital's capabilities are evaluated at the time of the presentation to determine the scope of services that must be offered. Full capabilities are required only during the hours when the emergency department is open. Hospitals with only part-time EDs should recognize that other areas of the hospital where patients may present with emergency conditions, such as walk-in clinics, would still be governed by EMTALA.

In order to accommodate small hospitals that operate their emergency department only part-time, CMS allows an exception for EMTALA obligations. CMS states:

---

[40] 42 C.F.R. § 482.12(f)(3).

> It is our policy that a hospital that offers emergency services on a regular, part-time basis is not considered to have an emergency department under section 1867 at the scheduled times when emergency services are not available. At those times only, the hospital is not subject to the requirements of section 1867 of the Act. The hospital would remain obligated at those times to meet the requirements of proposed § 482.50(c) for appraisals of emergency cases, initial treatment, and referral when appropriate. At all other times (that is, when emergency care is offered), the hospital is fully responsible for compliance with the statute (and with the implementing regulations at 42 C.F.R. § 489.24) and also would be obligated to meet the emergency services requirements set forth in proposed § 482.50(a) and (b).

> We expect that a hospital offering part-time emergency services will do so in good faith, and not open and close its emergency department selectively in an attempt to avoid meeting its statutory obligations to some patients based on their perceived inability to pay.[41]

Effective in October 2007, CMS requires that critical access hospitals and other hospitals that do not have physicians on duty 24/7 must provide the patient written notice of that fact and what the hospital's plan is to deal with emergencies when a physician is not on the premises. The rule was primarily aimed at specialty hospitals that typically did not have medical staff on premises 24/7 and increasingly were coming under criticism for transferring patients in the middle of the night to general hospitals if a patient deteriorated. If that patient requests transfer to a full-service hospital, the specialty hospital should arrange an appropriate transfer. If this transfer is a patient request and the patient has a stable medical condition, EMTALA does not govern and receiving hospitals are free to deny transfer. It is important for transferring hospitals to document fully that care was offered and the patient was not induced to request transfer. The hospital should request that the patient sign refusal of service forms.

Q 2:6   Patients on Hospital Property: How should a hospital handle a patient who is on hospital property but is not within the dedicated emergency department?

When a patient requests emergency care on hospital property but is outside the dedicated emergency department, the State Operations Manual states:

> If an individual is initially screened in a department or facility on-campus outside of the ED, the individual could be moved to another hospital department or facility on campus to receive further screening or stabilizing treatment without such movement being regarded as a transfer, as long as (1) all persons with the same medical condition are moved in such circumstances, regardless of their ability to pay for treatment; (2) there is bona fide medical reason to move the individual; and (3) appropriate medical personnel accompany the individual. The

---

[41] 62 Fed. Reg. 66,726, 66,741-742 (1997).

same is also true for an individual who presents to the dedicated emergency department (e.g., patient with an eye injury in need of stationary ophthalmology equipment located in the eye clinic) and must be moved to another hospital-owned facility or department on-campus for further screening or stabilizing treatment. The movement of the individual between hospital departments is not considered an EMTALA transfer under this section, since the individual is simply being moved from one department of a hospital to another department or facility of the same hospital.[42]

Cautions: A patient who has an emergency medical condition and is on hospital property outside of the dedicated emergency department but who is not already receiving care as an inpatient or outpatient is covered by the dictates of EMTALA. A visitor who passes out in the hospital parking lot, for instance, would fall into this category. CMS demands that the patient receive a medical screening examination while remaining on hospital property, consistent with the provision of the medical screening examination within the dedicated emergency department. CMS wants to see uniform practices where all patients with similar symptoms and conditions are similarly treated. A patient may be transported to an appropriate area of the hospital for further treatment as long as this is the routine practice and policy of the hospital. CMS does not want patients to be moved off hospital property for such care. The State Operations Manual states:

> Hospitals should not move individuals to off-campus facilities or departments (such as an urgent care center or satellite clinic) for a MSE. If an individual comes to a hospital-owned facility or department, which is off-campus and operates under the hospital's Medicare provider number, § 1867 (42 C.F.R. § 489.24) will not apply to that facility and/or department unless it meets the definition of a dedicated emergency department.[43]

If a hospital follows its own reasonable policies on how to respond to patients on hospital properties who request care for an emergency medical condition, then it has not violated EMTALA. In *Addiego v. City and County of San Francisco*,[44] Rina Addiego fell in the parking lot of California Pacific Medical Center (CPMC) and injured her hip. Although the patient was within 30 yards of the emergency department, the parking attendant, pursuant to hospital policy, called the hospital's security department. Security personnel arrived and proceeded to call 911 for paramedic services. After lying on the ground for about one hour, paramedics transported the patient to the hospital's emergency department where the patient was treated for a hip fracture and admitted to the hospital. Addiego filed a suit claiming that the delay in treatment exacerbated

---

[42] U.S. Dep't HHS, CMS, State Operations Manual, App. V, Emergency Medical Treatment and Labor Act (EMTALA) Interpretive Guidelines, Part II, Tag A-2406/C-2406 (revised 7/16/2010).

[43] U.S. Dep't HHS, Medicare Medicaid State Operations Manual, App. V, Emergency Medical Treatment and Labor Act (EMTALA) Interpretive Guidelines, Part II, Tag A-2406/C-2406 (revised 7/16/2010).

[44] No. C 05-04819 CRB (N.D. Cal. Feb. 17, 2006).

her injuries. She also alleges that the hospital violated EMTALA by not transporting her directly to the emergency department but rather called 911. The court noted that the plaintiff "does not cite any cases, however, that suggest EMTALA requires a hospital to use its own personnel to transport people requesting services from the parking garage to the emergency room, or, in the alternative, to send emergency room personnel to a parking lot to screen and stabilize a person requesting emergency services. And the language of EMTALA includes no such requirement." The court granted the defense's request to dismiss the EMTALA claim.

In early 2012, the HHS again considered the question of whether EMTALA applied to an inpatient admitted to a hospital. HHS concluded:

> if an individual "comes to the [hospital's] emergency department," as we have defined that term in regulation, and the hospital provides an appropriate medical screening examination and determines that an EMC exists, and then admits the individual in good faith in order to stabilize the EMC, that hospital has satisfied its EMTALA obligation towards that patient.[45]

Q 2:7 Private Clinics: Can EMTALA apply to physicians in a private clinic?

No. EMTALA applies only to physicians connected with an emergency department or facilities owned and operated by a hospital, not to physicians in private clinics. EMTALA does not apply to doctors' offices, public health centers, day surgery clinics, or any other facilities that are not owned by a hospital or operating under the hospital's OPPS billing.

Cautions: The Act governs only participating hospitals, off-site hospital facilities operating under the hospital's OPPS billing, and hospital-owned ambulances. In *King v. Ahrens*, the court ruled that a private clinic is not governed by EMTALA.[46] Franklin King was treated for chest pain at the private Ahrens Clinic. After an electrocardiogram and tests were performed and interpreted as normal, King was discharged for a gastrointestinal workup. King died two days later of a myocardial rupture from a missed myocardial infarction. The Eighth Circuit[47] held that the statutory language plainly restricted EMTALA to a hospital and ruled that King's family did not have a cause of action under EMTALA.

---

[45] 77 Fed. Reg. 5217 (Feb. 2, 2012). See **Appendix G** for the full text.

[46] King v. Ahrens, 16 F.3d 265, 270-71 (8th Cir. 1994).

[47] The Eighth Circuit covers Minnesota, North Dakota, South Dakota, Nebraska, Iowa, Missouri, and Arkansas. 28 U.S.C.A. § 41.

Q 2:8 No Dedicated Emergency Department: What if a hospital lacks a "dedicated emergency department"?

If none of a hospital's departments meets the definition of a "dedicated emergency department," the hospital is still bound by the Medicare CoPs, which require these departments to have policies and procedures in place to guide personnel on how to treat a person presenting there with an emergency medical condition. Additionally, if a Medicare-participating hospital has the specialized capabilities and capacity to treat a transfer patient, that hospital has an obligation to accept the transfer, regardless of whether it has a dedicated emergency department.

The Medicare CoPs, memorialized in the Code of Federal Regulations, state:

> If emergency services are not provided at a hospital, the governing body must assure that the medical staff has written policies and procedures for appraisal of emergencies, initial treatment, and referral where appropriate.[48]

The State Operations Manual states:

> Medicare **hospitals** that do not provide emergency services must meet the standard of § 482.12(f), which requires hospitals to have written policies and procedures for the appraisal of emergencies, initial treatment within its capability and capacity, and makes an appropriate referral to a hospital that is capable of providing the necessary emergency services.[49]

Cautions: Although specialty hospitals without dedicated emergency departments are not subject to EMTALA obligations when approached by individuals seeking initial examination or treatment for a medical condition, these hospitals are nevertheless obliged to accept appropriate patient transfers under EMTALA. In that aspect, their obligations do not differ from those of hospitals with dedicated emergency departments. CMS confirmed this policy in the final rule on Inpatient Prospective Payment Systems (IPPS) on August 18, 2006.[50] It stated:

> It has been CMS' longstanding policy that any Medicare-participant hospital with a specialized capability must, in accordance with section 1867(g) of the Act, accept, within the capacity of the hospital, an appropriate transfer from a requesting hospital. This policy has been applied to hospitals without regard to whether they have dedicated emergency departments. In fact, in the past, CMS has taken enforcement actions against hospitals with specialize capabilities that failed to accept appropriate transfers under EMTALA when the hospitals had the capacity to treat the transferred individuals.

---

[48] 42 C.F.R. § 482.12(f)(2).

[49] U.S. Dep't HHS, CMS, State Operations Manual, App. V, Emergency Medical Treatment and Labor Act (EMTALA) Interpretive Guidelines, Part II, Tag A-2406/C-2406 (revised 7/16/2010).

[50] 71 Fed. Reg. 47,870, 48,097 (2006).

The IPPS final rule specifically extends this EMTALA transfer obligation to for-profit, physician-owned "specialty hospitals" that have appeared in recent years. In its discussion concerning physician-owned specialty hospitals, CMS declined to impose on them any new on-call coverage, transfer requirements, or additional EMTALA obligations with respect to individuals approaching the hospitals as their initial point of entry into the medical system. CMS noted that Medicare CoPs already impose an obligation on all participating hospitals, including physician-owned limited service facilities, to have a physician on duty or on call at all times and to provide adequate physician services for hospital patients.

In sum, EMTALA primarily imposes obligations on hospitals participating in Medicare and operating a "dedicated emergency department," regardless of whether a formally designated emergency department exists. Federal Medicare regulations, however, require hospitals lacking dedicated emergency departments to establish policies and procedures for the assessment of presenting emergencies, provision of immediate assistance, and arrangement of transport to an appropriate hospital.[51] All Medicare-participating hospitals, even those without dedicated emergency departments, are obliged to accept an appropriate transfer if they possess the necessary capacity and capability that a transferring hospital lacks.

Q 2:9 Off-Campus Departments: Does EMTALA apply to hospital off-campus departments that are not dedicated emergency departments?

No. Unless that department meets the definition of a dedicated emergency department, the off-campus department does not have to abide by EMTALA's requirements, even if other departments in the hospital do. However, these off-campus departments remain bound by the Medicare CoPs, which require hospitals to have written policies and procedures that direct personnel in these off-campus departments on how to handle medical emergencies that arise.

The Medicare CoPs, memorialized in the Code of Federal Regulations, states:

> (3) If emergency services are provided at the hospital but are not provided at one or more off-campus departments of the hospital, the governing body of the hospital must assure that the medical staff has written policies and procedures in effect with respect to the off-campus department(s) for appraisal of emergencies and referral when appropriate.[52]

If, for example, a patient presents for physical therapy and develops chest pains, medical staff must have written policies defining how to proceed with assessing the patient's condition and referring him or her to the appropriate place.

---

[51] 42 C.F.R. § 482.12(e)(2).

[52] 42 C.F.R. § 482.12(f)(3).

Cautions: The State Operations Manual states:

> If a request were made for emergency care in a hospital department **off** the hospital's main campus that does not meet the definition of a dedicated emergency department, EMTALA would not apply. However, such an off-campus facility must have policies and procedures in place as how to handle patients in need of immediate care. For example, the off-campus facility policy may direct the staff to contact the emergency medical services/911 (EMS) to take the patient to an emergency department (not necessarily the emergency department of the hospital that operates the off-campus department, but rather the closest emergency department) or provide the necessary care if it is within the hospital's capability. Therefore, a hospital off-campus facility that does not meet the definition of a dedicated emergency department does not have an EMTALA obligation and not required to be staffed to handle potential EMC.[53]

This position represents a welcome change for hospitals. Previous proposals by CMS had ruled that all off-campus departments, including physical therapy, radiology, or laboratory sites, would have to comply with EMTALA's requirements,[54] including those for medical screening examination, stabilization, and transfer, as well as administrative requirements of signage, logs, and on-call lists. This created significant administrative difficulties for hospitals. While there is still ambiguity as to the criteria defining the term "dedicated emergency department," the restriction of EMTALA requirements to dedicated emergency departments, whether on- or off-campus, keeps many facilities that do not function and operate like a typical emergency department outside the scope of EMTALA.

Departments on the threshold remain the lingering problem. Some off-campus departments are not meant to be emergency care centers, yet seem to meet one of the three criteria of a dedicated emergency department. Primary care clinics, labor and delivery departments, and psychiatric clinics, for example, may satisfy the "one-third" rule. Because the one-third criterion does not include a specific methodology for making the necessary mathematical determination, hospitals now need to make a statistical analysis of patient visits to off-campus departments to assess whether the department meets this criterion. These hospitals must then decide if they should adjust non-scheduled services to avoid EMTALA complications.

Q 2:10   Hospital Property: What constitutes "hospital property"?

The definition of "hospital property" is expansive. The term hospital property includes the main hospital campus, which also encompasses the parking lot, sidewalk, and driveways, in addition to any parts of the hospital that are

---

[53] U.S. Dep't HHS, CMS, State Operations Manual, App. V, Emergency Medical Treatment and Labor Act (EMTALA) Interpretive Guidelines, Part II, Tag A-2406/C-2406 (revised 7/16/2010).

[54] U.S. Dep't HHS, CMS, State Operations Manual, App. V, Emergency Medical Treatment and Labor Act (EMTALA) Interpretive Guidelines, Part II, Tag A-2406/C-2406 (revised 7/16/2010).

within 250 yards of the main buildings. The definition also includes hospital-owned or -operated ambulances but excludes entities on the campus that are not part of the hospital, such as physician offices, skilled nursing facilities, rural health clinics, and so forth.

The State Operations Manual states:

> If an individual who is not a hospital patient comes elsewhere on **hospital property** (that is, the individual comes to the hospital but not to the dedicated emergency department), an EMTALA obligation on the part of the hospital may be triggered if either the individual requests examination or treatment for an emergency medical condition or if a prudent layperson observer would believe that the individual is suffering from an emergency medical condition.[55]

The Code of Federal Regulations defines hospital property and states that any individual on the property who requests treatment for a potential emergency condition will trigger EMTALA obligations:

> Hospital property means the entire main hospital campus as defined in Sec. 413.65(b) of this chapter, including the parking lot, sidewalk, and driveway, but excluding other areas or structures of the hospital's main building that are not part of the hospital, such as physician offices, rural health centers, skilled nursing facilities, or restaurants, shops, or other nonmedical facilities.[56]

CMS gives a definition of what constitutes a hospital campus:

> Generally, a hospital campus is defined in regulations as the physical area immediately adjacent to the hospital's main buildings, other areas and structures that are not strictly contiguous to the main buildings but are located within 250 yards of the main buildings, and any other areas determined on an individual case basis by the CMS regional office to be part of the hospital campus.[57] The term "hospital property" means the entire main hospital campus as defined in § 413.65(a), including the parking lot, sidewalk and driveway or hospital departments, including any buildings owned by the hospital that are within 250 yards of the hospital.[58]

The Final Regulations expressly preserve the 250-yard rule and retain the previous regulatory language. Generally, "hospital campus" is defined in regulations as the physical area immediately adjacent to the hospital's main buildings, other areas and structures that are not strictly contiguous to the main buildings but are located within 250 yards of the main buildings, and any other areas determined on an individual case basis by the CMS regional office to be

---

[55] U.S. Dep't HHS, CMS, State Operations Manual, App. V, Emergency Medical Treatment and Labor Act (EMTALA) Interpretive Guidelines, Part II, Tag A-2406/C-2406 (revised 7/16/2010).

[56] 42 C.F.R. § 489.24(b).

[57] 42 C.F.R. § 413.65(a)(2).

[58] U.S. Dep't HHS, CMS, State Operations Manual, App. V, Emergency Medical Treatment and Labor Act (EMTALA) Interpretive Guidelines, Part II, Tag A-2406/C-2406 (revised 7/16/2010).

part of the hospital campus.[59] Although CMS is not using the phrase "located within 250 yards of the hospital's main building" in EMTALA's section of the Code of Federal Regulations, CMS considers the concept intact since the definition of "campus" in the federal codes includes the 250-yard concept.[60] By referencing this section of the federal codes, CMS considers the 250-yard concept still applicable.[61] CMS considers only the parking lot, sidewalk, and driveway that are on hospital property to be part of the hospital for EMTALA purposes.[62] Hospitals do not have EMTALA obligations for any other non-hospital property located within 250 yards of the main building, such as public streets, restaurants, shops, etc.

> **Cautions:** The definitions of "comes to" and "emergency department" have been taken in the most expansive sense by CMS to prevent a hospital from avoiding EMTALA jurisdiction for patients who do not technically enter through the emergency department. If a patient presents with a medical emergency and is merely on hospital property, such as the parking lot, sidewalk, or driveway, or a hospital department within the 250-yard area of the main hospital building, he or she is considered to have "come to the hospital" and is protected by EMTALA requirements. Any person on hospital property who "requests" care for a possible emergency condition triggers EMTALA obligations for the hospital.

The major impetus for the creation of the 250-yard rule was an isolated incident where a teenage boy died across an alley from Ravenswood Hospital in Chicago when emergency department personnel refused to leave hospital property to provide care.[63] In May 1998, Christopher Sercye was shot during gang violence near the hospital. His friends assisted him to within half a block of Ravenswood's emergency department, where Christopher collapsed on the pavement. His friends dashed to the emergency department frantically begging for help. However, a hospital employee cited a hospital policy that forbade hospital staff from leaving hospital property to render care in medical situations off-campus. The hospital called the emergency 911 number and instructed the friends to await an ambulance.

The 911 dispatcher, however, was not able to dispatch ambulances to hospitals because policy barred EMS from being involved in what was perceived to be an interhospital transfer. A police officer arrived on the scene and attempted to get hospital personnel to assist the boy into the emergency department. They refused. After more than 25 minutes, the police supervisor on the scene authorized patrol officers to violate the standing order against medical intervention, and they carried the boy into the emergency department. The boy died within minutes. CMS cited Ravenswood for an EMTALA violation and fined

---

[59] 42 C.F.R. § 413.65(a)(2).

[60] 42 C.F.R. § 413.65(b).

[61] 68 Fed. Reg. 53,243 (2003).

[62] 42 C.F.R. § 489.24(b).

[63] Lola Smallwood, *Witnesses Say Hospital Refused to Help Dying Teen*, Chicago Tribune, May 18, 1998, Metro Chicago, at 1.

the hospital $40,000 even though the 250-yard rule was not in effect at the time. The hospital also had to settle a subsequent lawsuit for millions of dollars.

Q 2:11   Nonhospital-Owned Structures: Does EMTALA apply to nonhospital-owned structures within the 250-yard rule?

No. A hospital has no EMTALA obligation with respect to individuals who present to other areas or structures that may be located within 250 yards of the hospital's main building that are not part of the hospital (except areas like parking lots that serve the hospital).

The Code of Federal Regulations states:

> Hospital property means the entire main hospital campus as defined in § 413.65(b) of this chapter, including the parking lot, sidewalk and driveway, but excluding other areas or structures of the hospital's main building that are not part of the hospital, such as physician offices, rural health centers, skilled nursing facilities, or other entities that participate separately under Medicare, or restaurants, shops or other non-medical facilities.[64]

Cautions: There are many gray areas of the hospital where other entities lease space within the hospital for businesses catering to patients and visitors. Even though EMTALA does not apply in these areas, this does not mean that the hospital should not respond to medical emergencies that occur in these facilities.

In the past, only medically oriented businesses such as doctors' offices or skilled nursing facilities existed within hospital property. Now, fast food restaurants and other types of entities may be part of the main building. CMS has clarified that EMTALA requirements of medical screening examination, stabilization, and transfer do not apply in these entities. However, even though EMTALA does not apply, hospitals should still formulate policies addressing how to respond to medical emergencies in these entities.

Q 2:12   The 250-Yard Rule: How should a hospital formulate policy for the 250-yard rule?

When formulating a response policy for the 250-yard rule, hospitals need to consider the following:

- the safety of staff members to leave hospital property
- whether workers' compensation will cover injuries to staff off hospital property
- whether state "Good Samaritan" laws will protect staff members from liability when they come to the aid of off-property individuals

---

[64] 42 C.F.R. § 489.24(b).

- whether hospital liability insurance will cover or indemnify staff who commit negligence in the course of responding to an off-site emergency
- whether, when emergency department staff respond to an emergency 250 yards away, there will be sufficient staff left within the emergency department to care for patients who are already within the department
- how far off hospital property the emergency staff is expected to respond versus calling community EMS
- whether hospital staff are properly trained to provide emergency care in the streets outside the department
- whether the policy allows flexibility based on staff judgment
- what equipment needs to be brought to the scene
- which personnel are expected to respond (only RNs, or must the emergency physician also respond?)

Cautions: The 250-yard rule presents definite challenges and liabilities for the hospital. The hospital needs to be proactive and formulate specific policies and procedures for hospital personnel to follow whenever an emergency medical condition is perceived on hospital grounds.

The 250-yard rule presents numerous challenges to hospitals. The distance of 250 yards (750 feet) exceeds the length of two football fields. The logistics of requiring hospitals to attend to medical events outside the hospital building are problematic. Must the emergency physician and nurses abandon their patients in the emergency department to attend to a medical situation out in the streets, which may require extensive time (if the emergency staff is attending a cardiac arrest in the dedicated emergency department, must they divide staff to attend to a patient 250 yards away outside the hospital?). How is the hospital alerted to the patient's condition and notified to respond? What equipment will be provided? Are hospital personnel expected to drag a crash cart (crash carts hold vital medications and equipment to treat cardiac arrest and other critical resuscitations) through 250 yards of heavy snow to reach the patient? Will communications from the emergency site to the emergency department be provided? If personnel are endangered by violence in the streets, can they retreat and abandon the patient? Does hospital liability insurance cover employees who go out into the streets to treat patients?

Emergency staff members usually do not possess the special training of paramedics who have the training and experience to attend to medical situations in the field. Compromised airways, severe hemorrhage, neck injuries, unstable fractures, and gunshot wounds require specialized equipment and stabilization skills not normally possessed by emergency nurses. What special training should be provided to personnel? What are the liabilities for the hospital and hospital personnel when they go to the streets? Are they protected by the Good Samaritan statutes even though they are agents of the hospitals acting under a hospital policy? Such a complex issue involves many factors for hospital administrators to consider in developing response policies mandated by the regulations.

The hospital architect should prepare a site map that clearly lays out the 250-yard zone surrounding the outside walls and corners of the main hospital and all other buildings on the main campus of the hospital. All hospital-owned and -operated buildings, as well as immediately surrounding streets, alleys, sidewalks, lawns, and parking lots, are included in the covered areas. A hospital should have policies in place that would guide personnel to aid any patient who may collapse or show signs of an acute medical emergency in these areas. The hospital architect should also delineate areas within 250 yards that may not be accessible to hospital personnel, such as major highways, fenced areas, or areas blocked by natural barriers. In cases where different hospitals have overlapping 250-yard zones (in Chicago, Cook County Hospital and Rush Presbyterian Hospital are across the street from each other), agreements should be prepared between the two hospitals clarifying which hospital should respond to which areas. In addition, the hospital may formulate a new "code" such as a "code silver" announcement for the hospital intercom to cover such situations so that the medical team can respond.

Q 2:13 Hospital-Owned Ambulances: How does EMTALA apply to hospital-owned ambulances?

Hospital-owned ambulances are considered hospital property. Consequently, with limited exceptions, an individual "comes to" an emergency department once he or she enters a ground or air ambulance owned and operated by the hospital. The 2003 final rules amended previous rules governing EMTALA's applicability to hospital-owned ambulances. CMS stated in the 2003 final rules that a patient has "come to" a hospital for the purposes of EMTALA if the patient:

(5) Is in a ground or air ambulance owned and operated by the hospital for purposes of examination and treatment for a medical condition at a hospital's dedicated emergency department, even if the ambulance is not on hospital grounds. However, an individual in an ambulance owned and operated by the hospital is not considered to have "come to the hospital's emergency department" if—

(i) The ambulance is operated under communitywide emergency medical service (EMS) protocols that direct it to transport the individual to a hospital other than the hospital that owns the ambulance; for example, to the closest appropriate facility. In this case, the individual is considered to have come to the emergency department of the hospital to which the individual is transported, at the time the individual is brought onto hospital property;

(ii) The ambulance is operated at the direction of a physician who is not employed or otherwise affiliated with the hospital that owns the ambulance; or

(6) Is in a ground or air nonhospital-owned ambulance on hospital property for presentation for examination and treatment for a medical condition at a hospital's dedicated emergency department. However, an individual in a nonhospital-owned ambulance off

hospital property is not considered to have come to the hospital's emergency department, even if a member of the ambulance staff contacts the hospital by telephone or telemetry communications and informs the hospital that they want to transport the individual to the hospital for examination and treatment. The hospital may direct the ambulance to another facility if it is in "diversionary status," that is, it does not have the staff or facilities to accept any additional emergency patients. If, however, the ambulance staff disregards the hospital's diversion instructions and transports the individual onto hospital property, the individual is considered to have come to the emergency department.[65]

Cautions: This new ruling allows flexibility in proper patient care. For example, it would accommodate local disaster protocols that require ambulances to be diverted to appropriate hospitals in the system regardless of ambulance ownership. CMS specifies that an individual in an ambulance owned and operated by the hospital is not considered to have "come to the emergency department" if the ambulance is operated under communitywide EMS protocols or EMS protocols "mandated by State law" that direct it to transport the individual to a hospital other than the hospital that owns the ambulance.

When hospital EMS personnel on board the ambulance determine that transporting the patient to the owner hospital would put the patient's life or safety at risk, CMS recognizes that there may be some situations in which redirection of the ambulance is necessary. Under these circumstances, it would not be an EMTALA violation to transport the individual to the closest hospital capable of treating his or her condition. Additionally, this new ruling should release EMTALA obligations for hospitals that have ambulances and air-transport vehicles that provide taxi-service transports between other hospitals, neither of which is the home-based hospital. The ambulance or helicopter would be considered to be "on loan" to the other hospital, thereby transferring the direction of the ambulance to the other hospital.

In the event of a bioterrorist emergency, hospital ambulances may be redirected to other hospitals for other reasons, such as containing a biocontamination within a central location or a hazardous materials center hospital. CMS states that the Bioterrorism Act[66] authorizes the government to temporarily waive or modify the application of certain Medicare, Medicaid, and state Children's Health Insurance Program requirements, including requirements for the imposition of sanctions for the otherwise inappropriate transfer of an unstabilized individual, if the transfer arises out of the circumstances of the emergency. CMS provides an exception to EMTALA obligations during a national emergency by stating in Section 489.24(a)(2) of the Code of Federal Regulations:

---

[65] 68 Fed. Reg. 53,222, 53,262-263 (2003).

[66] Public Health Security and Bioterrorism Preparedness and Response Act of 2002 (Pub. L. No. 107-188) (2002).

Nonapplicability of provisions of this section. Sanctions under this section for inappropriate transfer during a national emergency do not apply to a hospital with a dedicated emergency department located in an emergency area, as specified in section 1135(g)(1) of the Act.[67]

CMS adds that in the event of such a national emergency, CMS would issue appropriate guidance to hospitals.

A federal district court ruled in *Hernández v. Starr County Hospital District*,[68] that a patient in a hospital-owned ambulance had effectively "come to the hospital." Hernández was an employee who sustained a work-related head injury that knocked him unconscious. Starr County Hospital's ambulance responded to the emergency call made on behalf of the unconscious employee. The employer instructed the ambulance personnel to transport the worker to Mission Hospital rather than Starr County Hospital, which owned the ambulance. The employer apparently directed the ambulance crew to the other hospital in the belief that Starr County Hospital did not have a neurology department. The ambulance personnel complied, transporting the worker to Mission Hospital. Hernández sued Starr County Hospital District under EMTALA, contending that the six-minute difference in travel time had adversely affected his medical condition.

The court agreed that the worker had "come to the [hospital's] emergency department" for the purposes of EMTALA. "Federal regulations, as promulgated by the Department of Health and Human Services, define 'comes to the emergency department,' to include an individual in the hospital's ambulance."[69] However, the court granted the hospital's motion for summary judgment on the grounds that the plaintiff failed to show that a "request was made" of the defendant hospital to provide examination or treatment for the plaintiff's alleged emergency medical condition. When the ambulance picked him up, Hernández was unconscious and unable to make a request. His supervisor told the emergency medical technicians (EMTs) to transport him to Mission Hospital, and it was reasonable for the EMTs to follow the instructions of the person in charge at the accident scene. The court concluded that although EMTALA is designed to prevent hospitals from rejecting patients seeking emergency help, it is not intended to force a hospital ambulance to bring a patient to that hospital despite a request that the patient be taken to a different hospital.

In *Hernández*, all the evidence supported the fact that someone other than the ambulance service determined the patient's destination. This is not always the case, and thus adequate documentation is essential to protect an ambulance service. When the patient or family requests a destination that does not conform to local system protocol or the "hospital-owned ambulance rule," CMS has advised hospital ambulances to obtain a refusal of services form (with risks and benefits) in the field to document that the patient, not the service, determined

---

[67] 42 C.F.R. § 489.24(a)(2).

[68] 30 F. Supp. 2d 970 (S.D. Tex. 1999).

[69] *Hernández*, 30 F. Supp. 2d 970, 972.

the patient's destination. CMS is skeptical of pre-printed risks and benefits, but it would seem that this is the best manner in which to create a risk and benefit statement to be used in the field.

The State Operations Manual states:

> If an individual is not on hospital property (which includes a hospital owned and operated ambulance), this regulation is not applicable. Hospital property includes ambulances owned and operated by the hospital, even if the ambulance is not on the hospital campus. An individual in a non-hospital owned ambulance, which is on hospital property is considered to have come to the hospital's emergency department. . . . If an individual is in an ambulance, regardless of whether the ambulance is owned by the hospital, a hospital may divert individuals when it is in "diversionary" status because it does not have the staff or facilities to accept any additional emergency patients at that time. However, if the ambulance is owned by the hospital, the diversion of the ambulance is only appropriate if the hospital is being diverted pursuant to community-wide EMS protocols. Moreover, if any ambulance (regardless of whether or not owned by the hospital) disregards the hospital's instructions and brings the individual onto hospital campus, the individual has come to the hospital and the hospital has incurred an obligation to conduct a medical screening examination for the individual.[70]

Q 2:14   Nonhospital-Owned Ambulances: How does EMTALA apply to nonhospital-owned ambulances?

In a typical course of events, an individual who calls 911 or contacts an Emergency Medical System (EMS) is loaded onto an ambulance by first responders. While en route to a nearby hospital, the ambulance staff places a call via telephone or telemetry to alert the hospital of the patient's condition, their arrival, and need for treatment. CMS and the circuit courts appear to have conflicting opinions on the issue of whether EMTALA applies to an individual in this situation.

CMS has stated that if a nonhospital-owned ambulance, while not yet on hospital property, contacts the hospital by telephone or telemetry, the individual on board is not considered to have "come to" the emergency department so as to trigger EMTALA obligations. This is not to say that such conduct is without consequences. CMS has observed that if a hospital not in diversionary status fails to accept a telephone or radio request by EMS for admission or transfer, the refusal could represent a violation of other federal or state requirements (e.g., Hill-Burton).[71] CMS also adds that if the ambulance arrives on the hospital

---

[70] U.S. Dep't HHS, CMS, State Operations Manual, App. V, Emergency Medical Treatment and Labor Act (EMTALA) Interpretive Guidelines, Part II, Tag A-2406/C-2406 (revised 7/16/2010).

[71] The Hospital Survey and Construction Act, Pub. L. No. 79-725, ch. 958, 60 Stat. 1040 (1946) (42 U.S.C. §§ 290 et seq.). Known as "The Hill-Burton Act," it was actually public works legislation designed to provide hospitals with new construction and improvement funds in light of a perceived shortage and to create construction jobs for the military personnel who were returning from World War II. Interestingly,

campus despite diversionary instructions, the individual is considered to have "come to" the emergency department and benefits from the protections of EMTALA from that point on.[72]

The First and Ninth Circuits, however, have concluded that if a nonhospital-owned ambulance calls ahead to a hospital that is not in diversionary status, that hospital is obligated by EMTALA to accept the individual on board. In short, in at least two circuits, mere telephone or telemetry contact by the EMT on a nonhospital-owned ambulance traveling toward a hospital is sufficient to qualify as "coming to" the emergency department.

Cautions: Emergency departments often divert ambulances to other hospitals even when the base hospital is not at capacity or on diversionary status. A patient may be diverted in the patient's best interest when his or her clinical presentation triggers a need for more specialized care than the hospital can offer. When a patient's injuries are severe or potentially severe because of the mechanism of the injury, diversion to a higher level of trauma care, such as a Level I trauma hospital or a tertiary hospital, is entirely appropriate to avoid delaying optimal care for the patient when a second transfer is needed. In addition, the emergency physician, while not on formal diversion status, may know, for example, that the CT scanner is down or that the neurosurgeon is in surgery.

The Seventh Circuit[73] was the first court of appeals to address this issue. In *Johnson v. University of Chicago*,[74] a federal district court in Illinois ruled that telemetry contact does not constitute "coming to" the emergency department under EMTALA because telemetry functions separately from the emergency department. Lenise Nelson, a two-month-old infant, stopped breathing at home. Emerald Johnson, Lenise's mother, telephoned the Chicago Fire Department on the 911 EMS telephone number. The fire department paramedics responded to the call, began cardiopulmonary resuscitation, loaded Lenise into an ambulance, and radioed the telemetry operator for the University of Chicago Hospital (UCH). Johnson lived just blocks from UCH in an area of almost 100 percent uninsured patient demographics. Denise McCall, an emergency nurse at UCH, advised the paramedics that UCH was on "partial bypass" because of full occupancy of the pediatric intensive care unit beds. There were, however, beds available in the emergency department to care for the child. Although Lenise was only minutes away from UCH, McCall instructed the paramedics to transport her to St. Bernard's Hospital, a hospital with no pediatric intensive care capacity located more than eight miles away. On arrival at St. Bernard's, Lenise was temporarily resuscitated. The child subsequently died after transfer

---

as with EMTALA within COBRA, a small section was inserted into the main body of the act that required hospitals receiving Hill-Burton funds to provide a "reasonable volume of services" to "persons unable to pay" and also services to "all persons residing in the territorial area of the [hospital]."

[72] 42 C.F.R. § 489.24(b)(4).

[73] The Seventh Circuit covers Wisconsin, Illinois, and Indiana. 28 U.S.C. § 41.

[74] 982 F.2d 230 (7th Cir. 1992).

to Cook County Hospital. Emerald Johnson filed suit against UCH for both EMTALA violation and medical malpractice under Illinois common law.

The plaintiff contended that a duty should arise under EMTALA because the patient was under the direction of the UCH emergency department by telemetry. On appeal, the Seventh Circuit considered whether telemetry contact was equivalent to "coming to the emergency room,"[75] making the University of Chicago liable under EMTALA even though the child never physically entered the hospital. All the major trauma centers in the Chicago-area emergency system immediately responded in alarm with *amicus curiae* briefs,[76] stressing that such a ruling would create havoc with the existing telemetry system. For example, during a disaster event, a central command hospital that diverted patients to other hospitals would be responsible for every patient so diverted. The court ultimately found that UCH was not liable because Lenise had never "come to" the UCH emergency room as required by EMTALA; her ambulance did not reach hospital property and had only called ahead to the telemetry center before it was diverted. As the Seventh Circuit critically noted, "a hospital-operated telemetry system is distinct from that hospital's emergency room."[77] Still, the court warned that the outcome might have been different if the plaintiffs had offered persuasive evidence that the diversion constituted a "scheme to dump patients."[78] The lesson from *Johnson* is that diversion should be based on emergency department capability and capacity, not on inpatient census.

Following the Seventh Circuit's lead, CMS refined its rules to mirror the holding of *Johnson*. The Code of Federal Regulations, 42 C.F.R. § 489.24(b)(4), now states:

> [A]n individual in a nonhospital-owned ambulance off hospital property is not considered to have come to the hospital's emergency department, even if a member of the ambulance staff contacts the hospital by telephone or telemetry communications and informs the hospital that they want to transport the individual to the hospital for examination and treatment. The hospital may direct the ambulance to another facility if it is in "diversionary status," that is, it does not have the staff or facilities to accept any additional emergency patients. If, however, the ambulance staff disregards the hospital's diversion instructions and transports the individual onto hospital property, the individual is considered to have come to the emergency department.[79]

---

[75] *Johnson*, 982 F.2d 230.

[76] *Amicus curiae* means, literally, "friend of the court. A person with strong interest in or views on the subject matter of a lawsuit, but not a party to the suit, may petition the court for permission to file a brief, ostensibly on behalf of a party but actually to suggest a rationale consistent with its own views." *Black's Law Dictionary* 82 (6th ed. 1990). *See* Fed. R. App. P. 29.

[77] *Johnson*, 982 F.2d 230. 233.

[78] *Johnson*, 982 F.2d 230.

[79] 42 C.F.R. § 489.24(b)(4).

The State Operations Manual states:

> An individual in a non-hospital owned ambulance not on the hospital's property is not considered to have come to the hospital's emergency department when the ambulance personnel contact "Hospital A" by telephone or telemetry communications.[80]

Subsequently, however, other circuits have departed from *Johnson*. These courts have interpreted the regulations in a manner that permits radio diversion of nonhospital-owned ambulances only when a hospital is in diversionary status.

The Ninth Circuit made this distinction in *Arrington v. Wong*.[81] In that case, Harold Arrington developed difficulty breathing while driving to work. An ambulance was dispatched to the scene, and EMTs initiated care for Arrington, who had respirations of 50 and could not speak more than a word or two between breaths. During transport to Queen's Medical Center, one of the EMTs spoke with Dr. Norbert Wong, the emergency physician at Queen's. Dr. Wong asked who the patient's private doctor was, and the EMT told him, "[the] patient is a Tripler patient [a hospital located five miles from Queen's], but since there was respiratory distress, we thought we'd come to a close facility."[82] Dr. Wong believed Arrington would be stable under the technicians' care and directed the technicians to drive the extra five miles to Tripler. However, Arrington suffered respiratory arrest several minutes after his arrival at Tripler and died. Arrington's family sued Queen's, Dr. Wong, the city and county of Honolulu as operators of the ambulance service, and the EMTs who treated Arrington in the ambulance, alleging violations of EMTALA. The U.S. District Court for the District of Hawaii found that the plaintiffs could not sue Queen's or its emergency physician under EMTALA because Arrington did not "come to Queen's."[83]

The Ninth Circuit reversed the trial court. Adopting the Webster's Dictionary definition of "comes to" (which includes "the process of coming" and "moving toward") to the CMS guidelines, the court of appeals concluded that Arrington "came to" Queen's emergency department when his ambulance began "moving toward" the hospital. In interpreting 42 C.F.R. § 489.24(b)(4), the Ninth Circuit emphasized that the provision's third sentence ("The hospital may direct the ambulance to another facility if it is in "diversionary status. . . .") qualified the second sentence ("An individual in a nonhospital-owned ambulance . . . is not considered to have come to the hospital's emergency department, even if a member of the ambulance staff contacts the hospital by telephone or telemetry communications. . . ."), such that hospitals may deny an individual access only if they are in diversionary status, even if the individual is in a nonhospital-owned ambulance and not on hospital property.[84] The Ninth Circuit reconciled

---

[80] U.S. Dep't HHS, CMS, State Operations Manual, App. V, Emergency Medical Treatment and Labor Act (EMTALA) Interpretive Guidelines, Part II, Tag A-2406/C-2406 (revised 7/16/2010).

[81] Arrington v. Wong, 237 F.3d 1066 (9th Cir. 2001).

[82] *Arrington*, 237 F.3d 1066, 1069.

[83] *Arrington*, 237 F.3d 1066, 1077.

[84] *Arrington*, 237 F.3d 1066, 1072.

this position with the Seventh Circuit's by pointing out that the defendant hospital in *Johnson* was on "partial bypass," which the Ninth Circuit equated with diversionary status.

Years later, the First Circuit followed suit. In *Morales v. Sociedad Española de Auxilio Mutuo y Beneficencia*,[85] Carolina Morales was diagnosed with a nonviable ectopic pregnancy. After Morales experienced severe abdominal pain and vomiting at work one day, her co-workers called an ambulance. After loading Morales inside, the ambulance headed for Hospital Español Auxilio Mutuo de Puerto Rico, where her obstetrician regularly practiced. The hospital did not own the ambulance or employ its paramedics. While in transit, the paramedics called ahead to the emergency department to notify the director, Dr. Salvador Marquez, of the plaintiff's condition and arrival. During the first and second calls, Dr. Marquez shared his suspicion that Morales had induced an abortion, said he was busy, and told the paramedics to call back. During the third call, Dr. Marquez asked about Morales' medical coverage and abruptly hung up after receiving no assurances that Morales was a member of the hospital's insurance plan. The paramedics took this as a refusal to treat Morales and took her to a different facility.

Initially, the district court rejected the Ninth Circuit's reasoning in *Arrington*. Rather than emphasizing the third sentence of 42 C.F.R. § 489.24(b)(4) (which permits hospitals in diversionary status to deny patients), the court believed that the second sentence (which stated that a nonhospital-owned ambulance calling ahead does not "come to" an emergency department) was the operative sentence. The First Circuit, on appeal, reversed. It found that the language of the regulations was muddled, contradictory, and of little assistance. As a result, the appeals court decided to rule according to the legislative intent driving EMTALA. Noting that EMTALA was designed to prevent hospitals from "dumping" patients, the First Circuit reasoned:

> If a hospital were allowed to turn away an individual while she was en route to the hospital under these facts, an uninsured or financially strapped person could be bounced around like a ping-pong ball in search of a willing provider. That result would be antithetic to the core policy on which EMTALA is based.[86]

The First Circuit concluded that given "an imprecise statute, an unenlightening regulation, and an absence of any clear agency interpretation of what that regulation means," summary judgment was not appropriate because a jury could have found that Morales had come to the hospital's emergency department within the purview of EMTALA.[87]

The stance of the First and Ninth Circuits greatly expands the reach of EMTALA and could have a tremendous impact on the EMS telemetry system. As *amici* have noted, a trauma center diverting ambulances to area hospitals under

---

[85] 524 F.3d 54 (1st Cir. 2008).

[86] *Morales*, 524 F.3d 54, 61.

[87] *Morales*, 524 F.3d 54, 61.

an area-wide disaster plan would be liable for all patients diverted (unless it was in diversionary status). How many hospitals would want to be the triage center with such liability hanging over their heads? The dissenting judges in *Arrington* and *Morales* vigorously argued that the regulations plainly state that individuals in nonhospital-owned ambulances do not "come to" the hospital's emergency department merely by calling ahead. As for the provision's third sentence, "the most plausible reading of the third sentence is that it is simply one scenario—when the hospital is in 'diversionary status'—under which the hospital may deny access to an individual in a non-hospital-owned ambulance that calls ahead, and not the only scenario under which it may deny access."[88] The dissenting judge in *Arrington* also criticized the majority's conflation of the term "comes to" with "move toward." He remarked, "[I]f we say come to court at 9 A.M., we mean 'be here,' we do not mean 'be in route.'"[89] Time will tell if other circuits find the majority or dissenting opinions in *Arrington* and *Morales* more persuasive.

Q 2:15 Ambulance Parking: Can an emergency department delay EMTALA obligations by "parking" patients?

No, a hospital's EMTALA obligations begin as soon as the patient arrives on hospital property regardless of when the patient is transferred onto a hospital cart.

The practice of "parking" is where hospitals delay EMS from transferring patients from the ambulance stretcher to a hospital cart, believing that the hospital's EMTALA obligations do not start until the patient is physically transferred to a hospital cart. CMS emphasizes that a hospital's EMTALA obligation begins as soon as the ambulance arrives on hospital property; physical transfer of the patient onto a hospital cart is irrelevant.

The State Operations Manual states:

> Hospitals that deliberately delay moving an individual from an EMS stretcher to an emergency department bed do not thereby delay the point in time at which their EMTALA obligation begins. Furthermore, such a practice of "parking" patients arriving via EMS, refusing to release EMS equipment or personnel, jeopardizes patient health and adversely impacts the ability of the EMS personnel to provide emergency response services to the rest of the community. Hospitals that "park" patients may also find themselves in violation of 42 C.F.R. 482.55, the Hospital Condition of Participation for Emergency Services, which requires that hospitals meet the emergency needs of patients in accordance with acceptable standards of practice.
>
> On the other hand, this does not mean that a hospital will necessarily have violated EMTALA and/or the hospital CoPs if it does not, in every instance, immediately assume from the EMS provider all responsibility

---

[88] *Morales*, 524 F.3d 54, 64 (*citing Arrington*, 237 F.3d 1066, 1076 (Fernández, F., dissenting)).

[89] *Arrington*, 237 F.3d 1066, n.2.

for the individual, regardless of any other circumstances in the ED. For example, there may be situations when a hospital does not have the capacity or capability at the time of the individual's presentation to provide an immediate medical screening examination (MSE) and, if needed, stabilizing treatment or an appropriate transfer. So, if the EMS provider brought an individual to the dedicated ED at a time when ED staff was occupied dealing with multiple major trauma cases, it could under those circumstances be reasonable for the hospital to ask the EMS provider to stay with the individual until such time as there were ED staff available to provide care to that individual. However, even if a hospital cannot immediately complete an appropriate MSE, it must still assess the individual's condition upon arrival to ensure that the individual is appropriately prioritized, based on his/her presenting signs and symptoms, to be seen by a physician or other QMP [qualified medical personnel] for completion of the MSE. The hospital should also assess whether the EMS provider can appropriately monitor the individual's condition.[90]

Cautions: As soon as an ambulance arrives on hospital property, regardless of whether the patient remains on the ambulance stretcher or is transferred to a hospital cart, EMTALA obligations begin. Hospitals are mistaken when they believe that they can delay the medical screening examination and stabilizing treatment by delaying the physical transfer of a patient to a hospital cart. If a patient suffers harm as a result of this delay in care, CMS makes it quite clear that this is an EMTALA violation.

CMS sent a memorandum on July 13, 2006, to State Survey Agency Directors concerning the issue of "parking" of ambulance patients. In the letter, CMS states:

> The Centers for Medicare & Medicaid Services (CMS) has learned that several hospitals routinely prevent Emergency Medical Service (EMS) staff from transferring patients from their ambulance stretchers to a hospital bed or gurney. Reports include patients being left on an EMS stretcher (with EMS staff in attendance) for extended periods of time. Many of the hospital staff engaged in such practice believes that unless the hospitals "take responsibility" for the patient, the hospital is not obligated to provide care or accommodate the patient. Therefore, they will refuse EMS requests to transfer the patient to hospital units.

> This practice may result in a violation of the Emergency Medical Treatment and Labor Act (EMTALA) and raises serious concerns for patient care and the provision of emergency services in a community. Additionally, this practice may also result in a violation of 42 C.F.R. § 482.55, the Conditions of Participation for Hospitals for Emergency Services, which requires that a hospital meet the emergency needs of patients in accordance with acceptable standards of practice.

> A hospital has an EMTALA obligation as soon as a patient "presents" at a hospital's dedicated emergency department, or on hospital property

---

[90] U.S. Dep't HHS, CMS, State Operations Manual, App. V, Emergency Medical Treatment and Labor Act (EMTALA) Interpretive Guidelines, Part II, Tag A-2406/C-2406 (revised 7/16/2010).

(as defined at 42 C.F.R. § 489.24(b)) other than the dedicated emergency department, and a request is made on the individual's behalf for examination or treatment of an emergency medical condition. A patient who arrives via EMS meets this requirement when EMS personnel request treatment from hospital staff. Therefore, the hospital must provide a screening examination to determine if an emergency medical condition exists and, if so, provide stabilizing treatment to resolve the patient's emergency medical condition. Once a patient presents to the dedicated emergency department of the hospital, whether by EMS or otherwise, the hospital has an obligation to see the patient, as determined by the hospital under the circumstances and in accordance with acceptable standards of care.

EMTALA obligations would also apply to a hospital that has accepted transfer of a patient from another facility, as long as it is an "appropriate transfer" under EMTALA. An appropriate transfer is one in which the transferring hospital provides medical treatment that minimizes risks to an individual's health and the receiving hospital has the capability and capacity to provide appropriate medical treatment and has agreed to accept transfer (42 C.F.R. § 489.24(e)(2)). Therefore, the expectation is that the receiving facility has the capacity to accept the patient at the time the transfer is effectuated. A hospital that delays the medical screening examination or stabilizing treatment of a patient who arrives via transfer from another facility, by not allowing EMS to leave the patient, could also be in violation of EMTALA.

CMS recognizes the enormous strain and crowding many hospital emergency departments face every day. However, this practice is not a solution. "Parking" patients in hospitals and refusing to release EMS equipment or personnel jeopardizes patient health and impacts the ability of the EMS personnel to provide emergency services to the rest of the community.[91]

CMS issued a clarification memorandum on this issue on April 27, 2007.[92] CMS clarified that the 2006 memorandum, quoted above, should not be interpreted to mean that a hospital cannot ever ask EMS staff to stay with an individual transported by EMS to the hospital when the hospital does not have the capacity or capability to immediately assume full responsibility for the individual. CMS stated in the 2007 memorandum:

> The memorandum was intended to address the specific concern that some hospital Emergency Department (ED) staff may deliberately delay the transfer of individuals from the EMS provider's stretcher to an ED bed under the mistaken impression that the ED staff is thereby relieved of their EMTALA obligation. However, it was reported to the TAG by hospital representatives that some EMS organizations have cited this memorandum as requiring hospitals to take instant custody of all

---

[91] Thomas E. Hamilton, *EMTALA—"Parking" of Emergency Medical Service Patients in Hospitals,* CMS S&C Memorandum to State Survey Agency Directors, No. 06-21 (July 13, 2006).

[92] Thomas E. Hamilton, *EMTALA Issues Related to Emergency Transport Services,* CMS S&C Memorandum to State Survey Agency Directors, No. 07-20 (Apr. 27, 2007).

individuals presenting via EMS transport at the hospital's dedicated emergency department.

The memorandum was intended to reinforce that the EMTALA responsibility of a hospital with a dedicated ED begins when an individual arrives on hospital property (ambulance arrival) and not when the hospital "accepts" the individual from the gurney. An individual is considered to have "presented" to a hospital when he/she arrives at the hospital's dedicated ED or on hospital property and a request is made by the individual or on his/her behalf for examination or treatment of an emergency medical condition. (42 C.F.R. 489.24(b)) Once an individual comes to the emergency department of the hospital, whether by EMS or otherwise, the hospital has an obligation to provide an appropriate medical screening examination and, if an emergency medical condition is determined to exist, provide any necessary stabilizing treatment or an appropriate transfer. (42 C.F.R. 489.24(a) and (b)). Failure to meet these requirements constitutes a potential violation of EMTALA.

On the other hand, this does not mean that a hospital will necessarily have violated EMTALA if it does not, in every instance, immediately assume from the EMS provider all responsibility for the individual, regardless of any other circumstances in the ED. For example, there may be situations when a hospital does not have the capacity or capability at the time of the individual's presentation to provide an immediate medical screening examination (MSE) and, if needed, stabilizing treatment or an appropriate transfer. So, if the EMS provider brought an individual to the dedicated ED at a time when ED staff was occupied dealing with multiple major trauma cases, it could under those circumstances be reasonable for the hospital to ask the EMS provider to stay with the individual until such time as there were ED staff available to provide care to that individual. However, even if a hospital cannot immediately provide a MSE, it must still triage the individual's condition immediately upon arrival to ensure that an emergent intervention is not required and that the EMS provider staff can appropriately monitor the individual's condition. All cases of this kind will be reviewed on a case-by-case basis and any decision regarding EMTALA compliance will be made by the CMS Regional Office only after a full review of all relevant facts and circumstances.

Q 2:16   Off-Campus Transport: How should the patient be transported from the off-campus site to the hospital's emergency department?

The 2005 revised Code of Federal Regulations does not address this issue; however the statements from the 2004 regulations should still apply:

Movement or appropriate transfer from off-campus departments—

(i) If the main hospital campus has the capability required by the individual and movement of the individual to the main campus would not significantly jeopardize the life or health of the individual, the personnel at the off-campus department must assist in arranging this movement. Movement of the individual to the main campus of the hospital is not considered a transfer under this section, since the individual is simply being moved from one department of a hospital to another department or facility of the same hospital.

(ii) If a transfer of an individual with a potential emergency condition to a medical facility other than the main hospital campus is warranted, either because the main hospital campus does not have the specialized capability or facilities required by the individual, or because the individual's condition is deteriorating so rapidly that taking the time needed to move the individual to the main hospital campus would significantly jeopardize the life or health of the individual, personnel at the off-campus department must, in accordance with protocols established in advance by the hospital, assist in arranging an appropriate transfer of the individual to a medical facility other than the main hospital. The protocols must include procedures and agreements established in advance with other hospitals or medical facilities in the area of the off-campus department to facilitate these appropriate transfers. Such a transfer would require:

a. That there be either a request by or on behalf of the individual as described in paragraph (d)(1)(ii)(A) of this section or a certification by a physician or a qualified medical person as described in paragraph (d)(1)(ii)(B) or (d)(1)(ii)(C) of this section; and

b. That the transfer comply with the requirements described in paragraph (d)(2) of this section.

(iii) If the individual is being appropriately transferred to another medical facility from the off-campus department, the requirement for the provision of medical treatment in paragraph (d)(2)(i) of this section would be met by provision of medical treatment within the capability of the transferring off-campus department.[93]

Cautions: When a patient presents to a provider-based off-campus site for an emergency medical condition, the off-campus site may find it necessary to transport the individual to the main hospital's emergency department either to complete the screening of the individual or to provide stabilizing treatment. CMS places the responsibility for transporting the patient to the emergency department from the off-campus site on the shoulders of the hospital. The hospital should have policies in place so that personnel at the off-campus site know the communication process required with the emergency department to transport the patient to the emergency department. Movement of the patient to the hospital's emergency department is not considered an EMTALA transfer because the individual is simply being

---

[93] 42 C.F.R. § 489.24(i)(3) (2004).

moved from one department of a hospital to another department or facility of the same hospital.[94]

When a patient needs transportation to the emergency department, the hospital must arrange the transport, either by the hospital's own transport services or by summoning an independently operated service that has agreed to provide transport for the hospital. If the individual insists on transporting him- or herself to the emergency department, the off-site department must document the individual's informed refusal of the offered transportation. If it is decided, in consultation with the main hospital's emergency department, that moving the patient to the main hospital would jeopardize the individual's life or health, the patient should be transferred according to EMTALA's appropriate transfer rules to the most appropriate hospital or other medical facility. Activating the EMS system by calling 911 does not excuse the hospital from its screening and stabilizing duties within its capabilities.

Q 2:17   Helipads: Does EMTALA apply to a hospital's helipad?

Unless there is a specific request for a medical screening examination, or the helicopter is transporting the patient to the hospital that owns the helipad for care, mere arrival of a helicopter on a hospital's helipad would not trigger EMTALA. The State Operations Manual states:

> The following two circumstances will not trigger EMTALA:
>
> - The use of a hospital's helipad by local ambulance services or other hospitals for the transport of individuals to tertiary hospitals located throughout the State does not trigger an EMTALA obligation for the hospital that has the helipad on its property when the helipad is being used for the purpose of transit as long as the sending hospital conducted the Medical Screening Examination prior to transporting the individual to the helipad for medical helicopter transport to a designated recipient hospital. The sending hospital is responsible for conducting the Medical Screening Examination prior to transfer to determine if an emergency medical condition exists and implementing stabilizing treatment or conducting an appropriate transfer. Therefore, if the helipad serves simply as a point of transit for individuals who have received a Medical Screening Examination performed prior to transfer to the helipad, the hospital with the helipad is not obligated to perform another Medical Screening Examination prior to the individual's continued travel to the recipient hospital. If, however, while at the helipad, the individual's condition deteriorates, the hospital at which the helipad is located must provide a Medical Screening Examination and stabilizing treatment within its capacity **if requested** by medical personnel accompanying the individual.
>
> - If as part of the EMS protocol, EMS activates helicopter evacuation of an individual with a potential emergency medical condition, the

---

[94] 42 C.F.R. § 489.24(i)(3) (2004).

hospital that has the helipad does not have an EMTALA obligation if they are not the recipient hospital, **unless a request** is made by EMS personnel, the individual or a legally responsible person acting on the individual's behalf for the examination or treatment of an emergency medical condition.[95]

Persons

Q 2:18   Any Individual: Which "individuals" are protected by EMTALA?

EMTALA obligations are triggered once "any individual (whether or not eligible for benefits under this subchapter) comes to the emergency department and a request is made on the individual's behalf."[96] Thus, EMTALA's protections extend beyond Medicare beneficiaries to any and all persons who come to the emergency department of a Medicare-participating hospital that operates a dedicated emergency department. "Any individual" includes not only the indigent but also all Medicare patients, minors, illegal aliens, managed care patients, private patients, intoxicated patients, and psychiatric patients.

The State Operations Manual states:

> Medicare participating hospitals that provide emergency services must provide a medical screening examination to any individual regardless of diagnosis (e.g., labor, AIDS), financial status (e.g., uninsured, Medicaid), race and color, national origin (e.g., Hispanic or Native American surnames), and/or disability, etc.[97]

Cautions: The courts have interpreted the statutory wording of "any individual" to mean that EMTALA can apply to any patient who comes to the emergency department, whether he or she is indigent, uninsured, insured, on Medicare, or a minor. In the past, emergency departments have sought guardian consent before treatment, but EMTALA now rules that a minor must be examined and stabilized or, if needed, transferred to another hospital for emergency stabilization without prior consent being obtained from a guardian. A hospital may violate EMTALA when it provides differential treatment to any patient for any reason.

The courts have uniformly interpreted the term "any individual" to mean that although EMTALA is a Medicare law under the Social Security Act, it is not limited to Medicare beneficiaries but applies to every patient who comes to the emergency department. The Code of Federal Regulations adds an economic

---

[95] U.S. Dep't HHS, CMS, State Operations Manual, App. V, Emergency Medical Treatment and Labor Act (EMTALA) Interpretive Guidelines, Part II, Tag A-2406/C-2406 (revised 7/16/2010).

[96] 42 U.S.C. § 1395dd(a).

[97] U.S. Dep't HHS, CMS, State Operations Manual, App. V, Emergency Medical Treatment and Labor Act (EMTALA) Interpretive Guidelines, Part II, Tag A-2406/C-2406 (revised 7/16/2010).

label to the phrase, stating: ". . . if an individual (whether or not eligible for Medicare benefits and regardless of ability to pay). . . ."[98]

On May 11, 2011, the U.S. District Court for the Northern District of California issued a decision granting a motion to dismiss, thus rejecting a mother's standing to bring her own cause of action under EMTALA for her minor daughter who was allegedly improperly discharged from Stanford Hospital.[99] The district court held that EMTALA's civil enforcement provision provides a private right of action only for the individual patient, not a non-patient third party, but noted that the mother could still bring an EMTALA claim on behalf of her daughter or assert a direct state law claim for negligent infliction of emotional distress.

The daughter of the Plaintiff was treated at Stanford Hospital for extreme pain following exploratory laparoscopic surgery and an appendectomy for abdominal pain at another hospital. Stanford Hospital refused to admit the daughter to inpatient pain management per the hospital's policy of not admitting anyone to inpatient pain management until failing "outpatient clinic." The Plaintiff asserted claims against Stanford Hospital under EMTALA, and the hospital moved to dismiss, arguing that the Plaintiff, as a non-patient third party, lacked standing to bring a direct EMTALA claim related to the treatment of her minor daughter. The Plaintiff asserted that the language of the EMTALA statute and authoritative precedent supported third-party standing.

In support of her claim for non-patient third-party standing, the Plaintiff relied on the Sixth Circuit's decision of *Moses v. Providence Hospital and Medical Center, Inc.*[100] In that case, the Sixth Circuit allowed a representative of the estate of a deceased woman to bring a claim under EMTALA. The deceased woman was murdered by her husband after the hospital allegedly prematurely released him. The Sixth Circuit commented that the "plain language of the civil enforcement provision of EMTALA contains very broad language regarding who may bring a claim: 'any individual who suffers personal harm as a direct result' of a hospital's EMTALA violation may sue," and it concluded that Congress did not intend for EMTALA's statutory scheme to apply to the same "individual" in all parts of the statute.

The district court here, however, decided not to follow *Moses* and, instead, found two federal district court decisions more persuasive. Those two decisions found the term "any individual," as used in EMTALA, to refer to the "individual patient," that being the individual for whose medical situation the emergency medical examination or treatment was sought. The district court reasoned that "[b]ecause Congress did limit expressly the persons to whom a hospital owes its EMTALA obligations, it was unnecessary for it to limit expressly the private right of action for enforcing these obligations." Overall, Stanford Hospital's motion to dismiss was granted, and the district court stated that "[e]xtending a private

---

[98] 42 C.F.R. § 489.24(a).

[99] Pauly v. Stanford Hosp., No. 10-CV-5582-JF (PSG) (N.D. Cal. May 11, 2011).

[100] 561 F.3d 580 (6th Cir. 2009).

right of action to a third party when the individual patient is still living would result in a significant expansion of liability for hospitals subject to EMTALA's provisions" and would be inconsistent with the statutory language.[101]

Q 2:19   Request: What constitutes a "request" for examination or treatment for a medical condition and who may make it?

Two different tests apply in determining whether an individual who comes to the hospital makes a "request" for emergency medical care:

1. If the individual makes a specific request (or a request is made on the individual's behalf) for examination or treatment of a medical condition; or

2. The individual's appearance or behavior would cause (or not cause) a "prudent layperson observer" to believe that examination or treatment for a medical condition is needed and that the individual would request that examination or treatment for him/herself if he or she were able to do so.[102]

The latter applies when an individual cannot make the request him- or herself, such as when the individual has passed out. The regulations further provide that an individual who can make the request but elects not to would not benefit from the "prudent layperson observer" requirement.

Cautions: The Act states: ". . . a *request* is made on the individual's behalf for examination or treatment for a medical condition." Anyone can make the "request" for medical care—the patient, a family member, a friend, a neighbor, a stranger, a babysitter, the police, or an illegal alien. Since EMTALA is a federal law that preempts state law, state laws that require prior permission to treat no longer apply. Parental consent is an example. Under EMTALA, a child qualifies as "any individual" and may request emergency care. EMTALA does not specify an "emergency" medical condition, so a request for care of any *medical* condition is covered. Additionally, in the absence of an actual request, CMS will presume a request exists if a prudent layperson observer would believe the individual needs examination or treatment for a medical condition.

The Act states: ". . . and a *request is made* on the individual's behalf for examination or treatment for a medical condition." The request does not have to be a formal verbal request since an individual may be so ill that he or she cannot request an examination and an individual who collapses on hospital grounds can trigger EMTALA. In these situations, CMS uses the prudent layperson standard. If a prudent layperson would believe that an individual has a medical condition that requires examination or treatment, this will trigger the offering of

---

[101] This case summary was written by Keith A. Mauriello, Partner, and Jessica T. Grozine, Associate, in the Healthcare Practice Group at Arnall Golden Gregory LLP, Atlanta, Georgia. It should not be construed as legal advice or opinion on specific matters.

[102] 68 Fed. Reg. 53,222, 53,234 (2003).

the MSE to that individual. Otherwise, anyone can make the request for the patient. However, CMS states that the standard would not be applied so broadly as to require a screening examination of an individual who was wheezing from a bad cough if that person was merely visiting a family member in the emergency department. CMS clarifies that, for individuals in the emergency department, the prudent layperson standard would not apply to "individuals who are fully capable of making a verbal request for examination or for a medical condition, but elect not to do so."[103]

A hospital procedural policy saved Fredonia Regional Hospital from an EMTALA civil liability suit. In *Cunningham v. Fredonia Regional Hospital*,[104] a family physician examined a patient in his office for chest pain and determined that the pain was not life threatening. That evening, the patient called the family physician's partner and complained that the pains were worse. This doctor told the patient to go to the emergency department for a pain shot. The emergency nurse gave the prescribed pain shot and sent the patient home. Later that night, the patient died of a myocardial infarction. The husband filed a lawsuit alleging that the hospital violated EMTALA by not providing an adequate MSE and not stabilizing an acute EMC. The hospital had two policies that could have applied to this patient. One was a chest pain policy that required all patients who are seen with "life-threatening symptoms of chest pain" to be examined by a physician. The other policy was a "determination of valid emergency illness/ injury policy" that allowed only nurse intervention with verbal physician contact when a patient is seen with "straightforward, straight diagnosis, and treatment with low complexity with low possibility of morbidity." The nurse claimed that she followed the second policy because she was in verbal contact with the ordering physician and the patient had already been examined by her physician. The district court determined that the emergency illness policy was applicable and rendered summary judgment in favor of the hospital.

The Tenth Circuit affirmed, finding that the hospital had followed its customary screening procedures. The court reasoned that the chest pain policy applied only when a patient was suffering "life-threatening symptoms of chest pain" and that this language would be superfluous if examination by a physician were required in every case of chest pain. The chest pain policy was inapplicable as long as the hospital personnel did not believe that the patient was suffering life-threatening chest pains or faced a high possibility of morbidity. In this case, the patient had not "requested" an examination for chest pain but merely presented for a prescribed pain shot ordered by her private physician.

This ruling is in agreement with most courts, in which EMTALA's stabilization requirement has been interpreted to apply only when the hospital actually detects an emergency condition, not when an emergency condition exists but is not diagnosed. Were it not for the existence of the emergency illness policy, the opposite ruling of an EMTALA violation could easily have been rendered. Still,

---

[103] 68 Fed. Reg. 53,222, 53,242 (2003).

[104] 98 F.3d 1349 (10th Cir. 1996).

emergency physicians should prudently offer MSEs to every patient who enters the emergency department.

However, CMS, unlike the court in *Cunningham*, would probably have no trouble citing this incident based on the surveyor's or physician review organization's (PRO's) determination that appropriate screening would have required the hospital to follow its normal chest pain protocol. An emergency department that ignores the possible implications of a set of symptoms such as chest pain or "worst headache of my life," regardless of what policies they believe support them, is likely to be cited for violations by CMS and to face a substantial fine from the Office of Inspector General (OIG).

Further, a hospital must be on notice of an individual's presentment and request for medical care. Absent notice, EMTALA does not apply. However, notice is tricky, and the standard of "reasonably knew or should have known" will probably apply. In this regard, a hospital's failure to have mechanisms in place so that personnel are readily able to identify, notify, and make emergency personnel aware and available to provide an MSE has to be factored into a hospital's claim that it did not have notice.

Q 2:20   If there is no "request:" What is the "prudent layperson" standard?

The regulations state:

> In the absence of such a request by or on behalf of the individual, a request on behalf of the individual will be considered to exist if a *prudent layperson* observer would believe, based on the individual's appearance or behavior, that the individual needs examination or treatment for a medical condition.[105]

Cautions: Although the statute states that an individual must make a request for examination or treatment for a medical condition, CMS states that such a "request" can be made when a prudent layperson observes that an individual needs emergency care. This situation occurs only when the patient is incapable of making the request him- or herself. It does not matter what a prudent layperson observes if a capable individual refuses care. Hospitals need to develop policies and procedures to respond when a prudent layperson determines that an individual on hospital property has an emergency condition.

In 1994, the American College of Emergency Physicians adopted a definition of emergency medicine policy statement that reads as follows:

> Emergency services are those health care services provided to evaluate and treat medical conditions of recent onset and severity that would

---

[105] 42 C.F.R. § 489.24(b)(1).

lead a prudent layperson, possessing an average knowledge of medicine and health, to believe that urgent and/or unscheduled care is required.[106]

In order to trigger EMTALA, a prudent layperson would have to identify a fairly obvious emergency medical condition, such as an individual passing out on hospital property. The "prudent layperson" standard is different from the objective "reasonable duty of care" standard of traditional medical liability law because it does not presume an average professional level of competency. This can affect liability in two contrary ways. In some cases, the standard may expand potential liability by precluding a defense based on lack of medical expertise; even nonmedical staff members such as secretaries will be held to the prudent layperson standard. But in other and perhaps more likely cases, the prudent layperson standard may reduce liability since symptoms that a prudent layperson may not be expected to interpret as serious (such as dizziness) will not trigger EMTALA protection, even if someone with medical training would (or should) have identified the danger.

Hospitals need to train their personnel who have any contact with the public to properly respond to prudent layperson perceived emergency conditions. Hospitals should establish policies where personnel in the emergency department must be contacted for directions on further medical response. Personnel should err on the side of caution so that medical response should be triggered even where the presence of a true emergency condition is questionable. Further, CMS guidance in this area will likely be unavailable until a specific incident is investigated.

> CMS states that the standard would not be applied so broadly as to require a screening examination of an individual who was wheezing from a bad cough if that person was merely visiting a family member in the emergency department. CMS clarifies that, for individuals in the emergency department, the prudent layperson standard would not apply to "individuals who are fully capable of making a verbal request for examination or for a medical condition, but elect not to do so."[107] CMS states that the prudent layperson standard is only a "legal standard" to be used to determine whether EMTALA was triggered and will be applied to the facts during an EMTALA review or investigation.[108] The standard applies at the time of the occurrence, not after the fact or some later day or time, which means that the application of the prudent layperson standard is at the time an individual presents to the hospital.

---

[106] www.ACEP.org.

[107] 68 Fed. Reg. 53,222, 53,242 (2003).

[108] 68 Fed. Reg. 53,222, 53,241-242 (2003).

Q 2:21   Discrimination: Must a patient prove discrimination for EMTALA liability?

In most cases, no. A patient does not need to prove discrimination or bad motive on the part of the hospital in order to succeed in an EMTALA lawsuit. An exception exists for claims filed in the Sixth Circuit[109] alleging a violation of EMTALA's "appropriate medical screening" requirement.

Cautions: While most courts have held that liability under EMTALA is not dependent on proof that the hospital had an economic motive or intent to discriminate, proof of such an improper motive may support a claim that the defendant's conduct constituted the type of patient dumping EMTALA was intended to remedy, rather than a random or inadvertent variance from standard procedures, which might not be actionable.

Early court cases reflected an attempt to construe EMTALA by its perceived intent rather than by the express language of the law and therefore applied EMTALA only to the indigent and those unable to pay. A key case following this "intent" approach was *Evitt v. University Heights Hospital,*[110] in which the court ruled that economic discrimination was necessary for an EMTALA violation. A patient's myocardial infarction was misdiagnosed as costochondritis, and the court concluded that her claim lay in the area of medical malpractice, an area traditionally regulated by state law.

Whether a motive for economic discrimination was necessary for a successful action under the Act became a hotly disputed topic in EMTALA litigation. In 1991, the Sixth Circuit issued the opinion that would act as the standard-bearer for the proposition that discrimination was a required element of an EMTALA violation. In *Cleland v. Bronson Health Care Group, Inc.,*[111] a child was discharged from the emergency department and died after a missed diagnosis of intussusception. The Sixth Circuit ruled that an EMTALA violation occurred only if a hospital acted with improper motives, such as discrimination on the basis of race, gender, ethnic group, politics, occupation, education, personal prejudice, drunkenness, or even spite.

By imposing an improper motivation requirement, the Sixth Circuit sought to prevent liability for EMTALA claims merely alleging physician negligence rather than the intentional dumping of protected individuals. This reasoning is in keeping with the legislative history of EMTALA, wherein Congress intended EMTALA to halt the denial of emergency care due to a patient's indigence or lack

---

[109] The Sixth Circuit covers Michigan, Ohio, Kentucky, and Tennessee. 28 U.S.C. § 41.

[110] 727 F. Supp. 495 (S.D. Ind. 1989). *See also* Nichols v. Estabrook, 741 F. Supp. 325, 330 (D.N.H. 1989) (finding that the congressional intent was "to provide some assurance that patients with emergency medical conditions will be examined and treated regardless of their financial resources"); Bryant v. Riddle Mem'l Hosp., 689 F. Supp. 490, 491 (E.D. Pa. 1988) (stating that EMTALA was enacted in order to combat the growing problem of patient-dumping); Thompson v. St. Anne's Hosp., 716 F. Supp. 8, 10 (N.D. Ill. 1989) (finding that EMTALA's legislative history "indicates that the statute is aimed at preventing hospitals not only from transferring indigent patients but also from simply rejecting them").

[111] 917 F.2d 266 (6th Cir. 1990).

of insurance. However, every other circuit to consider the issue has subsequently held, based on the text of the statute, that EMTALA may apply even when there is no bad motive on the hospital's part.

The first case applying the plain language of the Act to cover any patient was 1990's *Deberry v. Sherman Hospital Association.*[112] Veronica Deberry took her daughter, Shauntia, to Sherman Hospital's emergency because Shauntia had a fever and rash, along with irritability and lethargy, and her head tilted to the left. Shauntia was treated and discharged. Two days later, her condition worsened and she was brought back to the hospital. She was diagnosed with meningitis and eventually became deaf as a result of the disease. Veronica Deberry sued Sherman Hospital for violating EMTALA, alleging that Shauntia was discharged without her emergent medical condition being stabilized. Instead of looking at legislative intent, the court in *Deberry* departed from other courts by applying only EMTALA's plain language. Because the Act protects "any individual" who claims to have received improper emergency care, the court concluded it was not "free to change that language through a clandestine use of the legislative history."[113]

The court held that EMTALA did not mention indigence, inability to pay, or the hospital's motive as prerequisites to coverage and did not apply only to outright refusals to treat. The court ruled that the plaintiff's claim under EMTALA was proper even though the hospital had not "dump[ed]" the patient. Since the *Deberry* decision, most federal circuit courts of appeal have followed this reasoning and applied EMTALA's plain language to allow any patient to challenge his or her emergency treatment under EMTALA, whether or not there was economic discrimination.

In *Gatewood v. Washington Healthcare Corp.,*[114] for example, the D.C. Circuit[115] abandoned the discriminatory motive requirement for EMTALA. Mr. Gatewood, who was fully insured, arrived at Washington Healthcare complaining of chest pain radiating down his left arm. Dr. Mehlman, a resident, ordered blood tests, a chest X-ray, and an electrocardiogram (ECG). The tests were inconclusive, and Mr. Gatewood was discharged with a diagnosis of musculoskeletal chest pain. The next morning, Mr. Gatewood died from myocardial infarction. The D.C. Circuit ruled for the hospital, reasoning that a claim of misdiagnosis was not covered by EMTALA. The court established that EMTALA does not create sweeping federal liability for traditional state-based claims of negligence or malpractice. However, the court also explicitly rejected the discriminatory motive requirement, stating: "The motive for such departure (from standard screening procedures) is not important to this analysis, which applies whenever and for whatever reason a patient is denied the same level of

---

[112] 41 F. Supp. 1302 (N.D. Ill. 1990).

[113] *Deberry,* 741 F. Supp. 1302, 1307.

[114] 933 F.2d 1037 (D.C. Cir. 1991).

[115] Washington, D.C., has its own United States Court of Appeals called the D.C. Circuit. 28 U.S.C. § 41.

care provided others and guaranteed him or her by subsection 1395dd(a) (EMTALA)."[116]

In the 1994 case of *Power v. Arlington Hospital Association*,[117] the Fourth Circuit[118] adopted the position that "disparate" (different or non-uniform) treatment was sufficient to support an EMTALA action. Susan Power, a native of England who was not insured, had come to Arlington Hospital's emergency department complaining of pain in her left hip, abdomen, and back with radiation down her leg. She had chills and was unable to walk. After X-rays of the hip and urinary analysis were read as normal, she was released with a prescription for pain medication and a referral to an orthopedist with a discharge diagnosis of pain of unknown origin, possibly orthopedic or neurological in nature. She remained unable to walk. No blood work was done, nor was evaluation of the abdominal or back areas performed. Power returned the next day with septic shock and was admitted. Her disease eventually resulted in bilateral leg amputations, loss of sight in one eye, and severe pulmonary damage. Power brought suit against Arlington Hospital, alleging that it violated EMTALA by failing to provide her an "appropriate medical screening" when she first came to the emergency department. The case proceeded to trial, and the jury returned a verdict in favor of Susan Power on the EMTALA violation and awarded actual damages of $5 million.

The verdict was upheld on appeal. The Fourth Circuit adopted the D.C. Circuit's position from *Gatewood*, stating that "there is nothing in the statute itself that requires proof of indigence, inability to pay, or any other improper motive on the part of a hospital as a prerequisite to [EMTALA] recovery."[119] The court reasoned that a motive requirement would be unfair to the plaintiff because the statutory language did not demand it, the broad range of discriminatory motives suggested by the *Cleland* court posed no real limit at all, and the issue of the "proof predicament":

> having to prove the existence of an improper motive on the part of a hospital, its employees or its physicians, would make a civil EMTALA claim virtually impossible. We do not believe that proving the inner thoughts and prejudices of attending hospital personnel is required in order to recover under EMTALA.[120]

The Fourth Circuit held that in the absence of hospital policies and procedures, evidence of a deviation from standard of care (a negligence theory that brings EMTALA close to a malpractice statute) would be evidence of disparate treatment. The court placed the burden on the hospital to demonstrate that it

---

[116] *Gatewood*, 933 F.2d 1037, 1041.

[117] 42 F.3d 851 (4th Cir. 1994).

[118] The Fourth Circuit covers Maryland, West Virginia, Virginia, North Carolina, and South Carolina. 28 U.S.C. § 41.

[119] *Power*, 42 F.3d 851, 857.

[120] *Power*, 42 F.3d 851, 857.

followed the evaluation procedures it would have applied to anyone else in those circumstances.

Other circuits have followed suit. In 1995, the First Circuit in *Correa v. Hospital San Francisco* held that Carmen Gonzalez was denied an appropriate medical screening when she was ignored for hours in the waiting room after having complained of chest pains. The First Circuit held that "regardless of motive, a complete failure to attend a patient who presents a condition that practically everyone knows may indicate an immediate and acute threat to life can constitute a denial of an appropriate medical screening examination."[121] The court noted that "[t]he essence of this requirement is that there be some screening procedure, and that it be administered even-handedly."[122] Similarly, in 1996, the Eighth Circuit in *Summers v. Baptist Medical Center Arkadelphia* held that a showing of improper motive "would suffice to make out a case of inappropriate screening, but we cannot agree that such evidence of improper motivation is essential."[123] EMTALA was, in a sense, "a strict-liability provision. If a hospital fails to provide an appropriate medical screening examination, it is liable, no matter what the motivation was for this failure."[124]

On January 13, 1999, in *Roberts v. Galen of Virginia*, the United States Supreme Court weighed in on the matter, if only partially.[125] In *Roberts*, Humana Hospital transferred Wanda Johnson to a nursing home after six weeks of inpatient care for serious injuries suffered when she was run over by a truck. She developed urosepsis the day after transfer and was re-hospitalized at another hospital. When Johnson was refused state aid for her second set of hospital bills, her aunt, Jane Roberts, sued Humana Hospital for violation of EMTALA. Following the precedent it set in *Cleland*, the Sixth Circuit affirmed the district court's decision to dismiss the suit, ruling that Roberts lacked the required proof that Humana Hospital transferred Johnson because of an improper motive, such as discrimination based on indigence, race, or gender.[126] The Supreme Court reversed and remanded.

The Supreme Court distinguished *Cleland* from *Roberts* by noting that the *Cleland* court derived its improper motive test from the "appropriate medical screening" language of Section 1395dd(a). According to *Cleland*, the word "appropriate" regulated the motives underlying a hospital's actions, such that discriminatory or otherwise improper motives were barred.[127] *Roberts*, on the other hand, involved a violation of Section 1395dd(b), which requires a hospital to stabilize a patient but does not call for "appropriate" stabilization. Because the stabilization arm of EMTALA lacks an appropriateness requirement, the Supreme Court decided that *Cleland's* improper motive test was not relevant to

---

[121] Correa v. Hospital San Francisco, 69 F.3d 1184, 1193 (1st Cir. 1995).

[122] *Correa*, 69 F.3d 1184, 1192.

[123] Summers v. Baptist Med. Ctr. Arkadelphia, 91 F.3d 1132, 1138 (8th Cir. 1996).

[124] *Summers*, 91 F.3d 1132, 1137-38.

[125] Roberts v. Galen of Va., Inc., 525 U.S. 249 (1999).

[126] *Roberts*, 111 F.3d 405, 406-07, *rev'd by* 525 U.S. 249 (1999).

[127] *Cleland*, 917 F.2d 266, 272.

its analysis in *Roberts* and explicitly declined to rule on the correctness of *Cleland*'s rationale. However, the Supreme Court tellingly noted in dictum that the *Cleland* court's interpretation of Section 1395dd(a) conflicted with the law of all other circuits who have ruled on the matter.[128] The Supreme Court concluded that the text of Section 1395dd(b) could not be reasonably read to contain an express or implied "improper motive" requirement.

Under the precedent set by *Roberts*, a stabilization claim under EMTALA does not require proof of improper motive or discrimination on the part of the hospital, its staff, or physicians as a prerequisite for recovery. While *Roberts* does not bind lower courts analyzing the medical screening requirement of EMTALA, the tone of the Supreme Court's dictum, combined with the fact that all other circuits ruling on the issue have adopted a contrary stance, indicates that an improper motive test has no textual basis in other subsections of the statute. If the issue arises again, application of an improper motive test for other kinds of EMTALA claims is unlikely to withstand Supreme Court scrutiny. Notably, however, the Sixth Circuit alone still requires plaintiffs alleging a violation of the "appropriate medical screening" duty to make a showing of improper motive.[129] The CMS State Operations Manual also includes a statement that articulates the antidiscriminatory underpinnings of EMTALA: "Medicare participating hospitals that provide emergency services must provide a medical screening examination to any individual regardless of diagnosis (e.g., labor, AIDS), financial status (e.g., uninsured, Medicaid), race and color, national origin (e.g., Hispanic or Native American surnames), and/or disability, etc."[130]

Q 2:22   Illegal Immigrants: Does EMTALA apply to illegal immigrants?

Yes. The term "any individual" in EMTALA requires hospitals to provide emergency care to all patients who come to the emergency department, regardless of their immigration status.

Cautions: All EMTALA's threats of Medicare participation termination, OIG fines, civil suits, and other governmental agency involvement such as the Department of Civil Rights apply if a hospital denies care to illegal aliens.

Hospitals are required to provide emergency medical care to all individuals regardless of their immigration status in order to qualify for Medicare/Medicaid funding. Illegal immigrants tend to use emergency rooms as their principal source of medical care because they tend to be poor and lack private or

---

[128] *Roberts*, 525 U.S. 249, 253 n. 1 (1999), *citing Summers*, 91 F.3d 1132, 1137-38 (en banc); *Correa*, 69 F.3d 1184, 1193-94; Repp v. Anadarko Mun. Hosp., 43 F.3d 519, 522 (10th Cir. 1994); *Power*, 42 F.3d 851, 857; *Gatewood*, 933 F.2d 1037, 1041.

[129] Estate of Taylor v. Paul B. Hall Reg'l Med. Ctr., 182 F.3d 918 (6th Cir. 1999) (unpublished disposition) ("As the Supreme Court recently clarified, § 1395dd(b) claims—alleging a failure to stabilize an emergency patient—do not require an EMTALA plaintiff to prove that the defendant acted with an improper motive. Section 1395dd(a) claims, on the other hand—concerning the screening of emergency patients—carry with them the burden to demonstrate an improper motive on the part of defendant.") (internal citations omitted).

[130] U.S. Dep't HHS, CMS, State Operations Manual, App. V, Emergency Medical Treatment and Labor Act (EMTALA) Interpretive Guidelines, Part II, Tag A-2406/C-2406 (revised 7/16/2010).

employment insurance.[131] Between 1993 and 2003, 60 California hospitals were forced to close, and many scaled back their services due to outstanding bills for services rendered. It has been suggested that the Los Angeles County Trauma Care Network, one of the country's best emergency medical response organizations, was mostly dismantled as a result of EMTALA and the burden illegal immigrants placed on it.[132] The estimation is that hospitals collectively spend about $2 billion a year in unpaid medical expenses to treat undocumented immigrants.[133] The Parkland Health and Hospital system in Dallas reported $100 million in uncompensated care costs for people who couldn't prove U.S. citizenship between March 1, 2005, when it first started tracking this figure, and September 30, 2006. Undocumented women gave birth to about 30 babies every day at Parkland in fiscal year 2006. That's almost 70 percent of the 16,489 births at the hospital.[134] In 2007, Medi-Cal spent approximately $20 million on the care of 460 uninsured immigrants.[135]

In 2003, the Senate Finance Committee approved a bill that allocated funds to help hospitals with this illegal immigrant burden. Section 1011 of the Medicare Prescription Drug, Improvement and Modernization Act (MMA) allocated $1 billion over fiscal years 2005–2008 to reimburse hospitals, physicians, and ambulance providers for emergency care provided to undocumented aliens. Federal dollars allocated annually through Section 1011 total $250 million for fiscal years 2005 to 2008.[136] CMS published a final guidance on May 13, 2005.[137] The largest allocations in the 2005 fiscal year went to California, which received $70.8 million; Texas, $46 million; Arizona, $45 million; New York, $12.3 million; Illinois, $10.3 million; Florida, $8.7 million; and New Mexico, $5.1 million.[138] The problem is that to be eligible for Section 1011 funds, enrolled emergency department providers must document the undocumented status of uninsured patients who are unauthorized residents or other specified aliens who also are ineligible for Medicaid. This can be a difficult if not impossible task, as these patients may fear that revealing their undocumented status will jeopardize their living situation. It perhaps comes as no surprise, then, that nearly 75 percent of the available Section 1011 funds remain unclaimed.[139]

---

[131] Medeleine Pelner Cosman, *Illegal Aliens and American Medicine*, 10 J. Am. Physicians & Surgeons 6, 6 (2005).

[132] Medeleine Pelner Cosman, *Illegal Aliens and American Medicine*, 10 J. Am. Physicians & Surgeons 6, 6 (2005).

[133] Dana Canedy, *Hospitals Feeling Strain from Illegal Immigrants*, N.Y. Times, Aug. 22, 2002, at 116.

[134] Doug Trapp, American Medical Ass'n News, Jan. 8, 2007.

[135] Deborah Sontag, *Deported in Coma, Saved Back in U.S.*, N.Y. Times, Nov. 9, 2008, at A1, available at http://www.nytimes.com/2008/11.09/us09deport.html.

[136] The Centers for Medicare & Medicaid Services, FY 2007 State Allocations for Section 1011 of the Medicare Modernization Act, Federal Reimbursement for Emergency Health Services to Undocumented Aliens.

[137] 70 Fed. Reg. 25,578 (2005).

[138] Robert Pear, *United States Is Linking Status of Aliens to Hospital Aid*, N.Y. Times, Aug. 10, 2004, at A1.

[139] Laura Merisalo, *Editor's Corner*, 16 No. 8 Healthcare Registration 2.

Section 1011 is a patient access issue, as front-end registration employees (at Section 1011 enrolled facilities) must document that the organization did indeed provide emergency care to an undocumented alien and so is eligible to receive Section 1011 payment for that care. Patient access employees need to attest to certain items that lead them to believe a patient is an undocumented alien, without directly asking patients. Section 1011 presents a complex challenge for patient access, as the manner in which queries are made about an emergency patient's citizenship status is critical. If improperly handled, the provider organization may be in violation of civil rights issues and/or EMTALA.

Q 2:23   Outpatients: Does EMTALA apply to patients who come to the hospital for routine outpatient care?

No. The State Operations Manual states:

> If an individual is registered as an outpatient of the hospital and they present on hospital property but not to a dedicated emergency department, the hospital does not incur an EMTALA obligation with respect to that individual if they have begun to receive a scheduled course of outpatient care. Such an individual is protected by the hospital Conditions of Participation (CoPs) that protect patients' health and safety and to ensure that quality care is furnished to all patients in Medicare-participating hospital. If such an individual experiences an EMC while receiving outpatient care, the hospital does not have an obligation to conduct an MSE for that patient. As discussed in greater detail below, such a patient has adequate protections under the Medicare CoPs and state law.[140]

CMS changed the Code of Federal Regulations in Section 489.24(b) to state that an exception to EMTALA application would apply for an outpatient, defined as:

> [a]n individual who has begun to receive outpatient services as part of an encounter, as defined in Sec. 410.2 of this chapter, other than an encounter that the hospital is obligated by this section to provide. . . . [141]

Cautions: CMS has clarified that EMTALA does not apply to outpatients (as defined in 42 C.F.R. § 410.2) who are already under medical care and develop potential emergency conditions. An outpatient, for example, undergoing a biopsy procedure who develops hypotension would be treated directly by the anesthesiologist and/or the attending surgeon. EMTALA obligations such as transfer restrictions would not be activated. Importantly, CMS states further that even if an outpatient with an emergency medical condition is transported to the dedicated emergency department for further care, EMTALA is still not triggered. CMS feels that such an outpatient who

---

[140] U.S. Dep't HHS, CMS, State Operations Manual, App. V, Emergency Medical Treatment and Labor Act (EMTALA) Interpretive Guidelines, Part II, Tag A-2406/C-2406 (revised 7/16/2010).

[141] 68 Fed. Reg. 53,222, 53,240 (2003).

experiences what may be an emergency medical condition after the start of the outpatient encounter with a health professional would already have all the protections afforded to patients of a hospital under the Medicare hospital CoPs found in 42 C.F.R. § 482. Hospitals that fail to provide treatment to these patients already face termination of their Medicare provider agreements for a violation of the CoPs. CMS also states that these patients are already protected by state malpractice laws as well as under general rules of ethics governing the medical profession. Hospitals should draft specific policies to address situations where outpatients develop acute emergency conditions.

On September 2, 2009, the U.S. Court of Appeals for the Third Circuit affirmed the grant of summary judgment in a case previously decided in January 2008 by the U.S. District Court for the Eastern District of Pennsylvania. The court dismissed the EMTALA claim that several hospitals and physicians failed to stabilize and inappropriately transferred a patient when the patient with a high-risk pregnancy did not present in an emergent state and was not in an emergent state until she began to undergo a scheduled monitoring at the primary hospital.[142]

Because of her insulin-dependent diabetes, Torretti's pregnancy was high risk. Thus, Torretti's primary obstetrician, Dr. Patricia McConnell, referred Torretti to the Paoli Hospital Perinatal Testing Center for monitoring throughout the pregnancy. On May 23, Torretti drove to Paoli for the routine appointment, which included an ultrasound and a fetal non-stress test. The ultrasound showed excess amniotic fluid, and the non-stress test showed some contractions. Dr. Andres Gerson, a perinatologist, then referred Torretti to Lankenau Hospital for longer-term monitoring. Dr. Gerson did not feel that the situation was an emergency that would have required an ambulance. The Torrettis drove to Lankenau Hospital by car. Shortly after arriving at Lankenau Hospital, Torretti was placed on a monitor, which showed significant abnormalities. The baby, Christopher, was born via caesarean section, but he had severe brain damage.

The Torrettis sued the hospitals and doctors under EMTALA as well as state statutory and common-law claims. They asserted a federal question under EMTALA for inappropriate medical screening, stabilizing treatment, and transfer. The district court ruled that the Torrettis did not offer sufficient evidence to raise a reasonable inference that the defendants knew Torretti presented a medical emergency, and it thus granted the defense motion for summary judgment. The plaintiffs appealed the decision to the Third Circuit Court of Appeals.

In affirming the trial court's ruling, the appellate court reviewed EMTALA, as well as the Centers for Medicare & Medicaid Services (CMS) regulations promulgated to interpret and apply EMTALA. Turning to the regulations' interpretation of the statute, the court wrote:

---

[142] Torretti v. Main Line Hosps. Inc., 580 F.3d 168 (3d Cir. 2009).

EMTALA's requirements are triggered when an "individual" comes to the emergency department. An "individual" only "comes to the emergency department" if that person is not already a "patient." The Regulation defines "patient" . . . as "[a]n individual who has begun to receive outpatient services as part of an encounter." CMS explains that EMTALA does not apply to outpatients, even if during an outpatient encounter "they are later found to have an emergency medical condition . . . [and] are transported to the hospital's dedicated emergency department."[143]

The court then iterated the fact that Torretti came to Paoli for her scheduled appointment and routine monitoring but did not present as an emergency to the Paoli medical staff, thus concluding that Torretti's circumstances are not those contemplated by EMTALA coverage.

There are times when it would be prudent for a hospital to offer a medical screening examination even if a patient presented for outpatient care. Regardless of outpatient status, if a patient's condition or appearance would lead a prudent layperson to believe that an acute emergency medical condition may be present, a hospital should offer a medical screening examination. A patient who develops chest pain while waiting for laboratory tests, for example, would qualify for EMTALA examination. Outpatient status does not exempt a hospital from EMTALA obligations in these conditions. It is also key to understand that outpatient care must have already been initiated to excuse EMTALA obligations; thus, a patient who walks onto hospital property and collapses before the start of outpatient care is still protected by EMTALA.

Q 2:24   Inpatients: Does EMTALA apply to inpatients?

No. EMTALA obligations end for a hospital once a patient is admitted as an inpatient in good faith.

The Code of Federal Regulations states:

> If an emergency medical condition is determined to exist, (the hospital) must provide any necessary stabilizing treatment, as defined in paragraph (d) of this section, or an appropriate transfer as defined in paragraph (e) of this section. If the hospital admits the individual as an inpatient for further treatment, the hospital's obligation under this section ends, as specified in paragraph (d)(2) of this section.[144]

CMS defines "inpatient" in the Code of Federal Regulations as:

> an individual who is admitted to a hospital for bed occupancy for purposes of receiving inpatient hospital services as described in Sec. 409.10(a) of this chapter with the expectation that he or she will remain at least overnight and occupy a bed even though the situation later

---

[143] *Toretti*, 580 F.3d 168, 175.

[144] 42 C.F.R. § 489.24(a)(ii).

develops that the individual can be discharged or transferred to another hospital and does not actually use a hospital bed overnight.[145]

For emergency department patients who are admitted to the hospital, the Code of Federal Regulations at Section 489.24(d)(2) states:

(2) Exception: Application to inpatients.

   (i)   If a hospital has screened an individual under paragraph (a) of this section and found the individual to have an emergency medical condition, and admits that individual as an inpatient in good faith in order to stabilize the emergency medical condition, the hospital has satisfied its special responsibilities under this section with respect to that individual.

  (ii)   This section is not applicable to an inpatient who was admitted for elective (nonemergency) diagnosis or treatment.

 (iii)   A hospital is required by the conditions of participation for hospitals under Part 482 of this chapter to provide care to its inpatients in accordance with those conditions of participation.[146]

Cautions: The inpatient exception for EMTALA is an administrative decision by CMS. The courts are not bound by this interpretation and, in a civil suit, may still rule differently. In order for EMTALA's responsibility to end, the hospital must *formally* admit the patient to the hospital. Further, the stabilization process begun in the emergency department must continue in the inpatient wards.

The State Operations Manual emphasizes:

If an individual is admitted as an inpatient, EMCs must be stabilized either by the hospital to which an individual presents or the hospital to which the individual is transferred. If a woman is in labor, the hospital must deliver the baby and the placenta or transfer appropriately. She may not be transferred unless she, or a legally responsible person acting on her behalf, requests a transfer and a physician or other qualified medical personnel, in consultation with a physician, certifies that the benefits to the woman and/or the unborn child outweigh the risks associated with the transfer.[147]

EMTALA does not cover direct inpatient admissions even when sent through the emergency department by a private physician from his or her office, a nursing home, the patient's home, another hospital, or elsewhere. The Code of Federal Regulations states: "This section is not applicable to an inpatient who was admitted for elective (nonemergency) diagnosis or treatment."[148]

---

[145] 42 C.F.R. § 489.24(b).

[146] 42 C.F.R. § 489.24(d).

[147] U.S. Dep't HHS, CMS, State Operations Manual, App. V, Emergency Medical Treatment and Labor Act (EMTALA) Interpretive Guidelines, Part II, Tag A-2407/C-2407 (revised 5/29/2009).

[148] 42 C.F.R. § 489.24(d)(2)(ii).

Once the decision to admit is made, hospitals must document in the patient's chart and medical record the precise timing of such decision in order to define when EMTALA obligations end for that patient. Once admitted, even if the patient is still on hold in the emergency department waiting for an inpatient bed, EMTALA responsibilities end for that patient.[149] A patient placed in an observation unit attached to the emergency department has not been formally admitted as an inpatient, so the observation patients are still protected by EMTALA.

CMS agreed with the ruling of the Ninth Circuit in the 2002 case *Bryant v. Adventist Health System/west*[150] that an EMTALA patient stabilization requirement ends when an emergency room patient is admitted for inpatient care, absent evidence that the admission was done to avoid EMTALA requirements. In *Bryant*, David Bryant's parents brought him to the emergency department of Redbud Community Hospital because he had a respiratory infection. David was a severely disabled 17-year-old with the mental capacity of a young child. Dr. Robert Rosenthal, the emergency physician, interpreted David's chest x-ray as acute pneumonia. Dr. Rosenthal then treated David with an injection of the antibiotic Rocephin and discharged him once he appeared stable. The next day, a radiologist found the presence of a lung abscess on the chest x-ray. The hospital called the family to bring David back to the hospital. The hospital admitted David, but he eventually died from his illness. The family sued the hospital, alleging that the hospital violated EMTALA by discharging David in an unstable condition after the first emergency department visit and also by failing to stabilize his condition after admission to the hospital. The district court ruled for the hospital stating that Redbud Hospital could not be liable under EMTALA merely because its medical staff failed to detect an emergency medical condition. The district court also ruled that once Redbud admitted David for inpatient care, the family's remedies for David's alleged inadequate medical care were under state malpractice laws, not EMTALA. The court of appeals agreed, ruling that a hospital does not violate EMTALA if the hospital fails to detect or misdiagnose an emergency condition after an adequate screening examination. Further, the appeals court ruled that the patient stabilization requirements of EMTALA ended when a patient was admitted to the hospital for inpatient care.

In the final rules, CMS establishes that EMTALA will not apply to patients routinely admitted to the hospital.[151] By stating that EMTALA obligations end for an emergency department patient once the patient is admitted to the hospital, CMS went further than their proposed rules from May 2002. The proposed rule had stated that EMTALA would remain active for an emergency department patient admitted with an unstabilized emergency medical condition until that condition is stabilized. However, the 2003 final rules terminate EMTALA obligations once a patient is admitted to the hospital for further care,

---

[149] 68 Fed. Reg. 53,222, 53,244-248 (2003).

[150] 289 F.3d 1162 (9th Cir. 2002).

[151] 68 Fed. Reg. 53,222, 53,244-245 (2003).

regardless of whether the found EMC is stabilized. CMS reasoned that EMTALA protection is no longer needed once a patient is admitted to the hospital because he or she is then protected by state malpractice and tort laws, as well as the Medicare CoPs. CMS may terminate the Medicare provider agreement with a hospital for violations of CoPs.

The State Operations Manual states:

> A hospital continues to have a responsibility to meet the patient emergency needs in accordance with hospital CoPs at 42 CFR Part 482. The hospital CoPs protect individuals who are admitted, and they do not permit the hospital to inappropriately discharge or transfer any patient to another facility. The hospital CoPs that are most relevant in this case are as follows: emergency services; governing body; discharge planning; quality assurance; and medical staff.

> Hospitals are responsible for assuring that inpatients receive acceptable medical care upon admission. Hospital services for inpatients should include diagnostic services and therapeutic services for medical diagnosis, treatment, and care of the injured, disabled or sick persons with the intention of treating patients.[152]

CMS cautions that the patient must be admitted *in good faith* for further necessary medical care and that it is expected the patient will be admitted at least overnight. A hospital cannot admit a patient from the emergency department with an unstable condition only to immediately transfer him or her in an attempt to avoid EMTALA obligations. For example, a hospital cannot admit a patient in labor and then transfer her before delivery of the baby and placenta. CMS states in its State Operations Manual:

> If an individual is admitted as an inpatient, Emergency Medical Conditions must be stabilized either by the hospital to which an individual presents or the hospital must deliver the baby and the placenta or transfer appropriately. She may not be transferred unless she, or a legally responsible person acting on her behalf, requests a transfer and a physician or other qualified medical personnel, in consultation with a physician, certifies that the benefits to the woman and/or the unborn child outweigh the risks associated with the transfer.[153]

The State Operations Manual further warns: "If the surveyor discovers during the investigation that a hospital did not admit an individual in good faith with the intention of providing treatment (i.e., the hospital used the inpatient admission as a means to avoid EMTALA requirements), then the hospital is considered liable under EMTALA and actions may be pursued."[154] Finally, the Manual instructs its surveyors:

---

[152] U.S. Dep't HHS, CMS, State Operations Manual, App. V, Emergency Medical Treatment and Labor Act (EMTALA) Interpretive Guidelines, Part II, Tag A-2407/C-2407 (revised 5/29/2009).

[153] U.S. Dep't HHS, CMS, State Operations Manual, App. V, Emergency Medical Treatment and Labor Act (EMTALA) Interpretive Guidelines, Part II, Tag A-2407/C-2407 (revised 5/29/2009).

[154] U.S. Dep't HHS, CMS, State Operations Manual, App. V, Interpretive Guidelines for Responsibilities of Medicare Participating Hospitals in Emergency Cases, Part II, Tag A-2406/C-2406 (revised 7/16/2010).

If during an EMTALA investigation there is a question as to whether an individual was admitted so that a hospital could avoid its EMTALA obligation, the State Agency surveyor is to consult with Regional Office personnel to determine if the survey should be expanded to a survey of the hospital CoPs. After completion of the survey, the case is to be forwarded to the Regional Office for violation determination. If it is determined that the hospital admitted the individual solely for the purpose of avoiding its EMTALA obligation, then the hospital is liable under EMTALA and may be subject to further enforcement action.[155]

In *Morgan v. North Mississippi Medical Center,*[156] an EMTALA suit was allowed to proceed because a hospital's admission of a patient may have been subterfuge to avoid liability. On August 22, 2003, a man fell from a tree and sustained fractured ribs, fractured vertebrae, a dislocated shoulder, and a pulmonary contusion. The man, who did not have medical insurance, was treated at a nearby hospital and admitted to the hospital fur further care of his injuries. The hospital subsequently notified the man's wife that she would need to make financial arrangements for her husband's treatment. The wife did not make such arrangements. Nine days after admission, the hospital discharged the man despite ongoing medical difficulties. He was transported home by ambulance, physically carried into the house, and placed in bed. The man died twelve hours later from untreated injuries related to his fall. The wife filed a lawsuit against the hospital alleging violation of EMTALA. The court dismissed the wife's claim for failure to screen because she could not prove that the hospital's medical screening examination was any different from that afforded to others. However, the court allowed the claim on failure to stabilize to proceed, ruling that it was appropriate for a jury to decide whether the hospital's admission of the patient was a subterfuge to avoid EMTALA liability.

The Medicare CoPs require that the governing body of a hospital that participates in Medicare must ensure that its medical staff has written policies and procedures for appraising emergencies, initial treatment, and referral when appropriate. In a broader sense, the governing body must ensure that there is an effective, hospital-wide quality assurance program in place to evaluate the quality of care provided. In addition, the hospital must implement a discharge planning process that applies to all patients. Hospitals must also have an organized medical staff that operates under bylaws approved by the governing body that is responsible for the quality of care provided to the hospital's patients.

The consequence of a hospital's noncompliance with Medicare CoPs is equally as harsh as for EMTALA violations. Violation of Medicare's conditions of participation can, in rare circumstances, lead to termination of the hospital's Medicare provider agreement. More often, noncompliance leads to fines. Civil monetary fines totaling $5.6 million were imposed on 194 hospitals and 19 physicians between 1995 and 2000. Most fines prior to 2000 were less than

---

[155] U.S. Dep't HHS, CMS, State Operations Manual, App. V, Emergency Medical Treatment and Labor Act (EMTALA) Interpretive Guidelines, Part II, Tag A-2407/C-2407 (revised 5/29/2009).

[156] 403 F. Supp. 2d 1115 (S.D. Ala. 2005).

$25,000.[157] If, during an EMTALA investigation, a surveyor finds that it appears the CoPs were not met, the surveyor is instructed to contact the regional office for authorization to extend the investigation.[158]

In April 2008, CMS proposed to amend 42 C.F.R. § 489.24(f) to add a provision that when an individual covered by EMTALA is admitted as an inpatient and remains unstable to the point where the admitting hospital truly becomes unable to stabilize the emergency medical condition, then a receiving hospital with specialized capabilities able to treat the patient still has an EMTALA obligation to accept the patient on transfer. After receiving a barrage of negative feedback from the medical community, CMS reconsidered this provision and maintained the position that once admitted as an inpatient, EMTALA obligation ends for the admitting hospital as well as any other hospital that may have specialized capabilities to treat the patient on transfer.[159]

In early 2012, HHS once again considered the question of whether EMTALA applied to an inpatient admitted to a hospital. HHS concluded:

> if an individual "comes to the [hospital's] emergency department," as we have defined that term in regulation, and the hospital provides an appropriate medical screening examination and determines that an EMC exists, and then admits the individual in good faith in order to stabilize the EMC, that hospital has satisfied its EMTALA obligation towards that patient.[160]

Q 2:25   Prisoners: Do EMTALA requirements apply to prisoners brought to the emergency department by police?

Yes, EMTALA applies to prisoners brought to the dedicated emergency department.

The State Operations Manual states:

> Attention to detail concerning blood alcohol testing (BAT) in the ED is instrumental when determining if a MSE is to be conducted. If an individual is brought to the ED and law enforcement personnel request that emergency department personnel draw blood for a BAT only and does not request examination or treatment for a medical condition, such as intoxication and a prudent lay person observer would not believe that the individual needed such examination or treatment, then the EMTALA's screening requirement is not applicable to this situation because the only request made on behalf of the individual was for evidence. However, if for example, the individual in police custody was involved in a motor vehicle accident or may have sustained injury to him or

---

[157] R. Rockefeller, *The Emergency Medical Treatment and Active Labor Act*, Massachusetts Health and Hospital Law Manual, Vol. II, Ch. 12, § 12.15.

[158] U.S. Dep't HHS, CMS, State Operations Manual, App. V, Emergency Medical Treatment and Labor Act (EMTALA) Interpretive Guidelines, Part II, Tag A-2407/C-2407 (revised 5/29/2009).

[159] 73 Fed. Reg. 48,434, 48,655-660 (2008).

[160] 77 Fed. Reg. 5217 (Feb. 2, 2012). See **Appendix G** for the full text.

herself and presents to the ED a MSE would be warranted to determine if an EMC exists.

When law enforcement officials request hospital emergency personnel to provide clearance for incarceration, the hospital has an EMTALA obligation to provide a MSE to determine if an EMC exists. If no EMC is present, the hospital has met its EMTALA obligation and no further actions are necessary for EMTALA compliance.

Surveyors will evaluate each case on its own merit when determining a hospital's EMTALA obligation when law enforcement officials request screening or BAT for use as evidence in criminal proceedings. This principle also applies to sexual assault cases.[161]

Cautions: Technically, prisoners brought to the emergency department "only" for drug or alcohol testing would not be governed by EMTALA since such testing would fall under nonemergency services. However, hospitals would be prudent to offer a medical screening examination to all prisoners to avoid missing any occult emergency medical condition. Persons arrested for "drunk driving" or who are involved in car accidents or other altercations are actually not brought to the emergency department for blood alcohol testing; they are brought to the emergency department because the police noticed aberrant behavior and *suspected* it to be caused by alcohol intoxication. Alcohol intoxication should not automatically be presumed to be the cause of a patient's condition. CMS believes alcohol intoxication to be a "sufficiently severe medical symptom to warrant the label 'emergency medical condition,'[162] and therefore, an intoxicated individual has an Emergency Medical Condition until the hospital proves otherwise."

In *Gooch v. West Virginia Department of Public Safety, Raleigh General Hospital*,[163] Mr. Gooch had been diagnosed with bronchopneumonia and given an injection of penicillin by his private physician. The next day, Gooch was observed to be weaving in traffic on an interstate highway in Kentucky. A state trooper pulled Gooch over and arrested him on suspicion of drunken driving when a bottle of whisky was found in the car. The trooper brought Gooch to Raleigh General Hospital for a blood alcohol test. Gooch was not offered any medical examination or treatment. He was released the next day. The following day, Gooch was admitted to another hospital in West Virginia, where he died of complications of Streptococcal pneumonia.

The blood test taken at Raleigh General was negative for drugs and alcohol. Mrs. Gooch filed suit against Raleigh General and the West Virginia Department of Public Safety for negligence in the handling of her husband and violation of EMTALA by failing to provide an adequate medical screening examination. The West Virginia Supreme Court ruled for the defense, finding that there was nothing in the records "that would suggest that Mr. Gooch's appearance was

---

[161] U.S. Dep't HHS, CMS, State Operations Manual, App. V, Emergency Medical Treatment and Labor Act (EMTALA) Interpretive Guidelines, Part II, Tag A-2406/C-2406 (revised 7/16/2010).

[162] 59 Fed. Reg. 32,086, 32,107-108 (1994).

[163] 465 S.E.2d 628 (W. Va. 1995).

inconsistent with being under the influence or that would otherwise permit a rational trier of fact to conclude [that the initial] hospital personnel knew or reasonably should have known he was ill."[164] The court believed that Gooch's appearance in the emergency department did not trigger any concerns for a medical emergency condition; therefore, the hospital should not be held liable.

On the other hand, a Pennsylvania court ruled in 1996 that the estate of a man who died several days after a hospital had performed a blood alcohol test could sue the hospital under EMTALA.[165] On August 9, 1993, the Pennsylvania State Police took Raymond Felix to Montgomery Hospital Medical Center for a blood alcohol test. While there, Felix was lethargic and unable to sit up without assistance. He signed a "Consent to Hospital Care" form and the blood test was performed. After the test, Felix was placed in a holding cell at the police station. He was found without pulse or respiration the next morning and was transferred to the hospital, where he died of cerebral hypoxia complicating severe athero-sclerotic cardiovascular disease two days later. The main issue in the lawsuit was whether Felix "requested" an examination or treatment for a medical condition. The hospital argued that Felix had failed to request an examination, saying that police brought him to the emergency department for a blood alcohol test only. The court would not dismiss the suit, agreeing with the plaintiff's argument that Felix's signature on the consent-to-care form was evidence that he had sought treatment for a medical condition and that his lethargy and inability to sit up at the hospital without assistance provided additional evidence that he required medical care.

It would, therefore, be prudent for hospitals to ask every prisoner if he or she wants medical care. If the prisoner replies "yes" or cannot adequately reply because of incapacitation, the hospital needs to provide a medical screening examination. It is best to communicate this hospital policy to the local police in advance in order to avoid friction with local police who simply want a blood alcohol test and avoid delays. When the patient changes his or her mind and wants to be evaluated or demonstrates signs suggesting that he or she may need medical evaluation, CMS will expect an appropriate medical screening exami-nation to be given, even over the objections of the police. There are times when police insist on avoiding medical care since, under the constitution of most states, prisoners are treated at the expense of the state or county. In addition, medical care would require that the police wait much longer with the prisoner in the emergency department. Make it clear to the police that the hospital has a federal EMTALA obligation to provide a medical screening examination; if the police insist on removing the prisoner, then the hospital must make sure it has the appropriate documentation.

---

[164] *Gooch*, 195 W. Va. 357, 640.

[165] Evans v. Montgomery Hosp. Med. Ctr., No. CIV. A. 95-5039 (E.D. Pa. Apr. 30, 1996).

Q 2:26   Parental Consent: Does EMTALA apply to a minor who comes to the hospital for emergency care?

Yes. The term "any individual" also applies to a minor, so parental consent for a medical screening examination is not required if it delays the examination.

The State Operations Manual states:

> A minor (child) can request an examination or treatment for an EMC. The hospital is required by law to conduct the examination if requested by an individual or on the individual's behalf to determine if an EMC exists. Hospital personnel should not delay the MSE by waiting for parental consent. If after screening the minor, it is determined that no EMC is present, the staff can wait for parental consent before proceeding with further examination and treatment.[166]

Cautions: Appropriate medical screening examination and stabilizing care cannot be delayed for a minor because of parental consent. In the past, emergency departments usually sought parental consent before treating a minor who presented to the emergency department. Now, EMTALA mandates that a medical screening examination must be provided regardless of parental consent. If the medical screening examination reveals an emergency medical condition, the hospital is obligated by EMTALA to stabilize the minor, again regardless of parental consent. In fact, under EMTALA, a minor can be examined, treated, and even appropriately transferred to another hospital all without parental consent if the minor has an emergency medical condition. Of course, the hospital will continue to attempt contact with the parent or legal guardian during the course of examination and treatment. If the medical screening examination shows that the minor is stable without an emergency medical condition, then EMTALA requirements stop. The hospital may at its discretion continue to proceed with treatment or wait until parental consent is obtained.

The emergency community is aware of the case where a teenager brought his younger sister to the emergency department for a sore throat. The receptionist informed him that they would have to contact his parents in order to obtain parental consent because he was underage. Over the next hour, the teenager approached the receptionist several times saying that his sister's sore throat was getting worse. Each time, the teenager was told that his parents had not called back with consent. Finally, an emergency was called when the sister, still in the waiting room, developed acute airway obstruction from her epiglottitis. Because EMTALA applies to minors, the issue of parental consent is moot until a medical screening examination has been performed to establish whether an emergency medical condition exists or not. Only when the child has been deemed stable without an emergency medical condition can the hospital attempt to obtain parental consent for further care.

---

[166] U.S. Dep't HHS, CMS, State Operations Manual, App. V, Emergency Medical Treatment and Labor Act (EMTALA) Interpretive Guidelines, Part II, Tag A-2406/C-2406 (revised 7/16/2010).

Q 2:27　Inpatient Births: Does EMTALA apply to infants born while the mother is an inpatient?

No. Although a mother arriving at a birthing center for purposes of a medical screening examination may qualify for EMTALA application, once admitted for further care, the mother and the unborn fetus become inpatients and EMTALA does not apply.

Cautions: Once formally admitted, a mother and her unborn fetus become inpatients and EMTALA does not apply. However, prior to formal admission, a mother presenting to a birthing facility with an emergent delivery may still be covered by EMTALA requirements.

On January 24, 2008, the Wisconsin Court of Appeals affirmed that EMTALA's medical screening requirement does not apply to inpatients, including the case of a premature infant born after his mother was admitted to a hospital and taken to the hospital birthing center where the infant was birthed.[167]

Plaintiff Shannon Preston arrived at defendant Meriter Hospital on November 9, 1999, where she was admitted as an inpatient to Meriter's birthing center. More than ten hours later, Preston gave birth to a baby boy who weighed one and one-half pounds, which was not compatible with life absent resuscitative efforts. The baby was provided nursing care, but the hospital did not resuscitate or treat the child, who survived for two and one-half hours. Preston sued Meriter for medical negligence, for failing to obtain informed consent, for neglecting a patient, and for violating EMTALA. Preston appealed the dismissal and, in 2004, the Wisconsin Court of Appeals affirmed the lower court's ruling.[168]

Preston appealed to the Wisconsin Supreme Court, seeking a review of the appellate court ruling.[169] The Supreme Court reversed the dismissal "based on its determination that the phrase 'comes to the emergency department' applies to the hospital's birthing center as well as to its emergency room." However, the supreme court remanded the case for briefing on the issue of whether the EMTALA "screening requirement applies to inpatients or whether the newborn infant of a woman who is herself admitted to the hospital is also an inpatient by virtue of the mother's admission." On remand, the defendant moved for summary judgment on the inpatient issue, which the circuit court granted, noting that Preston's child became an inpatient at the same time as Preston and remained so until his subsequent death.

Preston then appealed this inpatient ruling. She argued that when the state's supreme court held that a "newborn has come to a birthing center for purposes of the screening requirement, the court implicitly held that the screening requirement continues to be in effect even after a patient's admission."[170] The appeals court, however, also saw that the higher court's question of the

---

[167] Preston v. Meriter Hosp., Inc. (Preston III), 747 N.W.2d 173 (Wis. App. Ct. 2008).

[168] Preston v. Meriter Hosp., Inc. (Preston I), 678 N.W. 2d 347 (Wis. App. Ct. 2004).

[169] Preston v. Meriter Hosp., Inc. (Preston II), 700 N.W. 2d 158 (Wis. 2005).

[170] *Preston III,* 747 N.W.2d 173, 177.

premature baby's inpatient status "could affect the validity of Preston's screening requirement claim."[171] The Wisconsin court decided that a hospital's obligation under EMTALA "ceases to apply once an individual has been admitted to a hospital for inpatient care." Upon admission, wrote the court, the patient's care "is then governed by state tort and medical malpractice law which all jurisdictions agree EMTALA was not intended to preempt."[172] The Wisconsin appellate court ruled that "when a hospital provides inpatient care to a woman that involves treating her fetus simultaneously, the unborn child is a second inpatient, admitted at the same time as the mother."[173] Thus the EMTALA screening requirement does not apply.

Q 2:28   The Born-Alive Infants Protection Act: Does EMTALA apply to infants born on hospital property when the mother is not an inpatient?

The Born-Alive Infants Protection Act (BAIPA) of 2002[174] adds to the United States Code a definition of the term "individual" that includes every infant who is born alive, at any stage of development. Therefore, newborn infants born on hospital property but who are not inpatients are "individuals" under EMTALA. Hospitals must provide such infants with an appropriate medical screening examination, stabilizing treatment, or an appropriate transfer.

BAIPA instructs that:

> [I]n determining the meaning of any Act of Congress, or of any ruling, regulation, or interpretation of the various administrative bureaus and agencies of the United States, the words "person," "human being," "child," and "individual," shall include every infant member of the species homo sapiens who is born alive at any stage of development.[175]

The statute goes on to define the term "born alive" with respect to the species homo sapiens, as any member of that species expelled or extracted:

> from his or her mother at any stage of development, who after such expulsion or extraction breathes or has a beating heart, pulsation of the umbilical cord, or definite movement of voluntary muscles, regardless of whether the expulsion or extraction occurs as a result of natural or induced labor, cesarean section or induced abortion.[176]

The State Operations Manual states:

> An infant that is born alive is a "person" and an "individual" under 1 U.S.C. 8(a) and the screening requirement of EMTALA applies to "any

---

[171] *Preston III*, 747 N.W.2d 173, 177.

[172] *Preston III*, 747 N.W.2d 173, 184, 187.

[173] *Preston III*, 747 N.W.2d 173, 188.

[174] Born-Alive Infants Protection Act (BAIPA) of 2002, 1 U.S.C. § 8 (Supp. III 2003).

[175] 1 U.S.C. § 8(a).

[176] 1 U.S.C. § 8(b).

individual" who comes to the emergency department. If an infant was born alive in a dedicated emergency department, and a request was made on that infant's behalf for screening for a medical condition (or if a prudent layperson would conclude, based on the infant's appearance or behavior, that the infant needed examination or treatment for a medical condition), the hospital and physician could be liable for violating EMTALA for failure to provide such a medical screening examination.[177]

If an infant is born alive elsewhere on the hospital's campus (i.e., not in the hospital's dedicated emergency department) and a prudent layperson observer would conclude, based on the born-alive infant's appearance or behavior, that the infant was suffering from an emergency medical condition, the hospital and its medical staff are required to perform a medical screening examination on the infant to determine whether or not an emergency medical condition exists. Whether in the DED or elsewhere on the hospital's campus, if the physician or other authorized qualified medical personnel performing the medical screening examination determines that the infant is suffering from an emergency medical condition, the hospital has an obligation under EMTALA to provide stabilizing treatment or an appropriate transfer. If the hospital admits the infant, its obligation under EMTALA ends.[178]

Cautions: Previously, physicians would not consider the delivery of a 20-week fetus as an emergency medical condition and, rather than provide futile intervention, would provide comfort for the newborn and support for the family. Now, the interaction of BAIPA and EMTALA forbids the normative ethical practice of offering discretionary palliative care for infants born at the soft edges of viability. The birth of a fetus at any age of gestation who maintains any signs of life is an "individual" with an "emergency medical condition" protected by all the requirements of EMTALA.

On April 22, 2005, CMS sent a notice to State Survey Agency Directors clarifying that because of BAIPA, EMTALA applies to all infants born alive regardless of gestational age or possibility of ultimate survival.[179] This letter provided guidance on the interaction of BAIPA and EMTALA. The letter explains:

Summary of the Born-Alive Infants Protection Act

The Born-Alive Infants Protection Act, Pub. L. 107-207, amended title 1 of the United States Code by defining the terms "person," "human being," "child," and "individual." In particular, the statute instructs that,

---

[177] U.S. Dep't HHS, CMS, State Operations Manual, App. V, Emergency Medical Treatment and Labor Act (EMTALA) Interpretive Guidelines, Part II, Tag A-2406/C-2406 (revised 7/16/2010).

[178] U.S. Dep't HHS, CMS, State Operations Manual, App. V, Emergency Medical Treatment and Labor Act (EMTALA) Interpretive Guidelines, Part II, Tag A-2406/C-2406 (revised 7/16/2010).

[179] Thomas E. Hamilton, *Interaction of the Emergency Medical Treatment and Labor Act (EMTALA) and the Born-Alive Infants Protection Act of 2002*, CMS S&C Memorandum to State Survey Agency Directors, No. 05-26 (Apr. 22, 2005).

> [i]n determining the meaning of any Act of Congress, or of any ruling, regulation, or interpretation of the various administrative bureaus and agencies of the United States, the words "person," "human being," "child," and "individual" shall include every infant member of the species homo sapiens who is born alive at any stage of development.

1 U.S.C. § 8(a).

The statute goes on to define the term "born alive" with respect to the species homo sapiens, as any member of that species expelled or extracted

> from his or her mother at any stage of development, who after such expulsion or extraction breathes or has a beating heart, pulsation of the umbilical cord, or definite movement of voluntary muscles, regardless of whether the expulsion or extraction occurs as a result of natural or induced labor, cesarean section or induced abortion.

1 U.S.C. § 8(b).

* * *

Interaction of the Born-Alive Protection Act and EMTALA

With the definition of the terms "person" and "individual" codified at 1 U.S.C. § 8, it is clear that there may be some circumstances where EMTALA protections can attach to an infant who is born alive, as that term is defined in 1 U.S.C. § 8(b). For example, assume that a hospital's labor and delivery department meets the definition of a "dedicated emergency department" under the new regulations. If an infant were born alive (again, as that term is defined in 1 U.S.C. § 8(b)) in that dedicated emergency department, and a request were made on that infant's behalf for screening for a medical condition (or if a prudent layperson would conclude, based on the infant's appearance or behavior, that the infant needed examination or treatment for an emergency medical condition and that a request would have been made for screening) the hospital and physician could be liable for violating EMTALA for failure to provide such a screening examination. This follows because the born-alive infant is a "person" and an "individual" under 1 U.S.C. § 8(a) and the screening requirement of EMTALA applies to "any individual" who comes to the emergency department.

Another example could occur were an infant to be born alive elsewhere on the hospital's campus (i.e., not in the hospital's dedicated emergency department) and a prudent layperson observer concluded, based on the born-alive infant's appearance or behavior, that the born-alive infant were suffering from an emergency medical condition. In such a circumstance, the hospital and its medical staff would be required to perform a medical screening examination on that born-alive infant to determine whether or not an emergency medical condition existed. If the hospital or its medical staff determined that the born-alive infant were suffering from an emergency medical condition, there would then arise an obligation to admit the infant, or to comply with either the stabilization requirement or the transfer requirement, or risk a finding of an EMTALA violation. This follows because the born-alive infant is a "person" and an "individual," as described above, and the stabilization and transfer requirements of EMTALA apply to "any individual" who comes to the hospital.

Finally, a third example could occur if the hospital were to admit a born-alive infant. As noted above, EMTALA does not apply to inpatients. Were an infant born alive and then admitted to the hospital, EMTALA would not apply to protect the infant in most circumstances. However, the CoPs described above clearly would apply to the infant once he or she was admitted to the hospital as an inpatient. If a hospital were to violate those CoPs, it would put at risk its Medicare provider agreement.

Conduct of Investigations

EMTALA is a complaint-driven statute. If you receive a complaint that suggests that a born-alive infant has been denied a screening examination, stabilizing treatment, or an appropriate transfer, you should treat that complaint as potentially triggering an EMTALA investigation of the hospital. Note that it is not necessary to determine that the hospital acted with an improper motive in any failure to provide a screening examination, stabilizing treatment, or an appropriate transfer in order to conclude that an EMTALA violation has occurred. The Supreme Court of the United States has held that a finding of improper motive is not required to conclude that an EMTALA violation has occurred.[180]

Specific Issues Arising When a Person "Comes to the Emergency Department"

Q 2:29 Use of Emergency Medical System: What is the appropriate use of the EMS or 911 system by the off-campus site?

An off-campus site may call in the local EMS or 911 system to help treat the patient if it is in the patient's best interest. However, simply calling 911 is not enough because using EMS does not excuse the off-campus site from providing the screening examination or stabilizing care within its capabilities. The EMS should be aware beforehand that it may be called to assist patients at these off-campus sites.

Cautions: CMS does not want the hospital to avoid its EMTALA duties by simply calling the EMS for every incident. CMS feels that personnel at the off-campus site may call in the EMS if it is evident that after the staff's best efforts to stabilize the patient, his or her condition continues to deteriorate and the instability of the patient's condition does not permit hospital staff to move the patient to the main hospital safely because doing so would significantly jeopardize the patient's life or health. Paramedics are specifically trained to respond to code or trauma situations at out-of-hospital sites

---

[180] Thomas E. Hamilton, *Interaction of the Emergency Medical Treatment and Labor Act (EMTALA) and the Born-Alive Infants Protection Act of 2002*, CMS S&C Memorandum to State Service Agency Directors, No. 05-26 (Apr. 22, 2005).

so using the EMS is appropriate. Even after calling in the EMS, the off-campus qualified medical personnel are still responsible for contacting the emergency department to notify it of the situation. The emergency department should assist in the disposition of the patient's treatment and record the patient in the hospital's emergency department log.

Q 2:30   Diversionary Status: May a hospital deny receiving a patient if it is in diversionary status?

A nonhospital-owned ambulance responding to an EMS call may sometimes attempt to transport a patient to a hospital in diversionary status. If the nonhospital-owned ambulance staff contacts a hospital by telephone or telemetry and the hospital is on diversionary status, the hospital is not required to accept additional patients, as these individuals have not yet "come to" the emergency department. If an individual is in an ambulance operated by a hospital on diversionary status, that hospital may also divert the ambulance, but only pursuant to community-wide EMS protocols.

In any case, if ambulance staff ignores diversion instructions and nevertheless arrives on a hospital campus, that patient is considered to have "come to" the emergency department, thus triggering EMTALA obligations.

The Code of Federal Regulations states:

> [A]n individual in a nonhospital-owned ambulance off hospital property is not considered to have come to the hospital's emergency department, even if a member of the ambulance staff contacts the hospital by telephone or telemetry communications and informs the hospital that they want to transport the individual to the hospital for examination and treatment. The hospital may direct the ambulance to another facility if it is in "diversionary status," that is, it does not have the staff or facilities to accept any additional emergency patients. If, however, the ambulance staff disregards the hospital's diversion instructions and transports the individual onto hospital property, the individual is considered to have come to the emergency department.[181]

The State Operations Manual states:

> An individual in a non-hospital owned ambulance not on the hospital's property is not considered to have come to the hospital's emergency department when the ambulance personnel contact "Hospital A" by telephone or telemetry communications. If an individual is in an ambulance, regardless of whether the ambulance is owned by the hospital, a hospital may divert individuals when it is in "diversionary" status because it does not have the staff or facilities to accept any additional emergency patients at that time. However, if the ambulance is owned by the hospital, the diversion of the ambulance is only appropriate if the hospital is being diverted pursuant to community-wide EMS protocols. Moreover, if any ambulance (regardless of whether

---

[181] 42 C.F.R. § 489.24(b)(4).

or not owned by the hospital) disregards the hospital's instructions and brings the individual onto hospital campus, the individual has come to the hospital and the hospital has incurred an obligation to conduct a medical screening examination for the individual.[182]

Cautions: Under local EMS rules and policies, a hospital converts to "diversionary" status for purposes of accepting patients when its resources are at capacity and it is unable to accommodate more patients. The phrase "comes to the emergency department" has created interpretive problems for the courts when telemetry is involved. A hospital must be careful about saying it is on diversion, when it is not at capacity, under the requirements of EMTALA. Therefore, a hospital must ensure that it does not enter diversionary status until it truly can no longer accommodate new patients after making a good faith effort to secure additional resources or space. Note that all unassigned beds are deemed available (hospital beds may not be held open for anticipated elective admissions or contingent in-house use).

Q 2:31   Waivers: Will sanctions for possible EMTALA violations be waived during a public health emergency?

Yes, CMS may waive sanctions during a public health emergency. If sanctions are waived, a hospital may redirect an individual who comes to the emergency department to an alternative location, pursuant to an emergency plan, without a screening exam or otherwise meeting EMTALA requirements prior to transfer.

On June 13, 2012, CMS issued two lengthy documents entitled "Emergency and Disaster-Related Policies and Procedures That May Be Implemented Only With a § 1135 Waiver"[183] and "Emergency-Related Policies and Procedures That May Be Implemented Without § 1135 Waivers."[184] Both documents contain a Section N that answers questions related to compliance with EMTALA during a health care emergency. The full text of Section N of each document may be found in **Appendix I**. These documents, in question-and-answer format, provide information regarding the waiver of EMTALA during a public health emergency. Neither document contains detailed citations to laws and regulations. What follows offers a detailed look as some of the most important legal sources.

---

[182] U.S. Dep't HHS, CMS, State Operations Manual, App. V, Emergency Medical Treatment and Labor Act (EMTALA) Interpretive Guidelines, Part II, Tag A-2406/C-2406 (revised 7/16/2010).

[183] U.S. Dep't HHS, *Emergency-Related Policies and Procedures That May Be Implemented Only with a § 1135 Waiver*, June 13, 2012, available at http://www.cms.gov/About-CMS/Agency-Information/Emergency/Downloads/MedicareFFS-EmergencyQsAs1135Waiver.pdf (accessed July 18, 2012).

[184] U.S. Dep't HHS, *Emergency-Related Policies and Procedures That May Be Implemented Without § 1135 Waivers*, June 13, 2012, available at http://www.cms.gov/About-CMS/Agency-Information/Emergency/Downloads/Consolidated_Medicare_FFS_Emergency_QsAs.pdf (accessed July 18, 2012).

CMS states:

> In accordance with Section 1135(b)(3) of the Act, hospitals and CAHs operating under an EMTALA waiver will not be sanctioned for:
>
> - Redirecting an individual who "comes to the emergency department," as that term is defined in § 489.24(b), to an alternate location for an MSE, pursuant to a State emergency preparedness plan or, as applicable, a State pandemic preparedness plan. Even when a waiver is in effect there is still the expectation that everyone who comes to the ED will receive an appropriate MSE, if not in the ED, then at the alternate care site to which they are redirected or relocated.
>
> - Inappropriately transferring an individual protected under EMTALA, when the circumstances of the transfer are necessitated by the circumstances of the declared emergencies. Transfers may be inappropriate under EMTALA for a number of reasons.
>
> However, even if a hospital/CAH is operating under an EMTALA waiver, the hospital/CAH would not be exempt from sanctions if it discriminates among individuals based on their ability to pay for services or on the source of their payment for services when redirecting or relocating them for the MSE by making inappropriate transfers.[185]

The Code of Federal Regulations was revised to state:

> (i) When a waiver has been issued in accordance with section 1135 of the Act that includes a waiver under section 1135 (b)(3) of the Act, sanctions under this section for an inappropriate transfer or for the direction or relocation of an individual to receive medical screening at an alternate location do not apply to a hospital with a dedicated emergency department if the following conditions are met:
>
> (A) The transfer is necessitated by the circumstances of the declared emergency in the emergency area during the emergency period.
>
> (B) The direction or relocation of an individual to receive medical screening at an alternate location is pursuant to an appropriate State emergency preparedness plan or, in the case of a public health emergency that involves a pandemic infectious disease, pursuant to a State pandemic preparedness plan.
>
> (C) The hospital does not discriminate on the basis of an individual's source of payment or ability to pay.
>
> (D) The hospital is located in an emergency area during an emergency period, as those terms are defined in section 1135(g)(1) of the Act.

---

[185] Thomas E. Hamilton, *Emergency Medical Treatment and Labor Act (EMTALA) Regulation Changes and H1N1 Pandemic Flu and EMTALA Waivers,* S&C Memorandum to State Survey Agency Directors, No. 10-05 (Nov. 6, 2009).

    (E)   There has been a determination that a waiver of sanctions is necessary.

  (ii) A waiver of these sanctions is limited to a 72-hour period beginning upon the implementation of a hospital disaster protocol, except that, if a public health emergency involves a pandemic infectious disease (such as pandemic influenza), the waiver will continue in effect until the termination of the applicable declaration of a public health emergency, as provided under section 1135(e)(1)(B) of the Act.[186]

The State Operations Manual states:

> In accordance with Section 1135(b)(3) of the Act, hospitals and CAHs operating under an EMTALA waiver will not be sanctioned for:
>
> - Redirecting an individual who "comes to the emergency department," as that term is defined at § 489.24(b), to an alternate location for an MSE, pursuant to a State emergency preparedness plan or, as applicable, a State pandemic preparedness plan. Even when a waiver is in effect there is still the expectation that everyone who comes to the ED will receive an appropriate MSE, if not in the ED, then at the alternate care site to which they are redirected or relocated.
>
> - Inappropriately transferring an individual protected under EMTALA, when the transfer is necessitated by the circumstances of the declared emergencies. Transfers may be inappropriate under EMTALA for a number of reasons.
>
> However, even if a hospital/CAH is operating under an EMTALA waiver, the hospital/CAH would not be exempt from sanctions if it discriminates among individuals based on their ability to pay for services, or the source of their payment for services when redirecting or relocating them for the MSE or when making inappropriate transfers.
>
> All other EMTALA-related requirements at 42 CFR 489.20 and EMTALA requirements at 42 CFR 489.24 continue to apply, even when a hospital is operating under an EMTALA waiver. For example, the statute does not provide for a waiver of a recipient hospital's obligation to accept an appropriate transfer of an individual protected under EMTALA. (As a reminder, even without a waiver, a hospital is obligated to accept an appropriate EMTALA transfer *only* when that recipient hospital has specialized capabilities required by the individual and the requisite capacity at the time of the transfer request.)
>
> Waiver of EMTALA requirements in accordance with a Section 1135 waiver does not affect a hospital's or CAH's obligation to comply with State law or regulation that may separately impose requirements similar to those under EMTALA law and regulations. Facilities are encouraged to communicate with their State licensure authorities as to the availability of waivers under State law.
>
> * * *

---

[186] 42 C.F.R. § 489.24(a)(2)(i)(ii).

In accordance with Section 1135 of the Act, an EMTALA waiver may be issued only when:

- The President has declared an emergency or disaster pursuant to the National Emergencies Act or the Robert T. Stafford Disaster Relief and Emergency Assistance Act; and

- The Secretary has declared a public health emergency (PHE) pursuant to Section 319 of the Public Health Service Act; and

- The Secretary has exercised his/her waiver authority pursuant to Section 1135 of the Act and notified Congress at least 48 hours in advance of exercising his/her waiver authority.

In exercising his/her waiver authority, the Secretary may choose to delegate to the Centers for Medicare & Medicaid Services (CMS) the decision as to which Medicare, Medicaid, or CHIP requirements specified in Section 1135 should be temporarily waived or modified, and for which health care providers or groups of providers such waivers are necessary. Specifically, the Secretary may delegate to CMS decision-making about whether and for which hospitals/CAHs to waive EMTALA sanctions as specified in Section 1135(b)(3).

In addition, in order for an EMTALA waiver to apply to a specific hospital or CAH:

- The hospital or CAH must activate its disaster protocol; and

- The State must have activated an emergency preparedness plan or pandemic preparedness plan in the emergency area, and any redirection of individuals for an MSE must be consistent with such plan. It is not necessary for the State to activate its plan statewide, so long as it is activated in the area where the hospital is located. It is also not necessary for the State plan to identify the specific location of the alternate screening sites to which individuals will be directed, although some may do so.

* * *

Except in the case of waivers related to pandemic infectious disease, an EMTALA waiver is limited in duration to 72 hours beginning upon activation of the hospital'/CAH's disaster protocol. In the case of a public health emergency (PHE) involving pandemic infectious disease, the genera EMTALA waiver authority will continue in effect until the termination of the declaration of the PHE. However, application of this general authority to a specific hospital/CAH or groups of hospitals and CAHs may limit the waiver's application to a date prior to the termination of the PHE declaration, since case-specific applications of the waiver authority are issued only to the extent they are necessary, as determined by CMS.

Furthermore, if a State emergency/pandemic preparedness plan is deactivated in the area where the hospital or CAH is located prior to the termination of the public health emergency, the hospital or CAH no longer meets the conditions for an EMTALA waiver and that hospital/CAH waiver would cease to be inn effect as of the deactivation date. Likewise, if a hospital or CAH deactivates its disaster protocol prior to the termination of the public health emergency, the hospital or CAH no longer meets the conditions for an EMTALA waiver and that hospital/ CAH waiver would cease to be in effect as of the deactivation date.

* * *

Section 1135 provides for waivers of certain Medicare, Medicaid, or CHIP requirements, including waivers of EMTALA sanctions, but only to the extent necessary, to ensure sufficient health care items and services are available to meet the needs of Medicare, Medicaid, and CHIP beneficiaries. The waivers also ensure that health care providers who provide such services in good faith but are unable to comply with one or more of the specified requirements may be reimbursed for such items and services and exempted from sanctions for noncompliance, absent any fraud or abuse.

When the Secretary has exercised his/her waiver authority and delegated to CMS decision-making about specific EMTALA waivers, CMS policy in exercising its authority for granting EMTALA waivers is as follows:

> **Localized Emergency Area:** In the case of localized disasters, such as those related to floods or hurricanes, CMS may exercise its discretion to advise hospitals/CAHs in the affected areas that they are covered by the EMTALA waiver, **without requiring individual applications for each waiver**. However, hospitals or CAHs that activate their disaster protocol and expect to take advantage of the area-wide waiver must notify their State Survey Agency (SA) at the time they activate their disaster protocol.

> **Nationwide Emergency Area:** In the case of a nationwide emergency area, CMS may also exercise its discretion to advise hospitals/CAHs in a specific geographical area(s) that they are covered by the EMTALA waiver **for a time-limited period**. CMS expects to do this only if the State has activated its emergency or pandemic preparedness plan in the affected area(s), and if there is other evidence of need for the waiver for a broad group of hospitals of CAHs. CMS will rely upon SAs to advise their CMS Regional Office (RO) whether and where a State's preparedness plan has been activated, as well as when the plan has been deactivated.

In the absence of CMS notification of area-wide applications of the waiver, hospitals/CAHs must contact CMS and request that the waiver provisions be applied to their facility. In all cases, the Act envisions that individuals protected under EMTALA will still receive appropriate MSEs somewhere (even if the MSE is not conducted at the hospital or CAH where they present), and that individuals who are transferred for stabilization of their emergency medical condition will be sent to a facility capable of providing stabilizing services, regardless of whether a waiver is in effect.

Unless CMS advises otherwise, in cases of a public health emergency involving pandemic infectious disease, hospitals/CAHs in areas covered by time-limited, area-wide applications of the EMTALA waiver that seek to extend the waiver's application to a later date within the waiver period (that is, within the period of the PHE declaration) must submit individual requests for extension. The requests must demonstrate their need for continued application of the waiver. Such requests must be received at least three calendar days prior to expiration of the time-limited waiver. Extensions of an EMTALA waiver in emergencies that do not involve pandemic infectious disease are not available.

* * *

Hospitals or CAHs seeking an EMTALA waiver must demonstrate to CMS that application of the waiver to their facility is necessary, and that they have activated their disaster protocol. CMS will confirm with the SA whether the State's preparedness plan has been activated in the area where the hospital or CAH is located. CMS will also seek to confirm when the hospital activated its disaster protocol, whether other measures may address the situation in a manner that does not require a waiver, and other factors important to the ability of the hospital to demonstrate that a waiver is needed.

* * *

EMTALA enforcement is a complaint-driven process. CMS will assess any complaints/allegations related to alleged EMTALA violations concerning the MSE or transfer during the waiver period to determine whether the hospital or CAH in question was operating under an EMTALA waiver at the time of the complaint, and, if so, whether the nature of the complaint involves actions or requirements not covered by the EMTALA waiver and warrants further on-site investigation by the SA.[187]

Cautions: The threat of bioterrorism or other public health emergencies has affected the response of emergency medical systems to disaster situations. Responding to a bioterrorism attack in the usual triage manner by dispersing affected individuals in ambulances to area hospitals may only spread the infective agent further into the community. Infected individuals who arrive at a hospital may need special considerations for the MSE and/or stabilization treatment for fear of introducing the infective agent into the hospital and endangering other patients and staff. This concern for containing the spread of any infective bioterrorism agent or other epidemic biologic agent may require special treatment patterns that could conflict with the mandates of EMTALA.

In response to a catastrophic public health event, it might be difficult or even impossible for hospital emergency departments and providers to comply with EMTALA's requirements due to factors such as overwhelming surges in patient volume, shortages in personnel and supplies, or disruptions in critical infrastructure. Following EMTALA's mandates in such instances may actually interfere with proper patient care. CMS recognizes this potential problem and has added the waiver of sanctions under such circumstances.

---

[187] U.S. Dep't HHS, CMS, State Operations Manual, App. V, Emergency Medical Treatment and Labor Act (EMTALA) Interpretive Guidelines, Part II, Tag A-2406/C-2406 (revised 7/16/2010).

Threats of biological terror attacks with, for example, anthrax after the terrorist attacks of September 11, 2001, along with a renewed fear of epidemic diseases such as Severe Acute Respiratory Syndrome (SARS) or a potential avian or H1N1 flu epidemic, have spurred critical reevaluation of comprehensive strategies for containing communicable diseases.[188] There may be cases in which state or local governments have developed community response plans that designate specific entities (hospitals, public health facilities, etc.) with responsibility for handling certain categories of patient in bioterrorism or other communitywide medical crisis situations. The transfer or referral of these patients in accordance with such a community plan would not violate the hospital's EMTALA obligations.[189]

This waiver of sanctions was created to accommodate cases in which state or local governments have developed community response plans that designate specific entities (hospitals, public health facilities, etc.) with responsibility for handling certain categories of patients in bioterrorism situations. Such plans are made in order to restrict the spread of a biohazardous agent to the community. Complying with these plans may cause conflicts with EMTALA's medical screening and stabilization as well as transfer requirements. This waiver of sanctions allows hospitals to comply with community emergency response plans without worrying about EMTALA conflicts.

Hospitals need to be aware that they should not use this sanction waiver to avoid basic EMTALA requirements. A patient's immediate medical needs should still be addressed. If a potentially exposed patient presents at the hospital, the patient should be assessed to make sure that he or she falls into the category for which the community has a specified screening site. Only after making such a reasonable determination can the patient be referred under the designated community plan. The situation at hand should dictate how extensive the medical screening examination and stabilization provided at the hospital should be before transferring to a central decontamination site. Every effort should be made to stabilize any obvious immediate emergency condition using available decontamination precautions before transferring the patient to a central designated site. CMS warns in its State Operations Manual:

> However, even if a hospital/CAH is operating under an EMTALA waiver, the hospital/CAH would not be exempt from sanctions if it discriminates among individuals based on their ability to pay for services, or the source of their payment for services when redirecting or relocating them for the MSE or when making inappropriate transfers.

> All other EMTALA-related requirements at 42 CFR 489.20 and EMTALA requirements at 42 CFR 489.24 continue to apply, even when a hospital is operating under an EMTALA waiver. For example, the statute does not provide for a waiver of a recipient hospital's obligation to accept an

---

[188] Steven D. Gravely, *Emergency Preparedness and Response: Legal Issues in a Changing World*, 17 Health Lawyer No. 3 at 2 (June 2005).

[189] Steven A. Pilovitz, Director Survey and Certification Group, Department of Health & Human Services, Letter to Regional Administrators of State Survey Agencies (Nov. 8, 2001), available at http://www.cms.hhs.gov.

appropriate transfer of an individual protected under EMTALA. (As a reminder, even without a waiver, a hospital is obligated to accept an appropriate EMTALA transfer only when that recipient hospital has specialized capabilities required by the individual and the requisite capacity at the time of the transfer request.)

Waiver of EMTALA requirements in accordance with a Section 1135 waiver does not affect a hospital's or CAH's obligation to comply with State law or regulation that may separately impose requirements similar to those under EMTALA law and regulations. Facilities are encouraged to communicate with their State licensure authorities as to the availability of waivers under State law.[190]

If CMS receives EMTALA complaints concerning events occurring during the waiver period, CMS states:

EMTALA enforcement is a complaint-driven process. CMS will assess any complaints/allegations related to alleged EMTALA violations concerning the MSE or transfer during the waiver period to determine whether the hospital or CAH in question was operating under an EMTALA waiver at the time of the complaint, and, if so, whether the nature of the complaint involves actions or requirements not covered by the EMTALA waiver and warrants further on-site investigation by the SA.[191]

The Public Health Security and Bioterrorism Preparedness and Response Act of 2002[192] authorizes the Secretary of HHS to waive sanctions for a violation of EMTALA where the violation is the result of an inappropriate transfer of an unstable patient if the transfer arises out of circumstances during a public health emergency (as defined by a Presidential declaration of emergency or disaster and a public health emergency declaration by the Secretary of HHS). The Code of Federal Regulations states: "Sanctions under this section for inappropriate transfer during a national emergency do not apply to a hospital with a dedicated emergency department located in an emergency area, as specified in section 1135(g)(1) of this Act"[193] Note that this law applies only to inappropriate transfers and the medical screening examination location, not to the stabilization arms of EMTALA. In addition, the waiver applies only to patients who are potential victims of the specific public health emergency, not to other patients who present to the hospital with other medical conditions. Lastly, this law does not extinguish the private right of action on the part of injured individuals.

---

[190] U.S. Dep't HHS, CMS, State Operations Manual, App. V, Emergency Medical Treatment and Labor Act (EMTALA) Interpretive Guidelines, Part II, Tag A-2406/C-2406 (revised 7/16/2010).

[191] U.S. Dep't HHS, CMS, State Operations Manual, App. V, Emergency Medical Treatment and Labor Act (EMTALA) Interpretive Guidelines, Part II, Tag A-2406/C-2406 (revised 7/16/2010).

[192] Pub. L. No. 107-188, 116 Stat. 627 (2002) (codified in scattered sections of the U.S. Code).

[193] 42 C.F.R. § 489.24(a)(2).

Q 2:32   Waiver: When can an EMTALA waiver be issued?

In accordance with Section 1135 of the Act, an EMTALA waiver may be issued only when:

- The President has declared an emergency or disaster pursuant to the National Emergencies Act or the Robert T. Stafford Disaster Relief and Emergency Assistance Act; and

- The Secretary has declared a public health emergency pursuant to Section 319 of the Public Health Service Act; and

- The Secretary has exercised his or her waiver authority pursuant to Section 1135 of the Act and notified Congress at least 48 hours in advance of exercising his or her waiver authority.

In the June 13, 2012, document entitled "Emergency and Disaster-Related Policies and Procedures That May Be Implemented Only With a § 1135 Waiver," CMS outlined the requirements that must be met before an EMTALA waiver is issued:

There are 5 prerequisites to a waiver of EMTALA sanctions under § 1135 of the Social Security Act. They are:

(1) The President declares an emergency or disaster under the Stafford Act or the National Emergencies Act,

(2) The Secretary of HHS declares a Public Health Emergency (PHE) under § 319 of the Public Health Service Act,

(3) The Secretary of HHS authorizes waivers under § 1135 of the Social Security Act and has delegated to CMS the specific authority to waive sanctions for certain EMTALA violations that arise as a result of the circumstances of the emergency,

(4) The hospital in the affected area has implemented its hospital disaster protocol, and

(5) CMS has determined that sufficient grounds exist for waiving EMTALA sanctions with respect to a particular hospital or geographic area. (Section 1135N-1).[194]

In exercising waiver authority the Secretary may choose to delegate to CMS the decision as to which Medicare, Medicaid, or CHIP requirements specified in Section 1135 should be temporarily waived or modified and for which health care providers or groups of providers such waivers are necessary. Specifically, the Secretary may delegate to CMS decision-making about whether and for which hospitals/CAHs to waive the EMTALA sanctions specified in Section 1135(b)(3).

---

[194] U.S. Dep't HHS, *Emergency-Related Policies and Procedures That May Be Implemented Only with a § 1135 Waiver*, June 13, 2012, http://www.cms.gov/About-CMS/Agency-Information/Emergency/Downloads/MedicareFFS-EmergencyQsAs1135Waiver.pdf (accessed July 18, 2012).

In addition, in order for an EMTALA waiver to apply to a specific hospital or CAH:

- The hospital or CAH must activate its disaster protocol; and
- The State must have activated an emergency preparedness plan or pandemic preparedness plan in the emergency area and any redirection of individuals for an MSE must be consistent with such plan. It is not necessary for the State to activate its plan statewide, so long as it is activated in the area where the hospital is located. It is not necessary for the State plan to identify the specific location of the alternate screening sites to which individuals will be directed, although some may do so.[195]

In the June 13, 2012, document entitled "Emergency-Related Policies and Procedures That May Be Implemented Without § 1135 Waivers,"[196] CMS answered the question "Has HHS issued any § 1135 waiver in the past that specifically address EMTALA|?"

> Since § 143 of the Public Health Security and Bioterrorism Preparedness and Response Act of 2002 amended § 1135 of the Social Security Act to add the waiver authority, § 1135 waivers have been issued for Hurricanes Katrina, Rita, Gustav and Ike, for the flooding in Iowa and Indiana during CY 2008, and for the flooding in North Dakota and Minnesota in CY 2009. In each emergency event, sanctions for certain types of EMTALA violations were waived for 72 hours after implementation of an affected hospital's disaster protocol. However, if a public health emergency were to involve a pandemic infectious disease, the Secretary could invoke his or her waiver authority under § 1135 to waive certain EMTALA sanctions and such an EMTALA waiver would continue in effect until the termination of the applicable public health emergency declaration (in accordance with § 1135(e)(1)(B) of the Act).[197]

In addition to the health emergencies noted by CMS in its June 13, 2012, "Emergency-Related Policies" document, HHS has also issued EMTALA waivers for the Missouri storms of 2011.[198]

In each case the waiver of sanctions for the specified EMTALA variations were waived for 72 hours after the implementation of the affected hospital's disaster protocol.

---

[195] Thomas E. Hamilton, *Emergency Medical Treatment and Labor Act (EMTALA) Regulation Changes and H1N1 Pandemic Flu and EMTALA Waivers*, CMS S&C Memorandum to State Services Agency Directors, No. 10-05 (Nov. 6, 2009).

[196] U.S. Dep't HHS, *Emergency-Related Policies and Procedures That May Be Implemented Without § 1135 Waivers*, June 13, 2012, available at http://www.cms.gov/About-CMS/Agency-Information/Emergency/Downloads/Consolidated_Medicare_FFS_Emergency_QsAs.pdf (accessed July 18, 2012).

[197] U.S. Dep't HHS, *Emergency-Related Policies and Procedures That May Be Implemented Without § 1135 Waivers*, June 13, 2012, Section N-4, http://www.cms.gov/About-CMS/Agency-Information/Emergency/Downloads/Consolidated_Medicare_FFS_Emergency_QsAs.pdf (accessed July 18, 2012).

[198] U.S. Dep't HHS, Office of the Secretary, *Waiver or Modification of Requirements under Section 1135 of the Social Security Act*, May 23, 2011, available at http://www.cms.gov/About-CMS/Agency-Information/Emergency/Downloads/Boehner-PHE.pdf (accessed July 18, 2012).

Q 2:33   Waivers: What are the limitations of an EMTALA waiver?

On June 13, 2012, CMS issued a document entitled "Emergency and Disaster-Related Policies and Procedures That May Be Implemented Only With a § 1135 Waiver."[199] This document, the relevant portion of which is reproduced in **Appendix I**, summarizes the key limitations on EMTALA waivers.

> Waivers of sanctions under the Emergency Medical Treatment and Labor Act (EMTALA) in the emergency area end 72 hours after implementation of the hospital's disaster plan. (If a public health emergency involves pandemic infectious disease, the waiver of sanctions under EMTALA is extended until the termination of the applicable declaration of a public health emergency.) (Section 1135N-2)
>
> Waivers for EMTALA (for public health emergencies that do not involve a pandemic disease) and HIPAA requirements are limited to a 72-hour period beginning upon implementation of a hospital disaster protocol. Waiver of EMTALA requirements for emergencies that involve a pandemic disease last until the termination of the pandemic-related public health emergency. (Section 1135N-3)

Even during emergency situations in which an EMTALA waiver is granted, hospitals must comply with all EMTALA requirements. However, under the Section 1135 waiver authority, the Secretary has the authority to waive sanctions if a hospital in the emergency area during the emergency period directs or relocates an individual to receive medical screening in an alternate location pursuant to either a state emergency preparedness plan or a state pandemic preparedness plan or transfers an individual who has not been stabilized if the transfer is necessitated by the circumstances of the declared emergency. These waivers are limited to a 72-hour period beginning upon implementation of a hospital's emergency or disaster protocol (unless the emergency involves a pandemic infectious disease) and, per Section 1135N-4, are not effective with respect to any action taken that discriminates among individuals on the basis of their source of payment or their ability to pay.

Q 2:34   Waivers: What is the process for seeking an EMTALA waiver?

On June 13, 2012, CMS issued a lengthy question-and-answer style document entitled "Emergency-Related Policies and Procedures That May Be Implemented Without § 1135 Waivers."[200] Section H of this document deals with EMTALA waivers. In answer to the question "What is CMS's procedure for addressing requests to waive EMTALA?," the following response was given:

---

[199] U.S. Dep't HHS, *Emergency-Related Policies and Procedures That May Be Implemented Only with a § 1135 Waiver*, June 13, 2012, available at http://www.cms.gov/About-CMS/Agency-Information/Emergency/Downloads/MedicareFFS-EmergencyQsAs1135Waiver.pdf (accessed July 18, 2012).

[200] U.S. Dep't HHS, *Emergency-Related Policies and Procedures That May Be Implemented Without § 1135 Waivers*, June 13, 2012, available at http://www.cms.gov/About-CMS/Agency-Information/Emergency/Downloads/Consolidated_Medicare_FFS_Emergency_QsAs.pdf (accessed July 18, 2012).

Because each emergency or disaster presents a unique set of circumstances, especially as they relate to the demand for emergency treatment, CMS calibrates its response to EMTALA-related issues to coincide with the nature of each emergency. But, in general, CMS handles these matters on a case-by-case basis. In an emergency or disaster, CMS, both centrally and through its Regional Offices, will open communications with affected State governments (especially the State Survey Agencies) and with providers, trade groups, and other stakeholders to learn about local conditions. In addition, the State survey agencies are responsible for reporting the status of health care providers affected by the emergency to their CMS Regional Office and CMS relies upon that information to make recommendations to the Secretary regarding the need for EMTALA waivers.[201]

In general, CMS policy in exercising authority for EMTALA waivers is as follows:

- **Localized Emergency Area:** In the case of localized disasters, such as those related to floods or hurricanes, CMS may exercise its discretion to advise hospitals/CAHs in the affected areas that they are covered by the EMTALA waiver, without requiring individual applications for each waiver. However, hospitals or CAHs that activate their disaster protocol and expect to take advantage of the area-wide waiver must notify their State Survey Agency (SA) at the time they activate their disaster protocol.

- **Nationwide Emergency Area:** In the case of a nationwide emergency area, CMS may also exercise its discretion to advise hospitals/CAHs in a specific geographical area(s) that they are covered by the EMTALA waiver *for a time-limited period.* CMS expects to do this only if the state has activated its emergency or pandemic preparedness plan in the affected area(s) and if there is other evidence of need for the waiver for a broad group of hospitals or CAHs. CMS will rely upon SAs to advise their CMS Regional Office (RO) whether and where a state's preparedness plan has been activated, as well as when the plan has been deactivated.

In the absence of CMS notification of area-wide applications of the waiver, hospitals/CAHs must contact CMS and request that the waiver provisions be applied to their facility. In all cases, individuals protected under EMTALA should still receive appropriate MSEs somewhere (even if the MSE is not conducted at the hospital or CAH where an individual presents), and individuals who are transferred for stabilization of their emergency medical condition should be sent to a facility capable of providing stabilizing services, regardless of whether a waiver is in effect.

Unless CMS advises otherwise, hospitals/CAHs in areas covered by time-limited, area-wide applications of the EMTALA waiver that seek to extend the

---

[201] U.S. Dep't HHS, *Emergency-Related Policies and Procedures That May Be Implemented Without § 1135 Waivers*, June 13, 2012, Section N-3, available at http://www.cms.gov/About-CMS/Agency-Information/Emergency/Downloads/Consolidated_Medicare_FFS_Emergency_QsAs.pdf (accessed July 18, 2012).

waiver's application to a later date must submit individual requests for extension. The requests must demonstrate their need for continued application of the waiver. Such requests must be received at least three calendar days prior to expiration of the time-limited waiver.

Hospitals or CAHs seeking an EMTALA waiver must demonstrate to CMS that application of the waiver to their facility is necessary and that they have activated their disaster protocol. CMS will confirm with the SA whether the state's preparedness plan has been activated in the area where the hospital or CAH is located. CMS will also seek to confirm when the hospital activated its disaster protocol, whether other measures may address the situation in a manner that does not require a waiver, and other factors important to the ability of the hospital to demonstrate that a waiver is needed.

Requests for EMTALA waivers should be submitted electronically to the appropriate CMS RO address indicated in the attachment. Additional information concerning the process for submitting all types of Section 1135 waiver requests to CMS may be found at: http://www.cms.hhs.gov/H1N1/Downloads/RequestingAWaiver101.pdf.[202]

Q 2:35   Non-Waiver: May hospitals set up alternate screening sites during a public health emergency without an official waiver?

Yes, CMS does provide hospitals with an option for managing extraordinary emergency department surges under existing EMTALA requirements without an official waiver.

On August 14, 2009, Thomas E. Hamilton, director of CMS's survey and certification group, issued a memorandum to state survey agency directors addressing requirements and options for hospitals experiencing an extraordinary surge in demand for emergency services.[203] This memorandum was in response to an expected H1N1 flu epidemic. The memorandum stated:

> II. *Options for Managing Extraordinary ED Surges Under Existing EMTALA Requirements (No Waiver Required)*
>
>   A. *Hospitals may set up alternative screening sites on campus*
>
>   • *The MSE does not have to take place in the ED. A hospital may set up alternative sites on its campus to perform MSEs.*
>
>   — *Individuals may be redirected to these sites after being logged in. The redirection and logging can even take place outside the entrance to the ED.*

---

[202] Thomas E. Hamilton, *Emergency Medical Treatment and Labor Act (EMTALA) Regulation Changes and H1N1 Pandemic Flu and EMTALA Waivers*, CMS S&C Memorandum to State Service Agency Directors, No. 10-05 (Nov. 6, 2009).

[203] Thomas E. Hamilton, *Emergency Medical Treatment and Labor Act (EMTALA) Requirements and Options for Hospitals in a Disaster*, CMS S&C Memorandum to State Service Agency Directors, No. 09-52 (Aug. 14, 2009).

The person doing the directing should be qualified (e.g., an RN) to recognize individuals who are obviously in need of immediate treatment in the ED.

- *The content of the MSE varies according to the individual's presenting signs and symptoms. It can be as simple or as complex, as needed, to determine if an EMC exists.*

- *MSEs must be conducted by qualified personnel, which may include physicians, nurse practitioners, physician's assistants, or RNs trained to perform MSEs and acting within the scope of their State Practice Act.*

- *The hospital must provide stabilizing treatment (or appropriate transfer) to individuals found to have an EMC, including moving them as needed from the alternative site to another on-campus department.*

B. ***Hospitals may set up screening at off-campus, hospital-controlled sites.***

- *Hospitals and community officials may encourage the public to go to these sites instead of the hospital for screening for influenza-like illness (ILI). However, a hospital may not tell individuals who have already come to its ED to go to the off-site location for the MSE.*

- *Unless the off-campus site is already a dedicated ED (DED) of the hospital, as defined under EMTALA regulations, EMTALA requirements do not apply.*

- *The hospital should not hold the site out to the public as a place that provides care for EMCs in general on an urgent, unscheduled basis. They can hold it out as an ILI screening center.*

- *The off-campus site should be staffed with medical personnel trained to evaluate individuals with ILIs.*

- *If an individual needs additional medical attention on an emergent basis, the hospital is required, under the Medicare Conditions of Participation, to arrange referral/ transfer. Prior coordination with local emergency medical services (EMS) is advised to develop transport arrangements.*

C. ***Communities may set up screening clinics at sites not under the control of a hospital***

- *There is no EMTALA obligation at these sites.*

- *Hospitals and community officials may encourage the public to go to these sites instead of the hospital for screening for ILI. However, a hospital may not tell individuals who have already come to its ED to go to the off-site location for the MSE.*

- *Communities are encouraged to staff the sites with medical personnel trained to evaluate individuals with ILIs.*

- *In preparation for a pandemic, the community, its local hospitals and EMS are encouraged to plan for referral and transport of individuals needing additional medical attention on an emergent basis.*

Cautions: As with an official waiver of sanctions for EMTALA deviations during a public health emergency, this allowance of alternate sites for the MSE applies only to patients who are potential victims of the specific public health emergency, not to other patients who present to the dedicated emergency department with other EMCs. In addition, this allowance of alternate screening sites does not extinguish a private right of action on the part of an injured individual.

Q 2:36   End of EMTALA Obligations: When do a hospital's EMTALA obligations end?

The State Operations Manual states:

A hospital's EMTALA obligation ends when a physician or qualified medical person has made a decision:

- That no emergency medical condition exists (even though the underlying medical condition may persist);

- That an emergency medical condition exists and the individual is appropriately transferred to another facility; or

- That an emergency medical condition exists and the individual is admitted to the hospital for further stabilizing treatment.[204]

Before the release of the 2003 final rules, there had been significant confusion as to when an EMTALA obligation ends once a hospital assumes EMTALA obligations for an individual. The Supreme Court ruling in *Roberts v. Galen of Virginia, Inc.*,[205] in which the Court ruled that EMTALA may still apply where a patient was discharged to a nursing home after two months of inpatient therapy, implied that there may be no end for an EMTALA obligation as long as the patient remains unstable or even develops new medical instabilities. Conversely, the Ninth Circuit held in *Bryant v. Adventist Health System/west*[206] that EMTALA's "stabilization requirement normally ends when a patient is admitted for inpatient care." The *Bryant* court focused on EMTALA's definition of "stabilized" and the fact that "the term is defined only in connection with the transfer of an emergency room patient." The court concluded that "the term stabilize was not intended to apply to those individuals who are admitted to a

---

[204] U.S. Dep't HHS, CMS, State Operations Manual, App. V, Emergency Medical Treatment and Labor Act (EMTALA) Interpretive Guidelines, Part II, Tag A-2407/C-2407 (revised 5/29/2009). *See also* 77 Fed. Reg. 5214 (Feb. 2, 2012), reproduced in **Appendix G**.

[205] 111 F.3d 405, *rev'd by* 525 U.S. 249.

[206] 289 F.3d 1162.

hospital for inpatient care." The court recognized that the Fourth Circuit followed the same approach, and it noted the Sixth Circuit's differing conclusion. The *Bryant* court supported its decision by stating that "Congress enacted EMTALA to create a new cause of action, generally unavailable under state tort law, for what amounts to failure to treat and not to duplicate preexisting legal protections," and "after an individual is admitted for inpatient care, EMTALA would be converted . . . into a federal malpractice statute, something it was never intended to be."[207]

CMS has clarified that once a hospital deems a patient stable after an appropriate MSE, EMTALA obligations end for that patient. CMS adds that an appropriate MSE does not guarantee an exact diagnosis and therefore an actual emergency medical condition may still exist. Remember that even if a hospital deems a patient stable, thus ending its EMTALA obligations, CMS may find during an investigation that the MSE was actually inappropriate or non-uniform. The final rule establishes that EMTALA obligations end with the admission of a patient even with an unstabilized emergency medical condition to the hospital, provided that the admission was made in good faith.

The problem with the "good faith" requirement for admission to the hospital is that the meaning of "good faith" is not clear and requires interpretation. What if an on-call specialist initially admits a patient in good faith but, after two days of care, decides that the still unstabilized patient should be transferred to a county hospital, perhaps influenced by the fact that the patient lacks insurance? Additionally, are hospitals with specialized services still required to accept transfers of unstabilized patients where the transferring hospital's EMTALA obligations have expired in view of the patient's inpatient status? Can receiving hospitals now refuse transfer of an unstabilized inpatient based on financial issues without violating EMTALA? Hospitals need to carefully evaluate their policies for the treatment of admitted patients with unstabilized emergency conditions to avoid EMTALA complications.

Until the point where EMTALA's obligations end, the treating medical staff should not be cognizant of the patient's financial status.[208] However, once EMTALA's obligations end, there is nothing in the law to prevent hospitals from asking for payment. For instance, a hospital may request payment for treatment

---

[207] *Bryant*, 289 F.3d 1162, 1168-69.

[208] The case of Harrison v. Christus St. Patrick Hosp., 430 F. Supp. 2d, 591 (W.D. La. 2006), is of some interest. On January 15, 2003, Autumn Harrison went to Christus St. Patrick Hospital's emergency room for treatment following a car accident. The hospital required Harrison to file a series of forms obligating her to pay the resulting medical expenses. Harrison had no applicable insurance and was never offered charity care or any need-based discount. She was subsequently billed $2,458.60 for services received. Harrison alleged that before uninsured patients are admitted to the emergency room, they are required to sign a contract promising to pay in full for medical care rendered; that by the enforcement of this requirement, the hospital had placed obstacles in the way of uninsured citizens who are trying to obtain health care. The court held that EMTALA does provide limited rights for civil enforcement by patients, but only with regard to patients who have suffered personal harm, as defined in 42 U.S.C. § 1395dd(d)(2)(A), as a direct result of a participating hospital's violation. The allegation that Harrison sought treatment and was made to sign a guarantee of payment did not suffice to state a claim for relief under EMTALA.

of a patient who presents with a routine sore throat once an appropriate MSE has ruled out EMCs such as tonsilar abscess, epiglottitis, and so on. In fact, the University of Colorado Hospital in Denver has a policy where the hospital requests a deposit toward the cost of care once the patient's condition is deemed stable with a non-emergent condition.[209]

---

[209] *Lawsuits Imply EMTALA Requires EDs to Admit All Uninsured Patients,* ED Manag., 16(8):85-7 (Aug. 2004).

Chapter 3

Medical Screening Examination

[T]he hospital must provide for an appropriate medical screening examination within the capability of the hospitals emergency department, including ancillary services routinely available to the emergency department, to determine whether or not an emergency medical condition (within the meaning of subsection (e)(1) of this section) exists.

42 U.S.C. § 1395dd(a)

If an individual comes to the emergency department requesting care, the Emergency Medical Treatment and Active Labor Act (EMTALA) requires that the hospital provide an appropriate medical screening examination (MSE). If the patient is found to have an emergency medical condition (EMC), the hospital must provide; stabilizing treatment and/or a transfer.

"Emergency medical condition" is defined as "acute symptoms of sufficient severity (including severe pain) such that the absence of immediate medical attention could reasonably be expected to result in—(i) placing the health of the individual . . . in serious jeopardy, (ii) serious impairment of bodily functions, or (iii) serious dysfunction of any bodily organ or part."[1] An emergency medical condition also includes a pregnant woman who is having contractions if there is inadequate time for a safe transfer to another hospital or if a transfer poses a threat to the health or safety of the mother or unborn child.[2]

---

[1] 42 C.F.R. § 1395dd(e)(1)(A).

[2] 42 C.F.R. § 1395dd(e)(1)(B).

The requirement for an appropriate MSE mandates that the hospital provide every patient seeking acute medical care with an examination to determine whether the patient has an emergency medical condition or is in active labor. The obligation to provide a screening exam is triggered when an individual comes to a hospital's dedicated emergency department or onto hospital property and requests an examination or treatment of a medical condition. In such a case, the hospital has incurred an obligation to provide an appropriate medical screening examination for the individual and, if an emergency medical condition is found, stabilizing treatment or an appropriate transfer. The purpose of the MSE is to determine whether or not an emergency medical condition exists.[3]

Once an individual comes to the emergency department, the issues raised by EMTALA include the appropriateness of the screening exam, finding an emergency, misdiagnosis, and patient consent or lack thereof.

Appropriateness of Screening

Q 3:1   The Medical Screening Examination: What constitutes a medical screening examination?

The CMS State Operations Manual states:

> A Medical Screening Examination is the process required to reach, with reasonable clinical confidence, the point at which it can be determined whether the individual has an Emergency Medical Condition or not. A Medical Screening Examination is not an isolated event. It is an ongoing process that begins, but typically does not end, with triage.[4]

Cautions: An MSE can range from a quick evaluation lasting a few seconds (a patient who complains of a sore throat and is in no obvious respiratory distress or appears nontoxic can quickly be deemed not a medical emergency) to a much longer evaluation (a patient with a headache may require extensive laboratory tests, a computed tomography scan of the head, and even a lumbar puncture evaluation before the physician can say that no acute medical emergency exists). Even after the emergency physician exhausts all available resources, there are times when a patient must be admitted without a definite determination that the patient does or does not have an EMC. For example, a patient with chest pain may be admitted without a definite determination of whether the pain is of cardiac etiology.

The exceptions where an EMTALA MSE is not required are:

- Admitted inpatients

---

[3] U.S. Dep't HHS, Centers for Medicare & Medicaid Servs. (CMS), State Operations Manual, App. V, Emergency Medical Treatment and Labor Act (EMTALA) Interpretive Guidelines, Part II, Tag A-2406/C-2406 (revised 7/16/2010).

[4] U.S. Dep't HHS, CMS, State Operations Manual, App. V, Emergency Medical Treatment and Labor Act (EMTALA) Interpretive Guidelines, Part II, Tag A-2406/C-2406 (revised 7/16/2010).

- Patients who arrive at the hospital for out-patient purposes even if that patient develops an EMC after the initiation of out-patient services
- Ambulances with patients on hospital property for the sole purpose of meeting a helicopter at the helipad for transport to another destination, so long as the ambulance or helicopter does not request an MSE

At what point does the MSE end and ongoing patient evaluation and care begin? In the past, CMS seemed to imply a distinction, when in the reality of clinical practice there often is not such a bright line. Patient care usually involves a continuum of assessment, testing, reassessment, and often retesting over time before a physician can reasonably be assured that a true medical emergency does or does not exist. The revised guidelines recognize that the MSE is usually an ongoing process rather than an isolated event.[5] However, this recognition still does not give any clear guidance on when EMTALA's MSE requirement ends.

The CMS State Operations Manual further states:

> Individuals coming to the emergency department must be provided a MSE appropriate to the individuals' presenting signs and symptoms, as well as the capability and capacity of the hospital. Depending on the individual's presenting signs and symptoms, an appropriate MSE can involve a wide spectrum of actions, ranging from a simple process involving only a brief history and physical examination to a complex process that also involves performing ancillary studies and procedures, such as (but not limited to) lumbar punctures, clinical laboratory tests, CT scans, and/or other diagnostic tests and procedures. The medical record must reflect continued monitoring according to the individual's needs until it is determined whether or not the individual has an Emergency Medical Condition and, if he/she does, until he/she is stabilized or appropriately transferred. There should be evidence of this ongoing monitoring prior to discharge or transfer.[6]

EMTALA does not specify what is to be included in screening procedures. Nor does it require that hospitals provide all necessary emergency treatment. Most courts hold that only if there is a discrepancy in treatment, or a lack of uniformity in treatment, can a charge of an inappropriate MSE be successful (see Q 3:3). It is up to the hospital to determine what the screening procedure will be. Having done so, it must apply the procedure equally to all patients.

The final rules of 2003 attempt to clarify what EMTALA's medical screening provision requires of a hospital. The final rules, while refraining from "dictating what type of medical screening examination is required for each individual who presents to the dedicated emergency department," proffer that the "screenings should be provided to each individual commensurate with the condition that is presented." Furthermore, the rules state that "the extent of the necessary

---

[5] U.S. Dep't HHS, CMS, State Operations Manual, App. V, Emergency Medical Treatment and Labor Act (EMTALA) Interpretive Guidelines, Part II, Tag A-2406/C-2406 (revised 7/16/2010).

[6] U.S. Dep't HHS, CMS, State Operations Manual, App. V, Emergency Medical Treatment and Labor Act (EMTALA) Interpretive Guidelines, Part II, Tag A-2406/C-2406 (revised 7/16/2010).

examination is generally within the judgment and discretion of the qualified medical personnel performing the examination." The final rules thus appear to promote a subjective standard for the medical screening requirement dependent on each individual patient's condition, an interpretation that is in accordance with the majority of the circuit courts. Moreover, the rules further match the majority of the circuit courts by stating that "EMTALA does not purport to establish a medical malpractice cause of action nor establish a national standard of care."[7]

Q 3:2 The Medical Screening Examination: What elements should a medical screening examination possess?

Based upon past citations by CMS, advisory letters from CMS, and past litigation, state enforcement agencies look for the following elements for a proper MSE:

- log entry with disposition;
- triage record;
- ongoing recording of vital signs;
- oral history;
- physical examination;
- use of all necessary available testing resources to check for an EMC;
- use of on-call physicians as needed;
- discharge or transfer vital signs; and
- adequate documentation of all the above.[8]

Cautions: The key element may be the last one requiring documentation. State enforcement agencies have the benefit of the "retroscope" when reviewing charts to assess proper medical screening. They may question why certain tests (e.g., CT scans) were not performed or why certain on-call specialists were not consulted. This second-guessing of a physician's decisions, which were performed amidst the stress of a chaotic emergency department, can be unfair. Emergency physicians may need to start documenting not only actual tests and procedures but also their reasoning as to why certain tests are not indicated or specialists not required.

The MSE is a process whose goal is to reasonably diagnose the presence or absence of a critical medical condition. If the original history and physical examination determine that the patient does not have an EMC or is stable, then EMTALA requirements end for that patient. However, any further ancillary studies or procedures required to reach that determination are considered to be part of the MSE process. It is important to note that on-call physicians, if needed, are part of this process. For example, if an emergency physician calls the on-call

---

[7] 68 Fed. Reg. 53,222, 53,244 (2003).

[8] Steven Frew, Cobra/EMTALA Resources, *Executive Summary*, vers. 3.0 (Sept. 2003); http://www.medlaw.com/handout.htm.

cardiologist because the examination and tests for a patient with chest pain are inconclusive, then the cardiologist's history, physical examination, and further procedures, such as a diagnostic angiogram, can be part of the MSE.

Q 3:3   "Appropriate Medical Screening Examination": What is an "appropriate" medical screening examination?

Congress defines the meaning of an "appropriate transfer" in Section 1395dd(c)(2) of EMTALA but does not specify what an "appropriate medical screening examination" should be, leaving the courts to provide judicial interpretations over the years. When tackling the challenge, one court remarked: "'Appropriate' is one of the most wonderful weasel words in the dictionary, and a great aid to the resolution of disputed issues in the drafting of legislation. Who, after all, can be found to stand up for 'inappropriate' treatment or actions of any sort?"[9]

Yet, over the years, circuit courts have more or less come to a consensus on how to assess the "appropriateness" of an MSE. The majority of circuits have adopted a "comparability" or "disparate treatment" test, which requires hospitals to apply their standard screening procedures uniformly to all patients presenting with similar clinical symptoms. That is, rather than judging an MSE according to its diagnostic accuracy or success, an MSE is "inappropriate" only if it was conducted in a manner deviating from the norm, given the medical circumstances of a patient.

The State Operations Manual states:

> The MSE must be the same MSE that the hospital would perform on any individual coming to the hospital's dedicated emergency department with those signs and symptoms, regardless of the individual's ability to pay for medical care. If a hospital applies in a nondiscriminatory manner (i.e., a different level of care must not exist based on payment status, race, national origin, etc.) a screening process that is reasonably calculated to determine whether an Emergency Medical Condition exists, it has met its obligations under EMTALA. If the MSE is appropriate and does not reveal an Emergency Medical Condition, the hospital has no further obligation under 42 C.F.R. § 489.24.[10]

According to a pattern jury instruction used by federal courts as an advisory template when directing juries on the issues they must decide:

> The term "appropriate medical screening examination" . . . means a screening to determine the existence of an emergency medical condition which is the same or similar to the screening provided to all patients

---

[9] Cleland v. Bronson Health Care Grp., Inc., 917 F.2d 266, 271 (6th Cir. 1990).

[10] U.S. Dep't HHS, CMS, State Operations Manual, App. V, Emergency Medical Treatment and Labor Act (EMTALA) Interpretive Guidelines, Part II, Tag A-406/C-406 (revised 7/16/2010).

presenting to the . . . emergency room complaining of the same condition or exhibiting the same symptoms or condition.[11]

Traditionally, legal scholarship on EMTALA divided courts into three different camps on the issue of defining "appropriate." Courts purportedly applied either (1) the comparability test, (2) the bad motive test, or (3) the capability test.[12] According to the academic literature, the comparability test provides that hospitals must uniformly apply screening examinations to patients with similar symptoms.[13] The bad motive test, used only in the Sixth Circuit, considers inappropriate any exam in which a hospital discriminates against an individual because of his or her race, sex, ethnicity, or disease; personal dislike of the patient; or the patient's occupation, politics, or cultural attributes.[14] The capability test, applied only in situations where a hospital lacks standard screening protocols, judges screening examinations against the capabilities of a particular hospital.[15]

In reality, these distinctions are artificial. To date, every circuit to rule on the issue of the appropriateness of an MSE under EMTALA agrees that a hospital satisfies the language of Section1395dd(a) so long as it acts toward a particular patient in the same way as it would toward other patients presenting with similar clinical symptoms. This includes the First, Fourth, Fifth, Sixth, Eighth, Ninth, Tenth, Eleventh, and D.C. Circuits.[16] While each circuit champions

---

[11] *See* 3C Kevin F. O'Malley et al., *Federal Jury Practice & Instructions* § 176.30 (5th ed. 2010).

[12] Dow Michael Edwards, *"Patient Dumping": Louisiana Revised Statute 40:2113.6 and the Emergency Medical Treatment and Active Labor Act (EMTALA)*, 27 S.U. L. Rev. 215, 219-220 (Spring 2000); Larry D. Weiss, *Current Status of the Patient Transfer Act (EMTALA) in the Fifth Circuit*, 43 Loy. L. Rev. 263, 272 (1987); Lawrence Singer, *Look What They've Done to My Law, MA: COBRA'S Implosion*, 33 Hous. L. Rev. 113, 137 (1996).

[13] *See* Correa v. Hospital San Francisco, 69 F.3d 1184, 1192 (1st Cir. 1995), *cert. denied*, 116 S. Ct. 1423 (1996).

[14] *See* Cleland v. Bronson Health Care Grp., 917 F.2d 266, 272 (6th Cir. 1990).

[15] *See* Power v. Arlington Hosp. Ass'n, 42 F.3d 851, 858 (4th Cir. 1994); Larry D. Weiss, *Current Status of the Patient Transfer Act (EMTALA) in the Fifth Circuit*, 43 Loy. L. Rev. 263, 272 (1987).

[16] *See* Gatewood v. Washington Healthcare Corp., 933 F.2d 1037, 1041 (D.C. Cir. 1991) ("[A] hospital fulfills the 'appropriate medical screening' requirement when it conforms in its treatment of a particular patient to its standard screening procedures. By the same token, any departure from standard screening procedures constitutes inappropriate screening in violation of the Emergency Act."); Correa v. Hospital San Francisco, 69 F.3d 1184, 1192-93 (1st Cir. 1995) ("[F]aulty screening, in a particular case, as opposed to disparate screening or refusing to screen at all, does not contravene the statute."); Baber v. Hospital Corp. of Am., 977 F.2d 872, 879 (4th Cir. 1992) ("[W]hile EMTALA requires a hospital emergency department to apply its standard screening examination uniformly, it does not guarantee that the emergency personnel will correctly diagnose a patient's condition as a result of this screening."); Marshall v. E. Carroll Parish Hosp. Serv., 134 F.3d 319, 323-24 (5th Cir. 1998) ("[A] treating physician's failure to appreciate the extent of the patient's injury or illness . . . may constitute negligence or malpractice, but cannot support an EMTALA claim for inappropriate screening. . . . It is the plaintiff's burden to show that the Hospital treated her differently from other patients"); Cleland, 917 F.2d 266, 272 ("If [the hospital] acts in the same manner as it would have for the usual paying patient, then the screening provided is 'appropriate' within the meaning of the statute."); Summers v. Baptist Med. Ctr. Arkadelphia, 91 F.3d 1132, 1139 (8th Cir. 1996) (en banc) ("[W]e hold that instances of 'dumping' or improper screening of patients for a discriminatory reason, or failure to screen at all, or screening a patient differently from other patients perceived to have the same condition, all are actionable under EMTALA. But instances of negligence in the screening or diagnostic process, or of mere faulty screening, are not."); Jackson v. East Bay Hosp., 246 F.3d 1248, 1255-56 (9th Cir. 2001) ("[A] hospital satisfies EMTALA's 'appropriate medical screening' requirement if it provides a patient with an examination

variations on this theme, all of them subscribe to a "disparate treatment" or "comparability" standard.

Granted, the Sixth Circuit can be distinguished from others in that it requires the plaintiff to make an additional evidentiary showing of improper motive, a rule established in *Cleland v. Bronson Health Care Group, Inc.*[17] Concerned that EMTALA's "appropriate medical screening examination" duty would be incorrectly interpreted to permit broad federal liability for violations typically covered by state malpractice law, the *Cleland* court reasoned that the term "appropriate" more accurately referred to the motives with which a hospital acts, rather than the substantive nature of a screening. This means that in order to prevail on an EMTALA screening claim, plaintiffs in the Sixth Circuit must prove that a hospital acted with an "inappropriate" motive, such as discrimination on the basis of race, sex, politics, occupation, education, personal prejudice, drunkenness, or even spite.[18] However, even the *Cleland* court announced that "[i]f [a hospital] acts in the same manner as it would have for the usual paying patient, then the screening provided is 'appropriate' within the meaning of the statute."[19] Rather than recognizing a different standard for the assessment of "appropriate," the Sixth Circuit's position is more accurately characterized as requiring uniformity in screening examinations, while specifically prohibiting departures from standard procedures due to improper motives. Although the additional motive requirement alters a plaintiff's burden of proof in the Sixth Circuit, this approach otherwise falls in line with that of other circuits requiring uniform treatment.

The capability test has come into play only on the rare occasions when a hospital lacks a standard screening protocol, thus leaving the district court to determine what procedures should have been in place in light of the capabilities of that particular hospital.[20] Even then, the underlying principle is uniformity. After determining what the appropriate MSE would have been in light of the

---

comparable to the one offered to other patients presenting similar symptoms . . . ."); Phillips v. Hillcrest Med. Ctr., 244 F.3d 790 (10th Cir. 2001) ("[A] hospital's obligation under EMTALA is measured by whether it treats every patient perceived to have the same medical condition in the same manner."); Holcomb v. Monahan, 30 F.3d 116, 117 (11th Cir. 1994) ("As long as a hospital applies the same screening procedures to indigent patients which it applies to paying patients, the hospital does not violate this section of the Act."); *see also* Torretti v. Main Line Hosps., Inc., 580 F.3d 168, 174 (3d Cir. 2009) (observing in dicta that "[l]iability is determined independently of whether any deficiencies in the screening or treatment provided by the hospital may be actionable as negligence or malpractice, as the statute was aimed at disparate patient treatment") (internal citation omitted).

[17] *See Cleland,* 917 F.2d 266.

[18] This rule survives Roberts v. Galen of Virginia, Inc., 525 U.S. 249 (1999). *See* Estate of Taylor v. Paul B. Hall Reg'l Med. Ctr., No. 98-5052, 182 F.3d 918 (6th Cir. July 15, 1999) (unpublished disposition).

[19] *See Cleland,* 917 F.2d 266, 272.

[20] *See* Power v. Arlington Hosp. Ass'n (Power II), 42 F.3d 851, 858 (4th Cir. 1994); Griffith v. Mt. Carmel Med. Ctr., 831 F. Supp. 1532, 1539-40 (D. Kan. 1993). The lone outlier is the 1993 case of Ruiz v. Kepler, 832 F. Supp. 1444, 1447-48 (D.N.M.1993), in which a district court found that a plaintiff's submitted affidavit was sufficient to create a genuine issue of material fact as to the adequacy of the defendant hospital's standard screening procedures, given the more thorough protocols of hospitals with comparable capabilities. This precluded a finding of summary judgment. In the nearly 20 years since this opinion was issued, no other court has cited it for the proposition that a plaintiff may challenge the adequacy of a hospital's standard screening protocols under § 1395dd(a) of EMTALA by comparing them to those of other hospitals. Indeed, this goes against the final rules and substantial jurisprudence

hospital's capabilities, district courts applying this test then considered whether the hospital departed from that screening standard.[21] While the issue of a hospital's capabilities enters the equation in the first stage of these calculations, the second stage, as with the majority of circuits, requires the court to consider whether that subjective standard was uniformly applied to the plaintiff, as it should have been to all other patients.

The comparability or disparate treatment standard is described concisely in *Phillips v. Hillcrest Medical Center.*[22] Martin Phillips presented to Hillcrest Medical Center's emergency room with chest pains and pneumonia-like symptoms. After an examination, the emergency physician prescribed medication and referred Phillips to an Oklahoma medical clinic for follow-up treatment. Several days later, Phillips went to another hospital because he was not improving. The second hospital admitted Phillips to the hospital and eventually diagnosed him with bacterial endocarditis. Phillips' condition worsened despite treatment and he eventually died from his cardiac infection. The family sued Hillcrest Medical Center for violation of EMTALA by not providing an appropriate MSE. Citing a number of sister circuits that had similarly interpreted Section1395dd(a) of ETMALA, the Tenth Circuit expressly adopted a uniform or disparate treatment standard for liability under the statute. It held that:

> a hospital's obligation to provide an emergency medical screening under EMTALA is measured by whether it treats every patient perceived to have the same medical condition in the same manner. "Disparate treatment" is simply another term for describing or measuring a hospital's duty to abide by its established procedures. Unless each patient, regardless of perceived ability to pay, is treated in a uniform manner in accordance with the hospital's existing procedures, EMTALA liability attaches.[23]

Under this standard, even delaying a screening examination, if delay is contrary to standard protocol, can amount to a violation of the "appropriate medical screening" duty. In 1995, the First Circuit in *Correa v. Hospital San Francisco* refused to overturn a jury's finding that 65-year-old Carmen Gonzalez was denied an appropriate medical screening when she was ignored for hours in the waiting room after having complained of chest pains. The defendant

---

consistently cautioning against the creation of a redundant "national standard of care." That is the realm of state malpractice law. It can safely be said that *Ruiz* is an anomaly.

[21] *See Power II*, 42 F.3d 851, 858 ("[A]bsent such standard protocols, an EMTALA claim may be established through proof of a failure to meet the standard of care *to which the Hospital adheres.*") (internal quotation marks and citations omitted); Power v. Arlington Hosp., 800 F. Supp. 1384, 1387 (E.D. Va.1992) ("[T]he issue is not whether the Hospital's treatment was adequate as measured against a malpractice standard of care, but rather whether the claimant received the same screening examination regularly provided to other patients in similar circumstances.") (internal citations omitted); *Griffith*, 831 F. Supp. 1532, 1539-40 ("Ultimately, [plaintiff] will have to prove that the screening provided to her husband was different than the screening Mount Carmel would have provided to another patient who had similar symptoms or a similar condition.").

[22] *Phillips*, 244 F.3d 790.

[23] *Phillips*, 244 F.3d 790, 797.

hospital's internal procedures required the monitoring of vital signs, compilation of a written chart, and immediate referral to an in-house physician for patients suffering from chest pains. In light of these standing protocols, the First Circuit held that the hospital's "delay in attending to the patient was so egregious and lacking in justification as to amount to an effective denial of a screening examination."[24] The court of appeals noted that while faulty screening does not violate EMTALA, disparate screening or "a refusal to follow regular screening procedures in a particular instance contravenes [EMTALA]."[25] To summarize, "[t]he essence of this requirement is that there be some screening procedure, and that it be administered even-handedly."[26]

> **Cautions:** Although all circuit courts that have interpreted Section1395dd(a) agree that an MSE is appropriate so long as it conforms to the hospital's standard screening protocols, the First and Ninth Circuits have explicitly added an additional requirement. Both circuits require that the MSE meet an objective level of adequacy. Specifically, in *Correa*, the First Circuit held that "[a] hospital fulfills its statutory duty to screen patients in its emergency room if it provides for a screening examination *reasonably calculated to identify critical medical conditions that may be afflicting symptomatic patients* and provides that level of screening uniformly to all those who present substantially similar complaints" (emphasis added).[27] Meanwhile, in *Jackson v. East Bay Hospital*, the Ninth Circuit declared that "a hospital satisfies EMTALA's 'appropriate medical screening' requirement if it provides a patient with an examination comparable to the one offered to other patients presenting similar symptoms, *unless the examination is so cursory that it is not 'designed to identify acute and severe symptoms that alert the physician of the need for immediate medical attention to prevent serious bodily injury'*" (emphasis added).[28]

The remaining circuits have not imposed objective standards of quality control on the screening procedures of hospitals as part of the "appropriateness" requirement. Rather, they appear to judge hospitals according to a subjective standard, which obligates a hospital to treat each patient in a nondisparate, uniform manner, within the individual capabilities of that hospital.[29] In contrast to the standard adhered to by the First and Ninth Circuits, this approach is more in keeping with CMS's interpretation of EMTALA, discussed below.

---

[24] Correa v. Hospital San Francisco, 69 F.3d 1184, 1193 (1st Cir. 1995).

[25] *Correa*, 69 F.3d 1184, 1192-93.

[26] *Correa*, 69 F.3d 1184, 1192. *See also* Hunt v. Lincoln County Mem'l Hosp., 317 F.3d 891, 894 (8th Cir. 2003); del Carmen Guadalupe v. Negron Agosto, 299 F.3d 15, 19 (1st Cir. 2002); Cruz-Queipo v. Hospital Espanol Auxilio Mutuo de P.R., 417 F.3d 67, 70 (1st Cir. 2005); Torretti v. Main Line Hosps., Inc., 580 F.3d 168, 173-74 (3d Cir. 2009).

[27] *Correa*, 69 F.3d 1184, 1192.

[28] *Jackson*, 246 F.3d 1248, 1256.

[29] Victoria K. Perez, *EMTALA: Protecting Patients First by Not Deferring to the Final Regulations*, 4 Seton Hall Cir. Rev. 149, 10 (2007).

CMS recognizes the great difficulties in judging uniformity of screening. When asked to define "appropriate medical screening examination," CMS replied:

> It is impossible to define in advance all of the circumstances in which an individual may come to a hospital emergency department. What constitutes an appropriate medical screening examination will vary according to the condition and past history of the individual and the capabilities of the hospital's emergency department—both its facilities and personnel . . . determinations about whether a hospital is in compliance with these regulations must be based on the facts in each individual case.[30]

In spite of the many difficulties in defining the uniformity of screening, the majority of circuits and now CMS have adopted the comparability or disparate treatment test, which requires all hospitals to apply uniform screening procedures to all individuals coming to the emergency room. A hospital will have provided appropriate screening if it acts in the same manner as it would have for the usual paying patient. Only if there is a discrepancy in treatment, or a complete lack of treatment, could EMTALA inappropriateness charges be successfully brought against the hospital. Mere de minimis deviations from a hospital's standard screening procedures, however, are insufficient to constitute an EMTALA violation. To be actionable under EMTALA, the deviations from a hospital's standard screening must be substantial, amounting to a failure to perform essential elements of the standard screening.

In early 2009, an administrative law judge (ALJ) sustained the imposition of the maximum allowable civil monetary penalty (CMP) against St. Joseph's Medical Center of Stockton, California. The Office of the Inspector General (OIG) of the Department of Health and Human Services (HHS) had previously levied a $50,000 penalty against St. Joseph's for egregious violations of the requirements of EMTALA. The case involved St. Joseph's failure to provide an MSE and stabilizing treatment to an 88-year-old man who had come to St. Joseph's emergency department. The man waited for nearly three hours without being examined by a physician. While his family repeatedly pleaded with the emergency room staff for help, the man's condition steadily deteriorated during the waiting period. The man eventually went into cardiopulmonary arrest and died in the waiting room without receiving any treatment. In sustaining the CMP of $50,000, the ALJ characterized St. Joseph's failures as "shocking" and "a complete collapse of the system of care [St. Joseph's] purported to offer emergency patients."[31]

---

[30] 59 Fed. Reg. 32,099 (1994).

[31] OIG Press Release, February 17, 2009, www.oig.hhs.gov/publications/docs/press/2009/emtala_st_josephs.pdf.

Another facility paid $50,000 in 2011 to resolve its liability[32] for allegations of failing to provide an appropriate MSE and treatment for a patient.[33] The patient presented to the emergency department of Texas's Dallas County Hospital District *d/b/a* Parkland Health and Hospital System (Parkland) with severe abdominal pain. After waiting for approximately 15 hours, the patient finally received a physical examination, and the physician determined that the patient required an electrocardiogram (EKG), laboratory studies, and imaging. Parkland never performed the EKG, nor did it perform any intravenous access or monitoring, and the patient died of a heart attack approximately three hours later. The OIG alleged that Parkland violated EMTALA by its delays in evaluation, treatment, and performance of diagnostic examinations.

In 2011, Santa Clara Valley Medical Center (SCVMC) in San Jose, California, agreed to pay $48,000 to resolve its liability[34] for violating EMTALA.[35] In April 2009, a 62-year-old male presented to SCVMC's emergency department complaining of dizziness, blurred vision, and fatigue. The man had been referred to SCVMC by a nearby urgent care facility. The urgent care facility suspected that based on severely low hemoglobin results, the patient was suffering from serious internal bleeding. The patient provided to a triage nurse at SCVMC his medical documents from the urgent care facility showing the abnormally low hemoglobin results. The triage nurse stated that the referral documents from the urgent care facility were difficult to read and that the patient did not appear to be in distress because he could walk. As a result, the patient was triaged as nonemergent and remained in the waiting room for seven hours while his heart rate steadily increased. There is no record that SCVMC notified a physician of the patient's heart rate. Ultimately, the patient died in the waiting room without receiving an MSE or stabilizing medical treatment.

In 2011, Piedmont Hospital (Piedmont) agreed to pay $50,000 to resolve its potential liability under EMTALA for failure to provide an appropriate MSE and stabilizing treatment for an individual who presented to Piedmont's emergency department for evaluation and treatment of an EMC. The individual made repeated requests for treatment for about eight hours, without success. The individual finally left Piedmont, went to another hospital, and was diagnosed and treated for deep vein thrombosis and pulmonary embolus.[36]

In 2012, Northside Hospital (Northside) in Florida agreed to pay $38,000 to resolve its liability[37] for OIG allegations that Northside violated EMTALA by failing to provide an appropriate MSE and stabilizing treatment to a patient with

---

[32] In each CMP case resolved through a settlement agreement, the settling party has contested the OIG's allegations and denied any liability. No CMP judgment or finding of liability has been made against the settling party.

[33] HHS Office of the Inspector General Semiannual Report to Congress—Fall 2011, Page III-13.

[34] SCVMC has contested the OIG's allegations and denied any liability. No CMP judgment or finding of liability has been made against SCVMC.

[35] HHS Office of the Inspector General Semiannual Report to Congress—Fall 2011, Page III-13.

[36] HHS Office of the Inspector General Semiannual Report to Congress—Spring 2012, Page III-19

[37] Northside has contested the OIG's allegations and denied any liability. No CMP judgment or finding of liability has been made against Northside.

a history of mitral valve replacement. The patient presented to Northside's emergency department by ambulance with flu symptoms and a high fever. A triage nurse instructed the patient to go home and to follow his primary care physician's orders. Two days later the patient presented again to Northside's emergency department and was admitted to its intensive care unit. On August 8, 2009, the patient died due to influenza A (H1N1).[38]

Q 3:4   Clinical Guidelines: Can a hospital's policies and clinical guidelines be used to test the "appropriateness" of a medical screening examination?

Yes. The plaintiff must show that he or she was treated in a non-uniform way from other patients. Any practice guideline or protocol implemented by the hospital can be used by the plaintiff to allege an EMTALA violation on the basis of a physician's failure to follow the guidelines uniformly.

Cautions: Any hospital practice guideline or protocol may be used by the plaintiff to support an allegation of an inappropriate MSE in an EMTALA violation case. Emergency physicians need to be thoroughly familiar with hospital guidelines and policies because deviation from such guidelines can be ruled an EMTALA violation through a non-uniform MSE. When a hospital prescribes internal guidelines for an MSE, these guidelines set the parameters for EMTALA compliance.

In *Summers v. Baptist Medical Center Arkadelphia*,[39] the Eighth Circuit reinstated a claim brought under EMTALA because a physician did not order a chest X-ray as required by the hospital's written guidelines. Summers was taken to a hospital emergency department by ambulance after a fall, allegedly complaining of severe pain in his head, back, and chest. The emergency physician ordered spinal X-rays but not a chest X-ray. On the basis of the spinal X-rays, the physician concluded that Summers had no fractures and discharged him. Two days later, Summers was diagnosed with a vertebral fracture, a sternal fracture, and multiple rib fractures complicated by bilateral hemopneumothoraces. Summers filed suit against the hospital. He claimed that he had complained of chest pain and that the hospital's guidelines called for a chest X-ray of any patient with chest pain. Because the emergency physician had not ordered a chest X-ray, argued Summers, there had been disparate treatment in violation of EMTALA.

The district court originally rendered summary judgment in favor of the hospital. On appeal, the Eighth Circuit reversed the decision. The court reasoned that EMTALA required a hospital to treat emergency patients in a uniform, nondiscriminatory manner on the basis of the presenting symptoms and complaints. Because the hospital had written guidelines that called for a chest X-ray for patients complaining of chest pain, the physician may have violated the hospital's standard screening procedures. Although the court en banc

---

[38] http://oig.hhs.gov/fraud/enforcement/cmp/patient_dumping.asp.

[39] *Summers*, 69 F.3d 902.

eventually reversed this decision, the message remains that a hospital's own written policies can be used to judge uniformity of medical examination.

In *Battle v. Memorial Hospital*,[40] hospital policy prevented the dismissal of a suit filed under EMTALA. Memorial Hospital treated a 15-month-old child who presented with fever, twitches, and sores on his tongue. The physician performed a lumbar puncture that was interpreted as normal. He discharged the child with diagnoses of febrile seizures, pneumonia, and an ear infection. The physician prescribed antibiotics. The next day, a second visit to the emergency department also resulted in a discharge, with new diagnoses of seizure disorder and pneumonia. The child returned to the hospital on the third day and was finally admitted, after which a rare form of viral encephalitis was diagnosed. The child ended up in a permanent vegetative state despite treatment. The hospital's emergency department nursing care standards manual stated that "infants and elderly are usually hospitalized if no definitive source for fever/infection is found." The court ruled that this policy precluded dismissal of the suit; the hospital may have violated EMTALA by not following its own manual.

In *Hoffman v. Tonnemacher*,[41] a patient sued the hospital for violation of EMTALA, as well as both the hospital and the physician for medical malpractice, after an emergency department physician failed to diagnose her bacterial infection. The patient went to the emergency room by ambulance at about 11:00 p.m., complaining of fever, chills, hyperventilation, cough, congestion, pain, numbness in her hands, nausea, and vomiting. The physician examined her and found that she had a fever of 102.3 degrees. The patient reported that her temperature had been 106 degrees earlier in the day. She also informed the physician of her medical history, which included a splenectomy and a heart murmur. The physician ordered chest X-rays and a urinalysis, both of which were negative, but did not order other tests such as a blood culture or a complete blood count. The physician diagnosed fever and viral bronchitis with a differential diagnosis of possible pneumonia. He discharged the patient with a prescription for an oral antibiotic.

The following afternoon, the patient returned to the emergency room in much worse condition. The emergency department physician diagnosed bacterial sepsis and immediately hospitalized the patient. The patient's sepsis progressed to systemic inflammatory response syndrome, and she developed serious complications. The patient survived, but doctors had to amputate six of her toes. The patient was discharged after two months in the hospital.

The hospital filed a motion for partial summary judgment, which the district court denied.[42] After further discovery, the hospital moved again for summary judgment, which the district court granted in part and denied in part. The patient's surviving claim alleged that the physician's screening examination constituted disparate treatment in violation of EMTALA because it failed to

---

[40] 228 F.3d 544 (5th Cir. 2000).

[41] Hoffman v. Tonnemacher, 593 F.3d 908 (9th Cir. 2010).

[42] Under Federal Rule of Civil Procedure 56(f).

comply with the hospital's EMTALA policy. Hospital policy obligated emergency physicians to address every item in the differential diagnosis. However, in a later motion for summary judgment, the court held that the patient could not show causation, as the results of a blood culture[43] would not have been available for two days, and the patient was stable for discharge.

Courts look to any relevant hospital policies and guidelines to determine appropriateness of the MSE. Emergency physicians should be thoroughly familiar with their hospital's guidelines and protocols for emergency patient care. These guidelines should be applied strictly and uniformly to all patients to avoid an EMTALA violation. Hospitals would be wise to word their guidelines with flexibility so that the guidelines do not come back to haunt them in the event of a lawsuit.

Q 3:5   Lack of Guidelines: What if a hospital does not have practice guidelines in place?

Without written practice guidelines, a physician's conduct will be judged by the applicable professional standard of care.

Cautions: EMTALA does not require a hospital to have practice guidelines, but once written, the guidelines can be used as a basis for an EMTALA violation. Although liability under EMTALA's screening provision may be based on a deviation from a hospital's standard screening procedures, a hospital cannot avoid liability by failing to have any such guidelines in place.

In *Power v. Arlington Physicians Group*,[44] the court said a hospital may not avoid liability under EMTALA by asserting that it has no standard emergency department procedures. The court held that "absent such standard protocols, an EMTALA claim may be established through proof of a failure to meet the standard of care to which the Hospital adheres."[45] A hospital may rebut a showing of differential treatment by presenting evidence that the physician in question exercised sound medical judgment in concluding that a particular procedure was not necessary under the circumstances of a specific case. The applicable professional standard of care could thereby enter into an EMTALA action as a defense, and in such a case, the claimant could then challenge the physician's judgment through expert testimony.

The court acknowledged that this inquiry might blur the distinction between a malpractice claim and an EMTALA claim but emphasized that the purpose of allowing this type of evidence in an EMTALA action would be to show disparate treatment rather than to establish a violation of the applicable medical standard of care.[46]

---

[43] At trial, the patient's medical expert said that a blood culture was necessary to rule out sepsis.

[44] 42 F.3d 851 (4th Cir. 1994).

[45] 42 F.3d 851, 858 (internal quotation marks and citations omitted).

[46] Some academics call the Fourth Circuit's approach in *Power* the "capability test." *See* Q 3:3 of this chapter.

In *Nolen v. Boca Raton Community Hospital,*[47] the Eleventh Circuit ruled that EMTALA does not require hospitals to have written guidelines. Anne Nolen was 22 weeks pregnant with triplets when she went to Boca Raton Community Hospital experiencing cramping. The hospital admitted her to the labor and delivery unit, where a fetal monitor was applied. Her doctor arrived about 70 minutes after her admission and examined her. Her doctor found that her cervix was neither dilated nor thinned and interpreted laboratory results as negative. The doctor eventually discharged Nolen, instructing her to keep her scheduled appointment with her perinatologist the next morning. The next morning, a doctor examined her and felt that she was entering preterm labor. Nolen was readmitted to the hospital where she stayed for two days before being transferred to another hospital with superior neonatal care. At the second hospital, she went into preterm labor. Her first baby was stillborn, and the other two babies were born alive but died within three weeks of birth. Nolen sued Boca Raton Community Hospital for violations of EMTALA. The trial court granted summary judgment for the hospital on all EMTALA claims. Nolen appealed, arguing that the trial court erred in finding that the screening provided by the hospital was appropriate, given that the hospital did not have a standard written screening procedure. The court found that EMTALA does not require such a written procedure so long as the patient is screened in a manner consistent with the screening other similarly situated patients receive.

If a hospital has practice guidelines in place, a physician who adheres to the guidelines can use this as a defense to a charge of disparate or inappropriate examinations in an EMTALA administrative case. Having a procedure in writing avoids ambiguity, allows every member of the team to review the procedure at his or her convenience, and, as would any written document, provides an excellent defense to liability in the event that the procedure's effectiveness is challenged. The adequacy of the practice guidelines then becomes an EMTALA compliance issue for the hospital in the event of a CMS investigation. Emergency personnel, including nurses and physicians, should thoroughly familiarize themselves with any practice guidelines adopted by their hospital. Any deviation from the practice guidelines should be explained in clear documentation in the hospital chart.

Q 3:6   Capability: What constitutes a hospital's "capability"?

EMTALA states that the hospital is to provide a medical screening "within the capability of the hospital's emergency department, including ancillary services routinely available to the emergency department."[48] The Code of Federal Regulations states that a hospital must provide:

---

[47] 373 F.3d 1151 (11th Cir. 2004).
[48] 42 U.S.C. § 1395dd(a).

> (i) Within the capabilities of the staff and facilities available at the hospital, for further medical examination and treatment as required to stabilize the medical condition.[49]

Cautions: A hospital's capabilities for examination and treatment are also assessed according to "ancillary services routinely available to the emergency department." These include the services of physicians in other departments. CMS gives an example: *"if a hospital has a department of obstetrics and gynecology, the hospital is responsible for adopting procedures under which the staff and resources of that department are available to treat a woman in labor who comes to its emergency department."*[50] Specialists such as ophthalmologists and psychiatrists, who may not have been on call in the past, are now obligated to take emergency calls. Physical capability is construed to include all sophisticated imaging techniques, as well as out-of-hospital specialty consultants. CMS explains that "Congress intended that the resources of the hospital and the staff generally available to patients at the hospital would be considered available for the examination and treatment of individuals coming to the hospital's emergency department, regardless of whether staff physicians had heretofore been obligated by the hospital to provide services to those coming to the hospital's emergency department."[51]

The State Operations Manual further states:

> Hospital resources and staff available to inpatients at the hospital for emergency services must likewise be available to individuals coming to the hospital for examination and treatment of an emergency medical condition because these resources are within the capability of the hospital. For example, a woman in labor who presents at a hospital providing obstetrical services must be treated with the resources available whether or not the hospital normally provides unassigned emergency obstetrical services.[52]

On July 13, 2011, the U.S. District Court for the District of Nevada granted Sunrise Hospital and Medical Center's (Sunrise Hospital) motion for summary judgment on the Plaintiffs' EMTALA claim.[53] This case arose out of the suicide of plaintiffs' decedent, Oscar Aniceto Mejia-Estrada. His relatives sued Sunrise Hospital and others for alleged EMTALA violations as well as state medical malpractice claims.

---

[49] 42 C.F.R. § 489.24(d)(i).

[50] 59 Fed. Reg. 32,086, 32,100 (June 22, 1994); U.S. Dep't HHS, CMS, State Operations Manual, App. V, Emergency Medical Treatment and Labor Act (EMTALA) Interpretive Guidelines, Part II, Tag A-2406/C-2406 (revised 7/16/2010).

[51] 59 Fed. Reg. 32,086, 32,100 (June 22, 1994); U.S. Dep't HHS, CMS, State Operations Manual, App. V, Emergency Medical Treatment and Labor Act (EMTALA) Interpretive Guidelines, Part II, Tag A-2406/C-2406 (revised 5/29/2009).

[52] U.S. Dep't HHS, CMS, State Operations Manual, App. V, Emergency Medical Treatment and Labor Act (EMTALA) Interpretive Guidelines, Part II, Tag A-2406/C-2406 (revised 7/16/2010).

[53] Esperanza v. Sunrise Hosp., Nos. 2:10-CV-01228-PMP-PAL, 2:10-CV-01983-PMP-GWG (D. Nev. July 13, 2011).

On July 25, 2008, Mr. Mejia-Estrada was transported to Sunrise Hospital's emergency room for displaying suicidal and homicidal tendencies. The doctor and staff who evaluated Mr. Mejia-Estrada found that he was not at risk and thus discharged him an hour after his arrival. Two days later, on July 27, Mr. Mejia-Estrada returned to the emergency room, accompanied by family members, for depression and anxiety. The evaluating doctor and nurse concluded that he did not have any physical illness or injury but assessed him as a suicide risk based on the complaints of depression and anxiety. At that time, the hospital did not offer psychiatric services or have a psychiatrist listed on the emergency room call roster. Therefore, Mr. Mejia-Estrada was moved to the Emergency Department Discharge Observation Unit for observation until he could receive the requisite evaluation, specifically from Southern Nevada Adult Mental Health, to determine whether he should be admitted to a psychiatric facility. More than seven hours later, Mr. Mejia-Estrada was found unresponsive and efforts to revive him were unsuccessful.

Relying on the Ninth Circuit's decision in *Baker v. Adventist Health, Inc.*,[54] the district court first explained that "EMTALA explicitly limits the screening examination that a hospital is required to provide to one that is within the capability of the hospital's emergency department." Based on this, the district court held that "[t]he record clearly establishes here that while Defendant Sunrise Hospital performed a medical screening of Mr. Mejia on July 27, 2008, it did not at that time have the capability to perform mental health screening." Accordingly, the district court found no genuine issue of material fact that Sunrise Hospital violated EMTALA by unfairly neglecting to provide a mental health screening. However, the district court refused to dismiss plaintiffs' medical malpractice claims and explained that "[t]he question, whether Sunrise Hospital and the other named Defendants adequately discharged their duty of care to protect against Mr. Mejia's suicide is the subject of Plaintiffs' claim of medical malpractice against Defendants in 2:10-CV-1983. This is not, however, determinative of Plaintiffs' EMTALA claim against Sunrise Hospital."

Note that in an earlier decision provided in this case,[55] the district court addressed the issue of whether state law peer review or similar privileges apply in an action alleging an EMTALA violation and state negligence and medical malpractice claims. Specifically, plaintiffs sought hospital reports regarding Mr. Mejia-Estrada's care, and Sunrise Hospital objected based on the state's peer review privileges. The district court agreed with an apparent majority of federal court decisions that in an action involving EMTALA and state law claims, a "federal district court should not refuse to apply state law privileges where information sought is relevant only to a claim or defense to which state law supplies the rule of decision." Given the uncertainty of the information contained in the reports, however, Sunrise Hospital was ordered to provide the district court such reports for an *in camera* review to determine

---

[54] 260 F.3d 987 (9th Cir. 2001).

[55] Guzman-Ibarguen v. Sunrise Hosp. & Med. Ctr., Nos. 2:10-cv-1228-PMP-GWF, 2:10-cv-1983-PMP-GWF (D. Nev. June 1, 2011).

whether the state law privileges applied or whether there was discoverable information relating to the EMTALA claims.[56]

Q 3:7   Qualified Personnel: Who can perform the medical screening examination?

The State Operations Manual states:

> Once an individual has presented to the hospital seeking emergency care, the determination of whether an emergency medical condition exists is made by the examining physician(s) or other qualified medical personnel of the hospital.[57]

The State Operations Manual further states:

> The Medical Screening Examination must be conducted by an individual(s) who is determined qualified by hospital by-laws or rules and regulations and who meets the requirements of § 482.55 concerning emergency services personnel and direction. The designation of the qualified medical personnel (QMP) should be set forth in a document approved by the governing body of the hospital. If the rules and regulations of the hospital are approved by the board of trustees or other governing body, those personnel qualified to perform the medical screening examinations may be set forth in the rules and regulations, or the hospital by-laws. It is not acceptable for the hospital to allow informal personnel appointments that could frequently change.[58]

Cautions: The examination does not have to be performed by a physician. Any individual who has been determined qualified by the hospital bylaws or rules and regulations and who meets the requirements of the interim rules may do so.[59] A physician is defined in Section 1861(r)(i) of the Act as:

> A doctor of medicine or osteopathy legally authorized to practice medicine and surgery by the State in which he performs such function or action. (This provision is not to be construed to limit the authority of a doctor of medicine or osteopathy to delegate tasks to other qualified health care personnel to the extent recognized under State law or a State's regulatory mechanism.)[60]

The designation of certain qualified individuals who may perform the initial MSE must be clearly stipulated in a a policy document approved by the

---

[56] This case summary was written by Keith A. Mauriello, Partner, and Jessica T. Grozine, Associate, in the Healthcare Practice Group at Arnall Golden Gregory LLP, Atlanta, Georgia. It should not be construed as legal advice or opinion on specific matters.

[57] U.S. Dep't HHS, CMS, State Operations Manual, App. V, Emergency Medical Treatment and Labor Act (EMTALA) Interpretive Guidelines, Part II, Tag A-2406/C-2406 (revised 7/16/2010).

[58] U.S. Dep't HHS, CMS, State Operations Manual, App. V, Emergency Medical Treatment and Labor Act (EMTALA) Interpretive Guidelines, Part II, Tag A-2406/C-2406 (revised 7/16/2010).

[59] 42 C.F.R. § 482.55.

[60] U.S. Dep't HHS, CMS, State Operations Manual, App. V, Emergency Medical Treatment and Labor Act (EMTALA) Interpretive Guidelines, Part II, Tag A–2409/C–2409 (revised 5/29/2009).

hospital's board of directors, such as hospital bylaws or a policy approved by the hospital's governing body. The delegation cannot be informal or arbitrary. The emergency department director, for example, may not informally designate who may perform the examination because that could frequently change.

CMS's general approach to nonphysician screening is to evaluate the system on a number of elements:

1. The level of nonphysician is approved for each individual department authorized to perform medical screening, such as emergency department, obstetrics, newborn nursery, employee health, etc., by the Board or in bylaws approved by the Board;

2. The scope of providing an MSE is within the scope of licensure for the individual involved, under state standards;

3. The individual nonphysician functions under medically approved protocols;

4. The protocols define the limits of the nonphysician's practice in providing an MSE and define objective criteria as to when the MSE must be performed by a physician; and

5. Individuals providing nonphysician MSEs are properly qualified, have appropriate competencies, are trained for the role, and are reviewed for quality on a regular basis.

CMS reserves the right to disagree with the hospital's choice. CMS, therefore, will rule on a case-by-case basis and may refuse to accept a hospital's determination of who is "qualified." A physician is ultimately responsible for any screening examination by a nonphysician, and the decisions of the nonphysician are often imputed to the sponsoring physician.

CMS seldom invalidates an entire policy on nonphysician screening when it disagrees with its application in a given situation. Most often, designations are not properly handled through the Board, or no formal policy on designation of QMP exists. In some cases, however, nonphysicians have exceeded their designated scope for providing MSEs or their scope of licensure. Examples include registered nurses or physician assistants who assessed multi-trauma patients when the protocol of the hospital required a physician examination, or a physician assistant who saw babies and young children in the emergency department but was licensed under state law to see only persons over the age of 12.

CMS looks very closely at the written requirements of the department and frequently requests personnel files to document that all criteria for personnel are met and documented in the files. Lapsed certifications, lack of current copies of licenses, or outright lack of privileges have resulted in citations on this basis.

A private attending physician rather than the on-duty emergency physician may perform the screening examination if he or she is in the emergency department and is privileged by the hospital to provide emergency services. General privileges may suffice if the scope can fairly be construed to encompass the emergency department. Private attending physicians are held to the same level of compliance for MSEs, testing, consults, admission, and transfers (including discharges) as an emergency physician. Noncompliance may inadvertently lead to violations for the nonemergency physician and the hospital.

Private patients presenting must be logged and triaged. If the private attending physician is delayed in getting to the emergency department to provide the MSE, the emergency physician should step in and perform the examination rather than accept the delay. If the patient is found to have no emergency condition, then further waiting for the private attending physician is reasonable within limits and conditioned on periodic observation notes. If the patient changes his or her mind about waiting for the private physician, the emergency physician should make every effort to see the patient, provide an MSE, and document all elements of the visit.

If a physician is present in the emergency department, he or she should not delegate the screening examination to a nonphysician. Such a practice is very risky; mistakes by nonphysicians have resulted in significant EMTALA penalties. When no physician is present in the emergency department, the qualified nonphysician may transfer a patient, but only after conferring with a physician by phone and having the physician co-sign the transfer order within a reasonable period after the transfer.[61]

The certification by a nonphysician for transfer is a potentially dangerous EMTALA situation if the physician could have come in to see and stabilize the patient within a reasonable time. In various citations, phone decisions to transfer have been faulted as failure or refusal of the on-call personnel to come in. Nonphysicians should not sign transfer documents unless the record clearly documents that the time necessary for the physician to respond would put the patient's safety at risk.

The American College of Emergency Physicians policy position states that a physician should perform the MSE.[62]

The Tenth Circuit[63] ruled in *Cunningham v. Fredonia Regional Hospital*[64] that a hospital did not violate EMTALA even though a nurse performed the MSE. On October 7, 1992, Wanda Cunningham saw Dr. Rindt, her family physician, for chest pain. After performing an ECG, Dr. Rindt determined that the chest pain was caused by bronchitis and was not cardiac in origin. That evening, Cunningham's husband consulted with Dr. Bacani about his wife's continued pain. Dr. Bacani referred the Cunninghams to the emergency department of Fredonia Regional Hospital, where he had left telephone orders for a pain shot. Only a nurse, not a physician, examined Mrs. Cunningham on her arrival at Fredonia. The nurse did not find any signs of an acute emergency and administered the

---

[61] 42 C.F.R. § 489.24.

[62] American College of Emergency Physicians, Hospital, Medical Staff, and Payer Responsibility for Emergency Department Patients (Sept. 1999).

[63] The Tenth Circuit covers Colorado, Kansas, New Mexico, Oklahoma, Utah, and Wyoming. 28 U.S.C. § 41.

[64] 98 F.3d 1349 (10th Cir. 1996).

pain shot. Mrs. Cunningham died that night in her sleep of a myocardial infarction. Mr. Cunningham sued, claiming that the hospital violated EMTALA by failing to comply with its own policy requiring a physician to examine patients with "life-threatening symptoms of chest pain." The hospital countered by presenting a second applicable policy that allowed nursing personnel to evaluate patients with medical conditions that have low complexity and low possibility of morbidity. The court declined to assess the adequacy of the hospital's policies under EMTALA.

The court concluded that courts may determine only whether a hospital followed its own policies, not whether the policies themselves constitute an appropriate screening policy under EMTALA. CMS, however, is not the slightest bit reluctant to subjectively evaluate the policies of a hospital and their relative adequacy in individual cases. Many hospitals have been cited on these types of issues. This again emphasizes that court decisions should not be taken as the final authoritative voice guiding hospital practices under EMTALA. One must also look to CMS standards or risk administrative sanctions.

Q 3:8   Triage: What is the difference between "triage" and a "medical screening examination"?

The State Operations Manual states:

> Triage entails the clinical assessment of the individual's presenting signs and symptoms at the time of arrival at the hospital, in order to prioritize when the individual will be seen by a physician or other qualified medical personnel (QMP).[65]

> If a hospital has an EMTALA obligation, it must screen individuals to determine if an emergency medical condition exists. It is not appropriate to merely "log-in" an individual and not provide a Medical Screening Examination. An MSE is the process required to reach, with reasonable clinical confidence, the point at which it can be determined whether the individual has an EMC or not. An MSE is not an isolated event. It is an ongoing process that begins, but typically does not end, with triage.[66]

Cautions: It is important to understand that initial first impressions, especially of a cursory nature with only vital signs and presenting complaint to guide the triage, cannot be the basis of an MSE. The MSE must be provided to every presenting patient and must be of sufficient scope to rule in or rule out the presence of a legally defined EMC. Triage was never intended to reach a diagnosis, and consequently it cannot be substituted for an MSE. As any emergency physician knows, even apparently minor presenting symptoms may turn out to be a medical emergency. A migraine headache could be a subarachnoid bleed. A stomachache could be appendicitis. A backache could

---

[65] U.S. Dep't HHS, CMS, State Operations Manual, App. V, Emergency Medical Treatment and Labor Act (EMTALA) Interpretive Guidelines, Part II, Tag A-2406/C-2406 (revised 7/16/2010).

[66] U.S. Dep't HHS, CMS, State Operations Manual, App. V, Interpretive Guidelines for Responsibilities of Medicare Participating Hospitals in Emergency Cases, Part II, Tag A407 (revised 5/29/2009).

be a dissecting aortic aneurysm. A sore throat could be epiglottitis. A child with a fever could have meningitis. Therefore, CMS expects that an MSE, not triage, will evaluate patients on a final basis. Triage is simply a process that applies general definitions of presenting signs and symptoms to say "this type of presentation should get first access for medical screening examination," whereas others necessarily wait in order of severity.

Triage involves the ranking of patients, who may or may not have an "emergency medical condition," in the order in which they will be seen according to a determination by a quick evaluation of the seriousness of their presenting signs and symptoms. The system was invented during the Napoleonic Wars as a way to sort injured soldiers on the battlefield so that the limited amount of time and effort available would not be wasted on treating the obviously hopeless or the walking wounded with minor injuries. Those who were seriously injured but not hopeless cases were treated first. An adaptation of the system has been adopted in almost every emergency department in the land as a practical way to maintain reasonable order in patient care.

Patients with presenting signs and symptoms indicative of serious illness (e.g., acute chest pain) are "taken straight back" without registration, so that immediate evaluation and care can be provided. They are assigned "John Doe" charts until patient demographic information can be obtained later. Those with less urgent presentations (e.g., a sprained ankle) are allowed to register first so that a hospital chart can be made up with an assigned patient identification number (all tests, X-rays, and procedures are ordered using this number as identification). This system has withstood the test of time and works well to facilitate a reasonable order for patient care that discriminates only by the apparent severity of patient illness. The validity of the system depends heavily on the scope of information obtained at the time of initial triage.

The hospital needs to document and maintain records for every triage interaction. The documentation cannot be disposed of if a patient decides to leave the dedicated emergency department before treatment. Without the benefit of documentation, a hospital will have a very difficult time proving compliance when an investigating surveyor accepts only the patient's account of what transpired during a visit. Triage notes should be subject to the same quality review for completeness and accuracy as the main hospital chart.

CMS does not specify who may perform the initial triage. However, since triage is essentially the initial component of an MSE, it is reasonable to assume that the requirement of "qualified personnel" would apply just as it does for an MSE. Specifically, secretaries, greeters, volunteers, security guards, and other non-medical personnel cannot perform triage.

Once triaged, a patient may wait in the waiting room if the patient does not present with emergent symptoms. However, if there is a prolonged wait, CMS will expect evidence of periodic reassessment of the patient's condition in the waiting room. A hospital should have policies and procedures covering appropriate reassessment of patients waiting for care. Reassessment care should be documented in the patient's chart.

On September 5, 2008, a Virginia district court denied defendant Danville Regional Medical Center of Virginia LLC's (DRMC) motion to dismiss a lawsuit, claiming the hospital violated EMTALA by not providing an appropriate MSE for more than 11 hours after triage.[67] On September 3, 2006, Everett Wayne Scruggs, the plaintiff, arrived at the DRMC emergency department complaining of "prolonged dry heaves over the past two days." An emergency registered nurse conducted the triage screening and prioritized Scruggs as a "non-urgent" patient. Approximately 11.5 hours after Scruggs had arrived at DRMC's emergency department, Dr. Ramon Gomez performed an MSE and ordered IV fluids, oxygen, cardiac monitoring, and laboratory tests to treat diabetic ketoacidosis. Nearly 40 minutes later, a nurse found the plaintiff "unresponsive and in cardiac and respiratory arrest." The staff successfully resuscitated Scruggs and admitted him for further care.

Seventeen months later, in February 2008, Mr. Scruggs filed suit alleging an EMTALA violation for DRMC's failure to provide an appropriate and prompt MSE. DRMC replied by asserting that the claim was one for "negligent triage and that EMTALA is not a substitute for state law medical negligence claims."[68] The district court found that triage is not equivalent to an EMTALA-required MSE, because triage "merely determines the order by which patients are seen in the emergency department." "Plaintiff clearly has outlined a claim within the realm of EMTALA," the court continued, "by asserting he did not receive an 'adequate' medical screening examination based on the eleven and one-half hour time period prior to receiving medical treatment. This is clearly more than a claim for negligent triage as proposed by Defendant at oral argument."[69] The court determined that the plaintiff's claim was sufficient under EMTALA and that the defendant's motion to dismiss was denied.

The *Scruggs* decision issues a note of caution to hospitals: reasonably limit delays for examination even when triage determines that a patient presentation is not emergent. Since the initiation of EMTALA in 1985, emergency department visits have increased by millions while more than a thousand emergency departments have closed. As more emergency departments become overwhelmed by the volume of presenting patients, this problem of delayed care will increase.

On June 9, 2011, the U.S. District Court for the District of Puerto Rico issued a decision denying Hospital Español Auxilio Mutuo de Puerto Rico's (Hospital Español) motion for partial summary judgment on an EMTALA claim asserted by the estate and family members of a deceased hospital patient.[70] On February 17, 2008, the patient presented to Hospital Español with chest pain, which was later confirmed to be an acute inferior myocardial infarction. She was admitted to Hospital Español for an emergency cardiac catheterization and an

---

[67] Scruggs v. Danville Reg'l Med. Ctr. of Va. LLC, No. 4.08CV00005 (W.D. Va. Sept. 5, 2008).

[68] *Scruggs*, No. 4.08CV00005 at *1.

[69] *Scruggs*, No. 4.08CV00005 at *4.

[70] Estate of Caillet-Bois v. Hospital Español Auxilio Mutuo De P.R., Civ. No. 09-1201(JP) (D.P.R. June 9, 2011).

angioplasty. The patient was discharged on March 4, 2008, but returned to the emergency room on March 8, 2008, again complaining of chest pain. At that time, she was triaged as an urgency level three, a less severe, lower priority than what testimony confirmed as being appropriate for chest pain cases. The triage was performed at 6:53 p.m., but, based on the triage classification, the patient was not aggressively evaluated and treated by the emergency room physician until 8:50 p.m., almost two hours later. The patient was admitted to Hospital Español and evaluated by another physician the next morning at 9:00 a.m. The patient died later that day.

The plaintiffs alleged that the intake procedure for Hospital Español violated EMTALA as the patient was improperly categorized as low priority and hospital staff disregarded chest pain protocols, thus failing to offer an adequate medical screening. While not admitting to any EMTALA violations, Hospital Español did not deny that such violations occurred but instead focused its motion solely on the issue of causation. The hospital specifically asserted that the plaintiffs did not have a viable EMTALA claim due to a failure to link the alleged EMTALA violations to the eventual demise of the patient.

Relying on the First Circuit Court's decision of *Cruz-Quiepo v. Hospital Español Auxilio Mutuo*,[71] which rejected a similar argument, the district court denied the motion, finding that:

> Hospitals do not generally cause the emergency conditions that they are called upon to identify during the initial screening process. Needless to say, that does not mean that a hospital's failure to appropriately screen a patient bears no causal relationship to the damages suffered by a patient as a result of deterioration in his or her condition that could have been avoided by an initial, appropriate screening. In this case, had the doctors followed its triage and chest pain protocols and provided [the patient] with an appropriate screening, they might have correctly and promptly identified her condition and treated her accordingly.

Based on the evidence in the light most favorable to the plaintiffs, the district court found that there was sufficient evidence for a reasonable jury to conclude that Hospital Español violated EMTALA in failing to provide an appropriate medical screening and that the violation caused damages to the patient.

In a footnote, the district court rejected consideration of Hospital Español's argument that EMTALA did not apply because the patient was not an emergency room patient when she died. The district court stated that the hospital failed to raise such argument at the outset of its motion for partial summary judgment, only raising it for the first time in its reply.[72]

---

[71] 417 F.3d 67 (1st Cir. 2005).

[72] This case summary was written by Keith A. Mauriello, Partner, and Jessica T. Grozine, Associate, in the Healthcare Practice Group at Arnall Golden Gregory LLP, Atlanta, Georgia. It should not be construed as legal advice or opinion on specific matters.

As recently as 2011, Santa Clara Valley Medical Center (SCVMC) in San Jose, California, agreed to pay $48,000 to resolve its liability for violating EMTALA.[73] In April 2009, a 62-year-old male presented to SCVMC's emergency department complaining of dizziness, blurred vision, and fatigue. The man had been referred to SCVMC by a nearby urgent care facility. The urgent care facility suspected that based on severely low hemoglobin results, the patient was suffering from serious internal bleeding. The patient provided to a triage nurse at SCVMC his medical documents from the urgent care facility showing the abnormally low hemoglobin results. The triage nurse stated that the referral documents from the urgent care facility were difficult to read and that the patient did not appear to be in distress because he could walk. As a result, the patient was triaged as nonemergent and remained in the waiting room for seven hours while his heart rate steadily increased. There is no record that SCVMC notified a physician of the patient's heart rate. Ultimately, the patient died in the waiting room without receiving an MSE or stabilizing medical treatment.

Q 3:9 Nonemergency Services: What level of screening is required for requests regarding nonemergency medical conditions?

EMTALA screening requirements apply regardless of whether a request for examination or treatment is made for an emergency, as opposed to a nonemergency, condition. Not all EMTALA screenings, however, need be equally extensive. CMS notes that "hospitals are not obligated to provide screening services beyond those needed to determine that there is no emergency."[74] While the appropriate level of screening varies according to the circumstances, the standard remains uniform; a hospital is obliged to perform only the level of screening required to determine whether the individual has an EMC as defined in the regulations.

In May 2002,[75] CMS proposed to amend the rule to reflect the above sentiment. The proposal was finalized in the final rules presented in the *Federal Register* in September 2003.[76] The amended Code of Federal Regulations now states:

> If an individual comes to a hospital's dedicated emergency department and a request is made on his or her behalf for examination or treatment for a medical condition, but the nature of the request makes it clear that the medical condition is not of an emergency nature, the hospital is required only to perform such screening as would be appropriate for any individual presenting in that manner, to determine that the individual does not have an emergency medical condition.[77]

---

[73] Reported by the Office of Inspector General on August 17, 2011, at http://oig.hhs.gov/fraud/enforcement/cmp/patient_dumping.asp. (accessed July 18, 2012).

[74] 67 Fed. Reg. 31,404, 31,473 (2002).

[75] Proposed Rules to Revise and Clarify EMTALA, 67 Fed. Reg. 31,404, 31,473 (2002).

[76] 68 Fed. Reg. 53,222, 53,234-238 (2003).

[77] 42 C.F.R. § 489.24(c).

The State Operations Manual states:

> Any individual with a medical condition that presents to a hospital's ED must receive a Medical Screening Examination that is appropriate for their medical condition. The objective of the Medical Screening Examination is to determine whether or not an emergency medical condition exists. This does not mean that all EMTALA screenings must be equally extensive. If the nature of the individual's request makes clear that the medical condition is not of an emergency nature, the Medical Screening Examination is reflective of the individual presenting complaints or symptoms. A hospital may, if it chooses, have protocols that permit a QMP [qualified medical personnel] (e.g., a request for a blood pressure check and that check reveals that the patient's blood pressure is within normal range). Once the individual is screened and it is determined the individual has only presented to the ED for a non-emergency purpose, the hospital's EMTALA obligation ends for that individual at the completion of the Medical Screening Examination. Hospitals are not obligated under EMTALA to provide screening services beyond those needed to determine that there is no emergency medical condition.

> For a hospital to be exempted from its EMTALA obligations to screen individuals presenting at its emergency department for non-emergency tests (e.g., individual has consulted with physician by telephone and the physician refers the individual to a hospital emergency department for a non-emergency test) the hospital must be able to document that it is only being asked to collect evidence, not analyze the test results, or to otherwise examine or treat the individual. Furthermore, a hospital may be exempted from its EMTALA obligations to screen individuals presenting to its dedicated emergency department if the individual had a previously scheduled appointment.

> If an individual presents to an ED and requests pharmaceutical services (medication) for a medical condition, the hospital generally would have an EMTALA obligation. Surveyors are encouraged to ask probing questions of the hospital staff to determine if the hospital in fact had an EMTALA obligation in this situation (e.g., did the individual present to the ED with an emergency medical condition and informed staff they had not taken their medication? Was it obvious from the nature of the medication requested that it was likely that the patient had an emergency medical condition?). The circumstances surrounding why the request is being made would confirm if the hospital in fact has an EMTALA obligation. If the individual requires the medication to resolve or provide stabilizing treatment of an emergency medical condition, then the hospital has an EMTALA obligation. Hospitals are not required by EMTALA to provide medication to individuals who do not have an emergency medical condition simply because the individual is unable to pay or does not wish to purchase the medication from a retail pharmacy or did not plan appropriately to secure prescription refills.

> If an individual presents to a dedicated emergency department and requests services that are not for a medical condition, such as preventive care services (immunizations, allergy shots, flu shots) or the gathering of evidence for criminal law cases (e.g., sexual assault, blood alcohol

test), the hospital is not obligated to provide a Medical Screening Examination under EMTALA to this individual.[78]

Cautions: In the past, hospitals were unsure about EMTALA obligations when patients arrived in the emergency department for obvious nonemergency treatments, such as suture removal. Can a hospital refer patients who present to the emergency department for such nonemergency services as preventive care services, pharmaceutical services, laboratory testing (which would include blood draws for law enforcement purposes), or X-rays to a primary care or specialty clinic for care of the nonemergency condition without violating EMTALA?

As indicated above, it would appear that hospitals are only obliged to conduct the screenings necessary to determine whether an emergency condition exists, given the information available to attending qualified medical personnel. For example, if an individual makes a request for such nonemergency care as the removal of sutures, brief questioning by qualified medical personnel to determine that no additional emergency condition exists will suffice as adequate screening.[79] Once the hospital determines, through an appropriate MSE, that a patient is stable and without an emergency medical condition, EMTALA obligations end.

Patients seeking only tests, as opposed to treatment, are not technically requesting "examination or treatment for a medical condition," so as to trigger EMTALA obligations. Therefore, they can be managed differently from regular emergency patients. The hospital should not put them through triage, take their vital signs, or create a regular emergency department chart. These patients should not sign the usual emergency treatment consent form. Rather, the patient should sign a nonemergency treatment form with language such as: "I do not request a medical screening exam to determine if I have an emergency medical condition, nor do I request treatment for a medical condition at this time. I understand that the hospital is willing to provide me with such examination and treatment should I ask for it."[80]

It is important to note that State Operations Manual suggestions that EMTALA exemptions exist for nonemergency testing are intended as guidance to its regional offices and surveyors. These suggestions have not been adopted by statute or regulation. In addition, CMS merely states that hospitals *may* be exempt from EMTALA for nonemergency services. The use of "may" suggests that nonemergency patient visits will be examined on a case-by-case basis.

After it has been determined that an emergency condition does not exist, the patient may be treated accordingly (suture removal by a nurse or administration

---

[78] U.S. Dep't HHS, CMS, State Operations Manual, App. V, Emergency Medical Treatment and Labor Act (EMTALA) Interpretive Guidelines, Part II, Tag A-2406/C-2406 (revised 7/16/2010).

[79] 67 Fed. Reg. 31,404, 31,473 (2002).

[80] Robert A. Bitterman, "Blood Alcohols, Labs, and Minor Treatments in the ED; Is a Medical Screening Exam Required by EMTALA?," Am. College of Emergency Physicians News, July 1998.

of outpatient medications such as IV antibiotics) or referred to the appropriate department (laboratory for blood draw, radiology for X-rays, pharmacy, physical therapy, etc.) or even discharged to an appropriate clinic or other care setting designated to properly provide the appropriate services. CMS cautions that it will review each case on an individual basis to assure that hospitals are not using this avenue to avoid EMTALA requirements.

Hospitals need to be cautious when private physicians send their patients to the dedicated emergency department "just" for some laboratory testing, X-rays, or medications (such as a pain shot for chronic migraines). A private physician cannot skirt EMTALA obligations by requesting such "courtesy" care. These are not truly outpatient services, so a hospital should still provide an EMTALA MSE to these patients.

Q 3:10   Triage Out of the Emergency Department of Non-emergent Patients: Can a hospital triage patients out of the emergency department to other care settings?

Yes. But the referral to another care setting must be on a medical basis, and all patients of similar conditions, complaints, and acuity must be referred uniformly.

Cautions: In order to relieve the congestion and long wait times for some patients who come to the emergency department for minor ailments, some emergency departments try to refer these patients to ambulatory care or urgent care settings where patients can be treated in a more expeditious manner, thereby allowing the emergency department to concentrate on treating patients with more serious medical conditions. This referral of patients cannot be based on insurance or revenue issues (economic triage). There must be a valid medical reason for referring the patient. The referral site should be on the same campus as the emergency department, and patients should be escorted to the referral site.

One system of "advanced" triage being used for medical screening was initially developed at the University of California, Davis.[81] The initial medical screening examiner—a highly trained mid-level provider—evaluates the patient according to a series of questions:

1. Chief symptom: Chronic condition, at risk, or a true emergency?
2. Vital signs?
3. Mental state: Evidence of change?
4. General appearance: Does the patient look sick?
5. Degree of pain: Does the patient have moderate or severe pain?
6. Skin: Evidence of dehydration, poor perfusion?
7. Focused physical examination results?

---

[81] Robert W. Derlet, *Prospective Identification and Triage of Nonemergency Patients out of an Emergency Department: A Five-Year Study*, 25 Ann. Emerg. Med. 215 (1995).

8. Ability to walk?

9. Pregnancy: Is the patient near term?

This process is not truly "triage," but rather a nonphysician MSE performed (uniformly!) on all patients who come to the emergency department requesting medical care. The person doing the examination asks no information about payer status, health maintenance organization membership, or insurance. The results of the examination are recorded on a screening examination form and become part of the patient's permanent medical record. If the examination triggers a need for physician intervention, laboratory tests, or X-rays, a formal examination is performed by the physician in the emergency department. If the screening examination triggers no concern for a medical emergency, the patient is determined to be "stable" and then processed as if EMTALA no longer applies. The nonemergency patient is then referred to an off-site care center that functions as the backup to the emergency department. On its surface, this system seems both to work well and to meet the screening examination requirements of CMS for UC Davis.

In reality, however, the system cannot be easily translated to other hospitals. The lack of highly trained mid-level personnel, the lack of extensive on-site clinics, and the risk of "triage-out" violations make it unsuitable for non-university settings. Those who attempt to substitute nonphysician screening and merge it with triage generally end up violating their own rules and facing citations or lawsuits. Although the UC Davis policy has worked well in its setting, it is not a panacea for complying with EMTALA for most hospitals in the United States.

Finding an Emergency

Q 3:11   Emergency Medical Condition: What constitutes an "emergency medical condition"?

The Act states:

The term "emergency medical condition" means—

(ii) a medical condition manifesting itself by acute symptoms of sufficient severity (including severe pain) such that the absence of immediate medical attention could reasonably be expected to result in:

    a)   placing the health of the individual (or, with respect to a pregnant woman, the health of the woman or her unborn child) in serious jeopardy,

    b)   serious impairment to bodily functions, or

    c)   serious dysfunction of any bodily organ or part; or

(iii) with respect to a pregnant woman who is having contractions—

a) that there is inadequate time to effect a safe transfer to another hospital before delivery, or

b) that transfer may pose a threat to the health or safety of the woman or the unborn child.[82]

Cautions: The importance of documenting whether an EMC exists cannot be overstated. The presence of an EMC triggers all EMTALA's requirements, obligations, certifications, penalties, and liabilities. On the other hand, the absence of a legally defined EMC releases the physician, hospital, and on-call specialists from all EMTALA requirements. Without an EMC, the patient may be discharged or transferred even for economic reasons without violating EMTALA. The determination of whether an EMC exists has enormous ramifications under EMTALA. Physicians should get in the habit of writing that "no emergency medical condition" exists or "emergency medical condition is stabilized" in every emergency patient chart when applicable. These notations, however, will not support a defense to legal or administrative actions if there are insufficient details of the history, physical findings, testing and results, and summary of the physician's thought process. CMS in particular looks to the chart to prove compliance with EMTALA, and an inadequately documented chart frequently results in citations.

CMS specifies that an EMC includes severe pain, psychiatric disturbances, or symptoms of substance abuse that, absent immediate medical attention, may reasonably be expected to result in serious jeopardy to health, serious impairment to bodily function, or serious dysfunction of any bodily organ or part.[83] Furthermore, CMS adds that some intoxicated individuals may meet the definition of people with an EMC because the absence of medical treatment may place their health in serious jeopardy or may result in serious impairment of bodily functions or serious dysfunction of a bodily organ. CMS reasons that it is not unusual for intoxicated individuals to have unrecognized trauma. Likewise, an individual expressing suicidal or homicidal thoughts or gestures, if determined to be dangerous to self or others, would be considered to have an EMC.

The problem with EMTALA's legal definition of a medical emergency is that it lacks significant relevancy to the way physicians practice and perceive patient care. Physicians see an EMC as one that is threatening to life or limb, and so they must be reeducated to understand and apply the legal definitions rather than the traditional medical definitions to comply with the EMTALA law. The practice of medicine is not an exact science. There is no exact point at which pain becomes "severe." Does a patient with a painful migraine have an EMC? What exactly does "serious dysfunction of any bodily function" or "serious dysfunction of any bodily organ or part" mean in the clinical context? At what point does an asthmatic have "serious dysfunction" of the lungs to qualify as an EMC? Regarding a diabetic with hyperglycemia, what blood sugar level constitutes an emergency? How high must a child's fever be? Ten different physicians will probably give ten different definitions for these statutory terms. How is a

---

[82] 42 U.S.C. § 1395dd(e)(1).

[83] 42 C.F.R. § 489.24(b).

physician to determine what type of "immediate medical attention" would not result in "serious dysfunctions" when the term "serious dysfunction" itself has imprecise meaning? Good clinical practice dictates that any patient who *may* be suffering from an EMC is still protected by EMTALA and warrants further examination and, if indicated, stabilizing treatment.

With the addition of the "pain scale" as a vital sign by the State of California and by the Joint Commission, self-described pain levels will be important indicators of whether severe pain is present. Although pain-scale self-reporting is very subjective, disregarding complaints above five on a scale of zero to ten may expose the case to CMS criticism or citation. In addition, severe pain is likely to be determined if the patient has no documented improvement in pain levels after taking medication, or when he or she is unable to function normally as a result of pain. A patient who cannot walk without assistance, stand upright because of stomach or back pain, or use his or her hands or who has a blinding headache will likely be considered to have severe pain within the meaning of EMTALA. Merely giving pain medication without a reasonable period of observation and documentation of improvement is not sufficient. Documenting pain without quantifying the level of pain and describing its location, nature, and any radiation will likewise leave the chart at risk for citation.

Q 3:12 Knowledge of Emergency Conditions: What if the hospital is unaware of an emergency medical condition?

If a hospital provides an appropriate MSE and the exact diagnosis is not revealed, the hospital cannot be held liable for not stabilizing a medical condition of which it is unaware.

Cautions: The Tenth Circuit[84] has held that a hospital may not be sued for violating EMTALA unless it had actual knowledge that the patient in question had an EMC. Numerous other court decisions agree that if the screening examination was appropriate but did not reveal an EMC, EMTALA was not violated. The hospital, however, is not excused from providing the normal care that it would provide any person presenting with similar symptoms. Therefore, knowledge of the symptoms may still result in liability if they are not pursued in the standard manner even if the physician fails to appreciate the ultimate diagnosis.

The Ninth Circuit goes further in establishing protections for patients, accounting for the possibility that a hospital might "intentionally fail to diagnose an emergency medical condition in order to avoid EMTALA's stabilization requirement."[85] It has held that a hospital may be found liable for violating EMTALA's "appropriate medical screening" requirement if the examination "is so cursory that it is not 'designed to identify acute and severe symptoms that alert the physician of the need for immediate medical

---

[84] The Tenth Circuit covers Colorado, Kansas, New Mexico, Oklahoma, Utah, and Wyoming. 28 U.S.C. § 41.

[85] Bryant v. Adventist Health Sys./West, 289 F.3d 1162, 1166 n. 3 (9th Cir. 2002).

attention to prevent serious bodily injury.'"[86] Similarly, the First Circuit requires that a screening examination be "reasonably calculated to identify critical medical conditions that may be afflicting symptomatic patients."[87]

A hospital is not liable for an EMTALA violation if it had no actual knowledge that an EMC existed. However, a hospital must demonstrate that it provided an appropriate screening examination to detect such a condition.[88] EMTALA, unlike traditional state negligence or malpractice law, does not provide a remedy for an inadequate or inaccurate diagnosis.

In *Urban v. King*,[89] the Tenth Circuit ruled that a hospital had no liability under EMTALA because of an absence of actual knowledge of an EMC. The patient, who was experiencing a high-risk pregnancy with twins, went to a hospital's obstetrics department for a stress test. The test was nonreactive, and the patient was allowed to return home. The next morning, a repeat stress test revealed no fetal movements and the absence of any heart activity in one fetus. A cesarean section was immediately performed, but one baby was stillborn and the other was born with brain damage. The mother filed suit against the hospital, alleging violation of EMTALA by releasing her without stabilization after the first test despite the existence of an EMC. The district court rendered summary judgment in favor of the hospital. The Tenth Circuit's ruling that a hospital's duty under EMTALA to provide stabilizing treatment arises only on the actual diagnosis of an EMC is in accord with rulings from other federal circuit courts that have considered the question.[90]

In *Green v. Reddy*,[91] the patient was treated in the emergency department of Susan B. Allen Memorial Hospital for injuries sustained in a motorcycle accident and then admitted to the intensive care unit. The emergency physician failed to diagnose a pneumothorax and a torn renal artery. The following morning, the patient's mother requested transfer to Wesley Medical Center in Wichita. The patient later had complications, including loss of his left kidney. A suit was filed for violation of EMTALA. A federal district court in Kansas ruled that although the hospital obviously knew that the patient had an EMC, it had no specific knowledge of the torn renal artery or pneumothorax before the patient was transferred. Accordingly, there was no need to question whether the hospital violated EMTALA by failing to stabilize those conditions before transfer.

---

[86] *Bryant*, 289 F.3d 1162, 1166 n.3.

[87] *Correa*, 69 F.3d 1184, 1192.

[88] In the majority of circuits, satisfaction of the "appropriate medical screening" duty requires a showing that a patient was treated in a uniform and nondisparate manner, according to standard screening protocol. The First and Ninth Circuits additionally require that a screening examination must reasonably be designed to identify severe symptoms or critical medical conditions. (*See* Q 3:3, "Appropriate Medical Screening Examination.")

[89] 43 F.3d 523 (10th Cir. 1994).

[90] *But see* Carodenuto v. N.Y.C. Health & Hosp. Corp., 593 N.Y.S.2d 442 (N.Y. Sup. Ct. 1992) (the court ruled that a hospital violates EMTALA if it discharges a patient without stabilizing an emergency medical condition, regardless of whether or not that condition has been diagnosed).

[91] 918 F. Supp. 329 (D. Kan. 1996).

In both these cases, CMS would be likely to issue citations if the record supported that the hospital had had reasonable notice of the condition. CMS would conclude that either the hospital policy or protocol on nonreactive stress tests would trigger a diagnosis of EMC or that the hospital failed to have an adequate set of policies and procedures. In the *Reddy* case, CMS would look at the adequacy of the testing and evaluation to determine whether the scope of the examination was appropriate to the presenting symptoms.

Whether a hospital knew about the presence of an EMC is not always clear. In the case of *Battle v. Memorial Hospital*,[92] Zeta Battle brought her 15-month-old son Daniel to his pediatrician on December 22, 1994, with fever and sores on his tongue. Dr. Reeves, the pediatrician, diagnosed an ear infection and tonsillitis, and prescribed antibiotics. That evening, Ms. Battle brought Daniel to the emergency department with possible seizures. A lumbar puncture was performed and results were normal. The emergency physician diagnosed Daniel with febrile seizure, prescribed a new course of antibiotics, and discharged Daniel. Three days later, Ms. Battle returned to the emergency department because of continued seizures. Dr. Aust, the emergency physician, administered Dilantin for a diagnosis of seizure disorder and discharged the patient with a prescription for Dilantin. The next day, Daniel returned to the emergency department with continued seizures and this time was admitted. A CT scan of the head was normal. An EEG was abnormal but was not read until a week later. On December 27, Dr. Akin evaluated Daniel and diagnosed him with viral encephalitis, possibly herpes simplex encephalitis. He started treatment with Acyclovir, but Daniel's condition continued to deteriorate and he left the hospital in February 1995 in a near vegetative state. Ms. Battle contended that Daniel was not admitted at the second emergency department visit because she was poor, African-American, and uninsured.

The Fifth Circuit ruled that the trial court had erred in granting summary judgment for the hospital on the stabilization issue. The court found that because Dr. Aust had written "seizure disorder" on the emergency room chart, a jury could have concluded from that evidence that Daniel's doctors knew he was suffering from an EMC, at least by the the patient's second visit. The court of appeals reasoned that seizures "of an unknown etiology" were an EMC "because deterioration is likely to occur."[93] In all fairness, however, the hospital knew about the seizure disorder but was not aware of the rare diagnosis of herpes encephalitis. How the seizure disorder should have been stabilized sounds like an issue of medical malpractice—what would a reasonable physician do? In any case, the Fifth Circuit ruled that this EMTALA stabilization question was an issue for the jury to decide.

---

[92] 228 F.3d 544.
[93] *Battle*, 228 F.3d 544, 559.

Misdiagnosis

Q 3:13   Misdiagnosis: What if an appropriate medical screening examination results in a misdiagnosis?

EMTALA is not a malpractice law, and courts are consistent in ruling that Congress did not intend to guarantee the accuracy of emergency care. Faulty screening, as opposed to disparate screening or refusing to screen at all, does not violate EMTALA. To qualify as appropriate, an MSE need only be uniform, reasonable, and made available to all similarly situated patients. Misdiagnoses, meanwhile, should be judged in state malpractice courts under negligence rules.

The CMS State Operations Manual states:

> The clinical outcome of an individual's condition is not a proper basis for determining whether an appropriate screening was provided or whether a person transferred was stable. However, the outcome may be a "red flag" indicating a more thorough investigation is needed. Do not make decisions based on clinical information that was not available at the time of stabilizing or transfer. If an individual was misdiagnosed, but the hospital utilized all of its resources, a violation of the screening requirement did not occur.[94]

Cautions: Courts have made the distinction that EMTALA governs non-uniform treatment, not incorrect treatment. In *Hunt v. Lincoln County Memorial Hospital*,[95] Lincoln County Memorial Hospital treated Joshua Hunt for a puncture wound to his right foot. The hospital cleaned the wound and gave Hunt a tetanus shot and wound care instructions. Later that month, the wound developed osteomyelitis and cellulitis. The family sued Lincoln County, claiming that the infection would not have occurred had Joshua received an appropriate MSE. The Eighth Circuit ruled that since the hospital personnel cared for Hunt as they would have cared for any other individual, the MSE was appropriate for EMTALA purposes. In short, a misdiagnosis is not in itself a violation of EMTALA.[96] However, hospitals need to ensure that patients are truly treated in a uniform manner because CMS will look to misdiagnoses as red flags and closely scrutinize hospital procedures.

Summers v. Baptist Medical Center Arkadelphia[97] is a prominent case dealing with the issue of whether a misdiagnosis can support a claim for violation of

---

[94] U.S. Dep't HHS, CMS, State Operations Manual, App. V, Emergency Medical Treatment and Labor Act (EMTALA) Interpretive Guidelines, Part II, Tag A-2406/C-2406 (revised 7/16/2010).

[95] 317 F.3d 891 (8th Cir. 2003); 15 Emerg. Dep't L., no. 2, 20 (Feb. 2003).

[96] Vickers v. Nash Gen. Hosp., 78 F.3d 139 (4th Cir. 1996) ("[T]he accuracy of the diagnosis is a question for state malpractice law, not EMTALA; the Act does not impose any duty on a hospital requiring that the screening result in a correct diagnosis.") (internal quotation marks and citations omitted); Baber v. Hosp. Corp., 977 F.2d 872, 880 (4th Cir.1992) ("The avowed purpose of EMTALA was not to guarantee that all patients are properly diagnosed, or even to ensure that they receive adequate care, but instead to provide an adequate first response to a medical crisis for all patients . . . .") (internal quotation marks and citations omitted).

[97] 69 F.3d 902 (8th Cir. 1995), *reh'g en banc*, 91 F.3d 1132 (1996).

EMTALA. On October 25, 1992, Harold Summers arrived at the emergency room at Baptist Medical Center by ambulance after he had fallen from a tree stand while hunting. Dr. Ferrell, the emergency physician, examined Summers and ordered spinal X-rays but not a chest X-ray. After review of the X-rays and further physical examination of Summers, Dr. Ferrell determined that Summers was stable for discharge. Dr. Ferrell ordered an injection for pain, prescribed muscle relaxants, and discharged Summers. Two days later, because of persistent pains, Summers went by ambulance to St. Bernard's Hospital, where further X-rays revealed a comminuted fracture of one of his vertebrae, a sternal fracture, and multiple rib fractures complicated by bilateral hemopneumothoraces. Summers filed a suit against Baptist claiming a violation of EMTALA for failing to provide an appropriate MSE. The district court awarded summary judgment for the hospital and the case was dismissed. However, on appeal, the court of appeals reversed the lower court's decision.

A panel of judges on the Eighth Circuit Court of Appeals initially held that the facts of the case would support a finding that a violation had occurred because (1) EMTALA requires that hospitals develop screening procedures to identify critical conditions and (2) the examining physician had admitted that a patient who complained of chest pain was a candidate for a chest X-ray that would have revealed the patient's injuries. However, the hospital requested a rehearing en banc, which was granted. After reargument and reconsideration, the court of appeals altered its course and found in favor of the hospital. It reinstated the decision of the district court, dismissing the EMTALA claim.

The en banc court noted that other courts have declared that EMTALA "is not a federal malpractice statute and does not set a national emergency health care standard; claims of misdiagnosis or inadequate treatment are left to the state malpractice arena."[98] The court stated that:

> in construing statutes that are less than explicit, the courts will not assume a purpose to create a vast new realm of federal law, creating a federal remedy for injuries that state tort law already addresses. If Congress wishes to take such a far-reaching step, we expect it to say so clearly. This is the rule, generally speaking, in interpreting federal criminal statutes.[99]

The court finally reasoned:

> An inappropriate screening examination is one that has a disparate impact on the plaintiff. Patients are entitled under EMTALA, not to correct or non-negligent treatment in all circumstances, but to be treated as other similarly situated patients are treated, within the hospital's capabilities. It is up to the hospital itself to determine what its screening procedures will be. Having done so, it must apply them alike to all patients.[100]

---

[98] *Summers*, 91 F.3d 1132, 1137.

[99] *Summers*, 91 F.3d 1132, 1137.

[100] *Summers*, 91 F.3d 1132, 1138.

In the *Summers* case and many subsequent cases in other circuits, courts have generally come to agree that EMTALA does not guarantee proper diagnosis or provide a federal remedy for medical diagnosis; it is not intended to duplicate preexisting legal protections but rather to create a new cause of action, generally unavailable under state law, for what amounts to failure to treat.

For example, in *Nelson v. Calvin*,[101] a district court in Kansas ruled in favor of the hospital because the plaintiff had failed to designate any expert witness who would testify that the hospital failed to follow its own standard screening procedures. The Salina Regional Health Center treated five-month-old Justin Nelson in the emergency department. After discharge, the child developed fulminating meningococcemia and died. The family sued the hospital for an EMTALA violation, claiming the hospital failed to provide an adequate MSE. The court ruled that EMTALA asks only whether the hospital adhered to its own procedures, not whether the procedures were adequate if followed. The question before the court was whether the hospital followed its own medical screening policies when it failed to obtain Justin's blood pressure and oxygen saturation level. The hospital's written policies did not define "a complete set of vital signs" for all patients and required oxygen saturation levels only "if appropriate." Since no expert witness would testify that the hospital did not follow its routine procedures, the court granted summary judgment for the hospital.

In sum, EMTALA does not require a "correct diagnosis" to measure up to a comparable standard of care. An individual cannot sue a hospital for poor treatment; rather, the person can sue only if he or she is treated differently than other patients. Courts have noted that an "uneasy intersection" exists between state law medical negligence claims and EMTALA claims. Under EMTALA, a hospital can escape liability by complying with its pre-existing standards even if the practical effect is an inadequate examination. The statute merely requires that a hospital perform an appropriate screening examination for an EMC; it does not provide a remedy for an inadequate or inaccurate diagnosis.[102] Moreover, EMTALA does not hold hospitals accountable for failing to stabilize conditions of which they were not aware or even those conditions of which they should have been aware. If it turns out that the hospital missed an EMC, that fact cannot be determined in hindsight to create EMTALA liability.

---

[101] No. 01-2021-CM (D. Kan. July 25, 2002). *See also Summers*, 91 F.3d 1132 (screening examination does not have to be correct or properly done, just uniform); Ingram v. Muskogee Reg'l Med. Ctr., 235 F.3d 500, 552 (10th Cir. 2000) (screening requirement is for limited purpose and does impose a duty of reasonable care).

[102] *See Phillip*, 244 F.3d 790, 798.

Patient Consent and Payment

Q 3:14 Refusal of Care: What if the patient refuses the medical screening examination or further treatment?

The Code of Federal Regulations states:

> A hospital meets the requirements of paragraph (d)(1)(ii) of this section with respect to an individual if the hospital offers to transfer the individual to another medical facility in accordance with paragraph (e) of this section and informs the individual (or a person acting on his or her behalf) of the risks and benefits to the individual of the transfer, but the individual (or a person acting on the individual's behalf) does not consent to the transfer. The hospital must take all reasonable steps to secure the individual's written informed refusal (or that of a person acting on his or her behalf). The written document must indicate the person has been informed of the risks and benefits of the transfer and state the reasons for the individual's refusal. The medical record must contain a description of the proposed transfer that was refused by or on behalf or the individual.[103]

CMS further clarifies in the State Operations Manual:

> The medical record should reflect that screening, further examination, and/or treatment was offered by the hospital prior to the individual's refusal.

> In the event an individual refuses to consent to further examination or treatment, the hospital must indicate in writing the risks/benefits of the examination and/or treatment; the reasons for refusal; a description of the examination or treatment that was refused; and the steps taken to try to secure the written, informed refusal if it was not secured.[104]

For an EMTALA investigation, the State Operations Manual instructs its surveyors:

> In cases where an individual (or person acting in the individual's behalf) withdrew the initial request for a medical screening examination (MSE) and/or treatment for an EMC and demanded his or her transfer, or demanded to leave the hospital, look for a signed informed refusal of examination and treatment form by either the individual (or a person acting on the individual's behalf) of the risks and benefits associated with the transfer or the patient's refusal to seek further care. If the individual (or person acting in the individual's behalf) refused to sign the consent form, look for documentation by the hospital personnel that states that the individual refused to sign the form. The fact that an individual has not signed the form is not, however, automatically a violation of the screening requirement. Hospitals must, under the

---

[103] 42 C.F.R. § 489.24(d)(5).

[104] U.S. Dep't HHS, CMS, State Operations Manual, App. V, Emergency Medical Treatment and Labor Act (EMTALA) Interpretive Guidelines, Part II, Tag A-2407/C-2407 (revised 5/29/2009).

regulations, use their best efforts to obtain a signature from an individual refusing further care.[105]

The State Operations Manual states:

> Hospitals may not attempt to coerce individuals into making judgments against their best interest by informing them that they will have to pay for their care if they remain, but that their care will be free or at low cost if they transfer to another hospital.

> An individual may only refuse examination, treatment, or transfer on behalf of the patient if the patient is incapable of making an informed choice for him/herself.[106]

In this age of emergency department overcrowding, patients sometimes leave the department before examination or while waiting for tests or other treatments. CMS does not force hospitals to take EMTALA responsibility for such situations. The State Operations Manual states:

> If a screening examination reveals an emergency medical condition and the individual is told to wait for treatment, but the individual leaves the hospital, the hospital did not dump the patient unless:

> - The individual left the emergency department based on a suggestion by the hospital, and/or
> - The individual's condition was emergent but the hospital was operating beyond its capacity and did not attempt to transfer the individual to another facility.

> If an individual leaves a hospital Against Medical Advice (AMA) or left without being seen (LWBS) on his or her own free will (no coercion or suggestion), the hospital is not in violation of EMTALA.[107]

However, EMTALA prohibits constructive as well as actual patient dumping. The practice of routinely keeping patients waiting so long that they leave without being seen by a medical staff member, particularly if the hospital does not try to determine and document why patients are leaving and to tell them that the hospital is prepared to provide an MSE if they stay, is considered unacceptable. A hospital's delay in attending to a patient can be so egregious and lacking in justification as to constitute an effective denial of a screening examination.[108]

On November 10, 1999, CMS put out a Special Advisory Bulletin that clarified the EMTALA obligation for hospitals when a patient leaves without notifying the

---

[105] U.S. Dep't HHS, CMS, State Operations Manual, App. V, Emergency Medical Treatment and Labor Act (EMTALA) Interpretive Guidelines, Part I, V, Task 3.

[106] U.S. Dep't HHS, CMS, State Operations Manual, App. V, Emergency Medical Treatment and Labor Act (EMTALA) Interpretive Guidelines, Part II, Tag A-2407/C-2407 (revised 5/29/2009).

[107] U.S. Dep't HHS, CMS, State Operations Manual, App. V, Emergency Medical Treatment and Labor Act (EMTALA) Interpretive Guidelines, Part II, Tag A-2406/C-2406 (revised 7/16/2010).

[108] *Correa*, 69 F.3d 1184, *cert. denied*, 517 U.S. 1136.

hospital.[109] For any patient who refuses further care or "leaves without being seen," the emergency staff must log and document who refused care, what time the hospital discovered that the patient left, retain all triage notes and additional records, and document attempts to obtain written refusal. If investigated by CMS, the hospital must show that the refusal of care was not due to delay of care caused by discriminatory reasons such economic/insurance status, race, color, nationality, and so on.

Q 3:15   Cost Information: What if a patient asks about costs or insurance coverage for his or her treatment?

CMS expects that the emergency department staff may answer questions about payment if the answer is known, but to reassure patients in no uncertain terms of the department's EMTALA obligations to provide an MSE and needed stabilization treatment for any emergency condition found.

In an advisory bulletin issued in 1999, CMS stated:

> With regard to a hospital's handling of patient inquiries regarding the patient's obligation to pay for emergency services, we recommended in the proposed bulletin that such questions be answered by qualified personnel. We also recommended that hospital staff encourage a patient who believes that he or she may have an emergency medical condition to defer any further discussions of financial responsibility until after the provision of an appropriate medical screening examination and the provision of stabilizing treatment if the patient's condition warrants it.

> This section does not suggest that a patient is not entitled to full disclosure, only that the hospital should always convey to the patient that screening and stabilization are its priorities regardless of the individual's insurance coverage or ability to pay and that the hospital should discuss, to the extent possible, the medical risks of leaving without a medical screening exam and/or stabilizing treatment.[110]

If a patient leaves the emergency department after being informed of potential costs, the hospital risks an EMTALA violation for that patient. The hospital has to walk a fine line when answering a patient's questions on costs or insurance coverage for his or her medical treatment. CMS feels that informing patients of the cost of care may be a hospital's way to coerce patients to leave the emergency department without a screening examination. CMS suggests that the hospital encourage patients to defer any questions on cost of care until after being treated. On the other hand, as consumers, patients are entitled to be informed of possible costs of their care so that they can make an informed judgment on seeking services. EMTALA obligates a hospital to provide care, but not free care. Patients may be billed subsequently for hundreds of dollars of care, which they may have elected to avoid if the medical condition was not truly emergent. Even a simple visit to the emergency department often generates

---

[109] OIG/HCFA Special Advisory Bulletin on the Patient Anti-Dumping Statute, 64 Fed. Reg. 61,353 (1999).

[110] 64 Fed. Reg. 61,353, 61,355 (1999).

a bill in the hundreds of dollars. A patient who presents to the emergency department with a simple sore throat might elect to wait to see his or her own physician the next day if the costs are known. This problem would arise mostly with patients who do not have any insurance coverage at all. Since they would have to pay the entire cost of care, they most certainly would want to have some idea of the costs involved. CMS's concerns about answering insurance coverage questions do not seem entirely valid. In most emergency departments, much of the care provided is uncompensated—so a patient with any kind of insurance is a welcome customer. Emergency departments would certainly never want to coerce any patient with insurance into leaving without treatment. Often, insurance companies reject payment for emergency care for what they perceive as non-emergent conditions. Emergency personnel are therefore hesitant to address cost questions at all due to EMTALA concerns. Additionally, a patient may perceive that vague responses by emergency staff on costs of care may be the hospital's attempt to impose expensive care on him or her.

Hospitals should train all their emergency department personnel on how to address patient questions on insurance coverage or costs. The hospital may want to formulate a response paper or brochure explaining costs as well as EMTALA obligations that the staff can give to the patient. In any case, all personnel should respond to such questions uniformly. Any further questions unanswered by the brochure or staff member should be referred to key personnel.

Q 3:16   Registration: When may a hospital obtain insurance information?

The Code of Federal Regulations in Section 489.24(d)(4) states:

(1) Delay in examination or treatment

   (i) A participating hospital may not delay providing an appropriate medical screening examination required under paragraph (a) of this section or further medical examination and treatment required under paragraph (d)(1) of this section in order to inquire about the individual's method of payment or insurance status.

   (ii) A participating hospital may not seek, or direct an individual to seek, authorization from the individual's insurance company for screening or stabilization services to be furnished by a hospital, physician, or nonphysician practitioner to an individual until after the hospital has provided the appropriate medical screening examination required under paragraph (a) of this section, and initiated any further medical examination and treatment that may be required to stabilize the emergency medical condition under paragraph (d)(1) of this section.

   (iii) An emergency physician or nonphysician practitioner is not precluded from contacting the individual's physician at any time to seek advice regarding the individual's medical history and needs that may be relevant to the medical treatment and screening of the patient, as long as this consultation does not inappropriately delay services required under paragraph (a) or paragraphs (d)(1) and (d)(2) of this section.

(iv) Hospitals may follow reasonable registration processes for individuals for whom examination or treatment is required by this section, including asking whether an individual is insured and, if so, what that insurance is, as long as that inquiry does not delay screening or treatment. Reasonable registration processes may not unduly discourage individuals from remaining for further evaluation.[111]

The registration process permitted in the dedicated emergency department typically consists of collecting demographic information, insurance information, whom to contact in an emergency, and other relevant information.[112]

Cautions: The almost infinite variations in patient presentations and registration processes make comprehension of this requirement of EMTALA difficult. Generally, at or prior to triage, the hospital should avoid obtaining any financial information and limit questions only to basic information such as name, address, and date of birth. Once triaged, if the hospital finds that the patient has symptoms that trigger concern for an EMC, the patient should be brought straight back to the treatment area without any registration delay. Registration may continue at the bedside for such patients as long as the MSE is not adversely affected. If triage does not reveal emergency concerns, then the patient may register routinely and wait in the waiting area for care. If the wait is long, the hospital should have policies and procedures for assessing the waiting patient on a regular basis.

An effective registration process that ensures EMTALA compliance should:

- Avoid seeking authorization from health plans or preparing patient financial responsibility forms prior to initiating the MSE or stabilizing medical services, but establish processes to ensure needed registration information is gathered at some point—at the patient bedside or by following up with patients after service. There is no urgency to obtain pre-authorizations for emergency services prior to those services being provided, regardless of health plan requirements. Federal law mandates that Medicare, managed care, and other health plans must pay for emergency services that are pursued by patients based on the "prudent layperson standard," which means that the need for emergency care is determined reasonable based on a patient's perspective of the need for that care at the time symptoms are present.

- Ensure emergency department patient access employees understand the facility's EMTALA obligations and how to respond to patients who inquire about financial issues prior to receiving an MSE or treatment. Emergency department registration employees always must reassure patients that

---

[111] 42 C.F.R. § 489.24(d)(4)(i), (ii), (iii), and (iv).

[112] U.S. Dep't HHS, CMS, State Operations Manual, App. V, Emergency Medical Treatment and Labor Act (EMTALA) Interpretive Guidelines, Part II, Tag A-2406/C-2406 (revised 7/16/2010).

their medical care and treatment come first and that any financial discussions can take place after the MSE.

- Document, to the greatest extent possible, patients who voluntarily choose to leave the emergency department without receiving an MSE. If patients indicate they plan to leave without receiving treatment, take steps to secure written, informed consent from patients who refuse the MSE and treatment. If patients leave without notifying staff, document when it was discovered the patient had left and retain all notes related to the patient presentation in the emergency department. Such documentation will prove invaluable should allegations of patient dumping arise.[113]

EMTALA did not initially address managed care issues because managed care was in its infancy when Congress passed EMTALA in 1985. Since then, managed care has become the dominant form of health care insurance and delivery. For years, the managed care requirement for prior authorization conflicted with EMTALA's dictate that all individuals who present to the hospital for care be provided an MSE and stabilizing care. Some emergency departments would transfer or discharge patients from the emergency department without treatment when the managed care company refused authorization. This practice resulted in numerous lawsuits as well as EMTALA violations and fines. In order to avoid EMTALA registration complaints and complications, hospitals may use the growing practice of bedside registration.

The State Operations Manual states:

> Hospitals should not delay providing a medical screening examination or necessary stabilizing treatment by inquiring about an individual's ability to pay for care. All individuals who present to a hospital and request an MSE for a medical condition (or have a request for an MSE made on their behalf) must receive that screening examination, regardless of the answers the individual may give to the insurance questions asked during the registration process. In addition, a hospital may not delay screening or treatment to any individual while it verifies the information provided.

> Hospitals may follow reasonable registration processes for individuals presenting with an EMC. Reasonable registration processes may include asking whether an individual is insured and, if so, what the insurance is, as long as this inquiry does not delay screening, treatment or unduly discourage individuals from remaining for further evaluation. The registration process permitted in the dedicated ED typically consists of collecting demographic information, insurance information, whom to contact in an emergency and other relevant information.

> If a managed care member comes to a hospital that offers emergency services, the hospital must provide the services required under the

---

[113] Patient Access and EMTALA Compliance, 18 No. 2 Healthcare Registration 3, Nov. 2008.

EMTALA statute without regard for the individual's insurance status or any prior authorization requirement of such insurance.[114]

HHS further mandated this requirement in a special advisory bulletin issued November 10, 1999.[115] The bulletin, issued jointly by the HHS OIG and CMS, emphatically states:

> Notwithstanding the terms of any managed care agreements between plans and hospitals, the anti-dumping statute continues to govern the obligations of hospitals to screen and provide stabilizing medical treatment to individuals who come to the hospital seeking emergency services regardless of the individual's ability to pay. While managed care plans have a financial interest in controlling the kinds of services for which they will pay, and while they may have a legitimate interest in deterring their enrollees from over-utilizing emergency services, no contract between a hospital and a managed care plan can excuse the hospital from its anti-dumping statute obligations. Once a managed care enrollee comes to a hospital that offers emergency services, the hospital must provide the services required under the anti-dumping statute without regard for the patient's insurance status or any prior authorization requirement of such insurance.[116]

CMS does not change the basic requirement of EMTALA that there must be no delay in the provision of an MSE or stabilizing treatment while obtaining insurance information. For example, the hospital may request to see the patient's insurance card as long as this does not delay the MSE. However, the wording allows concurrent communication with an insurance carrier as long as such action does not delay or negatively affect the patient's ongoing medical care. CMS also added the phrase "nonphysician" to accommodate the provision of emergency medical services by nonphysician practitioners such as nurse practitioners. The emergency physician may contact the patient's managed care provider at any time to discuss medical issues as needed in order to optimally care for the patient. This will not be seen as an attempt to contact the provider for authorization to treat. Such contact must not delay required examination or treatment. Reasonable registration processes may proceed concurrently with the patient's treatment as long as such action does not delay examination or treatment. CMS cautions that any information gathered by the registration process that reveals financial liability on the patient's part should never be used to coerce the patient to stop treatment. No copayment should be requested of the patient before the MSE. If the MSE shows that the patient has an EMC, no copayment should be requested until after treatment has begun.

In *Parker v. Salina Regional Health Center,*[117] the widow of a patient who died in the emergency department of a hospital sued the hospital alleging that the

---

[114] U.S. Dep't HHS, CMS, State Operations Manual, App. V, Emergency Medical Treatment and Labor Act (EMTALA) Interpretive Guidelines, Part II, Tag A-2408/C-2408 (revised 5/29/2009).

[115] OIG/HCFA Special Advisory Bulletin on the Patient Anti-Dumping Statute, 64 Fed. Reg. 61,353 (1999).

[116] 64 Fed. Reg. 61,353, 61,356 (Nov. 10, 1999).

[117] 463 F. Supp. 2d 1263 (D. Kan. 2006).

hospital had violated EMTALA as well as state law negligence claims. After waiting 20 minutes to be triaged, the patient collapsed while seated at the registration desk and died after receiving two hours of further emergency care. The widow claimed that the hospital violated EMTALA because the reception clerk asked for insurance information before the patient had been triaged, because the patient was not given an MSE upon arrival in the emergency department, and because the patient was made to wait 20 minutes before a screening exam was done.

The U.S. District Court of Kansas granted summary judgment to the hospital on the EMTALA claims holding that if any deviations from the emergency department policies and procedures occurred, they had been de minimis variations. The court noted that in resolving a "failure to screen" claim under EMTALA, the only thing that the courts should look to is whether the hospital adhered to its own procedures, not whether the procedures were adequate if followed.

While no published decisions have cited the Court's holding in *Parker*, at least one unpublished California decision followed *Parker's* holding. The court in *Jace v. Contra Costa County*[118] seemed to get to the heart of the issue when it stated that the EMTALA "no delay" requirement "does not mean a hospital cannot ask about insurance, only that it cannot delay provision of the screening examination."

Q 3:17 Co-pay: When may a hospital collect co-pays?

As with the entire registration and insurance information gathering process, the collection of co-pays must not delay the required MSE.

Cautions: EMTALA was born of the premise that emergency medical care cannot be denied to an individual based on his or her ability to pay for services. It is absolutely necessary that the screening examination, stabilizing treatment, and transfer decisions are not influenced by a patient's ability to pay the co-pay.

The issue of co-pays is not addressed in the State Operations Manual. It is reasonable to assume that the collection of co-pays follows a registration process that does not interfere with the timely administration of the MSE and stabilization process. It is imperative that the patient understand that continued examination and care are not conditioned on the collection of the co-pay. Any care should continue unhindered regardless of whether a patient can or cannot supply the co-pay.

---

[118] 2009 Cal. App. Unpub. LEXIS 6223 (Cal. App., 1st App. Dist., July 29, 2009).

Chapter 4

Treatment Required to Stabilize

If any individual (whether or not eligible for benefits under this title) comes to a hospital and the hospital determines that the individual has an emergency medical condition, the hospital must provide either—

(A) within the staff and facilities available at the hospital, for such further medical examination and such treatment as may be required to stabilize the medical condition, or

(B) for transfer of the individual to another medical facility in accordance with subsection (c).

42 U.S.C. § 1395dd(b)(1).

A hospital's duty to stabilize arises only when the hospital actually detects an emergency medical condition (EMC) in a patient.[1] The only permissible method of determining whether or not an "emergency medical condition" exists is by way of the "appropriate medical screening examination."

If an appropriate medical screening reveals no EMC, then EMTALA's stabilization requirement does not apply. EMTALA certification is not technically required for transfers of individuals who do not have an EMC, but the presence of a uniform system for transfers greatly reduces the risks of inadvertent violations.[2]

---

[1] *See* Vickers v. Nash Gen. Hosp., 78 F.3d 139 (4th Cir. 1996) A duty to stabilize arises when the screening exam reveals an emergency medical condition.

[2] U.S. Dep't HHS, Centers for Medicare & Medicaid Servs. (CMS), State Operations Manual, Appendix. V, Emergency Medical Treatment and Labor Act (EMTALA) Interpretive Guidelines, Part II, Tag A-2407/ C-2407 (revised 5/29/2009). Appendix V of the State Operations Manual is reproduced in **Appendix C** of this book.

If the medical screening reveals an EMC, the hospital may discharge its duty under EMTALA in one of three ways. First, the emergency department can provide the patient with treatment necessary to stabilize the EMC. Second, the hospital can admit the patient as an inpatient for further care. Third, if the hospital is unable to stabilize the patient either in the emergency department or by admission, it can transfer the patient appropriately to a facility that has the capability to stabilize the patient.

Determining whether a patient is stable presents a challenging intersection between law and medicine. EMTALA defines "stabilized" to mean, with respect to an EMC, that no material deterioration of the condition is likely to result from or occur during the transfer. With respect to labor, "stabilized" means that the woman has delivered (including the placenta).[3] The State Operations Manual states that a patient is deemed stabilized if the treating physician determines, within reasonable clinical confidence, that the EMC has been resolved or if the treating physician determines that the patient is "stable for transfer" or "stable for discharge."[4] However, physicians usually think of patient stability in terms of normal or abnormal vital signs. Predicting the stability of a particular patient hours in the future is outside usual medical thinking and can be difficult or impossible to determine.

This chapter deals with questions related to the duty to stabilize, the special case of stabilizing pregnant patients, and limits on stabilization.

Stabilizing Treatment

Q 4:1   Stabilization: What is EMTALA's stabilizing treatment requirement?

EMTALA states:

> (b)   Necessary stabilizing treatment for emergency medical conditions and labor
>
> >   (1)   In general
> >   If any individual (whether or not eligible for benefits under this subchapter) comes to a hospital and the hospital determines that the individual has an emergency medical condition, the hospital must provide either—
> >
> > >   (A)   within the staff and facilities available at the hospital, for such further medical examination and such treatment as may be required to stabilize the medical condition, or

---

[3] The Emergency Medical Treatment and Active Labor Act (EMTALA), Pub. L. No. 99-272, Title IX, § 9121(b), 100 Stat. 164 (codified as amended at 42 U.S.C. § 1395dd (1995)), at § 1395dd(e)(3)(B).

[4] U.S. Dep't HHS, CMS, State Operations Manual, App. V, Emergency Medical Treatment and Labor Act (EMTALA) Interpretive Guidelines, Part II, Tag A-2407/C-2407 (revised 5/29/2009).

   (B) for transfer of the individual to another medical facility in accordance with subsection (c) of this section.[5]

Once a medical screening examination (MSE) reveals an EMC, the hospital must provide care to stabilize that EMC before the patient can be discharged or transferred. Once a patient's EMC is stabilized, the hospital and physician have fulfilled their duties arising under EMTALA.[6] Their duties are also fulfilled if the patient refuses further examination or transfer. If no EMC is found, EMTALA no longer applies for that patient.

The State Operations Manual elaborates on the extent to which stabilizing treatment is required. It states:

> After the medical screening has been implemented and the hospital has determined that an emergency medical condition exists, the hospital must provide stabilizing treatment within its capability and capacity.
>
> Capabilities of a medical facility mean that there is physical space, equipment, supplies, and specialized services that the hospital provides (e.g., surgery, psychiatry, obstetrics, intensive care, pediatrics, trauma care).
>
> Capabilities of the staff of a facility means the level of care that the personnel of the hospital can provide within the training and scope of their professional licenses. This includes coverage available through the hospitals on-call roster.
>
> The capacity to render care is not reflected simply by the number of persons occupying a specialized unit, the number of staff on duty, or the amount of equipment on the hospital's premises. Capacity includes whatever a hospital customarily does to accommodate patients in excess of its occupancy limits. § 489.24(b). If a hospital has customarily accommodated patients in excess of its occupancy limits by whatever mean (e.g., moving patients to other units, calling in additional staff, borrowing equipment from other facilities), it has, in fact, demonstrated the ability to provide services to patients in excess of its occupancy limits.[7]

Cautions: A hospital must either (1) provide further medical examination and such treatment as may be required to stabilize the medical condition within the capabilities of the staff and facilities available at the hospital when the hospital determines that the individual has an EMC or (2) transfer the individual in accordance with the requirements of EMTALA.[8] Once it is established that a patient showed up at a hospital's emergency department (or any remote or off-site location, or within the hospital or the 250-yard zone

---

[5] 42 U.S.C. § 1395dd(b).

[6] In Green v. Touro Infirmary, 992 F.2d 537 (5th Cir.1993), the court found that the defendant infirmary met its obligations under EMTALA when it stabilized the patient's condition.

[7] U.S. Dep't HHS, CMS, State Operations Manual, App. V, Emergency Medical Treatment and Labor Act (EMTALA) Interpretive Guidelines, Part II, Tag A-2407/C-2407 (revised 7/16/2010).

[8] 42 C.F.R. § 489.24(d).

around the hospital) with an EMC, the hospital can be held in violation of EMTALA either (1) for failure to detect the nature of the emergency condition through inadequate screening procedures or (2) if the nature of the patient's emergency condition is detected, for failure to stabilize the condition before releasing or transferring the patient in violation of EMTALA criteria.[9]

As the following summary of enforcement actions suggests, violation of stabilization requirement in EMTALA has been aggressively enforced by the Office of the Inspector General.

In early 2009, an administrative law judge (ALJ) sustained the imposition of the maximum allowable civil monetary penalty (CMP) against St. Joseph's Medical Center of Stockton, California. The Office of the Inspector General (OIG) of the Department of Health and Human Services (HHS) had previously levied a $50,000 penalty against St. Joseph's for egregious violations of the requirements of EMTALA. The case involved St. Joseph's failure to provide an MSE and stabilizing treatment to an 88-year-old man who had come to St. Joseph's emergency department. The man waited for nearly three hours without being examined by a physician. While his family repeatedly pleaded with the emergency room staff for help, the man's condition steadily deteriorated during the waiting period. The man eventually went into cardiopulmonary arrest and died in the waiting room without receiving any treatment. In sustaining the CMP of $50,000, the ALJ characterized St. Joseph's failures as "shocking," and "a complete collapse of the system of care [St. Joseph's] purported to offer emergency patients."[10]

Another facility paid $50,000 in 2011 to resolve its liability[11] for allegations of failing to provide an appropriate MSE and treatment for a patient.[12] The patient presented to the emergency department of Texas's Dallas County Hospital District *d/b/a* Parkland Health and Hospital System (Parkland) with severe abdominal pain. After waiting for approximately 15 hours, the patient finally received a physical examination, and the physician determined that the patient required an electrocardiogram (EKG), laboratory studies, and imaging. Parkland never performed the EKG, nor did it perform any intravenous access or monitoring, and the patient died of a heart attack approximately three hours later. The OIG alleged that Parkland violated EMTALA by its delays in evaluation, treatment, and performance of diagnostic examinations.

In 2011, Santa Clara Valley Medical Center (SCVMC) in San Jose, California, agreed to pay $48,000 to resolve its liability[13] for violating

---

[9] *See* Deberry v. Sherman Hosp. Ass'n, 741 F. Supp. 1302 (N.D. Ill. 1990).

[10] OIG Press Release, February 17, 2009, available at www.oig.hhs.gov/publications/docs/press/2009/emtala_st_josephs.pdf.

[11] In each CMP case resolved through a settlement agreement, the settling party has contested the OIG's allegations and denied any liability. No CMP judgment or finding of liability has been made against the settling party.

[12] HHS Office of the Inspector General Semiannual Report to Congress—Fall 2011, Page III-13.

[13] SCVMC has contested the OIG's allegations and denied any liability. No CMP judgment or finding of liability has been made against SCVMC.

EMTALA.[14] In April 2009, a 62-year-old male presented to SCVMC's emergency department complaining of dizziness, blurred vision, and fatigue. The man had been referred to SCVMC by a nearby urgent care facility. The urgent care facility suspected that based on severely low hemoglobin results, the patient was suffering from serious internal bleeding. The patient provided to a triage nurse at SCVMC his medical documents from the urgent care facility showing the abnormally low hemoglobin results. The triage nurse stated that the referral documents from the urgent care facility were difficult to read, and that the patient did not appear to be in distress because he could walk. As a result, the patient was triaged as nonemergent, and remained in the waiting room for seven hours while his heart rate steadily increased. There is no record that SCVMC notified a physician of the patient's heart rate. Ultimately, the patient died in the waiting room without receiving an MSE or stabilizing medical treatment.

In 2011, Piedmont Hospital (Piedmont) agreed to pay $50,000 to resolve its potential liability under EMTALA for failure to provide an appropriate MSE and stabilizing treatment for an individual who presented to Piedmont's emergency department for evaluation and treatment of an EMC. The individual made repeated requests for treatment for about eight hours, without success. The individual finally left Piedmont, went to another hospital, and was diagnosed and treated for deep vein thrombosis and pulmonary embolus.[15]

In 2012, Northside Hospital (Northside) in Florida agreed to pay $38,000 to resolve its liability[16] for OIG allegations that Northside violated EMTALA by failing to provide an appropriate MSE and stabilizing treatment to a patient with a history of mitral valve replacement. The patient presented to Northside's emergency department by ambulance with flu symptoms and a high fever. A triage nurse instructed the patient to go home and to follow his primary care physician's orders. Two days later the patient presented again to Northside's emergency department and was admitted to its intensive care unit. On August 8, 2009, the patient died due to influenza A (H1N1).[17]

Q 4:2   Stabilization: What is the statutory meaning of the term "to stabilize"?

The Act states:

> The term "stabilized" means, with respect to an emergency medical condition described in paragraph (1)(A), that no material deterioration of the condition is likely, within reasonable medical probability, to result from or occur during the transfer of the individual from a facility,

---

[14] HHS Office of the Inspector General Semiannual Report to Congress—Fall 2011, Page III-13.

[15] HHS Office of the Inspector General Semiannual Report to Congress—Spring 2012, Page III-19.

[16] Northside has contested the OIG's allegations and denied any liability. No CMP judgment or finding of liability has been made against Northside.

[17] http://oig.hhs.gov/fraud/enforcement/cmp/patient_dumping.asp.

or, with respect to an emergency medical condition described in paragraph (1)(B), that the woman has delivered (including the placenta).[18]

The Code of Federal Regulations states:

> "Stabilized" means, with respect to an "emergency medical condition" as defined in this section under paragraph (1) of that definition, that no material deterioration of the condition is likely, within reasonable medical probability, to result from or occur during the transfer of the individual from a facility or, with respect to an "emergency medical condition" as defined in this section under paragraph (2) of that definition, that the woman has delivered the child and the placenta.

> "To stabilize" means, with respect to an "emergency medical condition" as defined in this section under paragraph (1) of that definition, to provide such medical treatment of the condition necessary to assure, within reasonable medical probability, that no material deterioration of the condition is likely to result from or occur during the transfer of the individual from a facility or that, with respect to an "emergency medical condition" as defined in this section under paragraph (2) of that definition, the woman has delivered the child and the placenta.[19]

A patient can be in critical condition and still be considered stabilized for purposes of EMTALA if no material deterioration of the condition is likely, within reasonable probability.[20] This is an objective standard. An EMTALA violation is not automatically found simply because a patient's condition deteriorated following discharge or transfer from the emergency department. Once a patient is considered "stabilized," the hospital and physician have fulfilled their duties arising under EMTALA.[21] A patient without an EMC may be treated routinely: admitted, discharged, or transferred without worrying about complying with EMTALA.

Cautions: A patient is deemed stabilized if the treating physician attending to the patient in the emergency department/hospital has determined, with reasonable clinical confidence, that the EMC has been resolved. A patient is considered stable for discharge (versus transfer) when a physician determines, with reasonable clinical confidence, that the patient has reached the point where his or her continued care, including diagnostic workup and/or treatment, could reasonably be performed on an outpatient basis, or later on an inpatient basis, provided the patient is given a plan for appropriate follow-up care with the discharge instructions.[22] Unfortunately, no clear formula exists, in either the legal profession or the medical profession, to determine whether a patient's condition should be considered stabilized. For

---

[18] 42 U.S.C. § 1395dd(e)(3)(A); 42 C.F.R. § 489.24(b).

[19] 42 C.F.R. § 489.24(b).

[20] Brooker v. Desert Hosp. Corp., 947 F.2d 412 (9th Cir. 1991).

[21] In Green v. Touro Infirmary, 992 F.2d 537 (5th Cir.1993), the court found that the defendant infirmary met its obligations under EMTALA when it stabilized the patient's condition.

[22] U.S. Dep't HHS, CMS, State Operations Manual, App. V, Emergency Medical Treatment and Labor Act (EMTALA) Interpretive Guidelines, Part II, Tag A-2407/C-2407 (revised 5/29/2009).

example, emergency physicians may disagree on whether a patient with a diagnosis of new-onset angina is stable enough for transfer, even though vital signs are normal and no ongoing chest pain is present. The astute emergency physician recognizes that the intent of the legislation is to promote cautious and conservative judgments before patient transfer or discharge.

CMS regional offices point out that diagnostic studies necessary to determine whether an EMC exists may not be deferred to outpatient testing or subsequent return to the hospital. This includes all diagnostic studies and procedures required by an on-call specialist to achieve the determination of stability.

This language is based to some extent on the concept of common negligence, which would consider whether a reasonable physician, under the same or similar circumstances, would have behaved in the same way and whether the steps taken to assess and treat the patient's EMC were adequate to confirm or rule out the existence of an emergency and to stabilize any emergency condition found to exist. As discussed in the introduction to this chapter, the term "stabilized" does not mean that the patient has normal vital signs. "Stabilized" as used in EMTALA is a statutory term that requires a physician to make a decision as to whether there is a significant probability that a patient may deteriorate. If a physician makes the wrong decision, a jury will decide whether he or she violated EMTALA.

Q 4:3   Responsibility: Who is responsible for determining the stability of a patient?

CMS's 2004 revised State Operations Manual states:

> Hospitals are responsible for treating and stabilizing, within their capacity and capability, any individual who presents him/herself to a hospital with an EMC. The hospital must provide care until the condition ceases to be an emergency or until the individual is properly transferred to another facility. An inappropriate transfer or discharge of an individual with an EMC would be a violation of EMTALA.
>
> If a hospital is alleged to have violated EMTALA by transferring an unstable individual without implementing an appropriate transfer according to § 489.24(e), and the hospital believes that the individual was stable (EMC resolved), the burden of proof is the responsibility of the transferring hospital. When interpreting the facts the surveyor should assess whether or not the individual was stable. Was it reasonable to believe that the transferring hospital should have been knowledgeable of the potential complications during transport? To determine whether the individual was stable and treated appropriately surveyors will request that the QIO [Quality Improvement Organization] physician review the case.
>
> If the treating physician is in doubt that an individual's EMC is stabilized, the physician should implement an appropriate transfer (see Tag

A-2409/C-2409) to prevent a potential violation of EMTALA, if his/her hospital cannot provide further stabilizing treatment.[23]

Cautions: The transferring hospital is solely responsible for the welfare of the patient until the patient arrives at the receiving hospital.

Some of the cases that led to the passage of EMTALA involved hospitals that transferred patients in dangerous unstable conditions to county hospitals. One study found that in Cook County Hospital, Chicago, patients were transferred in unstable states of clinical shock (systolic blood pressure less than 100 mm Hg), respiratory insufficiency (arterial partial pressure of oxygen less than 60 mm Hg), severe metabolic abnormalities (dangerous levels of blood sugar or electrolytes), acute complicated cerebral vascular accidents (intracranial hemorrhage), severe traumatic injuries (hypovolemic shock, unstable spinal fractures, flail chest, severe burns), acute abdominal conditions with signs of peritonitis or perforation, severe hypertension (blood pressure greater than 200/130), and potentially life-threatening infections.[24]

There will, of course, be instances where patients have to be transferred in an unstable condition. These are cases where the transferring hospital does not have the capabilities to stabilize the patient's condition (e.g., a hospital does not have a neurosurgeon on staff to operate on a patient with traumatic intracranial hemorrhage). In such a case, the patient will be unstable for transfer to a facility with the capabilities to treat the patient. CMS allows such transfers as long as the benefits of transfer outweigh the risks to the patient. Prior to any such transfer, the hospital must document that it has done all it can do within its capabilities to stabilize the patient's EMC as much as possible. This is the main purpose of the EMTALA certificate of transfer.

There may be times when a receiving hospital physician or the patient's private physician disagrees with a patient's transfer. CMS believes that the physician who is physically attending the patient in the emergency department has the top priority in making the final decision on transfer.

The reason for this interpretation is to prevent a primary physician of a managed care insurance company from insisting that a patient be transferred to an insurance-contracted hospital. The physician physically treating the patient in the emergency department has the final decision on whether the patient is stable for transfer or needs further stabilization or admission to the initial hospital.

---

[23] U.S. Dep't HHS, CMS, State Operations Manual, App. V, Emergency Medical Treatment and Labor Act (EMTALA) Interpretive Guidelines, Part II, Tag A-2407/C-2407 (revised 5/29/2009).

[24] Robert L. Schiff and David A. Ansell, *Transfers to a Public Hospital: A Prospective Study of 467 Patients*, 314 New Eng. J. Med. No. 9 (1986), 553.

Q 4:4   Inpatient Stabilization: Does EMTALA's stabilization requirement continue after a patient is admitted to the hospital?

According to CMS, the answer is no. The requirements of EMTALA end once a patient is admitted to the hospital from the emergency department as an inpatient. Further, hospitals are not subject to EMTALA requirements for patients admitted directly to the hospital for inpatient care. However, a hospital may be exposed to liability for failure to stabilize an admitted patient if that patient is able to show that his or her admission was a mere subterfuge to evade EMTALA liability.[25]

The application of EMTALA to inpatients was a source of great confusion prior to 2003. The confusion was fueled in 1999 when the U.S. Supreme Court decided *Roberts v. Galen of Virginia.*[26] There the Court held that a patient who had been hospitalized for 6 weeks could state a cause of action under EMTALA for her transfer to a skilled nursing facility. The high court never even mentioned the inpatient issue. By its silence, many observers intuited that the Supreme Court had tacitly determined that EMTALA did apply to inpatients.

In the final rules published in the *Federal Register* on September 9, 2003, CMS made clear that EMTALA does not apply to inpatients by amending the Code of Federal Regulations at Section 489.24(d)(2) to state:

> (2) Exception: Application to inpatients. (i) if a hospital has screened an individual under paragraph (a) of this section and found the individual to have an emergency medical condition, and admits that individual as an inpatient in good faith in order to stabilize the emergency medical condition, the hospital has satisfied its special responsibilities under this section with respect to that individual.

> (ii) This section is not applicable to an inpatient who was admitted for elective (nonemergency) diagnosis or treatment.[27]

Thus, under the final rules, EMTALA does not apply to inpatients who were admitted for non-emergent reasons or to patients who previously received an MSE.

Still, the issue of whether EMTALA applies to inpatients would not die. In April 2008 CMS proposed regulations concerning EMTALA's application to inpatients.[28] The proposed regulations, if adopted, would have further confused the inpatient issue. The proposed regulations suggested that "the obligation of EMTALA does not end for all hospitals once an individual has been admitted as an inpatient to the hospital where the individual first presented."[29]

---

[25] In Morgan v. North Miss. Med. Ctr., 458 F. Supp. 2d 1341 (S.D. Ala. 2006), the court affirmed the standard under which a patient's admission as an inpatient negates any EMTALA stabilization claim, unless the patient shows that his or her admission was not in good faith or was a mere subterfuge to evade liability.

[26] Roberts v. Galen of Va., Inc., 525 U.S. 249 (1999).

[27] 42 C.F.R. § 489.24(b).

[28] 73 Fed. Reg. 23,528, 23,668 (Apr. 30, 2008).

[29] 73 Fed. Reg. 23,670.

Ultimately CMS did not adopt its own proposal but adhered instead to the stance that EMTALA obligations end once a patient is admitted. Hospitals with specialized capabilities continue to have the obligation to accept the transfer of patients held in emergency departments and in need of emergency specialized care.[30]

The position that EMTALA does not apply to hospital inpatients was reaffirmed by Interpretive Guidelines released by CMS on March 6, 2009. The guidelines state[31]:

> [O]nce an individual is admitted in good faith to the admitting hospital, the admitting hospital has satisfied its EMTALA obligation with respect to that individual, even if the individual remains unstabilized, **and** a hospital with specialized capabilities does **NOT** have an EMTALA obligation to accept an appropriate transfer of that individual. However, it is important to note that this rule does not apply to individuals who are protected under EMTALA and placed in observation status rather than admitted as inpatients. These individuals are outpatients.

Despite these repeated determinations by the regulators, some courts remain unconvinced that EMTALA applies only to outpatients. In 2009, the Sixth Circuit decided *Moses v. Providence Hospital and Medical Center*.[32] In *Moses*, Providence Hospital admitted a man who had been taken to its emergency department after exhibiting various signs of psychological illness and threatening behavior toward his wife. The man was admitted to the hospital as an inpatient and was evaluated by at least four medical staff members. He was discharged six days later. Ten days after discharge, the discharged patient murdered his wife.

The *Moses* court overturned a Michigan district court's summary judgment ruling in favor of the hospital. The district court noted that CMS regulations state that following a good faith admission, the hospital's EMTALA obligations end. The Sixth Circuit, however, specifically rejected the defendants' reliance on the 2003 CMS regulation, stating that the regulation was contrary to the statutory language of EMTALA and Congressional intent.[33] The court held that admitting

---

[30] 73 Fed. Reg. 48,689 (Aug. 30, 2008) ("[I]f an individual with an unstable emergency medical condition is admitted, the EMTALA obligation has ended for the admitting hospital and even if the individual's emergency medical condition remains unstabilized and the individual requires special services only available at another hospital, the hospital with specialized capabilities does not have an EMTALA obligation to accept an appropriate transfer of that individual. However, we would like to emphasize that if an individual presents to a hospital with a dedicated emergency department and is found to have an emergency medical condition that requires stabilizing treatment which requires specialized treatment not available at the hospital where the individual presented, and has not been admitted as an inpatient, then another Medicare-participating hospital with the requisite specialized capabilities is obligated under EMTALA to accept the appropriate transfer of this individual so long as it has the capacity to treat the individual.").

[31] Dep't HHS, CMS, Inpatient Prospective Payment System (IPPS) 2009 Final Rule Revisions to Emergency Medical Treatment and Labor Act (EMTALA) Regulations (Mar. 6, 2009) (emphasis in original).

[32] 561 F.3d 573 (6th Cir. 2009).

[33] 561 F. 3d 573, 583-4.

the patient is not enough. The hospital may still be liable under EMTALA unless the EMC is stabilized and no further deterioration is likely.

In early 2012, HHS again considered the question of whether EMTALA applied to an inpatient admitted to a hospital and again decided it did not. HHS concluded:

> [I]f an individual "comes to the [hospital's] emergency department," as we have defined that term in regulation, and the hospital provides an appropriate medical screening examination and determines that an EMC exists, and then admits the individual in good faith in order to stabilize the EMC, that hospital has satisfied its EMTALA obligation towards that patient. We continue to believe that this policy is a reasonable interpretation of the EMTALA statute and is supported by several Federal courts that have held that an individual's EMTALA protections end upon admission as a hospital inpatient.[34]

Q 4:5   Inpatient Stabilization: Do newborns present a special case for which EMTALA's stabilization requirement does apply to inpatients?

While the majority of state and federal courts that have addressed the issue have found that EMTALA does not apply to inpatients,[35] some courts have demonstrated an inclination to ignore the 2003 CMS regulations and hold that that EMTALA does apply to infants born at a hospital.

In 2005, the Wisconsin Supreme Court, in *Preston v. Meriter Hospital*,[36] dealt with whether EMTALA applies to an infant born to an inpatient mother. Shannon Preston, 23 years old and 27 weeks pregnant, arrived at Meriter Hospital in Madison, Wisconsin, on November 9, 1999. She was admitted to Meriter's birthing center and gave birth to a boy weighing just 1½ pounds. Although the newborn could not survive without resuscitation and the administration of oxygen and fluids, Meriter did not resuscitate or treat him, and he died 2½ hours later. Preston sued Meriter for violating EMTALA, among other causes of action.[37]

The Wisconsin Circuit Court granted summary judgment in favor of Meriter, reasoning that EMTALA's screening requirement applied only to patients who present themselves at a hospital's emergency department and not to a newborn whose mother checked in at the hospital's birthing center. On appeal, the Wisconsin Supreme Court reversed, rejecting the lower court's analysis and holding that EMTALA's screening requirement also applied to the hospital's

---

[34] 77 Fed. Reg. 5217 (Feb. 2, 2012). See **Appendix G** for the full text.

[35] *See, e.g.,* Bryan v. Rectors & Visitors of UVA, 95 F.3d 349 (4th Cir. 1996); Bryant v. Adventist Health Sys., 289 F.3d 1162 (9th Cir. 2002); Harry v. Marchant, 291 F.3d 767 (11th Cir. 2002); Quinn v. BJC Health Sys., 364 F. Supp. 2d 1046 (E.D. Mo. 2005); Anderson v. Kindred Hosp., Case No. 1:05-cv-294 (E.D. Tenn. Mar. 24, 2008).

[36] 284 Wis. 2d 264, 700 N.W.2d 158 (Wis. 2005).

[37] Preston also brought claims for neglect, lack of informed consent, and malpractice. The trial court granted summary judgment in favor of Meriter on those claims.

birthing center. The court further held that by being born on hospital property (even if not in the emergency department), Preston's newborn "arrived" at Meriter Hospital, which triggered the hospital's duty to screen under EMTALA.

In 2007, a federal district court refused to apply the 2003 CMS regulations stating that EMTALA does not apply to inpatients, finding instead that the regulation was merely an interpretive rule that did not control judicial interpretation of EMTALA. The case was *Lima-Rivera v. UHS of Puerto Rico*,[38] and the court ruled that a hospital could be sued under EMTALA for failing to stabilize a newborn infant's EMC. In *Lima-Rivera*, a pregnant woman with an emergency condition and in labor presented to a hospital's emergency department. After she delivered her baby boy in the hospital's labor and delivery room, the infant was admitted to the hospital's regular nursery as an inpatient but shortly thereafter developed an unstable EMC and was taken to the critical care nursery. The following day, he was transferred in an unstable condition to another hospital, where he died within a day of the transfer.

Relying on a pre-2003 case,[39] the *Lima-Rivera* court held that the infant "presented" to the hospital when he was born in the operating room after a cesarean section and the hospital staff identified his EMC, which triggered EMTALA's stabilization and appropriate transfer requirement. In its holding, the court ignored the 2003 CMS regulations and applied EMTALA's stabilization and appropriate transfer requirement to an apparent inpatient.

The Born-Alive Infants Protection Act of 2002 (BAIPA)[40] added more complexity to the already challenging task of interpreting and correlating the requirements of EMTALA to in-hospital births. BAIPA is a federal law that defines the terms "individual"[41] and "born alive"[42] for the purpose of interpreting and applying all federal laws, including EMTALA. BAIPA's purpose is to ensure that infants who are separated from their mothers at any stage of development are treated as living beings if they have "a beating heart, pulsation of the umbilical cord, or definite movement of the voluntary muscles."[43] Newborn infants born on hospital property are therefore "individuals" under EMTALA.

---

[38] 476 F. Supp. 2d 92 (D. Puerto Rico 2007).

[39] Lopez-Soto v. Hawayek, 175 F.3d 170 (1st Cir. 1999).

[40] Born-Alive Infants Protection Act (BAIPA) of 2002, 1 U.S.C. § 8 (Supp. III 2003).

[41] "In determining the meaning of any Act of Congress, or of any ruling, regulation, or interpretation of the various administrative bureaus and agencies of the United States, the words 'person,' 'human being,' 'child,' and 'individual' shall include every infant member of the species homo sapiens who is born alive at any stage of development." 1 U.S.C. § 8(a).

[42] "As used in this section, the term 'born alive,' with respect to a member of the species homo sapiens, means the complete expulsion or extraction from his or her mother of that member, at any stage of development, who after such expulsion or extraction breathes or has a beating heart, pulsation of the umbilical cord, or definite movement of voluntary muscles, regardless of whether the umbilical cord has been cut, and regardless of whether the expulsion or extraction occurs as a result of natural or induced labor, cesarean section, or induced abortion." 1 U.S.C. § 8(b).

[43] 1 U.S.C. § 8(b).

In April 2005, CMS sent a notice to State Survey Agency Directors regarding the interaction of BAIPA and EMTALA[44] with the intent of clarifying circumstances in which EMTALA protects an infant who is "born alive."[45] The 2005 CMS guidance noted that if a hospital's labor and delivery department meets the definition of a "dedicated emergency department," then EMTALA would protect the infant born or delivered in such a setting if (1) a request were made for an emergency screening and stabilization or (2) a prudent layperson were to conclude that based on his or her appearance, the infant required emergency care.[46] CMS further noted that EMTALA screening and stabilization duties might be triggered "elsewhere on the hospital campus (i.e., not in the hospital's dedicated emergency department)" if a "prudent layperson observer concluded, based on the born-alive infant's appearance or behavior, that the born-alive infant were suffering from an emergency medical condition."[47] The 2005 CMS guidance implies that contrary to the 2003 regulations, CMS considers the health of the infant, not the setting of the care, to be the overriding priority in labor and delivery cases. If a prudent layperson were to recognize the need for screening and stabilization, the duty would attach regardless of where on the campus the birth occurred. While the guidance indicates that once the infant is transferred to inpatient care, EMTALA protections cease, the initial screening and stabilization duties may be applicable anywhere on a hospital campus.

The final answer to this question has yet to be written.

Q 4:6   Medical Discharge: When is a medical patient considered stable?

The CMS State Operations Manual states:

> If a hospital is unable to stabilize an individual within its capability, an appropriate transfer should be implemented. To be considered stable the emergency medical condition that caused the individual to seek care in the dedicated ED must be resolved, although the underlying medical condition may persist. For example, an individual presents to a hospital complaining of chest tightness, wheezing, and shortness of breath and has a medical history of asthma. The physician completes a medical screening examination and diagnoses the individual as having an asthma attack that is an emergency medical condition. Stabilizing treatment is provided (medication and oxygen) to alleviate the acute respiratory symptoms. In this scenario the EMC was resolved and the

---

[44] Thomas E. Hamilton, *Interaction of the Emergency Medical Treatment and Labor Act (EMTALA) and the Born-Alive Infants Protection Act of 2002,* CMS S&C Memorandum to State Survey Agency Directors, No. 05-26 (Apr. 22, 2005).

[45] As the term is defined under BAIPA, at 1 U.S.C. § 8(b).

[46] Thomas E. Hamilton, *Interaction of the Emergency Medical Treatment and Labor Act (EMTALA) and the Born-Alive Infants Protection Act of 2002,* CMS S&C Memorandum to State Survey Agency Directors, No. 05-26 (Apr. 22, 2005), at 5.

[47] Thomas E. Hamilton, *Interaction of the Emergency Medical Treatment and Labor Act (EMTALA) and the Born-Alive Infants Protection Act of 2002,* CMS S&C Memorandum to State Survey Agency Directors, No. 05-26 (Apr. 22, 2005), at 5-6.

hospital's EMTALA obligation is therefore ended, but the underlying medical condition of asthma still exists. After stabilizing the individual, the hospital no longer has an EMTALA obligation. The physician may discharge the individual home, admit him or her to the hospital, or transfer (the "appropriate transfer" requirement under EMTALA does not apply to this situation since the individual has been stabilized) the individual to another hospital depending on his or her needs. The preceding example does not reflect a change in policy, rather it is a clarification as to when an appropriate transfer is to be implemented to decrease hospitals risk of being in violation of EMTALA due to inappropriate transfers.[48]

The CMS State Operations Manual further states:

> An individual will be deemed stabilized if the treating physician or QMP (qualified medical personnel) attending to the individual in the emergency department/hospital has determined, within reasonable clinical confidence, that the emergency medical condition has been resolved.

For those individuals whose EMCs have been resolved, the physician or QMP has two options:

1. Discharge home with follow-up instructions. An individual is considered stable and ready for discharge when, within reasonable clinical confidence, it is determined that the individual has reached the point where his or her continued care, including diagnostic work-up and/or treatment, could be reasonably performed as an outpatient or later as an inpatient, provided the individual is given a plan for appropriate follow-up care as part of the discharge instructions. The EMC that caused the individual to present to the dedicated ED must be resolved, but the underlying medical condition may persist. Hospitals are expected within reason to assist/provide discharged individuals the necessary information to secure the necessary follow-up care to prevent relapse or worsening of the medical condition upon release from the hospital; or

2. Inpatient admission for continued care.[49]

Cautions: Once a patient's medical condition has been stabilized, EMTALA's obligations for that patient end so that the patient may be transferred or discharged without concerns about EMTALA violation. However, there are many instances when a patient's medical condition is not clearly stabilized. Patients with conditions such as asthma, atypical chest pain, nonspecific abdominal pains, and so on, may not have a definitive resolution even after examination and tests and treatment performed in the emergency department. Such conditions may worsen later after discharge. CMS's definition for "stable for discharge" allows a "reasonable" application to patient discharges so that if there is "reasonable clinical confidence" that a patient's

---

[48] U.S. Dep't HHS, CMS, State Operations Manual, App. V, Emergency Medical Treatment and Labor Act (EMTALA) Interpretive Guidelines, Part II, Tag A-2407/C-2407 (revised 5/29/2009).

[49] U.S. Dep't HHS, CMS, State Operations Manual, App. V, Emergency Medical Treatment and Labor Act (EMTALA) Interpretive Guidelines, Part II, Tag A-2407/C-2407 (revised 5/29/2009).

condition will not worsen, then he or she may be discharged for follow-up testing or care. A patient with an arm fracture, once properly stabilized by splinting, may be discharged for follow-up orthopedic care. Atypical chest pains, once acute myocardial infarction has been reasonably ruled out by testing, may be discharged for further outpatient testing such as cardiac stress testing. Nonspecific abdominal pain, once tests have reasonably ruled out an acute surgical condition (appendicitis), may be discharged for observation and follow-up care. Of course, if a patient suffers a bad outcome, CMS and the courts may apply the retroscope to determine whether the discharge was indeed "reasonable."

Q 4:7   Psychiatric Stability: When is a psychiatric patient considered "stable for transfer"?

The CMS State Operations Manual states:

> Psychiatric patients are considered stable when they are protected and prevented from injuring or harming him/herself or others. The administration of chemical or physical restraints for purposes of transferring an individual from one facility to another may stabilize a psychiatric patient for a period of time and remove the immediate Emergency Medical Condition but the underlying medical condition may persist and if not treated for longevity the patient may experience exacerbation of the Emergency Medical Condition. Therefore, practitioners should use great care when determining if the medical condition is in fact stable after administering chemical or physical restraints.[50]

A psychiatric patient may be made "stable" and no longer considered a threat to himself or herself or to others by medical treatment (e.g., tranquilizers) or by physical means (e.g., restraints or adequate physical control by ambulance personnel). A public psychiatric facility without adequate capacity to treat medical emergencies has the right to refuse a transfer if the patient has additional dangerous medical problems (e.g., acute overdose with signs of instability). A patient who is stable in a hospital with a large staff and available technical support may be considered unstable in a psychiatric hospital where close medical monitoring is less available. EMTALA terminology is now the law of the land so, before a psychiatric transfer, the prudent emergency physician should always document in the medical chart that "the patient is stable for psychiatric transfer because of" either (1) "medical evaluation," (2) "chemical restraints," or (3) "physical restraints."

Once a patient is deemed "stable," EMTALA no longer applies, and patients may be transferred to comply with state psychiatric transfer rules or even for economic reasons. The operative word for stabilizing psychiatric patients is "protected." A psychiatric patient is considered stable for transfer when, by use

---

[50] U.S. Dep't HHS, CMS, State Operations Manual, App. V, Emergency Medical Treatment and Labor Act (EMTALA) Interpretive Guidelines, Part II, Tag A-2407/C-2407 (revised 5/29/2009).

of either medication or physical restraints, the patient can be protected from hurting himself or herself or others.

Cautions: While the State Operations Manuel suggests use of "chemical or physical restraints for purposes of transferring an individual" to effect a stable transfer, great care must be exercised when following these recommendations. In 1998, CMS issued patient rights requirements[51] that included stiff restrictions on use of restraints and seclusion. Before a patient can be restrained for transfer, the provider must affirmatively document that no less-restrictive measures are feasible (such as retaining the patient at the initial hospital). Strict time limits on use of restraints and requirements for physician evaluation are also in place.

The standard set by CMS regarding use of restraint or sedation is:

> All patients have the right to be free from physical or mental abuse, and corporal punishment. All patients have the right to be free from restraint or seclusion, of any form, imposed as a means of coercion, discipline, convenience, or retaliation by staff. Restraint or seclusion may only be imposed to ensure the immediate physical safety of the patient, a staff member, or others and must be discontinued at the earliest possible time.[52]

The Interpretative Guidelines go on to say:

> The decision to use a restraint or seclusion is not driven by diagnosis, but by a comprehensive individual patient assessment. For a given patient at a particular point in time, this comprehensive individualized patient assessment is used to determine whether the use of less restrictive measures poses a greater risk than the risk of using a restraint or seclusion.[53]

Although the physician may be tempted to believe that the patient is not restrained, placing a patient on a stretcher and strapping him or her down such that he or she cannot release the straps constitutes restraint under this standard. Likewise, the physician may not appreciate that the placing of the patient in a room, an ambulance, or a squad car, from which he or she is not free to exit, is seclusion and is also strictly limited in usage. Indeed, strapping a patient to a cot, giving him or her drugs, and sending him or her out in an ambulance amounts to restraint and seclusion and demands that hospital personnel be in constant face-to-face observation of the patient during the transport.[54]

---

[51] U.S. Dep't HHS, CMS, State Operations Manual, App. A, Survey Protocol, Regulations and Interpretive Guidelines for Hospitals, § 482.13(e) (revised 12/22/2011).

[52] U.S. Dep't HHS, CMS, State Operations Manual, App. A, Survey Protocol, Regulations and Interpretive Guidelines for Hospitals, § 482.13(e) (revised 12/22/2011).

[53] U.S. Dep't HHS, CMS, State Operations Manual, App. A, Survey Protocol, Regulations and Interpretive Guidelines for Hospitals, Interpretive Guidelines § 482.13(e) (revised 12/22/2011).

[54] U.S. Dep't HHS, CMS, State Operations Manual, App. A, Survey Protocol, Regulations and Interpretive Guidelines for Hospitals, Interpretive Guidelines § 482.13(e)(1) (revised 12/22/2011).

Any time restraint or seclusion is used on a patient, it must be "the least restrictive intervention that will be effective to protect the patient, a staff member, or others from harm,"[55] be in "accordance with a written modification to the patient's plan of care,"[56] and be reviewed every four hours (or a shorter time period for a child).[57]

Q 4:8 Psychiatric Discharge: When is a psychiatric patient considered "stable for discharge"?

In the State Operations Manual, CMS states:

> Psychiatric patients are considered stable when they are protected and prevented from injuring or harming him/herself or others. The administration of chemical or physical restraints for purposes of transferring an individual from one facility to another may stabilize a psychiatric patient for a period of time and remove the immediate Emergency Medical Condition but the underlying medical condition may persist and if not treated for longevity the patient may experience exacerbation of the Emergency Medical Condition. Therefore, practitioners should use great care when determining if the medical condition is in fact stable after administering chemical or physical restraints.[58]

If, after an appropriate MSE, a hospital does not find an EMC as defined by EMTALA, then the patient is stable for discharge.

Cautions: In the case of *Pettyjohn v. Mission-St. Joseph's Health System, Inc.*,[59] Steven Pettyjohn went to St. Joseph's Hospital in Asheville, North Carolina, on August 23, 1997, with feelings of isolation and depression. Dr. Rita Ann Wilson Ogron examined him and found him to be physically stable. Dr. Carol Counts-Kuzma, the on-call psychiatric social worker, conducted a psychiatric profile and concluded that Pettyjohn was not in danger. Dr. Ogron offered to admit Pettyjohn, but he refused. Pettyjohn was discharged with instructions to resume taking lithium and to report to a psychiatric center. Six days later, Pettyjohn committed suicide. In a suit, Pettyjohn's parents claimed that his death resulted from the hospital's failure to stabilize his bipolar disorder before discharging him. The trial court granted summary judgment to the hospital. The appeals court noted that there was no evidence that the hospital treated Pettyjohn any differently than any other patient with similar symptoms. In addition, the hospital was not liable for not stabilizing a suicidal condition that was not apparent after an appropriate examination.

---

[55] U.S. Dep't HHS, CMS, State Operations Manual, App. A, Survey Protocol, Regulations and Interpretive Guidelines for Hospitals, Interpretive Guidelines § 482.13(e)(3) (revised 12/22/2011).

[56] U.S. Dep't HHS, CMS, State Operations Manual, App. A, Survey Protocol, Regulations and Interpretive Guidelines for Hospitals, Interpretive Guidelines § 482.13(e)(4) (revised 12/22/2011).

[57] U.S. Dep't HHS, CMS, State Operations Manual, App. A, Survey Protocol, Regulations and Interpretive Guidelines for Hospitals, Interpretive Guidelines § 482.13(e)(8) (revised 12/22/2011).

[58] U.S. Dep't HHS, CMS, State Operations Manual, App. V, Emergency Medical Treatment and Labor Act (EMTALA) Interpretive Guidelines, Part II, Tag A-2407/C-2407 (revised 5/29/2009).

[59] 21 Fed. Appx. 193 (4th Cir. 2001) (unpublished opinion).

The Pregnant Patient

Q 4:9   Labor: What is the definition of obstetric "labor" for EMTALA purposes?

"Labor" is defined in the Code of Federal Regulations as:

> . . . the process of childbirth beginning with the latent or early phase of labor and continuing through the delivery of the placenta. A woman experiencing contractions is in true labor unless a physician, certified nurse-midwife, or other qualified medical person acting within his or her scope of practice as defined in hospital medical staff bylaws and State law, certifies that, after a reasonable time of observation, the woman is in false labor.[60]

Congress specifically added obstetric labor to EMTALA in response to the case of Sharon Ford. In November 1985, Ford was in labor and went to Brookside Hospital's emergency department. She was seen in the waiting room by a nurse. Since Ford was a member of Health America Rockridge, a Medicaid HMO, she was referred to Samuel Merritt Hospital in Oakland, the HMO contract hospital. Merritt Hospital admitted her to the labor and delivery unit. Unfortunately, California was a week late in delivering the medical eligibility list to the Rockridge HMO so that Ford's name did not appear on the computerized list of those insured. Ford was again transferred, this time to Highland General Hospital, Oakland's county hospital. Shortly after arrival at Highland, Ford delivered a stillborn baby.[61]

Cautions: Any woman in active labor is generally considered unstable under EMTALA, preventing discharge or transfer, unless the transferring hospital has absolutely no capability to deliver the baby safely. Under that circumstance, transfer is permitted when the benefits of transfer outweigh the risk or when a legally responsible person acting on the patient's behalf requests the transfer. Hospitals that are not capable of handling high-risk deliveries or high-risk infants often have written transfer agreements with facilities capable of handling high-risk cases. The hospital must still meet EMTALA's requirements before transfer, making it imperative that the physician clearly document the explicit medical benefits of the transfer. CMS stipulates how to document the treatment of a patient in labor: "For pregnant women, the medical records should show evidence that the screening examination included ongoing evaluation of fetal heart tones, regularity and duration of uterine contractions, fetal position and station, cervical dilation, and status of the membranes, i.e., ruptured, leaking, intact."[62]

---

[60] 42 C.F.R. § 489.24(b).

[61] H.R. Rep. No. 100-531, at 6-7 (1988). *See* Andrew Jay McClurg, *Your Money or Your Life: Interpreting the Federal Act Against Patient Dumping*, 24 Wake Forest L. Rev. 173, 181 (1989). *See* Robert A. Bitterman, *Providing Emergency Care Under Federal Law: EMTALA*, American College of Emergency Physicians (2000).

[62] U.S. Dep't HHS, CMS, State Operations Manual, App. V, Emergency Medical Treatment and Labor Act (EMTALA) Interpretive Guidelines, Part I, V. Task 3—Record Review (revised 5/29/2009).

Essentially, any female in labor can go to any hospital in this country for delivery. If the hospital has the capability, EMTALA forces the hospital to deliver the baby. Since EMTALA is an unfunded mandate, this obligation can be a significant burden for on-call obstetricians working in indigent areas of this country. Only if the dangers of delivering the patient at the hospital outweigh the risks of transfer can a hospital avoid delivering the patient. In the State Operations Manual, CMS states:

- Regardless of practices within a State, a woman in labor may be transferred only if she or her representative requests the transfer and if a physician or other qualified medical personnel signs a certification that the benefits outweigh the risks. If the hospital does not provide obstetrical services, the benefits of a transfer may outweigh the risks. A hospital cannot cite State law or practice as the basis for transfer.

- Hospitals that are not capable of handling high-risk infants often have written transfer agreements with facilities capable of handling high-risk cases. The hospital must still meet the screening, treatment, and transfer requirements.[63]

Q 4:10   False Labor: What if the patient is in "false labor"?

Once a patient's labor is determined to be false, she is stable and EMTALA no longer applies. CMS had previously allowed only physicians to make the determination as to whether labor was false. As of August 18, 2006, a nurse midwife or other qualified medical practitioner other than a physician can make the false labor determination. CMS revised the regulations definition of labor to read:

> *Labor* means the process of childbirth beginning with the latent or early phase of labor and continuing through the delivery of the placenta. A woman experiencing contractions is in true labor unless a physician, certified nurse-midwife, or other qualified medical person acting within his or her scope of practice as defined in hospital medical staff by laws and State law, certifies that, after a reasonable time of observation, the woman is in false labor.[64]

Cautions: The regulations require a "reasonable time of observation." "Reasonable time" is not defined but is decided on a case-by-case basis. As with nonphysician practitioners performing MSEs, the Board must approve the category and the practitioner must be authorized to perform the screening examination in accordance with both state law and the hospital's rules concerning that practitioner's scope of practice or clinical privileges.

---

[63] U.S. Dep't HHS, CMS, State Operations Manual, App. V, Emergency Medical Treatment and Labor Act (EMTALA) Interpretive Guidelines, Part II, Tag A-2409/C-2409 (revised 5/29/2009).

[64] 71 Fed. Reg. 48,143 (2006); C.F.R. § 489.24(b).

CMS states in its State Operations Manual:

> Labor means the process of childbirth beginning with the latent or early phase of labor and continuing through the delivery of the placenta. A woman experiencing contractions is in true labor unless a physician, certified nurse-midwife, or other qualified medical person acting within his or her scope of practice as defined in hospital medical staff bylaws and state law certifies, after a reasonable time of observation, that the woman is in false labor.[65]

It was on the recommendation of the EMTALA Technical Advisory Group (TAG) that CMS adapted the regulations to allow nonphysicians to determine false labor. At its meeting held on June 15–17, 2005, the EMTALA TAG heard testimony from representatives of both physician and nonphysician professional societies regarding the competence of practitioners other than physicians to certify false labor. A representative of the American College of Nurse-Midwives stated that the then current requirement that allowed only a physician to certify false labor was overly restrictive and did not adequately recognize the training and competence of certified nurse-midwives. Testimony was also presented by the American College of Obstetricians and Gynecologists, which recommended amending the EMTALA regulations to allow certified nurse-midwives and other qualified medical persons to determine whether a woman is in false labor.

The hospital needs to be specific when formulating the required policies and procedures to guide the qualified medical person (QMP) on how to meet this requirement. The policy must clearly define the clinical standards that define false labor. A scoring system is not required but is probably helpful in checking off the clinical findings that define false labor. If there is dispute between the QMP and the attending obstetrician, then the obstetrician needs to come to the hospital to personally attend the patient. Discussions between the QMP and the obstetrician need to be fully documented.

Any discussion regarding false labor and the requirements of EMTALA should include an examination of the recent case of *Morin v. Eastern Maine Medical Center*,[66] the jury's verdict, and, in particular, the court's opinion. The lawsuit involved doctors at Eastern Maine Medical Center (EMMC) who sent a pregnant woman home from the emergency department knowing she was in labor and would soon expel her 16-week fetus, which doctors said had no heartbeat.

At approximately 4:30 a.m. on July 1, 2007, Lorraine Morin went to the emergency department at EMMC. Ms. Morin informed the registration clerk that she was 16 weeks pregnant, that she was having abdominal cramping, and that her primary care doctor, Pamela Gilmore, M.D., had told her to go to the hospital if she had any problems because of her high-risk pregnancy. Morin explained that her pregnancy was high risk as a result of her having previously had cervical cancer, a miscarriage, and a cone 2 biopsy. The patient gave the same

---

[65] 42 C.F.R. § 482.24(b).

[66] 780 F. Supp. 2d 84, 86 (D. Me. 2010).

information to the triage nurse and to Paul R. Reinstein, M.D., the emergency physician. Morin saw Dr. Reinstein at approximately 5:00 a.m. and his notes reflected that the patient had been experiencing contractions 10 minutes apart for the previous 20 hours.[67] Dr. Reinstein also reported that the patient had informed him that she had had one previous miscarriage, had given birth to two healthy children, and had pregnancy-induced hypertension.[68] Dr. Reinstein noted that although the patient had not noticed any bleeding, the nurse found some blood in her urine specimen.[69] After an ultrasound revealed a nonviable fetus, Dr. Reinstein referred Ms. Morin to Robert Grover, D.O., an obstetrical/gynecological doctor.

Dr. Grover performed a pelvic examination and another ultrasound and confirmed that the 16-week-old male fetus that Morin was carrying had no heartbeat. At 6:15 a.m., shortly after the examination, Dr. Grover discharged her, against her wishes and while she was still having contractions. Morin delivered her dead fetus in the bathroom of her home at around 9:00 p.m. later that day. The next morning, Morin called her obstetrician-gynecologist, Dr. Pamela Gilmore, who immediately admitted her to EMMC for surgery to stop her bleeding and to remove the remaining placenta.

Morin sued the hospital in U.S. District Court in Bangor, claiming EMTALA violations for failure to stabilize. After a three-day trial, the jury issued a verdict in favor of Morin, awarding her $50,000 in compensatory damages and $150,000 in punitive damages. The hospital appealed but settled with the plaintiff while the appeal was pending.

In his opinion, Chief U.S. District Judge John Woodcock observed that (1) EMTALA extends protection to a pregnant woman who is having contractions,[70] that (2) nothing in EMTALA limits this requirement depending on the viability of the fetus, and that (3) courts have extended EMTALA protections regardless of viability.[71] The court noted that Ms. Morin was 16 weeks pregnant when she arrived at the emergency room, that EMMC's medical records indicated she was experiencing "suprapubic cramps" while at EMMC and "having some contractions" when discharged,[72] and that, therefore, Morin appeared to fit within the plain language of EMTALA.[73]

---

[67] Morin, 780 F. Supp. 2d 84, 86.

[68] Morin, 780 F. Supp. 2d 84, 86.

[69] Morin, 780 F. Supp. 2d 84, 86.

[70] 42 U.S.C. § 1395dd(e)(1)(B).

[71] As examples, the court referenced Barrios v. Sherman Hosp., No. 06 C 2853, 2006 U.S. Dist. LEXIS 92146, 2006 WL 3754922, at *4 (N.D. Ill. 2006) (denying motion to dismiss EMTALA claim from a woman who was discharged after a miscarriage but prior to the delivery of the placenta); Thompson v. St. Anne's Hosp., 716 F. Supp. 8, 9 (N.D. Ill. 1989) (denying motion to dismiss EMTALA claim from a woman who alleged that she was not stabilized when she arrived at the emergency room 16-weeks pregnant and in active labor).

[72] Morin, 780 F. Supp. 2d 84, 93-94.

[73] Morin, 780 F. Supp. 2d 84, 94.

Judge Woodcock criticized the hospital for seeking to avoid the clear language of EMTALA[74] when it argued that Ms. Morin was diagnosed as having suffered a "missed abortion," not "as being in labor."[75] EMMC argued that because stabilization is required "only if the hospital determines that an emergency medical condition exists," the relevant inquiry is its diagnosis, not Ms. Morin's objective condition.[76] However, the court observed that EMTALA turns on a determination, not a diagnosis; that whether a patient is a pregnant woman having contractions is a fact, not a diagnosis. The court agreed that EMTALA would not apply if EMMC had not known either that Morin was pregnant or that she was having contractions.[77] But having determined that Ms. Morin was pregnant and having contractions, EMMC could not avoid EMTALA simply by assigning her a different diagnosis.

Judge Woodcock's opinion provides valuable insight as to how other courts may apply EMTALA in the future, given similar circumstances:

> EMMC's medical judgment does not trump the statute. If transfer of "a pregnant woman who is having contractions . . . may pose a threat to the health or safety of the woman or the unborn child," she has an "emergency medical condition" by law regardless of whether she has one by medicine.[78] EMMC is correct in pointing out that there may be tension between its determination and the statute's reach. The statute generally defines "emergency medical condition" in a fashion congruent with a common sense definition of the phrase. See, e.g., 42 U.S.C. § 1395dd(e)(1)(A)(i) (defining "emergency medical condition" as inter alia "a medical condition . . . such that the absence of immediate medical attention could reasonably be expected to result in the placing of the individual . . . in serious jeopardy"). However, the statute treats pregnant women differently and imposes a specific definition of "emergency medical condition," which may or may not comport with what a physician would determine. § 1395dd(e)(1)(B)(ii). Here, in the context of this motion, Ms. Morin has produced evidence that if believed by a jury would confirm she was pregnant when she presented to EMMC ER and was experiencing contractions. These facts, if proven, are sufficient to trigger the protections of EMTALA.

> EMMC responds that EMTALA's implementing regulations make distinctions on the basis of the viability of the fetus. [Citation] (citing 42 C.F.R. § 489.24(b)).[79] The regulations define "labor" as the process of

---

[74] 42 U.S.C. § 1395dd(e)(1)(B).

[75] *Morin*, 780 F. Supp. 2d 84, 94.

[76] *Morin*, 780 F. Supp. 2d 84, 94.

[77] The court referenced Brenord v. Catholic Med. Ctr. of Brooklyn & Queens, Inc., 133 F. Supp. 2d 179, 191-92 (E.D.N.Y. 2001) (granting summary judgment on EMTALA stabilization claim because hospital was unaware that pregnant woman was in labor).

[78] To be clear, the statute and the regulation do not tell physicians how to practice medicine. The question here is legal—whether EMTALA applies to a patient—not medical. If it does, legal consequences ensue; if it does not, they do not. The legal definitions do not direct the physicians or the hospital how to treat the woman medically, but they do direct the courts how she is to be treated legally.

[79] The court is uncertain and does not decide whether the regulation, which defines "labor," pertains to this portion of EMTALA. *Compare* 42 U.S.C. § 1395dd(e)(1)(B) (defining "emergency medical condition"

childbirth beginning with the latent or early phase of labor and continuing through the delivery of the placenta. A woman experiencing contractions is in true labor unless a physician, certified nurse-midwife, or other qualified medical person acting within his or her scope of practice as defined in hospital medical staff bylaws and State law, certifies that, after a reasonable time of observation, the woman is in false labor. 42 C.F.R. § 489.24(b). EMMC argues that "'labor' refers to 'the process of childbirth,' rather than defining it in a more general manner that could refer to missed abortions." [Citation] (quoting 42 C.F.R. § 489.24(b)). "In other words," says EMMC, "although section (e)(1)(B) refers to 'contractions,' it is clear that viewing the statutory scheme and its regulations as a whole, the protections of (e)(1)(B) apply to pregnant women who are experiencing contractions related to labor and childbirth, rather than cramping associated with a missed abortion." [Citation]

The Court is manifestly dubious about EMMC's stated fears that it will be inundated with pregnant women claiming that they are experiencing cramps and that EMTALA will require EMMC to stabilize them through delivery. Although EMMC argues that "[t]o avoid this absurd result," the Court must define labor to exclude missed abortions, EMMC never explains how doing so allows hospitals to discharge cramping pregnant women who "are not dilated enough to deliver." [Citation].

Moreover, the solution to EMMC's asserted dilemma is found in the implementing regulations, which allow hospitals to avoid EMTALA liability by certifying that a pregnant woman is in false labor. If a pregnant woman is having contractions, the regulations require that the hospital see her through delivery unless it concludes and certifies she is in false labor.

A straightforward reading of the regulation simply does not begin to support EMMC's questionable interpretation; there is no express or implicit requirement of viability. The regulation does not mention live birth. It focuses instead on the end result of the childbirth—the "delivery of the placenta," a phrase that encompasses both viable and nonviable fetuses.

EMMC further argues that because doctors certify when a patient is "in false labor," "Congress intended that, in application of EMTALA's requirements, physicians would be required to make certain medical judgments based on their medical education and experience." [Citation]. Because medical doctors do not define contractions at early stages of pregnancy as "labor," EMMC argues "there could have been no certification by a physician that Plaintiff was 'in false labor' because, medically, she would not have been considered by a physician to be in 'false labor' (much less labor)." [Citation].

The Court disagrees. Even though "false labor" is not defined, "labor" is. Regardless of what the physician may diagnose, the regulation says that a pregnant woman who is experiencing contractions is in true labor

---

as it applies to "a pregnant woman who is having contractions") *with* 42 C.F.R. § 489.24(b) (defining "labor" as "the process of childbirth beginning with the latent or early phase of labor and continuing through the delivery of the placenta").

unless the hospital certifies that she is in false labor. Medical professionals are presumably expected to certify "false labor" in reference to the regulation's definition of "labor," not an external medical definition. See *Burditt v. U.S. Dep't of Health and Human Services*, 934 F.2d 1362, 1369 (5th Cir. 1991) (stating that EMTALA's statutory definition "renders irrelevant any medical definition of active labor").[80]

Regarding EMMC's argument as a whole, the Court could not disagree more with EMMC at a most fundamental level. EMMC contends that the protections of the portion of EMTALA specific to pregnant women [pertain] only to women who seek medical assistance for pregnancies that result in the birth of a live infant and that the protections of the statute are unavailable for pregnant women who end up aborting. The Court is nonplussed at EMMC's disquieting notion that EMTALA and its regulations authorize hospital emergency rooms to treat women who do not deliver a live infant differently than women who do. EMMC's contention is not justified by the language of the statute or its implementing regulations and has disturbing policy implications. There is simply no suggestion that Congress ever intended such a harsh and callous result for women who, like Ms. Morin, are carrying a non-viable fetus.[81]

Q 4:11   Obstetric Stability: When is an obstetric patient considered "stable" under EMTALA?

A woman in labor is considered stable only if contractions stop, the baby and placenta are delivered, or a physician or other qualified medical person certifies that the labor is false. This definition makes it virtually impossible to transfer a woman in labor unless there is a distinct medical benefit to the transfer. EMTALA allows any patient who is in labor to come to any hospital and request obstetric care. The hospital is obligated to provide not only normal delivery but also any other care, including birth anesthesia, cesarean section, and, if necessary, intensive care for the mother or newborn as necessary until any EMC is stabilized.

Cautions: A patient with labor pains should be examined and evaluated by a physician before she is discharged or transferred.

In the case of *Williamson v. Roth*,[82] Brandy Williamson came to the emergency department of Citrus Memorial Hospital around 2:40 a.m. on September 22, 1996. She was pregnant and experiencing abdominal pains and an inability to urinate. An emergency nurse telephoned Dr. Stephen Roth and

---

[80] EMMC argues that *Burditt* is inapplicable because it was written under an earlier version of EMTALA in which "the threshold question was whether the woman was 'in labor.'" However, subsequent amendments strengthen, rather than undermine, *Burditt*'s conclusion. In the pre-1991 version of EMTALA, "active labor" was defined as "labor at a time when (B) there is inadequate time to effect safe transfer . . . or (C) a transfer may pose a threat to the health and safety of the patient." *Burditt*, 934 F.2d 1362, 1369. Because "labor" was not defined, the Fifth Circuit specified that "[a]ll agree that labor begins with the onset of uterine contractions."

[81] *Morin*, 780 F. Supp. 2d 84, 94-96.

[82] 120 F. Supp. 2d 1327 (M.D. Fla. 2000).

related Williamson's symptoms. Dr. Roth instructed the nurse to keep Williamson under observation. Williamson left the emergency department at 4:40 a.m. She returned at 8:30 a.m. with vaginal bleeding and worsening abdominal pain. Dr. Roth ordered an ultrasound, which revealed that Williamson's child had died due to placental abruption. Williamson filed suit, claiming a failure to conduct an adequate MSE and failure to stabilize under EMTALA. The failure to screen allegation was dropped because Williamson could not show that she was screened differently from other patients presenting with the same symptoms.

However, the hospital's own policies required that a patient in labor be examined by an obstetrician or physician before discharge. Williamson argued that if the hospital had followed its own procedures and required an obstetrician to evaluate her, the doctor would have been in a better position to properly evaluate the degree of her pain, its location, and the baby's well-being. The court agreed and allowed the failure-to-stabilize claim to proceed, reasoning that there was conflicting evidence on this issue. If the hospital had followed what the patient claimed were its established procedures, and had had her examined by an obstetrician before discharge, it might have avoided a lawsuit.

Ostensible injury does not have to occur for an EMTALA violation to exist. In *Owens v. Nacogdoches County Hospital,*[83] a pregnant woman without medical insurance presented to a local emergency room having contractions. She was directed to drive to another hospital in her boyfriend's car to be evaluated for labor. The woman arrived at the receiving hospital without incident, and neither she nor her unborn child suffered adverse outcomes. She filed a private EMTALA action against the original hospital. A federal district court in Texas ruled that, in this case, a private automobile was not the equivalent of an ambulance for purposes of EMTALA, and the transfer via private car violated the statute. In this case, the fact that the woman was experiencing contractions meant that she had an unstable EMC.

Limits on Stabilization

Q 4:12   Unable to Stabilize: Does EMTALA allow a hospital to deny stabilizing treatment?

No, not when a terminal illness is involved.

In a highly publicized decision (see below), the Fourth Circuit[84] ruled that if a patient comes to the hospital with an unstable medical condition, EMTALA obligates a physician to stabilize the condition regardless of whether the physician deems the type of stabilization appropriate.

---

[83] 741 F. Supp. 1269 (E.D. Tex. 1990).

[84] The Fourth Circuit covers Virginia, West Virginia, Maryland, North Carolina, and South Carolina. 28 U.S.C.A. § 41.

Cautions: On the surface, the term "to stabilize" appears fairly straightforward and reasonable. In *In re Baby K,*[85] the Fourth Circuit construed this as requiring a physician to provide medical "stabilization" that the physician may believe serves no therapeutic or palliative purpose, that the physician reasonably deems to be medically inappropriate and unethical, and that is contrary to broadly accepted standards of medical care.

Baby K was born with anencephaly. She was permanently unconscious with only brain stem support of organ functions and reflexes. Consistent with anencephaly, Baby K had respiratory difficulties requiring frequent respirator assistance. The hospital placed Baby K on a mechanical ventilator. The physicians recommended that Baby K be provided with only comfort care in the form of nutrition, hydration, and warmth. The physicians believed that ventilator treatment was medically inappropriate and urged Ms. H, the mother, to permit a "Do Not Resuscitate" order. Ms. H refused and insisted that the hospital provide Baby K with mechanical ventilation whenever the baby developed respiratory distress. After Ms. H's refusal, the treating physicians conferred with the hospital's ethics committee to override Ms. H's wishes. The ethics committee, composed of a family practitioner, a psychiatrist, and a minister, met with the treating physicians and concluded that the hospital should withdraw Baby K's ventilator because this treatment was futile in the committee's opinion.

Ms. H refused to withdraw aggressive treatment. Ms. H had a firm Christian faith that all life should be protected, and she believed God would work a miracle if that were God's will. Otherwise, she believed that God should decide the moment of Baby K's death, not other human beings. When Baby K's condition stabilized, the hospital transferred her to a nursing home. After several readmissions for mechanical ventilator treatment, the hospital filed for a declaratory judgment[86] to determine whether it had to continue providing Baby K with medical treatment that its physicians considered medically and ethically inappropriate.[87]

The hospital asked the court to create a futility or inhumanity exception to EMTALA. The court declined to do so, holding that such an exception would allow emergency departments to turn away anyone with a terminal health condition. The district court ruled[88] that the hospital was legally obligated to provide mechanical ventilation to Baby K under EMTALA, the Rehabilitation

---

[85] 832 F. Supp. 1022 (E.D. Va. 1993), *aff'd,* 16 F.3d 590 (4th Cir. 1994), *cert. denied,* 115 S. Ct. 91 (1994).

[86] Declaratory judgment is a "statutory remedy for the determination of a justifiable controversy where the plaintiff is in doubt as to his legal rights." A binding adjudication of the rights and status of litigants even though no consequential relief is awarded . . . . Such judgment is conclusive in a subsequent action between the parties as to the matters declared and, in accordance with the usual rules of issue preclusion, as to any issues actually litigated and determined. *Black's Law Dictionary* 409 (6th ed. 1990).

[87] *Baby K,* 832 F. Supp. 1022.

[88] *Baby K,* 832 F. Supp. 1022, 1031.

Act of 1973,[89] and the Americans with Disabilities Act.[90] In addition, the court held that Ms. H had a constitutional right to demand the treatment.[91]

The hospital appealed the case to the Fourth Circuit, which affirmed the district court's decision exclusively under EMTALA.[92] The Fourth Circuit first dismissed the hospital's argument that EMTALA merely required hospitals to provide uniform treatment to all patients exhibiting the same EMC. The court held that the "disparate treatment" standard applied only to "appropriate medical screening" claims, not stabilization claims.[93] The court then found that because it could not identify any "statutory language or legislative history evincing a Congressional intent to create an exception to the duty to provide stabilizing treatment when the required treatment would exceed the prevailing standard of medical care," the defendant hospital was bound to provide Baby K with stabilizing treatment even if it fell outside the bounds of standard medical care.[94] Finally, the court found unavailing the hospital's argument that because Virginia law does not require physicians to render medical treatment that they consider medically or ethically inappropriate, EMTALA cannot be construed to compel physicians to provide such care. The Fourth Circuit ruled that EMTALA preempts provisions of state law that directly conflict with it. To the extent that state law exempts physicians from providing care they consider inappropriate, then such laws are preempted by EMTALA.[95] The court conceded that "[w]e recognize the dilemma facing physicians who are requested to provide treatment they consider morally and ethically inappropriate, but we cannot ignore the plain language of the statute because to do so would 'transcend our judicial function.'"[96]

Q 4:13 Stabilization Refusal: Can a patient refuse stabilizing treatment?

EMTALA allows patients to refuse treatment. The Act states:

Refusal to consent to treatment:

> A hospital is deemed to meet the requirement of paragraph (1)(A) with respect to an individual if the hospital offers the individual the further medical examination and treatment described in that paragraph and informs the individual (or a person acting on the individual's behalf) of the risks and benefits to the individual of such examination and treatment, but the individual (or a person acting on the individual's

---

[89] Rehabilitation Act of 1973, 29 U.S.C. § 794.

[90] Americans with Disabilities Act of 1990, 42 U.S.C. §§ 12101-12213.

[91] *Baby K*, 832 F. Supp. 1022, 1030-31.

[92] *Baby K*, 16 F.3d 590, 592 n.2 (finding that EMTALA requires the hospital to provide stabilizing treatment and refusing to address the other federal statutes and the laws of Virginia).

[93] *Baby K*, 16 F.3d 590, 595-96.

[94] *Baby K*, 16 F.3d 590, 596.

[95] *Baby K*, 16 F.3d 590, 597.

[96] *Baby K*, 16 F.3d 590, 596 (internal quotation marks and citations omitted).

behalf) refuses to consent to the examination and treatment. The hospital shall take all reasonable steps to secure the individual's (or person's) written informed consent to refuse such examination and treatment.[97]

The hospital, therefore, has three responsibilities when a patient refuses treatment. The hospital must:

1. Offer the examination and treatment;

2. Inform the patient or surrogate of the risks and benefits of such examination and stabilizing treatment; and

3. Take all reasonable steps to secure the patient's or surrogate's written informed consent to refuse examination and treatment.

Cautions: The physician must document a description of the examination, treatment, or both, if applicable, that was refused by or on behalf of the individual. The hospital must take all reasonable steps to secure the individual's written informed refusal (or that of the person acting on his or her behalf). The written document should indicate that the person has been informed of the risks and benefits of the examination or treatment or both and specify exactly what the risks and benefits are.[98] Merely stating "risks and benefits explained to patient" does not suffice. Noting that the family consented is not sufficient. A signature of the refusing individual or person acting on his or her behalf must be present on the form, or the record must reflect those reasonable efforts made by the hospital to obtain the written refusal. Some hospitals have been cited for failure to obtain written refusals of care when patients walk out of the emergency department before an MSE because of long waits.

An authorized individual may refuse examination, treatment, or transfer on behalf of the patient only if the patient is incapable of making an informed choice for himself or herself.[99] Adequate documentation here is vital because there must be no indications that a patient was coerced into refusing care. Only a physician should be allowed to obtain any informed consent to refuse care. The burden of proof is on the hospital to prove that a patient affirmatively revoked his or her request for examination and treatment.

In some circumstances, however, a signed waiver is inadequate. In *Malave Sastre v. Hospital Doctors Center, Inc.,*[100] a patient who left the hospital after waiting more than five hours for an orthopedic surgeon to examine and treat her was allowed to proceed with a suit for EMTALA violation, notwithstanding her signing a release form before departing. Vianey Malave Sastre was brought to the emergency department of Doctors Center around 1:15 p.m. after being struck by a car. Malave had multiple traumas, including fractures to the right

---

[97] 42 U.S.C. § 1395dd(b)(2).

[98] 42 C.F.R. § 489.24(d)(3).

[99] U.S. Dep't HHS, CMS, State Operations Manual, App. V, Emergency Medical Treatment and Labor Act (EMTALA) Interpretive Guidelines, Part II, Tag A-2407/C-2407 (revised 5/29/2009).

[100] 93 F. Supp. 2d 105 (D.P.R. 2000).

leg. Dr. Felix Maldonado, the emergency physician, administered pain medications, ordered a single X-ray of the uninjured left leg, and consulted with Dr. Pedro Reyes Martinez, the orthopedic surgeon, who ordered admission to the hospital. Dr. Maldonado directed a paramedic to apply a posterior splint to Malave's injured leg, despite the paramedic's lack of training for the procedure. The paramedic failed to apply the proper wadding between the splint and the leg. Malave and her husband waited five more hours for the orthopedic surgeon to arrive but, frustrated with the wait, finally decided to leave the hospital at 9:30 p.m. They signed release forms and went to another hospital. At the second hospital, the splint was removed because of increased pain. The physician there found that the paramedic's error caused deep burns to Malave's leg. Malave had to undergo extensive skin grafts, lost significant movement in the leg, and had significant disfiguration.

Malave filed a suit against the hospital alleging an EMTALA violation for failure to screen and stabilize. The hospital argued Malave did not have a cause of action under EMTALA because she voluntarily signed a waiver before leaving and therefore refused treatment. The court refused to accept the proposition that after subjecting a patient to a wait of several hours to receive emergency medical care, the hospital can somehow be excused from liability just because a patient voluntarily signed herself out. The court declined to ignore the inexcusable delay in Malave's treatment, observing that EMTALA can be read to prohibit both actual and constructive dumping of patients.[101]

Q 4:14   Managed Care Refusal: What if a managed care organization refuses authorization for stabilizing treatment?

EMTALA does not allow any exemption for managed care refusal of authorization. An EMTALA violation occurs if a patient is released from the emergency department without an MSE or documentation of refusal of care because the patient's managed care insurance carrier refuses authorization for the visit.

Cautions: Emergency departments increasingly face the difficult situation in which a patient comes to the emergency department without contacting the managed care insurance carrier first. After arriving at the hospital, either the patient or the emergency department admissions clerk or other staff memeber calls the carrier for authorization. The hospital faces potential liability if the carrier refuses authorization and the hospital allows the patient to leave without an "adequate screening examination" or "treatment." CMS clearly indicates that a gatekeeper physician or managed care organization has no authority to deny care. At most, they can refuse to pay for care. This is an important distinction legally, although hospitals equate getting paid with providing care.

---

[101] *Sastre*, 93 F. Supp. 2d 105, 110-11.

The State Operations Manual states:

> If an individual seeking care is a member of a managed health care plan (e.g., HMO, PPO, or CMP) the hospital is obligated to comply with the requirements of § 489.24 regardless of the individual's payor source or financial status. The hospital is obligated to provide the services necessary to determine if an EMC is present and provide stabilizing treatment if indicated. This is true regardless if the individual is enrolled in a managed care plan that restricts its enrollees' choice of health care provider. EMTALA is a requirement imposed on hospitals, and the fact that an individual who comes to the hospital is enrolled in a managed care plan that does not contract with that hospital has no bearing on the obligation of the hospital to conduct an MSE and to at least initiate stabilizing treatment. A managed health care plan may only state the services for which it will pay or decline payment, but that does not excuse the hospital from compliance with EMTALA.[102]

In *Correa v. Hospital San Francisco*,[103] an EMTALA violation was found when Mrs. González was not provided an MSE before being allowed to leave the emergency department to go to the clinic designated as her primary care center by her medical insurance. González arrived at the emergency department of Hospital San Francisco (HSF) with dizziness, nausea, and chest pains. González was told to wait in the waiting room. No one took her vital signs or asked her any basic medical questions.

Her medical insurance would not have covered any emergency treatment received at HSF during the office hours of her primary care clinic. After waiting almost two hours, she was instructed to go to the primary care clinic. A nurse called Dr. Rojas at the primary care clinic to advise him that González would be coming to the clinic for treatment. Her condition worsened at the clinic, but Dr. Rojas did not have the staff or medications to treat her.

While waiting for an ambulance, González experienced cardiopulmonary arrest and died. Her son, Angel Correa, filed suit, and a jury awarded González's family $700,000. The First Circuit[104] affirmed the judgment and award, ruling that the plaintiff was successful in showing that:

> (1) the hospital is a participating hospital, covered by EMTALA, that operates an emergency department (or an equivalent treatment facility); (2) the patient arrived at the facility seeking treatment; and (3) the hospital either (a) did not afford the patient an appropriate screening in order to determine if she had an emergency medical condition, or (b) bade farewell to the patient whether by turning her away, discharging

---

[102] U.S. Dep't HHS, CMS, State Operations Manual, App. V, Emergency Medical Treatment and Labor Act (EMTALA) Interpretive Guidelines, Part II, Tag A-2407/C-2407 (revised 5/29/2009).

[103] 69 F.3d 1184 (1st Cir. 1995).

[104] The First Circuit covers Maine, New Hampshire, Massachusetts, Rhode Island, and Puerto Rico. 28 U.S.C.A. § 41.

her, or improvidently transferring her without first stabilizing the emergency medical condition.[105]

EMTALA states that no preauthorization, validation, or confirming of insurance may be sought by the hospital before completion of the MSE and initiation of stabilizing care. The hospital must offer to provide the MSE without any reference to money or to approval requirements of any insurance plan. If a patient declines an examination on the basis of the carrier's refusal of authorization, the hospital will be challenged to prove that the patient, not the hospital, independently contacted the insurance company. This needs to be well documented in the patient chart. The hospital should diplomatically require written refusal of treatment. If an EMC is at all suspected, the hospital should prudently do everything possible to convince the patient to stay for treatment regardless of payment and carefully document all these efforts and the conversations as they occur. If the patient insists on refusing care, this does not absolve the hospital of all EMTALA requirements. The hospital should help arrange for a safe transfer to a plan-provider hospital.

---

[105] *Correa,* 69 F.3d 1184, 1186. *See also* Miller v. Medical Ctr. of Sw. La., 22 F.3d 626 (5th Cir. 1994); Stevison v. Enid Health Sys., Inc., 920 F.2d 710 (10th Cir. 1990).

Chapter 5

Transfers

If an individual at a hospital has an emergency medical condition which has not been stabilized . . . the hospital may not transfer the individual unless—

(A) (i) the individual . . . after being informed . . . in writing requests transfer to another medical facility,

(ii) a physician . . . signed a certification . . . .

(B) the transfer is an appropriate transfer

(C) . . . the transferring hospital sends to the receiving facility all medical records . . . .

(D) . . . the transfer is effected through qualified personnel and transportation equipment . . . .

42 U.S.C. § 1395dd(c)

Congress did not pass EMTALA to prevent patient transfers. EMTALA's congressional intent was to protect indigent patients from dangerous transfers by requiring prior stabilization. In fact, the Centers for Medicare & Medicaid Services (CMS) states that if a hospital has exhausted all its capabilities in attempting to resolve the emergency medical condition (EMC), it must effect an appropriate transfer of the individual.[1] In addition, a hospital may transfer any patient even for economic reasons without violating EMTALA, provided no EMC

---

[1] U.S. Dep't HHS, Centers for Medicare & Medicaid Servs. (CMS), State Operations Manual, App. V, Emergency Medical Treatment and Labor Act (EMTALA) Interpretive Guidelines, Part II, Tag A-2407/ C-2407 (revised 5/29/2009).

exists. On the Congress floor, Senator David Durenberger stated: "This amendment does not prevent hospitals from making appropriate and safe transfers of patients for economic reasons."[2] The Act makes it clear that the restrictions on patient transfers apply only to patients who are "in emergency condition which has not been stabilized."[3]

The *Federal Register* explains that a hospital is responsible for providing care "until the condition ceases to be an emergency medical condition or until the patient is properly transferred to another facility."[4] Once a patient has been stabilized, the hospital has the option to either transfer the patient or simply discharge him or her without violating EMTALA.

However, as soon as an EMC is found, EMTALA stays in effect, and the hospital must provide the emergency patient with "such medical treatment of the condition as may be necessary to assure, within reasonable medical probability, that no material deterioration of the condition is likely to result from or occur during the transfer of the individual from a facility."[5]

Some courts have been confused by the transfer requirements of EMTALA, interpreting these requirements to prohibit transfers of unstabilized patients, when in fact EMTALA explicitly permits such transfers.[6] The State Operations Manual states:

> If the individual's condition requires immediate medical stabilizing treatment and the hospital is not able to attend to that individual because the emergency department is operating beyond its capacity, then the hospital should transfer the individual to a hospital that has the capability and capacity to treat the individual's EMC.[7]

The hospital may transfer unstabilized patients provided that it has done all that it can within its capabilities to first treat and stabilize the patient and that certain other statutory requirements are satisfied.[8] EMTALA squarely places the burden on the transferring hospital and physician to document explicitly and exactly that the receiving hospital has adequate resources to care for the patient and that the medical benefits of the transfer outweigh the risks.

In the 2003 final rules, CMS clarified that EMTALA only governs transfer of patients from a dedicated emergency department.[9] Transfers from a hospital's

---

[2] *See* 132 Cong. Rec. S13,904 (daily ed. Oct. 23, 1985).

[3] The Emergency Medical Treatment and Active Labor Act (EMTALA), Pub. L. No. 99-272, Title IX, § 9121(b), 100 Stat. 164 (codified as amended at 42 U.S.C. § 1395dd (1995)), at § 1395dd(c)(1).

[4] 53 Fed. Reg. 22,517 (1988).

[5] 42 U.S.C. § 1395dd(e)(3)(A).

[6] 42 U.S.C. § 1395dd(c).

[7] U.S. Dep't HHS, CMS, State Operations Manual, App. V, Emergency Medical Treatment and Labor Act (EMTALA) Interpretive Guidelines, Part II, Tag A-2407/C-2407 (revised 5/29/2009).

[8] 42 U.S.C. § 1395dd(c)(1).

[9] 68 Fed. Reg. 53,247 (Sept. 9, 2003).

inpatient wards are not governed by EMTALA but rather by Medicare's Conditions of Participation (CoPs). This ruling helps clarify the landscape of EMTALA by limiting EMTALA's governance to dedicated emergency departments.

In early 2012, the Department of Health and Human Services (HHS) again considered the question of whether EMTALA applied to an inpatient admitted to a hospital. HHS concluded:

> [I]f an individual "comes to the [hospital's] emergency department," as we have defined that term in regulation, and the hospital provides an appropriate medical screening examination and determines that an EMC exists, and then admits the individual in good faith in order to stabilize the EMC, that hospital has satisfied its EMTALA obligation towards that patient.[10]

In the same pronouncement, HHS also reaffirmed its prior position regarding "situations where a hospital seeks to transfer an individual, who was admitted by that hospital as an inpatient after coming to the hospital's dedicated emergency department with an EMC, to a hospital with specialized capabilities because the admitted inpatient continues to have an unstabilized EMC that requires specialized treatment not available at the admitting hospital."[11]

The HHS restated its position that "if an individual comes to the hospital's dedicated emergency department, is determined to have an EMC, is admitted as an inpatient, and continues to have an unstabilized EMC, which requires the specialized capabilities of another hospital, the EMTALA obligation for the admitting hospital has ended and a hospital with specialized capabilities also does not have an EMTALA obligation toward that individual."[12]

Obviously, not all transfers are covered by EMTALA. This chapter will consider which transfers are regulated by EMTALA; requirements to effect an EMTALA transfer; transportation between hospitals; EMTALA rules governing the receiving hospital; and patient consent.

EMTALA Transfers

Q 5:1   Transfer: What is EMTALA's definition of "transfer"?

The government defines "transfer" in the Code of Federal Regulations as:

> the movement (including the discharge) of an individual outside a hospital's facilities at the direction of any person employed by (or affiliated or associated, directly or indirectly, with) the hospital, but does not include such a movement of an individual who (i) has been

---

[10] 77 Fed. Reg. 5217 (Feb. 2, 2012). See **Appendix G** for the full text.

[11] 77 Fed. Reg. 5217 (Feb. 2, 2012).

[12] 77 Fed. Reg. 5217 (Feb. 2, 2012).

declared dead, or (ii) leaves the facility without the permission of any such person.[13]

Cautions: Once a patient is on hospital property, any movement of the patient to leave hospital property—whether by formal ambulance transfer to another facility, discharge from the hospital, referral to a health maintenance organization (HMO) office, or by simply encouraging the patient to leave on his or her own—is considered a "transfer" under EMTALA. Any patient movement to leave hospital property risks EMTALA violation, unless the patient has died, signs out against medical advice, or leaves the hospital without the hospital's permission or knowledge. The CMS State Operations Manual instructs surveyors to review the transfer logs for the entire hospital, examining the following for possible transfer violations:

- Transfers to off-site testing facilities and return;
- Death or significant adverse outcomes;
- Refusals of examination, treatment, or transfer;
- Patients leaving against medical advice (AMA);
- Returns to the emergency department within 48 hours; and
- Emergency department visits where the individual is logged in for an unreasonable amount of time before the time indicated for commencement of the medical screening examination.[14]

As soon as a patient is found to be stable either after an appropriate medical screening examination (MSE) or by stabilizing treatment, EMTALA no longer governs. Technically, therefore, the transfer of a stable patient is not controlled by EMTALA. Referral of a stable patient from the emergency department to a physician's office for follow-up would not need EMTALA certification. Transfer of stable patients to nursing homes or rehabilitation centers also would not need EMTALA certification. Transfer of stable patients to other sites for diagnostic testing or therapy would not require EMTALA certification. However, it would still be prudent for a hospital to treat all discharges and transfers uniformly with uniform transfer forms and packages to avoid confusion and possible violation.

Q 5:2 Movement Within Hospital Property: Does movement of a patient within hospital property constitute a "transfer"?

No. Movement of a patient from one area of the hospital to another that is contiguous with the hospital campus and operates under the hospital's Outpatient Perspective Payment System (OPPS) billing is not considered a transfer.

---

[13] 42 C.F.R. § 489.24(b).

[14] U.S. Dep't HHS, CMS, State Operations Manual, App. V, Emergency Medical Treatment and Labor Act (EMTALA) Interpretive Guidelines, Part II, Tag A-2409/C-2409 (revised 5/29/2009).

The State Operations Manual states:

> If an individual is initially screened in a department or facility on-campus outside of the ED, the individual could be moved to another hospital department or facility on-campus to receive further screening or stabilizing treatment without such movement being regarded as a transfer, as long as: (1) all persons with the same medical condition are moved in such circumstances, regardless of their ability to pay for treatment; (2) there is bona fide medical reason to move the individual; and (3) appropriate medical personnel accompany the individual. The same is also true for an individual who presents to the dedicated emergency department (e.g., patient with an eye injury in need of stationary ophthalmology equipment located in the eye clinic) and must be moved to another hospital-owned facility or department on-campus for further screening or stabilizing treatment. The movement of the individual between hospital departments is not considered an EMTALA transfer under this section, since the individual is simply being moved from one department of a hospital to another department or facility of the same hospital.[15]

Cautions: Movement of a patient to another area of hospital property that is contiguous to the hospital campus does not constitute a transfer under EMTALA. However, any movement to a noncontiguous or off-campus facility is considered a transfer and must meet statutory requirements. It may be the hospital's policy to direct all pregnant women to the labor and delivery area of the hospital. Hospitals may use other hospital areas, which are also used for inpatient or outpatient services, to provide emergency services. MSEs or stabilization may require ancillary services available only in areas or facilities of the hospital outside the emergency department. The movement is not considered a transfer under EMTALA as long as the patient is taken to a hospital-owned facility that (1) is contiguous (i.e., any area within the hospital or a hospital-owned facility on land that touches land where a hospital's emergency department sits) or part of the hospital "campus"; (2) is owned by the hospital; and (3) is operating under the hospital's OPPS billing. Movements of patients among remote sites and the main campus must be made in an appropriate manner.

The requirement of an identical OPPS provider number may cause problems if a facility does not operate under OPPS but the main hospital does. Physicians' offices may be defined as such a facility, provided they are located in a hospital-owned building that is contiguous or "on campus" and have been approved for OPPS status. However, what if they operate under a different entity of common ownership or are a joint venture between the hospital and a physician group? In those cases, they will not meet the requirements of OPPS and therefore are not the same entity as the hospital for EMTALA purposes.

The emergency department need not fulfill all EMTALA's appropriate transfer requirements of patient consent and certification before referring a patient across the hospital hall for cardiac stress testing for a possible unstabilized

---

[15] U.S. Dep't HHS, CMS, State Operations Manual, App. V, Emergency Medical Treatment and Labor Act (EMTALA) Interpretive Guidelines, Part II, Tag A-2406/C-2406 (revised 7/16/2010).

medical condition when, for example, a patient complains of chest pain. Under present OPPS guidelines, movement of a patient from one department of the hospital to another is not considered a transfer. And, if the cardiology department is leased to a private cardiology group, EMTALA does not apply to private physicians' offices.

Q 5:3   Transfer Agreement: What is a transfer agreement for off-campus sites?

A transfer agreement is an agreement designed to facilitate appropriate transfers from a provider-based off-campus site to a neighboring hospital that happens to be closer.

Cautions: There are times when a patient's condition is so critical that transfer to the closest hospital is in the patient's best interest even if that closest hospital is not the owner of the off-campus site. Transfer to a neighboring hospital may also be necessary if the transferring hospital does not have the specialized capabilities to treat the patient. CMS expects the owner hospital to have transfer agreements that establish protocols in advance with the neighboring hospital.

Protocols for such transfer agreements should include contact information and other relevant procedures to be followed when an emergency arises that necessitates such a transfer.[16] The recipient hospital needs to agree beforehand to such transfers because EMTALA mandates that a hospital with specialized capabilities may not refuse to accept such transfers.[17] The transfer would be considered an EMTALA transfer and must comply with all EMTALA requirements, such as certification and record transfer.

The State Operations Manual states:

> If an individual comes to a hospital-owned facility or department which is off-campus and operates under the hospital's Medicare provider number, § 1867 (42 C.F.R. § 489.24) will not apply to that facility and/or department unless it meets the definition of a dedicated emergency department.

> If, however, such a facility does meet the definition of a dedicated ED, it must screen and stabilize the patient to the best of its ability or execute an appropriate transfer if necessary to another hospital or to the hospital on whose Medicare provider number it is operated. Hospital resources and staff available at the main campus are likewise available to individuals seeking care at the off campus facilities or departments within the capability of the hospital. Movement of the individual to the main campus of the hospital is not considered a transfer since the individual is simply being moved from one department of a hospital to another department or facility of the same hospital. In addition, a transfer from such an entity (i.e., an off-campus facility that meets the definition of a

---

[16] 42 C.F.R. § 489.24(i)(3)(ii).
[17] 42 C.F.R. § 489.24(e).

dedicated ED) to a nonaffiliated hospital (i.e., a hospital that does not own the off-campus facility) is allowed where the facility at which the individual presented cannot stabilize the individual and the benefits of transfer exceed the risks of transfer. In other words, there is no requirement under EMTALA that the individual be always transferred back to the hospital that owns and operates the off-campus dedicated ED. Rather, the requirement of EMTALA is that the individual be transferred to an appropriate facility for treatment.[18]

Q 5:4   Unstable Transfers: In which instances may an unstable patient be transferred?

There are only two instances in which an unstable patient may be transferred. They are (1) when the hospital does not have the capacity or capability to stabilize the patient and the benefits to be received by transfer to another hospital outweigh the risk of transfer and (2) when the patient (or his or her representative) insists on transfer even after being informed of the risks of transfer and the hospital's obligations under EMTALA. According to the State Operations Manual, a hospital may appropriately transfer a patient before it has "used and exhausted all of its resources available if the individual requests the transfer to another hospital for his or her treatment and refuses treatment at the sending hospital."[19]

The second method of appropriate transfer of an unstable patient is the more straightforward of the two. It occurs when a patient or his or her representative insists on transfer. The regulations require that the patient's request be in writing and indicate the reasons for the request. The documentation must also reflect that the patient (or patient's representative) was aware of the risks and benefits of the transfer. Hospitals should develop a refusal of transfer form for patients to sign when they refuse to be transferred.

The first method of appropriate transfer imposes greater obligations on the hospital. It occurs when the transferring hospital lacks the capability or capacity to stabilize the patient, and the benefits of transfer outweigh the risks. Before transfer, however, the transferring hospital is obligated to provide stabilizing treatment within its capability and capacity to minimize the risks to the patient during transport. The State Operations Manual states:

> If a hospital is alleged to have violated EMTALA by transferring an unstable individual without implementing an appropriate transfer according to § 489.24(e), and the hospital believes that the individual was stable (EMC resolved), the burden of proof is the responsibility of the transferring hospital. When interpreting the facts the surveyor should assess whether or not the individual was stable. Was it reasonable to believe that the transferring hospital should have been knowledgeable

---

[18] U.S. Dep't HHS, CMS, State Operations Manual, App. V, Emergency Medical Treatment and Labor Act (EMTALA) Interpretive Guidelines, Part II, Tag A-2406/C-2406 (revised 7/16/2010).

[19] U.S. Dep't HHS, CMS, State Operations Manual, App. V, Emergency Medical Treatment and Labor Act (EMTALA) Interpretive Guidelines, Part II, Tag A-2407/C-2407 (revised 7/16/2010).

of the potential complications during transport? To determine whether the individual was stable and treated appropriately surveyors will request that the QIO physician review the case.

If the treating physician is in doubt that an individual's EMC is stabilized, the physician should implement an appropriate transfer (see Tag A-2409/C-2409) to prevent a potential violation of EMTALA, if his/her hospital cannot provide further stabilizing treatment.[20]

. . .

Assessment of whether the transferring hospital with the requisite capabilities lacked the capacity to provide stabilizing treatment or the recipient hospital lacked the capacity to accept an appropriate transfer requires a review of the hospital's general practices in adjusting its capacity. If a hospital generally has a record of accommodating additional patients by various means, such as moving patients from one unit to another, calling in additional staff, and temporarily borrowing additional equipment from other facilities, then that hospital would be expected under EMTALA to take reasonable steps to respond to the treatment needs of an individual requiring stabilizing treatment for an emergency medical condition. The determination of a hospital's capacity would depend on the case-specific circumstances and the hospital's previous implementation of capacity management actions.[21]

Hospitals need not expand their resources or offer more services; EMTALA focuses only on "existing capabilities." CMS has taken a rigid position on capabilities of the transferring hospital to avoid hospital searches for excuses to transfer. For example, if a hospital has the ability to stabilize a patient by delivering a baby through a normal, uncomplicated vaginal delivery by a family physician, even though it lacks an obstetrics department, then it must do so rather than transfer the individual to another hospital. If the hospital has accommodated patients in the past "by whatever means," including calling in additional staff, then "it has demonstrated the ability to provide services to patients in excess of its occupancy limit."[22]

CMS has stated that "[w]hen a hospital has exhausted all of its capabilities in attempting to resolve the EMC, it must effect an appropriate transfer of the individual."[23] CMS uses the term "must" transfer when an EMC persists. Yet medical conditions often exist in states of continuum in which there is not a clear point when an emergency does or does not exist. An emergency that seems stabilized can become unstable very quickly. This begs the question: after exhausting its capabilities, "must" a hospital transfer a patient whose EMC persists but could possibly be stabilized with further evaluation and care? Transportation by ambulance adds risks and dangers of its own. If the hospital

---

[20] U.S. Dep't HHS, CMS, State Operations Manual, App. V, Emergency Medical Treatment and Labor Act (EMTALA) Interpretive Guidelines, Part II, Tag A-2407/C-2407 (revised 5/29/2009).

[21] U.S. Dep't HHS, CMS, State Operations Manual, App. V, Emergency Medical Treatment and Labor Act (EMTALA) Interpretive Guidelines, Part II, Tag A-2411/C-2411 (revised 7/16/2010).

[22] 59 Fed. Reg. 32,086, 32,105 (1994).

[23] U.S. Dep't HHS, CMS, State Operations Manual, App. V, Emergency Medical Treatment and Labor Act (EMTALA) Interpretive Guidelines, Part II, Tag A-2407/C-2407 (revised 5/29/2009).

chooses to be courageous by further intervention only to have a poor outcome, does the hospital violate this dictate? The CMS answer appears to be that where the capabilities and capacity of the hospital are clearly exceeded, the transfer must be made. It still falls on a physician to certify that the risks of transfer are outweighed by the benefits to be obtained at the destination hospital. If there is adequate documentation that the risks of transfer are too severe, CMS and the Peer Review Organization (PRO) reviewer are likely to accept the decision not to transfer. It is much more problematic when the patient clearly needs transfer and the attending physician does not want to relinquish the patient or the billing by transfer. That issue then falls on administration or the medical executive committee (MEC) to enforce reasonable standards of professional practice by means of the hospital's disciplinary process.

Cautions: Although hospitals are required to stabilize emergency patients, EMTALA does not require them to perform the impossible. There will, of course, be instances when hospitals do not have the capability to stabilize patients with serious EMCs. These patients will then have to be transferred in an unstable condition, with no guarantees that there will be no "material deterioration" in the medical condition. These are cases where the transferring hospital does not have the capabilities to stabilize the patient's condition (e.g., a hospital does not have a neurosurgeon on staff to operate on a patient with traumatic intracranial hemorrhage). In such a case, the patient will be unstable for transfer to a facility with the capabilities to treat the patient. CMS allows such transfers as long as the benefits of transfer outweigh the risks to the patient. Prior to any such transfer, the hospital must document that it has done all it can do within its capabilities to stabilize the patient's EMC as much as possible. This is the main purpose of the EMTALA certificate of transfer. The situation is not to be taken lightly; some cases that led to the original passage of EMTALA involved hospitals that transferred patients in dangerous unstable conditions to county hospitals.

Claims arising from the transfer of unstable patients are common and costly. In the case of *Smith v. Botsford General Hospital*,[24] the hospital was convicted of violating EMTALA by failing to stabilize a patient who died while en route to another facility. Kelly Smith, a 33-year-old man weighing approximately 600 pounds, fractured his left leg during a rollover car accident. An ambulance transported Smith to Botsford Hospital, where physicians diagnosed an open comminuted left femur fracture. Botsford decided to transfer Smith to another hospital because it felt that it did not have the capabilities to treat a patient of Smith's size. While en route to the other hospital, Smith developed hemorrhagic shock and died. Andrea Smith sued Botsford Hospital for failure to stabilize her husband with blood transfusions before transfer. The jury found in favor of the plaintiff and awarded $35,000 for economic damages and $5,000,000 for noneconomic damages. On appeal, the Sixth Circuit found that Michigan's cap of $359,000 on noneconomic damages for malpractice suits applied to this case.

---

[24] 419 F.3d 513 (6th Cir. 2005).

However, strict compliance with statutory requirements, despite a tragic turn of events during transfer, will prevent liability under EMTALA. In *Martin v. Ohio County Hospital Corporation*,[25] Billie C. Shreve was injured in an automobile accident and transported to Ohio County Hospital for emergency treatment. The nurse and attending emergency physician, diagnosing hemorrhagic shock, believed Shreve was in need of a surgeon. No surgeon was available at the hospital, nor was one called. Instead, the emergency physician ordered blood transfusions and a CT scan to identify the site of hemorrhaging and then sent the films to a radiologist at another hospital for review. Over four hours later, Shreve was finally transferred to another hospital. She died from her hemorrhagic shock en route. Shreve's estate filed a lawsuit alleging medical negligence and EMTALA violations.

Although Shreve's estate prevailed on the tort claims, the Kentucky Supreme Court found that the hospital was entitled to a directed verdict in its favor on the EMTALA claim because it met all the Act's requirements. Although the court appeared to doubt whether the physician and hospital staff performed within the appropriate standard of care, it concluded that:

> those questions are not covered by this statute. By its terms, [EMTALA] is a strict liability statute: it asserts what a hospital *must* do, and creates liability for any failure. If a hospital does not follow the requirements of the statute, it is liable . . . . On the other hand, if the hospital has complied with the statute's requirements, it is not material under the statute how well it did them—that is a different cause of action, likely for negligence.[26]

The court found that the hospital had thoroughly complied with EMTALA's mandates. The hospital recognized that a medical emergency existed, recognized that the surgeon on call was unavailable, undertook stabilizing treatment by transfusing the patient to counter her blood loss, and then attempted to determine the source of the bleeding with a CT scan. After this, a physician "began the process of transferring the patient to another hospital, and completed and signed the Certificate of Transfer as required by the statute."[27] Having followed, to the word, the statutory requirements of EMTALA, the hospital could not be found liable for a violation of the Act.

On April 8, 2011, the First Circuit Court of Appeals affirmed a federal district court's granting of summary judgment in favor of Centro Medico del Turabo d/b/a Hospital HIMA San Pablo Fajardo and its insurer HIMA San Pablo Captive Insurance Company Limited (collectively Hospital) in an action involving allegations that the Hospital violated EMTALA by transferring the plaintiffs' son (patient) without delivering the best treatment before the transfer.[28] The district

---

[25] 295 S.W.3d 104, 113 (Ky. Sup. Ct. 2009).

[26] *Martin*, 295 S.W.3d 104, 113.

[27] *Martin*, 295 S.W.3d 104, 113.

[28] Ramos-Cruz v. Centro Medico del Turabo d/b/a Hosp. HIMA San Pablo Fajardo, No. 10-1203 (1st Cir. Apr. 8, 2011).

court found that the Hospital complied with EMTALA's transfer requirements and the First Circuit affirmed.

In 2006, the patient arrived at the Hospital with abdominal problems and was diagnosed with upper gastrointestinal bleeding. The Hospital did not have gastroenterologic services available, so the emergency room physician arranged to have the patient transferred to another hospital. The patient was transferred and died approximately 36 hours later. On the "Clinical Summary and Examination at the Moment of Transfer" form, the physician wrote "Gastroenterologist" to explain the benefits of the transfer.

When a patient is transferred, EMTALA requires the physician to sign a certification that "the medical benefits reasonably expected from the provision of appropriate medical treatment of another facility outweigh the increased risks to the individual." The First Circuit found that the physician's note of "Gastroenterologist" was "merely a summary statement of the more explicit explanation that [the Patient] needed a gastroenterologist, none was present at the Hospital, and, therefore, [the Patient] needed to be transferred, because the benefits of a gastroenterologist outweighed the dangers of transportation."[29]

The plaintiffs conceded that the Hospital followed standard transfer procedures but argued that "if the hospital does not deliver the feasible specific treatment that is best, whatever it may be in a given circumstance, it violates EMTALA." The First Circuit found that the Hospital provided appropriate pre-transfer treatment and "provided for transfer in the best interests of the patient." The First Circuit also stated that (1) EMTALA is violated when a hospital fails to follow its standard procedures, not by providing allegedly faulty treatment, and (2) the plaintiffs' position "would create a federal malpractice cause of action" allowing an unstabilized patient to sue in federal court any time correct care is not provided prior to transfer, which is inconsistent with jurisprudence and Congressional intent. The First Circuit concluded that the Hospital "provided for the transfer in the best interests of the patient."[30]

Q 5:5   Labor: When can a patient who is in labor be transferred?

The CMS State Operations Manual states:

Women in Labor

- Regardless of practices within a State, a woman in labor may be transferred only if she or her representative requests the transfer and if a physician or other qualified medical personnel signs a certification that the benefits outweigh the risks. If the hospital does not provide obstetrical services, the benefits of a transfer may outweigh

---

[29] *Ramos-Cruz*, No. 10-1203.

[30] *Ramos-Cruz*, No. 10-1203. This case summary was written by Keith A. Mauriello, Partner, and Jessica T. Grozine, Associate, in the Healthcare Practice Group at Arnall Golden Gregory LLP, Atlanta, Georgia. It should not be construed as legal advice or opinion on specific matters.

the risks. A hospital cannot cite State law or practice as the basis for transfer.

- Hospitals that are not capable of handling high-risk infants often have written transfer agreements with facilities capable of handling high-risk cases. The hospital must still meet the screening, treatment, and transfer requirements.[31]

Congress specifically added obstetric labor to EMTALA in response to the case of Sharon Ford. In November 1985, Ford went to Brookside Hospital's emergency department in labor. A nurse saw her in the waiting room. Since Ford was a member of Health America Rockridge, a Medicaid HMO, she was referred to Samuel Merritt Hospital in Oakland, the HMO contract hospital. Merritt Hospital admitted her to the labor and delivery unit. Unfortunately, California was a week late in delivering the medical eligibility list to the Rockridge HMO, so Ford's name did not appear on the computerized list of those insured. Ford was again transferred, this time to Highland General Hospital, Oakland's county hospital. Shortly after arrival at Highland, Ford delivered a stillborn baby.[32]

Cautions: Any woman in active labor is generally considered unstable under EMTALA, preventing discharge or transfer unless the transferring hospital has absolutely no capability to deliver the baby safely. Under that circumstance, transfer is permitted when the benefits of transfer outweigh the risk or when a legally responsible person acting on the patient's behalf requests the transfer. Hospitals that are not capable of handling high-risk deliveries or high-risk infants often have written transfer agreements with facilities capable of handling high-risk cases. The hospital must still meet EMTALA's requirements before transfer, making it imperative that the physician clearly documents the explicit medical benefits of the transfer.

In *Owens v. Nacogdoches County Hospital*,[33] the court, in holding the defendant hospital liable for the transfer of a woman in active labor to another hospital in violation of EMTALA, found that the fact that the transferee hospital had a neonatal unit while the transferor hospital did not, failed to justify the transfer. In this case, the plaintiff, a 16-year-old indigent whose pregnancy was full-term, presented herself at the emergency room of the defendant hospital after she began to experience labor pains. She was examined by a physician under contract with the defendant hospital who discharged her 30 minutes later with instructions that she go to another hospital four hours away. In defense of his decision, the transferring physician argued that he felt that the benefits of sending the plaintiff to the transferee hospital outweighed the risks involved because the transferee hospital had facilities that were better equipped to deal with high-risk patients. The court, after examining the physician's testimony

---

[31] U.S. Dep't HHS, CMS, State Operations Manual, App. V, Emergency Medical Treatment and Labor Act (EMTALA) Interpretive Guidelines, Part II, Tag A-2409/C-2409 (revised 5/29/2009).

[32] H.R. Rep. No. 100-531, at 6-7 (1988). *See* Andrew Jay McClurg, *Your Money or Your Life: Interpreting the Federal Act Against Patient Dumping*, 24 Wake Forest L. Rev. 173, 181 (1989). *See* Robert A. Bitterman, *Providing Emergency Care Under Federal Law: EMTALA*, American College of Emergency Physicians (2000).

[33] 741 F. Supp. 1269 (E.D. Tex. 1990).

and the testimony of several medical experts, determined that this argument was not persuasive. First, the court noted the risks the physician thought justified the transfer, which included problems that might be associated with poor nutrition, a potential for the plaintiff to have a growth-retarded baby, a possibility that the plaintiff might require a cesarean section, and the possibility that the plaintiff might have Acquired Immune Deficiency Syndrome (AIDS). However, the physician admitted that poor nutrition was not corrigible during labor, that the defendant hospital could have provided the nutrition necessary to counteract growth retardation, and that he could have competently delivered a growth-retarded baby; that he was fully capable of performing a cesarean section; and that he had no reason to suspect that the plaintiff had AIDS. Next, the court weighed these risks against the dangers associated with travel delivery, which were found to include separation of the placenta, drop in fetal heart rate, hemorrhaging, cord prolapse, and the death of both mother and child. Based on expert medical testimony, the court concluded that the risks associated with sending a frightened adolescent girl on a four-hour trip by private car were markedly more severe than those of admitting her for delivery and that, as a result, the defendant hospital was not justified in transferring the plaintiff.

Although it does not involve transfer issues, the recent case of *Morin v. Eastern Maine Medical Center,*[34] and the court's opinion regarding the application of EMTALA to pregnant women must be seriously considered. The lawsuit involved doctors at Eastern Maine Medical Center (EMMC) who sent a pregnant woman home from the emergency department knowing she was in labor and would soon expel her 16-week fetus, which doctors said had no heartbeat.

At approximately 4:30 a.m. on July 1, 2007, Lorraine Morin went to the emergency department at Eastern Maine Medical Center (EMMC). Morin informed the registration clerk that she was 16-weeks pregnant, that she was having abdominal cramping, and that her primary care doctor, Pamela Gilmore, M.D., had told her to go to the hospital if she had any problems due to her high-risk pregnancy. Morin explained that her pregnancy was high risk as a result of her having previously had cervical cancer, a miscarriage, and a cone 2 biopsy. The patient gave the same information to the triage nurse and to Paul R. Reinstein, M.D., the emergency physician. Morin saw Dr. Reinstein at approximately 5:00 a.m. and his notes reflected that the patient had been experiencing contractions 10 minutes apart for the previous 20 hours.[35] Dr.Reinstein also reported that the patient had informed him that she had had one previous miscarriage, had given birth to two healthy children, and had pregnancy-induced hypertension.[36] Dr. Reinstein noted that although the patient had not noticed any bleeding, the nurse found some blood in her urine specimen.[37] After

---

[34] 780 F. Supp. 2d 84, 86 (D. Me. 2010).

[35] *Morin*, 780 F. Supp. 2d 84, 86.

[36] *Morin*, 780 F. Supp. 2d 84, 86.

[37] *Morin*, 780 F. Supp. 2d 84, 86.

an ultrasound revealed a nonviable fetus, Dr. Reinstein referred Ms. Morin to Robert Grover, D.O., an obstetrical-gynecological doctor.

Dr. Grover performed a pelvic examination and another ultrasound and confirmed that the 16-week-old male fetus that Morin was carrying had no heartbeat. At 6:15 a.m., shortly after the examination, Dr. Grover discharged her, against her wishes and while she was still in contractions. Morin delivered her dead fetus in the bathroom of her home later that day at around 9:00 p.m. The next morning, Morin called her obstetrician-gynecologist, Dr. Pamela Gilmore, who immediately admitted her into EMMC for surgery to stop her bleeding and to remove the remaining placenta.

Morin sued the hospital in U.S. District Court in Bangor, claiming EMTALA violations for failure to stabilize. After a three-day trial, the jury issued a verdict in favor of Morin, awarding her $50,000 in compensatory damages and $150,000 in punitive damages. The hospital appealed but settled with the plaintiff while the appeal was pending.

In his opinion, Chief U.S. District Judge John Woodcock observed that (1) EMTALA extends protection to a pregnant woman who is having contractions,[38] that (2) nothing in EMTALA limits this requirement depending on the viability of the fetus, and that (3) courts have extended EMTALA protections regardless of viability.[39] The court noted that Morin was 16-weeks pregnant when she arrived at the emergency room, that EMMC's medical records indicated that she was experiencing "suprapubic cramps" while at EMMC and "having some contractions" when discharged,[40] and that therefore Morin appeared to fit within the plain language of EMTALA.[41]

Judge Woodcock criticized the hospital for seeking to avoid the clear language of EMTALA[42] when it argued that Morin was diagnosed as having suffered a "missed abortion," not "as being in labor."[43] EMMC argued that because stabilization is required "only if the hospital determines that an emergency medical condition exists," the relevant inquiry is its diagnosis, not Morin's objective condition.[44] However, the court observed, EMTALA turns on a determination, not a diagnosis; that whether a patient is a pregnant woman having contractions is a fact, not a diagnosis. The court agreed that EMTALA would not apply if EMMC had not known either that Morin was pregnant or that

---

[38] 42 U.S.C. § 1395dd(e)(1)(B).

[39] As examples, the court referenced Barrios v. Sherman Hosp., No. 06 C 2853, 2006 U.S. Dist. LEXIS 92146, 2006 WL 3754922, at *4 (N.D. Ill. 2006) (denying motion to dismiss EMTALA claim from a woman who was discharged after a miscarriage but prior to the delivery of the placenta); Thompson v. St. Anne's Hosp., 716 F. Supp. 8, 9 (N.D. Ill. 1989) (denying motion to dismiss EMTALA claim from a woman who alleged that she was not stabilized when she arrived at the emergency room 16-weeks pregnant and in active labor).

[40] *Morin*, 780 F. Supp. 2d 84, 93-94.

[41] *Morin*, 780 F. Supp. 2d 84, 94.

[42] 42 U.S.C. § 1395dd(e)(1)(B).

[43] *Morin*, 780 F. Supp. 2d 84, 94.

[44] *Morin*, 780 F. Supp. 2d 84, 94.

she was having contractions.[45] But having determined that Morin was pregnant and having contractions, EMMC could not avoid EMTALA simply by assigning her a different diagnosis.

Judge Woodcock's opinion provides valuable insight as to how other courts may apply EMTALA in the future, given similar circumstances:

> EMMC's medical judgment does not trump the statute. If transfer of "a pregnant woman who is having contractions . . . may pose a threat to the health or safety of the woman or the unborn child," she has an "emergency medical condition" by law regardless of whether she has one by medicine.[46] EMMC is correct in pointing out that there may be tension between its determination and the statute's reach. The statute generally defines "emergency medical condition" in a fashion congruent with a common sense definition of the phrase. See, e.g., 42 U.S.C. § 1395dd(e)(1)(A)(i) (defining "emergency medical condition" as inter alia "a medical condition . . . such that the absence of immediate medical attention could reasonably be expected to result in the placing of the individual . . . in serious jeopardy"). However, the statute treats pregnant women differently and imposes a specific definition of "emergency medical condition," which may or may not comport with what a physician would determine. § 1395dd(e)(1)(B)(ii). Here, in the context of this motion, Ms. Morin has produced evidence that if believed by a jury would confirm she was pregnant when she presented to EMMC ER and was experiencing contractions. These facts, if proven, are sufficient to trigger the protections of EMTALA.
>
> EMMC responds that EMTALA's implementing regulations make distinctions on the basis of the viability of the fetus. [Citation] (citing 42 C.F.R. § 489.24(b)).[47] The regulations define "labor" as the process of childbirth beginning with the latent or early phase of labor and continuing through the delivery of the placenta. A woman experiencing contractions is in true labor unless a physician, certified nurse-midwife, or other qualified medical person acting within his or her scope of practice as defined in hospital medical staff bylaws and State law, certifies that, after a reasonable time of observation, the woman is in false labor. 42 C.F.R. § 489.24(b). EMMC argues that "'labor' refers to 'the process of childbirth,' rather than defining it in a more general manner that could refer to missed abortions." [Citation] (quoting 42 C.F.R. § 489.24(b)). "In other words," says EMMC, "although section (e)(1)(B) refers to 'contractions,' it is clear that viewing the statutory scheme and its

---

[45] The court referenced Brenord v. Catholic Med. Ctr. of Brooklyn & Queens, Inc., 133 F. Supp. 2d 179, 191-92 (E.D.N.Y. 2001) (granting summary judgment on EMTALA stabilization claim because hospital was unaware that pregnant woman was in labor).

[46] To be clear, the statute and the regulation do not tell physicians how to practice medicine. The question here is legal—whether EMTALA applies to a patient—not medical. If it does, legal consequences ensue; if it does not, they do not. The legal definitions do not direct the physicians or the hospital how to treat the woman medically, but they do direct the courts how she is to be treated legally.

[47] The Court is uncertain and does not decide whether the regulation, which defines "labor," pertains to this portion of EMTALA. *Compare* 42 U.S.C. § 1395dd(e)(1)(B) (defining "emergency medical condition" as it applies to "a pregnant woman who is having contractions"), *with* 42 C.F.R. § 489.24(b) (defining "labor" as "the process of childbirth beginning with the latent or early phase of labor and continuing through the delivery of the placenta").

regulations as a whole, the protections of (e)(1)(B) apply to pregnant women who are experiencing contractions related to labor and child-birth, rather than cramping associated with a missed abortion." [Citation]

The Court is manifestly dubious about EMMC's stated fears that it will be inundated with pregnant women claiming that they are experiencing cramps and that EMTALA will require EMMC to stabilize them through delivery. Although EMMC argues that "[t]o avoid this absurd result," the Court must define labor to exclude missed abortions, EMMC never explains how doing so allows hospitals to discharge cramping pregnant women who "are not dilated enough to deliver." [Citation].

Moreover, the solution to EMMC's asserted dilemma is found in the implementing regulations, which allow hospitals to avoid EMTALA liability by certifying that a pregnant woman is in false labor. If a pregnant woman is having contractions, the regulations require that the hospital see her through delivery unless it concludes and certifies she is in false labor.

A straightforward reading of the regulation simply does not begin to support EMMC's questionable interpretation; there is no express or implicit requirement of viability. The regulation does not mention live birth. It focuses instead on the end result of the childbirth—the "deliv-ery of the placenta," a phrase that encompasses both viable and nonviable fetuses.

EMMC further argues that because doctors certify when a patient is "in false labor," "Congress intended that, in application of EMTALA's requirements, physicians would be required to make certain medical judgments based on their medical education and experience." [Citation]. Because medical doctors do not define contractions at early stages of pregnancy as "labor," EMMC argues "there could have been no certification by a physician that Plaintiff was 'in false labor' because, medically, she would not have been considered by a physician to be in 'false labor' (much less labor)." [Citation].

The Court disagrees. Even though "false labor" is not defined, "labor" is. Regardless of what the physician may diagnose, the regulation says that a pregnant woman who is experiencing contractions is in true labor unless the hospital certifies that she is in false labor. Medical profes-sionals are presumably expected to certify "false labor" in reference to the regulation's definition of "labor," not an external medical definition. See *Burditt v. U.S. Dep't of Health and Human Services*, 934 F.2d 1362, 1369 (5th Cir. 1991) (stating that EMTALA's statutory definition "ren-ders irrelevant any medical definition of active labor").[48]

---

[48] EMMC argues that *Burditt* is inapplicable because it was written under an earlier version of EMTALA in which "the threshold question was whether the woman was 'in labor.'" [Citation]. However, subsequent amendments strengthen, rather than undermine, *Burditt*'s conclusion. In the pre-1991 version of EMTALA, "active labor" was defined as "labor at a time when (B) there is inadequate time to effect safe transfer . . . or (C) a transfer may pose a threat to the health and safety of the patient." *Burditt*, 934 F.2d at 1369. Because "labor" was not defined, the Fifth Circuit specified that "[a]ll agree that labor begins with the onset of uterine contractions." [Citation] The court found further support for its definition in the fact that "Congress explicitly recognized this definition of 'labor' in revising EMTALA." [Citation] (citing 42 U.S.C.A. § 1395dd(e)(1)(B) (West Supp. 1991)). In other words, *Burditt* concluded that

Regarding EMMC's argument as a whole, the Court could not disagree more with EMMC at a most fundamental level. EMMC contends that the protections of the portion of EMTALA specific to pregnant women [pertain] only to women who seek medical assistance for pregnancies that result in the birth of a live infant and that the protections of the statute are unavailable for pregnant women who end up aborting. The Court is nonplussed at EMMC's disquieting notion that EMTALA and its regulations authorize hospital emergency rooms to treat women who do not deliver a live infant differently than women who do. EMMC's contention is not justified by the language of the statute or its implementing regulations and has disturbing policy implications. There is simply no suggestion that Congress ever intended such a harsh and callous result for women who, like Ms. Morin, are carrying a non-viable fetus.[49]

Q 5:6   Off-Campus Transfers: Does EMTALA govern a hospital's transfers from off-campus facilities?

A patient transfer from a hospital's own off-campus facility to the main hospital campus is not an EMTALA transfer. In addition, transfer of a patient from such an off-campus facility to a nonaffiliated hospital is not governed by EMTALA unless the off-campus facility meets the definition of a dedicated emergency department.

The State Operations Manual states:

> Hospitals should not move individuals to off-campus facilities or departments (such as an urgent care center or satellite clinic) for a MSE. If an individual comes to a hospital-owned facility or department, which is off-campus and operates under the hospital's Medicare provider number, § 1867 (42 CFR 489.24) will not apply to that facility and/or department unless it meets the definition of a dedicated emergency department.

> If, however, such a facility does not meet the definition of a dedicated ED, it must screen and stabilize the patient to the best of its ability or execute an appropriate transfer if necessary to another hospital or to the hospital on whose Medicare provider number it is operated. Hospital resources and staff available at the main campus are likewise available to individuals seeking care at the off-campus facilities or departments within the capability of the hospital. Movement of the individual to the main campus of the hospital is not considered a transfer since the individual is simply being moved from one department of a hospital to another department or facility of the same hospital. In addition, a

---

Congress gave "labor" a nonmedical statutory definition despite the fact Congress left the term undefined. As *Burditt* recognized, its conclusion was affirmed by subsequent revisions to EMTALA, which redefined coverage of pregnant women in relation to EMTALA. Other cases have since applied *Burditt*'s conclusion to the current version of EMTALA. *See* Torretti v. Paoli Mem'l Hosp., Civil Action No. 06-3003, 2008 U.S. Dist. LEXIS 6263, 2008 WL 268066, at *4 (E.D. Pa. Jan. 29, 2008) (quoting *Burditt* for the conclusion that EMTALA's statutory definition "renders irrelevant any medical definition of active labor").

[49] *Morin*, 780 F. Supp. 2d 84, 94-96.

transfer from such an entity (i.e., an off-campus facility that meets the definition of a dedicated ED) to a nonaffiliated hospital (i.e., a hospital that does not own the off-campus facility) is allowed where the facility at which the individual presented cannot stabilize the individual and the benefits of transfer exceed the risks of transfer. In other words, there is no requirement under EMTALA that the individual be always transferred back to the hospital that owns and operates the off-campus dedicated ED. Rather, the requirement of EMTALA is that the individual be transferred to an appropriate facility for treatment.[50]

Cautions: In January 2001, CMS presented OPPS regulations[51] that require qualifying off-campus hospital sites to comply with EMTALA regulations. These regulations specify appropriate transfers from such sites. Moving a patient to the main hospital to provide medical care not available at the off-campus site should be undertaken if the resources at the remote site are inadequate to care for the patient. Movement of the patient to the hospital's emergency department is not considered an EMTALA transfer because the individual is simply being moved from one department of a hospital to another department or facility of the same hospital. However, when transporting the patient to a facility other than the main campus hospital is required because (1) the main hospital campus does not have the capability required by the patient or (2) the time needed to transport to the main campus rather than a closer hospital could significantly jeopardize the patient's health, the transfer is an EMTALA transfer if the facility meets the definition of a dedicated emergency department, with the same certification and communication requirements as if the patient were being transferred from the main emergency department of the hospital.

In the final rules of September 9, 2003, CMS specifically allows transfers to a nonaffiliated hospital when such a transfer is in the patient's best interest. CMS states in the *Federal Register*:

> Both under past and current rules, a transfer from an urgent care center to a nonaffiliated hospital is allowed under EMTALA where the facility at which the individual presented cannot stabilize the individual and the benefits of transfer exceed the risks of transfer and certain other regulatory requirements are met. Thus, our rules permit a satellite facility covered under the definition of dedicated emergency department, in this example, to screen and determine whether the case is too complex to be treated on site, that a lengthy ambulance ride to an affiliated hospital would present an unacceptable risk to the individual, and then conclude that the benefit of transfer exceeds the risk of transfer. In this case, the satellite facility could then transfer the individual to an appropriate nearby medical facility.[52]

---

[50] U.S. Dep't HHS, CMS, State Operations Manual, App. V, Emergency Medical Treatment and Labor Act (EMTALA) Interpretive Guidelines, Part II, Tag A-2406/C-2406 (revised 7/16/2010).

[51] 42 C.F.R. § 489.24(i).

[52] 68 Fed. Reg. 53,232 (Sept. 9, 2003).

Many hospitals have off-campus facilities such as urgent care centers and ambulatory care centers. If these facilities meet the definition of a dedicated emergency department, then they need to be aware of this ruling. CMS places the responsibility for transporting the patient from the off-campus site to the emergency department on the shoulders of the hospital. The hospital should have policies in place so that personnel at the off-campus site know the communication process required with the emergency department to transport the patient to the emergency department. The personnel at the off-campus site should also be trained in filling out proper EMTALA certification papers should they need to transfer to a facility other than the main hospital campus.

If the off-campus facility is a non-clinical facility (e.g., an MRI facility, a physical therapy department, etc.), then EMTALA does not govern, but proper policies and procedures should still be in place to address acute clinical emergent conditions. The personnel at these sites also need to be educated in how and when it is appropriate to call the 911 EMS system for emergency conditions.

The State Operations Manual states:

> If a request were made for emergency care in a hospital department off the hospital's main campus that does not meet the definition of a dedicated emergency department, EMTALA would not apply. However, such an off-campus facility must have policies and procedures in place as to how to handle patients in need of immediate care. For example, the off-campus facility policy may direct the staff to contact the emergency medical services/911 (EMS) to take the patient to an emergency department (not necessarily the emergency department of the hospital that operates the off-campus department, but rather the closest emergency department) or provide the necessary care if it is within the hospital's capability. Therefore, a hospital off-campus facility that does not meet the definition of a dedicated emergency department does not have an EMTALA obligation and is not required to be staffed to handle potential EMCs.[53]

Q 5:7 Round-trip Transfers: What if a patient is transferred to another hospital for diagnostic services with the intention of returning to the first hospital?

Transfers to another hospital for necessary specialty testing with the intent of returning to the original hospital afterward are permitted by CMS. EMTALA compliance with transfer requirements must still be met by the transferring hospital.

Cautions: Occasionally, hospitals transfer patients to another facility for specialized testing, such as magnetic resonance imaging (MRI) or cardiac

---

[53] U.S. Dep't HHS, CMS, State Operations Manual, App. V, Emergency Medical Treatment and Labor Act (EMTALA) Interpretive Guidelines, Part II, Tag A-2406/C-2406 (revised 7/16/2010).

angiography. The transferring hospital still needs to have an EMTALA-compliant transfer with documentation, certification, and acceptance by the receiving hospital. The benefits still need to outweigh the risks of transfer. CMS clarifies:

> If an individual is moved to a diagnostic facility located at another hospital for diagnostic procedures not available at the transferring hospital, and the hospitals arrange to return the individual to the transferring hospital, the transfer requirements must still be met by the sending hospital. The recipient hospital is not obligated to meet the EMTALA transfer requirements when implementing an appropriate transfer back to the transferring hospital. However, it is reasonable to expect the recipient hospital with the diagnostic capability to communicate (e.g., telephonic report or documentation within the medical record) with the transferring hospital its findings of the medical condition and a status report of the individual during and after the procedure.[54]

During an investigation, the CMS team examines these transfers carefully, specifically reviewing records for:

- Transfers to off-site testing facilities and return;
- Gaps, return cases, or nonsequential entries in the log;
- Refusals of examination, treatment, or transfer;
- Patients leaving against medical advice (AMA); and
- Returns to the emergency department within 48 hours.[55]

The receiving hospital also bears responsibility for such transfers even though the patient technically is being transferred solely for testing. The receiving hospital needs to comply with EMTALA requirements for central logging and documentation just as if it were receiving a regular transfer. The receiving hospital should be available to treat any emergency condition that arises while the patient is being tested. The receiving hospital should also prudently assume further treatment for a patient if testing reveals an EMC and any transfer back to the original hospital would jeopardize the patient's safety. One approach would be to register all such transfer patients in the receiving hospital's emergency department where the emergency physician can adequately evaluate the patient's condition and test results before safe return to the original hospital.

CMS allows the transfer document from the sending facility to function as a "round trip ticket" so long as the testing facility does not identify an EMC.

---

[54] U.S. Dep't HHS, CMS, State Operations Manual, App. V, Emergency Medical Treatment and Labor Act (EMTALA) Interpretive Guidelines, Part II, Tag A-2409/C-2409 (revised 5/29/2009).

[55] U.S. Dep't HHS, CMS, State Operations Manual, App. V, Emergency Medical Treatment and Labor Act (EMTALA) Interpretive Guidelines, Part I, IV, Task 2 (revised 5/29/2009).

Q 5:8   Lateral Transfers: Are "lateral" transfers to another hospital for admission allowed?

Yes. If the patient has a stable medical condition, transfer to another hospital is allowed under EMTALA. If the patient has an unstable EMC, there must be a medical benefit to the transfer. The State Operations Manual states:

> Lateral transfers, that is, transfers between facilities of comparable resources and capabilities, are not required by § 489.24(f), because the benefits of such a transfer would not be likely to outweigh the risks of the transfer, except when the transferring hospital has a serious capacity problem, a mechanical failure of equipment, or similar situations, such as loss of power or significant flooding.[56]

Cautions: A lateral transfer involves the transfer of patients between hospitals of equal capacity and capability. Once a patient is deemed stable after an appropriate MSE or stabilizing treatment, EMTALA no longer applies and a patient may be transferred to another hospital for any reason. Managed care companies often request that a patient be transferred to a hospital that has contracted with the managed care organization for hospital care. EMTALA does not prohibit transfers to a second hospital of equal or even lesser capacity and capability as long as the patient has been stabilized according to EMTALA's definition for stability.

The transferring hospital needs to be very sure that the patient is stable. In CMS's words:

> A patient is stable for transfer from one facility to a second facility when the treating physician attending to the patient has determined, within reasonable clinical confidence, that the patient is expected to leave the hospital and be received at the second facility with no material deterioration in his or her medical condition, and the treating physician reasonably believes the receiving facility has the capability to manage the patient's medical condition and any reasonably foreseeable complication of that condition.[57]

Since the patient is stable and EMTALA no longer applies, the statutory requirements for such a transfer do not technically need to meet CMS's definition of an "appropriate" transfer. The burden of responsibility is on the transferring physician and hospital if the patient experiences medical deterioration and harm en route. Note, however, that CMS citations are not limited to those cases of adverse outcome. CMS routinely cites on the basis of whether the transfer inappropriately placed the patient at risk.

---

[56] U.S. Dep't HHS, CMS, State Operations Manual, App. V, Emergency Medical Treatment and Labor Act (EMTALA) Interpretive Guidelines, Part II, Tag A-2411/C-2411 (revised 5/29/2009).

[57] U.S. Dep't HHS, CMS, State Operations Manual, App. V, Emergency Medical Treatment and Labor Act (EMTALA) Interpretive Guidelines, Part II, Tag A-2407/C-2407 (revised 5/29/2009).

Q 5:9 Consultation Transfers: May a hospital transfer a patient to another hospital for specialty consultation?

A hospital may not transfer a patient to another hospital for specialty consultation if there is any question of a patient's stability or presence of an EMC unless the patient specifically requests the transfer and understands the risks. Once a patient is stable, EMTALA no longer applies and such transfers are therefore allowed.

Cautions: Managed care organizations may request that only specialists who have contracted with the managed care organization be consulted. As with admission transfers, a patient who has been stabilized and will not experience any foreseeable deterioration during the transfer may be transferred for consultation because EMTALA no longer technically applies once a patient has been stabilized. However, this practice is fraught with danger. EMTALA establishes a duty on the first hospital to provide on-call specialists for emergency consultation. If the emergency physician is transferring the patient to another hospital for a specialist there to determine whether an EMC exists, then the patient has not truly been "stabilized" under EMTALA. CMS may view such transfers as EMTALA violations.

An on-call specialist at the original hospital, even without contract to the managed care organization, must provide the consultation to either determine whether an EMC exists or to stabilize a recognized emergency condition. On-call specialists who refuse to respond to a call to treat a patient with an EMC because of managed care contract issues risk EMTALA violation. The emergency physician would be prudent to avoid all such transfers.

Q 5:10 Refusal to Transfer: What EMTALA liability arises from a refusal or failure to transfer a patient?

EMTALA has no provision for a civil suit premised on a hospital's refusal to transfer or discharge a patient. In *Fraticelli-Torres v. Hospital Hermanos*, the First Circuit held that "[a] hospital's negligent medical decision not to transfer a critical patient promptly to another hospital to receive necessary treatment might trigger state-law medical malpractice liability, but it could not constitute an EMTALA anti-dumping violation."[58] The First Circuit came to this conclusion by interpreting the express terms of EMTALA, which restrict the circumstances under which one hospital may transfer an unstabilized patient to another hospital but do "not impose any positive obligation on a covered hospital to transfer a critical patient under particular circumstances to obtain stabilization at another hospital."[59]

The issue also arose when a plaintiff class sued a New Orleans hospital for injuries and deaths of patients that occurred during the Hurricane Katrina

---

[58] Fraticelli-Torres v. Hospital Hermanos, 300 Fed. Appx. 1, 8 (1st Cir. 2008).
[59] *Fraticelli-Torres*, 300 Fed. Appx. 1, 6.

disaster in August/September 2005.[60] During the hurricane, roughly 1,000 people were trapped in the hospital. Despite the rescue efforts made to evacuate the building, many patients remained trapped inside for an extended period. In total, approximately 35 patients died and many were injured. In the case *Preston v. Tenet Healthsystem Memorial Medical Center, Inc.*, various patients and relatives of the deceased and allegedly injured filed a suit against the hospital in district court and petitioned for class certification. The complaint alleged, *inter alia*, that the hospital violated EMTALA by leaving some patients behind after deciding to evacuate others. The plaintiffs claimed federal subject matter jurisdiction on the basis of this claim. The U.S. District Court for the Eastern District of Louisiana concluded that no viable cause of action under EMTALA existed for a hospital's refusal to transfer or discharge a patient.[61] Because the court lacked federal subject matter jurisdiction over the case, it remanded the action to state court.

Like the First Circuit, the Louisiana district court reasoned that EMTALA was designed to prevent situations in which a doctor or hospital refuses to provide emergency medical treatment to a patient who is unable to pay for the medical services. Essentially, EMTALA provides for civil monetary penalties against hospitals and doctors who improperly transfer or discharge ("dump") emergency room patients, who are then injured by their improper transfer or discharge. Because none of the patients in *Preston* was transferred or discharged, or injured by improper transfer or discharge, the district court concluded that there was no actionable claim under EMTALA. The court noted that this determination was consistent with the legislative intent behind EMTALA, as the statute was not intended to be used as a federal malpractice statute.[62]

It bears noting that CMS has stated that "[w]hen a hospital has exhausted all of its capabilities in attempting to resolve the [emergency medical condition], it must effect an appropriate transfer of the individual."[63] The obligation imposed by the word "must" is unclear, particularly in situations where transfer may exacerbate the patient's condition. As always, it falls on a physician to certify that the risks of transfer are outweighed by the benefits to be obtained at the destination hospital. If there is adequate documentation that the risks of transfer are too severe, CMS will likely accept a decision not to transfer. If a patient in clear need of a transfer is denied transfer by a physician who does not wish to relinquish the patient or the billing for inappropriate reasons, the responsibility falls on the hospital's disciplinary process to enforce reasonable standards of professional practice.

---

[60] Preston v. Tenet Healthsystem Mem'l Med. Ctr., Inc., 463 F. Supp. 2d 583 (E.D. La. 2006), *aff'd by* 485 F.3d 804 (5th Cir. 2007).

[61] The definition of "reverse dumping" adopted by the *Preston* plaintiffs differed from the definition used by the Tenth Circuit in *St. Anthony Hospital,* 309 F.3d 680, where "reverse dumping" described refusals by emergency departments to accept an appropriate transfer of a patient requiring the hospital's specialized capabilities. In contrast, the plaintiff class in *Preston* applied the term to the defendant hospital's failure to transfer or discharge patients. 463 F. Supp. 2d 583, 595.

[62] *Preston,* 463 F. Supp. 2d 583, 595.

[63] U.S. Dep't HHS, CMS, State Operations Manual, App. V, Emergency Medical Treatment and Labor Act (EMTALA) Interpretive Guidelines, Part II, Tag A-2407/C-2407 (revised 5/29/2009).

Q 5:11   Inability to Transfer: Does a hospital incur EMTALA liability for unsuccessful transfer attempts?

No. EMTALA does not require that a hospital have a procedure in place guaranteeing transfer of patients.

Cautions: In the case of *Dabney v. H.C.A. Fort Walton Beach Medical Center,*[64] the United States District Court for the Northern District of Florida granted a hospital's motion to dismiss a case involving EMTALA brought against it by a patient who presented to its emergency department and required a neurosurgical consult. On August 12, 2005, the plaintiff was transported by EMS to the defendant hospital after being found on the floor in his home. After examination and tests, it was determined that the patient required a neurosurgical consult. The hospital had a neurosurgeon scheduled to be on call, but when called for the consult, the neurosurgeon advised that he was unable to come due to illness. The hospital did not have any backup neurosurgeon to cover for the unavailable on-call neurosurgeon. The hospital attempted to obtain consent for transfer of the patient to three nearby hospitals but all refused to accept the transfer. The hospital had no pre-arranged interhospital transfer agreement with any nearby hospital. The patient alleged a violation of EMTALA because the hospital lacked such agreements.

The court observed that EMTALA does not require a hospital to have a transfer agreement when an on-call physician is unavailable, nor does it require that a hospital have a procedure in place guaranteeing transfer of a patient. It also noted that to be successful under EMTALA, the patient must allege that the hospital could have successfully transferred him or her to a reasonably available hospital but did not take that course of action. Because the patient in this case did not make such allegations, the court granted the hospital's motion to dismiss.

Q 5:12   Community Disaster Plans: May a hospital transfer patients according to local EMS community-wide plans?

Yes. A hospital may provide transfer of patients according to community-wide plans. The hospital must still provide EMTALA screening and stabilization, but the transfer or referral of these individuals in accordance with a community response plan that designates specific hospitals or areas to handle certain categories of patients during a catastrophic event would not result in a violation of EMTALA.

The CMS State Operations Manual states:

> If community wide plans exist for specific hospitals to treat certain EMCs (e.g., psychiatric, trauma, physical or sexual abuse), the hospital must meet its EMTALA obligations (screen, stabilize, and or appropriately transfer) prior to transferring the individual to the community plan

---

[64] No. 3:07cv331/RS/EMT (N.D. Fla. Oct. 22, 2007).

hospital. An example of a community wide plan would be a trauma system hospital. A trauma system is a comprehensive system providing injury prevention services and timely and appropriate delivery of emergency medical treatment for people with acute illness and traumatic injury. Those systems are designed so that patients with catastrophic injuries will have the quickest possible access to an established trauma center or a hospital that has the capabilities to provide comprehensive emergency medical care. These systems ensure that the severely injured patient can be rapidly cared for in the facility that is most appropriately prepared to treat the severity of injury.

Community plans are designed to provide an organized, pre-planned response to patient needs to assure the best patient care and efficient use of limited health care resources. Community plans are designed to augment physician's care if the necessary services are not within the capability of the hospital but does not mandate patient care nor transfer patterns. Patient health status frequently depends on the appropriate use of the community plans. The matching of the appropriate facility with the needs of the patient is the focal point of this plan and assures every patient receives the best care possible. Therefore, a sending hospital's appropriate transfer of an individual in accordance with community wide protocols in instances where it cannot provide stabilizing treatment would be deemed to indicate compliance with § 1867.[65]

In addition, for bioterrorism events, the State Operations Manual states:

In accordance with Section 1135(b)(3) of the Act, hospitals and CAHs operating under an EMTALA waiver will not be sanctioned for:

- Redirecting an individual who "comes to the emergency department," as that term is defined at § 489.24(b), to an alternate location for an MSE, pursuant to a State emergency preparedness plan or, as applicable, a State pandemic preparedness plan. Even when a waiver is in effect there is still the expectation that everyone who comes to the ED will receive an appropriate MSE, if not in the ED, then at the alternate care site to which they are redirected or relocated.

- Inappropriately transferring an individual protected under EMTALA, when the transfer is necessitated by the circumstances of the declared emergencies. Transfers may be inappropriate under EMTALA for a number of reasons.

However, even if a hospital/CAH is operating under an EMTALA waiver, the hospital/CAH would not be exempt from sanctions if it discriminates among individuals based on their ability to pay for services, or the source of their payment for services when redirecting or relocating them for the MSE or when making inappropriate transfers.

All other EMTALA-related requirements at 42 CFR 489.20 and EMTALA requirements at 42 CFR 489.24 continue to apply, even when a hospital is operating under an EMTALA waiver. For example, the statute does not provide for a waiver of a recipient hospital's obligation to accept an

---

[65] U.S. Dep't HHS, CMS, State Operations Manual, App. V, Emergency Medical Treatment and Labor Act (EMTALA) Interpretive Guidelines, Part II, Tag A-2407/C-2407 (revised 5/29/2009).

appropriate transfer of an individual protected under EMTALA. (As a reminder, even without a waiver, a hospital is obligated to accept an appropriate EMTALA transfer *only* when that recipient hospital has specialized capabilities required by the individual and the requisite capacity at the time of the transfer request.)

Waiver of EMTALA requirements in accordance with a Section 1135 waiver does not affect a hospital's or CAH's obligation to comply with State law or regulation that may separately impose requirements similar to those under EMTALA law and regulations. Facilities are encouraged to communicate with their State licensure authorities as to the availability of waivers under State law.

* * *

In accordance with Section 1135 of the Act, an EMTALA waiver may be issued only when:

- The President has declared an emergency or disaster pursuant to the National Emergencies Act or the Robert T. Stafford Disaster Relief and Emergency Assistance Act; and

- The Secretary has declared a public health emergency (PHE) pursuant to Section 319 of the Public Health Service Act; and

- The Secretary has exercised his/her waiver authority pursuant to Section 1135 of the Act and notified Congress at least 48 hours in advance of exercising his/her waiver authority.

In exercising his/her waiver authority, the Secretary may choose to delegate to the Centers for Medicare & Medicaid Services (CMS) the decision as to which Medicare, Medicaid, or CHIP requirements specified in Section 1135 should be temporarily waived or modified, and for which health care providers or groups of providers such waivers are necessary. Specifically, the Secretary may delegate to CMS decision-making about whether and for which hospitals/CAHs to waive EMTALA sanctions as specified in Section 1135(b)(3).

In addition, in order for an EMTALA waiver to apply to a specific hospital or CAH:

- The hospital or CAH must activate its disaster protocol; and

- The State must have activated an emergency preparedness plan or pandemic preparedness plan in the emergency area, and any redirection of individuals for an MSE must be consistent with such plan. It is not necessary for the State to activate its plan statewide, so long as it is activated in the area where the hospital is located. It is also not necessary for the State plan to identify the specific location of the alternate screening sites to which individuals will be directed, although some may do so.

* * *

Except in the case of waivers related to pandemic infectious disease, an EMTALA waiver is limited in duration to 72 hours beginning upon activation of the hospital's/CAH's disaster protocol. In the case of a public health emergency (PHE) involving pandemic infectious disease, the genera EMTALA waiver authority will continue in effect until the termination of the declaration of the PHE. However, application of this general authority to a specific hospital/CAH or groups of hospitals and CAHs may limit the waiver's application to a date prior to the termination of the PHE declaration, since case-specific applications of the waiver authority are issued only to the extent they are necessary, as determined by CMS.

Furthermore, if a State emergency/pandemic preparedness plan is deactivated in the area where the hospital or CAH is located prior to the termination of the public health emergency, the hospital or CAH no longer meets the conditions for an EMTALA waiver and that hospital/ CAH waiver would cease to be inn effect as of the deactivation date. Likewise, if a hospital or CAH deactivates its disaster protocol prior to the termination of the public health emergency, the hospital or CAH no longer meets the conditions for an EMTALA waiver and that hospital/ CAH waiver would cease to be in effect as of the deactivation date.

* * *

Section 1135 provides for waivers of certain Medicare, Medicaid, or CHIP requirements, including waivers of EMTALA sanctions, but only to the extent necessary, to ensure sufficient health care items and services are available to meet the needs of Medicare, Medicaid, and CHIP beneficiaries. The waivers also ensure that health care providers who provide such services in good faith but are unable to comply with one or more of the specified requirements may be reimbursed for such items and services and exempted from sanctions for noncompliance, absent any fraud or abuse.

When the Secretary has exercised his/her waiver authority and delegated to CMS decision-making about specific EMTALA waivers, CMS policy in exercising its authority for granting EMTALA waivers is as follows:

> **Localized Emergency Area:** In the case of localized disasters, such as those related to floods or hurricanes, CMS may exercise its discretion to advise hospitals/CAHs in the affected areas that they are covered by the EMTALA waiver, **without requiring individual applications for each waiver**. However, hospitals or CAHs that activate their disaster protocol and expect to take advantage of the area-wide waiver must notify their State Survey Agency (SA) at the time they activate their disaster protocol.

> **Nationwide Emergency Area:** In the case of a nationwide emergency area, CMS may also exercise its discretion to advise hospitals/CAHs in a specific geographical area(s) that they are covered by the EMTALA waiver **for a time-limited period**. CMS expects to do this only if the State has activated its emergency or pandemic preparedness plan in the affected area(s), and if there is other evidence of need for the waiver for a broad group of hospitals of CAHs. CMS will rely upon SAs to advise their CMS Regional Office (RO) whether and where a State's preparedness plan has been activated, as well as when the plan has been deactivated.

In the absence of CMS notification of area-wide applications of the waiver, hospitals/CAHs must contact CMS and request that the waiver provisions be applied to their facility. In all cases, the Act envisions that individuals protected under EMTALA will still receive appropriate MSEs somewhere (even if the MSE is not conducted at the hospital or CAH where they present), and that individuals who are transferred for stabilization of their emergency medical condition will be sent to a facility capable of providing stabilizing services, regardless of whether a waiver is in effect.

Unless CMS advises otherwise, in cases of a public health emergency involving pandemic infectious disease, hospitals/CAHs in areas covered by time-limited, area-wide applications of the EMTALA waiver that seek to extend the waiver's application to a later date within the waiver period (that is, within the period of the PHE declaration) must submit individual requests for extension. The requests must demonstrate their need for continued application of the waiver. Such requests must be received at least three calendar days prior to expiration of the time-limited waiver. Extensions of an EMTALA waiver in emergencies that do not involve pandemic infectious disease are not available.

* * *

Hospitals or CAHs seeking an EMTALA waiver must demonstrate to CMS that application of the waiver to their facility is necessary, and that they have activated their disaster protocol. CMS will confirm with the SA whether the State's preparedness plan has been activated in the area where the hospital or CAH is located. CMS will also seek to confirm when the hospital activated its disaster protocol, whether other measures may address the situation in a manner that does not require a waiver, and other factors important to the ability of the hospital to demonstrate that a waiver is needed.

* * *

EMTALA enforcement is a complaint-driven process. CMS will assess any complaints/allegations related to alleged EMTALA violations concerning the MSE or transfer during the waiver period to determine whether the hospital or CAH in question was operating under an EMTALA waiver at the time of the complaint, and, if so, whether the nature of the complaint involves actions or requirements not covered by the EMTALA waiver and warrants further on-site investigation by the SA.[66]

   The Public Health Security and Bioterrorism Preparedness and Response Act of 2002[67] authorizes the Secretary of HHS to waive sanctions for a violation of EMTALA where the violation is the result of an inappropriate transfer of an unstable patient if the transfer arises out of circumstances during a public health emergency (as defined by a Presidential declaration of emergency or disaster and a public health emergency declaration by the Secretary of HHS). This law

---

[66] U.S. Dep't HHS, CMS, State Operations Manual, App. V, Emergency Medical Treatment and Labor Act (EMTALA) Interpretive Guidelines, Part II, Tag A-2406/C-2406 (revised 7/16/2010).

[67] Pub. L. No. 107-188, 116 Stat. 627 (2002) (codified in scattered sections of the U.S. Code).

applies only to inappropriate transfers, not to the MSE or stabilization arms of EMTALA. In addition, this law does not extinguish the private right of action on the part of injured individuals. In 2001, when anthrax was a problem, Steven A. Pelovitz, Director for the CMS Survey and Certification Group, sent a note to Regional Administrators clarifying that there may be situations where referral of a potentially exposed patient prior to the actual examination is appropriate. He gave an example of a potentially exposed patient presenting at an undesignated hospital. After questioning the patient and making a determination that the patient falls into the category for which the community has a specified screening site, the patient may be referred to the designated community facility.[68]

Requirements for Transfer

Q 5:13   Transfer Requirements: What are EMTALA's transfer requirements?

A hospital may not transfer an individual with an unstable EMC except under the following circumstances as outlined in the Code of Federal Regulations:

> (e) *Restricting transfer until the individual is stabilized*—(1) General. If an individual at a hospital has an emergency medical condition that has not been stabilized (as defined in paragraph (b) of this section), the hospital may not transfer the individual unless—
>
> (1) The transfer is an appropriate transfer (within the meaning of paragraph (e) (2) of this section; and
>
>> (A) The individual (or a legally responsible person acting on the individual's behalf) requests the transfer, after being informed of the hospital's obligations under this section and of the risk of transfer. The request must be in writing and indicate the reasons for the request as well as indicate that he or she is aware of the risks and benefits of the transfer;
>>
>> (B) A physician (within the meaning of section 1861(r)(1) of the Act) has signed a certification that, based upon the information available at the time of transfer, the medical benefits reasonably expected from the provision of appropriate medical treatment at another medical facility outweigh the increased risks to the individual or, in the case of a woman in labor, to the woman or the unborn child, from being transferred. The certification must contain a summary of the risks and benefits upon which it is based; or
>>
>> (C) If a physician is not physically present in the emergency department at the time an individual is transferred, a qualified medical person (as determined by the hospital in its by-laws or rules and regulations) has signed a certification described in paragraph (e)(1)(ii)(B) of this section after a

---

[68] *Question and Answer Relating to Bioterrorism and EMTALA*, CMS letter to Regional Administrators, Steven A. Pelovitz, Ref: S&C-02-04.

physician (as defined in section 1861(r)(1) of the Act) in consultation with the qualified medical person, agrees with the certification and subsequently countersigns the certification. The certification must contain a summary of the risks and benefits upon which it is based.[69]

Cautions: Technically, EMTALA governs a transfer only when it involves a patient with an unstable EMC. However, a hospital should treat all transfers (whether stable or unstable) uniformly as if EMTALA governs, so that no unstable patient is inadvertently transferred without EMTALA certification requirements. The medical profession recognizes that seemingly stable patients can become unstable without warning. Patients are often transferred from a hospital for a variety of reasons: the patient's private physician and records are at his or her own hospital closer to home, the transfer is to a skilled nursing facility for rehabilitation, or the receiving hospital has specialized equipment or physicians. For whatever reason, the majority of transfers are non-EMTALA transfers of stable patients. However, hospitals should get in the habit of obtaining patient consent and filling out EMTALA certificates for every transfer from the emergency department in order to avoid possible citations.

The American College of Emergency Physicians' policy statement on appropriate inter-hospital patient transfers provides a valuable guideline when considering transfers:

- The optimal health and well being of the patient should be the principal goal of patient transfer.

- Emergency physicians and hospital personnel should abide by applicable laws regarding patient transfer. All patients should be provided a Medical Screening Examination (MSE) and stabilizing treatment within the capacity of the facility before transfer. If a competent patient requests transfer before the completion of the MSE and stabilizing treatment, these should be offered to the patient and documented. Hospital policies and procedures should articulate these obligations and ensure safe and efficient transfer.

- The transferring physician should inform the patient or responsible party of the risks and the benefits of transfer and document these. Before transfer, patient consent should be obtained and documented whenever possible.

- The hospital policies and procedures and/or medical staff bylaws should identify the individuals responsible for and qualified to perform MSEs. The policies and procedures or bylaws must define who is responsible for accepting and transferring patients on behalf of the hospital. The examining physician at the transferring hospital will use his or her best judgment regarding the condition of the patient when determining the timing of transfer, mode of transportation, level of care provided during transfer, and the destination of the patient.

---

[69] 42 C.F.R. § 489.24(e).

- Transfers are effected through qualified personnel and transportation equipment, as required, including the use of necessary and medically appropriate life support measures during the transfer.

- Agreement to accept the patient in transfer should be obtained from a physician or responsible individual at the receiving hospital in advance of transfer. When a patient requires a higher level of care other than that provided or available at the transferring facility, a hospital with the capability to provide a higher level of care may not refuse any request for transfer.

- An appropriate medical summary and other pertinent records should accompany the patient to the receiving facility or be electronically transferred as soon as is practical.

- When transfer of patients is part of a regional plan to provide optimal care at a specialized medical facility, written transfer protocols and interfacility agreements should be in place.[70]

Q 5:14   The Appropriate Transfer: What is an "appropriate" EMTALA transfer?

The Code of Federal Regulations describes an "appropriate" transfer as:

A transfer to another medical facility will be appropriate only in those cases in which—

(i)   The transferring hospital provides medical treatment within its capacity that minimizes the risks to the individual's health and in the case of a woman in labor, the health of the unborn child;

(ii) The receiving facility—

(A)   Has available space and qualified personnel for the treatment of the individual; and

(B)   Has agreed to accept transfer of the individual and to provide appropriate medical treatment;

(iii) The transferring hospital sends to the receiving facility all medical records (or copies thereof) related to the emergency condition which the individual has presented that are available at the time of the transfer, including available history, records related to the individual's emergency medical condition, observations of signs or symptoms, preliminary diagnosis, results of diagnostic studies or telephone reports of the studies, treatment provided, results of any tests and the informed written consent or certification (or copy thereof) required under paragraph (e)(1)(ii) of this section, and the name and address of any on-call physician (described in paragraph (g) of this section) who has refused or failed to appear within a reasonable time to provide necessary stabilizing treatment. Other records (e.g., test results not yet available or

---

[70] ACEP Policy Statement, *Appropriate Interhospital Patient Transfer* (Feb. 2009), available at http://www.acep.org/practres.aspx?id=32334.

historical records not readily available from the hospital's files) must be sent as soon as practicable after transfer; and

(iv) The transfer is effected through qualified personnel and transportation equipment, as required, including the use of necessary and medically appropriate life support measures during the transfer.[71]

Cautions: The four requirements of an "appropriate" transfer are applied only if the transfer is to another medical facility. In other words, the hospital has the alternative of either (1) providing treatment to stabilize the EMC and subsequently admitting, discharging, or transferring the individual or (2) appropriately transferring an unstabilized individual to another medical facility if the EMC still exists. There is no "third" option of simply "referring" the individual away after performing step one (treatment to minimize the risk of transfer) of the four transfer requirements of an appropriate transfer.[72] In addition, the Act leaves the final say on whether a transfer was appropriate by stating that an appropriate transfer "meets such other requirements as the Secretary may find necessary in the interest of the health and safety of individuals transferred."[73]

The responsibility to ensure a transfer within these provisions rests with the transferring hospital and physician. Fulfillment of these provisions needs to be clearly articulated on the EMTALA transfer certificate.

Further, the transfer must be accomplished through qualified personnel and transportation equipment, including the use of necessary and medically appropriate life support measures during the transfer.[74] In *Burditt v. U.S. Department of HHS*,[75] the court affirmed a $20,000 civil penalty assessed against a physician by HHS. The patient presented to DeTar Hospital in labor and suffering from dangerously high blood pressure. She had received no prenatal care and had no means to pay for medical services. Dr. Burditt was called since he was next on the hospital's rotating call list of physicians. Over the phone, he ordered the patient to be transferred to a hospital 170 miles away.

Before the patient was transferred, Dr. Burditt came to the hospital. He briefly examined the patient and signed the certification required by EMTALA. The patient transfer was commenced by ambulance with an obstetrical nurse and an emergency medical technician present. Although stocked with standard supplies, the ambulance was not stocked with any equipment or supplies that might be needed for obstetrical care during the estimated two hour trip. Approximately 40 miles into the 170 mile trip, the child was delivered. Without so much as a baby blanket, the ambulance sought supplies at a nearby hospital and then returned to DeTar Hospital, where the trip had originated.

---

[71] 42 C.F.R. § 489.24(e)(2).

[72] U.S. Dep't HHS, CMS, State Operations Manual, App. V, Emergency Medical Treatment and Labor Act (EMTALA) Interpretive Guidelines, Part II, Tag A-2409/C-2409 (revised 5/29/2009).

[73] 42 U.S.C. § 1395dd(c)(2)(E).

[74] 42 U.S.C. § 1395dd (c)(2)(D).

[75] 934 F.2d 1362 (5th Cir. 1991); *see also* Cherukuri v. Shalala, 175 F.3d 446 (6th Cir. 1999).

The question of *Burditt's* violation of EMTALA depended on the manner in which the transfer was accomplished.[76] Once the need for transfer has been properly certified, the method of transfer must be effected through qualified personnel and transportation equipment.[77] The *Burditt* court held that the Act required using personnel and equipment that a reasonable physician would consider appropriate to safely transport that particular patient.[78] "Standard" equipment or the minimum equipment required to meet state licensing requirements is not necessarily sufficient to comply with EMTALA. The *Burditt* court concluded that "[w]e thus read 'transportation equipment' to include all physical objects reasonably medically necessary for safe patient transfer."[79]

Appropriate transportation also includes the type of transport used. In *Smith v. James*,[80] the court denied a motion for summary judgment finding a jury question in the issue of whether a patient should have been transferred with the use of an air ambulance rather than surface ambulance. In *Smith*, a burn patient went into respiratory arrest while being transported by ground. The *Smith* court said the patient should have been transported by air. However, in some instances, the hospital and its staff may not be able to dictate either the method of transportation or the services provided by the transporter. Recognizing this, the court in *Wey v. Evangelical Community Hospital*[81] found that transfer by private car met the hospital's obligations since the use of an ambulance was neither required nor necessary by the patient's condition.

As for whether a hospital has violated its obligation to provide a transfer patient "treatment within its capacity that minimizes the risks to the individual's health" in compliance with the Act,[82] the Tenth Circuit, in *Ingram v. Muskogee Regional Medical Center*,[83] has held that the plaintiff must show a departure from the hospital's standard procedures.

In *Ingram*, an ambulance brought LaTasha Ingram, who had a gunshot wound to her chest, to the emergency department at Muskogee Regional Medical Center. There, Dr. Gregory, the on-call surgeon, determined that she needed cardiovascular surgery. Because his hospital did not have a cardiovascular surgeon, Gregory arranged a transfer to St. Francis Hospital in Tulsa. Ingram died shortly after arrival at the Tulsa hospital. Ingram's family sued Muskogee Regional for an inappropriate transfer under EMTALA. Ingram's family claimed that chest tubes should have been inserted prior to transfer. The hospital claimed that chest tubes would have increased bleeding into the chest during transfer. The court reasoned that it could find no reason not to construe the "appropriate transfer" language in the same fashion as the language in

---

[76] *Burditt*, 934 F.2d 1362, 1372.

[77] 42 U.S.C. § 1395dd(c)(2)(D).

[78] *Burditt*, 934 F.2d 1362, 1372.

[79] *Burditt*, 934 F.2d 1362, 1373.

[80] 895 F. Supp. 875 (S.D. Miss. 1995).

[81] 833 F. Supp. 453, 466 (M.D. Pa. 1993)

[82] 42 U.S.C. § 1395dd(c)(2)(A); 42 C.F.R. § 489.24(e)(2)(i).

[83] 235 F.3d 550 (10th Cir. 2000); 13 Emerg. Dep't L. 1, p. 4.

EMTALA's "appropriate medical screening" provision, given the similarity in the two sections and the lack of a meaningful distinction between "capability" (used in the screening provision) and "capacity." Because the Tenth Circuit had previously ruled that a screening examination was "inappropriate" only if it deviated from standard protocol, it held that whether the hospital appropriately "provided medical treatment within its capacity" should be measured by whether it complied with its standard procedures. The court of appeals affirmed the district court's grant of summary judgment because Ingram's family failed to produce evidence that Dr. Gregory violated any existing hospital procedure or requirement by not inserting chest tubes.

On April 8, 2011, the First Circuit Court of Appeals affirmed a federal district court's granting of summary judgment in favor of Centro Medico del Turabo d/b/a Hospital HIMA San Pablo Fajardo and its insurer HIMA San Pablo Captive Insurance Company Limited (collectively Hospital) in an action involving allegations that the Hospital violated EMTALA by transferring the plaintiffs' son (the patient) without delivering the best treatment before the transfer.[84] The district court found that the Hospital complied with EMTALA's transfer requirements and the First Circuit affirmed.

In 2006, the patient arrived at the Hospital with abdominal problems and was diagnosed with upper gastrointestinal bleeding. The Hospital did not have gastroenterologic services available, so the emergency room physician arranged to have the patient transferred to another hospital. The patient was transferred and died approximately 36 hours later. On the "Clinical Summary and Examination at the Moment of Transfer" form, the physician wrote "Gastroenterologist" to explain the benefits of the transfer.

When a patient is transferred, EMTALA requires the physician to sign a certification that "the medical benefits reasonably expected from the provision of appropriate medical treatment of another facility outweigh the increased risks to the individual." The First Circuit found that the physician's note of "Gastroenterologist" was "merely a summary statement of the more explicit explanation that [the Patient] needed a gastroenterologist, none was present at the Hospital, and, therefore, [the Patient] needed to be transferred, because the benefits of a gastroenterologist outweighed the dangers of transportation."[85]

The plaintiffs conceded that the Hospital followed standard transfer procedures but argued that "if the hospital does not deliver the feasible specific treatment that is best, whatever it may be in a given circumstance, it violates EMTALA." The First Circuit found that the Hospital provided appropriate pre-transfer treatment and "provided for transfer in the best interests of the patient." The First Circuit also stated that (1) EMTALA is violated when a hospital fails to follow its standard procedures, not by providing allegedly faulty treatment, and (2) the plaintiffs' position "would create a federal malpractice

---

[84] Ramos-Cruz v. Centro Medico del Turabo d/b/a Hosp. HIMA San Pablo Fajardo, No. 10-1203 (1st Cir. Apr. 8, 2011).

[85] *Ramos-Cruz*, No. 10-1203, at 5.

cause of action" allowing an unstabilized patient to sue in federal court any time correct care is not provided prior to transfer, which is inconsistent with jurisprudence and Congressional intent. The First Circuit concluded that the Hospital "provided for the transfer in the best interests of the patient."[86]

If the patient has not been stabilized, then the following six conditions must be met before transferring the patient:

1. physician certification that the expected medical benefits of transfer outweigh the risks of transfer (there must be a benefit because transfer to a comparable facility that offers no additional medical benefit is not allowed unless the patient specifically requests such a transfer);

2. patient consent (the patient must understand the reason for and risks of the transfer);

3. attempt made by the transferring hospital, within its capability, to stabilize the patient to minimize any risks during transfer;

4. agreement by the receiving facility to the transfer, assuring its capacity and capability to treat the transferred patient;

5. delivery of all medical records to the receiving hospital; and

6. transfer made with qualified personnel and transportation equipment.

Q 5:15   Authority to Decide: Who may decide when a patient is appropriate for transfer?

The attending physician has the authority to decide when a patient is appropriate for transfer. If a physician is not physically present at the time of transfer, then qualified personnel (as determined by hospital bylaws or other board-approved documents) in consultation with a physician can determine whether a patient is stable for transfer.[87]

Cautions: Individuals other than physicians may sign the EMTALA transfer certificate. However, these individuals must be identified in hospital bylaws, rules and regulations, or another board-approved document. If a nonphysician signs a certificate, the approving physician must countersign the certificate. Hospital bylaws or policies and procedures should describe the maximum amount of time allowed to obtain a physician's countersignature.[88]

As noted in previous comments, resort to phone transfer authorization in the emergency department is appropriate only when the time necessary for the on-call to respond would jeopardize the safety of the patient.

---

[86] *Ramos-Cruz*, No. 10-1203, at 5. This case summary was written by Keith A. Mauriello, Partner, and Jessica T. Grozine, Associate, in the Healthcare Practice Group at Arnall Golden Gregory LLP, Atlanta, Georgia. It should not be construed as legal advice or opinion on specific matters.

[87] 42 C.F.R. § 489.24(d)(ii)(C).

[88] U.S. Dep't HHS, CMS, State Operations Manual, App. V, Emergency Medical Treatment and Labor Act (EMTALA) Interpretive Guidelines, Part II, Tag A-2407/C-2407 (revised 5/29/2009).

The State Operations Manual states:

> Under certain circumstances qualified medical personnel other than a physician may sign the certification. A qualified medical person (QMP) may sign the certification of benefits versus risks of a transfer only after consultation with a physician who agrees with the transfer. The physician must subsequently countersign the certification. The physician's countersignature must be obtained within the established time frame according to hospital policies and procedures. Hospital by-laws or rules or regulations must specify the criteria and process for granting medical staff privileges to QMPs, and in accordance with the hospital or CAH Conditions of Participation, each individual QMP must be appropriately privileged.[89]

A hospital cannot force a physician to transfer patients. In fact, EMTALA regulations protect a physician who refuses a transfer in the patient's best interest:

> A participating hospital may not penalize or take adverse action against a physician or a qualified medical person described in paragraph (d)(1)(ii)(C) of this section because the physician or qualified medical person refuses to authorize the transfer of an individual with an emergency medical condition that has not been stabilized, or against any hospital employee because the employee reports a violation of a requirement of this section.[90]

Q 5:16   EMTALA Certificate: What is EMTALA's transfer certificate requirement?

The CMS State Operations Manual states:

> The regulation requires an express written certification. Physician certification cannot simply be implied from the findings in the medical record and the fact that the patient was transferred.[91]

Cautions: EMTALA requires a written certification for all unstabilized transfers. Physician certification cannot be implied from the medical record and the fact that the patient was transferred. The transfer certificate must meet EMTALA requirements and needs to be filled out at the time of transfer. Technically, EMTALA requires certification only if an individual has an EMC that has not been stabilized. However, a hospital would be prudent to fill out certificates for every transfer.

---

[89] U.S. Dep't HHS, CMS, State Operations Manual, App. V, Emergency Medical Treatment and Labor Act (EMTALA) Interpretive Guidelines, Part II, Tag A-2409/C-2409 (revised 5/29/2009).

[90] 42 C.F.R. § 489.24(e)(3).

[91] U.S. Dep't HHS, CMS, State Operations Manual, App. V, Emergency Medical Treatment and Labor Act (EMTALA) Interpretive Guidelines, Part II, Tag A-2409/C-2409 (revised 5/29/2009).

The CMS State Operations Manual further states:

> The certification must state the reason(s) for transfer. The narrative rationale need not be a lengthy discussion of the individual's medical condition reiterating facts already contained in the medical record, but it should give a complete picture of the benefits to be expected from appropriate care at the receiving (recipient) facility and the risks associated with the transfer, including the time away from an acute care setting necessary to effect the transfer. The risks and benefits certification should be specific to the condition of the patient upon transfer.
>
> This rationale may be included on the certification form or in the medical record. In cases where the individual's medical record does not include a certification, give the hospital the opportunity to retrieve the certification. Certifications may not be backdated.[92]

The important elements that must be included are found in the following sample certificate:

(1) Patient condition:

❏ The patient is stable so that, within reasonable medical probability, no material deterioration of the patient's condition is likely to result from the transfer.

❏ The patient is unstable, but the expected medical benefits of transfer outweigh potential risks associated with the transfer.

(2) Benefits of transfer:

❏ Specific benefit of transfer: _____

❏ Specialized equipment and/or services at receiving facility:

❏ Continuity of care

❏ Patient requests transfer:

    ❏ Reason: _____

Benefits of transfer explained to:

    ❏ patient   ❏ family   ❏ other Relationship: _____

(3) Risks of transfer:

❏ Risks of transfer include:

    ❏ deterioration in condition: _____

    ❏ transportation risks: _____

Risks of transfer explained to:

    ❏ patient   ❏ family   ❏ other Relationship: _____

---

[92] U.S. Dep't HHS, CMS, State Operations Manual, App. V, Emergency Medical Treatment and Labor Act (EMTALA) Interpretive Guidelines, Part II, Tag A-2409/C-2409 (revised 5/29/2009).

(4) Receiving hospital:

❑ Receiving facility: _____

❑ Receiving facility has capacity to treat patient

❑ Receiving facility agrees to accept the transfer

❑ Accepting physician: _____

❑ Accepting facility representative: _____

❑ Receiving facility provided with all appropriate medical records and test results

❑ Report called to receiving facility

❑ Name of person receiving report: _____

(5) Mode of transportation:

❑ Private vehicle

❑ Ambulance with appropriate equipment

❑ Transported by: _____

❑ Accompanying qualified personnel: _____

(6) Patient consent:

Transfer requested by:

   ❑ Patient

   ❑ Physician

   ❑ Other _____

❑ I acknowledge that I understand the risks and benefits of the transfer and therefore consent to transfer.

Patient/legally responsible individual signature: _____

Witness: _____Date/Time: _____

(7) Transferring physician certification:

I certify that I have explained the risks and benefits of transfer to the patient. On the basis of information available to me at the time of transfer, the medical benefits reasonably expected from the provisions of appropriate medical treatment at another medical facility outweigh the increased risk to the individual and, in the case of labor, to the unborn child.

Signature: _____

The statement of risks and benefits is often the source of EMTALA citations. Use of a purely "check the box" form is not permitted by CMS, and such forms must contain at least one handwritten risk and benefit.

The physician must understand that the reason for transfer is not the same as the benefit of transfer. Hospitals have been cited for benefits listed as "higher level of care," "to PICU," "to Trauma Center," and "equipment not available here." What then should be listed as benefits?

CMS expects the statement of benefits to answer the question "What exactly can be provided at the destination hospital that cannot be provided here?" Although the examples of unacceptable benefits given above may seem reasonable to physicians, they are generic in nature and do not identify the exact service, specialty care, level of care, or equipment the patient needs that is not currently available at the transferring facility. If, for example, the transfer is for a magnetic resonance imaging (MRI) when the transferring facility has an MRI, then an explanation such as "the MRI is down" is necessary.

Under the risks section, physicians typically minimize the stated risks. If the patient's risks include death or disability, then those risks must be expressly stated. Failure to list known risks in details sufficient for the patient to understand will result in citation, possible fines, and possible civil liability for the hospital and the physician. Often physicians simply put "none," which is almost always cited as not entered in good faith. Preprinted risks such as traffic accidents, although helpful, are not enough. Again, a handwritten statement of risks must be entered. At the very least, all transfers pose the risk of increased pain from the vibration, jolting, and bouncing encountered in a routine ambulance transport.

Q 5:17 Certification Violation: How can a hospital violate the EMTALA certification provisions?

In *Burditt*,[93] the court held that a hospital may violate the certification provisions in four ways:

1. The hospital fails to secure the required signature from the appropriate medical personnel on a certification form;
2. The signer has not actually deliberated and weighed the medical risks and the medical benefits of transfer before executing the certification;
3. The signer makes an improper consideration a significant factor in the certification decision; or
4. The signer concludes in the weighing process that the medical risks outweigh the medical benefits of transfer yet signs a certification that the opposite is true.[94]

Certification is not required for patients who do not have an EMC or who have been stabilized before transfer such that they are not at risk to deteriorate from or during transport. However, a hospital would be prudent to uniformly complete EMTALA certificates on every transfer as a precaution. The hospital should educate the medical staff on the risks and proper completion of EMTALA certificates of transfer.

---

[93] *Burditt*, 934 F.2d 1362, 1370.
[94] *Burditt*, 934 F.2d 1362, 1370.

Q 5:18   Signing Certificates: Must a physician sign the transfer certificate?

Yes, but....

The Code of Federal Regulations states:

> If a physician is not physically present in the emergency department at the time an individual is transferred, a qualified medical person (as determined by the hospital in its bylaws or rules and regulations) has signed a certification described in paragraph (e)(1)(ii)(B) of this section after a physician (as defined in section 1861(r)(1) of the Act) in consultation with the qualified medical person, agrees with the certification and subsequently countersigns the certification. The certification must contain a summary of the risks and benefits upon which it is based.[95]

Medicare regulations require that phone or verbal orders be signed within 24 hours for injectables and biologic substances and within a reasonable period for other orders. The maximum time for compliance is 30 days from discharge or the arrival of the CMS investigators, whichever occurs first.

Cautions: The hospital should have policies and procedures in place that stipulate who can and who cannot authorize transfers. Transferring physicians should be educated on EMTALA responsibilities and penalties.

A transferring physician's responsibilities were addressed in *Sterling v. Johns Hopkins Hospital.*[96] In *Sterling,* a pregnant woman, Laverne Sterling, entered the Peninsular Regional Medical Center (PRMC) exhibiting various symptoms indicating her pregnancy was in danger. The next day, with her condition worsening, Sterling came under the care of Dr. Gray, who ordered lab work and rendered a presumptive diagnosis of severe pre-eclampsia and potential HELLP syndrome. When this diagnosis was confirmed, Dr. Gray initiated the process of transferring Sterling to another hospital because PRMC did not have a neonatal intensive care unit and her condition potentially required the premature delivery of her child.[97]

Dr. Gray spoke with the attending physician at Johns Hopkins, Dr. Adib Khouzami and informed him of the patient's diagnosis and her lab results. After agreeing with Gray's diagnosis, Dr. Khouzami asserted that Hopkins had the resources available to care for the patient and would accept the patient. The doctors further agreed Sterling would be transported by ambulance per regional guidelines, even though Dr. Gray had initially requested transport via helicopter. During her trip to Johns Hopkins, Sterling became unresponsive. The ambulance was diverted to Memorial Hospital in Easton, Maryland, where a

---

[95] 42 C.F.R. § 489.24(e)(1)(ii)(C).
[96] 145 Md. App. 161, 802 A.2d 440 (2002).
[97] *Sterling,* 802 A.2d 440, 442.

cesarean section was performed. In the process, Sterling suffered an intraventricular hemorrhage that resulted in her death two days later.[98]

The *Sterling* court held that a physician-patient relationship was never established between Dr. Khouzami and Sterling, and therefore neither Khouzami nor Johns Hopkins could be held liable in negligence.[99] While recognizing that the creation of a physician-patient relationship was not predicated on the existence of an express contract or direct contact between the parties, the court nonetheless determined that Dr. Khouzami had not implied his consent to enter into a physician-patient relationship with Sterling even though he had accepted the request to transfer her to Hopkins.[100] The court stated:

> Dr. Khouzami owed no independent consultive duty to PRMC, its staff or patients with respect to the care and treatment of individual patients. . . . [W]hile Dr. Khouzami did conclude that the diagnosis and treatment given to Ms. Sterling at PRMC was appropriate, he did not give any advice that would cause Dr. Gray or the staff at PRMC to rely on his expertise. Dr. Khouzami, in essence, merely conveyed the fact that Johns Hopkins had the facilities and staff to treat that appellant if she was transferred.[101]

Holding that the transferring physician has the primary responsibility if a patient deteriorates during transfer, the *Sterling* court analysis focused on (1) the existence of a relationship between the consulting doctor and the facility providing care that would require the consulting doctor to provide advice; (2) the degree to which the consultation given affected the course of treatment; and (3) the relative ability and independence of the immediate care provider to implement his or her own decision.

The transferring physician should consult with administration, discuss the disposition with his or her on-call specialists, and assure that the hospital resources are inadequate to treat the patient prior to authorization. There should be protocols for securing proper transportation (basic transport, advanced life support, or air transport), any necessary accompanying equipment and/or personnel (e.g., qualified nurse), and all medications to be given or procedures to be performed (e.g., IV antibiotics for sepsis, airway stabilization) prior to transfer. Remember, the patient's well-being is entirely the responsibility of the transferring hospital until the patient physically arrives at the receiving hospital. Leaving the medical staff to arbitrarily transfer patients without knowledge of the EMTALA ramifications could expose the hospital to EMTALA violations.

The EMTALA transfer certificate information must be based on information available at the time of transfer, not a prior history and physical. Just prior to leaving the hospital, the hospital personnel should take a last set of vital signs and review all labs, X-rays, and other test results to reassess patient stability.

---

[98] *Sterling,* 802 A.2d 440, 443.

[99] *Sterling,* 802 A.2d 440, 458.

[100] *Sterling,* 802 A.2d 440, 446.

[101] *Sterling,* 802 A.2d 440, 458.

Any change in the patient's condition since the last communication with the receiving facility should be communicated to the receiving facility.

Q 5:19 Medical Records: What medical records must the transferring hospital provide?

The CMS State Operations Manual states:

> Necessary medical records must accompany individuals being transferred to another hospital. If a transfer is in an individual's best interest, it should not be delayed until records are retrieved or test results come back from the laboratory. Whatever medical records are available at the time the individual is transferred should be sent to the receiving (recipient) hospital with the patient. Test results that become available after the individual is transferred should be telephoned to the receiving (recipient) hospital, and then mailed or sent via electronic transmission consistent with HIPAA provisions on the transmission of electronic data.
>
> Documentation in the medical records should identify the services that were performed before transfer.[102]

Cautions: An appropriate transfer requires a transferring hospital to send specific medical records along with the patient to the receiving hospital. The transferring physician needs to keep meticulous records to justify any unstable transfer and to maintain compliance with EMTALA. In addition to documenting the clinical history, physical examination, test results, and disposition in the chart, the transferring physician must also include the following items if applicable:

1. **Record of patient refusal of treatment**: The hospital must document that the physician offered treatment and explained the risks and benefits of treatment. The records should reflect that all reasonable steps were taken to secure the patient's or surrogate's written informed consent to refuse such examination and treatment;[103]

2. **Record of patient refusal of transfer**: The hospital chart must indicate that the patient has been informed of the risks and benefits of the transfer and should state the reasons for the individual's refusal. The chart must contain a description of the proposed transfer that was refused by or on behalf of the individual;[104]

---

[102] U.S. Dep't HHS, CMS, State Operations Manual, App. V, Emergency Medical Treatment and Labor Act (EMTALA) Interpretive Guidelines, Part II, Tag A-2409/C-2409 (revised 5/29/2009).

[103] U.S. Dep't HHS, CMS, State Operations Manual, App. V, Emergency Medical Treatment and Labor Act (EMTALA) Interpretive Guidelines, Part II, Tag A-2409/C-2409 (revised 5/29/2009).

[104] U.S. Dep't HHS, CMS, State Operations Manual, App. V, Emergency Medical Treatment and Labor Act (EMTALA) Interpretive Guidelines, Part II, Tag A-2409/C-2409 (revised 5/29/2009).

3. **Transfer certification**: The transferring physician must complete a certificate of transfer in accordance with EMTALA requirements, recording the patient's consent to transfer and justification for the transfer;[105]

4. **Failure of the on-call physician to respond**: EMTALA requires a transferring physician to record on the hospital chart the name and address of any on-call physician who refused to respond to a call for assistance to treat an EMC, thus necessitating the transfer.[106]

Receiving Hospitals

Q 5:20   Receiving Hospitals: What are EMTALA's requirements for a receiving hospital?

The receiving facility must have adequate space, equipment, and qualified personnel to treat the individual before agreeing to accept the transfer. Having accepted transfer, the receiving facility is obligated to provide appropriate medical treatment.[107] After the patient's arrival at the receiving hospital, all provisions of EMTALA that had applied to the transferring hospital are now applicable to the receiving hospital.

Cautions: All hospitals, not just university hospitals or major teaching centers, can be receiving hospitals for EMTALA purposes. The only requirement for the receiving hospital is that it possesses the space, equipment, and qualified personnel to treat a patient's EMC that the transferring hospital lacks. Receiving hospitals need to recognize that once they accept the patient, they then assume all EMTALA responsibilities, including the MSE, stabilizing care, and transfer restrictions.

Hospitals should prepare policies and procedures for receiving patients so as to avoid complications. A short list of items that need to be addressed includes:

- Who can and cannot accept transfers on the hospital's behalf. Hospitals should specify in writing who has the authority to accept or refuse transfers. These individuals should be educated on the requirements and ramifications of EMTALA. Accepting a transfer shifts all EMTALA requirements to the receiving hospital upon patient arrival. (The patient's care is the responsibility of the transferring hospital while en route.) Refusing a transfer may put the hospital at risk for equally serious "reverse dumping" violations;

- Distinct procedures guiding acceptance of transfer. The accepting physician should contact the hospital administrative representative, check whether space is available (e.g., are operating rooms available) and equipment is operational (e.g., CT scanner is not down for repair), consult

---

[105] 42 U.S.C. § 1395dd(c)(2).

[106] 42 U.S.C. § 1395dd(c)(2)(C); 42 C.F.R. § 489.24(d)(iii).

[107] 42 U.S.C. § 1395dd(c)(2)(B).

the pertinent on-call specialist for availability and acceptance, determine which department (e.g., emergency department or specialty unit) should accept the patient, and so on;

- Specific guidelines for a hospital's basis for refusing a transfer, such as lack of space or resources, down equipment, unavailable personnel, etc., should be in writing for reference;

- Acceptance/rejection certificates. Just as there are transfer EMTALA certificates, hospitals should have acceptance/rejection certificates to document the details of the transfer request. This certification should document information from the requesting hospital (e.g., name of hospital, physician calling, and patient; condition of patient; time and date) as well as reasons for acceptance or refusal of the transfer;

- Educational sessions on EMTALA responsibilities for all personnel who would have input into or contact with transfer procedures. Physicians and nurses are obvious choices, but secretaries, telephone operators, and administrative staff also should be educated.

CMS measures the "capacity" of a recipient hospital similarly to that of the transferring hospital. The CMS State Operations Manual states:

> Assessment of whether the transferring hospital with the requisite capabilities lacked the capacity to provide stabilizing treatment, or of whether the recipient hospital lacked the capacity to accept an appropriate transfer, requires a review of the hospital's general practices in adjusting its capacity. If a hospital generally has a record of accommodating additional patients by various means, such as moving patients from one unit to another, calling in additional staff, and temporarily borrowing additional equipment from other facilities, then that hospital would be expected under EMTALA to take reasonable steps to respond to the treatment needs of an individual requiring stabilizing treatment for an emergency medical condition. The determination of a hospital's capacity would depend on the case-specific circumstances and the hospital's previous implementation of capacity management actions.[108]

Q 5:21 Recipient Hospitals: What are the responsibilities of a recipient hospital?

A recipient hospital is obligated to accept a transfer request if a patient is in need of specialized capabilities offered by the recipient hospital and the recipient hospital has the capacity to receive the patient. The Code of Federal Regulations states:

> (f) *Recipient hospital responsibilities.* A participating hospital that has specialized capabilities or facilities (including, but not limited to, facilities such as burn units, shock-trauma units, neonatal intensive care units, or (with respect to rural areas) regional referral centers, which,

---

[108] U.S. Dep't HHS, CMS, State Operations Manual, App. V, Emergency Medical Treatment and Labor Act (EMTALA) Interpretive Guidelines, Part II, Tag A-2411/C-2411 (revised 5/29/2009).

for purposes of this subpart, means hospitals meeting the requirements of referral centers found at § 412.96 of this chapter) may not refuse to accept from a referring hospital within the boundaries of the United States an appropriate transfer of an individual who requires such specialized capabilities or facilities if the receiving hospital has the capacity to treat the individual. This requirement applies to any participating hospital with specialized capabilities, regardless of whether the hospital has a dedicated emergency department.[109]

Cautions: Even if both the sending and the receiving hospitals have similar capabilities and facilities, a patient may require service beyond the capability of the sending hospital at the time of the transfer (e.g., if a hospital's neurosurgeon is unavailable because he is already occupied with a prolonged surgical procedure) if these services are available at the recipient hospital. In that instance, the recipient hospital is obligated to accept the patient from the sending hospital.

The interpretive guidelines are clear that a recipient hospital has to accept the patient only if:

> the patient requires the specialized capabilities of the hospital in accordance with this section. If the transferring hospital wants to transfer a patient because it has no beds or is overcrowded, but the patient does not require any specialized capabilities, the receiving . . . hospital is not obligated to accept the patient.

> If the patient required the specialized capabilities of the intended receiving . . . hospital, and the hospital had the capability and capacity to accept the transfer but refused, this requirement has been violated.[110]

Q 5:22 Hospital Refusals: May a receiving hospital refuse an appropriate transfer?

If a transfer is "appropriate," then the only valid reason for a hospital to refuse the transfer is if it lacks the specialized capabilities to treat the patient. A hospital with specialized capabilities or facilities may not refuse to accept an appropriate transfer of an individual who requires such specialized capabilities or facilities if the hospital has the capacity to treat the individual. Such a refusal would be considered a "reverse dumping." However, receiving hospitals do not have an EMTALA obligation to accept transfers from inpatient units of another hospital even when that patient has an unstable EMC.[111] Receiving hospitals are not required to accept transfers from hospitals located outside the United States.

The Act states:

> A participating hospital that has specialized capabilities or facilities (such as burn units, shock-trauma units, neonatal intensive care units,

---

[109] 42 C.F.R. § 489.24(f).

[110] U.S. Dep't HHS, CMS, State Operations Manual, App. V, Emergency Medical Treatment and Labor Act (EMTALA) Interpretive Guidelines, Part II, Tag A-2411/C-2411 (revised 5/29/2009).

[111] 73 Fed. Reg. 48,434 (Aug. 19, 2008).

or (with respect to rural areas) regional referral centers as identified by the Secretary in regulation, shall not refuse to accept an appropriate transfer of an individual who requires such specialized capabilities or facilities if the hospital has the capacity to treat the individual.[112]

The Code of Federal Regulations states:

Recipient hospital responsibilities. A participating hospital that has specialized capabilities or facilities (including, but not limited to, facilities such as burn units, shock-trauma units, neonatal intensive care units, or, with respect to rural areas, regional referral centers (which, for purposes of this subpart, mean hospitals meeting the requirements of referral centers found at § 412.96 of this chapter)) may not refuse to accept from a referring hospital within the boundaries of the United States an appropriate transfer of an individual who requires such specialized capabilities or facilities if the receiving hospital has the capacity to treat the individual.

(1) The provisions of this paragraph (f) apply to any participating hospital with specialized capabilities, regardless of whether the hospital has a dedicated emergency department.

(2) The provisions of this paragraph (f) do not apply to an individual who has been admitted to a referring hospital under the provisions of paragraph (d)(2)(i) of this section.[113]

Cautions: If a receiving hospital has the resources and personnel to treat a patient while a transferring hospital lacks those same capabilities, then it has no recourse but to accept the transfer.

In a letter to its regional administrators, CMS writes:

A recipient hospital is obligated to accept a transfer request if a patient is in need of specialized capabilities offered by the recipient hospital and the recipient hospital has the capacity to receive the patient. Even if both the sending and the receiving hospitals have similar capabilities and facilities, a patient may require service beyond the capability of the sending hospital [at the time of the transfer], if these services are available at the recipient hospital. In that instance, the recipient hospital is obligated to accept the patient from the sending hospital.[114]

There is no specific distance limitation, although hospitals may refuse a transfer if the transfer is from a hospital located outside the United States. The State Operations Manual states:

There is no EMTALA obligation for a Medicare-participating hospital with specialized capabilities to accept transfers from hospitals located outside the boundaries of the United States. In accordance with Section 210(i) of the Social Security Act, the term "United States," when used in

---

[112] 42 U.S.C. § 1395dd(g).

[113] 42 C.F.R. § 489.24(f).

[114] Letter to Associate Regional Administrator, DMSO, CMS Ref: S&C-02-06.

a geographical sense, means the States, the District of Columbia, the Commonwealth of Puerto Rico, the Virgin Islands, Guam, and American Samoa. Hospitals that request transfers must recognize that the appropriate transfer of individuals with unstabilized emergency medical conditions that require specialized services should not routinely be made over great distances, bypassing closer hospitals with the needed capability and capacity.[115]

A recipient hospital may refuse a transfer if it lacks the capability and/or capacity to accommodate the patient.

The State Operations Manual states:

A participating hospital that has specialized capabilities or facilities may not refuse to accept from a referring hospital an appropriate transfer of an individual who requires such specialized capabilities or facilities. This assumes that, in addition to its specialized capabilities the recipient hospital has the capacity to treat the individual, and that the transferring hospital lacks that capability or capacity. This requirement applies to any participating hospital with specialized capabilities, regardless of whether the hospital has a dedicated emergency department.

A hospital with specialized capabilities or facilities includes, but is not limited to, facilities such as burn units, shock-trauma units, or neonatal intensive care units. With respect to rural areas, this includes regional referral centers that meet the requirements of referral centers found at 42 CFR 412.96.[116]

The receiving hospital can never base its decision of refusal on financial information. The State Operations Manual states:

This requirement applies equally to both the referring and the receiving (recipient) hospital. Therefore, it may be a violation if the receiving hospital delays acceptance of the transfer of an individual with an unstabilized Emergency Medical Condition pending receipt or verification of financial information. It would not be a violation if the receiving hospital delayed acceptance of the transfer of an individual with a stabilized Emergency Medical Condition pending receipt or verification of financial information because EMTALA protections no longer apply once a patient is stabilized.[117]

The basis for this requirement stems from cases that came to light during the early years of EMTALA's governance. In Detroit, an unconscious 32-year-old woman who had been robbed and beaten in the head with a baseball bat was

---

[115] U.S. Dep't HHS, CMS, State Operations Manual, App. V, Emergency Medical Treatment and Labor Act (EMTALA) Interpretive Guidelines, Part II, Tag A-2411/C-2411 (revised 5/29/2009).

[116] U.S. Dep't HHS, CMS, State Operations Manual, App. V, Emergency Medical Treatment and Labor Act (EMTALA) Interpretive Guidelines, Part II, Tag A-2411/C-2411 (revised 5/29/2009).

[117] U.S. Dep't HHS, CMS, State Operations Manual, App. V, Emergency Medical Treatment and Labor Act (EMTALA) Interpretive Guidelines, Part II, Tag A-2408/C-2408 (revised 5/29/2009).

brought to an emergency department by ambulance. The hospital lacked a neurosurgeon who could treat the patient's serious head injuries. The emergency physician called 14 different hospitals in southern Michigan seeking emergency neurosurgical care for the patient. Seven hospitals refused the transfer outright and the other seven refused because of a lack of insurance confirmation. The patient ultimately was admitted to the original hospital and died within a few days. Later, it was found that the patient worked for a Detroit automobile company and had excellent Blue Cross insurance coverage.[118]

Another case arising in Detroit involved a man whose jaw was shattered by a gunshot wound. Because he had no insurance, no hospital in southern Michigan would approve transfer to provide the necessary surgery. After 19 hours of transfer refusals, the patient left the original facility and went to another facility for care. Upon his arrival, that facility was then obligated by EMTALA to treat him.[119] In response to cases such as these, Congress amended EMTALA in 1989 to require higher-level facilities to accept transfer patients when they had the ability to manage the patients' emergency conditions.[120]

On-call specialists whose services are required cannot refuse transfer if they are available. The fact that a hospital may not have a contract with the patient's managed care plan does not matter. Hospitals may not refuse patients from a different county or state (including out-of-state Medicaid patients). However, hospitals do not have to accept requests for transfer from facilities outside the boundaries of the United States.[121]

Some specialty hospitals have complained that referring community hospitals take advantage of EMTALA by cherry-picking and choosing whom they will keep and whom they will transfer—that is, they may choose to keep paying patients but find reasons to transfer nonpaying patients who may require specialized care. When a hospital believes that it may have received a patient as a result of false certification of the patient for transfer, it is obligated to report the offending hospital within the requirements of the law. However, it is hard for receiving hospitals to determine at the moment whether a requesting hospital truly lacks the capability or capacity to stabilize a patient. The University of Mississippi Medical Center in Jackson took the drastic action of announcing that it may decide not to accept transfers from other facilities on a case-by-case basis when it believes that the requesting facility has the resources to care for the patient. The Mississippi Medical Center experienced a $20 million increase in the amount of indigent or uncompensated care from fiscal year 2003 to fiscal

---

[118] Governor's Task Force on Access to Healthcare, State of Michigan, July 29, 1989 (testimony of Robert A. Bitterman, M.D.).

[119] Governor's Task Force on Access to Healthcare, State of Michigan, July 29, 1989 (testimony of Robert A. Bitterman, M.D.).

[120] 1990 Amendments, Pub. L. No. 101-508, Title IV, §§ 4008-(b)(1)-(3)(A), 4207(a)(1)(A), (2), (3), (k)(3), 104 Stat. 1388-44,1388-117,1388-124 (enacted Nov. 5, 1990, effective on Jan. 5, 1991 and May 5, 1991) (codified in 42 U.S.C.A. § 1395dd (West Supp. 1991).

[121] 42 C.F.R. § 489.24(e); U.S. Dep't HHS, CMS, State Operations Manual, App. V, Emergency Medical Treatment and Labor Act (EMTALA) Interpretive Guidelines, Part II, Tag A-2411/C-2411 (revised 5/29/2009).

year 2004. Most of the increased cost was due to lower level trauma care transferred from other hospitals.[122] The University of Mississippi Medical Center is putting itself in danger of violating EMTALA. It is not up to the hospital being asked to accept a transfer to decide that the hospital seeking transfer is fully capable of treating the patient in question. If the university refuses a valid transfer where the transferring hospital truly lacked the resources to treat a patient, then the university would be guilty of the violation of "reverse dumping." It would be better for the administrators of the hospitals to communicate beforehand. The university would be better suited to let the transferring hospitals know in no uncertain terms that the university is mandated to report to CMS any inappropriate transfer where the transferring hospital actually had the resources to treat the patient. The transferring hospitals would think twice before transferring with this threat of an investigation by CMS.

A transferring hospital has no affirmative duty imposed by EMTALA to report a hospital that refuses to accept the transfer of an EMTALA patient, in violation of EMTALA, when that hospital could have provided the needed specialized care.

Q 5:23 Reverse Dumping: What happens if a receiving hospital with specialized capabilities refuses an appropriate transfer?

A hospital with specialized capabilities or facilities (including, but not limited to, facilities such as burn units, shock-trauma units, neonatal intensive care units, or, in rural areas, regional referral centers) may not refuse an appropriate transfer if the patient requires the hospital's specialized capabilities and the hospital has the capacity to treat the individual. Such a practice is known as "reverse dumping." HHS can impose large fines for violation of EMTALA's reverse dumping provision.

The provision states:

> A participating hospital that has specialized capabilities or facilities (such as burn units, shock-trauma units, neonatal intensive care units, or (with respect to rural areas) regional referral centers as identified by the Secretary in regulation, shall not refuse to accept an appropriate transfer of an individual who requires such specialized capabilities or facilities if the hospital has the capacity to treat the individual.[123]

Cautions: Traditionally, the medical profession sees transfers for specialized care primarily to tertiary care teaching hospitals with specialized facilities such as trauma centers, burn units, spinal units, and so on. However, over the years, community hospitals have evolved to possess many of the specialty care capabilities that teaching hospitals used to exclusively provide. After a recent ruling by the HHS, any community

---

[122] *Desperate to Stop the Flow of Red Ink, Level I Trauma Center Will Deny Transfers*, ED Manag., 17(3):25-7 (Mar. 2005).
[123] 42 U.S.C. § 1395dd(g).

hospital with special services is now a referral center for any other hospital that does not have that special service.

In *Inspector General v. St. Anthony Hospital*, CMS imposed a fine of $25,000 on an Oklahoma hospital that refused to receive an appropriate patient transfer from another hospital for emergency surgery.[124] On April 8, 1995, a 65-year-old male was involved in an automobile accident on a highway outside of Oklahoma City. At 4:50 p.m., he was taken to the emergency department at Shawnee Regional Hospital, a small hospital about 35 miles outside of Oklahoma City. Dr. Kent Thomas initially treated the patient and endorsed care to Dr. Carl Spengler at 7:00 p.m. It was determined that the patient had fractures of his spine and ribs but more importantly had paralysis of his legs. Since Shawnee Hospital did not have the resources to treat such a major trauma, Dr. Spengler arranged ground transfer to University Hospital. However, after being boarded onto an ambulance, the patient developed mental confusion, hypotension, and cyanosis of his lower extremities. Dr. Spengler determined that the patient had a serious aortic injury that required immediate surgery. Dr. Spengler returned the patient to the emergency department and continued stabilization treatments. Due to the critical nature of the patient, Dr. Spengler arranged air-ambulance transport to University Hospital. The Medi-Flight helicopter arrived at Shawnee, but University Hospital called Dr. Spengler and informed him that all operating suites were occupied with present surgery so that they could not accommodate the transfer. Dr. Spengler made a series of phone calls attempting to find a hospital with a vascular surgeon who could provide the surgery. Dr. Spengler eventually spoke with Dr. Scott Lucas, the on-call thoracic-vascular surgeon at St. Anthony Hospital, an Oklahoma City community hospital with specialized surgical facilities. Dr. Lucas refused Dr. Spengler's request for transfer to St. Anthony Hospital. Ultimately, the patient was transferred to Presbyterian Hospital in Oklahoma City, where aortography revealed that he had suffered traumatic occlusion of the abdominal aorta. The patient was taken immediately to surgery for revascularization of his lower extremities. The patient's condition deteriorated during the next several days, and, following bilateral above-knee amputations, he died on April 11, 1995.

In May 1998, the HHS Office of Inspector General (OIG) notified St. Anthony Hospital that it sought to impose a $50,000 civil monetary penalty against it based "on a determination that St. Anthony Hospital failed to accept the appropriate transfer of the patient on Saturday, April 8, 1995"—in other words, reverse dumping. In June 2000, the Departmental Appeals Board of the HHS upheld the imposition of the civil monetary penalty against St. Anthony Hospital for violation of EMTALA's reverse-dumping provisions. St. Anthony filed an appeal to the United States Court of Appeals, Tenth Circuit. The Tenth Circuit denied St. Anthony's appeal.[125]

Notably, Dr. Lucas, the refusing surgeon at St. Anthony, was not liable for violating EMTALA. There is no provision in EMTALA where a private on-call

---

[124] Inspector General v. St. Anthony Hosp., HHS Dep't Appeals Bd., No. CR620 (Dec. 1999).

[125] St. Anthony Hosp. v. U.S. Dep't HHS, 309 F.3d 680, 713 (10th Cir. 2002).

specialist at a receiving hospital must accept the patient. The risk is held entirely by the hospital in reverse-dumping cases. An on-call specialist violates EMTALA only when he or she refuses to attend a patient who is already physically at the on-call specialist's hospital. Although on-call specialists have no personal obligation under EMTALA to accept transfers, they should be aware of the legal risks to their hospital when they refuse transfers.

The ruling in *St. Anthony* imposes a duty on every hospital with special services to accept the transfer of patients with an unstable EMC from any other hospital that lacks such services. Specialists such as neurosurgeons who had previously been on call only for their own hospitals are now effectively on call for all area hospitals that seek to transfer unstable patients to them. EMTALA does not even require hospitals to seek transfer to tertiary centers first. A simple telephone call for transfer triggers the EMTALA obligation for the receiving hospital. At present, there are not even any geographic limitations to the request for transfer,[126] so that any hospital anywhere within the United States can request transfer to another hospital anywhere else within the United States. Community hospitals that did not see themselves as referral centers now become *de facto* referral centers that cannot refuse a call for transfer of an EMTALA patient.

The EMTALA Technical Advisory Group has collected testimony indicating that some hospitals are taking advantage of EMTALA on-call allowances by maintaining marginal on-call coverage. The hospitals believe that by doing so EMTALA allows them to transfer patients they cannot immediately care for. Receiving hospitals are reluctant to challenge transfer requests for fear of being accused of a reverse-dumping EMTALA violation. Although EMTALA allows receiving hospitals to report inappropriate transfers, very few receiving hospitals do so.

Q 5:24   Specialty Hospitals: Do specialty hospitals without dedicated emergency departments have to accept appropriate transfer requests?

Yes. CMS states that any Medicare-participating hospital with a specialized capability, in accordance with EMTALA's specialized capabilities,[127] must accept, within the capacity of the hospital, an appropriate transfer from a requesting hospital. This policy applies to the specialized hospital without regard to whether it has a dedicated emergency department.

---

[126] The only limitation is expressed in the CMS State Operations Manual: "There is no EMTALA obligation for a Medicare-participating hospital with specialized capabilities to accept transfers from hospitals located outside the boundaries of the United States. In accordance with Section 210(i) of the Social Security Act, the term 'United States,' when used in a geographical sense, means the States, the District of Columbia, the Commonwealth of Puerto Rico, the Virgin Islands, Guam, and American Samoa." CMS State Operations Manual, Appendix V – Interpretive Guidelines – Responsibilities of Medicare Participating Hospitals in Emergency Cases, Interpretive Guideline to § 489.24(f) Recipient Hospital Responsibilities. (Rev. 46, Issued: 05-29-09, Effective/Implementation: 05-29-09)

[127] 42 U.S.C. § 1395cc(g).

Cautions: Specialty hospitals are defined as stand-alone, single-specialty facilities not within the walls of a full-service hospital. Physicians have created a host of such for-profit, physician-owned specialty hospitals around the country. One of the criticisms of specialty hospitals has been that many of them do not have dedicated emergency departments, which reduces the amount of care they must provide to indigent patients and allows them to avoid the financial impact of complying with EMTALA.[128] However, specialty hospitals do have EMTALA obligations with respect to accepting transfers of patients from other hospitals. CMS stated that receiving hospitals with special capabilities must accept the transfer of an individual with an unstable EMC regardless of whether the individual is received through the hospital's dedicated emergency department. Due to specialty hospitals' expertise and high-tech equipment for the treatment of the conditions in which they specialize, they would qualify as hospitals with special capabilities.

The EMTALA Technical Advisory Group addressed this issue of EMTALA applicability to specialty hospitals in 2005. CMS commented in the *Federal Register*:

> At its meeting held on October 26-28, 2005, the EMTALA TAG heard testimony from representatives of physician groups, hospital associations, and others regarding EMTALA compliance by specialty hospitals that typically do not have dedicated emergency departments. After extensive consideration and discussion of the issues raised and views presented, the members of the EMTALA TAG voted to recommend to the Secretary that hospitals with specialized capabilities (as defined in § 489.24(f) of the regulations) that do not have a dedicated emergency department be bound by the same responsibility to accept an appropriate transfer under EMTALA as hospitals with a dedicated emergency department.
>
> We agree with the EMTALA TAG's assessment.[129]

In response to the EMTALA TAG's recommendation, CMS proposed changes to the EMTALA regulations on April 25, 2006, as part of the fiscal year 2007 Inpatient Prospective Payment System (IPPS) proposed rule.[130] In its proposed changes, CMS noted that the revision would not require hospitals without dedicated emergency departments to open emergency departments, nor would it impose any EMTALA obligations on those hospitals with respect to individuals who come to the hospital as their initial point of entry into the medical system seeking an MSE or treatment for a medical condition. By its proposed revision, CMS sought only to clarify that any Medicare-participating hospital with specialized capabilities had EMTALA obligations as per the specialized capabilities provision.

---

[128] Anne S. Kimbol, *The Debate Over Specialty Hospitals: How Physician-Hospital Relationships Have Reached a New Fault Line Over These "Focused Factories,"* 38 J. Health L. 633 (2005).

[129] 71 Fed. Reg. 48,097 (Aug. 18, 2006).

[130] 71 Fed. Reg. 24,118 (Apr. 25, 2006).

The Code of Federal Regulations now states:

(f) *Recipient hospital responsibilities.* A participating hospital that has specialized capabilities or facilities (including, but not limited to, facilities such as burn units, shock-trauma units, neonatal intensive care units, or (with respect to rural areas) regional referral centers, which, for purposes of this subpart, means hospitals meeting the requirements of referral centers found at § 412.96 of this chapter) may not refuse to accept from a referring hospital within the boundaries of the United States an appropriate transfer of an individual who requires such specialized capabilities or facilities if the receiving hospital has the capacity to treat the individual. (1) This requirement applies to any participating hospital with specialized capabilities, regardless of whether the hospital has a dedicated emergency department.[131]

This means that if a hospital does not have the capacity or capability to stabilize an EMC but a specialty hospital does possess the capacity and capability, the specialty hospital cannot refuse the requested appropriate transfer of the patient. Specialty hospitals will need to institute some form of physician backup to accommodate such transfers. CMS states:

While physician-owned limited service hospitals certainly are required to maintain compliance with the hospital conditions of participation, those regulations set forth in 42 C.F.R. Part 482 do not include an explicit on-call requirement. Thus, we are not including a revision in this final rule to include the specific change requested by the commenter. However, we note that the conditions of participation relating to a hospital's governing body at § 482.12(c)(3) require that all Medicare-participating hospitals have a doctor of medicine or osteopathy either on duty or on call at all times. In addition, the governing body condition of participation and the condition of participation for medical staff found at § 482.22 include various other requirements that make the hospital governing body and medical staff accountable for providing adequate physician services for hospital patients. These requirements also apply to physician-owned limited service facilities, including those that do not operate emergency departments, on the same basis as to community and other hospitals.[132]

On August 18, 2006, CMS clarified in the IPPS final rule that all Medicare-participating hospitals have an obligation to accept an appropriate transfer, regardless of whether the hospital has a dedicated emergency department, if the hospital has specialized capabilities and capacity to treat the patient. By emphasizing the applicability of EMTALA transfer obligations to hospitals with specialized capabilities, CMS is making clear that the analysis of whether the hospital has a dedicated emergency department or not is irrelevant. The IPPS final rule specifically extends the EMTALA transfer obligation to physician-owned specialty hospitals that participate in Medicare. In its discussion concerning physician-owned specialty hospitals, CMS declined to impose any new

---

[131] 42 C.F.R. § 489.24(f).

[132] 71 Fed. Reg. 48,098 (Aug. 18, 2006).

on-call coverage or transfer requirements on such specialty hospitals. CMS notes that Medicare CoPs already impose an obligation on all participating hospitals, including physician-owned limited service facilities, to have a physician on duty or on call at all times and to provide adequate physician services for hospital patients.[133]

CMS affirmatively stated that the EMTALA transfer obligations of hospitals with specialized capabilities do not require such hospitals to open a dedicated ED if they do not have one. Nor does the IPPS final rule impose any additional EMTALA obligations on those hospitals without dedicated emergency departments with respect to walk-in patients who initially go to such hospitals seeking examination or treatment for a medical condition.

Q 5:25   Equal Capabilities: May a receiving hospital with equal capabilities refuse a transfer request?

Yes. A receiving hospital without specialized capabilities, but rather the same capabilities as the transferring hospital, may refuse transfer.

Cautions: EMTALA does not address lateral transfers between hospitals of equal capabilities, so a hospital without specialized units may refuse transfers regardless of appropriateness. If the transferring hospital wants to transfer a patient because it has no beds or is overcrowded, but the patient does not require any "specialized" capabilities, the receiving (recipient) hospital is not obligated under EMTALA to accept the patient.

CMS has stated in the past:

> Recipient hospitals only have to accept a patient if the patient requires the specialized capabilities of the hospital in accordance with this section and the hospital has the capacity to treat the individual. If the transferring hospital wants to transfer a patient, but the patient does not require any "specialized" capabilities, the receiving (recipient) hospital is not obligated to accept the patient unless the individual presents at the recipient hospital. If the patient required the specialized capabilities of the intended receiving (recipient) hospital, and the hospital has the capability and capacity to accept the transfer, but refused, this requirement has been violated.

> Lateral transfers, that is, transfers between facilities of comparable resources, are not sanctioned by § 489.24 because they would not offer enhanced care benefits to the patient except where there is a mechanical failure of equipment, no ICU beds available, or similar situations. However, if the sending hospital has the capability but not the capacity, the individual would most likely benefit from the transfer.[134]

---

[133] 71 Fed. Reg. 48,096-097 (Aug. 18, 2006).

[134] U.S. Dep't HHS, CMS, State Operations Manual, App. V, Emergency Medical Treatment and Labor Act (EMTALA) Interpretive Guidelines, Part II, Tag A-2411/C-2411 (revised 5/29/2009).

Although this comment has been removed from the most recent revision of the State Operations Manual, CMS has not indicated a change in this ruling. Note that CMS considers the availability of specific equipment, specialties, services, or levels of care that are not available at the sending hospital "specialty capabilities" of the receiving hospital. If equipment breaks down, an on-call physician is not available because he or she is in surgery, or the hospital does not have a specialist in the needed area of practice, the requested receiving facility must accept.

In *Fingers v. Jackson-Madison County General Hospital District*,[135] 15-year-old Kinon B. Fingers arrived at Bolivar Community Hospital with an accidental, self-inflicted gunshot wound. Because Bolivar did not have a surgeon available, the emergency department physician, Dr. Mark Dixon, attempted to transfer Kinon to another hospital. Dr. Dixon first contacted Jackson-Madison County General Hospital, which refused to accept Kinon's transfer. Dr. Dixon then contacted McNairy County General Hospital, Shelby County Health Care Corporation d/b/a The Regional Medical Center, Methodist Hospital of Fayette County, and LeBonheur Children's Medical Center concerning the possible transfer of Kinon. All refused to accept his transfer. Dr. Dixon again contacted Jackson-Madison, which again refused Kinon's transfer. Two hours after his arrival at Bolivar, Kinon died. Kinon's mother, Sandra Fingers, filed suit alleging that the hospitals violated EMTALA by refusing an appropriate transfer. The claims against Bolivar, McNairy, and Jackson-Madison were voluntarily dismissed. The court addressed the remaining claims against defendants Shelby, LeBonheur, and Methodist.

The court agreed that EMTALA obligates only hospitals with specialized capabilities (such as burn units, shock-trauma units, neonatal intensive care units or, with respect to rural areas, regional referral centers as identified by the Secretary in regulation)[136] to accept appropriate transfers. Because Fingers could not show that the defendant hospitals had specialized capabilities that Bolivar Community Hospital lacked, the appellate court affirmed the district court's ruling to dismiss the suit.

In contrast to the court's holding in *Fingers*, many understand federal law to require courts to defer to the interpretation of regulatory agencies unless the interpretation patently contravenes the law. By CMS standards, the availability of the specialist created an obligation to accept the patient. Use causation in relying on the *Fingers* decision.

Failure to accept transfer is clearly on the HHS and OIG's radar. In the OIG's Spring 2011 Semiannual Report to Congress,[137] three of the four reported EMTALA cases dealt with failure to receive transfers. Mobile Infirmary, in the state of Alabama, paid $45,000 to resolve allegations that it had improperly

---

[135] 101 F.3d 702 (6th Cir. 1996).

[136] 42 U.S.C. § 1395dd(g).

[137] HHS Office of the Inspector General Semiannual Report to Congress—Spring 2011, *available at* http://oig.hhs.gov/reports-and-publications/archives/semiannual/2011/spring/spring2011_semiannual.pdf.

refused to accept a patient transferred from another hospital. The patient came to the transferring hospital's emergency department complaining of severe abdominal pain, which required immediate specialized surgical intervention that was not available at the transferring hospital. Mobile Infirmary purportedly refused to accept the transfer, even though it had the capacity and specialized capabilities to treat the patient's condition. The patient was finally transferred to a hospital 60 miles away. The patient's condition deteriorated en route, which necessitated that he be transported by Life Flight helicopter to the receiving hospital, where he later died.[138] In Texas, Houston Northwest Medical Center (HNMC) paid $40,000 to resolve allegations that it failed to provide an appropriate MSE or stabilizing treatment and inappropriately transferred a pregnant woman who came to HNMC while having contractions. HNMC transferred the patient by ambulance to a hospital nearly two hours away. The patient went into active labor en route and ended up being diverted to a closer hospital.[139] In Florida, Port St. Lucie Hospital, an inpatient mental health facility, paid $19,000 to resolve allegations that it refused to accept a patient from a transferring hospital. A nurse at Port St. Lucie allegedly refused to accept the transfer of a patient with acute psychosis because the nurse believed the patient was uninsured.[140]

Q 5:26   Inpatient Transfers: Must a receiving hospital with specialized capabilities accept an EMTALA patient who had been admitted as an inpatient at another hospital?

No. Once a hospital admits an EMTALA patient as an inpatient, and even though the patient remains unstabilized with an EMC the admitting hospital determines that it does not have the capability to treat, receiving hospitals with specialized capabilities to treat the condition are not obligated by EMTALA to accept a transfer.

Cautions: The inpatient exception for EMTALA is an administrative decision by CMS. The courts are not bound by this interpretation and, in a civil suit, may still rule differently. In order for EMTALA's responsibility to end, the hospital must *formally* admit the patient to the hospital. Further, the stabilization process begun in the emergency department must continue in the inpatient wards. In addition, individuals who are placed in observation status are not inpatients, even if they occupy a bed overnight. Therefore, placement in observation status of an individual who came to the hospital's dedicated emergency department does not terminate the EMTALA obligations of that hospital or a recipient hospital toward the individual.[141]

---

[138] HHS Office of the Inspector General Semiannual Report to Congress—Spring 2011, III 14.

[139] HHS Office of the Inspector General Semiannual Report to Congress—Spring 2011, III 14.

[140] HHS Office of the Inspector General Semiannual Report to Congress—Spring 2011, III 14-15.

[141] U.S. Dep't HHS, CMS, State Operations Manual, App. V, Emergency Medical Treatment and Labor Act (EMTALA) Interpretive Guidelines, Part II, Tag A-2411/C-24011 (revised 5/29/2009).

EMTALA, in its nondiscrimination section, states that a participating hospital with specialized capabilities or facilities (such as burn units, shock-trauma units, neonatal intensive care units, or, with respect to rural areas, regional referral centers as identified by the Secretary in regulation) shall not refuse to accept an appropriate transfer of an individual who requires these specialized capabilities or facilities if the hospital has the capacity to treat the individual.[142] CMS has decided that this nondiscrimination section does not apply to inpatients. Even though CMS decided that once an individual is admitted as an inpatient receiving hospitals do not have an EMTALA obligation to accept transfer of that individual, receiving hospitals should not use this ruling to avoid appropriate transfers.

In April 2008, CMS stated that it believed receiving hospitals with specialized capabilities ought to have an EMTALA obligation to receive appropriate transfers even though the patient is an inpatient in another hospital. CMS proposed to revise its regulations to address the situation of an individual (1) who presents to a hospital that has a dedicated emergency department and who is determined to have an unstabilized EMC; (2) who is admitted to the hospital as an inpatient; and (3) for whom the hospital subsequently determines that stabilizing his or her EMC requires specialized care available only at another hospital. CMS believed that it is appropriate to propose to clarify that the nondiscrimination section of EMTALA continues to apply so as to protect even an individual admitted as an inpatient to the admitting hospital who has not been stable since becoming an inpatient. CMS believed that this proposed clarification was necessary to ensure that EMTALA protections are continued for individuals who are not otherwise protected by the Medicare CoPs.[143]

In August 2008, CMS reversed its decision after receiving numerous comments from concerned physicians and hospitals on this proposed ruling. Commenters expressed concerns that admitting hospitals would abuse the proposal in order to dump many marginally stabilized patients on receiving hospitals for economic reasons. Commenters expressed concern that tertiary hospitals would become overburdened by the uncontrolled transfer of such patients. CMS recognized that patients admitted under EMTALA would have different transfer rights than a patient who was directly admitted without using the dedicated emergency department. CMS also recognized significant difficulties in addressing new definitions for inpatient instability, inpatient capabilities, appropriate inpatient transfers, and so on. In considering all the concerns and inequities presented for receiving hospitals, CMS also recognized that, at that time, there was not a known problem with tertiary hospitals refusing appropriate transfers of patients from the inpatient services. After considering the many comments for and against the proposal, CMS concluded that a hospital with specialized capabilities does **not** have an obligation under EMTALA to accept transfer of inpatients.[144] In the *Federal Register*, CMS stated:

---

[142] 42 U.S.C. § 1395dd(g).

[143] 73 Fed. Reg. 23,668-71 (Apr. 30, 2008).

[144] 73 Fed. Reg. 48,434-458 (Aug. 19, 2008).

Due to the many concerns that the commenters raised which are noted above, we believe it is appropriate to finalize a policy to state that if an individual with an unstable emergency medical condition is admitted, the EMTALA obligation has ended for the admitting hospital and even if the individual's emergency medical condition remains unstabilized and the individual requires special services only available at another hospital, the hospital with specialized capabilities does not have an EMTALA obligation to accept an appropriate transfer of that individual.[145]

Accordingly, CMS has revised EMTALA at Section 489.24(f) to state that it does not apply to an individual who has been admitted under Section 489.24(d)(2)(i).[146]

In early 2012, HHS once again considered the question of whether EMTALA applied to an inpatient admitted to a hospital. This statement reaffirmed the position that admission ends all obligations under EMTALA. HHS concluded:

If an individual "comes to the [hospital's] emergency department," as we have defined that term in regulation, and the hospital provides an appropriate medical screening examination and determines that an EMC exists, and then admits the individual in good faith in order to stabilize the EMC, that hospital has satisfied its EMTALA obligation towards that patient.[147]

Q 5:27   Reporting Requirement: Must a hospital report receiving an inappropriate transfer?

Yes. In an effort to increase reports of dumping violations, Congress amended EMTALA so that a receiving hospital is mandated to report any perceived EMTALA violations it receives, or else be subject to EMTALA penalties.[148]

The receiving hospital must report transfer violations within 72 hours. The State Operations Manual states:

A hospital (recipient) that suspects it may have received an improperly transferred (transfer of an unstable individual with an emergency medical condition who was not provided an appropriate transfer according to § 489.24(e)(2)) individual is required to promptly report the incident to CMS or the state Agency (SA) within 72 hours of the occurrence. If a recipient hospital fails to report an improper transfer, the hospital may be subject to termination of its provider agreement according to 42 C.F.R. § 489.53(a).

Surveyors are to look for evidence that the recipient hospital knew or suspected the individual had been to a hospital prior to the recipient

---

[145] 73 Fed. Reg. 48,659-660 (Aug. 19, 2008).

[146] 73 Fed. Reg. 48,659 (Aug. 19, 2008).

[147] 77 Fed. Reg. 5217 (Feb. 2, 2012). See **Appendix G** for the full text.

[148] 42 C.F.R. § 489.20(m).

hospital, and had not been transferred in accordance with § 489.24(e).
Evidence may be obtained in the medical record or through interviews
with the individual, family members or staff.[149]

Cautions: Hospitals are mandated to report perceived dumping by transferring hospitals. CMS orders that hospitals make a report whenever they have
"a reason to believe that a violation has occurred, regardless of whether the
receiving hospital believes the sending hospital violated the law intentionally
or with any ill motive."[150] Further, CMS orders hospitals "to have and enforce
policies and procedures to require its employees and staff physicians to
report to the administration instances where an individual has been inappropriately transferred under this statute."[151] Any physician who receives a
perceived inappropriate transfer should report the incident to the hospital's
legal counsel. A hospital that neglects to report an inappropriate transfer
exposes itself to fines of $50,000 per occurrence, as well as termination of its
Medicare provider agreement.[152]

The 72-hour rule published in the State Operations Manual[153] now puts
significant pressure on receiving hospitals. It is not always clear whether a
transfer is inappropriate. How is a receiving hospital to know of the capacities
and capabilities of transferring hospitals? Was the transferring hospital really at
full capacity? Was the on-call physician really unavailable? Could the transferring hospital really have treated the patient appropriately? EMTALA prohibits
receiving hospitals from refusing transfers; now the receiving hospital must
determine within 72 hours whether the transfer was appropriate or face the
penalties attached to EMTALA.

Transportation Between Hospitals

Q 5:28   Mode of Transfer: Does a transfer have to be made by an ambulance?

The fourth requirement for an appropriate transfer mandates that the transfer
be "effected through qualified personnel and transportation equipment, as
required, including the use of necessary and medically appropriate life support
measures during the transfer."[154] The wording of "as required" allows transfer
by means other than a full ambulance. If there is any question about patient
safety, the patient should be transferred by ambulance. However, in cases

---

[149] U.S. Dep't HHS, CMS, State Operations Manual, App. V, Emergency Medical Treatment and Labor Act
(EMTALA) Interpretive Guidelines, Part II, Tag A-2401/C-2401 (revised 5/29/2009).

[150] 59 Fed. Reg. 32,106 (1994).

[151] 59 Fed. Reg. 32,106 (1994).

[152] 42 C.F.R. § 489.24(f); 42 C.F.R. § 489.53(a) and (b)(1)(ii).

[153] U.S. Dep't HHS, Medicare Medicaid State Operations Manual, App. V, Emergency Medical Treatment
and Labor Act (EMTALA) Interpretive Guidelines, Part II, Tag A-2401/C-2401 (revised 5/29/2009).

[154] 42 U.S.C. § 1395dd(c)(2).

where a patient's well-being would not be jeopardized, other means of transportation besides an ambulance may be acceptable.

Cautions: EMTALA regulations state that "[t]he transfer is effected through qualified personnel and transportation equipment, as required, including the use of necessary and medically appropriate life support measures during the transfer."[155] In *Burditt v. United States Department of Health and Human Services*, the court held that these objective provisions require a hospital to use "personnel and transportation equipment that a reasonable physician would consider appropriate to transfer a patient."[156]

In *Burditt*,[157] the Court affirmed a $20,000 civil penalty assessed against a physician by HHS. The patient presented to the DeTar Hospital in labor and suffering from dangerously high blood pressure. She had received no prenatal care and had no means to pay for medical services. Dr. Burditt was called since he was next on the hospital's rotating call-list of physicians. Over the phone, he ordered the patient to be transferred to a hospital 170 miles away.

Before the patient was transferred, Dr. Burditt came to the hospital. He briefly examined the patient and signed the certification required by EMTALA. The patient transfer was commenced by ambulance with an obstetrical nurse and an emergency medical technician present. Although stocked with standard supplies, the ambulance was not stocked with any equipment or supplies that might be needed for obstetrical care during the estimated two hour trip. Approximately 40 miles into the 170 mile trip, the child was delivered. Without so much as a baby blanket, the ambulance sought supplies at a nearby hospital and then returned to DeTar Hospital, where the trip had originated.

The question of *Burditt's* violation of EMTALA depended on the manner in which the transfer was accomplished.[158] Once the need for transfer has been properly certified, the method of transfer must be effected through qualified personnel and transportation equipment.[159] The *Burditt* court held that EMTALA requires using personnel and equipment that a reasonable physician would consider appropriate to safely transport that particular patient.[160] "Standard" equipment or the minimum equipment required to meet state licensing requirements is not necessarily sufficient to comply with EMTALA. The *Burditt* court concluded, "We thus read 'transportation equipment' to include all physical objects reasonably medically necessary for safe patient transfer."[161]

Appropriate transportation includes the type of transport used. In *Smith v. James*,[162] the court denied a motion for summary judgment finding a jury

---

[155] 42 C.F.R. § 489.24(d)(2)(iv).

[156] *Burditt*, 934 F. 2d 1362, 1372.

[157] *Burditt*, 934 F.2d 1362; *see also* Cherukuri v. Shalala, 175 F.3d 446 (6th Cir. 1999).

[158] *Burditt*, 934 F.2d 1362, 1372.

[159] 42 U.S.C. § 1395dd(c)(2)(D).

[160] *Burditt*, 934 F.2d 1362, 1372.

[161] *Burditt*, 934 F.2d 1362, 1373.

[162] Smith v. James, 895 F. Supp. 875 (S.D. Miss. 1995).

question in the issue of whether a patient should have been transferred with the use of an air ambulance rather than surface ambulance. In *Smith*, a burn patient had a respiratory arrest while transported by ground. The *Smith* court said the patient should have been transported by air. However, in some instances, the hospital and its staff may not be able to dictate either the method of transportation or the services provided by the transporter. Recognizing this, the a federal district court in Pennsylvania found in *Wey v. Evangelical Community Hospital*[163] that transfer by private car met the hospital's obligations since the use of an ambulance was neither required by nor necessary for the patient's condition. Christopher Wey was transported to Evangelical Community Hospital by ambulance after a bicycle accident. Wey had pre-existing idiopathic thrombocytopenic purpura and was HIV positive. The emergency physician diagnosed a bimalleolar fracture and dislocation of the right ankle. The physician was unsuccessful in trying to reduce the dislocation.

The physician informed Wey that transfer to a specialist and possible surgery would be necessary to treat the injury. Wey was also informed that the hospital did not provide ambulance services and that a private ambulance would cause extra expense. Wey agreed to private automobile transportation to the Veterans Administration Medical Center, where his injuries were treated. Wey then filed suit alleging violation of EMTALA because of an inappropriate transfer, which caused him pain and suffering. In *Wey*, the court ruled that the defendant hospital fulfilled its burden under EMTALA by stabilizing Wey's ankle. The court further held that transfer by personal car was allowable even though the patient was not able to comply with directions to keep the injured limb elevated and even though he suffered pain for some time because the pain medication administered at the transferring hospital wore off. The plaintiff had provided no expert testimony that such transportation was medically inappropriate.

CMS, on the other hand, has cited transfers by private vehicle. A private vehicle provides no safety, appropriate medical personnel, or appropriate equipment and fails in those regards to meet the literal requirements of an appropriate transfer. However, a patient who is mentally and legally capable of making a decision may sign a refusal of ambulance transport. Clear details of all possible risks need to be noted on the refusal form.

Transportation that would jeopardize the patient's condition is prohibited. In *Owens v. Nacogdoches County Hospital*,[164] a federal district court in Texas ruled that an automobile with no medical equipment, whose only occupant other than the indigent patient in labor was her boyfriend, was not the equivalent of an "ambulance" for purposes of EMTALA. Justification of transfer with or without qualified personnel and transportation equipment must be documented in detail.

CMS regulations on ambulance payment went into effect on January 1, 2001. These standards indicate that the level of care specified by the transferring

---

[163] 833 F. Supp. 453, 466 (M.D. Pa. 1993).
[164] 741 F. Supp. 1269 (E.D. Tex. 1990).

physician in EMTALA cases is the level that should be reimbursed. CMS now recognizes the following levels of ambulance transport:

a. **Basic Life Support (BLS)**—Transportation by ground ambulance vehicle and medically necessary supplies and services, plus the provision of BLS ambulance services. The ambulance must be staffed by an individual who is qualified in accordance with State and local laws as an emergency medical technician-basic (EMT-Basic). These laws may vary from State to State. For example, only in some States is an EMT-Basic permitted to operate limited equipment on board the vehicle, assist more qualified personnel in performing assessments and interventions, and establish a peripheral intravenous (IV) line.

b. **Advanced Life Support, Level 1 (ALS1)**—Transportation by ground ambulance vehicle, medically necessary supplies and services and either an ALS assessment by ALS personnel or the provision of at least one ALS intervention.

- **ALS assessment** is an assessment performed by an ALS crew as part of an emergency response that was necessary because the patient's reported condition at the time of dispatch was such that only an ALS crew was qualified to perform the assessment. An ALS assessment does not necessarily result in a determination that the patient requires an ALS level of service.

- **ALS intervention** means a procedure that is, in accordance with State and local laws, required to be furnished by ALS personnel.

- **ALS personnel** means an individual trained to the level of the emergency medical technician-intermediate (EMT-Intermediate) or paramedic. The EMT-Intermediate is defined as an individual who is qualified, in accordance with State and local laws, as an EMT-Basic and who is also qualified in accordance with State and local laws to perform essential advanced techniques and to administer a limited number of medications. The EMT-Paramedic is defined as possessing the qualifications of the EMT-Intermediate and also, in accordance with State and local laws, as having enhanced skills that include being able to administer additional interventions and medications.

c. **Advanced Life Support, Level 2 (ALS2)**—Either transportation by ground ambulance vehicle, medically necessary supplies and services, and the administration of at least three medications by intravenous push/bolus or by continuous infusion, excluding crystalloid, hypotonic, isotonic, and hypertonic solutions (Dextrose, Normal Saline, Ringer's Lactate); or transportation, medically necessary supplies and services, and the provision of at least one of the following ALS procedures:

- Manual defibrillation/cardioversion
- Endotracheal intubation
- Central venous line
- Cardiac pacing
- Chest decompression

- Surgical airway
- Intraosseous line

d. **Specialty Care Transport (SCT)**—Interfacility transportation of a critically injured or ill beneficiary by a ground ambulance vehicle, including medically necessary supplies and services, at a level of service beyond the scope of the EMT-Paramedic. SCT is necessary when a beneficiary's condition requires ongoing care that must be furnished by one or more health professionals in an appropriate specialty area, for example, nursing, emergency medicine, respiratory care, cardiovascular care, or a paramedic with additional training.

e. **Paramedic ALS Intercept (PI)**—EMT-Paramedic services furnished by an entity that does not furnish the ground ambulance transport, provided the services meet the requirements specified in § 410.40(c) of this chapter.

f. **Fixed Wing Air Ambulance (FW)**—Transportation by a fixed wing aircraft that is certified as a fixed wing air ambulance and such services and supplies as may be medically necessary.

g. **Rotary Wing Air Ambulance (RW)**—Transportation by a helicopter that is certified as an ambulance and such services and supplies as may be medically necessary.[165]

The general categories of appropriate transport for field response are not conclusive for EMTALA transports.

Q 5:29 Ambulance Equipment: Can transportation by an inadequately equipped ambulance violate EMTALA?

Yes. If an ambulance is not equipped to treat the medical emergency at hand, it can be considered an inappropriate transfer. The physician at the sending hospital (not the receiving hospital) has the responsibility of determining appropriate mode, equipment, and attendants for transfer.[166]

The CMS State Operations Manual states:

> Emergency medical technicians may not always be "qualified personnel" for purposes of transferring an individual under these regulations. Depending on the individual's condition, there may be situations in which a physician's presence or some other specialist's presence might be necessary. The physician at the sending hospital (and not the receiving hospital) has the responsibility to determine the appropriate mode, equipment, and attendants for transfer.
>
> While the sending hospital is ultimately responsible for ensuring that the transfer is [e]ffected appropriately, the hospital may meet its

---

[165] 42 C.F.R. § 414.605; 67 Fed. Reg. 9100, 9106 (2002).

[166] U.S. Dep't HHS, CMS, State Operations Manual, App. V, Emergency Medical Treatment and Labor Act (EMTALA) Interpretive Guidelines, Part II, Tag A-2409/C-2409 (revised 5/29/2009).

obligations as it sees fit. These regulations do not require that a hospital operate an emergency medical transportation service.[167]

Cautions: The Code of Federal Regulations states that the transfer be "effected through qualified personnel and transportation equipment, as required, including the use of necessary and medically appropriate life support measures during transfer."[168] EMTs may not always be "qualified personnel" for purposes of transferring an individual under EMTALA. Depending on the circumstances, a physician's or some other specialist's presence might be mandatory. The physician at the sending hospital has the responsibility to determine appropriate mode, equipment, and attendants for transfer.[169]

EMTALA requires that any transfer of a patient be effected through qualified personnel and transportation equipment that a reasonable physician would consider appropriate for safely transporting a patient under those conditions known to the transferring physician. In *Burditt*,[170] the court ruled that Dr. Burditt was appropriately fined because he approved patient transportation via an ill-equipped ambulance.

Rosa Rivera arrived in the emergency department of DeTar Hospital in Victoria, Texas, in labor, hypertensive, and with membranes ruptured. Dr. Burditt, the on-call obstetrician, was notified, but he refused to attend the patient and ordered that she be transferred to John Sealy Hospital in Galveston, Texas, 170 miles away.

The hospital administrator informed Dr. Burditt that according to hospital regulations and federal law, Dr. Burditt would have to examine the patient and arrange for transfer himself. Dr. Burditt examined Rivera and found a blood pressure reading of 210/130. Dr. Burditt persisted in arranging transfer to John Sealy Hospital. When presented with EMTALA transfer papers, Dr. Burditt signed the certificate but did not fill in the required reasons for the transfer.

Forty miles into the 170-mile trip to John Sealy, an accompanying obstetrical nurse, Anita Nichols, delivered Rivera's baby. The ambulance was diverted to Guanado Hospital because of Rivera's excessive bleeding. There, Nichols telephoned Burditt and informed him of the birth. Burditt continued to insist that Rivera be transferred to John Sealy. Instead, per Rivera's wishes, Nichols returned Rivera to DeTar. Burditt refused to see Rivera because she had failed to proceed to John Sealy in accordance with his instructions.

The hospital found another physician to treat Rivera, who recovered after a three-day hospital stay. In *Burditt*, the court found that Dr. Burditt violated EMTALA by (1) transferring Rivera without complying with the certification

---

[167] U.S. Dep't HHS, CMS, State Operations Manual, App. V, Emergency Medical Treatment and Labor Act (EMTALA) Interpretive Guidelines, Part II, Tag A-2409/C-2409 (revised 5/29/2009).

[168] 42 C.F.R. § 489.24(d)(2)(iv).

[169] U.S. Dep't HHS, CMS, State Operations Manual, App. V, Emergency Medical Treatment and Labor Act (EMTALA) Interpretive Guidelines, Part II, Tag A-2409/C-2409 (revised 5/29/2009).

[170] *Burditt*, 934 F.2d 1362, 1372.

requirement[171] and (2) transferring Rivera in an ambulance with neither the medical personnel to perform a cesarean section nor the equipment, such as a fetal heart monitor, that might have been necessary given the patient's condition.[172] The court upheld a $20,000 civil fine against Burditt by the OIG. It is important to note that Rivera suffered no significant injury and that the baby was healthy; no medical malpractice or negligence was alleged. Burditt's violation of the technical certification provisions of EMTALA and refusal to provide stabilizing care were sufficient for penalty. The hospital was fined $5,000 for failure to effectively ensure that the on-call physician complied with the law.

Q 5:30   Air Transport: Does EMTALA apply to patient transfers by helicopter or airplane?

Yes. EMTALA applies to all patient transfers whether by air or ground. The same rules apply as for ground ambulances.

Cautions: When a hospital calls an air transport to transport a patient for an appropriate transfer to the base hospital for care, the same rules apply as for ground ambulance transfer. These appropriate transfers require (1) EMTALA certification, (2) patient consent, (3) stabilizing treatment, (4) acceptance by the receiving facility, (5) sending medical records, and (6) qualified personnel and equipment for the transport. It is important for the transferring physician to document that the transfer is an EMTALA certified inter-facility transfer to a higher level of care. The 2001 regulations that affect ambulance service payments under Medicare and Medicaid require that when requesting a helicopter or fixed wing air ambulance, the transferring physician must document that the nearest hospital with appropriate facilities (1) is inaccessible by land vehicle or at a great distance or that there are other obstacles (e.g., heavy traffic), and/or (2) that the patient's medical condition is not appropriate for transport by either basic life support or advanced life support ground ambulance.

Q 5:31   Use of a Helipad: Does an air transport that simply uses a hospital's property as a landing site trigger EMTALA obligations for the hospital?

No. Helicopters and ambulances entering hospital grounds for the sole purpose of conveying a patient from or to another hospital do not trigger EMTALA obligations.

Cautions: If a helicopter lands on the helipad of one hospital solely for the patient to be transported immediately by ground ambulance to another hospital pursuant to a community-wide protocol (or if an ambulance comes to the helipad to meet a helicopter to take the patient to a trauma center or

---

[171] *Burditt*, 934 F.2d 1362, 1371.

[172] *Burditt*, 934 F.2d 1362, 1372.

other destination), the patient should not be considered to have "come to" the hospital that owns the helipad for purposes of triggering EMTALA obligations. CMS has indicated in guidance letters and public presentations that it will not hold the helipad owner hospital liable under EMTALA unless the air medical crew or ground ambulance crew request medical assistance for the patient.

Hospital-owned and -operated air transport presents interesting EMTALA difficulties. If a hospital-owned and -operated air transport arrives at the scene of an accident and places an unstable patient within the air transport vehicle for pre-hospital transport, that patient triggers EMTALA obligations for the hospital just as if an unstable patient enters a hospital-owned ground ambulance. The patient is deemed to have "come to" the hospital that owns the air transport vehicle and must be transported to the owner-hospital for an MSE and stabilization. What if a patient's condition warrants a diversion to another hospital before arriving at the owner-hospital? Logically, if a patient's condition deteriorates unexpectedly during transport, diversion to the closest proper facility for emergency stabilizing assistance should be allowed, because the "transfer" would involve a distinct medical benefit for the patient. A hospital-owned air transport vehicle might elect to transport the patient to a different hospital that possesses specialized facilities or capabilities such as spinal cord units or burn units. Also, hospital-owned air transports sometimes function as "taxi" services by transporting a patient from one hospital to another, neither of which is the owner hospital. CMS should allow such exceptions where the hospital-owned air transport team would be operating under community-wide protocols that determine the destination of the patient based on condition or acuity.

The Interpretive Guidelines state:

- The use of a hospital's helipad by local ambulance services or other hospitals for the transport of individuals to tertiary hospitals located throughout the State does not trigger an EMTALA obligation for the hospital that has the helipad on its property when the helipad is being used for the purpose of transit as long as the sending hospital conducted the Medical Screening Examination prior to transporting the individual to the helipad for medical helicopter transport to a designated recipient hospital. The sending hospital is responsible for conducting the Medical Screening Examination prior to transfer to determine if an emergency medical condition exists and implementing stabilizing treatment or conducting an appropriate transfer. Therefore, if the helipad serves simply as a point of transit for individuals who have received a Medical Screening Examination performed prior to transfer to the helipad, the hospital with the helipad is not obligated to perform another Medical Screening Examination prior to the individual's continued travel to the recipient hospital. If, however, while at the helipad, the individual's condition deteriorates, and a request is made for medical care, the hospital at which the helipad is located must provide its own Medical Screening Examination and stabilizing treatment within its capacity if requested by medical personnel accompanying the individual.

- If as part of the EMS protocol, EMS activates helicopter evacuation of an individual with a potential emergency medical condition, the hospital that has the helipad does not have an EMTALA obligation if they are not the recipient hospital, *unless a request* is made by EMS personnel, the individual or a legally responsible person acting on the individual's behalf for the examination or treatment of an emergency medical condition.[173]

Q 5:32   Specific Transport: May a hospital condition its acceptance of an EMTALA transfer based on a specific transport service?

No. The State Operations Manual states:

> A hospital with specialized capabilities or facilities that has the necessary capacity to treat an individual with an emergency medical condition may not condition or attempt to condition its acceptance of an appropriate transfer of an individual protected under EMTALA on the use of a particular mode of transport or transport service. It is the treating physician at the transferring hospital who decides how the individual is transported to the recipient hospital and what transport service will be used, since this physician has assessed the individual personally. The transferring hospital is required to arrange transport that minimizes the risk to the individual who is being transferred, in accordance with the requirements of § 489.24(e)(2)(B)(iv).[174]

Cautions: Hospitals may discuss the proper mode of transport, but the final decision on mode of transport rests with the attending physician who is transferring the patient because he or she is in the best position to assess the condition of the patient for proper transport. A receiving hospital cannot refuse the transport even when it disagrees with this decision.

In a memorandum sent to its State Survey Agency Directors,[175] CMS stated:

> The Emergency Medical Treatment and Labor Act Technical Advisory Group (EMTALA TAG) received testimony indicating that instances have occurred where a hospital has refused to accept an appropriate transfer of an individual with an emergency medical condition unless the sending hospital used an air medical service owned by the receiving hospital for the transfer. The EMTALA TAG recommended that the Centers for Medicare & Medicaid Services (CMS) issue guidance on this matter.

---

[173] U.S. Dep't HHS, CMS, State Operations Manual, App. V, Emergency Medical Treatment and Labor Act (EMTALA) Interpretive Guidelines, Part II, Tag A-2406/C-2406 (revised 5/29/2009).

[174] U.S. Dep't HHS, CMS, State Operations Manual, App. V, Emergency Medical Treatment and Labor Act (EMTALA) Interpretive Guidelines, Part II, Tag A-2411/C-2411 (revised 5/29/2009).

[175] Thomas E. Hamilton, *EMTALA Issues Related to Emergency Transport Services*, Ref: S&C-07-20, Center for Medicaid and State Operations/Survey and Certification Group, April 27, 2007.

It is a violation of the EMTALA requirements for a receiving hospital to condition its acceptance of an appropriate transfer of an individual with an EMC upon the sending hospital's use of a particular transport service to accomplish the transfer. Specifically, 42 C.F.R. § 489.24(f) reads in pertinent part as follows:

> Recipient hospital responsibilities. A participating hospital that has specialized capabilities . . . may not refuse to accept from a referring hospital within the boundaries of the United States an appropriate transfer of an individual who requires such specialized capabilities or facilities if the receiving hospital has the capacity to treat the individual.

If in the course of an EMTALA investigation there is evidence that a hospital with specialized capabilities or facilities and the necessary capacity to treat an individual with an EMC conditioned, or attempted to condition, its acceptance of an appropriate transfer of the individual on the use by the sending hospital of a particular transport service instead of the transport arrangements made by the attending physician at the sending hospital, then the receiving hospital is to be cited for violation of EMTALA Tag A-2411/C-2411.

Patient Consent

Q 5:33   Patient Refusal: What if the patient refuses the transfer?

An individual has the legal right to refuse transfer, but the hospital must fulfill some requirements to avoid liability under EMTALA. If the patient refuses transfer for whatever reason, the hospital needs to do the following:

- Take all reasonable steps to secure the individual's written informed refusal,
- Inform the individual of the risks and benefits of transfer and document in the medical record the reasons for the individual's refusal, and
- Describe the nature of the proposed transfer that was refused.

The Code of Federal Regulations states:

> Refusal to consent to treatment. A hospital meets the requirements of paragraph (d)(1)(i) of this section with respect to an individual if the hospital offers the individual the further medical examination and treatment described in that paragraph and informs the individual (or a person acting on the individual's behalf) of the risks and benefits to the individual of the examination and treatment, but the individual (or a person acting on the individual's behalf) does not consent to the examination or treatment. The medical record must contain a description of the examination, treatment, or both if applicable, that was refused by or on behalf of the individual. The hospital must take all reasonable steps to secure the individual's written informed refusal (or that of the person acting on his or her behalf). The written document

should indicate that the person has been informed of the risks and benefits of the examination or treatment, or both.[176]

The Act states:

> A hospital is deemed to meet the requirement of paragraph (1) with respect to an individual if the hospital offers to transfer the individual to another medical facility in accordance with subsection (C) of this section and informs the individual (or a person acting on the individual's behalf) of the risks and benefits to the individual of such transfer, but the individual (or a person acting on the individual's behalf) refuses to consent to the transfer. The hospital shall take all reasonable steps to secure the individual's (or person's) written informed consent to refuse such transfer.[177]

Cautions: The hospital chart and refusal form must indicate that the patient has been informed of the risks and benefits of the transfer and list those risks and benefits. The refusal must also state the reasons for the individual's refusal. The chart must contain a description of the proposed transfer that was refused by or on behalf of the individual.[178]

If the patient refuses transfer, the hospital must still provide ongoing treatment and care to the best of its ability. Refusal of transfer does not authorize the hospital to deny care or discharge the patient. The hospital personnel and/or physician who countersigns the refusal of transport should document that the patient has the mental capacity (not intoxicated, delusional, or mentally incapacitated by disease) to make the refusal. If there are any doubts concerning the patient's ability to speak for him- or herself, the hospital should act in the best interest of the patient.

It is vital that the hospital document fully in the medical record. Documentation needs to include the medical staff's attempts to dissuade the individual from refusing a recommended transfer. The nature of the proposed transfer that was refused should also be documented, ideally including the name of the facility proposed to receive the transfer and the proposed transportation plan. An entry as simple as "transfer to St. Elsewhere by ambulance for treatment of injuries was refused" will help overcome any allegation that no transfer was offered in violation of EMTALA. The State Operations Manual states:

> For individuals who refuse to consent to a transfer, the hospital staff must inform the individual of the risks and benefits and document the refusal and, if possible, place a signed informed consent to refusal of the transfer in the individual's medical record.[179]

---

[176] 42 C.F.R. § 489.24(d)(3).

[177] 42 U.S.C. § 1395dd(b)(3).

[178] 42 C.F.R. § 489.24(d)(5).

[179] U.S. Dep't HHS, CMS, State Operations Manual, App. V, Emergency Medical Treatment and Labor Act (EMTALA) Interpretive Guidelines, Part II, Tag A-2408/C-2408 (revised 5/29/2009).

Q 5:34   Patient Demands Transfer: What if a patient insists on a transfer?

A patient who is mentally capable of the decision may be accommodated with a transfer for any reason. However, it would be the hospital's burden to show that all dangers involved and the hospital's EMTALA obligations have been explained and understood by the patient. Documentation is vital.

Cautions: If a patient requests a transfer for any reason, a hospital may appropriately transfer that patient before the transferring hospital has used and exhausted all its available resources. A patient who is mentally and legally capable can always refuse treatment. As with any patient actions against medical advice, it is incumbent on the hospital to explicitly document that a physician or qualified medical person has explained the possible risks involved. If a patient still insists on transfer, the hospital may comply. The receiving hospital must still be notified of the transfer and must agree to accept the transfer.

The State Operations Manual states:

> A transfer may be made at the request of the individual with an EMC or of a person legally responsible for that individual. The hospital must assure that the individual or legally responsible person is first informed of the hospital's obligations under EMTALA, e.g., its obligation to provide stabilizing treatment within its capability and capacity, regardless of the individual's ability to pay. The hospital must also assure that the individual has been advised of the medical risks associated with transfer. After the hospital has communicated this information, the individual's request for a transfer must be in writing. The request must include the reason(s) why the transfer is being requested and a statement that the individual is aware of the risks and benefits associated with the transfer. The individual or individual's representative must sign the written request.[180]

The hospital is well advised to have a specific form for patient-initiated transfers. The form should include a statement of the hospital's obligations under the law, a statement of the risks of transfer, a statement of the benefits of staying at the hospital, and any benefits of transfer. Again, the hospital must obtain the signature of the patient if he or she is capable of signing—that is, this is another form of refusal of services. In the event that another person signs the request, the reason that the patient is not signing should appear in the record. If all parties refuse or are unable to sign, the form should be completed in its entirety with a notation of all reasonable efforts made by the hospital to obtain written confirmation.

---

[180] U.S. Dep't HHS, CMS, State Operations Manual, App. V, Emergency Medical Treatment and Labor Act (EMTALA) Interpretive Guidelines, Part II, Tag A-2409/C-2409 (revised 5/29/2009).

Q 5:35 Patient Leaves: What if a patient leaves the hospital on his or her own accord?

CMS's 2009 revised State Operations Manual explains:

> If a screening examination reveals an Emergency Medical Condition and the individual is told to wait for treatment, but the individual leaves the hospital, the hospital did not "dump" the patient unless:
>
> (1) The individual left the emergency department based on a "suggestion" by the hospital,
>
> (2) The individual's condition was an emergency, but the hospital was operating beyond its capacity and did not attempt to transfer the individual to another facility, or
>
> (3) If an individual leaves a hospital against medical advice (AMA) or left without being seen (LWBS), on his or her own free will (no coercion or suggestion), the hospital is not in violation of EMTALA.[181]

Cautions: CMS does not want the hospital to either actively or passively coerce the patient into leaving by increasing the waiting time or by not using its specialized care resources for the patient. Emergency departments and specialists are often strained to capacity by an overwhelming number of patients arriving at the emergency department in a short period of time. There sometimes seems to be a nebulous line between trying to treat and stabilize a patient in a timely manner and straining the emergency department's resources beyond capacity. If a patient leaves after a long wait because the emergency department is very busy or because other patients' more critical medical conditions take priority, this is not an EMTALA violation unless the patient was coerced to leave.

CMS has cited various hospitals for delays when patients left without being seen. The issues in these cases revolved around whether the patient's departure was influenced by staff comments such as "you could get seen sooner at St. Elsewhere," whether references to the fact that their insurance might not pay for the visit were made, or whether the patients were properly reassessed periodically as they waited in the emergency department waiting or treatment areas. When patients left with the knowledge of the hospital staff, several cases were cited for failure to obtain written refusal of care.

If an individual leaves a hospital AMA or LWBS on his or her own free will (no coercion or suggestion), the hospital is not in violation of EMTALA. However, EMTALA prohibits constructive as well as actual patient dumping. The practice of routinely keeping patients waiting so long that they leave without being seen by a medical staff member, particularly if the hospital does not try to determine and document why patients are leaving and to tell them that the hospital is prepared to provide an MSE if they stay, is considered

---

[181] U.S. Dep't HHS, CMS, State Operations Manual, App. V, Emergency Medical Treatment and Labor Act (EMTALA) Interpretive Guidelines, Part II, Tag A-2406/C-2406 (revised 5/29/2009).

unacceptable. A hospital's delay in attending to a patient can be so egregious and lacking in justification as to constitute an effective denial of a screening examination.[182]

In instances when patients leave the emergency department without notifying staff, the hospital should document when it was discovered that the patient had left, and all notes related to the patient presentation to the emergency department should be retained. The OIG underscores that even when patients voluntarily leave the department, "the burden rests with the hospital to show that it has taken appropriate steps to discourage an individual from leaving the hospital without evaluation."[183]

---

[182] Correa v. Hospital San Francisco, 69 F.3d 1184 (1st Cir. 1995), *cert. denied*, 517 U.S. 1136 (1996); *see also* Malave Sastre v. Hospital Doctors Ctr., Inc., 93 F. Supp. 2d 105 (D.P.R. 2000).

[183] 64 Fed. Reg. 61,359 (Nov. 19, 1999).

Chapter 6

Hospital Compliance with EMTALA

Look for evidence that the procedures and policies for emergency medical services (including triage of patients) are established, evaluated, and updated on an ongoing basis.

Instructions for an Investigating Team, CMS, State Operations Manual[1]

Below is a sample EMTALA Compliance Checklist:

A. **Entrances and Signage**

1. Identify and review all entrances to the emergency department that can be utilized by persons presenting for treatment.

2. Are signs posted that give information about the person's right to a Medical Screening Examination regardless of ability to pay?

3. Are signs posted in the entrances, waiting areas, registration, triage and treatment areas?

4. Are signs clearly visible from a distance of 20 feet or the expected vantage point of the patron?

5. Are signs in the languages of the population(s) most frequently served by the facility?

6. Is the waiting area visible to triage staff so that patients can be monitored?

---

[1] U.S. Dep't HHS, Centers for Medicare & Medicaid Servs. (CMS), State Operations Manual, App. V, Investigation Procedures for Responsibilities of Medicare Participating Hospitals in Emergency Cases, Part 1.

B. **Triage**

1. Where is triage performed and how are patients directed there?

2. When is triage performed? [Best practice is prior to registration]

3. What happens if someone leaves before or after triage?

4. Are patients informed to notify staff if condition worsens or if they choose to leave (so that Informed Refusal of Care can be documented)?

5. Confirm that Informed Refusal of Care forms are located in close proximity to waiting area.

C. **Registration**

1. What information is obtained?

2. Where is it documented?

3. When is the central log initiated?

4. Confirm that Medical Screening Examination and treatment are not being delayed for registration; however, if patient triaged is non-emergent, reasonable registration process can begin.

5. Do registration staff have scripts to address patients who insist on discussing insurance coverage prior to Medical Screening Examination?

6. Confirm that preauthorization of services with insurers is not occurring until after the Medical Screening Examination.

D. **Medical Screening Examination**

1. Do physicians or Qualified Medical Providers (QMPs) document when the Medical Screening Examination has been completed?

2. Are ancillary services used as needed to evaluate the presenting complaint and determine if an Emergency Medical Condition exists?

E. **Stabilizing Treatment**

1. Is it performed within the capability of the facility and staff?

2. Confirm that all physicians are presenting to the facility when called and in compliance with the timeframe set forth in the facility policy.

3. Is there a communication process between the clinical staff and registration staff so that any required prior authorization can be sought once stabilization has been initiated?

F. **Transfers Out**

1. Audit transfer paperwork to confirm that all transfers of individuals with unstabilized Emergency Medical Conditions are initiated either by (a) a written request for transfer or (b) a physician certification regarding the medical necessity for the transfer. [Documentation for the foregoing must be included in the medical record and a copy sent to the receiving hospital.]

   a. If the transfer is requested, do forms allow clear documentation of the request and that the risks and benefits of transfer were discussed with the patient? [Form used to document requested transfers should include a brief statement of the hospital's obligations under EMTALA. Reason for request by patient must be documented as well.]

    b. How does the physician certify that the benefits of transfer outweigh the risks? [Focus should be on the patient's complaints, symptoms and diagnosis.]

2. Do facility policies and procedures define documentation standards and the facility person(s) responsible for:

    a. Identifying a receiving physician at the receiving hospital;

    b. Obtaining acceptance of the patient by the receiving hospital; and

    c. Sending pertinent medical records with the patient?

3. Do available forms provide a place for the physician to write an order for the transfer and describe transportation staffing and equipment requirements?

4. If a transfer occurs due to an on-call physician's failure to appear, are the name and address of the physician included in the records sent to the receiving hospital?

G. Transfers In

1. Has the facility established a transfer request log to capture the following information regarding requested transfers into the facility: (a) date and time of request; (b) facility requesting transfer; (c) services requested/reason for transfer; (d) service availability at receiving hospital; (e) whether transfer accepted or denied and (f) if applicable, reason for denial?

H. Documentation Review

1. Audit central log for disposition and compliance with additional state law requirements (e.g., documentation of chief complaint, time of arrival and time of disposition).

2. Review Bylaws (or Rules and Regulations) to confirm indication of who may perform a Medical Screening Examination. If a nonphysician is authorized to perform a Medical Screening Examination, confirm that the required credentials, competencies and practices standards/protocols are identified.

3. Review physician on-call list to verify that it reflects coverage of services available to inpatients. Physicians must be listed by name rather than practice group.

4. Review triage and reassessment policy.

5. Confirm that EMTALA policy has been updated to reflect 2003 regulatory changes and 2009 interpretive guidance changes, for example:

    a. Definition of "comes to the emergency department";

    b. Definition of "dedicated emergency department";

    c. Concept of "prudent layperson observer";

   d. Changes in obligations for non-dedicated emergency department off-campus departments;

   e. Cessation of EMTALA obligations upon inpatient admission; and

   f. Requirement that back-up arrangements for on-call coverage be documented in policies.

When the Centers for Medicare & Medicaid Services (CMS) investigates allegations of EMTALA violations, it first looks to compliance with recordkeeping and policy requirements. The hospital should diligently maintain proper records and adopt all required policies to avoid CMS sanctions. CMS does not offer any guidelines on specific wordings for hospital EMTALA policies. It would be difficult to create a "boilerplate" policy for hospitals given the great variance of hospital emergency personnel, community needs, and emergency department capabilities and capacities. However, certain basic elements, as shown in the sample checklist above, need to be incorporated into any policy. At a minimum, the policy must state the hospital's responsibilities under EMTALA, the qualifications of medical screening personnel, the manner in which the medical screening examination (MSE) is to be performed, the way an emergency medical condition (EMC) is to be treated, the hospital locations where the MSE can be performed, the responsibilities of on-call physician specialists, the transfer responsibilities, and the maintenance of central logs.

Hospital Policies

Q 6:1   Hospital Policies: What written hospital policies does EMTALA require?

EMTALA requires a hospital to:

1. Adopt a compliance policy to ensure compliance with EMTALA.[2]

2. Adopt a policy setting forth which medical personnel are qualified to perform the MSE.[3]

3. Maintain a list of on-call physicians.[4]

4. Post signs informing the public of the hospital's EMTALA obligations.[5]

5. Maintain a central log of all individuals who come to the emergency department.[6]

6. Keep records of persons transferred to or from the hospital for at least five years from date of transfer.[7]

---

[2] The Emergency Medical Treatment and Active Labor Act (EMTALA), Pub. L. No. 99-272, Title IX, § 9121(b), 100 Stat. 164 (1986) (codified as amended at 42 U.S.C. § 1395dd (1995)), at § 1395cc(a)(1)(I)(i).

[3] 42 C.F.R. § 489.24(a).

[4] 42 U.S.C. § 1395cc(a)(1)(I)(iii).

[5] 42 U.S.C. § 1395cc(a)(1)(I)(iii).

[6] 42 C.F.R. § 489.20(r)(3).

[7] 42 U.S.C. § 1395cc(a)(1)(I)(ii).

7. Adopt a policy guiding emergency departments on the course of action when an on-call physician is unable to respond to a call to help stabilize an EMTALA patient.[8]

The State Operations Manual instructs investigators to confirm that hospitals have taken the following measures:

- Adopt and enforce policies and procedures to comply with the requirements of 42 C.F.R. § 489.24;

- Post signs in the emergency department specifying the rights of individuals with emergency medical conditions and women in labor who come to the emergency department for health care services, and indicate on the signs whether the hospital participates in the Medicaid program;

- Maintain medical and other records related to individuals transferred to and from the hospital for a period of five years from the date of the transfer;

- Maintain a list of physicians who are on call to provide treatment necessary to stabilize an individual with an emergency medical condition;

- Maintain a central log on each individual who comes to the emergency department seeking treatment and indicate whether these individuals:
  - Refused treatment,
  - Were refused treatment,
  - Were treated, admitted, stabilized, and/or transferred or discharged.

- Provide for an appropriate medical screening examination;

- Provide necessary stabilizing treatment for emergency medical conditions and labor within the hospital's capability and capacity;

- Provide an appropriate transfer of an unstabilized individual to another medical facility if:
  - The individual (or person acting on his or her behalf), after being informed of the risks and the hospital's obligations, requests a transfer;
  - A physician has signed the certification that the benefits of the transfer of the patient to another facility outweigh the risks; or
  - A qualified medical person (as determined by the hospital in its bylaws or rules and regulations) has signed the certification after a physician, in consultation with that qualified medical person, has made the determination that the benefits of the transfer outweigh the risks and the physician countersigns in a timely manner the certification. (This last criterion applies if the responsible physician is not physically present in the emergency department at the time the individual is transferred.

---

[8] 42 C.F.R. § 489.24(j)(2)(i).

- Provide treatment to minimize the risks of transfer;

- Send all pertinent records to the receiving hospital;

- Obtain the consent of the receiving hospital to accept the transfer;

- Ensure that the transfer of an unstabilized individual is effected through qualified personnel and transportation equipment, including the use of medically appropriate life support measures;

- Medical screening examination and/or stabilizing treatment is not delayed to inquire about payment status;

- Accept appropriate transfer of individuals with an emergency medical condition if the hospital has specialized capabilities or facilities and has the capacity to treat those individuals; and

- Not penalize or take adverse action against a physician or a qualified medical person because the physician or qualified medical person refuses to authorize the transfer of an individual with an emergency medical condition that has not been stabilized or against any hospital employee who reports a violation of these requirements.[9]

Cautions: The CMS guidelines for surveyors conducting an EMTALA investigation call for the team to focus initially on the hospital's compliance with EMTALA's required policies and procedures. The team checks for proper hospital policies, on-call physician lists, and posted signs. When CMS conducts an investigation of a hospital, the investigators want to easily review a "central log" of all emergency patients who come to the hospital, regardless of the location of their arrival at the hospital.[10] Therefore, hospitals should designate a particular place to keep logs that are sent from all locations that meet the definition of a "dedicated emergency department" as defined in the 2003 final rules.[11]

Q 6:2 Compliance Policy: What should an EMTALA compliance policy state?

A compliance policy needs to address the responsibilities of hospitals and what treatment and services must be provided to be in compliance with EMTALA. The compliance policy should address the following:

- Hospitals must provide an appropriate MSE to all individuals seeking emergency services to determine the presence or absence of an EMC, either by a physician or other qualified medical personnel, as specified in medical staff bylaws, rules and regulations, or policy and procedures.

- Hospitals must stabilize the EMC of the individual, within the capabilities of the staff and facilities available at the hospital, prior to discharge or

---

[9] U.S. Dep't HHS, CMS, State Operations Manual, App. V, Investigation Procedures for Responsibilities of Medicare Participating Hospitals in Emergency Cases, Part 1.

[10] 42 C.F.R. § 489.20(r)(3).

[11] 68 Fed. Reg. 53,262 (2003).

transfer. Obstetric patients with contractions are considered unstable until delivery of baby and placenta.

- An unstable patient cannot be transferred unless the patient (or a person acting on his or her behalf) requests the transfer, the transfer benefits outweigh the risks, and the transfer is in the best medical interest of the patient. In the event of transfer, the hospital must:
  - — Stabilize within the hospital's capabilities to minimize the risk of the transfer;
  - — Obtain the acceptance of the receiving hospital;
  - — Send all pertinent medical records available at the time of the transfer to the receiving hospital; and
  - — Effect the transfer through qualified persons and transportation equipment (including life support measures).
- A receiving hospital with specialized capabilities must accept a patient transfer unless that acceptance would exceed its capability and capacity for providing care.
- Hospitals are responsible for ensuring that on-call physicians respond within a reasonable period of time.
- The transferring hospital must send the name and address of any on-call physician who refused to respond or failed to make a timely response without good cause along with the transfer records of any patient transferred as a result of that refusal or lack of timely response.
- Prior to screening and stabilization, the hospital emergency department may follow normal registration processes, as long as staff does not delay care or discourage the patient from further treatment and as long as prior authorization is not received before screening or commencing stabilizing treatment is allowed.
- Conspicuous signage must be posted in the emergency department stating the rights of individuals under EMTALA and whether the hospital participates in the Medicaid program. The hospital must also maintain a 24-hour/7-day (24/7) on-call schedule of physicians taking call for the emergency department.

Cautions: It is strongly recommended that all policies include a restatement of the EMTALA definitions of "emergency medical condition," "stability," and "transfer." This listing helps clarify for staff that routine medical usage for these terms is not sufficient.

Q 6:3   Medical Screening Policy: What should the policy on medical screening examination state?

EMTALA requires that every individual who comes to the hospital requesting acute care be given an appropriate MSE. It is important to establish who performs this examination, as well as what, how, where, when, and why.

What?

The hospital policy should start with its EMTALA obligations by minimally stating:

- Any individual who comes to the hospital emergency department requesting examination or treatment shall be provided with an appropriate MSE.
- The hospital shall not discriminate against any individual when providing an MSE.
- The purpose of the MSE is to determine whether an individual has an EMC.

Who?

The hospital bylaws or rules and regulations must formally identify which hospital personnel with what qualifications may perform the initial MSE. The hospital's governing body must formally approve this delegation of personnel; the delegation cannot be informal, ad hoc, or arbitrary.

The policy should cover not only those who can perform the examination but also the scope of patients on whom the examination must be performed. Patients who come only for testing or outpatient care may be excluded from EMTALA policies.[12] Patients who come to the dedicated emergency department for nonemergency services are also not covered by EMTALA.[13]

The EMTALA policy should minimally state:

- An MSE may be performed by an emergency physician or other nonphysician practitioner who is qualified to conduct the examination and is approved by the hospital board.
- A list of the categories of QMPs who have been approved by the hospital board to provide the screening examination is attached.

How?

Any policy must outline how, on arrival, patients are to be provided with an appropriate MSE. At present, in most emergency departments, the patient first sees a triage nurse as the initial intervention in the medical care process. CMS does not consider triage to be an MSE. The policy should distinguish the triage process from medical screening, detail when and how registration information may be requested, and provide for periodic reassessment of patients who are waiting for care. A standard triage protocol should be implemented and followed to avoid issues of inconsistent practice and procedure as potential discriminatory treatment.

---

[12] 68 Fed. Reg. 53,263 (2003).
[13] 68 Fed. Reg. 53,263 (2003).

The EMTALA policy should minimally state:

- The emergency department triage is not an MSE.
- The MSE shall include ancillary services routinely available to the emergency department.
- The MSE must be uniform for patients presenting with similar symptoms.

Where?

The policy should identify contiguous locations in the hospital where the emergency medical examination may take place. If, for instance, the hospital has an ambulatory care center, urgent care center, psychiatric intake, obstetrics ambulatory clinic, or orthopedic clinic where patients may come for acute care, the hospital must assess these locations to see whether they fall under the CMS definition of "dedicated emergency department." If so, the policy should include these locations as official sites where the emergency medical examination may take place and address any specific requirements or procedures associated with the use of these sites. Off-site locations need not have policies and procedures identical to those of the main emergency department because of the need to tailor the policies to the staff and capabilities at the off-site location.

Once a policy is formulated, the hospital must be consistent in compliance. If, for example, the hospital generally refers obstetric patients to the labor and delivery area, then all patients requiring obstetric care must be directed there. Any exceptions to the location(s) of the MSE should be carefully delineated in the policy and based on medical needs, not, for instance, on insurance status or whether the patient has a private physician at the institution.

The EMTALA policy should minimally state:

- The hospital will provide an appropriate MSE for any individual who comes to its dedicated emergency department.
- An individual is also considered to have come to the hospital emergency department if the individual is on hospital property (including its parking lot, driveway, or sidewalk) and is requesting care for what may be an EMC. Hospital property is the hospital's campus, defined as an area that is 250 yards around the main hospital building, but it does not include other areas or structures of the main hospital building that are not a part of the hospital, such as physician offices, rural health centers, skilled nursing facilities, or other entities that participate separately in Medicare.

When?

EMTALA has the following "no-delay" clause:

> A participating hospital may not delay providing an appropriate medical screening examination required under paragraph (a) of this section or further medical examination and treatment required under subsection

(b) of this section in order to inquire about the individual's method of payment or insurance status.[14]

Policies on what information may be obtained during registration should be in place to conform to the Department of Health and Human Services (HHS) Office of Inspector General's (OIG's) guidance. Policies should prohibit contacting any insurer, managed care organization, or gatekeeper, or taking action to verify insurance, before the MSE. The policies should also specify the process to be followed if the patient asks about insurance coverage.

The policy should minimally state:

- There shall be no delay in providing an MSE.
- For patients who are enrolled in a managed care plan, prior authorization from the plan shall not be required or requested before providing an MSE.

Why?

The policy should minimally state:

- The purpose of the MSE is to determine whether an individual is experiencing an EMC.
  - An "emergency medical condition" is a condition manifesting symptoms (including severe pain, psychiatric disturbances and/or symptoms of substance abuse) which, in the absence of immediate medical attention, is likely to cause serious dysfunction or impairment to a bodily organ or function or serious jeopardy to the health of the individual or unborn child.
  - A pregnant woman who is having contractions is considered to be in an "emergency medical condition" if there is not enough time to safely transfer the woman prior to delivery or a transfer would pose a threat to the woman or her unborn child.

Q 6:4 Stabilization Policy: What should the hospital EMTALA policy state concerning stabilization?

The hospital EMTALA policy on stabilization and treatment should minimally state:

- If any individual comes to the hospital and the hospital determines that the individual has an EMC, the hospital must provide either—
  - Within the staff and facilities available at the hospital, for such further medical examination and such treatment as may be required to stabilize the medical condition, or
  - For transfer of the individual to another medical facility if the hospital lacks the capability or capacity to treat the patient.

---

[14] 42 C.F.R. § 489.24(d)(4)(i).

- A patient is considered to be stabilized when the treating physician has determined, with reasonable clinical confidence, that the patient's EMC has been resolved.

Q 6:5 Transfer Policy: What should the hospital EMTALA policy state concerning transfer?

The hospital EMTALA policy on patient transfer should minimally state;

- A patient in an EMC may be transferred to another medical facility before stabilization if:
  — After being informed of the risks of transfer and of the hospital's obligation to treat the EMC, the individual requests to be transferred, or
  — The transfer is an appropriate transfer. Based on the information available at the time of transfer, the physician determines that the medical benefits to be received at another medical facility outweigh the risks to the patient of being transferred (including, in the case of a woman in labor, the risks to the unborn child) and a certification to this effect is signed by the physician.
- The consent of the receiving hospital must be obtained and documented in the patient's medical record before transfer. The receiving hospital must have the capability and capacity to treat the individual's EMC.
- The hospital shall provide all available medical records as well as the name and address of any on-call physician who has refused or failed to provide necessary stabilizing treatment.
- The transfer shall be effected through qualified personnel and transportation equipment, as required, including the use of necessary and medically appropriate life support measures during the transfer.

Q 6:6 EMTALA Signage: What is the EMTALA signage responsibility?

The Code of Federal Regulations states:

In the case of a hospital as defined in Sec. 489.24(b):

(1) To post conspicuously in any emergency department or in a place or places likely to be noticed by all individuals entering the emergency department, as well as those individuals waiting for examination and treatment in areas other than traditional emergency departments (that is, entrance, admitting area, waiting room, treatment area), a sign (in a form specified by the Secretary) specifying rights of individuals under Section 1867 of the Act with respect to examination and treatment for emergency medical conditions and women in labor; and

(2) To post conspicuously (in a form specified by the Secretary) information indicating whether or not the hospital or rural primary care hospital (e.g., critical access hospital) participates in the Medicaid program under a State plan approved under Title XXIX . . . ;[15]

The State Operations Manual adds:

To comply with the requirements hospital signage must at a minimum:

- Specify the rights of individuals with EMCs and women in labor who come to the emergency department for health care services;
- Indicate whether the facility participates in the Medicaid program;
- The wording of the sign(s) must be clear and in simple terms and language that are understandable by the population served by the hospital; and
- The sign(s) must be posted in a place or places likely to be noticed by all individuals entering the emergency department as well as those individuals waiting for examination and treatment (e.g., entrance, admitting area, waiting room, treatment area).[16]

Cautions: The final rules specify that the signs should be posted "in a place or places likely to be noticed by all individuals entering the emergency department, as well as those individuals waiting for examination and treatment (e.g., entrance, admitting area, waiting room, treatment area)." Additionally, if the hospital serves a significant number of Hispanic patients, the signs must also be in Spanish.[17] The Office of Civil Rights requires signage and critical documents to be translated into non-English languages. Signs should be in each language representing a significant population in the geographical area served by the hospital. State laws, Joint Commission standards, and federal regulations on Limited English Proficiency may all apply, and the burden will be on the hospital to meet the most demanding of the rules applicable to that hospital. The hospital should have existing demographic data to demonstrate the actual level in its service area of populations speaking a language other than English. Signs posted in foreign languages must be of the same size and general locations as those in English.

Signs in general waiting areas must be clearly visible and readable from a distance of 20 feet. Signs in registration cubicles, treatment rooms, or other small areas must be clearly readable from the patient's perspective.

Signs must be posted in all areas that meet CMS's definition of "dedicated emergency department." Signs should be readable from a distance of 20 feet or generally be about 18 to 20 inches high.

---

[15] 42 C.F.R. § 489.20(q)(1) and (2).

[16] U.S. Dep't HHS, CMS, State Operations Manual, App. V, Emergency Medical Treatment and Labor Act (EMTALA) Interpretive Guidelines, Part II, Tag A-2402/C-2402 (revised 5/29/2009).

[17] U.S. Dep't HHS, CMS, State Operations Manual, App. V, Emergency Medical Treatment and Labor Act (EMTALA) Interpretive Guidelines, Part II, Tag A-2402/C-2402 (revised 5/29/2009).

Signs that conflict with the EMTALA language or raise issues of finances are not permitted. Signs that refer to requirements to contact the insurance carrier, refer to co-pays, or otherwise indicate financial criteria are frequently cited by CMS. In Kansas, for example, Medicaid rules required signs to be posted stating that if the visit turned out not to be a true emergency, the patient would be responsible for the bill. Failure to post the sign resulted in the hospital not being paid. Nevertheless, the Kansas City Regional Office of CMS determined that the sign violated EMTALA and had to come down. (It also violated the Balanced Budget Act requirement that Medicaid payments be based on the "prudent lay person" standard and not on the final diagnosis as an emergency.)

Q 6:7   EMTALA Sign Text: What text should the EMTALA signage include?

The EMTALA signs should state:

You have the right to receive, within the capabilities of this hospital's staff and facilities:

— An appropriate Medical Screening Examination,
— Necessary Stabilizing Treatment (including treatment for an unborn child), and if necessary,
— An appropriate Transfer to another facility even if you cannot pay or do not have medical insurance or you are not entitled to Medicare or Medicaid.

This hospital (does/does not) participate(s) in the Medicaid program.[18]

Q 6:8   On-Call List: How does the hospital meet its on-call physician list responsibility?

The hospital must maintain "a list of physicians who are on call for duty after the initial examination to provide further evaluation and/or treatment necessary to stabilize an individual with an emergency medical condition."[19]

The Code of Federal Regulations states:

Availability of on-call physicians. In accordance with the on-call list requirements specified in Sec. 489.20(r)(2), a hospital must have written policies and procedures in place—

(1) To respond to situations in which a particular specialty is not available or the on-call physician cannot respond because of circumstances beyond the physician's control; and

(2) To provide that emergency services are available to meet the needs of individuals with emergency medical conditions if a hospital elects to—

---

[18] 59 Fed. Reg. 32,127 (1994).
[19] 42 C.F.R. § 489.20(r)(2).

(i) Permit on-call physicians to schedule elective surgery during the time that they are on call;

(ii) Permit on-call physicians to have simultaneous on-call duties; and

(iii) Participate in a formal community call plan. Notwithstanding participation in a community call plan, hospitals are still required to perform medical screening examinations on individuals who present seeking treatment and to conduct appropriate transfers. The formal community plan must include the following elements:

  (A) A clear delineation of on-call coverage responsibilities; that is when each hospital participating in the plan is responsible for on-call coverage.

  (B) A description of the specific geographic area to which the plan applies.

  (C) A signature by an appropriate representative of each hospital participating in the plan.

  (D) Assurances that any local and regional EMS system protocol formally includes information on community on-call arrangements.

  (E) A statement specifying that even if an individual arrives at a hospital that is not designated as the on-call hospital, that hospital still has an obligation under Sec. 489.24 to provide a medical screening examination and stabilizing treatment within its capability, and that hospitals participating in the community call plan must abide by the regulations under Sec. 489.24 governing appropriate transfers.

  (F) An annual assessment of the community call plan by the participating hospitals.[20]

The State Operations Manual states:

> Section 1866(a)(1) of the Act states, as a requirement for participation in the Medicare program, that hospitals must maintain a list of physicians who are on-call for duty after the initial examination to provide treatment necessary to stabilize an individual with an Emergency Medical Condition. This on-call list requirement is a general provider agreement requirement for all hospitals and is thus technically an "EMTALA-related" requirement rather than a specific requirement of the EMTALA portion of the Act. When determining compliance with the on-call list requirement as part of an EMTALA survey it must be remembered that the on-call list requirement applies not only to hospitals with dedicated emergency departments, but also to hospitals subject to EMTALA requirements to accept appropriate transfers. (See discussion of § 489.24(f).) The on-call list clearly identifies and ensures that the

---

[20] 42 C.F.R. § 489.24(j).

hospital's personnel is prospectively aware of which physicians, including specialists and subspecialists, are available to provide stabilizing treatments for individuals with emergency medical conditions.

The list of on-call physicians must be composed of physicians who are current members of the medical staff or who have hospital privileges. If the hospital participates in a community call plan then the list must also include the names of physicians at other hospitals who are on-call pursuant to the plan. The list must be up to date, and accurately reflect the current privileges of the physicians on-call. Physician group names are not acceptable for identifying the on-call physician. Individual physician names are to be identified on the list with their accurate contact information.

Hospital administrators and the physicians who provide the on-call services have flexibility regarding how to configure an on-call coverage system. Several options to enhance this flexibility are permitted under the regulations. It is crucial, however, that hospitals are aware of their responsibility to ensure that they are providing sufficient on-call services to meet the needs of their community in accordance with the resources they have available. CMS expects a hospital to strive to provide adequate specialty on-call coverage consistent with the services provided at the hospital and the resources the hospital has available (73 FR 48662).[21]

Cautions: The on-call physician records need to be maintained indefinitely because CMS does not provide a limit on how long these records must be kept. CMS investigations always involve a request to review the roster of the medical staff by areas of practice and the on-call schedules to confirm that all areas are reflected in the call list.

The on-call list requirement is designed to ensure that the emergency department is aware of which physicians and specialties are available to provide the treatment necessary to stabilize individuals with EMCs. EMTALA does not require all physicians or specialties to be present at all times on a hospital's on-call list. However, all medical specialties represented on the medical staff should be available for emergency services through the call list. If a hospital offers a service to the public, the service should be available to the emergency department through on-call coverage.

A hospital must have in place policies and procedures that define the responsibility of on-call physicians to respond, examine, and treat patients with EMCs and that establish expected response times for on-call physicians. Because EMTALA does not specify an exact on-call response time, hospital policies on this issue should avoid specific response times and use terminology such as "reasonable." Response time should be dictated by the degree of severity of the EMC. CMS investigators will substitute their own view of "reasonableness" for that of the physician if the hospital does not formally establish response times. Hospitals are responsible for ensuring that on-call

---

[21] U.S. Dep't HHS, CMS, State Operations Manual, App. V, Emergency Medical Treatment and Labor Act (EMTALA) Interpretive Guidelines, Part II, Tag A-2404/C-2404 (revised 5/29/2009).

physicians respond when called and, in addition, respond within a reasonable period of time so that patient welfare is not endangered. When an on-call request is made, even those patients deemed "non-emergent" in a medical terminology sense must receive an appropriate bedside presentation by the on-call physician within a reasonably prompt period of time. Designation of STAT and routine response times have been acceptable to CMS in various plans of correction on this issue.

Besides on-call policies and medical staff bylaw rules, the hospital should have quality assurance programs to enforce compliance with EMTALA. Hospital failure to discipline offending physicians who do not respond reasonably to calls from the emergency department may incite CMS to apply penalties if a hospital is investigated.

CMS attempted to give hospitals flexibility in providing on-call coverage "in accordance with the resources available to the hospital, including the availability of on-call physicians."[22] This "resources available" language is broad and ambiguous. One hospital with three orthopedic surgeons on staff may take this to mean that they will provide 24/7 coverage for the emergency department. Another hospital with three orthopedic surgeons who are not willing to take call every other night may interpret its resources as providing coverage for only four or five days per week. Hospitals may also use this "resources available" clause to eliminate or decrease on-call coverage, rather than pay physicians to take call. Does this language mean that hospitals are only required to maintain a list of the physicians who have voluntarily or contractually agreed to take call? It is unclear how CMS surveyors will ultimately interpret the meaning of "best meets the needs of the hospital's patients who are receiving services required under this section in accordance with the resources available to the hospital, including the availability of on-call physicians." The language of the statute states "to maintain a list of physicians who are on-call"; it does not say that the hospital must provide a defined level of services by on-call physicians.

The availability of physicians on call was one of the basic reasons that the original EMTALA law was amended to specifically note the on-call obligation. Emergency physicians during the early EMTALA years attempted to comply with the law but were often frustrated by the lack of willing response by specialists. CMS recognized this and imposed specific obligations for call. For a number of years, this improved specialist availability. In the late 1990s, however, specialists in large urban areas reverted to a view that on-call coverage is a hospital problem and that physicians are doing the hospital a favor by taking call. This has been aggravated by physicians' awareness of the substantial penalties associated with failure to respond to a call in a timely manner as required by EMTALA and other demands of the law that had been there all along, but of which they remained ignorant.

---

[22] 42 C.F.R. § 489.24(j).

Although it would be unrealistic to ignore the fact that on-call physicians are balking at call and in some cases demanding compensation, these activities must be viewed in context. Like taxes, many mandates of government are not acceptable to everyone, and least of all to those who bear the greatest burden. The law, however, does not beg approval; it demands compliance. For hospitals, it demands that call lists be generated. For physicians, it demands call duties and compliance. And when physicians fail to comply, EMTALA ultimately requires removal of hospital privileges. How individual hospitals and staff arrange their system remains their option, as long as it meets the basic EMTALA requirements:

1. All areas of practice are reflected on the call list.
2. When there are insufficient physicians in an area of practice to provide full call, each physician in that area assumes a reasonable response obligation.
3. The call list prospectively assigns call obligations.
4. The call list is published or otherwise made known to physicians.
5. The call list can be used to retrospectively identify call obligations.
6. The obligation to respond to the bedside is addressed.
7. Timely response is specified.
8. The system is monitored for quality and enforced by the medical staff.

The policy should clarify that when specialty physicians are on call during their own office hours, it is generally unacceptable to refer emergency cases to their offices for examination and treatment if an unstable EMC exists. Any request for the on-call specialist to come in to see a patient dictates that the on-call specialist must come to the hospital to examine the patient. An on-call physician may also violate EMTALA by directing that the patient be transferred to another hospital where the on-call physician prefers to treat the patient, so hospital policy must address this issue as well.

Under the 2000 Outpatient Prospective Payment System (OPPS) requirements, the physician practice and space must be hospital-owned and qualified under the OPPS for hospital billing.

CMS accepts a referral to a specialist's office when there is a distinct medical benefit, such as to an ophthalmologist with specialized equipment not available at the emergency department. Such a referral should be treated as an EMTALA transfer with all statutory certification requirements. Any referral out of the emergency department to a specialist must be for distinct medical reasons—not for economics or convenience—and effected with full transfer compliance.

It is important to note that there are no reported cases concerning the failure of a hospital to properly maintain a list of on-call physicians or failure to have an adequate number of physicians or specialists. Hospitals, especially small and rural ones, do not violate EMTALA merely because they do not have the appropriate specialist on call. Indeed, they do not necessarily violate EMTALA if they have *no* specialist on call. Even if the available specialist on call refuses to perform stabilizing procedures because he or she feels incompetent, the hospital will not be found liable if the hospital makes an "appropriate transfer." Hospitals will be found liable, however, when they are capable and well-staffed, yet refuse to accept a transfer, or "reverse dump."[23]

In accordance with the statutory language, courts have taken into consideration the plight of small or ill-equipped hospitals when deciding EMTALA cases. For example, in *Vargas v. Del Puerto Hospital*,[24] a patient brought a civil action against a small rural California hospital with no specialists available or on call and only one physician available in the emergency room. The court held that the hospital was not liable under EMTALA when it transferred an unstable patient to a pediatric intensive-care unit. The physician made an appropriate transfer because he genuinely weighed the risks and benefits and determined that the child needed pediatric intensive care that was not available at the hospital. Similarly, in *Hines v. Adair County Public Hospital District Corp.*,[25] another private action, a Kentucky hospital that had no orthopedist on call was not found liable when the on-call physician did not perform needed surgery, which resulted in amputation of the patient's leg. The on-call physician instead performed a temporary procedure and scheduled an appointment for the patient with an orthopedist. The court held that an appropriate screening within this hospital's capability consisted only of "readying Plaintiff for an appointment with a specialist," which the on-call physician did.

Logs and Patient Records

Q 6:9   The Central Log: What are EMTALA's central log requirements?

The Code of Federal Regulations states that a hospital must maintain:

> A central log on each individual who comes to the emergency department, as defined in Sec. 489.24(b), seeking assistance and whether he or she refused treatment, was refused treatment, or whether he or she was transferred, admitted and treated, stabilized and transferred, or discharged.[26]

Regarding the rules for the central log, the State Operations Manual states:

> The purpose of the central log is to track the care provided to each individual who comes to the hospital seeking care for an emergency medical condition.

> Each hospital has the discretion to maintain the log in a form that best meets the needs of the hospital. The central log includes, directly or by reference, patient logs from other areas

---

[23] Erin M. McHugh, *The New EMTALA Regulations and the On-call Physician Shortage: In Defense of the Regulations*, 37 J. Health L. 61 (Winter 2004).

[24] No. CV-F-94-5201-REC-DBL, 1996 WL 684501 (E.D. Cal. Nov. 7, 1996).

[25] 827 F. Supp. 426 (W.D. Ky. 1993).

[26] 42 C.F.R. § 489.20(r)(3).

of the hospital that may be considered dedicated emergency departments, such as pediatrics and labor and delivery where a patient might present for emergency services or receive a medical screening examination instead of in the "traditional" emergency department. These additional logs must be available in a timely manner for surveyor review. The hospital may also keep its central log in an electronic format.

Review the dedicated emergency department log covering at least a six month period that contains information on all individuals coming to the emergency department and check for completeness, gaps in entries or missing information.[27]

Cautions: The hospital must maintain a central log on each individual who comes to the dedicated emergency department seeking medical care, showing whether the individual refused treatment or was refused treatment, or whether the individual was transferred, admitted, stabilized and transferred, or discharged.[28] The central log must include, directly or by reference, patient logs from other areas of the hospital that meet the definition of dedicated emergency department, such as ambulatory care, pediatrics, psychiatry, and labor and delivery, where a patient might come for emergency services other than in the emergency department.

A hospital must create a log entry and chart for every patient who comes to the emergency department whether the patient was ultimately treated or not (patients may leave due to long waiting times, leave against medical advice, and so on). If a hospital neglects to produce a chart or log entry, CMS would accept a patient's account of events that transpired during his or her visit. The burden will be on the hospital in such cases to prove compliance without the benefit of any chart documentation.

In *Hutchinson v. Greater Southeast Community Hospital*,[29] Willie Joe Hunter came to Greater Southeast Community Hospital with weakness and headaches. Dr. Kenneth Larsen examined Hunter and assessed his condition as nonemergency. Dr. Larsen arranged for a taxicab to transfer Hunter to the District of Columbia General Hospital (D.C. General). Hunter was later found aimlessly wandering the streets in a confused state and was taken to D.C. General, where he died of a missed subarachnoidal hemorrhage.

Dr. Larsen's documentation on the chart was cursory. Joyce Hutchinson, Hunter's wife, filed suit against the hospital and physician for violating EMTALA. Hutchinson argued that because the hospital had a charting policy that requires history, physical, and conclusions to be documented, Dr. Larsen violated his own hospital's documentation policies. The plaintiff contended that the medical record supported an inference that Dr. Larsen did not provide an adequate screening examination.

---

[27] U.S. Dep't HHS, CMS, State Operations Manual, App. V, Emergency Medical Treatment and Labor Act (EMTALA) Interpretive Guidelines, Part II, Tag A-2405/C-2405 (revised 5/29/2009).

[28] 42 C.F.R. § 489.20(r)(3).

[29] 793 F. Supp. 6, 10 (D.D.C. 1992).

The court in *Hutchinson* ruled that inadequate documentation was not enough to violate EMTALA, but "the total absence of a record that a patient received a screening examination by a physician would support a claim of (EMTALA) violation."[30]

CMS, on the other hand, routinely cites medical records in which the details are insufficient to prove an adequate MSE was performed. Records have also been found to amount to an EMTALA violation when the record is illegible.

The Joint Commission requirements dictate a control register or log of every individual visiting an emergency department. To track compliance with EMTALA, CMS now requires that all hospitals, including those not accredited by the Joint Commission, maintain such a log of patients. A chart must be created to document activity even for patients who leave the emergency department after their managed care plan refuses authorization.

Patients coming to the emergency department for outpatient procedures, scheduled return visits, and scheduled testing must be logged, but an MSE is not required. When there is any question about the nature of the visit, many hospitals have a separate form that specifies that the patient is not requesting a medical evaluation in the emergency department.

Q 6:10   The Central Log: What are EMTALA's recordkeeping requirements?

The Code of Federal Regulations states that a hospital must maintain:

> A central log on each individual who "comes to the emergency department," as defined in § 489.24(b), seeking assistance and whether he or she refused treatment, was refused treatment, or whether he or she was transferred, admitted and treated, stabilized and transferred, or discharged.[31]

Cautions: A hospital must maintain a central log on each individual who comes for medical assistance that shows whether the individual refused treatment or was refused treatment, or whether the individual was transferred, admitted and treated, stabilized and transferred, or discharged.[32]

The medical records must include:

1. A record of refusal of treatment with documentation of explanatory details.[33]

2. A record of refusal of transfer with documentation of explanatory details.[34]

---

[30] *Hutchinson*, 793 F. Supp. 6.

[31] 42 C.F.R. § 489.20(r)(3).

[32] 42 C.F.R. § 489.20(r)(3).

[33] 42 U.S.C. § 1395dd(b)(2).

[34] 42 U.S.C. § 1395dd(b)(3).

3. A record of the transfer consent or certification.[35]

4. A copy of records accompanying a transfer and details of all records to be sent to the receiving hospital.[36]

5. A record documenting the failure of on-call physicians to provide medical care.[37]

State surveyors will want to review the central log at the beginning of the investigation and will expect that the log be sequential, complete, organized, and in a compliant format. A hospital should develop policies and procedures regarding log location and maintenance. Although referred to as the "central" log, individual departments may keep separate logs as long as each log is readily accessible to a state surveyor. Surveyors may request to see logs as far back as five years.

Q 6:11   Maintaining Records: How long must the hospital keep records of EMTALA transfers?

The Code of Federal Regulations states:

In the case of a hospital as defined in § 489.24(b) (including both the transferring and receiving hospitals), to maintain—

(1) Medical and other records related to individuals transferred to or from the hospital for a period of 5 years from the date of transfer.[38]

Cautions: The State Operations Manual states:

The medical records of individuals transferred to or from the hospital must be retained in their original or legally reproduced form in hard copy, microfilm, microfiche, optical disks, computer disks, or computer memory for a period of five years from the date of transfer.[39]

For patients in labor, CMS even mandates how medical records need to be documented. In the State Operations Manual, CMS states: "For pregnant women, the medical records should show evidence that the screening examination included ongoing evaluation of fetal heart tones, regularity and duration of uterine contractions, fetal position and station, cervical dilation, and status of the membranes, i.e., ruptured, leaking, intact."[40] Emergency physicians need to document labor the same way as do obstetricians.

---

[35] 42 U.S.C. § 1395dd(c)(1).

[36] 42 U.S.C. § 1395dd(c)(2)(C).

[37] 42 U.S.C. § 1395dd(c)(2)(C).

[38] 42 C.F.R. § 489.20(r)(1).

[39] U.S. Dep't HHS, CMS, State Operations Manual, App. V, Emergency Medical Treatment and Labor Act (EMTALA) Interpretive Guidelines, Part II, Tag A-2403/C-2403 (revised 5/29/2009).

[40] U.S. Dep't HHS, CMS, State Operations Manual, App. V, Interpretive Guidelines for Responsibilities of Medicare Participating Hospitals in Emergency Cases, Part I, V. Task 3—Record Review (revised 5/29/2009).

Reporting and Billing

Q 6:12   Reporting Responsibilities: What are the reporting responsibilities of the receiving hospital?

The new hospital must report transfer violations within 72 hours. The State Operations Manual states:

> A hospital (recipient) that suspects it may have received an improperly transferred (transfer of an unstable individual with an emergency medical condition who was not provided an appropriate transfer according to § 489.24(e)(2)) individual is required to promptly report the incident to CMS or the state Agency (SA) within 72 hours of the occurrence. If a recipient hospital fails to report an improper transfer, the hospital may be subject to termination of its provider agreement according to 42 C.F.R. § 489.53(a).

> Surveyors are to look for evidence that the recipient hospital knew or suspected the individual had been to a hospital prior to the recipient hospital, and had not been transferred in accordance with § 489.24(e). Evidence may be obtained in the medical record or through interviews with the individual, family members or staff.[41]

Cautions: CMS makes it mandatory for a receiving hospital to report a suspected inappropriate transfer and puts a 72-hour time limit on the receiving hospital to report such transfers. Congress added the mandatory reporting requirement in September 1995. CMS believed that many incidences of improper transfers were not being reported. To improve on the reporting of violations, the receiving hospital is faced with termination of its Medicare provider agreement if it does not report suspected violations.[42] EMTALA allows a receiving hospital that incurs economic loss to sue the transferring hospital for damages,[43] but few hospitals have done so to date. CMS interpreted this as meaning that many EMTALA violations were left unreported because hospitals were hesitant to report each other. To force compliance with this reporting requirement, CMS chose to threaten receiving hospitals with the same sanctions for which transferring hospitals are liable.[44] Hospitals have been cited by CMS for failure to report other hospitals that transferred patients inappropriately.[45]

---

[41] U.S. Dep't HHS, CMS, State Operations Manual, App. V, Emergency Medical Treatment and Labor Act (EMTALA) Interpretive Guidelines, Part II, Tag A-2401/C-2401 (revised 5/29/2009).

[42] 42 C.F.R. §§ 489.20(m), 489.53(a)(10) (1999) (making failure of a transferee hospital to report a basis for termination of the transferee hospital).

[43] 42 U.S.C. § 1395dd(d)(2)(B).

[44] 42 C.F.R. §§ 489.20(m), 489.53(a)(10) and (b)(1)(ii).

[45] S.A. Frew, *Hospitals Cited for Failure to Report Transfer Violations*, Frew Consulting Letter, 6(2):3 (1999); S.A. Frew, *The First Hospital Cited for Failure to Report COBRA Transfer Violation*, Emergency Physicians Monthly (Oct. 1996).

Q 6:13   Collecting Co-pays: Can a hospital collect insurance co-pays without violating EMTALA?

Yes. But as with the registration process, collecting co-payments must not delay the screening or treatment requirements of EMTALA.

Cautions: There is no wording under the EMTALA statute or in CMS's guidelines that precludes a hospital from collecting co-pays from patients. However, the hospital needs to be very careful that such activity does not delay needed screening examinations or stabilization care. Additionally, such activity can never induce patients to leave without examination or treatment.

In an attempt to limit overuse of the emergency department by patients for non-emergency conditions, some insurance companies require patients to pay a co-payment for emergency department care. CMS has a basic requirement that there must be no delay in the provision of an MSE or stabilizing treatment. This requirement is aimed at the registration process but would also include any process to obtain payment for care. Hospitals should not post signs requesting co-pays as this would conflict with EMTALA signage and potentially induce patients to leave before treatment. The timing of the request for co-pay is vital since the collection of co-payments must never be used to deny care or induce the patient to leave before care.

Of the 20 alleged EMTALA violations in 2005, three were directly linked to emergency department front-end registration processes and resulted in fines totaling $65,000. One hospital allegedly requested an emergency patient to pay $85 prior to receiving an MSE. Another facility declined to treat a patient due to lack of insurance. In the third instance, an emergency department registration employee asked the mother of a young child in need of emergency medical care to make a $2,150 deposit prior to providing the child with treatment.[46]

---

[46] *OIG 2007 Work Plan*, Healthcare Reg. 16(3):7.

Chapter 7

EMTALA Enforcement

Any individual who suffers personal harm as a direct result of a participating hospitals violation of a requirement of this section may, in a civil action against the participating hospital, obtain those damages available for personal injury under the law of the State in which the hospital is located, and such equitable relief as is appropriate.

42 U.S.C. § 1395dd(d)(2)(A)

The U.S. Department of Health and Human Services (HHS) is responsible for enforcing EMTALA. This duty is divided between two of its agencies: (1) the Centers for Medicare & Medicaid Services (CMS), the agency that runs the federal Medicare program, and (2) the Office of Inspector General (OIG), the office charged with promoting the efficiency, effectiveness, and integrity of the HHS programs. CMS is responsible for Medicare terminations; the OIG, for imposing fines.

The enforcement of EMTALA is a complaint-driven process. The investigation of a hospital's policies, procedures, and processes and any subsequent sanctions are initiated by a complaint.[1] When one of CMS's ten regional offices (ROs) receives an EMTALA complaint judged worthy of investigation, the RO refers the complaint to the respective state hospital-licensing agency, which

---

[1] U.S. Dep't HHS, Centers for Medicare & Medicaid Servs. (CMS), State Operations Manual, App. V, Interpretive Guidelines for Responsibilities of Medicare Participating Hospitals in Emergency Cases, Part 1, 1 (revised 5/29/2009).

forms a survey team to investigate. The survey team then makes an unannounced on-site investigation of the hospital. The on-site investigation includes an entrance conference with the hospital; a review of the emergency department log and a sample of patient records, including the complaint case; interviews with hospital staff and physicians involved in the incident; and an exit conference. The survey agency is required to make a report to the RO within 15 days of completing the investigation.

If the medical judgment or physician action is in question, and in the view of the survey agency a physician review is necessary to determine whether an EMTALA violation occurred, the survey agency can recommend that the RO obtain such a review. Appropriate physician review, which must occur within five days, may be performed under contract with a Quality Improvement Organization (QIO) by physician reviewers who are board certified and have experience in peer review. At least one of the physician-reviewers must be drawn from the same specialty as the physician whose care is under review. In some areas, this may be complicated by the regulatory requirement that a panel of QIO reviewers cannot include a physician who is in direct economic competition with the practitioner being considered for a sanction or who otherwise has a substantial bias for or against that practitioner.

The CMS regional office retains the authority to make the initial determination as to whether or not EMTALA has been violated. If a violation is confirmed, the only remedy available to a CMS RO is to initiate the process to terminate the hospital's Medicare provider agreement. The RO can place the hospital on either a 23-day termination track for violations that represent an immediate and serious threat to patient health and safety or a 90-day termination track for other violations. In all but the rarest cases, if the facility submits a plan of correction[2] and CMS accepts it within these time frames, the termination process ends.

If the RO determines that a hospital has violated EMTALA, it sends a notification letter and a statement of deficiencies to the hospital, along with explanations of possible penalties, such as termination from the Medicare provider program and/or fines.

The following list contains examples from the State Operations Manual of what surveyors should be looking for:

- Any time delivery of a baby occurs during transfer, obtain a copy of all available records and refer the case for review to the QIO physician reviewer;
- If you are unsure whether qualified personnel and/or transportation equipment were used to effectuate a transfer, review the hospital's transfer policies, and obtain a copy of the medical record and transfer records;

---

[2] A plan of correction is a written plan submitted by a health care facility on CMS Form 2567 (Statement of Deficiencies and Plan of Correction).

- In cases where treatment is rendered to stabilize an emergency medical condition (EMC), the medical records should reflect the medically indicated treatment necessary to stabilize it, the medications, treatments, surgeries and services rendered, and the effect of treatment on the individual's emergency condition or on the woman's labor and the unborn child;

- The medical records should contain documentation such as: medically indicated screenings, tests, mental status evaluation, impressions, and diagnoses (supported by a history and physical examination, laboratory, and other test results) as appropriate;

- For pregnant women, the medical records should show evidence that the screening examination included ongoing evaluation of fetal heart tones, regularity and duration of uterine contractions, fetal position and station, cervical dilation, and status of the membranes, i.e., ruptured, leaking, intact;

- For individuals with psychiatric symptoms, the medical records should indicate an assessment of suicide or homicide attempt or risk, orientation, or assaultive behavior that indicates danger to self or others.

- In cases where an individual (or person acting in the individual's behalf) withdrew the initial request for a medical screening examination (MSE) and/or treatment for an EMC and demanded his or her transfer, or demanded to leave the hospital, look for an informed refusal of examination and treatment form signed by either the individual or a person acting on the individual's behalf of the risks and benefits associated with the transfer or the patient's refusal to seek further care. If the individual (or person acting in the individual's behalf) refused to sign the consent form, look for documentation by the hospital personnel that states that the individual refused to sign the form. The fact that an individual has not signed the form is not, however, automatically a violation of the screening requirement. Under the regulations, hospitals must use their best efforts to obtain a signature from an individual refusing further care.

- Examine the ambulance trip reports in questionable transfer cases (if available). These records can answer questions concerning the appropriateness of a transfer and the stability of the individual during the transfer.

- Appropriate record review should also be conducted at the receiving (or recipient) hospital if the alleged case and any other suspicious transfer cases involve the transfer or movement of the individual to another hospital.[3]

When the CMS determines that an EMTALA violation has occurred, it also forwards the case to the OIG for a possible assessment of civil monetary penalties. The OIG focuses on compliance with the specific EMTALA statutory requirements, such as a failure to provide a screening examination or authorizing an inappropriate transfer, and has the authority to assess civil monetary

---

[3] U.S. Dep't HHS, CMS, State Operations Manual, App. V, Interpretive Guidelines for Responsibilities of Medicare Participating Hospitals in Emergency Cases, Part I, V, Task 3 (revised 5/29/2009).

penalties only for these statutory violations. The OIG can impose a civil monetary penalty of up to $50,000 per violation ($25,000 for a hospital with fewer than 100 beds). In addition, any physician, including an on-call physician, who negligently violates EMTALA may be fined a maximum of $50,000 and excluded from the Medicare program by the OIG. If the OIG does impose a civil monetary penalty, that action is subject to administrative and judicial review.

The emotions aroused by the media coverage of dumping were intense before EMTALA enactment in 1986. These feelings were reflected in draconian penalties originally proposed by the House Ways and Means Committee, which drafted EMTALA. The penalties recommended for physicians included criminal penalties of up to $100,000 and/or up to one year of imprisonment. Furthermore, if the patient died as a result of the transfer, the Committee called for a fine of up to $250,000 and a five-year term of imprisonment. Fortunately, cooler heads prevailed before passage of EMTALA. Among others, Bruce D. Janiak, MD, then-president of the American College of Emergency Physicians, communicated with Representative Peter W. Rodino, Jr., chairman of the House Judiciary Committee, and raised serious concerns about the proposed statute and its severe penalties.

The Judiciary Committee decided that the proposed sanctions were indeed unnecessarily severe and in fact raised serious constitutional questions under the due process clause. The Ways and Means Committee listened to the words of caution and adopted the recommended changes, striking the criminal sanctions against physicians and reducing the civil monetary penalties.[4] The retained civil monetary penalties are still stiff, however, and termination of Medicare funds would effectively close many hospitals with significant Medicare volume and could end a physician's career. These significant sanctions continue to emphasize the very serious concern that CMS and OIG have about noncompliance with EMTALA.

In addition to governmental penalties, EMTALA allows two avenues for civil lawsuits. An individual who suffers personal harm as a direct result of an EMTALA violation may sue the hospital (but not the physician) for damages and equitable relief.[5] In addition, a medical facility that suffers a financial loss as a direct result of another participating hospital's EMTALA violation may sue the offending hospital for damages and equitable relief.[6] The two-year statute of limitations for bringing such lawsuits is not tolled by a patient's minority.[7] The exposure to civil liability and to governmental penalties poses major difficulties for hospitals, especially in times of economic restraints. This, of course, underscores the need for hospitals to carefully address compliance issues to prevent violations and reduce risk of liability.

---

[4] H.R. Rep. No. 99-241, pt. 3, at 7 (1986) (from the report by the Senate Committee on the Judiciary, Sept. 11, 1985).

[5] The Emergency Medical Treatment and Active Labor Act (EMTALA), Pub. L. No. 99-272, Title IX, § 9121(b), 100 Stat. 164 (codified as amended at 42 U.S.C. § 1395dd (1995)), at § 1395dd(d)(2)(A).

[6] 42 U.S.C. § 1395dd(d)(2)(B).

[7] Vogel v. Linda, 23 F.3d 78 (4th Cir. 1994).

Under the statute, the OIG and CMS share responsibility for enforcement. CMS is authorized to terminate hospitals from the Medicare program, and the OIG may assess civil fines for violations. Enforcement of EMTALA by the OIG was slow in the early years after enactment.[8] The sluggish early level of enforcement was partly because the proposed regulations to implement the law were not published until 1988, and the final regulations were not published until 1994, almost a decade after the original law was signed by President Reagan.

The OIG has commented that it has no way of knowing how much dumping occurs because "it can only act on what is reported to it."[9] For example, hospital officials said they may not always report possible cases of patient dumping because they are reluctant to jeopardize their relationships with other hospitals in their community. They need to maintain a positive working relationship with other hospitals and sometimes they rely on other facilities for patient referrals.[10] From 1986 to 1994, 1,729 investigations of EMTALA complaints were made, 412 hospitals were cited for noncompliance with EMTALA, and 27 hospitals and 6 physicians were fined for violations. Hospital fines ranged from $1,500 to $150,000. Physician fines ranged from $2,500 to $20,000. Seven hospitals—but no physicians—were terminated from the Medicare program.[11]

Enforcement incidents increased significantly in the late 1990s. In 1995, 356 citations were issued nationwide, including 212 MSE violations and 97 transfer violations. In the first half of 1996, 127 violations were recorded; 56 (44 percent) related to MSEs and 62 (49 percent) related to transfer violations.[12] From 1995 through 2000, the OIG imposed fines totaling more than $5.6 million on 194 hospitals and 19 physicians. The majority of hospital fines were $25,000 or less. The highest settlement for an EMTALA violation was $148,000, paid by the 447-bed University of Kansas Medical Center, Kansas City, in 1999. By 2001, a total of 28 physicians were fined by the OIG for EMTALA violations,[13] and there were an average of 400 investigations per year since CMS issued EMTALA regulations in 1994. About half resulted in confirmed violations.[14] For example, in December 1997, community hospitals in Millville and Bridgeton, New Jersey, had their emergency departments closed temporarily by CMS because of EMTALA violations.[15] In the years 2002 through 2006, OIG pursued 110 cases,

---

[8] Equal Access to Health Care: Patient Dumping: Hearings Before the Subcomm. on Human Resources and Intergovernmental Relations to the House Comm. on Government Operations, H.R. Rep. No. 100-531, at 8 (1988).

[9] *Health Care: Public Citizen Calls HHS Enforcement of Patient Dumping Act "Tragic Failure,"* 79 Daily Rep. for Execs. (BNA) A14 (Apr. 24, 1991) (quoting Judy Holtz, OIG spokeswoman).

[10] Report to Congressional Committees, United States General Accounting Office GAO, June 2001 Emergency Care, EMTALA, Implementation and Enforcement Issues (hereinafter GAO Report).

[11] Robert J. Levine, *An Analysis of Federally Imposed Penalties for COBRA Violations,* 28 Ann. Emerg. Med. 45 (July 1996).

[12] Robert W. Derlet, *Managed Care and Emergency Medicine: Conflicts, Federal Law, and California Legislation,* 30 Ann. Emerg. Med. 292 (Sept. 1997).

[13] GAO Report (June 2001).

[14] GAO Report (June 2001).

[15] *On-Call Consultants Present EMTALA Risks for the ED,* 10 Emerg. Dep't Mgmt. 37, 42 (Apr. 1998).

recovering more than $3.1 million. By 2006, 13 hospitals had been terminated from Medicare.[16]

The OIG reports settlements related to patient dumping on its website.[17] Summarizing the settlements reported for calendar years 2007 to 2011 suggests how active the OIG has been in civil enforcements.

Year	No. of Settlements	Total Penalties Collected
2007	14	$301,250
2008	8	$277,500
2009	7	$350,000
2010	7	$264,000
2011	10	$535,500

There was a perception in the early 2000s that different CMS ROs exhibited inconsistent levels of aggressiveness in their pursuit of EMTALA violations. Physicians practicing emergency care in Chicago, for example, should have the same liability under EMTALA as physicians in Los Angeles. However, a 2001 report of the OIG confirmed that citation rates varied from 22 percent in some regions to 66 percent in others. The OIG called for greater centralized oversight of the ROs, greater reliance on QIO review of medical issues before citation, and an improvement in collection and organization of records.[18] In addition to variability among ROs, there appears to be variability across years. One hopes this relates to the number of violations brought to the attention of the OIG rather than factors with only limited relationship to the number and severity of statutory violations.

Administrative Enforcement Process

Q 7:1   Investigation Initiation: How is an EMTALA investigation initiated?

The enforcement procedure is a complaint-driven process. Any individual or organization may make a complaint of possible EMTALA violations to CMS, and a full investigation by CMS can be initiated by a single complaint. Sources of complaints include the following:

- A patient or any individual,
- A hospital that received an improper transfer,
- A self-report from the hospital, or

---

[16] Charlotte S. Yeh MD, *EMTALA Anti-Dumping*, lecture at The National Congress on the Un and Under Insured, Washington, D.C., Dec. 10, 2007.

[17] Office of Inspector General, HHS, *Patient Dumping*, available at http://www.oig.hhs.gov/fraud/enforcement/cmp/patient_dumping.asp (accessed Aug. 6, 2012).

[18] OEI-09-98-02213, 1/01.

- A state surveyor performing a licensure or recertification survey.

The RO evaluates all complaints and refers to the state agency (SA) those that warrant SA investigation. The SA or the RO sends a letter to the complainant acknowledging the complaint and informing the complainant of whether an investigation is warranted. The SA's responsibility is to verify whether a violation of 42 C.F.R. § 489.24 and/or the related requirements at 42 C.F.R. § 489.20 occurred and whether there were other violations.[19]

> Complainants, if known, receive a letter of acknowledgment from the SA or RO. Do not disclose the identity of complainants. When information obtained during the investigation appears to be in conflict with the information supplied by the complainant, consult with the complainant, if this can be done without disclosing the person's identity.[20]

Cautions: Complaints are received by CMS ROs and state survey agencies and can be generated by several sources, including a patient, another hospital, or a report from the hospital itself. In addition, a state surveyor may identify a potential EMTALA violation while performing a hospital licensing or recertification survey. A hospital that receives an improper transfer is required to report the offending transferring hospital to CMS or risk penalties. The complaint is forwarded to one of the ten CMS ROs. RO personnel evaluate the complaint and decide whether an investigation is warranted. The RO then refers the complaint to the respective state's hospital-licensing agency, department of health, or similar state agency and authorizes the state agency to form an investigation team and conduct an unscheduled facility-wide survey. The investigation team must make an unannounced on-site investigation of the hospital within five working days. The purpose of the investigation is to ascertain whether a violation took place, to determine whether the violation constitutes an immediate and serious threat to patient health and safety, to identify any patterns of violations at the facility, and to assess whether the facility has policies and procedures to address the provisions of the EMTALA law.[21]

Q 7:2   CMS Investigation: What constitutes a routine complete investigation by CMS?

The RO gives an initial verbal authorization to the SA to investigate the EMTALA allegation and then completes Form CMS-1541A in ACTS (Aspen Complaint/Incidents Tracking System). If the RO identifies Medicare conditions or standards it wants the SA to survey, related to the EMTALA allegation at a deemed hospital, the RO completes Form CMS-2802 in ACTS. If the RO identifies

---

[19] U.S. Dep't HHS, CMS, State Operations Manual, Chapter 5, Complaint Procedures, Sec. 5430.1 (Rev. 50, 07/10/09).

[20] U.S. Dep't HHS, CMS, State Operations Manual, Chapter 5, Complaint Procedures, Sec. 5440.3 (Rev. 50, 07/10/09).

[21] U.S. Dep't HHS, CMS, State Operations Manual, App. V, Investigation Procedures for Responsibilities of Medicare Participating Hospitals in Emergency Cases, Part 1, I (revised 5/29/2009).

conditions or standards it wants the SA to survey related to the EMTALA allegations at a non-deemed hospital, it directs the SA to conduct a survey by completing Form CMS-1541A in ACTS.[22]

The SA selects surveyors with a background in the profession or area to be investigated. Preferably, the surveyors should have acute care training and experience. All surveyors must be adequately trained in the evaluation of 42 C.F.R. § 489.24 cases. Physicians should have experience in peer review.[23]

Allegations of EMTALA violation against a non-deemed or deemed hospital represent a probable immediate jeopardy to the next individual who comes to the hospital requesting examination and treatment for an emergency medical condition (EMC). Therefore, the investigation should be completed within five working days after receipt of the telephone authorization from the RO. The onsite investigation must be conducted on consecutive working days. The survey must be completed on time and should not be interrupted by other activities. No investigations are to be announced.[24]

The state survey team, at a minimum, assesses that the hospital takes the following measures:

- Adopts and enforces policies and procedures to comply with the requirements of 42 C.F.R. § 489.24;
- Posts signs in the emergency department specifying the rights of individuals with EMCs and women in labor who come to the emergency department for health care services, and indicates on the signs whether the hospital participates in the Medicaid program;
- Maintains medical and other records related to individuals transferred to and from the hospital for a period of five years from the date of the transfer;
- Maintains a list of physicians who are on call to provide treatment necessary to stabilize an individual with an EMC;
- Maintains a central log on each individual who comes to the emergency department seeking treatment and indicate whether these individuals:
  - Refused treatment,
  - Were denied treatment,
  - Were treated, admitted, stabilized, and/or transferred or were discharged.[25]
- Provides for an appropriate MSE;

---

[22] U.S. Dep't HHS, CMS, State Operations Manual, Chapter 5, Complaint Procedures, Sec. 5430.2 (Rev. 50, 07/10/09).

[23] U.S. Dep't HHS, CMS, State Operations Manual, Chapter 5, Complaint Procedures, Sec. 5440.1 (Rev. 50, 07/10/09).

[24] U.S. Dep't HHS, CMS, State Operations Manual, Chapter 5, Complaint Procedures, Sec. 5440.2 (Rev. 50, 07/10/09).

[25] U.S. Dep't HHS, CMS, State Operations Manual, App. V, Investigation Procedures for Responsibilities of Medicare Participating Hospitals in Emergency Cases, Part 1, I (revised 5/29/2009).

- Provides necessary stabilizing treatment for EMCs and labor within the hospital's capability and capacity;
- Provides an appropriate transfer of an unstabilized individual to another medical facility if:
  — The individual (or person acting on his or her behalf) after being informed of the risks and the hospital's obligations requests a transfer,
  — A physician has signed the certification that the benefits of the transfer of the patient to another facility outweigh the risks, or
  — A qualified medical person (as determined by the hospital in its by-laws or rules and regulations) has signed the certification after a physician, in consultation with that qualified medical person, has made the determination that the benefits of the transfer outweigh the risks and the physician countersigns in a timely manner the certification. (This last criterion applies if the responsible physician is not physically present in the emergency department at the time the individual is transferred.
- Provides treatment to minimize the risks of transfer;
- Sends all pertinent records to the receiving hospital;
- Obtains the consent of the receiving hospital to accept the transfer;
- Ensures that the transfer of an unstabilized individual is effected through qualified personnel and transportation equipment, including the use of medically appropriate life support measures;
- Does not delay MSE and/or stabilizing treatment in order to inquire about payment status;
- Accepts appropriate transfer of individuals with an EMC if the hospital has specialized capabilities or facilities and has the capacity to treat those individuals; and
- Does not penalize or take adverse action against a physician or a qualified medical person (QMP) because the physician or QMP refuses to authorize the transfer of an individual with an EMC who has not been stabilized, or against any hospital employee who reports a violation of these requirements.[26]

In addition, CMS must notify a hospital when an investigation has officially ended. EMTALA states: "NOTICE UPON CLOSING AN INVESTIGATION.—The Secretary shall establish a procedure to notify hospitals and physicians when an investigation under this section is closed."[27]

Cautions: The focus of the investigation is on the initial allegation of EMTALA violation, as well as on the discovery of any additional violations. Even if the allegation of violation is not confirmed, the survey team will still look for assurance that the hospital's policies and procedures, physician

---

[26] U.S. Dep't HHS, CMS, State Operations Manual, App. V, Investigation Procedures for Responsibilities of Medicare Participating Hospitals in Emergency Cases, Part 1, I (revised 5/29/2009).

[27] 42 U.S.C. § 1395dd(d)(4).

certifications of transfers, etc., are in compliance. If the allegations of violation seem to be confirmed, the investigation continues, with an emphasis on the hospital's compliance within the last six months.[28] Although many initial cases are not ultimately cited, it is important to realize that the entirety of the hospital's compliance comes under scrutiny in a CMS investigation, and this often leads to multiple, unrelated citations. The state agency provides input but has no decision-making power in the case. CMS may still cite a hospital even though the hospital passed the survey team's inspection.

The surveyors will conduct interviews in order to gather information. The State Operations Manual gives specific guidelines on interviews:

> To obtain a clear picture of the circumstances surrounding a suspected violation of the special responsibilities of Medicare hospitals in emergency cases, it is necessary to interview facility staff. For example, you may be able to gather a great deal of information from the admitting clerk in the emergency department, the nurses on shift at the time the individual sought treatment, and the Director of Quality Improvement in the hospital to name a few. You may also need to interview witnesses, the patient, and/or the patient's family. The physician(s) involved in the incident should be interviewed. Document each interview you conduct on a blank sheet of paper or SA worksheet and label it "Summary of Interviews." Include the following information, as appropriate, in your notes for each interview:
>
> - The individual's job title and assignment at the time of the incident;
> - Relationship to the patient and/or reason for the interview; and
> - Summary of the information obtained.
>
> Appropriate interviews should also be conducted at the receiving hospital in cases of transfer or movement of the individual to another hospital.[29]

The hospital has very few rights when it comes to EMTALA investigation. Once an EMTALA investigation has begun, the hospital should:

- Cooperate with the survey team. Trying to argue the hospital's innocence, denying documents for confidentiality reasons, or any delaying tactics can only harm the hospital;
- Hospital counsel should be involved immediately upon notice of an EMTALA investigation;
- Hospital's corporate compliance officer or committee should be involved from the beginning. The compliance officer and committee should review the EMTALA Interpretive guidelines and be familiar with the contents;

---

[28] U.S. Dep't HHS, CMS, State Operations Manual, App. V, Interpretive Guidelines for Responsibilities of Medicare Participating Hospitals in Emergency Cases, Part 1 (revised 5/29/2009).

[29] U.S. Dep't HHS, CMS, State Operations Manual, App. V, Interpretive Guidelines for Responsibilities of Medicare Participating Hospitals in Emergency Cases, Part I, VI, Task 4 (revised 5/29/2009).

- Initiate an EMTALA file, which should include all charts reviewed by the surveyors, people interviewed, what was discussed at the interviews, minutes of meetings with the surveyors, and any action taken by the surveyors;
- Start corrective actions immediately after learning of violations perceived by the surveyors at the exit conference;
- Monitor and record all efforts at corrective actions. CMS will specifically review monitoring actions taken based on the hospital's plan of correction when the re-survey is conducted;
- Involve the hospital board since CMS will not accept any plan of correction unless fully authorized by the board.

Q 7:3 Basis of Violation: How can hospitals be found in violation of EMTALA?

Hospitals can be found in violation of EMTALA and/or their Medicare Provider Agreement if they fail to:

- Comply with hospital policies and procedures that address the EMTALA provisions;
- Report suspected inappropriate transfers (this applies to receiving hospitals);
- Post required signs;
- Maintain transfer records for five years;
- Maintain a list of on-call physicians;
- Maintain a central log on each individual that comes to the hospital seeking emergency services;
- Provide appropriate medical screening;
- Provide stabilizing treatment;
- Provide examination or treatment without a delay in order to inquire about payment status;
- Provide appropriate transfer;
- Provide whistleblower protections;
- Meet receiving hospital responsibilities (nondiscrimination).[30]

Q 7:4 Required Information: What will the investigation team demand to see at the beginning of the investigation?

The State Operations Manual states:

A brief entrance conference must be held with the CEO/president of the hospital (or his or her designee) and any other staff the CEO considers

---

[30] GAO Report, *Emergency Care—EMTALA Implementation and Enforcement Issues* (June 2001), GAO-01-747.

appropriate to explain the nature of the allegation, the purpose of the investigation, and the requirements against which the complaint will be investigated. The identity of the complainant and patient must always be kept confidential unless written consent is obtained. Ask the CEO to have the staff provide you with the following information (as appropriate):

1. Dedicated ED logs for the past 6–12 months;

2. The dedicated ED policy/procedures manual (review triage and assessment of patients presenting to the ED with emergency medical conditions, assessment of labor, transfers of individuals with emergency medical conditions, etc.);

3. Consent forms for transfers of unstable individuals;

4. Dedicated ED committee meeting minutes for the past 12 months;

5. Dedicated ED staffing schedule (physicians for the past three months and nurses for the last four weeks) or as appropriate;

6. Bylaws/rules and regulations of the medical staff;

7. Minutes from medical staff meetings for the past 6 to 12 months;

8. Current medical staff roster;

9. Physician on-call lists for the past six months;

10. Credential files (to be selected by you) that include the director of the emergency department and emergency department physicians. Review of credentials files is optional. However, if there has been a turnover in significant personnel (e.g., the ED director) or an unusual turnover of ED physicians, or a problem is identified during record review of a particular physician's screening or treatment in the ER, credentials files should be obtained and reviewed;

11. Quality Assessment and Performance Improvement (QAPI) Plan (formally known as Quality Assurance);

12. QAPI minutes (request the portion of the quality improvement minutes and plan which specifically relates to EMTALA regulations. If a problem is identified that would require a more thorough review, additional portions of the quality improvement plan and minutes may be requested for review);

13. List of contracted services (request this list if a potential violation of §§ 1866 and 1867 of the Act is noted during the investigation and the use of contracted services is questioned);

14. Dedicated ED personnel records (optional);

15. In-service training program records, schedules, reports, etc.;

16. Ambulance trip reports and memoranda of transfer, if available (to be selected by you if the cases you are reviewing concern transfers);

17. Ambulance ownership information and applicable state/regional/ community EMS protocols.

In addition, if the case you are investigating occurred prior to the timeframes mentioned, examine the above records for a three-month period surrounding the date of the alleged violation.[31]

Cautions: A hospital should cooperate fully with providing the above items to the investigators. The clock is ticking toward either the 23-day or 90-day termination penalty, and any delay only penalizes the hospital by limiting hospital response times. Even items that the hospital perceives as privileged, such as quality review committee minutes, peer review reports, and other confidential information, should be provided. Laws regarding privilege and confidentiality are state statutes that the federal government does not have to comply with. Medicare contract rules and federal regulations specifically make all this material available to the federal investigators.

A hospital may want to prepare for a possible EMTALA investigation by performing a dry-run response. Every item on this list, or information on where the information can be immediately found, should be filed in a special EMTALA folder. A hospital may want to have EMTALA drills at least annually for the emergency department administration. By having this minimum information for an investigation team, the hospital can save invaluable time for responding to the complaint itself rather than scrambling to gather the needed information.

Q 7:5   Conclusion of Investigation: What occurs at the conclusion of an investigation?

In its State Operations Manual complaint procedures, CMS instructs its investigators:

> After the investigation is concluded, complete a Form CMS-1541B (Exhibit 137). If one or more of the provisions of EMTALA are not met, complete Form CMS-2567, using "Principles of Documentation." Describe in detail the facts of each individual case. In addition, specify whether the hospital was aware of the problem and took steps to remedy it prior to the survey. If a SA physician was a member of the investigation team, include the medical review of the case. Use the "Physician Review Outline for Emergency Care Obligations of Medicare Hospitals," (Exhibit 138) for this purpose. In addition, complete Form CMS-562. All the forms must be signed, showing the professional titles of all participating surveyors, and dated.

> A hospital may have multiple sites listed under its Medicare provider number. These sites may not be in close proximity of each other and each site may have its own dedicated emergency department (DED). In cases where the alleged EMTALA violation is against a specific site of the hospital, the surveyors should focus their survey investigation at the hospital site mentioned in the complaint intake. However, the surveyors should review all EMTALA related Policies and Procedures of all sites of the hospital. The surveyors need to survey the other sites of the hospital

---

[31] U.S. Dep't HHS, CMS, State Operations Manual, App. V, Investigation Procedures for Responsibilities of Medicare Participating Hospitals in Emergency Cases, Part 1, III, Task 1 (revised 5/29/2009).

if the survey findings indicate that the potential EMTALA violation maybe widespread.[32]

It is usually desirable and appropriate to conduct an exit conference. The surveyor(s) may outline the basic facts uncovered during the onsite investigation. However, the surveyor(s) must inform the hospital that the RO makes the final compliance determination, and the determination is often made with information obtained after the onsite investigation. Do not reveal the complainant and do not venture an opinion on what determination the RO might make. The exit conference should include a description of the process that is followed if the RO determines that a violation has occurred.[33]

Q 7:6   Information Entitled to Hospital: Which details of the complaint is the hospital entitled to see?

Once the hospital receives the complaint, the RO is encouraged to share with the providers being investigated as much information as possible regarding the complaint and the investigation of the hospital, according to the Privacy Act and the Health Insurance Portability and Accountability Act (HIPAA). The RO may also include any facts about the violation, a copy of any medical reviews (the identity of the reviewer must be deleted), and the identity of the patient involved (not the identity of the complainant or source of the complaint). CMS will determine whether the violation constitutes immediate jeopardy to patient health and safety. The hospital has the opportunity to present evidence to CMS that it believes demonstrates its compliance and the opportunity to comment on evidence CMS believes demonstrates the hospital's noncompliance. CMS ROs retain delegated enforcement authority, and final enforcement decisions are made there.[34]

Cautions: This information is seldom available at the initial phase of the investigation and generally is not provided before the plan of correction is required. The hospital, then, must address the concerns of the citation promptly and without reference to details of the review.

Hospital efforts to correct errors or misunderstandings, or to supplement the record, are usually best addressed in the plan of correction and not by disputes with the regulators before submission of a plan. Debates with ROs typically waste valuable time that is better spent on the plan of correction and often exacerbate the RO's impression that the hospital is not willing to comply.

---

[32] U.S. Dep't HHS, CMS, State Operations Manual, Chapter 5, Complaint Procedures, Sec. 5440.4 (Rev. 50, 07/10/09).

[33] U.S. Dep't HHS, CMS, State Operations Manual, Chapter 5, Complaint Procedures, Sec. 5440.5 (Rev. 50, 07/10/09).

[34] U.S. Dep't HHS, CMS, State Operations Manual, App. V, Investigation Procedures for Responsibilities of Medicare Participating Hospitals in Emergency Cases, Part 1, II (revised 5/29/2009).

In a letter to an HHS Committee on Regulatory Reform looking at EMTALA, Rich Pollack, the executive vice president of the American Hospital Association, noted that providers are not provided true due process:

> Under current enforcement policy for EMTALA, a hospital under investigation cannot make a reasonable challenge to a CMS's Regional Office finding that the hospital did not comply with the law. Under the routinely used "fast track," a hospital is notified that it has been found out of compliance and will be terminated from the Medicare program in 23 days unless it develops a plan of correction that is acceptable to the regional office. Under such severe time restraints, no hospital can risk termination by trying to convince its regional CMS office that there was not a violation of EMTALA. In addition, such a challenge would potentially alienate the regional office staff that accept or reject a plan of correction. We believe it is necessary to create due process for hospitals before the agency can issue a public notice of termination and proceed with a termination letter.[35]

Q 7:7 Investigation Report: What recommendations does the inspecting team make after the initial investigation?

At the end of an investigation, CMS instructs its investigative team:

> Transmit the results of the investigation and your recommendations to the RO through ACTS (ASPEN Complaint Tracking System) within 10 working days following completion of the onsite survey, if it appears there may be an EMTALA violation. If there appears to be no violation, this time frame may be extended to 15 working days, in order to allow the SA additional processing time.

> Transmit the following materials to the RO through ACTS:

- Form CMS-562, "Medicare/Medicaid/CLIA Complaint Form";
- Form CMS-1541B, "Responsibilities of Medicare Participating Hospitals in Emergency Cases Investigation Report." Recommend one or more of the actions below on the form:
  - **None**—This means the complaint was not substantiated;
  - **In Compliance, but Previously Out of Compliance**—This means that the hospital identified the problem on its own and took effective corrective action prior to the investigation. In addition to this recommendation, document on the Form CMS-2567 when the hospital identified the violation or a similar problem, the corrective action taken, and the date of such action. Also, document that the hospital has had no violations or similar problems for at least the past 6 months.
  - **Recommend Termination (23 calendar day track)**—This means that the hospital is out of compliance with 42 CFR 489.20(l), (m),

---

[35] Rick Pollack, letter to the HHS Advisory Committee on Regulatory Reform, May 3, 2002, available at http://www.hospitalconnect.com/aha.

(q) or (r) and the violation presents an immediate jeopardy to patient health and safety;

— **Recommend Termination (90 calendar day track)**—This means that the hospital is out of compliance with 42 CFR 489.24 or the related requirements at 42 CFR 489.20 (l), (m), (q) or (r), but the violation does not present an immediate jeopardy to patient health and safety;

— **Request Physician Review**—This means that it is recommended that the RO obtain a medical review of the case;

— **Possible Discrimination**—This means that it is believed that discrimination occurred based on financial status, race, color, nationality, handicap, or diagnosis.

- Form CMS-670, "Survey Team Composition and Workload Report;"
- Form CMS-2567, "Statement of Deficiencies and POC (Plan of Correction);"

NOTE: If the hospital had identified the deficiency and took corrective action prior to the investigation, indicate on the Form CMS-2567 that the requirement was not met. However, indicate on the Form CMS-2567 and the narrative report that the hospital took corrective action prior to the investigation, what action was taken, and for how long the hospital has been in compliance.

- Physician Review Outline for Emergency Care Obligations of Medicare Hospital (if physician review was done by SA);
- Complaint investigation narrative;
- Copies of pertinent hospital policies and procedures that relate to the identified deficiencies;
- Summary listing of all patients comprising the sample, including an explanation of how and why the cases were selected for review;
- Summary of interviews.

Transmit the following to the RO by overnight mail:

- Copies of medical records for substantiated cases, medical records of individuals named in the complaints, and other medical records for which a QIO review is requested;
- Certification of benefits versus risks of the transfer, if this is a transfer case.[36]

After completing an investigation, the team leader assures that the following additional documentation has been prepared for submission:

At a minimum, [the survey team will] identify:

- The name of each individual chosen to be a part of the sample and the date of their request for services;

---

[36] U.S. Dep't HHS, CMS, State Operations Manual, Chapter 5, Complaint Procedures, Sec. 5450 (Rev. 50, 07/10/09).

- Any individual identifier codes used as a reference to protect the individual's confidentiality;
- The reason for including the individual in the sample (e.g., unstabilized transfer, lack of screening, lack of treatment, failure to stabilize, diagnosis, race, color, financial status, handicap, nationality); and
- A copy of the medical record(s) for all individuals for whom the hospital violated the provisions in 42 C.F.R. § 489.24.

Also identify:

- How the sample was selected;
- The number of individuals in the sample; and
- Any overall characteristics of the individuals in the sample, such as race, color, nationality, handicap, financial status, and diagnosis.[37]

Q 7:8   Regional Office Review: What procedures does the RO follow upon receipt of the investigation report?

RO review of investigation proceeds as follows:

Upon receiving the case from the SA, the RO has 10 working days to review the investigation findings. The RO requests a 5-day advisory medical review of the case by the QIO to determine if there is an EMTALA violation. The RO has 5 working days to review the case upon return from the QIO. With this information, and any other additional information, the RO determines whether the hospital complied with the EMTALA requirements and determines whether the violation constitutes an immediate jeopardy to patient health and safety.

Prior to determining compliance or noncompliance, the RO is encouraged to confer with the State Agency, and may confer with the hospital's representatives. The RO shares as much data as possible in accordance with current Privacy Act requirements.[38]

The RO must determine the following:

- **Hospital Is In Compliance—No Past Violation.** If the RO determines that the allegation is not substantiated and that the hospital is in compliance with 42 CFR 489.24 and/or the related requirements at 42 CFR 489.20, the RO notifies the hospital and forwards a copy of the letter to the SA. If the SA received the complaint, it notifies the complainant that the complaint was not substantiated. If the RO received the complaint, the RO notifies the complainant.
- **Hospital Is In Compliance—Past Violation, No Termination.** If the RO determines that the allegation was substantiated, but the hospital had identified the violation on its own, took effective corrective action prior to the investigation, and has had no EMTALA violations

---

[37] U.S. Dep't HHS, CMS, State Operations Manual, App. V, Investigation Procedures for Responsibilities of Medicare Participating Hospitals in Emergency Cases, Part 1, X (revised 5/29/2009).

[38] U.S. Dep't HHS, CMS, State Operations Manual, Chapter 5, Complaint Procedures, Sec. 5460 (Rev. 50, 07/10/09).

for at least the past 6 months, termination action is not initiated. The RO notifies the hospital via a "Past Violation—No Termination Letter." The SA receives a copy of the letter through ACTS. The RO or SA sends a letter to the complainant regarding the outcome of the investigation. Although no termination action is taken, the RO refers past violations of 42 CFR 489.24 to the OIG for assessment of civil monetary penalties (CMPs) if warranted.

- **Hospital Is Not In Compliance—Immediate Jeopardy to Patient Health and Safety.** If the RO determines that the hospital is not in compliance and the violation represents an immediate jeopardy to patient health and safety, the RO follows a 23 calendar-day termination process. The termination procedures in § 3010 are followed. Uncorrected deficiencies that resulted in a violation of 42 CFR 489.24 may pose an immediate jeopardy to people seeking emergency care. The RO notifies the complainant that the complaint was substantiated. It also informs the hospital in writing of the specific violations via a preliminary determination letter, and sends the hospital a copy of Form CMS-2567. The SA receives a copy of the letter through ACTS.

- **Hospital Is Not In Compliance—Situation Does Not Pose an Immediate Jeopardy to Patient Health and Safety.** If the RO determines that the hospital is not in compliance with the EMTALA requirements, but the violation does not pose an immediate jeopardy to patient's health and safety, or the hospital took corrective action after the investigation to remove the immediate jeopardy, the RO follows a 90 calendar-day termination process. The termination procedures in § 3012 are followed. The RO notifies the complainant that the complaint was substantiated. The RO informs the hospital, in writing, of the specific violations via a preliminary determination letter and sends the hospital a copy of Form CMS-2567. The SA receives a copy of the letter through ACTS.[39]

Q 7:9   Quality Improvement Organization: What is the role of the Quality Improvement Organization?

Quality Improvement Organizations (QIOs, which were previously known as Peer Review Organizations (PROs)) function as non-binding advisors to CMS and OIG on whether EMTALA violations can be proven. CMS submits cases to QIOs for five-day reviews prior to issuing a citation. The reviewing physician for the QIO evaluates the patient condition and medical aspects of compliance. The QIO reviews the clinical aspects of the case, not whether EMTALA was violated.

The Act states:

CONSULTATION WITH PEER REVIEW ORGANIZATIONS,—In considering allegations of violations of the requirements of this section in imposing sanctions under paragraph (1) or in terminating a hospital's

---

[39] U.S. Dep't HHS, CMS, State Operations Manual, Chapter 5, Complaint Procedures, Sec. 5460.1 to5460.4 (Rev. 50, 07/10/09).

participation under this title, the Secretary shall request the appropriate utilization and quality control peer review organization (with a contract under part B of title XI) to assess whether the individual involved had an emergency medical condition which had not been stabilized, and provide a report on its findings. Except in the case in which a delay would jeopardize the health or safety of individuals, the Secretary shall request such a review before effecting a sanction under paragraph (1) and shall provide a period of at least 60 days for such review. Except in the case in which a delay would jeopardize the health or safety of individuals, the Secretary shall also request such a review before making a compliance determination as part of the process of terminating a hospital's participation under this title for violations related to the appropriateness of a medical screening examination, stabilizing treatment, or an appropriate transfer as required by this section, and shall provide a period of 5 days for such review. The Secretary shall provide a copy of the organization's report to the hospital or physician consistent with confidentiality requirements imposed on the organization under such part B.[40]

The Code of Federal Regulations states:

> (h) *Consultation with Quality Improvement Organizations (QIOs)*—(1) *General*. Except as provided in paragraph (h)(3) of this section, in cases where a medical opinion is necessary to determine a physician's or hospital's liability under section 1867(d)(1) of the Act, CMS requests the appropriate QIO (with a contract under Part B of the title XI of the Act) to review the alleged section 1867(d) violation and provide a report on its findings in accordance with paragraph (g)(2)(iv) and (v) of this section. CMS provides to the QIO all information relevant to the case and within its possession or control. CMS, in consultation with the OIG, also provides to the QIO a list of relevant questions to which the QIO must respond in its report.
>
> (2) Notice of review and opportunity for discussion and additional information. The QIO shall provide the physician and hospital reasonable notice of its review, a reasonable opportunity for discussion, and an opportunity for the physician and hospital to submit additional information before issuing its report. When a QIO receives a request for consultation under paragraph (g)(1) of this section, the following provisions apply—
>
>> (i) The QIO reviews the case before the 15th calendar day and makes its tentative findings.
>>
>> (ii) Within 15 calendar days of receiving the case, the QIO gives written notice, sent by certified mail, return receipt requested, to the physician or the hospital (or both if applicable).

---

[40] 42 U.S.C. § 1395dd(d)(3).

(iii) (A) The written notice must contain the following information:

(1) The name of each individual who may have been the subject of the alleged violation.

(2) The date on which each alleged violation occurred.

(3) An invitation to meet, either by telephone or in person, to discuss the case with the QIO, and to submit additional information to the QIO within 30 calendar days of receipt of the notice, and a statement that these rights will be waived if the invitation is not accepted. The QIO must receive the information and hold the meeting within the 30-day period.

(4) A copy of the regulations at 42 C.F.R. § 489.24.

(B) For purposes of paragraph (g)(2)(iii)(A) of this section, the date of receipt is presumed to be 5 days after the certified mail date on the notice, unless there is a reasonable showing to the contrary.

(iv) The physician or hospital (or both where applicable) may request a meeting with the QIO. This meeting is not designed to be a formal adversarial hearing or a mechanism for discovery by the physician or hospital. The meeting is intended to afford the physician and/or the hospital a full and fair opportunity to present the views of the physician and/or hospital regarding the case. The following provisions apply to that meeting:

(A) The physician and/or hospital has the right to have legal counsel present during that meeting. However, the QIO may control the scope, extent, and manner of any questioning or any other presentation by the attorney. The QIO may also have legal counsel present.

(B) The QIO makes arrangements so that, if requested by CMS or the OIG, a verbatim transcript of the meeting may be generated. If CMS or OIG requests a transcript, the affected physician and/or the affected hospital may request that CMS provide a copy of the transcript.

(C) The QIO affords the physician and/or the hospital an opportunity to present, with the assistance of counsel, expert testimony in either oral or written form on the medical issues presented. However, the QIO may reasonably limit the number of witnesses and length of such testimony if such testimony is irrelevant or repetitive. The physician and/or hospital, directly or through counsel, may disclose patient records to potential expert witnesses without violating any nondisclosure requirements set forth in part 476 of this chapter.

(D) The QIO is not obligated to consider any additional information provided by the physician and/or the hospital after the meeting, unless, before the end of the meeting, the QIO then allows the physician and/or the hospital an additional period of time, not to exceed 5 calendar days from the meeting, to submit the relevant information to the QIO.

(v) Within 60 calendar days of receiving the case, the QIO must submit to CMS a report on the QIO's findings. CMS provides copies to the OIG and to the affected physician and/or the affected hospital. The report must contain the name of the physician and/or the hospital, the name of the individual, and the dates and times the individual arrived at and was transferred (or discharged) from the hospital. The report provides expert medical opinion regarding whether the individual involved had an emergency medical condition, whether the individual's emergency medical condition was stabilized, whether the individual was transferred appropriately, and whether there were any medical utilization or quality of care issues involved in the case.

(vi) The report required under paragraph (h)(2)(v) of this section should not state an opinion or conclusion as to whether section 1867 of the Act or § 489.24 has been violated.

(3) If a delay would jeopardize the health or safety of individuals or when there was no screening examination, the QIO review described in this section is not required before the OIG may impose civil monetary penalties or an exclusion in accordance with section 1867(d)(1) of the Act and 42 C.F.R. part 1003 of this title.

(4) If the QIO determines after a preliminary review that there was an appropriate medical screening examination and the individual did not have an emergency medical condition, as defined by paragraph (b) of this section, then the QIO may, at its discretion, return, the case to CMS and not meet the requirements of paragraph (h) except for those in paragraph (h)(2)(v).

(i) Release of QIO assessments. Upon request, CMS may release a QIO assessment to the physician and/or hospital, or the affected individual, or his or her representative. The QIO physician's identity is confidential unless he or she consents to its release. (See Sections 476.132 and 476.133 of this chapter.)[41]

Cautions: The investigating state agency may recommend a physician review to the RO if the agency feels that a medical judgment or physician action is in question. Before the OIG receives a case from CMS, the case must first have been reviewed by a state QIO with physician reviewers who are board certified and have experience in peer review to answer any questions of medical judgment or treatment that may have led to the complaint. The RO will provide the QIO with all information relevant to the case. The QIO examines the medical records in the case and completes a physician review form for each medical record reviewed. The form addresses such issues as whether the patient had an EMC, whether the patient received an appropriate medical screening examination (MSE), whether the patient's EMC was stabilized at the time of transfer, and whether the hospital provided an appropriate transfer. The QIO is not asked to determine whether an EMTALA violation occurred. Physician review may also be provided by other qualified physicians, such as physicians who are employees of the state survey agency or CMS RO and physicians who have contracts with state or local medical societies. The QIO with which CMS consults must provide the accused physician and/or hospital with written notice of its review, a reasonable opportunity to discuss the case with the QIO, and an opportunity to offer additional information before the QIO completes its report. The QIO must submit a written report of its findings to CMS within 60 days of receiving a case. The regulation indicates that CMS is to provide copies of the QIO's report to the OIG and to the physician and/or hospital involved, if requested.[42] The QIO physician's identity is confidential unless the physician consents to its release.

According to the State Operations Manual, the purpose of a professional medical review (physician review) is to provide peer review using information available to the hospital at the time the alleged violation took place. Physician review is required prior to the imposition of civil monetary penalties or the termination of a hospital's Medicare provider agreement to determine any of the following:

- The screening examination was appropriate. Under EMTALA, the term "appropriate" does not mean "correct," in the sense that the treating emergency physician is not required to correctly diagnose the individual's medical condition. The fact that a physician may have been negligent in his or her screening of an individual is not necessarily an EMTALA violation. When used in the context of EMTALA, "appropriate" means that

---

[41] 42 C.F.R. § 489.24(h), (i).

[42] 42 C.F.R. § 489.24(h).

the screening examination was suitable for the symptoms presented and conducted in a nondisparate fashion. Physician review is not necessary when the hospital did not screen the individual.

- The individual had an EMC. The physician should identify what the condition was and why it was an emergency (e.g., what could have happened to the patient if the treatment was delayed).

- In the case of a pregnant woman, there was inadequate time to effect a safe transfer to another hospital before delivery, or the transfer posed a threat to the health and safety of the woman or the unborn child.

- The stabilizing treatment was appropriate within a hospital's capability. Note that the clinical outcome of an individual's medical condition is not the basis for determining whether an appropriate screening was provided or whether the person transferred was stabilized.

- The transfer was effected through qualified personnel and transportation equipment, including the use of medically appropriate life support measures.

- When applicable, the on-call physician's response time was reasonable.

- The transfer was appropriate for the individual because the individual requested the transfer or because the medical benefits of the transfer outweighed the risk.[43]

Q 7:10   Other Agencies: Can an EMTALA allegation be expanded to involve other governmental agencies?

Yes. CMS routinely shares any EMTALA complaint with all other governmental agencies that may have been violated, such as the Office of Civil Rights (OCR), and state licensure boards of those professionals involved in a cited incident. CMS also regularly shares such complaints with the Joint Commission, which CMS has designated a deeming authority for hospitals.[44]

The CMS State Operations Manual instructs its investigators:

> If you suspect emergency services are being denied based on diagnosis (e.g., AIDS), financial status, race, color, national origin, or handicap, refer the cases to the RO. The RO will forward the cases to the Office of Civil Rights (OCR) for investigation of discrimination.[45]

---

[43] U.S. Dep't HHS, CMS, State Operations Manual, App. V, Interpretive Guidelines for Responsibilities of Medicare Participating Hospitals in Emergency Cases, Part I, VIII, Task 6, Professional Medical Review (revised 5/29/2009).

[44] The Joint Commission accredits and certifies more than 19,000 health care organizations and programs in the United States. Its accreditation and certification are recognized nationwide as symbols of quality that reflect an organization's commitment to meeting certain performance standards. Hospitals accredited by The Joint Commission may choose to be deemed as meeting Medicare and Medicaid certification requirements.

[45] U.S. Dep't HHS, CMS, State Operations Manual, App. V, Investigation Procedures for Responsibilities of Medicare Participating Hospitals in Emergency Cases, Part 1, I (revised 5/29/2009).

Cautions: Even if the hospital is able to come to a satisfactory resolution with CMS after an investigation and acceptance of a plan of correction, hospitals may face further disciplinary actions. CMS sends each complainant a letter acknowledging receipt of the complaint, advising the complainant of his or her rights to consider independently the EMTALA civil enforcement provisions, and stating that CMS will refer the complaint for further investigation if it determines that the matter falls under the jurisdiction of another agency. For example, if CMS determines that a patient's civil rights have been violated, it will then refer the patient to the OCR.[46] Hospitals and physicians should be aware that any violation against these other agencies may subject them to criminal prosecution under the civil rights acts.

In *Howe v. Hull*,[47] Dr. Hull, the on-call physician, refused to admit an AIDS patient with a severe drug reaction into the hospital. The patient had to be transferred to another hospital, where he recovered. The patient filed an action against the hospital and Dr. Hull, alleging violations of the Americans with Disabilities Act (ADA), the Federal Rehabilitation Act (FRA), and EMTALA. The court denied a defense motion for summary judgment on the EMTALA claim, determining that a reasonable jury could find that the patient was provided a lesser degree of care because of his HIV status.[48] The court also upheld the ADA and FRA claims. A jury awarded compensatory damages of $62,000 and punitive damages of $150,000 against the physician and $300,000 against the hospital.

In addition, during an investigation, state surveyors look for quality-of-care issues other than EMTALA violations. If other quality-of-care issues arise during the investigation, the surveyors will report this to the RO for further investigation. The State Operations Manual instructs its surveyors:

> Quality of care review performed either by the State Agency or other physicians must not delay processing of a substantiated EMTALA violation. If during the course of the investigation, you identify possible quality of care issues other than those related to the provisions of this regulation, obtain a copy of the patient's medical record and send the case to the Regional Office for referral to the appropriate Quality Improvement Organization (QIO). Contact the Regional Office if the hospital refuses to provide a copy of the medical record.[49]

---

[46] U.S. Dep't HHS, CMS, State Operations Manual, App. V, Investigation Procedures for Responsibilities of Medicare Participating Hospitals in Emergency Cases, Part 1, I (revised 5/29/2009).

[47] 874 F. Supp. 779 (N.D. Ohio 1994).

[48] *Howe*, 874 F. Supp. 779, 785.

[49] U.S. Dep't HHS, CMS, State Operations Manual, App. V, Interpretive Guidelines for Responsibilities of Medicare Participating Hospitals in Emergency Cases, Part I, I (revised 5/29/2009).

Q 7:11   Previous Violations: Does the Office of Inspector General consider previous EMTALA actions?

The OIG may consider not only previous EMTALA violations but also any previous instances of possible violation in determining fines and sanctions against a hospital.

Cautions: In the March 18, 2002, *Federal Register*,[50] the OIG expanded the enforcement process of EMTALA. Previously, regulations allowed the OIG to consider only prior history of offenses in considering penalties. Now the OIG can consider also other "instances," described as previous instances that did not lead to convictions, or judicial or administrative decisions. Such consideration of these "offenses" means hospitals may find themselves under OIG scrutiny more than once for the same incidents considered not to be violations by a court or by an administrative law judge (ALJ). Thus, the method of determining civil monetary penalties will impose greater fines on hospitals with multiple "instances" rather than treating them like those with a single violation. Accordingly, hospitals with multiple previous investigations need to be particularly vigilant.

Q 7:12   Whistleblower Protection: Does EMTALA provide protection for persons who report an EMTALA violation?

Yes. EMTALA has a "whistleblower" clause that protects reporting individuals from reprisal.

The Act states:

> A participating hospital may not penalize or take adverse action against a qualified medical person described in subsection (c)(1)(A)(iii) or a physician because the person or physician refuses to authorize the transfer of an individual with an emergency medical condition that has not been stabilized or against any hospital employee because the employee reports a violation of a requirement of this section.[51]

Cautions: This clause was added so that employees are free to report an EMTALA violation without fearing reprisals by the hospital. For instance, when an on-call physician fails to respond to a call for assistance from the emergency physician and a transfer is therefore conducted, the emergency physician is obligated by EMTALA to write down the name of the offending on-call physician in the chart. The hospital cannot penalize the emergency physician for doing this. A hospital also cannot penalize a physician who refuses to transfer a patient if the physician believes that the transfer is not appropriate.

The scope of the protection, however, does not clearly protect those who advocate for EMTALA compliance in a general sense. Although there have

---

[50] 67 Fed. Reg. 11, 928 (2002) (to be codified in 42 C.F.R. Pts. 1001, 1003, 1005, and 1008).

[51] 42 U.S.C. § 1395dd(i).

been successful recoveries for these types of cases, the time and expense are significant. This has, in fact, caused some physicians to submit to processes that are noncompliant rather than lose their employment. CMS has rarely stepped in to protect staff in these situations, but in a few instances has cited hospitals for violations of the "whistleblower" provisions.

In *Fotia v. Palmetto Behavioral Health,* [52] Doug Fotia, a licensed clinical social worker hired as an emergency assessment worker by Palmetto Health, sued the hospital claiming that the hospital retaliated against him for reporting an EMTALA violation. Fotia had assessed a suicidal patient who had been stabilized at another hospital that was not equipped to treat the patient's psychiatric condition. A physician had already certified the transfer to Palmetto Health, which specialized in psychiatric care and had an open bed. According to Fotia, a Palmetto Health administrator informed him that the hospital had already taken its share of unfunded patients and that the patient should be transferred to the Medical University of South Carolina. Fotia did so but argued that this action constituted a violation of EMTALA. A week later, Fotia was terminated by Palmetto Health, ostensibly because there had been complaints about him. Palmetto Health argued that individuals were not granted the right to bring a civil action for financial loss by the whistleblower protection provision. Palmetto Health also asserted that Fotia had not suffered personal harm or injury because, under South Carolina tort law, wrongful discharge is not a personal injury. Palmetto Health further argued that Fotia had failed to state a claim, based on violation of EMTALA, because he had not made a report of an EMTALA violation. The court rejected all Palmetto Health's arguments to dismiss the suit.

Q 7:13　Actual Medical Emergency: Does a patient need to have an actual medical emergency to charge an EMTALA violation?

No. A plaintiff only has to show that a hospital violated the provisions of EMTALA, without having to show that the patient had an actual medical emergency at the time of arrival. No adverse outcome is required for EMTALA administrative citations. Civil lawsuits, however, require proof that the violation caused injury to the patient.

Cautions: EMTALA does not require that patients show that they in fact suffered from an EMC when they arrived at the emergency department to establish a violation. For example, a patient may come for care of a simple sprained finger, but if the hospital treats him or her in a discriminatory manner, the hospital may violate EMTALA. EMTALA directs participating hospitals to provide appropriate medical screening to all who come to the emergency department. To prove violation of the screening provisions of EMTALA, patients need not prove that they actually suffered from an emergency condition when they first arrived because failure to appropriately screen, by itself, is sufficient for violation when other elements are met.

---

[52] 317 F. Supp. 2d 638 (D.S.C. 2004).

However, to file a civil lawsuit against a hospital, the patient needs to show that he or she suffered an injury as a direct result of the EMTALA violation.[53]

EMTALA requires hospitals to provide appropriate medical screening to all who enter a hospital's emergency department, whether or not they exhibit a medical emergency when they arrive. In *Correa v. Hospital San Francisco*,[54] the hospital argued that Mrs. González, the patient, did not have an actual EMC when she came to the emergency department, and therefore her discharge to the primary clinic was appropriate. The court in *Correa* ruled that EMTALA does not require that the patient have an EMC, stating:

> The statute by its terms directs a participating hospital to provide an appropriate screening to all who come to its emergency department. Thus, to prove a violation of EMTALA's screening provisions, a plaintiff need not prove that she actually suffered from an emergency medical condition when she first came through the portals of the defendant's facility; the failure appropriately to screen, by itself, is sufficient to ground liability as long as the other elements of the cause of action are met.[55]

Q 7:14   Actual Injury: Does a patient have to suffer actual injury for an EMTALA violation to occur?

No. The government may apply penalties for EMTALA violations even when the patient does not suffer injury. A civil lawsuit, however, requires actual injury.[56]

Cautions: It is very important to remember that liability under EMTALA is not grounded in traditional negligence concepts. A patient does not have to suffer injury as a result of a hospital's or physician's actions for penalties to be applied. As long as a hospital or physician is found to have violated EMTALA's statutory requirements, the government may apply penalties. If a patient suffers harm, he or she may file a civil lawsuit against the hospital.

An EMTALA claim does not rest on any proof that a hospital or physician was negligent but is predicated on compliance with the provisions of the EMTALA statute that make the hospital or physician strictly liable for any personal harm that directly results from that violation.[57] Arguing a case under EMTALA is easier for a plaintiff's attorney than arguing a malpractice case because the four basic elements of a negligence malpractice suit need not be proved: duty, breach of a standard of care, proximate cause, and injury. The attorney needs to show only that the hospital was in noncompliance with EMTALA and that the client was injured as a result of this noncompliance. As noted in the *Baby K* case

---

[53] 42 U.S.C. § 1395dd(3).

[54] 69 F.3d 1184, 1191 (1st Cir. 1995).

[55] *Correa*, 69 F.3d 1184, 1193.

[56] 42 U.S.C. § 1395dd(3).

[57] Griffith v. Mt. Carmel Med. Ctr., 842 F. Supp. 1359 (D. Kan. 1994).

discussed earlier (see Q 4:11), issues of medical standard of care or medical ethics are not material to EMTALA.

If CMS performs a formal investigation of the specific violation, it actually does much of the investigative work for the attorney because the attorney can use all CMS's investigative data in his or her legal arguments. The suit is filed in federal court, where the time to trial is generally much shorter than in state courts. Federal courts are generally recognized as being more lenient to plaintiffs. Finally, even if a plaintiff's attorney wins a negligent malpractice suit in a state court, he or she may then additionally file an EMTALA suit in federal court, providing another avenue for compensation.

Q 7:15 Multiple Violators: What if more than one person was responsible for an EMTALA violation?

In any case where it is determined that more than one person was responsible, each such person may be held liable for the penalty and an assessment may be imposed against one such person or jointly and severally[58] against two or more persons. The aggregate amount of the assessment collected may not exceed the amount that could be collected if only one person were responsible so that the patient cannot collect double compensation.[59]

The OIG, therefore, will apportion a single maximum fine among the responsible physicians. The hospital, however, will be fined separately, and the total of the two types of fines may exceed the total fine that could individually have been assessed against just the hospital or just the physician.

In civil litigation, this means that the total damages sustained by the patient are paid only once, and liability is divided among the defendants as the jury or law provides.

Q 7:16 Public Notice: When does CMS file a public notice of a threatened Medicare termination?

For a 23-day termination track, a public notice is provided to the press, radio, and television on the 21st day. For a 90-day termination track, the public notice is provided on the 70th day.

Cautions: Public notice of an EMTALA investigation and threat of Medicare termination would create major public relations problems for any hospital. A hospital's reputation in the community is of vital importance. Fortunately, CMS does not publish the "notice of proposed termination" unless the hospital fails to take corrective action before the end of the termination

---

[58] "Jointly and severally" means that liability is on more than one person, responsible together and individually. The person who has been harmed can "sue one or more of the parties to such liability separately, or all of them together at his option." *Black's Law Dictionary* 837 (6th ed. 1990). The wronged person can recover from both/all of the wrongdoers or from just one of the wrongdoers (if he or she goes after both/all of them; however, he or she does not receive double compensation).

[59] 42 C.F.R. § 1003.102(d)(1)(2).

process. By taking corrective action within the given time frame, the hospital can avoid public notice of the violation. This is a strong incentive for hospitals to move quickly and comply with corrective actions.

Before 1993, the settlements negotiated by the OIG routinely included non-disclosure clauses in which the government agreed not to publicize the case affirmatively. This saved many hospitals from severe public relations quandaries. The government discontinued the secrecy policy in 1992, and current OIG policy is to include a community outreach provision in all settlements with hospitals. The outreach provision typically requires the hospital to run ads in local newspapers notifying the public that the hospital's emergency department is open to all members of the community, regardless of ability to pay. Some critics believe that this provision is still insufficient to punish hospitals that violate EMTALA because the public is not informed that the hospital was investigated for an alleged EMTALA violation.[60] However, similar clauses are common in all types of legal settlements and are intended to dispose of potential litigation without a trial or formal finding by a jury or court. All settlements are available through freedom of information requests, thereby protecting public interest access to the information.

Q 7:17   Left Without Being Seen: Could a hospital be found in violation of EMTALA if a patient voluntarily leaves the waiting room before being examined?

Yes, if it can be shown that the hospital coerced or prompted the patient to leave before an MSE could be performed.

CMS's 2009 revised State Operations Manual explains:

> If a screening examination reveals an Emergency Medical Condition and the individual is told to wait for treatment, but the individual leaves the hospital, the hospital did not "dump" the patient unless:
>
> (1) The individual left the emergency department based on a "suggestion" by the hospital, and/or
>
> (2) the individual's condition was emergent, but the hospital was operating beyond its capacity and did not attempt to transfer the individual to another facility.
>
> (3) If an individual leaves a hospital against medical advice (AMA) or left without being seen (LWBS), on his or her own free will (no coercion or suggestion), the hospital is not in violation of EMTALA.[61]

In its November 10, 1999, Special Advisory Bulletin, CMS stated:

---

[60] *See* Dame, *The Emergency Medical Treatment and Active Labor Act,* at 18.

[61] U.S. Dep't HHS, CMS, State Operations Manual, App. V, Emergency Medical Treatment and Labor Act (EMTALA) Interpretive Guidelines, Part II, Tag A-2406/C-2406 (revised 7/16/2010).

Since every patient who presents seeking emergency services is entitled to a screening examination, a hospital could violate the patient anti-dumping statute if it routinely keeps patients waiting so long that they leave without being seen, particularly if the hospital does not attempt to determine and document why individual patients are leaving, and reiterate to them that the hospital is prepared to provide a medical screening if they stay.[62]

Presently, U.S. emergency departments are overwhelmed with the number of patients seeking emergency care. According to a report by the Centers for Disease Control and Prevention (CDC) issued in April 2002, emergency department visits rose from 95 million in 1997 to 108 million in 2000—a jump of 14 percent—while at the same time the number of emergency departments fell from 4,005 to 3,934, a decrease of about 2 percent.[63] With more patients and fewer emergency departments, the waiting times have increased proportionally. The CDC reports that the number of emergency department visits rose to 119.2 million in 2006. See the CDC Web site (http://www.cdc.gov/nchs) for current information.

The closure and consolidation of hospitals around the country has reduced the number of emergency departments in suburban and urban areas and has even left some rural areas without facilities at all. Increasing numbers of patients use the emergency department as their primary source of care because of lack of insurance or difficulty obtaining appointments in a timely manner. The number of elderly relying on Medicare is also growing, but the number of physicians willing to take Medicare patients is shrinking because of low reimbursements.[64]

This situation leaves emergency physicians and hospitals between a rock and a hard place. The increasing number of patients visiting fewer emergency departments strains hospitals' resources. Patients are kept waiting not because of intentional disregard but rather an inability to see every patient in a timely manner. The hospital has no control over who leaves the waiting room without stationing a guard or other personnel. Yet if a patient leaves the emergency department for any reason, the hospital and the emergency physician face potential EMTALA violations.

Q 7:18 Discoverability: Are peer review files and quality assurance committee reports discoverable in an EMTALA lawsuit or investigation?

Yes. All peer review and quality assurance committee information is discoverable during an EMTALA lawsuit or investigation.

---

[62] OIG/HCFA [now CMS] Special Advisory Bulletin on the Patient Anti-Dumping Statute, 64 Fed. Reg. 61,356 (Nov. 10, 1999).

[63] "National Hospital Ambulatory Medical Care Survey: 2000 Emergency Department Summary," Centers for Disease Control and Prevention, available at http://www.cdc.gov/nchs/pressroom/02news/emergency.htm.

[64] Victoria Stagg Elliott, *Emergency Physicians Warn of a System Close to the Brink,* American Medical Association, AMNews (May 13, 2002).

Cautions: There is no protection from discovery for peer review or quality assurance committee minutes during an EMTALA investigation or lawsuit. EMTALA is a federal law and therefore federal laws provide the rules of discovery in regard to EMTALA. Usually, negligence medical malpractice cases are adjudicated in state courts and are therefore governed by state peer review privileges. Federal courts do not have to recognize state peer view protections.

The case of *Atteberry v. Longmont United Hospital*[65] illustrates this lack of protection. An ambulance brought Scott Atteberry to Longmont United Hospital's emergency department after Atteberry was involved in a motorcycle accident. He was in hypovolemic shock from internal hemorrhages. After three hours of treatment in the emergency department, Dr. Leonard, the trauma surgeon, arranged for transfer of Scott by helicopter to St. Anthony's Hospital in Denver. Scott suffered cardiac arrest and died in the helicopter en route to St. Anthony's Hospital. Ms. Atteberry, Scott's mother, filed a lawsuit against Longmont United Hospital asserting that her son should not have been transferred out of the emergency department and that the transfer to St. Anthony's Hospital violated EMTALA in that Dr. Leonard did not stabilize Scott before transfer and did not fill out any EMTALA transfer certification.

During the discovery phase of the suit, the plaintiff's lawyers sought the release of all credentialing files, peer review files, and quality assurance committee reports pertaining to Scott Atteberry's medical care. Longmont Hospital objected to the production requests, asserting that the requested information was confidential and protected from discovery by (1) the Health Care Quality Improvement Act, (2) the Colorado state peer review privilege, and (3) the Colorado state quality management privilege, among other doctrines.

The *Atteberry* court reasoned that neither the U.S. Supreme Court nor the Tenth Circuit Court of Appeals has recognized a medical peer review or medical risk management privilege under federal common law. The court also reasoned that Congress did not create an analogous federal privilege when it enacted the Health Care Quality Improvement Act. The court cited the language in another case, noting "Congress spoke loudly with its silence in not including a privilege against discovery of peer review materials in the Health Care Quality Improvement Act."[66] The court concluded, "Every legislative and controlling judicial indication is that federal policy, under these circumstances, opposed recognition of the quality management and peer review privileges enacted by the state of Colorado." The *Atteberry* court ruled that the requested materials were all discoverable and ordered Longmont United Hospital to produce all documents requested.

Discovery in the federal courts is governed by the Federal Rules of Civil Procedure. There are no quality committee confidentiality protections for this

---

[65] 221 F.R.D. 644 (D. Colo. June 15, 2004).

[66] Health Care Quality Improvement Act of 1986, § 402, 42 U.S.C.A. § 11101.

federal law. Federal courts do not have to abide by state peer review confidentiality laws. State laws restricting discovery for medical peer review and quality management committees are not applicable in medical malpractice cases heard in federal courts. Even during the investigation phase, when CMS presents to the hospital for an EMTALA complaint, CMS is entitled to view minutes from quality assurance committees. Hospitals and physicians would be wise to practice caution in what they say and document in their quality assurance committees when they review EMTALA-type cases.

In the case of *Southard v. United Regional Health Care System*,[67] the plaintiff in an EMTALA lawsuit requested the discovery of records of patients other than the plaintiff for the past year in order to ascertain whether the plaintiff patient's treatment was uniform with that provided to other patients with similar clinical presentations. The district court for the Northern District of Texas noted that under EMTALA, a hospital must provide an appropriate medical screening measured by comparison to other patients presenting to the emergency department. Because the plaintiffs tied their discovery requests to symptoms presented, tests run, and diagnoses made on other patients for a one-year period immediately preceding the death involved in this case, the court concluded that the requests struck a fair balance among alternative extremes and were crucially relevant for the plaintiffs to make the appropriate comparison mandated under EMTALA. The court found that the documents requested by the plaintiff were relevant, indeed, crucial, for the plaintiff to make the appropriate comparison mandated under EMTALA. Therefore, the court concluded that the defendant's objections to the discovery were overruled.

Q 7:19 Hospital Response: How should a hospital respond to an EMTALA investigation?

When notified of an EMTALA investigation, the hospital should:

- Cooperate with the survey team. The clock is ticking on either the 23-day or 90-day termination track. There is no time to argue with the survey team or refuse to provide documents.

- Contact hospital counsel. Hospital counsel should be involved from the beginning to provide legal advice and support.

- Involve the hospital's corporate compliance officer and/or committee. Meeting EMTALA's requirements or rectifying violations is all part of the hospital's corporate compliance obligations.

- Read the Guidelines. The Guidelines outline what the surveyors are to look for.

- Start a file. Document all the charts reviewed by the surveyors, all the people interviewed, and all other actions taken by the survey team. Talk to the people interviewed to find out what was discussed.

---

[67] No. 7:06-CV-011-R (N.D. Tex. Aug. 14, 2007).

- Do not attempt to retaliate. Do not waste time trying to figure out who reported the alleged violation to CMS. At this point, there is nothing to be done about that, and any retaliatory action is going to be viewed very badly by CMS. Do not make the hospital's situation worse.

- Learn everything you can at the exit conference with the surveyors.

- Educate all parts of the hospital. Inform all involved physicians, staff, management, and the Board about EMTALA and the plan of correction being instituted by the hospital.

- Monitor to make sure corrective actions are working. CMS will specifically review monitoring actions taken based on the hospital's plan of correction when the re-survey is conducted.

- Fully inform the hospital's Board of Directors about the allegations, the investigation, and corrective action. The Board must approve the plan of correction or CMS will not accept it as complete and fully authorized.

- Finally, do not assume that the hospital is out of the woods. Even if the hospital is able to come to a satisfactory resolution with CMS, the OIG can investigate the matter and so can the Office for Civil Rights, if the surveyors reported that discriminatory actions were taken against patients based on financial status, race, color, nationality, handicap, or diagnosis.[68]

While the majority of hospitals manage to avert Medicare termination by CMS and civil monetary penalties by OIG, the ordeal of undergoing an EMTALA investigation is enormous. There is major expenditure of monies, staff time, and angst. Hospitals are well advised to do all they can to avoid an EMTALA investigation.

Administrative Penalties

Q 7:20   Penalties: What are the possible administrative penalties for violating EMTALA?

The possible penalties for violating EMTALA are:

- A hospital may be fined between $25,000 and $50,000 per violation ($25,000 limit for hospitals with fewer than 100 beds).

- A physician may be fined $50,000 per violation.

- A hospital may be terminated from its Medicare provider agreement.

- A physician may be excluded from Medicare and Medicaid programs.

- A patient who suffers personal injury from the violation may sue the hospital in civil court.

- A receiving facility, having suffered financial loss as a result of another hospital's violation of EMTALA, can bring suit to recover damages.

---

[68] See EMTALA and On-call Problems Workbook, Horty Springer Publications, 2006.

Cautions: CMS intensified its EMTALA investigations in the late 1990s. The OIG filed a report to Congress in 2002 which showed that during the first ten years of EMTALA, approximately $1.8 million in settlements and judgments was collected in total. However, beginning in 1998, with more aggressive enforcement, OIG imposed $1.83 million in fines in 54 cases, including four against physicians. Enforcement continued to increase for 1999 with approximately $2.7 million in judgments and settlements from 95 hospitals and 2 physicians. In 2000, total fines were $1.17 million in 54 cases, and five penalties were imposed on physicians, two of whom were emergency physicians.[69] The OIG collected over $1 million in fines annually from 1998 to 2000. Between 1997 and 2001, 13 physicians paid an average of $19,967 in fines.[70] Between 1997 and 1999, it has been estimated that 527 hospitals were determined by HHS to be noncompliant with EMTALA.[71] Between 1986 and 1996, six hospitals had their Medicare certifications revoked, four of which were later recertified.[72]

Each year the OIG publishes settlements resulting in monetary penalties. Some of the settlements are included in the OIG's Semiannual Report to Congress published in the spring and fall of each year.[73] The Semiannual Report usually contains only selected examples of settlements for patient dumping. However, the OIG website[74] contains what appears to be a complete list of all civil penalty settlements by year.

The OIG website reports the following 2012 settlements through July 2012:

> 05-31-2012—Texas County Memorial Hospital (TCMH), Texas, agreed to pay $20,000 to resolve its liability for Civil Monetary Penalties under the patient dumping statute. The OIG alleged that TCMH failed to provide an adequate medical screening examination for a minor. Specifically, the minor presented to TCMH's emergency department (ED) and was accompanied by a family member. TCMH's registration clerk informed the family member that the minor should be treated by her family physician rather than be admitted to TCMH's ED. The minor left TCMH without receiving a medical screen.

> 03-07-2012—Northside Hospital (Northside), Florida, agreed to pay $38,000 to resolve its liability for Civil Monetary Penalties under the patient dumping statute. The OIG alleged that Northside failed to

---

[69] Office of Inspector General, Department of Health and Human Services, Semi-annual reports to Congress, available at http://www.oig.hhs.gov/publications/semiannual.asp.

[70] Tanya Albert, *Consumer Group Finds Hundreds of EMTALA Violations,* AMednews, American Medical Association (July 30, 2001).

[71] K. Blalock & S.M. Wolfe, *Questionable Hospitals*, Public Citizen Health Research Group Web site, available at http://www.citizen.org/questionablehospitals.

[72] Lauren Dame & Sidney M. Wolfe, Public Citizen Health Research Group, *Patient Dumping in Hospital Emergency Rooms* 3 (1996).

[73] Office of the Inspector General, Department of Health and Human Services, Semiannual Report to Congress, available at http://oig.hhs.gov/reports-and-publications/semiannual/index.asp (accessed Aug. 6, 2012).

[74] Office of the Inspector General, Department of Health and Human Services, *Patient Dumping*, available at http://www.oig.hhs.gov/fraud/enforcement/cmp/patient_dumping.asp (accessed Aug. 6, 2012).

provide an appropriate medical screening examination and stabilizing treatment to a patient with a history of mitral valve replacement. Specifically, the patient presented to Northside's emergency department (ED) by ambulance with flu symptoms and a high fever. A triage nurse instructed the patient to go home and to follow his primary care physician's orders. Two days later the patient presented again to Northside's ED and was admitted to their intensive care unit. On August 8, 2009, the patient died due to influenza A (H1N1).

02-10-2012—Fort Lauderdale Hospital, Inc. (FLH), Florida, agreed to pay $45,000 to resolve its liability for Civil Monetary Penalties under the patient dumping statute. The OIG alleged that FLH failed to provide an appropriate medical screening examination and stabilizing treatment to an autistic patient that presented to FLH's emergency department after physically attacking his mother. A clinical psychologist asked for the patient's insurance information. FLH did not accept the patient's insurance and the patient's mother was instructed to take the patient to another facility. The patient was seen at another facility and admitted for six days due to a diagnosis of depression.[75]

Q 7:21   Civil Monetary Penalties: How does the Office of Inspector General impose penalties for EMTALA violations?

EMTALA grants the Office of Inspector General the power to impose civil monetary penalties (CMPs) against noncompliant hospitals.

Cautions: The OIG may decide to assess CMPs for a violation of EMTALA even if the hospital comes into compliance, the hospital submits an acceptable plan of correction, and CMS decides not to terminate the hospital's Medicare provider agreement.

Guidelines for referring a case to OIG are found in the State Operations Manual, Complaint Procedures:

CMS refers appropriate cases to the OIG for investigation. Periodically, OIG will advise us of the criteria they would prefer CMS to use in referring cases. Examples of the types of case that may be referred include:

1. **Financial Screening**—The hospital and/or responsible physician refused to examine or treat a person based on the person's insurance status or inability to pay a fee. The financial basis for the decision must be clearly supported by evidence in the file, e.g., documented policy, interview reports.

2. **Patient with Trauma or Acute Emergency Condition**—The hospital and/or responsible physician (including an on-call physician who failed to come to the hospital) failed to screen, stabilize, or appropriately transfer (or, in the case of a hospital with specialized capabilities or facilities, refused to accept an appropriate transfer

---

[75] Office of the Inspector General, Department of Health and Human Services, *Patient Dumping*, available at http://www.oig.hhs.gov/fraud/enforcement/cmp/patient_dumping.asp (accessed Aug. 6, 2012).

of) a person with trauma, e.g., a severe head injury, or other acute emergency condition, e.g., heart attack or stroke, requiring immediate and substantial medical intervention.

3. **High Risk Event (such as Birth) Occurs Prior to Arrival at Another Hospital**—The hospital and/or responsible physician discharged or refused to screen/treat a person who gave birth (or is subject to another high risk medical event) prior to arriving at another hospital (especially if transport is by private vehicle).

4. **Death or Serious Harm Results from Dump**—The evidence in the file (including the QIO Review) demonstrates that the dumping violation caused serious medical harm or death to the victim of the violation.

5. **Egregious Violation Prioritized by CMS**—CMS concludes that a CMP is appropriate because of the seriousness of the violation (the person must have had an emergency medical condition) and other relevant factors, e.g., long history of noncompliance, hospital policy resulting in violations, pattern of serious violations, knowing and willful violation. This category is for those cases that CMS determines are very serious and merit a CMP but do not fit within other categories identified by OIG.[76]

The OIG operates within the same agency as CMS but is independent and operates separately from CMS. The OIG looks to see whether a violation has occurred on legal standards rather than CMS's quality enforcement standards. After the QIO reports its views on the medical judgment and treatment provided, the OIG may either close the case or decide whether monetary penalties are applicable. The OIG must analyze the QIO report and any other information available for evidence of aggravating and mitigating circumstances, applicable regulations, and EMTALA case law. Most of the cases in which a hospital ends up paying a CMP are voluntarily settled by the OIG and the hospital or physician. The settlement agreement typically includes a "No Admission of Liability" clause stating that "[t]his Agreement shall not be construed as an admission of liability or wrongdoing on the part of Respondent."[77] The OIG may impose a penalty for EMTALA violations against:

1. any participating hospital with an emergency department that

   a. knowingly[78] violates the statute on or after August 1, 1986; or

---

[76] U.S. Dep't HHS, CMS, State Operations Manual, Chapter 5, Complaint Procedures, Sec. 5480.2 (Rev. 50, 07/10/09).

[77] Lauren A. Dame, *The Emergency Medical Treatment and Active Labor Act: The Anomalous Right to Health Care*, 8 Health Matrix 3, 15-16 (Winter 1998).

[78] "The use of the word ['knowingly'] in an indictment is equivalent to an averment that the defendant knew what he was about to do, and, with such knowledge, proceeded to do the act charged." *Black's Law Dictionary* 872 (6th ed. 1990). Initially, hospitals could violate EMTALA by "knowingly" violating the statute. This was changed in 1991 to "negligently."

    b. negligently[79] violates the statute on or after May 1, 1991[80]

2. any responsible physician who:

    a. knowingly violates the statute on or after August 1, 1986;

    b. negligently violates the statute on or after May 1, 1991;

    c. signs a certification if the physician knew or should have known that the benefits of transfer to another facility did not outweigh the risks of such a transfer; or

    d. misrepresents an individual's condition or other information, including a hospital's EMTALA obligations.[81]

A California hospital was ordered by the OIG to pay a penalty of $50,000 for failing to provide required emergency care for a patient who died in the emergency department.[82] In a January 30, 2009, decision, ALJ Steven T. Kessel (Departmental Appeals Board, Civil Remedies Division) sustained the OIG's determination that St. Joseph's Medical Center in Stockton, California, violated EMTALA by failing to provide an MSE and stabilizing treatment for the patient. The OIG issued a press release to highlight the fact that St. Joseph's pursued litigation before an ALJ, which is a relatively unusual situation.

The patient was brought to St. Joseph's emergency department by members of his family. After about an hour and a half, the triage nurse checked the patient but was unable to take his temperature because his tongue was swollen. However, the triage nurse classified the patient as "routine" and sent the patient back to the waiting room. The patient's condition deteriorated, and an hour later, a family member notified the nurse that he might be having a heart attack. The emergency department charge nurse instructed a technician to put the patient on a cardiac monitor and to administer oxygen. However, the instructions were not followed. After another half hour, the patient demonstrated serious breathing problems. When a medical team arrived, the patient was in full cardiopulmonary arrest, and the team was unable to resuscitate the patient, who died an hour later.

In his decision, the ALJ stated that the failure to provide the patient with a timely screening examination was "shocking" in light of the facts that were known to St. Joseph's staff the night the patient died. He also noted that the events that took place show that St. Joseph's staff "botched horribly" the

---

[79] "A person acts negligently with respect to a material element of an offense when he should be aware of a substantial and unjustifiable risk that the material element exists or will result from his conduct. The risk must be of such a nature and degree that the actor's failure to perceive it, considering the nature and purpose of his conduct and the circumstances known to him, involves a gross deviation from the standard of care that a reasonable person would observe in the actor's situation." *Black's Law Dictionary* 1035 (6th ed. 1990). In 1990, Congress changed the word describing the way for hospitals to violate EMTALA from "knowingly" to "negligently" so that hospitals cannot plead innocence due to ignorance of EMTALA's requirements.

[80] Pub. L. No. 101-508, § 4008(b)(1) (1990), 42 U.S.C. § 1395dd(d)(1)(A).

[81] 42 U.S.C. § 1395dd(d)(B).

[82] St. Joseph's Med. Ctr. v. OIG, Departmental Appeals Bd., Civil Remedies Div., Dec. No. CR1895, 1/30/09.

care they gave to the patient. "This case demonstrates that OIG will impose the maximum civil monetary penalty for egregious violations of the requirements of EMTALA," HHS OIG Daniel R. Levinson said.

The ALJ was not persuaded by St. Joseph's argument that EMTALA is not a federal malpractice statute that makes hospitals liable for all negligence committed in emergency rooms. The ALJ determined that the evidence supported a conclusion that the hospital's staff grossly neglected the patient's needs and failed to provide him with a screening examination even after being told that the patient was having difficulty breathing.

Judge Kessel wrote, "EMTALA does not excuse a hospital for failing to perform a screening examination where that failure is the consequence of the hospital's staff's gross negligence. EMTALA is unequivocal. A hospital must provide a screening examination to every individual who comes to its emergency department requesting treatment. There is no 'negligence' exception to the law." He determined that the evidence proved that St. Joseph's manifested a high level of culpability for its neglect of the patient and also found additional evidence that underscored both the hospital's culpability and the seriousness of its EMTALA violation. The ALJ also found that the person performing triage on the patient was not qualified, under St. Joseph's own criteria, to perform triage. "This may have been the first instance of an EMTALA violation by [St. Joseph's]," the ALJ concluded. "But, if so, it is so egregious as to merit a maximum civil money penalty in and of itself."[83]

Q 7:22   Civil Monetary Penalties: What penalties may the Office of Inspector General impose?

For an EMTALA violation, the Act allows:

(1) Civil Monetary Penalties.

A participating hospital that negligently violates a requirement of this section is subject to a civil money penalty of not more than $50,000 (or not more than $25,000 in the case of a hospital with less than 100 beds) for each such violation. The provisions of section 1320a-7a of this title (other than subsections (a) and (b) shall apply to a civil money penalty under this subparagraph in the same manner as such provisions apply with respect to a penalty or proceeding under section 1320a-7a (a) of this title.

(B) Subject to subparagraph (C), any physician who is responsible for the examination, treatment, or transfer of an individual in a participating hospital, including a physician on-call for the care of such an individual, and who negligently violates a requirement of this section, including a physician who—

(i) signs a certification under subsection (c)(1)(A) of this section that the medical benefits reasonably to be expected from a transfer to

---

[83] *St. Joseph's Med. Ctr.*, Dec. No. CR1895 (Jan. 30, 2009).

> another facility outweigh the risks associated with the transfer, if
> the physician knew or should have known that the benefits did not
> outweigh the risks, or
>
> (ii) misrepresents an individual's condition or other information,
> including a hospital's obligations under this section,
>
> is subject to a civil money penalty of not more than $50,000 for each
> such violation and, if the violation is (2) gross and flagrant or is
> repeated, to exclusion from participation in this subchapter and State
> health care programs. The provisions of section 1128A (other than the
> first and second sentences of subsection (a) and subsection (b)) shall
> apply to a civil money penalty and exclusion under this subparagraph in
> the same manner as such provisions apply with respect to a penalty,
> exclusion, or proceeding under section 1128A(a).[84]

Although EMTALA grants the OIG the power to impose fines, the OIG also has the discretion not to fine providers. The amount of OIG fines has increased. In fiscal year 1997, the OIG fined 14 hospitals a total of $500,000. By the end of fiscal year 2000, the OIG fined 48 hospitals $1.2 million. Still, the number of EMTALA cases in which the OIG imposes a civil monetary penalty represents a small fraction of the total number of confirmed violations. Between January 1, 1995, and March 20, 2001, the OIG declined to impose a civil monetary penalty in 61 percent of cases forwarded to the office by CMS.[85]

The OIG must follow a specific procedure to obtain civil monetary damages. First, the OIG initiates the case by issuing a demand letter describing the sanction sought.[86] The respondent hospital or physician has the right to request a hearing before an ALJ within HHS.[87] In such a hearing, the respondent may present evidence and the ALJ issues a written decision. The ALJ decision may be appealed both administratively and in federal court.[88]

The OIG has discretion to decide whether to assess CMPs, and OIG officials state that their major concern is encouraging future compliance with EMTALA and deterring future violations. When the OIG receives a case from CMS, it first determines whether there is a violation of the EMTALA statute; it declines cases that do not involve specific EMTALA statutory violations. To make this decision, the OIG relies on the state survey report, the QIO review, and information collected by CMS. When a case involves a violation of the EMTALA statute, the OIG can decide either to pursue CMPs or exercise prosecutorial discretion and not impose a fine. In making this decision and in determining the amount of a fine, the OIG considers several factors, including the seriousness of the patient's condition, the nature of the violation, the culpability of the hospital or physician,

---

[84] 42 U.S.C. § 1395dd(d).

[85] *Small Share of Patient Dumping Nets Fines: Mitigating Factors Get Hospitals Off Hook*, Health Care Pol'y, at 1502 (Oct. 2, 2001).

[86] U.S. Dep't HHS, Office of Inspector General, Background on Civil Monetary Penalties, available at http://oig.hhs.gov/fraud/enforcement/cmp/index.asp.

[87] 42 C.F.R. § 1005.2(a).

[88] DHHS Office of Inspector General, Background on Civil Monetary Penalties, available at http://oig.hhs.gov/fraud/enforcement/cmp/index.asp.

and the effect of the penalty on the hospital's ability to provide care. For example, if a hospital emergency department was aware that it had a problem with on-call coverage and did not attempt to resolve the coverage shortage, OIG would consider the hospital culpable. If, however, an on-call physician refused to come in despite being told by the hospital of his or her obligation, OIG would consider the hospital's culpability to be far smaller.[89]

The number of EMTALA cases in which the OIG imposes a civil monetary penalty represents a small fraction of the total number of confirmed violations.[90] From January 1, 1995, through March 30, 2001, the OIG processed a total of 605 EMTALA violation cases; 237 were settled and 368 were declined. Overall, the OIG has declined about 61 percent of the violation cases forwarded by CMS. The OIG states that it would not be accurate to conclude from the fact that the OIG decided not to assess fines in some cases that CMS had erred in its conclusion that a violation had occurred. As a prosecutor's office, the OIG states that it always considers a range of issues in deciding whether an additional enforcement action is warranted. Some of the major factors that may influence its decision include the seriousness of the violation, CMS enforcement activity that has already occurred, additional information discovered during the 60-day QIO review or brought to the OIG's attention by the hospital (whether or not the hospital has been privately sued for its actions[91]), and even previous "instances" where a hospital may have been investigated for EMTALA violation but was not cited.[92] It is important to note that several violations may occur within the treatment of a single patient or other violations may be found during the investigation, so the final penalty may accumulate up to several hundred thousand dollars for a single patient incident.

Once the OIG decides to pursue a CMP, it tries to negotiate a settlement amount with the hospital. If a settlement cannot be reached, the OIG initiates the administrative process to collect the CMP amount it considers appropriate. If the hospital appeals the OIG action, the case is resolved at an administrative hearing. However, this rarely occurs; there have been fewer than ten administrative hearings. From 1995 through 2000, the OIG collected more than $5.6 million in fines from 189 hospitals and 19 physicians. The money collected from CMPs is deposited in the Medicare trust fund. Between 1997 and 1998 there was a dramatic increase in the number of cases settled and the amount of fines collected. From 1995 to 1997, the OIG settled an average of about 16 cases per year and collected about $997,000 total in fines. From 1998 to 2000, it settled an average of 55 cases per year and collected about $4.7 million in fines. According to the OIG, these increases reflected additional OIG staffing that resulted in the

---

[89] GAO Report (June 2001).

[90] *Small Share of Patient Dumping Nets Fines: Mitigating Factors Get Hospitals Off Hook,* Health Care Pol'y, at 1502 (Oct. 2, 2001).

[91] GAO Report (June 2001).

[92] 67 Fed. Reg. 11,928 (2002) 42 C.F.R. § 1003.106.

elimination of a backlog of cases rather than a surge in confirmed EMTALA violations.[93]

The OIG has the authority to assess CMPs against physicians, and it examines the activities of the individual physician involved in every case forwarded by CMS. The OIG pursues a case against a physician only if it considers the physician largely responsible for the violation. Overall, the OIG has sought civil monetary penalties from 28 physicians and collected $412,500; it generally does not pursue a physician unless clearly culpable behavior is involved, such as an on-call physician refusing to come to the hospital to treat a patient when asked by the hospital.[94]

Q 7:23 Medicare Termination: What are the circumstances under which CMS may terminate a hospital's Medicare agreement?

The Code of Federal Regulations states:

> *Termination of provider agreement.* If a hospital fails to meet the requirements of paragraph (a) through (f) of this section, CMS may terminate the provider agreement in accordance with § 489.53.[95]

CMS may terminate the Medicare provider agreement of any hospital that:

1. Violates the MSE, stabilization and treatment, or transfer requirements of the Act;
2. Has specialized capabilities and refuses to accept an appropriate transfer;
3. Fails to post signs conspicuously in the hospital outlining the hospital's responsibilities and individual's rights under the Act;
4. Fails to maintain medical and other records related to transferred individuals for a period of five years;
5. Fails to maintain a list of on-call physicians;
6. Fails to keep a central log on each individual who seeks treatment in the emergency department;
7. Fails to report that it may have received an individual transferred by another hospital in violation of the Act.[96]

Essentially, CMS can terminate a hospital's Medicare provider agreement for any violation of EMTALA. Whether the EMTALA violation is major or minor, CMS has only one remedy available to it—Medicare termination.

---

[93] GAO Report (June 2001).

[94] GAO Report (June 2001).

[95] 42 C.F.R. § 489.24(g).

[96] 42 C.F.R. § 489.53(b)(1) and (2).

Q 7:24   Medicare Termination Process: What is the process by which CMS terminates a hospital's Medicare provider agreement?

The State Operations Manual Complaints Procedure instructs the RO of procedures for termination process:

> In cases where the RO determined that an immediate jeopardy existed, after a 5-day QIO advisory review has been completed, the RO follows the termination procedures in § 3010. The processing timeframes are the maximum allowed. The termination procedures are not postponed or stopped unless evidence of correction of the deficiencies or proof that the violation did not exist is provided by the hospital to the RO. The RO forwards the supporting documents to the QIO (for a 60 day QIO review) in order to provide a medical opinion on the case. The RO refers the case to the OIG that has the responsibility for assessment of CMPs against the hospital and/or physician and physician exclusion provisions for violations of 42 CFR 489.24. The case is also referred to the Office for Civil Rights (OCR) because OCR may take action under the Hill-Burton Subpart G Community Services regulations at 42 CFR 124.603(b)(1).

> The termination track starts on the date that the RO makes the determination of noncompliance with 42 CFR 489.24. It is the date of the preliminary determination letter. The letter is forwarded to the hospital by the fastest method available (fax, e-mail or telephone). In addition, a written letter follows up by mail. The preliminary determination letter informs the hospital of:

> - The RO's findings based on the investigation and the results of medical review;

> - The projected termination date (the 23rd calendar day from the date of the preliminary determination letter);

> - The date on which the RO issues a Notice of Termination Letter and notifies the public (at least two calendar days, but no more than four calendar days prior to the termination date); and

> - That the hospital may avoid the termination action and notice to the public by either providing acceptable POCs (Plan of Correction) for the deficiencies or by successfully showing that the deficiencies did not exist. In either case, the necessary information must be furnished to the CMS RO in time for the SA to verify the corrections before the projected termination date.

> If, during the resurvey, the SA finds that the provider had implemented systems and processes to ensure that the likelihood of further violation is remote and there is adequate evidence that the provider is in compliance with the requirements, the termination action is rescinded and the provider is put back in compliance.

> If during the resurvey, the SA finds that the provider has not adequately implemented systems and processes to ensure compliance, the RO gives the hospital an additional 67 days or a total of 90 days (23 plus 67) to achieve compliance.

> This allows the hospital time to prove that the corrective action is good for the long-term (i.e., the corrective action is adequate to ensure that no

further violations will occur). The RO directs the SA to conduct a second survey by the 60th calendar day. On the resurvey, the surveyor(s) reviews patients' emergency department (ED) records and other relevant documents for the period since the last survey to assess continued compliance. If the hospital fails to achieve compliance, it is terminated from the Medicare program. The RO sends the complainant a letter reporting the final results of the investigation.

If the termination takes place and the hospital desires to become re-certified as a Medicare provider, the hospital must provide reasonable assurance that compliance will be maintained. The procedures at § 2016 are followed.[97]

The authority to terminate a Medicare provider agreement has been delegated from the HHS through the CMS administrator to the CMS ROs. CMS designed the termination authority under EMTALA so that prompt action may be taken to protect the public from any potential harm. Termination proceedings do not require QIO review.

CMS has the option of enforcing a 90-day termination track or a 23-day fast-track termination. When CMS determines that a violation poses an immediate and serious threat to patient health and safety, a hospital is placed on a 23-day fast-track termination schedule.[98] The determination of whether a violation poses an immediate and serious threat to the public is made entirely at the discretion of the CMS RO. When CMS determines that no immediate threat to public safety exists, the RO initiates a 90-day termination schedule.[99]

Documentation errors typically receive 90-day notices, whereas those relating to medical screening, stabilization, on-call response, and transfer generally receive 23-day notices. When substantial corrections have been made before the CMS visit, citations may not be issued at all, or the hospital may receive a 90-day notice.

A hospital may avoid termination of its Medicare provider agreement by demonstrating to CMS's satisfaction that it has in place effective policies and procedures to prevent a recurrence. Although this process is generically referred to as a "Plan of Correction," the proper CMS term is a "credible allegation of compliance." The name difference is significant. Under plans of correction situations for most hospitals, the plan promises future actions to address the issue. In an EMTALA situation, the plan details the corrections that have been made and future plans to ensure that violations do not occur in the future.

The OIG remains free to seek CMPs against the hospital and/or physician for the violation of EMTALA.

Medicare termination is such a harsh penalty that CMS has been hesitant to apply it arbitrarily and works to help ensure that the institution makes the

---

[97] U.S. Dep't HHS, CMS, State Operations Manual, Chapter 5, Complaint Procedures, Sec. 5470.1 (Rev.50, 07/10/09).

[98] 42 C.F.R. § 489.53(c)(2)(ii).

[99] 42 C.F.R. § 489.53(c)(1).

corrections necessary to remain in the program. Occasionally, hospitals remain reticent on compliance, and the situation proceeds to termination.

Q 7:25   Immediate and Serious Threat: What constitutes an "immediate and serious threat to patient health and safety"?

CMS's 1998 revised State Operations Manual describes "immediate and serious threat" as a situation that prevents individuals from getting MSEs and/or a lack of treatment that makes use of both the capacity and capability of the hospital's full resources, as guaranteed under EMTALA. Illustrations of such situations include:

- failure to provide appropriate medical screening or stabilizing treatment;
- failure of an on-call physician to respond appropriately;
- improper transfer; and
- evidence of a denial of MSEs and/or treatment to persons with EMCs as a direct result of requesting prior authorization from a managed care organization before medical assessment of the patient's condition.[100]

Likewise, the manual provides examples of noncompliance that usually do not pose an immediate and serious threat, including:

- a transfer that was appropriate, but not signed or dated by the physicians;
- an appropriate, functioning central log that on one particular day was not fully completed; or
- a missing written hospital policy that is nonetheless being implemented.[101]

Violations that pose an immediate and serious threat to patients are handled under the 23-day termination track. Violations that do not pose an immediate and serious threat to patients trigger the 90-day Medicare termination track.

Q 7:26   The 23-Day Termination Track: What is the 23-day Medicare provider termination track?

When the CMS RO determines that an immediate and serious threat to patient health or safety exists, termination procedures are completed within 23 calendar days.

The Code of Federal Regulations states:

    (c)   Notice of termination—

          (1)   Timing: Basic rule—Except as provided in paragraph (d)(2) of this section, CMS gives the provider notice of termination at least 15 days before the effective date of termination of the provider agreement.

---

[100] U.S. Dep't HHS, CMS, State Operations Manual, App. V, v-ix-B (1998).

[101] U.S. Dep't HHS, CMS, State Operations Manual, App. V, v-ix-B (1998).

(2)   Timing exceptions: Immediate jeopardy situations—(i) Hospital with emergency department. If CMS finds that a hospital with an emergency department is in violation of Sec. 489.24, paragraphs (a) through (e), and CMS determines that the violation poses immediate jeopardy to the health or safety of individuals who present themselves to the hospital for emergency services, CMS—

     (a)   Gives the hospital a preliminary notice indicating that its provider agreement will be terminated in 23 days if it does not correct the identified deficiencies or refute the finding; and

     (b)   Gives a final notice of termination, and concurrent notice to the public, at least 2, but not more than 4, days before the effective date of termination of the provider agreement.[102]

Cautions: The 23-day termination track proceeds as follows:

- Day 1: This is the date on which the RO makes the determination of an EMTALA violation that poses an immediate and serious threat to patient health and safety. A preliminary determination letter is immediately sent to the hospital. The letter reviews the findings of the investigation, the projected termination date (the 23d day from the date of the preliminary determination letter), the date on which the RO will issue a Notice of Termination letter and notify the public (at least two days, but no more than four days before the termination date), and notification that the hospital may avoid the termination action and notice to the public either by providing credible evidence of correction of the deficiencies or by successfully showing that the deficiencies did not exist. The plan of correction generally must be submitted no more than 14 days after notification to allow CMS review and a return inspection visit to validate the corrective actions have been achieved.

- Day 21: A public notice is published. This public notice may be made through a newspaper notice or a press release to the radio and television stations serving the area.

- Day 23: Termination from Medicare takes effect unless compliance has been achieved or the threat to public safety has been removed.

In addition to undergoing the CMS termination procedures, the case is referred to the OIG, which has the responsibility for imposing other civil penalties for violation of EMTALA. The case is also referred to the OCR, because OCR may take action under the Hill-Burton Subpart G Community Services regulations.[103] If the hospital alleges compliance or provides credible evidence that the immediate and serious threat to patient health and safety has been removed after initiation of termination action, the RO may switch from the 23-day termination procedures to the 90-day track to allow the hospital time to prove that the corrective action is good for the long term.

---

[102] 42 C.F.R. § 489.53(d).

[103] 42 C.F.R. § 124.603(b)(1).

Previously, any EMTALA violation triggered a 23-day notice to complete a corrective plan. At present, CMS recognizes that if the violation involves "medical care" versus "administrative" violations, then the 23-day track is appropriate. In contrast, alleged administrative violations (e.g., failure to post conspicuous signs about patients' rights under EMTALA or to maintain proper transfer records) do not need QIO review and often follow a 90-day track.

Q 7:27   The 90-Day Termination Track: What is the 90-day Medicare provider termination track?

When the CMS RO determines that a violation has occurred but there is no immediate and serious threat to patient health and safety, the 90-day termination track is initiated.

The 90-day termination track proceeds as follows:

- Day 1: This is the date on which the RO makes the determination of EMTALA violation. A preliminary determination letter and procedure schedule is sent to the offending hospital.
- Between Day 45 and Day 60: An unannounced return inspection can be anticipated.
- Day 70: The RO sends a Notice of Termination letter to the hospital and a copy to the state Medicaid agency if the hospital also participates in the Medicaid program.
- Day 75: The public notice is published. The RO notifies the public of the proposed termination action by the most expeditious means available. A newspaper notice or a press release to the radio and television stations serving the area are all appropriate options. The notice must be made 15 days prior to the effective date of termination.
- Day 90: Termination takes effect unless compliance has been achieved or the threat has been removed.

As with the 23-day track, reports are forwarded to the OIG and the OCR. Once a hospital submits an acceptable plan of correction, the termination process is discontinued.

Examples of noncompliance that usually do not pose an immediate jeopardy to public safety are:

1. A transfer that was appropriate but not signed or dated by the physician;
2. An appropriate functioning central log that on one particular day is not fully completed; and
3. A written hospital policy that is missing but is nonetheless being implemented.[104]

---

[104] U.S. Dep't HHS, CMS, State Operations Manual, App. V, Interpretive Guidelines for Responsibilities of Medicare Participating Hospitals in Emergency Cases, Part I, VIII, Task 7.B, Professional Medical Review (revised 5/29/2009).

The fact that the hospital has completed a plan of correction should not be interpreted to mean that the hospital admits violating the EMTALA requirements. However, the hospital is included on the log of facilities with EMTALA violations, with the notation that an acceptable plan of correction was received by CMS and termination action was stopped.[105]

Q 7:28   Physician Penalties: What EMTALA penalties may the Inspector General apply to physicians?

If a physician is deemed to have violated EMTALA, the Inspector General may:

1. Impose a civil money penalty of not more than $50,000 for each knowing violation occurring on or after December 22, 1987.[106]

2. Impose a civil money penalty of not more than $50,000 for each negligent violation occurring on or after May 1, 1991.[107]

3. Additionally, CMS may terminate a practitioner from the Medicare/Medicaid/state health programs if the physician's EMTALA violation is gross and flagrant or is repeated.[108]

The Act states:

> Subject to subparagraph (C), any physician who is responsible for the examination, treatment, or transfer of an individual in a participating hospital, including a physician on-call for the care of such an individual, and who negligently violates a requirement of this section, including a physician who—signs a certification under subsection (c)(1)(A) of this section that the medical benefits reasonably to be expected from a transfer to another facility outweigh the risks associated with the transfer, if the physician knew or should have known that the benefits did not outweigh the risks, or misrepresents an individual's condition or other information, including a hospital's obligations under this section, is subject to a civil money penalty of not more than $50,000 for each such violation and, if the violation is gross and flagrant or is repeated, to exclusion from participation in this subchapter and State health care programs. The provisions of section 1320a-7a of this title (other than the first and second sentences of subsection (a) and subsection (b)) shall apply to a civil money penalty and exclusion under this subparagraph in the same manner as such provisions apply with respect to a penalty, exclusion, or proceeding under section 1320a-7a(a) of this title.[109]

Cautions: Although infrequently, federal investigators will process EMTALA charges against physicians. In December 2011, a physician who

---

[105] U.S. Dep't HHS, CMS, State Operations Manual, Chapter 5, Complaint Procedures, Sec. 5460.4 (Rev. 50, 07/10/09).

[106] 42 C.F.R. § 1003.103(e)(2)(ii).

[107] 42 C.F.R. § 1003.103(e)(2)(iii).

[108] 42 U.S.C. § 1395dd(d)(1)(B).

[109] 42 U.S.C. § 1395dd(d)(1)(B).

refused to accept an appropriate transfer while on call agreed to pay $35,000 in CMPs. In February 2009, an on-call physician who failed to respond to a request to come to the emergency department to treat a patient who presented with an open leg fracture agreed to pay $35,000.[110] As these recent results suggest, the most commonly prosecuted violations involve the failure of on-call physicians to show when called for emergencies.

Q 7:29   On-Call Penalties: Do EMTALA penalties apply to on-call physicians?

Yes. The Act states:

> If, after an initial examination, a physician determines that the individual requires the services of a physician listed by the hospital on its list of on-call physicians (required to be maintained under section 1866(a)(1)(I)) and notifies the on-call physician and the on-call physician fails or refuses to appear within a reasonable period of time, and the physician orders the transfer of the individual because the physician determines that without the services of the on-call physician the benefits of transfer outweigh the risks of transfer, the physician authorizing the transfer shall not be subject to a penalty under subparagraph (B). However, the previous sentence shall not apply to the hospital or to the on-call physician who failed or refused to appear.[111]

Cautions: If the on-call physician refuses to provide services in a medical emergency, the emergency physician who then is forced to transfer the patient is relieved of liability and the on-call physician becomes liable for penalties. The on-call physician may also be added to a civil lawsuit against the hospital because on-call physicians can be deemed agents of the hospital.

In *McDougal v. Lafourche Hospital*,[112] a federal district court in Louisiana held that a hospital could recover damages from an independent staff physician who was directly responsible for an EMTALA violation.

In *McDougal*, Tonya McDougal, 34 weeks pregnant and with vaginal bleeding, went to Thibodaux Hospital by ambulance. Dr. Blanch ordered that McDougal be transferred to a state hospital. Although the fetus was alive at Thibodaux, the fetus was dead upon arrival at the state hospital. McDougal filed a suit against Thibodaux Hospital for violating EMTALA. Thibodaux Hospital filed a third-party complaint against Dr. Blanch and his insurer for contribution or indemnity, alleging that any liability that it suffered was the result of Dr.Blanch's actions or inaction. The Louisiana District Court rejected Dr. Blanch's motion to dismiss this third-party claim, reasoning:

---

[110] Office of Inspector General, *Patient Dumping,* http://www.oig.hhs.gov/fraud/enforcement/cmp/patient_dumping.asp.

[111] 42 U.S.C. § 1395dd(d)(1)(C).

[112] No. 92-2006 (E.D. La. May 24, 1993).

The Act does not provide for contribution or indemnity, but it explicitly states that it does "not preempt any State or local law requirement, except to the extent that the requirement directly conflicts with a requirement of this section." 42 U.S.C. § 1395dd(f). There is no direct conflict on this issue because the Act is silent. No one has cited any case law, and I have found none, that addresses this issue. Contrary to plaintiff's contention, I find that a claim for contribution or indemnity would likely increase compliance with the statute because the party actively at fault would be forced to bear the financial burden of any violation. Absent controlling precedent to the contrary, the hospital which is only "technically" at fault may assert its state law claim against the doctor who is "actively" at fault. Accordingly, the motion to dismiss the third-party claim is denied.[113]

Administrative Waivers and Appeals

Q 7:30   Waiver of Sanctions: Can HHS waive sanctions for EMTALA violations for national health emergencies?

Yes. The Public Health Security and Bioterrorism Preparedness and Response Act of 2002 authorizes the Secretary of HHS to waive sanctions for a violation of EMTALA where the violation is the result of an inappropriate transfer of an unstable patient if the transfer arises out of circumstances relating to a public health emergency (as defined by a Presidential declaration of emergency or disaster and a public health emergency declaration by the Secretary of HHS).[114]

Cautions: The waiver of sanctions by HHS is limited to inappropriate transfers of unstable patients during a public health emergency declaration. The law does not change the underlying EMTALA duties, nor does it extinguish the private right of action on the part of injured individuals. Furthermore, the law does not affect a hospital's MSE obligations.[115]

On August 22, 2007, CMS published the Hospital Inpatient Prospective Payment System (IPPS) final rule that implemented a change to the EMTALA regulations: "special responsibilities of Medicare hospitals in emergency cases under EMTALA." The IPPS rule, pursuant to amendments to Section 1135(b) of the Act, clarifies that the waiver of sanctions under Section 489.24(a)(2) includes those for:

- The inappropriate transfer of an individual who has not been stabilized. Pursuant to the Act the inappropriate transfer must arise out of the circumstances of the emergency; or

---

[113] *McDougal,* No. 92-2006, 1 (E.D. La. May 25, 1993).

[114] Pub. L. No. 107-188, 116 Stat. 627 (2002) at 143.

[115] Sara Rosenbaum, *Finding a Way Through the Hospital Door: The Role of EMTALA in Public Health Emergencies,* 31 J.L. Med. & Ethics, 590-601 (2003).

- The direction or relocation of an individual to receive an MSE at an alternate location pursuant to an appropriate state emergency preparedness plan or state pandemic preparedness plan. If a state emergency preparedness plan or pandemic preparedness plan has been activated in the emergency area, then the direction or relocation of individuals for MSEs is considered to be pursuant to a state plan.

Section 1135(g)(1) of the Act defines an "emergency area" as a geographical area in which, and an "emergency period" as the period during which, there exists:

- An emergency or disaster declared by the President pursuant to the National Emergencies Act or the Robert T. Stafford Disaster Relief and Emergency Assistance Act; *and*
- A public health emergency declared by the Secretary pursuant to Section 319 of the Public Health Service Act.

The waiver of sanctions applies only to hospitals:

- With dedicated emergency departments; and
- Located in an emergency area during an emergency period; and
- When the Secretary has exercised his or her waiver authority pursuant to Section 1135 of the Act.

In addition, the Act and the regulations at Section 489.24(a)(2) limit the duration of the waiver from EMTALA enforcement to 72 hours in most cases. The 72-hour period begins with the implementation of a hospital disaster protocol. In the case of an infectious pandemic disease, however, the waiver continues past the 72 hours and remains in effect until termination of the declaration of a public health emergency as described in Section 1135(e)(1)(B) of the Act.

When all the above conditions exist, then the RO may issue an advisory notice that hospitals with dedicated emergency departments in the emergency area will not, during the emergency period, be subject to EMTALA sanctions for:

- Redirecting individuals seeking an MSE when a state emergency preparedness plan or a pandemic preparedness plan has been activated in the emergency area; or
- Inappropriate transfers arising out of the circumstances of the emergency.

The RO notice will also indicate that the waiver of sanctions will be for the 72-hour period starting with each hospital's activation of its hospital disaster protocol. However, the 72-hour period may not in any case start before the effective date of the Secretary's public health emergency declaration. In the case of an infectious pandemic disease, however, the RO notice will indicate that the waiver may continue past the 72-hour period and remain in effect until termination of the declaration of public health emergency as described in Section 1135(e)(1)(B) of the Act.

EMTALA complaints alleging violations by a hospital in an emergency area during an emergency period related to failure to provide an MSE or to an inappropriate transfer must first be reviewed by the RO to determine whether a waiver of sanctions was in effect. The review may require some preliminary investigation, usually by telephone. If the review indicates a waiver was in effect for that hospital at the time of the complaint, then the RO will not authorize the State Agency to conduct an EMTALA investigation of the complaint.[116]

Q 7:31   Appeals Process: What appeals rights does the hospital have?

Realistically, because of the severity of Medicare termination and time restraints of the 23-day or 90-day termination tracks, the hospital has a very limited ability to appeal an EMTALA violation.

Cautions: The hospital essentially has no realistic appeals process. Once CMS initiates either the 23- or 90-day termination process, the hospital has no pre-termination appeals rights under EMTALA. The hospital has only two choices: submit a plan of correction acceptable to CMS in the time provided or go to termination. Once terminated, the hospital may then appeal, but Medicare benefits are not paid to the hospital during any appeals process. The appeals process includes a hearing before an ALJ, then an appeal to the national appeals board, and from there a direct appeal to the U.S. Circuit Court of Appeals for the jurisdiction in which the hospital is located. The appeals process takes up to three years, and bankruptcy will generally close a hospital long before its appeals process is completed. There has been no determination of whether a Chapter 11 bankruptcy filing by a hospital would stay the termination of benefits. Negative publicity associated with the termination process is considered to be detrimental to a hospital.

Hospital Surveys

Q 7:32   The One-Third Rule: What will the surveyors look for to determine whether a hospital meets the one-third rule?

The State Operations Manual instructs surveyors:

> To determine if a hospital department is a dedicated emergency department because it meets the "one-third requirement" described above (i.e., the hospital, in the preceding year, had at least one-third of all of its visits for the treatment of EMCs on an urgent basis without requiring a previously scheduled appointment) the surveyor is to select a representative sample of patient visits that occurred the previous calendar year in the area of the hospital to be evaluated for status as a dedicated emergency department. This includes individuals who may present as

---

[116] U.S. Dep't HHS, CMS, State Operations Manual, App. V, Emergency Medical Treatment and Labor Act (EMTALA) Interpretive Guidelines, Part II, Tag A-2406/C-2406 (revised 7/16/2010).

unscheduled ambulatory patients to units (such as labor and delivery or psychiatric units of hospitals) where patients are routinely admitted for evaluation and treatment. The surveyors will review the facility log, appointment roster and other appropriate information to identify patients seen in the area or facility in question. Surveyors are to review 20–50 records of patients with diagnoses or presenting complaints, which may be associated with an emergency medical condition (e.g., cardiac, respiratory, pediatric patients (high fever, lethargic), loss of consciousness, etc.). Surveyors have the discretion (in consultation with the regional office) to expand the sample size as necessary in order to adequately investigate possible violations or patterns of violations. Do not allow the facility staff to select the sample. Review the selected cases to determine if patients had an emergency medical condition and received stabilizing treatment. If at least one-third of the sample cases reviewed were for the treatment of EMCs on an urgent basis without requiring a previously scheduled appointment, the area being evaluated is a dedicated emergency department, and therefore, the hospital has an EMTALA obligation. Hospitals that may meet this one-third criterion may be specialty hospitals (such as psychiatric hospitals), hospitals without "traditional" emergency departments, and urgent care centers. In addition, it is not relevant if the entity that meets the definition of a dedicated ED is not located on the campus of the main hospital.[117]

Further, the State Operations manual gives guidelines to determine whether a department meets the one-third criteria:

For each case, the surveyors should answer three questions.

1. Was the individual an outpatient? If not, what was his or her status (e.g., inpatient, visitor or other)?

2. Was the individual a walk-in (unscheduled appointment)?

3. Did the individual have an EMC, and receive stabilizing treatment?

(*Note*—an affirmative *yes* must be present for both parts of this question for the case to be counted toward fulfillment of the one-third criterion. If *no* is answered for any part of this question, the criterion was *not met*, and select no for the overall answer).

All questions must have an answer of yes to confirm that the case is included as part of the percentage (one-third) to determine if the hospital has a dedicated emergency department. If one-third of the total cases being reviewed receive answers of "yes" to the three questions above, then the hospital has an EMTALA obligation.[118]

Cautions: Hospitals need to be vigilant in deciding whether certain of their departments meet the definition of a dedicated emergency department for EMTALA applicability. A hospital may consider a department not to be a

---

[117] U.S. Dep't HHS, CMS, State Operations Manual, App. V, Interpretive Guidelines for Responsibilities of Medicare Participating Hospitals in Emergency Cases, Part 1, IV, Task 2 (revised 5/29/2009).

[118] U.S. Dep't HHS, CMS, State Operations Manual, App. V, Interpretive Guidelines for Responsibilities of Medicare Participating Hospitals in Emergency Cases, Part 1, IV, Task 2 (revised 5/29/2009).

dedicated emergency department because (1) it is not licensed as an emergency department; (2) the department does not hold itself out as a place for emergency care; and (3) more than two-thirds of its patients have scheduled appointments. Surveyors do not determine the one-third rule based on the entire patient visits for the year but rather on a review of 20 to 50 charts. In fact, the choice of which charts are reviewed is biased toward emergency care since the surveyors are instructed to pick only charts of patients with diagnoses or presenting complaints associated with EMCs. A department may have only 10 percent actual non-scheduled patient visits, but the surveyors may find that over one-third of the charts selected meet the requirement for the one-third rule. In addition, patient visit censuses vary significantly from year to year so that the hospital needs to keep a close track of how many patients present without appointments. This one-third rule presents confusion and added burdens in compliance for hospitals.

Q 7:33   Case Selection: How do surveyors select charts to review?

The State Operations Manual gives the following instructions:

> Even though a single occurrence is considered a violation a sample is done to identify additional violations and/or patterns of violations.
>
> A. **Sample Size.** Select 20-50 records to review in depth, using the selection criteria described below. The sample is not intended to be a statistically valid sample and the sample selection should be focused on potential problem areas. The sample size should be expanded as necessary in order to adequately investigate possible violations or patterns of violations.
>
> B. **Sample Selection.** The type of records sampled will vary based on the nature of the complaint and the types of patients requesting emergency services. Do not allow the facility staff to select the sample. Use the emergency department log and other appropriate information, such as patient charts, to identify:
>
> - Individuals transferred to other facilities;
> - Gaps, return cases, or nonsequential entries in the log;
> - Refusals of examination, treatment, or transfer;
> - Patients leaving against medical advice or left without being seen (LWBS); and
> - Patients returning to the emergency department within 48 hours.
>
> Sample selection requires that:
>
> 1. You identify the number of emergency cases seen per month for each of the 6 months preceding the survey. Place this information on Form CMS-1541B, "Responsibilities of Medicare Participating Hospitals in Emergency Cases Investigation Report," (Exhibit 137).
> 2. You identify the number of transfers of emergency patients to other acute care hospitals per month for each of the preceding 6 months. Review in-depth, transfers of patients where it appears that the

transferring hospital could have provided continuing medical care. Place this information on Form CMS-1541B.

3. You include the complaint case(s) in the sample, regardless of how long ago it occurred. Select other cases at the time of the complaint in order to identify patterns of hospital behavior and to help protect the identity of the patient.

4. If the complaint case did not involve an inappropriate transfer (e.g., the complaint was for failure to provide an adequate screening examination, or a hospital with specialized capabilities refused an appropriate transfer), you identify similar cases and review them.

5. If you identify additional violations, determine, if possible, whether there is a pattern related to:

- Diagnosis (e.g., labor, AIDs, psych);
- Race;
- Color;
- Type of health insurance (Medicaid, uninsured, under-insured, or managed care);
- Nationality; or
- Disability[119]

Civil Lawsuits

Q 7:34   Civil Liability: What is the civil liability for a hospital found in violation of EMTALA?

The Act states:

> Any individual who suffers personal harm as a direct result of a participating hospital's violation of a requirement of this section may, in a civil action against the participating hospital, obtain those damages available for personal injury under the law of the State in which the hospital is located, and such equitable relief as is appropriate.[120]

Cautions: In addition to the governmental monetary penalties and threat of Medicare termination enforced by OIG and CMS, a hospital found in violation of EMTALA is open to a civil lawsuit brought either by an individual against a hospital or by one hospital against another.[121] Even where CMS and OIG determine that there was no violation of EMTALA, individuals who believe that they were harmed by the hospital's actions may still bring an EMTALA lawsuit. While a federal agency's decision may be to exonerate a hospital's actions, it does not preclude a patient's lawsuit based on EMTALA.

---

[119] U.S. Dep't HHS, CMS, State Operations Manual, App. V, Interpretive Guidelines for Responsibilities of Medicare Participating Hospitals in Emergency Cases, Part 1, IV, Task 2 (revised 5/29/2009).

[120] 42 U.S.C. § 1395dd(d)(2)(A).

[121] 42 U.S.C. § 1395dd(d)(2)(A)-(B).

A patient who suffers personal harm as a direct result of the violation may file suit against the hospital for damages allowable to an individual plaintiff under the laws of the state in which the hospital is located.[122] A hospital (such as the receiving hospital) suffering a financial loss directly resulting from another hospital's violation of the Act may also sue the offending hospital for damages allowable under the law of the state in which the hospital is located.[123]

Hospital liability has greatly expanded under EMTALA. Under EMTALA, hospitals are directly, not vicariously, liable for physician actions. The hospital is now legally responsible for the negligent acts of its medical staff in the treatment, discharge, or transfer of all patients who present with a medical emergency. In the past, hospitals were relatively immune from the actions of medical staff because a plaintiff lawyer would have to prove apparent agency or medical malpractice to show hospital liability. The hospital's liability under EMTALA is not grounded on tort concepts: EMTALA plaintiffs' claims do not rest on any proof that the hospital was negligent but are predicated on the hospital's violation of the federal statute that makes hospitals strictly liable for any personal harm that directly (proximately) results from that violation.[124]

In an ordinary malpractice suit, the plaintiff must prove that the physician's breach of the standard of care proximately caused damages to the patient. In contrast, the plaintiff in an EMTALA lawsuit need only prove that the emergency department departed from its standard screening procedures and the patient suffered an injury as a consequence. If the plaintiff proves disparate treatment, then the hospital is strictly liable for any resulting damages.

Q 7:35 Jurisdiction: Which courts hold jurisdiction over EMTALA civil suits?

The federal courts hold jurisdiction over EMTALA claims (state courts generally hear malpractice claims). If plaintiffs elect to bring an EMTALA suit in state court, the defense can seek removal to federal court if it believes removal would be in its best interest.

Cautions: Although EMTALA does not specify whether an action under the Act is to be brought in the state or federal courts, the courts have determined that Congress intended to create concurrent jurisdiction. In addition, it has been held that courts with federal jurisdiction over EMTALA claims may exercise ancillary jurisdiction over pendent state medical malpractice claims arising out of the same nucleus of operative facts.

---

[122] 42 U.S.C. § 1395dd(d)(2)(A).

[123] 42 U.S.C. § 1395dd(d)(2)(B).

[124] Griffith v. Mt. Carmel Med. Ctr., 842 F. Supp. 1359 (D. Kan. 1994).

Because EMTALA is a federal statute, federal courts (as opposed to state courts) have subject matter jurisdiction[125] over EMTALA cases. In *Thornton v. Southwest Detroit Hospital*,[126] the Sixth Circuit[127] affirmed federal jurisdiction by interpreting the legislative history of EMTALA as clearly demonstrating Congress's intent for federal courts to have subject matter jurisdiction over actions brought pursuant to EMTALA. In *Jones v. Wake County Hospital System*[128] the defendants argued that a North Carolina District Court did not have jurisdiction to hear an EMTALA claim. The district court stated that federal district courts have subject matter jurisdiction in "all civil actions arising under the Constitution, laws, or treaties of the United States."[129] The U.S. Supreme Court has interpreted this language to mean that federal courts have jurisdiction in all cases where a well-pleaded complaint shows that "federal law creates the cause of action" or where the "plaintiff's right to relief necessarily depends on resolution of a substantial question of federal law."[130]

In *Bryant v. Riddle Memorial Hospital*[131] the court, after considering the legislative history and the overall purpose of EMTALA, determined that the Act provides for a private cause of action in federal court. The court noted that the Act expressly allows for civil enforcement of its provisions through a private cause of action in Section 1395dd(d)(3)(A), but that it does not mention in what forum a party can bring such action. The court then engaged in an extensive examination of the legislative history surrounding the enactment of the statute and finally concluded that Congress intended to allow a Section 1395dd action to be brought in federal court. In order to determine Congress's intent, the court considered various congressional committee reports, including a report by the House Committee on Ways and Means stating that "[a]ny persons or entity adversely and directly affected by a participating hospital's violation of these requirements may bring an action, in an appropriate state or Federal District Court, for damages to the person arising from the violation and for other relief as may be appropriate to remedy the violation or deter subsequent violations."[132] The court also noted that the Senate Judiciary Committee, after concurring with the findings of the House Ways and Means Committee, clarified the Act's enforcement provisions, stating in another report that "state courts will have concurrent jurisdiction to hear and decide actions brought under [Section 1395dd], and . . . the Act allows an aggrieved party to bring an action in federal or state court."[133] Finally, the court noted that the Judiciary Committee

---

[125] "Subject matter jurisdiction" is a term that "refers to a court's power to hear and determine cases of the general class or category to which the proceedings in question belong; the power to deal with the general subject involved in the action." *Black's Law Dictionary* 1425 (6th ed. 1990).

[126] 895 F.2d 1131 (6th Cir. 1990).

[127] The Sixth Circuit covers Michigan, Ohio, Kentucky, and Tennessee. 28 U.S.C. § 41.

[128] 786 F. Supp. 538 (E.D.N.C. 1991).

[129] 28 U.S.C. § 1331 (Supp. 1991).

[130] *Jones,* 786 F. Supp. 538, 542.

[131] 689 F. Supp 490 (E.D. Pa 1988).

[132] *Bryant,* 689 F. Supp. 490, 492.

[133] *Bryant,* 689 F. Supp. 490, 493.

proposed an amendment, which was subsequently defeated, that would have stricken the federal cause of action. The court concluded that it was "therefore clear that both the Senate and the House agreed to provide a federal cause of action and to instruct both state and federal courts to apply state law when determining damages."[134]

Federal courts offer certain advantages for plaintiffs' lawyers. Federal courts have a reputation for being more lenient to plaintiffs and are less congested, so cases go to trial sooner. Federal law has liberal "notice pleading" rules, grants wide latitude in admitting expert testimony, and gives broad subpoena power.[135]

Plaintiffs' lawyers may report an EMTALA violation to CMS for CMS to initiate an investigation. The plaintiffs' lawyers then obtain the details of the investigation under the Freedom of Information Act[136] and use the information in their lawsuit against the hospital. Injured patients save substantial time, money, and effort by allowing CMS to perform investigations for them. In addition, if CMS finds the hospital guilty of an EMTALA violation, the objective finding improves the chances of an early, reasonable settlement that serves the best interests of the claimant and ultimately the defendants. If CMS does not find an EMTALA violation, unnecessary or potentially frivolous pleadings are avoided.

Q 7:36 Civil Lawsuit: What elements must be proven in court to sustain an EMTALA civil suit?

To make a prima facie case[137] for damages under EMTALA, the plaintiff must prove the following:

First, the hospital is a participating (Medicare) hospital, covered by EMTALA, that operates an emergency department (or an equivalent treatment facility).

A civil action under EMTALA may be based on the "screening" provisions, the "stabilization" provisions, or both.[138]

Establishing a prima facie case in an action for violation of EMTALA's screening provisions generally requires proof that:

---

[134] *Bryant*, 689 F. Supp. 490, 493.

[135] Barry R. Furrow, *Indigent Patients: Dumping the Fiscally Impaired*, 21 J.L. Med. & Ethics 2 (Summer 1993).

[136] The Freedom of Information Act, 5 U.S.C. § 552. The Freedom of Information Act provides for making information held by federal agencies available to the public unless it comes within one of the specific categories of matters exempt from public disclosure.

[137] Prima facie: Latin for "at first sight." In law, a *prima facie* case consists of sufficient evidence in the type of case to get a plaintiff past a motion for directed verdict in a jury case or motion to dismiss in a nonjury case; it is the evidence necessary to require a defendant to proceed with his case. *Black's Law Dictionary* 825 (abridged 6th ed. 1991).

[138] 8 Causes of Action 2d 629 (2007).

1. The patient came to the defendant's emergency department and requested examination or treatment and

2. The defendant failed to provide an "appropriate medical screening," that is, the same screening that the hospital would have provided for any other patient with similar symptoms in similar circumstances.

Establishing a prima facie case in an action for violation of EMTALA's stabilization provisions generally requires proof that:

1. The patient was physically present in the hospital;

2. The defendant determined that the patient had an "emergency medical condition"; and

3. The defendant failed to "stabilize" the patient, that is, to provide treatment to assure, within reasonable medical probability, that no material deterioration of the patient's condition would be likely to occur or, in cases of pregnancy, that the patient would not be likely to deliver, in the course of transfer from the hospital.

The Act states under the section on Civil Enforcement:

> (A) Personal harm.—Any individual who suffers personal harm as a direct result of a participating hospital's violation of a requirement of this section may, in a civil action against the participating hospital, obtain those damages available for personal injury under the law of the State in which the hospital is located, and such equitable relief as is appropriate.[139]

Cautions: It must be emphasized that an EMTALA plaintiff need not prove negligence or malpractice, only that the hospital violated the statutory requirements of EMTALA and that this violation resulted in injury. The most important elements of proof for both parties frequently will involve the existence of any disparity between the medical screening provided in the plaintiff's case and the screening procedures usually followed by the defendant in similar cases, whether the defendant determined that the patient had an EMC, whether the defendant provided adequate treatment within its capability to stabilize the patient's condition, and whether the defendant complied with the statutory provisions for an appropriate transfer of an unstabilized patient.

In defense, the hospital needs to show that the patient was provided an "appropriate" MSE that was uniform to that provided any other patient presenting with similar complaints. In defense of the stabilization requirement, the hospital may show that:

1. The defendant did not determine that the patient had an EMC;

2. The patient's EMC was stabilized; and/or

3. The conditions for an unrestricted or appropriate transfer were satisfied, even if the patient had an EMC.

---

[139] 42 U.S.C. § 1395dd(d)(2)(A).

There is also no requirement that the hospital be first cited for an EMTALA violation by CMS. The plaintiff may bring his or her case whether or not there has been a CMS investigation and whether or not a citation was issued. Although the issuance of a citation is not conclusive in civil litigation, it typically is a strong predictor of the plaintiff's success in civil litigation.

First, a hospital needs to show that it provided an "appropriate" MSE. The majority of circuits have adopted the comparability test, which requires screening examinations to be uniform for all patients presenting with similar clinical pictures.

In the revised State Operations Manual, CMS states:

> The Medical Screening Examination must be the same Medical Screening Examination that the hospital would perform on any individual coming to the hospital's dedicated emergency department with those signs and symptoms, regardless of the individual's ability to pay for medical care. If a hospital applies in a nondiscriminatory manner (i.e., a different level of care must not exist based on payment status, race, national origin, etc.) a screening process that is reasonably calculated to determine whether an EMC exists, it has met its obligations under EMTALA. If the MSE is appropriate and does not reveal an EMC, the hospital has no further obligation under 42 CFR 489.24.[140]

In spite of the many difficulties in defining the uniformity of screening it appears that the majority of circuits and now CMS are adopting the comparability test as the underlying principle that EMTALA requires all hospitals to apply uniform screening procedures to all individuals coming to the emergency room. A hospital will have provided appropriate screening if it acts in the same manner as it would have for the usual paying patient. Only if there is a discrepancy in treatment, or a lack of uniformity in treatment, could EMTALA inappropriateness charges be successfully brought against the hospital. The minority of the circuits, including the First and Ninth Circuits, follow an objectively reasonable standard. This standard requires that a hospital provide its patients with a screening examination "reasonably calculated to identify critical medical conditions that may be afflicting symptomatic patients and provides that level of screening uniformly to all those who present substantially similar complaints." In contrast, the majority of the circuits, including the Sixth, Eighth, Tenth, Eleventh, and D.C. Circuits, follow a subjective standard. The subjective standard requires that a hospital treat each patient in a nondisparate uniform manner, within the individual capabilities of that hospital.[141] Mere de minimis deviations from a hospital's standard screening procedures, however, are insufficient to constitute an EMTALA violation. To be actionable under

---

[140] U.S. Dep't HHS, CMS, State Operations Manual, App. V, Emergency Medical Treatment and Labor Act (EMTALA) Interpretive Guidelines, Part II, Tag A-2406/C-2406 (revised 5/29/2009).

[141] Victoria K. Perez, *EMTALA: Protecting Patients First by Not Deferring to the Final Regulations*, 4 Seton Hall Cir. Rev. 149, p. 10 (2007).

EMTALA, the deviations from a hospital's standard screening must be substantial, amounting to a failure to perform essential elements of the standard screening.

Second, a hospital needs to show that it met the stabilization requirement of EMTALA before discharging or transferring the patient. The elements of a civil claim under EMTALA for failure to stabilize include that the hospital had actual knowledge that a patient was suffering from an "emergency medical condition"; that the hospital did not, within the limits of the staff and facilities available at the hospital, provide for necessary stabilizing treatment before transfer or discharge so that the transfer or discharge was not medically reasonable under the circumstances; and that the patient suffered personal harm as a direct result. EMTALA mandates stabilizing treatment only for diagnosed EMCs and only such treatment as can be provided within the capabilities of the staff and facilities available at the hospital. EMTALA thus imposes liability for a failure to stabilize a patient only if an EMC is actually discovered, rather than for negligent failure to discover and treat such a condition.

Third, a hospital needs to show that the transfer of a patient was appropriate. When a hospital needs to transfer an unstable patient because it does not have the capability to stabilize the patient, it must meet the requirements for an "appropriate transfer." The transfer requires a certification that the benefits of transfer outweigh the risks, arrangement for acceptance by the receiving hospital, and the provision of treatment, personnel, and equipment appropriate to the patient's medical needs to effect the transfer.

Q 7:37   Civil Suit Against the Physician: May the patient file an EMTALA civil suit against the treating physician?

No. EMTALA does not provide for legal actions by individuals against emergency physicians. The Act states that "[a]ny individual who suffers personal harm as a direct result of a participating hospital's violation of a requirement of this section may, in a civil action against the participating *hospital*."[142] The text of EMTALA is silent regarding a private right of action against physicians. The legislative history, however, clearly states the intent that there should be no private right of action against physicians:

> The Committee amendment makes it clear that the section authorizes only two types of actions for damages. The first of these could be brought by the individual patient who suffers harm as a direct result of a hospital's failure to appropriately screen and stabilize, or properly transfer the patient . . . (within the meaning of [the Act]) or a woman in active labor. It also clarifies that actions for damages may be brought only against the hospital which has violated the requirements of [the Act].[143]

---

[142] 42 U.S.C. § 1395dd(d)(2)(A).

[143] Lawrence Bluestone, *Straddling the Line of Medical Malpractice: Why There Should Be a Private Cause of Action Against Physicians Via EMTALA*, 28 Cardozo L. Rev. 2829 (2007).

Because EMTALA mentions only the participating hospital in its language, the courts interpret this absence of reference to physicians as an example of intent by Congress to excuse physicians from civil suits that arise from EMTALA. Individual plaintiffs do not have a cause of action against the treating emergency physician under EMTALA. The Committee on Ways and Means stated that private actions for damages could be brought only against the hospital.[144] In *Eberhardt v. City of Los Angeles*,[145] where the plaintiff sued the physician, alleging violation of EMTALA by discharging the patient in an unstable mental condition, the court held that the private right of action created by EMTALA applies only to hospitals and does not extend to individual physicians. In reaching this conclusion, the court pointed out that EMTALA contains a civil enforcement provision that authorizes the assessment of administrative monetary penalties against both hospitals and physicians who violate the statute. In contrast, the provision of EMTALA that establishes a private right of action[146] for civil damages on behalf of injured patients refers only to hospitals and does not mention physicians.

In the court's view, this statutory language reflected a clear intent to limit the private remedy to hospitals. If Congress had wanted physicians to be liable, then legislators would have added the wording into the statute. However, physicians should be aware that if a hospital suffers losses as a result of the physician's individual actions, the hospital can turn around and sue the emergency physician for recovery.

EMTALA actions against the hospital also often involve state malpractice claims against physicians and the hospital. When the plaintiff files suit in federal court, this results in state claims being tried in federal court before juries that have heard repeated emphasis on EMTALA legal obligations. Defenses based on "standard of care" arguments typically fail to overcome the clearly mandated standards of EMTALA.

Q 7:38 Civil Suit Against a Transferring Hospital: May a receiving hospital file an EMTALA civil suit against a transferring hospital for an inappropriate transfer?

Yes. EMTALA does allow a receiving hospital to recoup its financial losses from an inappropriate transfer by filing a civil suit against the transferring hospital.

The Act states:

> (B) Financial loss to other medical facility: Any medical facility that suffers a financial loss as a direct result of a participating hospital's violation of a requirement of this section may, in a civil action against

---

[144] H.R. Rep. No. 99-241, pt. 3, at 6-8 (1985).

[145] 62 F.3d 1253 (9th Cir. 1995).

[146] Right of action means "[t]he right to bring suit; a legal right to maintain an action, growing out of a given transaction or state of facts and based thereon. Right of action pertains to remedy and relief through judicial procedure." *Black's Law Dictionary* 1325 (6th ed. 1990).

the participating hospital, obtain those damages available for financial loss, under the law of the State in which the hospital is located, and such equitable relief as is appropriate.[147]

At the time of this writing, the author has been unable to find documentation showing that hospitals have pursued this legal avenue.

Q 7:39   Civil Suit by Heirs: May the heirs of a patient who dies sue the hospital under EMTALA?

Depending on the laws of the state, the heirs of a patient who dies of an alleged EMTALA violation may sue the hospital under EMTALA.

Cautions: Because patients can sue a hospital under the laws of the state in which the hospital is located, any state that allows heirs to sue for medical malpractice toward a deceased family member also allows suits under EMTALA.

In *Alvarez-Pumarejo v. Municipality of San Juan,*[148] Rosa Alvarez-Pumarejo and her daughters sued under EMTALA for damages resulting from the accidental injuries and death of her husband, Julio. The hospital argued that any claim under EMTALA is limited to the patient. However, the court ruled that EMTALA allows state law to govern whether the lawsuit transfers to the heirs of a patient. Because Puerto Rico's Civil Code allows a lawsuit to pass to the heirs of the injured person, a claim under EMTALA also passes on to the eligible heirs. On the other hand, if a state does not allow heirs to sue for a patient's injuries for negligent malpractice, then the same rule would apply to EMTALA claims.

Q 7:40   Statute of Limitations: What is the statute of limitations for EMTALA?

The Act states:

> No action may be brought under this paragraph more than two years after the date of the violation with respect to which the action is brought.[149]

This two-year statute of limitations has no exceptions. The two-year statute of limitations for bringing such actions, for example, is not tolled by a patient's minority.[150]

Cautions: Although state law notice of claim requirements may apply, EMTALA itself contains a two-year statute of limitations. In *HCA Health Services of Indiana, Inc. v. Gregory,*[151] an Indiana appeals court held that a

---

[147] 42 U.S.C. § 1395dd(d)(2)(B).

[148] 972 F. Supp. 86 (D.P.R. 1997).

[149] 42 U.S.C. § 1395dd(d)(2)(C).

[150] *Vogel,* 23 F.3d 78.

[151] 596 N.E.2d 974 (Ind. Ct. App. 1992).

patient had to file an EMTALA suit within EMTALA's two-year statute of limitations, regardless of whether the Indiana Department of Insurance first ruled on the claim as mandated by state law.

A hospital discharged an infant patient, who died shortly thereafter. The patient's mother filed a complaint with the Indiana Department of Insurance, alleging that the hospital violated EMTALA. She did this pursuant to the state's Medical Malpractice Act, which requires that patients submit medical malpractice claims to the Department and receive a decision before filing a complaint in either state or federal court. When the EMTALA statute of limitations on the patient's claim expired, the Department of Insurance still had not issued a decision on the mother's complaint. The appeals court dismissed the mother's claim, ruling that the EMTALA statute of limitations preempts state law procedure. The court noted that when state law interferes with or is contrary to federal law, federal law governs. The court concluded that the state-imposed waiting period that prohibits patients from filing suit does in fact conflict with EMTALA's statute of limitations. The court also found it significant that EMTALA clearly states that its provisions directly preempt conflicting state law. The state procedures apply, the court concluded.

Q 7:41 Punitive Damages: May punitive damages be assessed against a hospital that violates EMTALA?

Yes. Punitive damages may be assessed if the laws of the state where the hospital is located allow for such damages.

Cautions: EMTALA provides that an individual who suffers harm as a result of an EMTALA violation may obtain against the participating hospital those damages available for personal injury under the laws of the state in which the hospital is located.

In the case of *Maziarka v. St. Elizabeth Hospital*,[152] the court dismissed the plaintiff's request for punitive damages against a hospital under EMTALA, holding that a plaintiff can recover punitive damages under the Act, but only if the law in the state in which the hospital is located also provides that punitive damages are recoverable. In this case, the plaintiff alleged that the defendant hospital violated EMTALA by improperly transferring him. The hospital argued that his complaint was not a malpractice claim but rather one for a violation of a federal statute providing its own basis for relief. The court stated that it found no merit in this argument since Illinois law provided that punitive damages were not recoverable in healing art and legal malpractice cases.

---

[152] No. 88 C 6658 (N.D. Ill. Feb. 16, 1989).

Chapter 8

EMTALA and On-Call Physicians

Each hospital must maintain an on-call list of physicians on its medical staff in a manner that best meets the needs of the hospital's patients who are receiving services required under this section in accordance with the resources available to the hospital, including the availability of on-call physicians.

42 C.F.R. § 489.24(j)(1).

In the September 9, 2003, *Federal Register*, the Centers for Medicare & Medicaid Services (CMS) put forth its comments on the final rules concerning the on-call issue. The tremendous variations in hospital on-call resources and physician specialty situations across the country make it virtually impossible to specify exactly how hospitals and physicians must provide on-call services. This nebulous area of EMTALA's application to on-call coverage has evolved into a significant area of contention, confusion, and controversy. CMS, therefore, has extended flexible requirements so that hospitals are relatively free to provide the on-call services in a manner that they see fit as long as the process is reasonable. The State Operations Manual states:

> Section 1866(a)(1)(I)(iii) of the Act states, as a requirement for participation in the Medicare program, that hospitals must maintain a list of physicians who are on-call for duty after the initial examination to provide treatment necessary to stabilize an individual with an emergency medical condition. This on-call list requirement is a general provider agreement requirement for all hospitals and is thus technically an "EMTALA-related" requirement rather than a specific requirement of the EMTALA portion of the Act. When determining compliance with the on-call list requirement as part of an EMTALA survey it must be remembered that the on-call list requirement applies not only to hospitals with dedicated emergency departments, but also to hospitals subject to EMTALA requirements to accept appropriate transfers. (See discussion of § 489.24(f).) The on-call list clearly identifies and ensures

that the hospital's personnel is prospectively aware of which physicians, including specialists and subspecialists are available to provide stabilizing treatments for individuals with emergency medical conditions.[1]

CMS in 2008 deleted the old language "in a manner that best meets the needs of the hospital's patients" and replaced it with "in accordance with the resources available to the hospital."[2] CMS expects that all specialty services provided by a hospital should be represented in the on-call roster. Yet CMS sets no minimum call requirements and has already stated that it cannot mandate physicians to take calls. The highly variable situations involving on-call coverage for the nation's 3,000 hospitals due to geographic location (urban versus suburban versus rural), lack of availability of certain specialists such as neurosurgeons, the growing reluctance of physicians to assume on-call responsibilities, and physicians limiting their credentials make it very difficult for the government to provide comprehensive rules. This is a pressure cooker issue that will explode eventually.

The final rules remain more favorable to physicians than to hospitals. The problem remains that EMTALA mandates hospitals to provide and enforce on-call schedules but does not require physicians to provide such services. This creates significant tensions between hospitals and their medical staffs. In the present health care climate, physicians are more and more reluctant to provide such services, because of both the physical and financial burdens that on-call duties bring and the possibility of extending their malpractice liability. In addition, the high costs of malpractice premiums are forcing many specialists to decertify certain hospital privileges. The Institute of Medicine's June 2006 report titled "Hospital-Based Emergency Care: At the Breaking Point" describes components that have contributed to the on-call problem. These components include the supply of specialists, compensation, quality of life, professional liability costs, and EMTALA requirements. The Institute of Medicine recommends that Congress appoint a commission to examine and act on the factors responsible for the declining availability of emergency services before a crisis situation occurs.[3]

EMTALA creates a paradigm shift in how on-call physicians view their duty to provide care when called on in a medical emergency. Traditionally, staff physicians viewed their emergency department on-call duties as a favor to the hospital in return for the privilege of being a member of the medical staff. The on-call duties were usually flexible in regard to response time, method of providing care, and location of care. It was generally up to the on-call physician, in his or her capacity as a specialist, to decide how the care should be provided. Neither the hospital nor the government set any specific guidelines for how this

---

[1] U.S. Dep't HHS, Centers for Medicare & Medicaid Servs. (CMS), State Operations Manual, App. V, Emergency Medical Treatment and Labor Act (EMTALA) Interpretive Guidelines, Part II, Tag A-2404/C-2404 (revised 5/29/2009).

[2] 42 C.F.R. § 489.2(r)(2).

[3] *Hospital-Based Emergency Care: At the Breaking Point,* The Institute of Medicine, June 2006, available at http://www.IOM.edu.

care was to be provided. There were no legal risks to being on call, other than malpractice suits arising from direct patient care, as with any other patient. This system worked well in most hospitals for many years. However, the system changed dramatically after a few specialists chose to renege on their ethical responsibility to provide proper patient care while on call, leading to the creation of EMTALA.

Congress enacted EMTALA in 1985 primarily in response to denial-of-care incidents for patients in emergency situations, a number of which involved on-call physicians who refused to provide care. The case that finally drew national and Congressional attention to the issue involved an on-call specialist.

On January 28, 1985, paramedics brought Eugene Barnes, a 32-year-old male, to Brookside Hospital's emergency department with a penetrating stab wound to the scalp. The emergency physician called the on-call neurosurgeon for help, but the neurosurgeon refused to come to the hospital. The emergency physician had to call three other hospitals: Contra Costa County Hospital, Alameda County's Highland General Hospital, and finally San Francisco General Hospital, which agreed to accept Barnes. Barnes was transferred four hours after his arrival at Brookside. San Francisco General immediately operated on Barnes, but he died three days later.[4]

The case ignited a blitz of nationwide media coverage. Local television stations, as well as Dan Rather on the "CBS Nightly News," broadcast the story to the public. Newspapers and magazines eagerly pursued the story and wrote extensive exposés involving other cases of emergency care denial, suggesting that this type of patient care denial was widespread. The practice of denying patient care in emergency departments eventually gained the moniker of "patient dumping." Multiple egregious anecdotes describing patient dumping offended the national conscience. An indignant Congress responded by introducing the EMTALA legislation. President Reagan signed the legislation into law on April 7, 1986, as part of the Comprehensive Omnibus Budget Reconciliation Act of 1986.[5]

Congress originally enacted EMTALA to target hospitals and emergency departments rather than on-call physicians. However, it became apparent that unstable transfers from the emergency department were often necessitated by the refusal of on-call physicians to provide care. The infamous 1986 case of *Burditt v. United States Department of Health and Human Services*[6] occurred when the on-call obstetrician, Dr. Burditt, refused to provide care for a hypertensive patient who was in labor. Dr. Burditt ultimately had to pay a fine of $20,000 levied by the Department of Health and Human Services (HHS), which was affirmed by the Fifth Circuit.

---

[4] Equal Access to Health Care: Patient Dumping: Subcommittee on Human Resources and Intergovernmental Relations to the House Comm. on Government Operations, H.R. Rep. No. 531, 100th Cong., 2d Sess., at 6-7 (1988).

[5] The Consolidated Omnibus Budget Reconciliation Act of 1985, Pub. L. No. 99-272, § 9121, 100 Stat. 82 (1986).

[6] Burditt v. U.S. Dep't HHS., 934 F.2d 1362, 1372 (5th Cir. 1991).

In Detroit, an emergency physician treated a 32-year-old female who sustained severe head injuries after being beaten over the head with a baseball bat during a robbery. The emergency physician tried to transfer the patient because he had no neurosurgeon on staff. Fourteen different hospitals in southeastern Michigan refused the transfer because the patient apparently had no insurance. The patient was finally admitted to the original hospital and died.[7]

In response to these and other cases, Congress amended EMTALA in 1989 to require that hospitals provide on-call coverage and that tertiary hospitals with specialist capabilities accept transfers if they have the capacity. With this amendment, on-call physicians joined hospitals and emergency departments as targets for EMTALA citations. In no other area of medicine has EMTALA created a greater and more confusing impact than in the law involving on-call physicians. Every physician who provides on-call services to a hospital must become familiar with EMTALA's mandates, as well as the legal and financial risks for violations.

Doctors no longer view on-call duty as a privilege or responsibility but as an inconvenient physical and financial burden. By accepting on-call duties, physicians face more malpractice risks because they are usually called in to treat very ill, dangerously unstable patients with whom they have no prior relationship. While EMTALA does not mandate that physicians provide on-call services, once they assume on-call duty, they face EMTALA fines and risk being dropped from Medicare participation. They are often paid slowly, underpaid, or not paid at all for dragging themselves out of bed in the middle of the night. After an exhausting night on call, they may have to cancel scheduled surgery the next day, which compounds economic loss and is unfair for the patient whose surgery was canceled. Family and personal time is sacrificed for the provision of this uncompensated care. Doctors who choose to work in underserved areas shoulder a particularly heavy economic burden, and being forced to add more nonpaying patients to the load may be enough to force them to practice elsewhere. As a result, many low compensation areas now have an increasing shortage of physicians, particularly specialists, willing to serve on-call.

On an occasional basis, such burdens are accepted as necessary evils in a doctor's life. However, if this type of burden becomes routine, is it any wonder that specialists cry "enough!" in frustration? Physicians have come to resent the intrusion into their professional and personal lives, not to mention financial losses, brought on by on-call demands. The fact that EMTALA penalizes hospitals, not doctors, for failing to provide on-call coverage sometimes forces hospitals to provide incentives for physicians to take on-call duties.

Some hospitals have resorted to paying physicians to be on call in order to fulfill EMTALA's requirements. A survey by the California chapter of the American College of Emergency Physicians revealed that 45 percent of hospitals

---

[7] Governor's Task Force on Access to Healthcare, State of Michigan. July 29, 1989 (testimony of Robert A. Bitterman, MD).

in California were forced to pay physicians a stipend to be on call.[8] Hospitals have paid from $100 to $1,000 per day for specialists to take calls, although many hospitals in these lean times are finding it difficult to come up with money for on-call doctors. According to a 2004 survey by the American College of Physician Executives, out of 818 responses, (1) 46 percent pay for some call; (2) 44 percent do not pay for call; (3) 22 percent are considering paying for call; (4) 64 percent struggle to get specialists; and (5) 29 percent report no problem.[9] A 2006 American College of Emergency Physicians survey of more than 1,300 responding hospitals revealed a deteriorating picture. Responding hospitals reported that 73 percent of emergency directors felt that on-call specialist coverage was inadequate, compared with 66 percent in a 2004 survey; 51 percent reported deficiencies in coverage because specialists had left their hospitals to practice elsewhere; 36 percent of hospitals had to pay on-call specialists for coverage compared to 8 percent in the 2004 survey. The practice of paying physicians for on-call services creates a slippery slope where other physicians will also demand to be paid for on-call service. The hospital board of directors may try to mandate on-call coverage as part of medical staff privileges. However, when pushed, physicians may elect to simply leave the hospital for another without mandates. Physicians are also resorting to joining specialty hospitals that do not have the restrictions and demands of a full-service general hospital. Small hospitals can rarely afford to lose the income and services of scarce specialists. Physicians may choose to limit their credentials (neurosurgeons choosing to de-credential their intracranial privileges for head trauma), request frequent leave of absence, or give up their active staff privileges in favor of courtesy privileges. In any case, some state laws prohibit hospitals from unilaterally amending medical staff bylaws.

Many states have tried to alleviate the on-call shortage by enacting laws mandating payment for emergency services by managed care organizations (MCOs). For example, a Texas statute requires health maintenance organizations (HMOs) to pay for emergency care services performed by non-network physicians and providers, regardless of whether the physician has a relationship with the HMO.[10] The statute adopts a "prudent layperson" standard for the purpose of determining whether an emergency condition exists. In addition, the statute requires coverage for post-stabilization care. State laws of this sort may help to alleviate the on-call physician shortage by mandating compensation to on-call physicians. States have also placed affirmative duties on physicians with regard to serving on call. Many states set maximum response times for on-call physicians. For example, the maximum response time for an emergency is 30 minutes in Missouri, New Jersey, and West Virginia. In addition, state medical malpractice law may impose obligations on on-call physicians. In Missouri,

---

[8] L.A. Johnson, *Results of the On-Call Backup Survey: Searching for Solutions to a Serious Public Health Problem,* California ACEP Lifeline, 3, 10 (Feb. 1999).

[9] Bill Steiger, *ACPE Poll Physician Leaders Distressed by Specialist Shortage: On Call Pay Controversial,* The Physician Executive (May-June 2005).

[10] *See* Tex. Ins. Code Ann. Art. 3.70-3C § 5 (Vernon 1997) (Emergency Care Provisions).

on-call physicians have a tort duty to respond to emergencies and to notify the hospital when they cannot respond.[11]

Emergency department use continues to grow each year while hospitals' capacity and services continue to decrease. The ultimate solution for many hospitals would be to close their emergency departments (although EMTALA requirements may still apply to hospitals without a formal emergency department). Many hospitals, especially in California, have resorted to this final solution. The California Medical Association released a report showing that 50 emergency departments in California have closed since 1990. By the end of 2000, just 355 of the state's 568 acute care hospitals still had emergency departments.[12] By burdening hospitals with the load of uncompensated emergency care, the unfunded EMTALA mandate may have the unfortunate unintended effect of limiting that very care.

The on-call issue is no doubt the most significant battleground between the federal government and hospitals/physicians on mandated EMTALA care. Given the flexibility that CMS has extended in the final rules, some hospitals may try to take advantage of this flexibility and overly limit on-call responsibilities for its medical staff. If too much of this occurs, leading to dangerous conditions for patients with emergency medical conditions EMCs), then CMS will have to respond with more restrictions. Physicians continue to devise ways to avoid emergency department services. Neurosurgeons have decredentialed intracranial privileges in order to avoid treating head trauma or intracranial bleeds (areas of high malpractice risks). Orthopedic surgeons have decredentialed hand surgery or other complicated fractures. Even primary-care physicians have relinquished all hospital privileges and practice only office-based care to avoid taking emergency department calls. Specialists are also relinquishing membership in community hospital medical staffs in order to stay only at tertiary care referral centers where specialty call can be more broadly shared. As with the closing of numerous hospitals and emergency departments, EMTALA may ultimately have the paradoxical effect of limiting the very care that it was created to enforce. A 2007 survey of California emergency department directors suggests emergency on-call specialist availability and the ability to transfer for higher level of care have worsened since the passage of the EMTALA final rule in 2003.[13] If Congress and/or CMS continue to use a heavy hand with more restrictions, mandatory laws, and punitive actions rather than address the real issue of uncompensated care, then the situation will only worsen.

---

[11] Erin M. McHugh, *The New EMTALA Regulations and the On-call Physician Shortage in Defense of the Regulations*, 37 J. Health L. 61, Winter 2004.

[12] "California Emergency Services Incur $400 Million in Losses," ACEP News, 20 (Apr. 2001), 4 at 1.

[13] Larry J. Baraff MD, *On-Call Specialists and Higher Level of Care Transfers in California Emergency Departments,* Acad. Emerg. Med. 15(4): 329-36, Apr. 2008.

Hospital Duties

Q 8:1   On-Call Requirement: Does EMTALA govern on-call physicians?

Absolutely. Congress extended EMTALA to specifically include on-call physicians in the 1989 EMTALA amendments.[14]

The Medicare provider agreement statute concerning EMTALA states:

> (a)   Filing of agreement; eligibility for payment; charges with respect to items and services
>
> > (1)   Any provider of services . . . shall be qualified to participate under this subchapter and shall be eligible for payments under this subchapter if it files with the Secretary an agreement—
> >
> > > (I)   In the case of a hospital or rural primary care hospital—
> > >
> > > > (i)   To adopt and enforce a policy to ensure compliance with the requirements of section 1395dd [EMTALA] of this title and to meet the requirements of such section,
> > > >
> > > > (ii)   To maintain medical and other records related to individuals transferred to or from the hospital for a period of five years from the date of transfer, and
> > > >
> > > > (iii)   To maintain a list of physicians who are on call for duty after the initial examination to provide treatment necessary to stabilize an individual with an "emergency medical condition."[15]

The State Operations Manual states:

> Section 1866(a)(1)(I)(iii) of the Act states, as a requirement for participation in the Medicare program, that hospitals must maintain a list of physicians who are on-call for duty after the initial examination to provide treatment necessary to stabilize an individual with an emergency medical condition. This on-call list requirement is a general provider agreement requirement for all hospitals and is thus technically an "EMTALA-related" requirement rather than a specific requirement of the EMTALA portion of the Act. When determining compliance with the on-call list requirement as part of an EMTALA survey it must be remembered that the on-call list requirement applies not only to hospitals with dedicated emergency departments, but also to hospitals subject to EMTALA requirements to accept appropriate transfers. (See discussion of § 489.24(f).) The on-call list clearly identifies and ensures

---

[14] 42 U.S.C. § 1395dd(g). Congressional amendments in 1989. Pub L. No. 101-239, Title VI, §§ 6003(g)(3)(D)(XIV), 6211(a)-(h), 103 Stat 2154, 2245 (enacted Dec. 19, 1989, effective July 1, 1990) (codified in 42 U.S.C.A. § 1395dd (West Supp. 1991).

[15] 42 U.S.C. § 1395cc.

that the hospital's personnel is prospectively aware of which physicians, including specialists and subspecialists, are available to provide stabilizing treatments for individuals with emergency medical conditions.[16]

In addition, CMS requires hospitals to write policies covering on-call coverage. In the interpretive guidelines, CMS states:

> A hospital must have written on-call policies and procedures and must clearly define the responsibilities of the on-call physician to respond, examine and treat patients with an EMC. Among other things, the policies and procedures must address the steps to be taken if a particular specialty is not available or the on-call physician cannot respond due to circumstances beyond his/her control (e.g., transportation failures, personal illness, etc.). The policies and procedures must also ensure that the hospital provides emergency services that meet the needs of an individual with an EMC if the hospital chooses to employ any of the on-call options permitted under the regulations, i.e., community call, simultaneous call, or elective procedures while on-call. In other words, there must be a back-up plan to these optional arrangements. For instance, some hospitals may employ the use of "jeopardy" or back-up call schedules to be used only under extreme circumstances. The hospital must be able to demonstrate that hospital staff is aware of and able to execute the back-up procedures.[17]

Cautions: CMS specifically includes on-call physicians as part of the ancillary services to be used to provide an appropriate medical screening examination (MSE). EMTALA requires that lists of on-call physicians who would be available to provide emergency care be maintained and posted in the emergency department.[18] On-call physicians must realize that they are liable for civil monetary penalties (CMPs) and termination from Medicare and state health care programs for EMTALA violations.[19]

On-call issues and refusal of specialist physicians to respond to a call from the emergency department made up the number-two source of EMTALA violation citations in the country as of 1998.[20] These citations ranged from lack of a call system or one that does not cover all required services to physician failure or refusal to come to the hospital in a timely manner or failure to accept transfers mandated by EMTALA. In spite of a rising number of on-call citations, the majority of on-call physicians have only a marginal understanding of their EMTALA-mandated duties and risks. Hospitals need to make a concerted effort to educate their medical staffs on EMTALA in order to reduce risks of violation.

---

[16] U.S. Dep't HHS, CMS, State Operations Manual, App. V, Emergency Medical Treatment and Labor Act (EMTALA) Interpretive Guidelines, Part II, Tag A-2404/C-2404 (revised 5/29/2009).

[17] U.S. Dep't HHS, CMS, State Operations Manual, App. V, Emergency Medical Treatment and Labor Act (EMTALA) Interpretive Guidelines, Part II, Tag A-2404/C-2404 (revised 5/29/2009).

[18] 42 C.F.R. § 489.20(r)(2).

[19] 59 Fed. Reg. 32,086, 32,090 (1994).

[20] See *On-Call Consultants Present EMTALA Risks for the ED*, 10 Emerg. Dep't Mgmt. 37 (Apr. 1998).

A determination of whether a hospital meets its on-call obligations includes all relevant factors, including the following:

- The number of physicians on staff;
- The number of physicians in a particular specialty;
- Other demands on these physicians;
- The frequency with which the hospital's patients typically require the services of on-call physicians;
- Vacations, conferences, and days off; and
- The provisions the hospital has made for situations in which a physician in the specialty is not available or the on-call physician is unable to respond.[21]

CMS intended this "all relevant factors" test to give hospitals and physicians some flexibility in terms of on-call coverage. However, inevitably, some specialists will take advantage of this flexibility to limit their responsibilities. Hospitals need to be on guard to prevent large gaps in on-call coverage in spite of the availability of an adequate number of specialists.

Q 8:2 On-Call Responsibility: Whose responsibility is it to provide on-call coverage?

CMS places the responsibility of ensuring on-call coverage squarely on the shoulders of the hospital.

The State Operations Manual stipulates:

> Section 1866(a)(1)(I)(iii) of the Act states, as a requirement for participation in the Medicare program, that hospitals must maintain a list of physicians who are on-call for duty after the initial examination to provide treatment necessary to stabilize an individual with an emergency medical condition. This on-call list requirement is a general provider agreement requirement for all hospitals and is thus technically an "EMTALA-related" requirement rather than a specific requirement of the EMTALA portion of the Act. When determining compliance with the on-call list requirement as part of an EMTALA survey it must be remembered that the on-call list requirement applies not only to hospitals subject to EMTALA requirements to accept appropriate transfers. (See discussion of § 489.24(f).) The on-call list clearly identifies and ensures that the hospital's personnel is prospectively aware of which physicians, including specialists and subspecialists, are available to provide stabilizing treatment for individuals with emergency medical conditions.[22]

---

[21] Interpretive Guidelines, § 489.24(j)(1), at 21.

[22] U.S. Dep't HHS, CMS, State Operations Manual, App. V, Emergency Medical Treatment and Labor Act (EMTALA) Interpretive Guidelines, Part II, Tag A-2404/C-2404 (revised 5/29/2009).

Cautions: In addition to written policies, the hospital must post conspicuously in the emergency department a written list of on-call physicians and be able to provide the list to CMS investigators at any time. All specialties and subspecialties represented by the active medical staff must be included on the daily on-call list for the emergency department. CMS gives the example that "if a hospital has a department of obstetrics and gynecology, the hospital is responsible for adopting procedures under which the staff and resources of that department are available to treat a woman in labor who comes to its emergency department."[23] Specialists such as ophthalmologists and psychiatrists, who may not have been on call in the past, are now obligated to take emergency calls. Sub-specialists such as cardiologists, pulmonologists, and neurologists should be on the call list. The governing body of a hospital without an emergency department must still provide written policies and procedures for appraisal of emergencies, initial treatment, and transfer for patients who may present with EMCs.[24]

Courts have taken into consideration the plight of small or ill-equipped hospitals when deciding EMTALA cases. Hospitals are not found liable under EMTALA merely because they do not have an appropriate specialist on call. For example, in *Vargas v. Del Puerto Hospital*,[25] a patient brought a civil action against a small rural California hospital with no specialists available or on call and only one physician available in the emergency room. The court held that the hospital was not liable under EMTALA when it transferred an unstable patient to a pediatric intensive-care unit. The physician made an appropriate transfer because he genuinely weighed the risks and benefits and determined that the child needed pediatric intensive care that was not available at the hospital.

Similarly, in *Hines v. Adair County Public Hospital District Corp.*,[26] another private action, a Kentucky hospital that had no orthopedist on-call was not found liable when the on-call physician did not perform needed surgery, which resulted in the amputation of the patient's leg. The on-call physician instead performed a temporary procedure and scheduled an appointment for the patient with an orthopedist. The court held that an appropriate screening with *this* hospital's capability consisted only of "readying Plaintiff for an appointment with a specialist," which the on-call physician did.

The hospital needs to follow up policies with enforcement. A California court of appeal has ruled that a hospital properly removed a physician from its emergency "call panel" after the physician admitted a patient in active labor and then declined to provide treatment to her because his malpractice insurance did not cover patients admitted through the emergency department. In *Hongsathavij v. Queen of Angels/Hollywood Presbyterian Medical Center*,[27] Dr. Hongsathavij had contracted with Los Angeles County to provide prenatal, obstetric, and

---

[23] 59 Fed. Reg. 32,100 (1994).

[24] 42 C.F.R. § 482.12(f)(2).

[25] No. CV-F-94-5201-REC-DBL (E.D. Cal. Nov. 7, 1996).

[26] 827 F. Supp. 426 (W.D. Ky. 1993).

[27] 73 Cal. Rptr. 2d 695 (Cal. App. 2d 1998).

newborn services to patients whose care was then paid for by the county. Dr. Hongsathavij was a member of the medical center's on-call panel for obstetrics.

Other physicians understood that on-call coverage meant treatment of all walk-in patients, including both county-covered and non-county patients. However, Dr. Hongsathavij viewed the call panel as a panel only for county-covered patients and did not want to treat non-county patients in the emergency department. Dr. Hongsathavij did not carry malpractice insurance for non-county patients. Treating only county patients would require no malpractice insurance because the county would indemnify him.

On January 23, 1991, a 29-year-old patient came to the emergency department in premature labor with active vaginal bleeding, no prior prenatal care, and a history of drug abuse. Dr. Hongsathavij admitted the patient to the labor and delivery ward but refused to treat her when he discovered that she was not a county-referred patient. Dr. Hongsathavij never called a substitute physician, thus forcing a hospital administrator to find another physician to take care of the patient. The medical center removed Dr. Hongsathavij from the emergency call panel. Hongsathavij sued for reinstatement. The trial court dismissed his suit.

The appellate court agreed with the ruling, reasoning that Hongsathavij's contention that he was not subject to the requirements of EMTALA because he was purportedly not on call for non-county patients flew in the face of the intent of EMTALA. Hongsathavij was not at liberty under EMTALA to accept an emergency department patient and then reject her because she had no means to pay for services and no means to indemnify him for malpractice.

Q 8:3 Hospital On-Call Responsibilities: How should a hospital fulfill its EMTALA on-call responsibilities?

Under EMTALA, the on-call system is the responsibility of the hospital. A hospital needs to:

- Formally address the mandates of EMTALA's on-call requirements in its medical staff bylaws or rules and regulations.
- Maintain an emergency department on-call roster that represents the medical specialty services available at the hospital.
- Post the daily on-call list of specialists in the emergency department. EMTALA mandates that the hospital maintain a record of this list for five years.
- Provide continuous education, as required by CMS, for the medical staff concerning the mandates of EMTALA. This education should be mandatory as a condition of staff privileges for all new as well as existing medical staff members. The medical staff physicians need to understand the liabilities that they as well as the hospital face if found in violation of EMTALA.

Cautions: The sentinel case which sparked a social uproar that led to the creation of EMTALA in 1985 involved an on-call neurosurgeon who refused to come to the emergency room to treat a patient with a life-threatening medical condition. A hospital is directly (not vicariously) liable under EMTALA if harm comes to any patient due to a failure in its on-call system. A hospital could face a costly and burdensome CMS investigation, monetary fines, civil suits, and finally disbarment from the Medicare program if an on-call physician fails his or her obligations. Hospitals need to take their on-call responsibilities very seriously.

A hospital has significant responsibilities to maintain its on-call responsibilities under EMTALA. The hospital and the medical staff must decide exactly which physicians must take call and how often. The emergency department must know prospectively whether it does or does not have a particular specialty available for each 24-hour period. This is critically important information for notifying Emergency Medical Services (EMS) in the local community of the services available, for transferring patients to other hospitals, and for accepting or rejecting patients in transfer from other hospitals. The hospital needs to explicitly define the duties and responsibilities of the physicians when they do take call so that everyone knows in advance exactly what it means to be "on-call" for the hospital. The hospital needs to formulate policies to define exactly what on-call responsibilities are, how to change call coverage, reasonable response times, procedures to follow when unable to respond, on-call exemptions, simultaneous calls, appropriate transfers, and community call plans if applicable.

Hospital policy should also define the actions the emergency department should take if the on-call physician refuses to come to the department when requested or fails to respond to a call. A chain of command (including administration) should be available for the emergency physician to call for back-up. Transferring a patient to another hospital if an on-call physician fails his or her duty is an unquestionable violation of EMTALA, so any such transfer should be a last-ditch option.

Q 8:4   Payment: Can hospitals pay a physician to take on-call duty?

Yes. Payment for on-call services is allowed. EMTALA mandates hospitals to provide on-call services but does not stipulate how the hospitals should arrange that service.

Cautions: Many hospitals have already begun to assume the burden of paying specialists to take on-call duties. Paying one group of specialists to be on call can start a slippery slope where other groups will also demand payment to be on call. The economic demands of paying for on-call services have threatened the financial viability of some hospitals. In addition, there is the possibility of violations of Stark and anti-kickback laws where criminal charges could result. If the hospitals do not lay proper groundwork for on-call responsibilities (such as response time, arranging back-up if the specialist schedules elective surgery, taking charity care, etc.), then in spite of payment, some hospitals find that response times and availability do not improve.

The next major battleground for EMTALA will be the struggle between hospitals, which must maintain economic solvency, proper patient care, and regulatory compliance, on one side and, on the other side, physician specialists who want to maintain their practice free of emergency on-call demands that would cut into their revenue and interrupt their life-style (time spent away from their practice or home life), especially if they must respond nights and on weekends and holidays. The battle between hospital and physician specialists has found its way into the courts.

In 2001, Neurosurgeons at Lehigh Valley Health Network sued the hospital demanding payment for on-call services.[28] The court dismissed this suit ruling that hospitals can hold physicians to hospital bylaws.

In 2005, Charleston Area Medical Center and a group of cardiac surgeons filed legal actions against each other.[29] The surgeons complained that the hospital was attempting to enforce trauma call coverage with possible loss of privileges. The surgeons also complained about payment to neurosurgeons being unfair and that the hospital required the physicians to follow transfer rules regulating locations for surgery. The hospital retaliated with a federal suit of its own alleging that the physicians were engaged in federal antitrust violations.[30] The issues in the cases were eventually reduced to whether a physician could sue Charleston Area Medical Center for the termination of his staff privileges. On appeal, the Fourth District ruled the hospital was protected by the Health Care Quality Improvement Act.[31]

Thirteen gastroenterologists at the Loxahatchee, Florida, Palms West Hospital quit practicing at the hospital February 1, 2006, when their demands for a $1,000 per day on-call stipend were refused by the hospital.[32]

A 2006 American College of Emergency Physician survey[33] of thousands of emergency departments revealed that 36 percent of respondents were paying stipends for on-call coverage. A survey by the American College of Physician Executives revealed that out of 818 responses, 46 percent pay for some call while 22 percent are considering paying for call and 64 percent struggle to get specialists to take call.[34] *The Physician Executive* also reported average daily

---

[28] Neurosurgical Assocs. v. Lehigh Valley Health Network 2001 U.S. Dist. LEXIS 284 (E.D. Pa. 2001).

[29] Stephen A. Frew, *Battle Over On-Call Requirements Turns Bloody*, MedLaw.com at http://www.medlaw.com/healthlaw/EMTALA/courtcases/battle-over-oncall-requir.shtml. (Feb. 2, 2006).

[30] Charleston Area Med. Ctr. v. Rashid, No. 2:2005cv01181, (S.D. W. Va., filed Dec. 28, 2005), http://www.jonesday.com/files/upload/CAMC%20Complaint.pdf.

[31] Wahi v. Charleston Area Med. Ctr., 562 F 3d 599 (4th Cir., 2009).

[32] Stephen A. Frew, *13 Specialists Quit Hospital Over On-Call Issues Following EMTALA Citation*, MedLaw.com at http://www.medlaw.com/healthlaw/EMTALA/other/13-specialists-quit-hospi.shtml (Feb. 14, 2007).

[33] *On-Call Specialist Coverage in U.S. Emergency Departments*, American College of Emergency Physicians, ACEP Survey of Emergency Department Directors, Apr. 2006.

[34] Bill Steiger, *ACEP Poll: Physician Leaders Distressed by Specialist Shortage; On Call Pay Controversial*, The Physician Exec., May-June 2005.

stipends compiled by HealthCare Appraiser in Delray Beach, Florida, ranged from $164 for pediatricians up to $2,500 for neurosurgeons and orthopedists.[35]

Before offering stipends for on-call services, hospitals need to be systematic. First, the hospital should assemble a task force composed of pertinent members of the medical staff, administration, and hospital Board. This task force needs to operate in good faith and be open-minded to solve the problem with a commitment to compromise. First of all, the task force should educate the medical staff and all involved on how EMTALA works and the penalties it imposes. Concrete data are a must to determine exactly what services are needed. The data should ascertain information that includes:

- who is taking call and how much call each physician took over the past two or three years;
- how often each physician responds to the emergency department calls;
- how often each physician must come to the hospital;
- the insurance status of patients treated by each physician;
- the level of intensity of care provided;
- financial data that would show how payment would impact the hospital's economic bottom line; and
- any other way in which hospitals can reward a physician for on-call duties short of stipends.

The task force should define physician expectations such as how much call is expected, what response time is reasonable, and whether elective surgery can be scheduled. The hospital needs to define exactly what services are expected for payment such as:

- specifics on response to emergency department calls;
- follow-up visits in the office;
- staying in Medicare and/or Medicaid;
- charity care policy; and
- noncompetition at surgery centers.
- The various methods of payment include:
- per diem for coverage;
- payment only when physicians are called in;
- hourly rate variations, stipends for taking call above an expected level; and
- a lower flat rate for carrying a beeper and a higher second rate for responding.

Some innovative hospitals have decided to use a new model for payment, such as non-qualified deferred compensation for on-call coverage.

---

[35] Maureen Glabman, *Specialist Shortage Shakes Emergency Rooms; More Hospitals Forced to Pay for Specialist Care*, The Physician Exec., May-June 2005.

Q 8:5   Anti-kickback Violation: Can payment to on-call physicians violate the anti-kickback statute?

Yes. Hospitals that have a problem scheduling on-call services with specialists can choose to offer pay for on-call services. However, improper structure of such payments may be a violation of the anti-kickback statute.

Cautions: The hospital needs to take care to structure payment policies carefully; if the hospital formulates its on-call payment improperly, violation of the anti-kickback statute may be interpreted. In an Advisory Opinion issued on September 27, 2007,[36] the Office of Inspector General (OIG) gave suggestions on how hospitals should formulate their on-call payment policies in order to avoid conflict with the anti-kickback statute. In this advisory, Lewis Morris, Chief Counsel to the Inspector General, responded to a hospital's query on the issue by stating:

> We are writing in response to your request for an advisory opinion regarding the physicians' on-call coverage and uncompensated care arrangement employed by a medical center (the "Arrangement"). Specifically, you have inquired whether the Arrangement constitutes grounds for the imposition of sanctions under the exclusion authority at section 1128(b)(7) of the Social Security Act (the "Act"), or the civil monetary penalty provision at section 1128A(a)(7) of the Act, as those sections relate to the commission of acts described in section 1128B(b) of the Act, the Federal anti-kickback statute.

> **I. FACTUAL BACKGROUND**

> [Name redacted] (the "Medical Center") is a tax-exempt, not-for-profit medical center located in [location redacted], with a charitable mission to help the poor and less fortunate. As required by state law, the Medical Center operates an emergency department (the "ED") that always remains open and accepts all people regardless of their ability to pay. Nearly one in four patients visiting the ED has no form of health insurance, whether private or governmental. Underinsured and uninsured patients often present through the ED and move on to follow-up care as Medical Center inpatients. Approximately one in ten of the uninsured patients who present at the ED are subsequently admitted to the Medical Center for further care.

> According to the Medical Center, prior to the Arrangement, the growing financial burdens of uncompensated patient care and malpractice insurance costs, as well other factors, had depleted the local supply of various types of physicians providing ED on-call coverage and uncompensated inpatient follow-up care for patients that initially presented at the ED. Physicians in some specialties, in fact, proved altogether unwilling to provide ED on-call services without compensation. The lack of available physicians constrained the Medical Center's ability to meet community needs.

---

[36] *See* http://oig.hhs.gov/fraud/advisoryopinions/2007.asp.

The Medical Center consequently had to transfer ED patients to other medical facilities both for emergency treatment and necessary inpatient care that might have been handled more conveniently and efficiently at the Medical Center. Given the special role of the ED in caring for the underinsured and uninsured, the shortage of available physicians hindered the Medical Center in fulfilling its charitable mission. As a result, the Medical Center formed an ad hoc committee comprised of Board Members, as well as leading staff and administration. The committee studied the problem of physician unwillingness to take calls to the ED, to provide inpatient care to patients admitted through the ED, and to provide inpatient consultative services for uninsured patients while on-call. Under the Arrangement, developed along the lines of the committee's recommendations, physicians on the Medical Center's staff in certain medical specialties provide ED on-call coverage, respond to patient emergencies in the ED, and provide inpatient care for uninsured patients. All the physicians on the Medical Center staff within the relevant specialties is offered the opportunity to contract for two-year terms under the Arrangement. The basic obligations under the Arrangement include the following:

(1) Participation in Call Rotation—At the beginning of each month the medical staff department or division head for each relevant specialty establishes a call rotation schedule for his or her specialty. Physicians within each specialty who participate in the Arrangement divide the monthly call obligation as equally as possible.

(2) Inpatient Care and Consultative Services—Physicians are obligated to provide inpatient care to any patient seen at the ED while on-call, if the patient is admitted to the Medical Center. This obligation applies regardless of the patient's ability to pay for the care delivered and continues until the patient is properly discharged.

(3) Timely Response to Calls—Physicians are required to respond to calls from the ED in a reasonable time. The Medical Center monitors response times to ensure that the Arrangement does not lengthen the Medical Center's historically short response times. All participating physicians must adjust their work schedules and lifestyles accordingly.

(4) Cooperation with Care Management/Risk Management and Quality Initiatives—Physicians are required to collaborate with the Medical Center's Care Management Staff and participate in the initiatives of the Medical Center's Risk Management and Performance Improvement Committees on issues including discharge planning, utilization issues, and review of observation patients.

(5) Medical Record Completion—Physicians are required to document their services in timely medical records for all patients seen under the Arrangement.

Different quality of care criteria are monitored under the program. The Arrangement calls on the Medical Center to take specific measures to ensure that different aspects of performance does not deteriorate under the Arrangement. Physicians who fail to adhere to requirements or refuse to cooperate with the oversight and planning of the Medical

Center's Care Management, Risk Management, and Performance Improvement Committees have their payments under the Arrangement suspended until they demonstrate compliance. Continuation of noncompliance will result in termination of the physician's involvement with the Arrangement.

Physicians participating in the Arrangement are paid a per diem rate for each day spent on-call at the ED, except for one and one-half days that each physician must contribute gratis to the rotation schedule monthly (amounting to eighteen days contributed annually by each).

The *per diem* rate varies based on two factors: physician specialty and whether call coverage is on a weekday or a weekend (to reflect the fact that weekend availability places a greater demand on the physician). The difference in *per diem* rates among specialties is based on the following factors:

(1) Severity of illness typically encountered by that specialty in treating a patient presenting at the ED;

(2) Likelihood of having to respond when on-call at the ED;

(3) Likelihood of having to respond to a request for inpatient consultative services for an uninsured patient when on-call; and,

(4) Degree of inpatient care typically required of the specialty for patients that initially present at the ED.

The Medical Center has certified that the *per diem* rates paid under the Arrangement are, and will be, fair market value for the services provided and are not, and will not, take into account in any way the volume or value of referrals or business generated between the parties. The Medical Center engaged [name redacted] (the "Consultant"), an independent health care industry consultancy, to provide advice on, among other things, the reasonableness of the per diem rates paid under the Arrangement. The Consultant's analysis incorporated both publicly available data and proprietary data concerning practices and pay rates at dozens of medical facilities. The Consultant developed benchmarks from the data and then compared the Arrangement to both the data and the benchmarks.

The details of the Consultant's analysis, as well as its conclusions that the per diem rates meet acceptable industry standards and represent fair market value for the services provided, were set out in an opinion letter, a copy of which was provided to OIG.

The Medical Center has certified that since the Arrangement was instituted, the ED is running much more efficiently. Physician responses to on-call requests have improved dramatically. The ED physicians have indicated to the management of the Medical Center that the cooperation they receive from on-call physicians has improved significantly. Patient survey results indicate that overall satisfaction with the ED has increased as well.

II. LEGAL ANALYSIS

A. Law

The anti-kickback statute makes it a criminal offense knowingly and willfully to offer, pay, solicit, or receive any remuneration to induce or reward referrals of items or services reimbursable by a Federal health care program. See § 1128B(b) of the Act. Where remuneration is paid purposefully to induce or reward referrals of items or services payable by a Federal health care program, the anti-kickback statute is violated. By its terms, the statute ascribes criminal liability to parties on both sides of an impermissible "kickback" transaction. For purposes of the anti-kickback statute, "remuneration" includes the transfer of anything of value, directly or indirectly, overtly or covertly, in cash or in kind. The statute has been interpreted to cover any arrangement where one purpose of the remuneration was to obtain money for the referral of services or to induce further referrals. *United States v. Kats*, 871 F.2d 105 (9th Cir. 1989*); United States v. Greber*, 760 F.2d 68 (3d Cir.), cert. denied, 474 U.S. 988 (1985).

Violation of the statute constitutes a felony punishable by a maximum fine of $25,000, imprisonment up to five years, or both. Conviction will also lead to automatic exclusion from Federal health care programs, including Medicare and Medicaid. Where a party commits an act described in section 1128B(b) of the Act, the OIG may initiate administrative proceedings to impose civil monetary penalties on such party under section 1128A(a)(7) of the Act. The OIG may also initiate administrative proceedings to exclude such party from the Federal health care programs under section 1128(b)(7) of the Act.

The Department of Health and Human Services has promulgated safe harbor regulations that define practices that are not subject to the anti-kickback statute because such practices would be unlikely to result in fraud or abuse. See 42 C.F.R. § 1001.952. The safe harbors set forth specific conditions that, if met, assure entities involved of not being prosecuted or sanctioned for the arrangement qualifying for the safe harbor.

However, safe harbor protection is afforded only to those arrangements that precisely meet all of the conditions set forth in the safe harbor.

The safe harbor for personal services and management contracts, 42 C.F.R. § 1001.952(d), is potentially applicable to the Arrangement. The personal services and management contracts safe harbor provides protection for personal services contracts if all of the following seven standards are met:

(i) the agreement is set out in writing and signed by the parties;

(ii) the agreement covers and specifies all of the services to be provided;

(iii) if the services are to be performed on a periodic, sporadic, or part-time basis, the agreement exactly specifies the schedule, length, and charge for the performance intervals;

(iv) the agreement is for not less than one year;

(v) the aggregate amount of compensation is set in advance, is consistent with fair market value in arms-length transactions and is not determined in a manner that takes into account the volume or value of any referrals or business otherwise generated between the parties for which payment may be made by Medicare, Medicaid, or other Federal health care programs;

(vi) the services performed under the agreement do not involve the counseling or promotion of a business arrangement or other activity that violates any Federal or State law; and

(vii) the aggregate services contracted for do not exceed those which are reasonably necessary to accomplish the commercially reasonable business purpose of the services.

B. Analysis

1. On-Call Coverage Issues

We are aware that hospitals increasingly are compensating physicians for on-call coverage for hospital emergency rooms. We are mindful that legitimate reasons exist for such arrangements in many circumstances, including: compliance with EMTALA obligations; scarcity of certain physicians within a hospital's service area; or access to sufficient and proximate trauma services for local patients. Simply put, depending on market conditions, it may be difficult for hospitals to sustain necessary on-call physician services without providing compensation for on-call coverage. Notwithstanding the legitimate reasons for such arrangements, on-call coverage compensation potentially creates considerable risk that physicians may demand such compensation as a condition of doing business at a hospital, even when neither the services provided nor any external market factor (e.g., a physician shortage) support such compensation. Similarly, payments by hospitals for on-call coverage could be misused to entice physicians to join or remain on the hospital's staff or to generate additional business for the hospital. As noted in our Supplemental Compliance Program Guidance for Hospitals:

> The general rule of thumb is that any remuneration flowing between hospitals and physicians should be at fair market value for actual and necessary items furnished or services rendered based upon an arm's-length transaction and should not take into account, directly or indirectly, the value or volume of any past or future referrals or other business generated between the parties. 70 Fed. Reg. 4858, 4866 (January 31, 2005).

Thus, with respect to compensation for on-call coverage, the key inquiry is whether the compensation is: (i) fair market value in an arm's-length transaction for actual and necessary items or services; and (ii) not determined in any manner that takes into account the volume or value of referrals or other business generated between the parties. We believe it should be possible for parties to structure on-call payment arrangements that are consistent with this standard and therefore pose minimal risk under the statute. Moreover, in many cases, it should be possible to structure on-call coverage compensation to satisfy the personal services safe harbor at 42 CFR 1001.952(d). There is a substantial risk that improperly structured payments for on-call coverage could be used to disguise unlawful remuneration.

Covert kickbacks might take the form of payments that exceed fair market value for services rendered (In some circumstances not present here, a physician offering to provide call coverage at below fair market value rates might also implicate the statute, if one purpose of the arrangement is to induce referrals.) or payments for on-call coverage not actually provided. Moreover, depending on the circumstances, problematic compensation structures that might disguise kickback payments could include, by way of example:

(i) "lost opportunity" or similarly designed payments that do not reflect bona fide lost income;

(ii) payment structures that compensate physicians when no identifiable services are provided;

(iii) aggregate on-call payments that are disproportionately high compared to the physician's regular medical practice income; or

(iv) payment structures that compensate the on-call physician for professional services for which he or she receives separate reimbursement from insurers or patients, resulting in the physician essentially being paid twice for the same service.

Each on-call coverage arrangement must be evaluated based on the totality of its facts and circumstances.

2. The Arrangement

The safe harbor for personal services and management contracts, 42 C.F.R. § 1001.952(d), is potentially applicable to the Arrangement. However, this safe harbor requires that the aggregate amount of compensation be set in advance. Because the Hospital's monthly payments to participating physicians can vary from month to month, the Arrangement does not fit squarely within the terms of the safe harbor, and we must analyze it for compliance with the anti-kickback statute by taking into account the totality of facts and circumstances.

For a combination of the following reasons, we believe the Arrangement presents a low risk of fraud and abuse.

First, the Medical Center has certified that the payments are fair market value for actual services needed and provided, without regard to referrals or other business generated between the parties. We rely on this certification in issuing this opinion. We note that several features of the Arrangement appear to support the certification. The *per diem* rate paid to physicians appears tailored to reflect the burden on a physician and the likelihood that a physician in a particular specialty will actually be required to respond while on-call, as well as the likelihood that he or she will have to provide uncompensated treatment, and the likely extent of that treatment. Moreover, the Arrangement places additional demands on the physician beyond the actual time spent on-call. The physician's obligation to provide care to any patient seen while on-call begins in the ED. In the event that the patient is admitted to the Medical Center, the physician's obligation to provide inpatient care continues until the patient's discharge. Throughout this time, which varies depending on the patient's condition and finances, the physician remains at risk of having to furnish additional services for no additional payment.

The physician is also required to provide eighteen days of uncompensated care annually as part of the overall Arrangement. Furthermore, the physician assumes responsibility for medical recordkeeping, and for cooperation with Medical Center care and risk management and performance improvement efforts. In sum, the per diem payments under the Arrangement are tailored to cover substantial, quantifiable services, a large portion of which are furnished to uninsured patients in the ED and afterwards. They sharply contrast with payments that are less plainly tied to tangible physician responsibilities, and which may represent little more than illicit payments for referrals.

Additional aspects of the Medical Center's methodology for establishing the *per diem* amount also lower the risk that the Arrangement is a vehicle to disguise payments for referrals.

The *per diem* payments are administered uniformly for all doctors in a given specialty without regard to the individual physician's referrals to, or other business generated for, the Medical Center. Indeed, the only variable in calculating the per diem rate within a specialty is whether the on-call service is performed on a weekday or on the weekend. This appears reasonable because, when on-call, physicians need to make themselves available in short response times. They must adjust their work schedules and lifestyles to accommodate the Arrangement, an accommodation that typically involves a greater imposition over the weekend.

The difference in *per diem* rates among specialties is based on the different extent of the uncompensated responsibilities that likely fall on physicians from each specialty under the Arrangement. Factors considered in calculating the rates include the severity of illness that physicians in a given specialty typically encounter when on-call; the likelihood they will need to respond to an ED call; the likelihood they will provide on-call care for an uninsured patient; and the degree of inpatient care they typically provide patients admitted from the ED.

An independent third-party valuation of the services provided under the Arrangement concluded that the compensation allotted in the per diem payments is within the fair market value range for the services provided.

Second, the circumstances giving rise to the Arrangement suggest that the Medical Center had a legitimate, unmet need for on-call coverage and uncompensated care physician services. Prior to entering into the Arrangement, the ED was understaffed for lack of capable and willing physicians. Prior to the Arrangement, the Medical Center resorted to the outsourcing of emergency care and other related treatment to other medical facilities. These circumstances lower the risk that the Arrangement was instituted as a way to funnel unlawful remuneration to physicians for referrals.

Third, the Arrangement includes features that further minimize the risk of fraud and abuse. The Arrangement is offered uniformly to all physicians in the relevant specialties. Monthly call obligations in each specialty are divided as equally as possible, a practice that suggests that call scheduling is not being used to selectively reward the highest referrers. Physicians must provide inpatient follow-up care to any patient seen on the ED while on-call, if the patient is admitted to the Medical Center. This obligation applies regardless of the patient's ability to pay for care and lessens the risk that physicians might "cherry-pick" only those emergency room patients that are likely to be lucrative. Moreover, the requirement that the on-call physicians document their services in medical records promotes transparency and accountability. In short, as structured, the Arrangement appears to contain safeguards sufficient to reduce the risk that the remuneration is intended to generate referrals of Federal health care program business. Moreover, the Arrangement promotes an obvious public benefit in facilitating better emergency on-call and related uncompensated care physician services at the Medical Center. Since the institution of the Arrangement, the Medical Center has seen greater efficiency in the ED, improved on-call physician performance, and achieved greater overall patient satisfaction. These advances should, in turn, aid the Medical Center in better fulfillment of its charitable mission. Finally, the Arrangement is structured so that all costs are absorbed by the Medical Center and that none accrue to Federal health care programs.

In light of the totality of facts and circumstances presented, we conclude that we would not subject the Health System to administrative sanctions under sections 1128(b)(7) or 1128A(a)(7) of the Act (as those sections relate to the commission of acts described in section 1128B(b) of the Act) in connection with the Arrangement. Finally, we note that nothing in this opinion should be construed to require a medical center or other facility to pay for on-call coverage. To the contrary, on-call coverage compensation should be scrutinized closely to ensure that it is not a vehicle to disguise payments for referrals.

III. CONCLUSION

Based on the facts certified in your request for an advisory opinion and supplemental submissions, we conclude that while the Arrangement could potentially generate prohibited remuneration under the anti-kickback statute, if the requisite intent to induce or reward referrals of Federal health care program business were present, the OIG will not impose administrative sanctions on the Medical Center under sections 1128(b)(7) or 1128A(a)(7) of the Act (as those sections relate to the commission of acts described in section 1128B(b) of the Act) in connection with the Arrangement. This opinion is limited to the Arrangement and, therefore, we express no opinion about any ancillary agreements or arrangements disclosed or referenced in your request letter or supplemental submissions.

IV. LIMITATIONS

The limitations applicable to this opinion include the following:

• This advisory opinion is issued only to [name redacted], the requestor of this opinion. This advisory opinion has no application to, and cannot be relied upon by, any other individual or entity.

- This advisory opinion may not be introduced into evidence in any matter involving an entity or individual that is not a requestor of this opinion.

- This advisory opinion is applicable only to the statutory provisions specifically noted above. No opinion is expressed or implied herein with respect to the application of any other Federal, state, or local statute, rule, regulation, ordinance, or other law that may be applicable to the Arrangement, including, without limitation, the physician self-referral law, section 1877 of the Act.

- This advisory opinion will not bind or obligate any agency other than the U.S. Department of Health and Human Services.

- This advisory opinion is limited in scope to the specific arrangement described in this letter and has no applicability to other arrangements, even those which appear similar in nature or scope.

- No opinion is expressed herein regarding the liability of any party under the False Claims Act or other legal authorities for any improper billing, claims submission, cost reporting, or related conduct.

This opinion is also subject to any additional limitations set forth at 42 C.F.R. Part 1008. The OIG will not proceed against [name redacted] with respect to any action that is part of the Arrangement taken in good faith reliance upon this advisory opinion, as long as all of the material facts have been fully, completely, and accurately presented, and the Arrangement in practice comports with the information provided. The OIG reserves the right to reconsider the questions and issues raised in this advisory opinion and, where the public interest requires, to rescind, modify, or terminate this opinion. In the event that this advisory opinion is modified or terminated, the OIG will not proceed against [name redacted] with respect to any action taken in good faith reliance upon this advisory opinion, where all of the relevant facts were fully, completely, and accurately presented and where such action was promptly discontinued upon notification of the modification or termination of this advisory opinion.

An advisory opinion may be rescinded only if the relevant and material facts have not been fully, completely, and accurately disclosed to the OIG.

Q 8:6 Compensation for Non-Paying Patients: Can a hospital compensate on-call physicians specifically for treating patients who are indigent or uninsured?

Yes. Instead of a per diem payment for taking on-call duty, a hospital may choose to compensate an on-call physician only for treating patients who are indigent or uninsured.

Cautions: In an Advisory Opinion on May 14, 2009,[37] the OIG opined that under very specific conditions a hospital may compensate on-call physicians only for those patients who are indigent or have no insurance. The OIG emphasizes that such plans still require careful scrutiny to avoid fraud and abuse violations.

In this Advisory Opinion, a 400-bed general hospital requested an opinion from OIG on a proposed arrangement in which the hospital would amend the hospital by-laws to allow participating on-call physicians to submit claims to the hospital for payment for services rendered to certain indigent and uninsured patients treated in the emergency department as part of the physician's on-call duties. Under the proposed arrangement, on-call physicians will be eligible for compensation for seeing patients presenting to the hospital's emergency department who are deemed "Eligible Patients." In order to qualify as an Eligible Patient, an individual must have no sponsoring insurance plan that includes Medicare, Medicaid, Workers' Compensation, private commercial insurance, a hospice program, and/or motor vehicle accident or home owner's insurance policy. Under the proposal, after a physician treats an Eligible Patient, the physician will submit a completed claim request form to the hospital. Physicians receiving compensation under the proposal would agree to waive all billing or collection rights, as well as claims against any third-party payer or the Eligible Patient, for services rendered.

Under the proposed arrangement, physicians would be compensated according to the following plan:

- Emergency consultations on an Eligible Patient presenting: $100 flat fee.
- Care of Eligible Patients admitted as inpatients from the emergency department: $300 per admission.
- Surgical procedure or procedures performed on an Eligible Patient admitted from the emergency department: $350 flat fee.
- Endoscopy procedure or procedures performed on an Eligible Patient admitted from the emergency department: $150 flat fee.

The OIG approved the plan but reiterated its concerns for potential fraud and abuse violations. In its approval, OIG reasoned as follows:

> First, the Hospital has certified that the payment amounts are within the range of fair market value for services rendered, without regard to referrals or other business generated between the parties. We rely on this certification in issuing this opinion. Several features of the Proposed Arrangement only will allow payments for tangible services that physicians render pursuant to their on-call duties, such as surgical or endoscopy procedures. No "lost opportunity" or other amorphous payments will be made under the Proposed Arrangement, and unlike some on-call arrangements that pay regardless of actual emergency department calls, the Proposed Arrangement only reimburses

---

[37] Office of Inspector General, OIG Adv. Op. No. 09-05 (May 14, 2009), available at http://oig.hhs.gov/fraud/docs/advisoryopinions/2009/AdvOpn09-05.pdf.

physicians for time they actually spend providing services in the Emergency Department. In addition, physicians only will be able to seek payment for services rendered to uninsured patients, a limitation that eliminates the risk that a physician could be paid twice for the same service by collecting under the Proposed Arrangement and receiving separate reimbursement from an insurer. This feature of the Proposed Arrangement is protected by rigorous safeguards: patient eligibility will be determined by reference to an objective standard—qualification for [state program redacted] as determined independently by [state agency redacted]—verified by the Hospital's Patient Accounting Department, and fortified by a detailed claims request process that includes a waiver of the physician's billing rights. Furthermore, physicians participating in the Proposed Arrangement will be at risk for furnishing additional services without compensation because their obligation will extend to providing follow-up care in the Hospital for Eligible Patients admitted through the Emergency Department. Finally, the rates that will be paid to physicians participating in the Proposed Arrangement appear to be scrupulously tailored to reflect the value of services actually provided in four distinct categories. These four payment rates reflect the variation in the level of service in the four payment categories, and each payment rate is uniform for all physician specialties. In sum, the payments under the Proposed Arrangement are tailored to cover substantial, quantifiable services, all of which will be furnished to uninsured patients that present to the Hospital's Emergency Department. These payments sharply contrast with payments that are less plainly tied to tangible physician responsibilities, and which may represent little more than illicit payments for referrals.

Second, the circumstances giving rise to the Proposed Arrangement suggest that the Hospital has a legitimate rationale for revising its on-call coverage policy. The Hospital reports that there are weeks when it does not have needed specialists on-call, that its [specialty practice group redacted] has reduced its on-call coverage to the minimum allowed under the Hospital's Medical Staff By-laws, citing the lack of compensation for on-call coverage, and that it is having to outsource its Emergency Department obligations. These factors, set against the backdrop of a medical staff that the Hospital describes as disliking on-call coverage because of its disruptive nature, liability issues, and lack of compensation, provide a reasonable basis for the Proposed Arrangement and reduce the risk that it will be used as a way to funnel unlawful remuneration to physicians for referrals.

Third, the Proposed Arrangement includes features that further minimize the risk of fraud and abuse. The Proposed Arrangement will be offered uniformly to all physicians and will impose tangible responsibilities on them. For instance, physicians must respond within 30 minutes to a request from the Hospital's Emergency Department when consulted, evaluate the patient in person, and provide such additional evaluation and care as is clinically appropriate. Moreover, the method of scheduling on-call coverage will be governed by the Hospital's Medical Staff By-laws, will be uniform within each department or specialty, and appears to be an equitable policy that will not be used to selectively reward the highest referrers. In addition, the requirement that on-call physicians' claims for payment include the date of service, description of service, dollar amount, patient's full name, and patient's social security number promotes transparency and accountability, and helps ensure that physicians are only paid for services rendered to Eligible Patients.

Fourth, the Proposed Arrangement appears to be an equitable mechanism for the Hospital to compensate physicians who actually provide care that the Hospital must furnish to be eligible for [state program redacted] funding. In this way, the Proposed Arrangement may stanch additional defections from on-call duties, and forestall additional on-call shortages. This would promote an obvious public benefit in facilitating better emergency on-call and related uncompensated care physician services at the Hospital, the sole provider of acute care, inpatient hospital services in [county and state redacted].

In short, as structured, the Proposed Arrangement appears to contain safeguards sufficient to reduce the risk that the remuneration is intended to generate referrals of Federal health care program business. In light of the totality of facts and circumstances presented, we conclude that we would not subject the Hospital to administrative sanctions under sections 1128(b)(7) or 1128A(a)(7) of the Act (as those sections relate to the commission of acts described in section 1128B(b) of the Act) in connection with the Proposed Arrangement.

Finally, we note that nothing in this opinion should be construed to require a hospital or other facility to pay for on-call coverage. To the contrary, on-call coverage compensation should be scrutinized closely to ensure that it is not a vehicle to disguise payments for referrals.[38]

Q 8:7 Inability to Respond: What if the on-call specialist is occupied and cannot respond?

The Code of Federal Regulations added provisions in 2003 under "Availability of On-call Physicians," which state:

(2) The hospital must have written policies and procedures in place:

(i) To respond to situations in which a particular specialty is not available or the on-call physician cannot respond because of circumstances beyond the physician's control; and

(ii) To provide that emergency services are available to meet the needs of patients with emergency medical conditions if it elects to permit on-call physicians to schedule elective surgery during the time that they are on call or to permit on-call physicians to have simultaneous on-call duties.[39]

On-call physicians may continue to see patients in their private practice and perform elective surgery unless the physician is on call at a critical-access hospital.

---

[38] Office of Inspector General, OIG Adv. Op. No. 09-05 (May 14, 2009).
[39] 42 C.F.R. § 489.24(j)(2)(i) & (ii).

CMS allows some leeway in excusing on-call physicians from responding to the emergency department. In the final rules discussion, CMS states: "The hospital must have policies and procedures to be followed when a particular specialty is not available or the on-call physician cannot respond because of situations beyond his or her control."[40] The written policies and procedures should:

- Address how dedicated emergency departments should respond to situations in which a particular specialty is not available or the on-call physician cannot respond because of circumstances beyond the physician's control, and
- Provide that emergency services are available to meet the needs of patients with EMCs if the hospital elects to permit on-call physicians to have simultaneous on-call duties at multiple facilities.

The State Operations Manual states:

> Hospitals are permitted to allow physicians to perform elective surgery or other procedures while they are on-call. Hospitals are also permitted to adopt a policy that does not allow physicians to perform elective surgery or other procedures while they are on-call. (Critical Access Hospitals (CAHs) should be aware that if they reimburse physicians for being on-call, there are Medicare payment policy regulations, outside the scope of EMTALA requirements, that the CAH might want to consider before making a decision to permit on-call physicians to schedule elective procedures.)

> When a physician has agreed to be on-call at a particular hospital during a particular period of time, but also has scheduled elective surgery or an elective diagnostic or therapeutic procedure during that time as permitted by hospital policy, that physician and the hospital must have planned back-up in the event the physician is called while performing elective surgery and is unable to respond to an on-call request in a reasonable time.[41]

Cautions: CMS does not require specialists to be on call at all times. CMS realizes that specialist physicians must attend to their private practices. CMS will allow valid excuses for not being able to respond to a call from the emergency department, but physicians should be aware that if they are investigated, CMS will go as far as checking surgery logs to verify the excuse. If a patient is undergoing surgery or would otherwise be jeopardized by the physician's response to the emergency department, the physician may be excused from response in that individual case. Additionally, elective surgeries cannot be "stacked" to render the physician continuously unavailable during call. In such cases, the physician would be expected to interrupt the schedule and "bump" elective cases as necessary to accommodate the emergency case under EMTALA. The on-call physician should arrange for a

---

[40] 68 Fed. Reg. 53,250 (2003).

[41] U.S. Dep't HHS, CMS, State Operations Manual, App. V, Emergency Medical Treatment and Labor Act (EMTALA) Interpretive Guidelines, Part II, Tag A-2404/C-2404 (revised 5/29/2009).

back up (if possible), alert the emergency department concerning when and whom to contact while he or she is in surgery, and inform the emergency department when he or she is through with surgery and once again available. If the on-call physician cannot arrange back up (if, for example, he or she is the only specialist on staff), then the hospital should have contingency transfer policies and/or agreements with neighboring hospitals.

Steven A. Pelovitz, then director for CMS's Survey and Certification Group, sent a memorandum to the regional offices, state survey agency personnel, and hospitals regarding EMTALA's on-call requirements:[42]

> Except in the case of Critical Access Hospitals (See 42 C.F.R. § 413.70), CMS has not issued any rule or interpretative guidelines that prohibit a physician from performing surgery while on-call. A hospital may have such a policy to prohibit elective surgery by on-call physicians to better serve the needs of its patients seeking treatment for a potential emergency medical condition; CMS recognizes that hospitals need to have flexibility in developing a method of providing coverage for such patients. Nevertheless, we would expect that if a physician has agreed to be on-call at a particular hospital during a particular period of time, but has also scheduled elective surgery during that time, that physician would have a planned back-up in the event that they are called while performing elective surgery. We anticipate that surveyors would recognize that physicians and hospitals need flexibility in developing a back-up plan that the back-up plan needs to be developed in the best interests of the community.[43]

CMS specifically allows on-call physicians to perform surgery on their own patients while on call, understanding that while in surgery, the physician would be unavailable to the emergency department. The State Operations Manual states:

> Physicians are not prohibited from performing surgery while on call. The only exception applies to Critical Access Hospital (CAH) staff. On-call physicians who are reimbursed for being on call at CAHs cannot provide services at any other provider or facility. However, a hospital may have its own internal policy prohibiting elective surgery by on call physicians to better serve the needs of its patients seeking treatment for a potential emergency medical condition. When a physician has agreed to be on call at a particular hospital during a particular period of time, but has also scheduled elective surgery during that time, that physician and the hospital should have planned backup in the event that he/she is called while performing elective surgery and is unable to respond to the

---

[42] Steven A. Pelovitz, *On-call Requirements—EMTALA*, CMS memorandum June 13, 2002, Ref: #S&C-02-34.

[43] Steven A. Pelovitz, *On-call Requirements—EMTALA*, CMS memorandum June 13, 2002, Ref: #S&C-02-34.

situation or the implementation of an appropriate EMTALA transfer according to § 489.24(e).[44]

The State Operations Manual instructs its surveyors that:

> If a physician who is on call does not come to the hospital when called, but rather repeatedly or typically directs the patient to be transferred to another hospital where the physician can treat the individual, the physician may have violated EMTALA. Surveyors are to assess all facts of the case prior to making a recommendation to the RO as to whether the physician violated EMTALA. Surveyors are to consider the individual needs and the physician circumstances, which may have an impact upon the case. Each case is to be viewed on its own merit and specific facts.[45]

Q 8:8 Continuous Coverage: Does EMTALA require a hospital to have continuous on-call coverage 365 days a year?

No. The amount of on-call coverage depends on the physician resources available to the hospital. CMS states in the *Federal Register*:

> Medicare does not set requirements on how frequently a hospital's staff of on-call physicians are expected to be available to provide on-call coverage; that is a determination to be made between the hospital and the physicians on its on-call roster. We are aware that practice demands in treating other patients, conferences, vacations, days off, and other similar factors must be considered in determining the availability of staff. We also are aware that some hospitals, particularly those in rural areas, have stated that they incur relatively high costs of compensating physician groups for providing on-call coverage to their emergency departments, and that doing so can strain their already limited financial resources. CMS allows hospitals flexibility to comply with EMTALA obligations by maintaining a level of on-call coverage that is within their capability.[46]

CMS further states:

> We do not believe it would be appropriate for CMS to prescribe levels of on-call coverage; on the contrary, these matters should be worked out between individual hospitals and their medical staff. Therefore, we have not included any provision on the level of on-call coverage hospital may require.[47]

---

[44] U.S. Dep't HHS, CMS, State Operations Manual, App. V, Emergency Medical Treatment and Labor Act (EMTALA) Interpretive Guidelines, Part II, Tag A-2404/C-2404 (revised 3/21/2008).

[45] U.S. Dep't HHS, CMS, State Operations Manual, App. V, Emergency Medical Treatment and Labor Act (EMTALA) Interpretive Guidelines, Part II, Tag A-2404/C-2404 (revised 5/29/2009).

[46] 68 Fed. Reg. 53,250-251 (2003).

[47] 68 Fed. Reg. 53,254 (2003).

In addition, the State Operations Manual states:

> CMS expects that a hospital should strive to provide adequate on-call coverage consistent with the services provided at the hospital and the resources the hospital has available, including the availability of specialists. (42 FR 48662). CMS does not have specified requirements regarding how frequently on-call physicians are expected to be available to provide on-call coverage. However, CMS recognizes that in order to supply safe and effective care it would not be prudent for a hospital to expect one physician to be on-call every day of the week, every week of the year. There is also no pre-determined ratio CMS uses to identify how many days a hospital must provide medical staff on-call coverage for a particular specialty based on the number of physicians on staff for that particular specialty. In particular, CMS has no rule stating that whenever there are at least three physicians in a specialty, the hospital must provide 24-hour/7-day coverage in that specialty.[48]

Cautions: If a hospital has limited on-call specialist services, policies should be drafted to specify when and what kind of specialty services cannot be provided. The hospital needs to ensure that specialists take a reasonable amount of call. When these services cannot be provided, the hospital should have transfer policies, cross-coverage policies, and transfer agreements with nearby hospitals that have the capability to accommodate the needs of the patient. It is imperative that the hospital personnel be absolutely consistent in complying with the hospital's own policies and not use transfer agreements as a means of convenience.

Hospitals must not misuse CMS's extension of flexible on-call requirements to limit on-call services when they have the capability to provide comprehensive on-call coverage. One hospital may interpret the "available resources" to require its three orthopedic surgeons to provide 24/7 coverage, while another similar hospital with the same capability may provide limited coverage because its orthopedic surgeons are unwilling to take call so often. Whatever level of on-call service is provided, hospitals need to assure that the services are available equally to all who present to the emergency department regardless of payment issues.

Q 8:9   Exemptions to On-Call Service: Does EMTALA allow a hospital to provide exemptions to on-call duties for its medical staff?

Yes. Reasonable exemptions for traditionally accepted reasons are allowed by EMTALA. CMS states in the 2003 Preamble to the Regulations:

> We understand that some hospitals exempt senior medical staff physicians from being on call. This exemption is typically written into the hospital's medical staff bylaws or the hospital's rules and regulations, and recognizes a physician's active years of service (for example, 20 or more years) or age (for example, 60 years of age or older), or a combination of both. We wish to clarify that providing such exemptions

---

[48] U.S. Dep't HHS, CMS, State Operations Manual, App. V, Emergency Medical Treatment and Labor Act (EMTALA) Interpretive Guidelines, Part II, Tag A-2404/C-2404 (revised 5/29/2009).

to members of hospitals' medical staff does not necessarily violate EMTALA. On the contrary, we believe that a hospital is responsible for maintaining an on-call list in a manner that best meets the needs of its patients as long as the exemption does not affect patient care adversely. Thus CMS allows hospitals flexibility in the utilization of their emergency personnel.[49]

The State Operations Manual states:

> There is no EMTALA or Medicare provider agreement requirement for all physicians on the medical staff and/or having hospital privileges to take call. A hospital policy allowing exemptions to medical staff members (e.g., senior physicians) would not in and of itself violate EMTALA-related Medicare provider agreement requirements. However, if a hospital permits physicians to selectively take call only for their own established patients who present to the ED for evaluation, then the hospital must be careful to assure that it maintains adequate on-call services, and that the selective call policy is not a substitute for the on-call services required by the Medicare provider agreement.[50]

Cautions: Hospitals should not take advantage of this allowance and "game" the system—i.e., write hospital bylaws and policies so liberally that unreasonable exemptions are allowed such as exempting physicians at the early age of 50 or after only 10 years of staff duty or for other reasons, such as being a medical staff officer. Even if a physician qualifies for senior call exemption, if providing that exemption jeopardizes patient care (i.e., only two specialists on staff and exemption will leave only one specialist available for call), the hospital board should decide whether partial or no exemption be granted based on patient needs. CMS specifically stated in the Preamble that "we believe that a hospital is responsible for maintaining an on-call list in a manner that best meets the needs of its patients *as long as the exemption does not affect patient care adversely.*" CMS will probably evaluate exemptions on a case-by-case basis and probably disallow overly generous exemption policies. CMS states in the *Federal Register*: "We will continue to investigate such situations in response to complaints and will take appropriate action if the level of on-call coverage is unacceptably low."[51]

Some physicians have attempted to avoid on-call obligations by requesting reappointment to the Courtesy Staff instead of the Active Staff or by limiting certain privileges (e.g., an orthopedic surgeon requesting no hand surgery). The hospital needs to be diligent when it suspects that such tactics are being used to avoid on-call responsibilities. Granting such requests may put added burdens on other physicians in that specialty to cover the lost services. The hospital needs to take a proactive stance and work with the department chief to see whether relinquishment of privileges would create an unreasonable hardship on the

---

[49] 68 Fed. Reg. 53,251 (2003).

[50] U.S. Dep't HHS, CMS, State Operations Manual, App. V, Emergency Medical Treatment and Labor Act (EMTALA) Interpretive Guidelines, Part II, Tag A-2404/C-2404 (revised 5/29/2009).

[51] 68 Fed. Reg. 53,252 (2003).

remaining specialists. The hospital Board, after evaluating the impact of such requests, should make the final decision on whether to grant any limitation of privileges that would affect on-call coverage and patient safety.

Q 8:10 Predetermined Ratio of On-Call Coverage: Does EMTALA require a predetermined ratio of days of on-call coverage per number of physicians available in a certain specialty?

No. The State Operations Manual states:

> CMS expects that a hospital should strive to provide adequate on-call coverage consistent with the services provided at the hospital and the resources the hospital has available, including the availability of specialists. (42 FR 48662). CMS does not have specified requirements regarding how frequently on-call physicians are expected to be available to provide on-call coverage. However, CMS recognizes that in order to supply safe and effective care it would not be prudent for a hospital to expect one physician to be on-call every day of the week, every week of the year. There is also no pre-determined ratio CMS uses to identify how many days a hospital must provide medical staff on-call coverage for a particular specialty based on the number of physicians on staff for that particular specialty. In particular, CMS has no rule stating that whenever there are at least three physicians in a specialty, the hospital must provide 24-hour/7-day coverage in that specialty.[52]

CMS states in the 2003 final rules that:

> We also note that there is no predetermined "ratio" that CMS uses to identify how many days a hospital must provide medical staff on-call coverage based on the number of physicians on staff for that particular specialty. In particular, CMS has no rule stating that whenever there are at least three physicians in a specialty, the hospital must provide 24-hour/7-day coverage in that specialty. Generally, in determining EMTALA compliance, CMS will consider *all relevant factors*, including the number of physicians on staff, other demands on these physicians, the frequency with which the hospital's patients typically require services of on-call physicians, and the provisions the hospital has made for situations in which a physician in the specialty is not available or the on-call physician is unable to respond.[53]

---

[52] U.S. Dep't HHS, CMS, State Operations Manual, App. V, Emergency Medical Treatment and Labor Act (EMTALA) Interpretive Guidelines, Part II, Tag A-2404/C-2404 (revised 3/21/2008).

[53] 68 Fed. Reg. 53,251 (2003).

CMS comments in the *Federal Register*:

> [We] do not believe it would be practical or equitable to attempt to adopt more prescriptive rules on such matters as the number of hours per week physicians must be on call or the numbers of physicians needed to fulfill on-call responsibilities at particular hospitals. We believe these are local decisions that can be made reasonably only at the individual hospital level through coordination between the hospitals and their staffs of physicians.[54]

Cautions: Hospitals must not take advantage of this interpretation by CMS to "game" the law and allow medical specialists to take too few on-call days. Hospitals should be able to explain why they allow limitations in the number of on-call days for medical specialists on the hospital staff. Valid reasons would be a limited number of specialists in that field; limited capabilities of specialists (e.g., an orthopedic surgeon who does not perform surgery on pediatric patients); allowance of reasonable times for physician vacations; medical education conferences; personal emergencies; and so on. Limiting the number of on-call days for specialists who simply do not want to be on call because of inconvenience would probably not be acceptable. CMS states in the 2003 Preamble that it intends to use the "all relevant factors" test to determine whether hospitals are complying with its EMTALA on-call requirements. CMS further states: "We understand the concerns expressed by the commentators about possible reductions in access to on-call services and wish to emphasize that the proposals are not intended to signal any change in CMS's position regarding hospitals' responsibility to comply with EMTALA."[55]

Although hospitals would welcome more specific regulations on this matter in order to comply with EMTALA mandates, it would be very difficult for CMS to devise regulations mandating that specific numbers of physicians be on call at a given time. CMS cannot know the intricate details of the day-to-day operations, variations in staffing, and community on-call needs of the thousands of hospitals across the country. Any attempt to be specific on numbers of physicians covering specific days on call would probably result in confusion and discontent far greater than this flexible recommendation.

Q 8:11   Referral Agreements: Does EMTALA require hospitals to have referral agreements with other hospitals?

CMS explains in the *Federal Register*:

> We agree that it is appropriate for hospitals to have referral agreements with other hospitals to facilitate appropriate transfers of patients who require specialty physician care that is not available within a reasonable period of time at the hospital to which the patient is first

---

[54] 68 Fed. Reg. 53,253 (2003).
[55] 68 Fed. Reg. 53,253 (2003).

presented. Hospitals that cannot maintain full-time on-call coverage in specific medical specialties would also keep local EMS staff advised of the times during which certain specialties will not be available, thereby minimizing the number of cases in which individuals must be transferred due to lack of complete on-call coverage. However, we are not mandating the maintenance of such agreements in this final rule. Even though such agreements may be desirable, we recognize that hospitals may be unable, despite their best efforts, to secure such advance agreements from specialty hospitals.[56]

Cautions: Although CMS does not require referral agreements between hospitals, it would still be prudent for hospital administrations and medical staff representatives to meet and discuss referrals between their hospitals. Referral hospitals and receiving hospitals should agree what would be acceptable as far as types of patients to transfer in order to avoid EMTALA violations. A list of transfer criteria, specific phone numbers to call, contact personnel, type of transportation, and so on would be helpful. Administrators on call should be aware of such agreements. The medical staff on-call physicians and emergency physicians should also be well aware of items on such agreements. These agreements would help to avoid questionable transfers that might force receiving hospitals to report the incident to CMS (triggering an EMTALA investigation) and thereby create ill-will between the hospitals.

Q 8:12 Community Call Plan: Are community call plans allowed by EMTALA?

Yes. CMS allows hospitals in a geographic area to fulfill their EMTALA on-call requirements through participation in a community call plan (CCP). CMS adopted the community call plans and amended the regulations governing the on-call list effective October 1, 2008. The rules were part of the FY 2009 Inpatient Prospective Payment System (IPPS) final rule.[57]

Cautions: CMS does not define the geographic size, composition, or structure of a community call system. Not every hospital within a geographic area needs to participate in the CCP. The CCP may involve all or only some of the specialties available. For example, neurosurgeons may participate in a CCP, but each hospital may retain its own on-call orthopedic surgeon. A single hospital in the system may be designated a destination for a particular specialty, but a specialist cannot simply transfer a patient to that hospital for his or her convenience. There still needs to be a medical benefit to the transfer. Hospitals need to be careful to treat all patients within a CCP the same without regard to insurance or payment issues. A hospital with a full compliment of physicians in a specific specialty should not use the CCP to reduce call responsibilities for its medical staff.

---

[56] 68 Fed. Reg. 53,251 (2003).

[57] www.cms.gov/AcuteinpatientPPS/downloads/CMS-1390F.

CMS adopted the CCP as a practical response to hospital needs. In rural areas where there is a shortage of certain specialists, such as neurosurgeons, hospitals often share a specialist's on-call services. CMS clarifies that this practice is allowed, stating:

> We believe that providing hospitals with flexibility in maintaining on-call will allow for, as well as encourage, more specialists to participate in on-call for hospitals. We agree with the commenters that this proposal is especially important to rural hospitals that may have previously had difficulty obtaining specialty coverage for their emergency departments.[58]

The State Operations Manual states:

Permitted On-Call Options

Community Call Plan

CMS permits hospitals to satisfy their on-call obligations through participation in a community call plan (CCP). It is strictly voluntary. Under such a community on-call plan, a hospital may augment its on-call list by adding to it physicians at another hospital. There are different ways a CCP could be organized. For example, if there are two hospitals that choose to participate in community call, Hospital A could be designated as the on-call facility for the first 15 days of the month and Hospital B could be designated as the on-call facility for the remaining days of the month. Alternatively, Hospital A could be designated as on-call for cases requiring specialized interventional cardiac care, while Hospital B could be designated as on-call for neurosurgical cases.

Ideally, a CCP could allow various physicians in a certain specialty in the aggregate to be on continuous call (24 hours a day, 7 days a week) without putting a continuous call obligation at the participating hospitals on any one physician. Even if this ideal cannot be achieved, given the resources of the participating hospitals, at a minimum, hospitals choosing to participate in a CCP should be able to provide more on-call specialty coverage than they would on their own.

The plan must clearly articulate which on-call services will be provided on which dates/times by each hospital participating in the plan. Furthermore, the [dedicated emergency department] in each hospital must have specific information based on the allocation of on-call responsibilities in the plan readily available as part of the on-call list, so that personnel who are providing required services to individuals protected under EMTALA know which specialists based in which hospital(s) are available on-call to provide the necessary specialist services.

Participation in a community call plan does not mean that on-call physicians must travel from the hospital where they practice to the hospital needing their on-call services. Instead, this arrangement facilitates appropriate transfers to the hospital providing the specialty on-call services pursuant to the plan. The hospital where the individual initially presents still has an EMTALA obligation to conduct a medical screening examination, and, for individuals found to have an emergency medical condition, to provide stabilizing treatment within its capability and

---

[58] 73 Fed. Reg. 48,664 (Aug. 19, 2008).

capacity. However, when the individual is appropriately transferred pursuant to a CCP for further stabilizing treatment, it can generally be assumed that the transferring hospital has provided treatment within its capability and capacity and that its on-call list is adequate for that specialty. For example, if an individual requires the services of a neurologist on a date when the neurologist on-call pursuant to the CCP is based at hospital B, and that neurologist is part of hospital A's on-call list, then a transfer to hospital B to obtain the services of the neurologist on-call would be in order, assuming all other transfer requirements have been met.

In those cases where, for example, hospitals A and B participate in a CCP and a physician who is a member of the medical staff or has privileges at both hospitals is on-call directly at hospital B, but only indirectly through the CCP to hospital A, there is no regulatory prohibition against the on-call physician going to hospital A to provide the stabilizing treatment, rather than transferring the individual to hospital B. The treating and on-call physician might consider which approach is in the best interests of the patient and also maintains the availability of the on-call specialist pursuant to the CCP.

The regulations establish a number of specific requirements for community call plans:

- The plan must include the geographic parameters of the on-call coverage, indicating what patient origin areas the plan expects to service (e.g. certain communities, counties, regions, municipalities). CMS does not stipulate geographic criteria that a community call plan must meet, since the intent of the plan is to promote flexibility amongst the participating hospitals in developing a call plan that best meets the needs of their communities and utilizes the resources within the region. Similarly, there is no requirement that all hospitals within a defined geographic area must participate in the community call plan.

Regardless of the geographic specifications of the community call plan, the existence of a CCP in a specific area does not eliminate the EMTALA obligations of hospitals with respect to making appropriate transfers. Among other things this means that:

- Hospitals participating in the community call plan are not relieved of their recipient hospital obligations to accept appropriate transfers from hospitals not participating in the plan.
- Non-participating hospitals must accept appropriate transfers, regardless of whether the transferring hospital participates in a CCP with the recipient hospital or any other hospital.
- Non-participating hospitals must provide stabilizing treatment within their capability and capacity before seeking to transfer an individual to another hospital, regardless of whether the recipient hospital is providing on-call services to other hospitals pursuant to a CCP.

In other words, all Medicare-participating hospitals must fulfill their transfer responsibilities under EMTALA, notwithstanding the presence or absence of a transfer agreement and regardless of whether the transferring or recipient hospital is participating in a formal community call plan (73 FR 48667).

- The community call plan for each participating hospital must show evidence that the duly authorized representative of each hospital has officially signed the plan. The regulations do not require that the plan be signed by an appropriate representative as part of the annual assessment, but it is expected that updated signatures would be included in any subsequent revision of the CCP.

- The delivery of pre-hospital medical services is quite varied throughout the country and there are no specific EMTALA requirements that pertain to development of EMS protocols. However, if there are EMS protocols in effect in part or all of the areas served by the CCP, then there must be an attestation by the CCP-participating hospitals that the CCP arrangement information has been communicated to the EMS providers and will be updated as needed so that EMS providers have the opportunity to consider this information when developing protocols. In addition, hospitals which are in the process of developing and refining their own CCPs may want to consider including input from the EMS providers that serve their DEDs so as to facilitate the efficient implementation of the CCP. For communities that do not have formalized EMS protocols, hospitals participating in a CCP would still be well-advised to inform individual EMS providers of the CCP arrangements amongst the hospitals in the geographic area specified in the plan.

- The formal language of the CCP must contain a statement that each hospital participating in the CCP will continue to follow the regulations requiring the provision of MSEs, and stabilizing treatment for individuals determined to have EMCs.

- Hospitals must conduct an annual reassessment of their CCP, including an analysis of the specialty on-call needs of the communities for which the CCP is effective (73 FR 48665). It is expected that the CCP would expand specialty coverage to the communities served by the plan and improve, within the hospitals' capabilities and capacities, the adequacy of the on-call list for the hospitals participating in the plan. CMS expects the annual assessment to support a Quality Assurance/Performance Improvement approach to the functioning of the CCP, and that hospitals would, as necessary and feasible, adjust the CCP based on the annual reassessment. Hospitals participating in the CCP have flexibility to determine how to design and implement the assessment.[59]

In order to formally establish a community call plan, hospitals in the specified geographic area must meet together and formulate such a specific policy. The policy should delineate the geographic area, the specialty to be covered, specific physicians who will participate in the plan, times when each hospital is participating, and coordination with the local EMS. The policy should include contingency plans in the event that the on-call physician is not available.

---

[59] U.S. Dep't HHS, CMS, State Operations Manual, App. V, Emergency Medical Treatment and Labor Act (EMTALA) Interpretive Guidelines, Part II, Tag A-2404/C-2404 (revised 5/29/2009).

The responsibility of maintaining the call list, notifying physicians of when they are on call, quality assurance plans, credentialing physicians, and other implementation specifics should also be addressed in the policy.

In devising a formal CCP, CMS requires the following elements:

- The community call plan would include a clear delineation of on-call coverage responsibilities, that is, each hospital participating in the plan is responsible for on-call coverage.

- The community call plan would define the specific geographic area to which the plan applies.

- The community call plan would be signed by an appropriate representative of each hospital participating in the plan.

- The community call plan would ensure that any local and regional EMS system protocol formally includes information on community on-call arrangements.

- Hospitals participating in the community call plan would engage in an analysis of the specialty on-call plan in the community for which the plan is effective.

- The community call plan would include a statement specifying that even if an individual arrives at the hospital that is not designated as the on-call hospital, that hospital still has an EMTALA obligation to provide a medical screening examination and stabilizing treatment within its capability, and hospitals participating in community on-call must abide by the EMTALA regulations governing appropriate transfers.

- There would be an annual reassessment of the community call plan by the participating hospitals.[60]

If a hospital participates in a CCP, CMS requires the hospital to maintain "[a]n on-call list of physicians who are on the hospital's medical staff or who have privileges at the hospital, or who are on the staff or have privileges at another hospital participating in a formal community call plan, in accordance with the resources available to the hospital."[61]

CMS provides examples of what can constitute "community call":

> For example, if there are two hospitals that choose to participate in community call, Hospital A could be designated as the on-call facility for the first 15 days of each month and Hospital B could be designated as the on-call facility for the remaining days of each month. Alternately, Hospital A could be designated as on-call for cases requiring specialized interventional cardiac care, while Hospital B could be designated as on-call for neurosurgical cases. Based on the proposal, we anticipated that hospitals and their communities would have the flexibility to develop a plan that reflects their local resources and needs. Such a community on-call plan would allow various physicians in a certain

---

[60] 42 C.F.R. § 489.24(j).

[61] 42 C.F.R. § 489.20(r).

specialty in the aggregate to be on continuous call (24 hours a day, 7 days a week), without putting a continuous call obligation on any one physician. We note that, generally, if an individual arrives at a hospital other than the designated on-call facility, is determined to have an unstabilized emergency medical condition, and requires the services of an on-call specialist, the individual would be transferred to the designated on-call facility in accordance with the community call plan.[62]

Q 8:13   Policies: What on-call policies does EMTALA require of the hospital?

The medical staff bylaws, rules and regulations, or policies and procedures must define the responsibility of on-call physicians to respond, examine, and treat patients with EMCs. In addition, the medical staff and hospital should have policies and procedures to be followed when a particular specialty is not available or the on-call physician cannot respond because of situations beyond his or her control.

Cautions: CMS requires that every hospital formulate a policy to address the issue of on-call coverage for emergency medical care. The policy should require that all specialties and subspecialties represented by the active medical staff be included on the daily emergency on-call list. This on-call list must be conspicuously posted in the emergency department at all times. The policy should address the issue of reasonable response times. The State Operations Manual instructs investigating teams to specifically "review the hospital's policy with respect to response time of the on-call physician. Hospitals are responsible for ensuring that on-call physicians respond within a reasonable period of time."[63] The policy should also address conflicts between the emergency department physician and the on-call specialist. For instance, if the emergency physician feels that the patient is unstable and cannot be discharged while the on-call physician disagrees, then there should be a chain of command where a neutral third party, such as the chairperson of the department, medical staff president, or administrative officer on duty, can be called for resolution. If the hospital has inadequate staff to be on call 24 hours a day, 7 days a week, then transfer policies to area hospitals or tertiary centers should be addressed. The policy should address a proper course of action, including disciplinary actions (if needed) for on-call specialists who abuse the on-call policy requirement. CMS wants to see that on-call policies are enforced. Failure of the hospital to supervise on-call specialists and enforce on-call policies exposes the hospital to violation even if a policy is in place.

It is important to note that there are no reported cases concerning the failure of a hospital to properly maintain a list of on-call physicians or failure to have an adequate number of physicians or specialists. Hospitals, especially small and

---

[62] 73 Fed. Reg. 48,663 (2008).

[63] U.S. Dep't HHS, CMS, State Operations Manual, App. V, Emergency Medical Treatment and Labor Act (EMTALA) Interpretive Guidelines, Part II, Tag A-2404/C-2404 (revised 5/29/2009).

rural ones, do not violate EMTALA merely because they do not have the appropriate specialist on call. Indeed, they do not necessarily violate EMTALA if they have *no* specialist on call. Even if the available specialist on call refuses to perform stabilizing procedures because he or she feels incompetent, the hospital will not be found liable if the hospital makes an "appropriate transfer." Hospitals will be found liable, however, when they are capable and well staffed, yet refuse to accept a transfer, or "reverse dump."[64]

In accordance with the statutory language, courts have taken into consideration the plight of small or ill-equipped hospitals when deciding EMTALA cases. For example, in *Vargas*,[65] a patient brought a civil action against a small rural California hospital with no specialists available or on call and only one physician available in the emergency room. The court held that the hospital was not liable under EMTALA when it transferred an unstable patient to a pediatric intensive-care unit. The physician made an appropriate transfer because he genuinely weighed the risks and benefits and determined that the child needed pediatric intensive care that was not available at the hospital. Similarly, in *Hines*,[66] another private action, a Kentucky hospital that had no orthopedist on call was not found liable when the on-call physician did not perform needed surgery, which resulted in the amputation of the patient's leg. The on-call physician instead performed a temporary procedure and scheduled an appointment for the patient with an orthopedist. The court held that an appropriate screening within this hospital's capability consisted only of "readying Plaintiff for an appointment with a specialist," which the on-call physician did.

Q 8:14   Calling 911: Can a specialty hospital call 911 as a substitute for providing emergency services?

No. A hospital is not in compliance if it uses 911 as a substitute for providing emergency services required by the Medicare Conditions of Participation (CoPs).

Cautions: In an April 26, 2007 memorandum to its State Survey Agency Directors, CMS addressed this issue by stating:

- All hospitals are required to appraise medical emergencies, provide initial treatment and referral when appropriate, regardless of whether the hospital has an emergency department.

- A hospital is not in compliance with the Medicare Conditions of Participation (CoPs) if it relies on 9-1-1 services to provide appraisal or initial treatment of individuals in lieu of its own capability to do so.

In this memorandum we affirm and explain current regulatory requirements pertaining to a hospital's ability to meet the emergency needs of individuals.

---

[64] Erin M. McHugh, *The New EMTALA Regulations and the On-call Physician Shortage: In Defense of the Regulations*, 37 J. Health L. 61, Winter 2004.

[65] *Vargas*, No. CV-F-94-5201-REC-DBL.

[66] *Hines*, 827 F. Supp 426.

Any hospital participating in Medicare, regardless of the type of hospital and regardless of whether the hospital has an emergency department must have the capability to provide basic emergency care interventions.

Requirements Applicable to All Hospitals (except Critical Access Hospitals)

The following Medicare hospital Conditions of Participation (CoPs) apply to all participating hospitals (except Critical Access Hospitals) and provide a foundation for safe care for all persons, including those with emergency care needs. Critical Access Hospitals (CAHs) are governed by regulations separate from those governing hospitals, and may be found at 42 C.F.R. § 485.618.

- **Physician On Duty or On Call:** The Governing Body CoP at 42 C.F.R. § 482.12(e)(3) requires hospitals to have a physician either on duty (onsite) or on call at all times.

- **A Responsible Physician for Each Patient:** The Governing Body CoP at 42 C.F.R.§ 482.12(c)(4) requires that an MD/DO is responsible for the care of each Medicare patient with respect to any medical or psychiatric problem that is present on admission or that develops during the hospitalization.

- **RN Supervision & Availability 24/7:** The Nursing Service CoP at 42 C.F.R. § 482.23(b) requires hospitals to provide 24-hour nursing services furnished by or supervised by an RN, that an RN supervise and evaluate the care of each patient, and that an RN be immediately available, when needed, to provide bedside care to any patient.

- **Right to Care in a Safe Setting:** The Patients' Rights CoP at 42 C.F.R. § 482.13(c)(2) states: "the patient has a right to receive care in a safe setting."

- **Governing Body Ensures Accountability:** The Governing Body CoP at 42 C.F.R. § 482.12(a)(5) states: "[The governing body must:] ensure that the medical staff is accountable to the governing body for the quality of care provided to patients."

- **Medical Staff-Organized & Accountable:** The Medical Staff CoP at 42 C.F.R. § 482.22(b) states: "The medical staff must be well organized and accountable to the governing body for the quality of care provided to patients."

- **Quality Assessment and Performance Improvement (QAPI):** The CoP at 42 C.F.R. § 482.21(e) requires that the hospital's governing body, medical staff, and administrative officials are responsible and accountable for ensuring that clear expectations for safety and established and that adequate resources are allocated for reducing risk to patients.

- **Appraisal, Initial Treatment, Referral:** The governing Body CoP at 42 C.F.R. § 482.12(f)(2) states: "If emergency services [i.e., department] are not provided at the hospital, the governing body must assure that the medical staff has written policies and procedures for **appraisal of emergencies, initial treatment, and referral when appropriate.**" [emphasis added]

- **Off-Campus Locations:** For hospitals that do have an emergency department(s) but also have off-campus hospital location(s) that do not have an emergency department, the governing body must still assure that the medical staff has written policies and procedures for each off-campus location's appraisal of emergencies and referral when appropriate (42 C.F.R. § 482.12(f)(3).

Explanation of Appraisal, Initial Treatment, and Referral

We emphasize that hospitals without emergency departments must nonetheless have appropriate policies and procedures in place for addressing individuals' emergency care needs 24 hours per day and 7 days per week, including the following:

- **Appraisal of Persons with Emergencies:** A hospital must have medical staff policies and procedures for conducting appraisals of persons with emergencies. The policies and procedures must take into account all of the other CoP requirements mentioned above and ensure that:

  - An RN is immediately available, as needed, to provide bedside care to any patient and that,

  - Among such RN(s) who are immediately available at all times, there must be an RN(s) who is/are qualified, through a combination of education, licensure, and training, to conduct an assessment that enables the to recognize the fact that a person has a need for emergency care.

    The polices and procedures for appraisal should provide that the MD/DO (on-site or on-call) would directly provide appraisals of emergencies or provide medical direction of onsite staff; conducting appraisals.

- **Initial Treatment:** A hospital must have medical staff policies and procedures for providing the initial treatment needed by persons with emergency conditions. Among the RN(s) who must be available at all times in a hospital, there must be RN(s) who are qualified, through a combination of education, licensure and training, to provide initial treatment to a person experiencing a medical emergency. The on-site or on-call physician could provide initial treatment directly or provide medical oversight and direction to other staff. This requirement, taken together with the other regulatory requirements described above, suggests that a prudent hospital would evaluate the patient population the hospital routinely cares for in order to anticipate potential emergency care scenarios and develop the policies, procedures, and staffing that would enable it to provide safe and adequate initial treatment of an emergency.

- **Referral when Appropriate:** A hospital must have medical staff policies and procedures to address situations in which a person's emergency needs may exceed the hospital's capabilities. The policies and procedures should be designed to enable hospital staff members who respond to emergencies to (a) recognize when a person requires a referral or transfer and (b) assure appropriate handling of the transfer. This includes arrangement for appropriate transport of the patient. Further, in accordance with the Discharge Planning CoP at 42 C.F.R. § 482.43(d), the hospital must transfer patients to appropriate facilities, i.e., those with the appropriate capabilities to handle the patient's condition. The regulation also requires that necessary medical information be sent along with the patient being transferred. This enables the receiving hospital to treat the medical emergency more efficiently.

What Is an Emergency?

The hospital CoPs do not include a definition of a medical emergency. However, the Emergency Medical Treatment and Labor Act (EMTALA) statute and regulations offers insight into emergency medical conditions. Although this definition is tailored to the specific requirements of EMTALA, it also might be a helpful reference when considering a hospital's compliance with the regulatory requirements for emergency services. This definition is attached as Appendix A, but please observe the cautionary note provided at the end.

Hospitals with Emergency Departments—Other Specific Requirements:

Hospitals are not required to have an emergency department. The regulations refer to this as "offering emergency services" and the term "offer emergency services" is treated in the regulations as synonymous with having an emergency department. In accordance with the Governing Body CoP at 42 C.F.R. § 482.12(f)(1), a hospital that offers emergency services (i.e., has an Emergency Department) must be in compliance with the Emergency Services CoP at 42 C.F.R. § 482.55, including the following requirements:

- **Meeting Emergency Needs of Patients:** "The hospital must meet the emergency needs of patients in accordance with acceptable standards of practice." (42 C.F.R. § 482.55)

- **Direction by Qualified Medical Staff:** "The services must be organized under the direction of a qualified member of the medical staff." (42 C.F.R. § 482.55(a)(1))

- **Integration with Other Departments:** "The services must be integrated with other departments of the hospital." (42 C.F.R. § 482.55(a)(2))

- **Supervision:** "The emergency services must be supervised by a qualified member of the medical staff" (42 C.F.R. § 482.55(b)(1))

- **Adequate Personnel Qualified in Emergency Care:** "There must be adequate medical and nursing personnel qualified in emergency care to meet the written emergency procedures and needs anticipated by the facility." (42 C.F.R. § 482.55(b)(2))

Patient Transportation and Emergency Medical Services (EMS)

A hospital may arrange transportation of the referred patient by several methods, including using the hospital's own ambulance service, the receiving hospital's ambulance service, a contracted ambulance service, or, in extraordinary circumstances, alerting EMS via calling 9-1-1 to obtain transport does not, however, relieve the hospital of its obligation to arrange for the patient's transfer to an appropriate facility and to provide the necessary medical information along with the patient.

A hospital policy or practice that relies on calling 9-1-1 in order for EMS to substitute its emergency response capabilities for those the hospital is required to maintain, as described above, is not consistent with the Medicare CoPs. For example, a hospital may not rely upon 9-1-1 to provide appraisal and initial treatment of medical emergencies that occur at the hospital. Such policy or practice should be considered as condition-level non-compliance with the applicable; CoP, 42 C.F.R. § 482.55 or 42 C.F.R. § 482.12(f).

Surveys

Surveyors are to evaluate each hospital's capability to address emergencies as required by the applicable regulations. In addition to complying with the requirements in the CoPs referenced on pages 1-2 of this memorandum, hospitals with emergency departments must comply with 42 C.F.R. § 482.55 and the EMTALA requirements at 42 C.F.R. § 489.24. Hospitals without emergency departments must comply with 42 C.F.R. § 482.12(f)(2). Surveyors should consider the discussion above when determining hospital compliance with these requirements. Hospitals that do not demonstrate full compliance with these requirements may be placing their patient's safety at significant risk. Condition-level noncompliance with 42 C.F.R. § 482.55 also indicates condition-level noncompliance with 42 C.F.R. § 482.12(f)(1). Hospitals that are not in compliance with emergency services requirements in 42 C.F.R. § 482.12 or 42 C.F.R. § 482.55 should also be carefully surveyed for compliance with the closely-related CoPs that are referenced in this memo, and areas of noncompliance with these CoPs should also be cited, as appropriate.[67]

Physician Duties

Q 8:15   On-Call Responsibilities: What are the EMTALA responsibilities for on-call physicians?

On-call physicians need to fully understand their EMTALA responsibilities:

- On-call physicians or other qualified medical personnel (QMP) must respond to the hospital when requested to attend to patients in a timely manner and complete an MSE or provide stabilizing care unless circumstances beyond the physician's control prevent a response.

- The transferring physician must discuss the case with the receiving hospital's authorized representative and obtain agreement to accept the

---

[67] Thomas E. Hamilton, *Provision of Emergency Services—Important Requirements for Hospitals,* Dep't of Health & Human Services, Center for Medicaid and State Operations/Survey and Certification Group, Ref: S&C-07-19, Apr. 26, 2007.

patient in transfer. (All hospitals with specialized capabilities, including physician specialists, have a responsibility to accept a transfer when such transfer is necessary to stabilize an EMC.)

- On-call physicians, who may be on call at another hospital simulta-neously, must not request that a patient be transferred to a second hospital for the physician's convenience.
- On-call physicians who, as part of their routine responsibilities, are charged with the duty to accept patients transferred from other facilities may not refuse any unstable transfer as long as their hospital has the capability and capacity to provide treatment.

Cautions: The on-call specialist must provide reasonable on-call services when called on for an EMC and respond within a reasonable period of time when called to the emergency department. Physicians whose names appear on the on-call list are responsible for finding a suitable replacement if they cannot be available for duty and for updating the on-call list with the replacement physician's name and other appropriate information. They need to understand the extensive liabilities that they expose themselves as well as the hospital to if they fail their duty.

Physicians' EMTALA obligations are derived from their contractual relation-ship with a hospital. In the case of hospital-based physicians such as emergency physicians, the contract is one of employment or independent contractor. Hospitals must have policies and procedures to respond to situations when a particular specialty is not available. The medical staff bylaws, rules and regulations, or policies and procedures should define the responsibility of on-call physicians to respond, examine, and treat patients with EMCs. The medical staff and hospital must have policies and procedures to be followed when a particular specialty is not available or the on-call physician cannot respond because of situations beyond his or her control. The physician is presumed to know and accept these obligations concurrent with acceptance of staff appointment.

Physicians need to take their on-call duties very seriously. Physicians will be permitted to be on call simultaneously for more than one hospital and to schedule elective surgery or other medical procedures during on-call times. Unreasonable delays in response to calls from the emergency department resulting in patient injury are EMTALA violations that can subject the on-call physician to all of EMTALA's penalties. On-call physicians cannot engage in delay tactics such as debating with the emergency department physician on the necessity of coming to the hospital, ordering that the patient be transferred to another hospital because of severity or scope of condition, asking about payment status, offering only office follow-up, and insisting on another special-ist consult before coming to the hospital. The emergency department physician has the ultimate authority in deciding whether the specialist needs to come to the hospital to help stabilize the patient. If the on-call physician refuses to come to the hospital and the emergency physician is forced to transfer the patient for emergency care, EMTALA mandates that the name and phone number of the refusing on-call physician be documented on the chart so that the receiving hospital can report the on-call physician.

In *Millard v. Corrado*,[68] Dr. Joseph Corrado was scheduled to be on call at Audrain Medical Center's emergency department. However, without notifying the hospital, he attended a medical conference 30 miles away. Due to his unavailability, a trauma patient had to be transferred to another hospital. The patient sued Dr. Corrado, alleging that the delay caused material injury. The Missouri Court of Appeals reversed the trial court's summary judgment for Dr. Corrado, declaring that public policy and the foreseeability of harm dictated that a physician who places himself on on-call status be available to treat patients within a reasonable period of time, notify the hospital of his unavailability, or supply a qualified replacement.

Q 8:16   Response Time: What is a reasonable response time by the on-call physician?

When it revised the Guidelines in 2004, CMS continued its policy of not defining what it means by a "reasonable response time." However, the 2009 Guidelines now require hospitals to provide that definition. The Guidelines state that expected response time should be stated in actual minutes in the hospital's policies.

The State Operations Manual states:

> If a physician who is on-call, either directly, or indirectly pursuant to a CCP, refuses or fails to appear at the hospital where he/she is directly on call in a reasonable period of time, then that physician as well as the hospital may be found to be in violation of EMTALA. Likewise, if a physician who is on-call typically directs the individual to be transferred to another hospital instead of making an appearance as requested, then that physician as well as the hospital may be found to be in violation of EMTALA. While CMs' enforcement of the EMTALA section of the Act and regulations and the EMTALA-related provisions of the provider agreement section of the Act and regulations are directed solely against hospitals, it is important to note that Section 1867 of the Act also provides for the Office of the Inspector General (OIG) to levy civil monetary penalties or take other actions against hospitals or physicians for EMTALA violations. CMS refers cases it has investigated to the OIG when CMS finds violations that appear to fall within the OIG's EMTALA jurisdiction. Section 1867(d)(1)(C) of the Act specifically provides for penalties against both a hospital and the physician when a physician who is on-call either fails to appear or refuses to appear within a reasonable period of time. Thus, a hospital would be well-advised to establish in its on-call policies and procedures specific guidelines—e.g., the maximum number of minutes that may elapse between receipt of a request and the physician's appearance for what constitutes a

---

[68] 14 S.W.3d 42 (Mo. App. Ct. 1999).

reasonable response time, and to make sure that its on-call physicians and other staff are aware of these time-sensitive requirements.[69]

Cautions: The hospital and the on-call physician may be subject to an EMTALA violation if he or she fails or refuses to appear within a reasonable period of time without a valid excuse when called by an emergency department physician, and the emergency physician then has to order a transfer, determining that without the timely services of the on-call physician the benefits of transfer outweigh the risks.[70] EMTALA obligates the emergency physician to write on the transfer form the name and address of any on-call physician who fails to provide needed services to stabilize a patient. The receiving hospital that received the unstable patient is also obligated under EMTALA to report the transferring hospital and on-call physician to the federal government.[71] Failure to report the on-call physician subjects the emergency physician as well as the receiving hospital to EMTALA penalties. CMS included this regulation because of the perception that lack of on-call specialist response necessitated many unstable transfers and that these transfers were routinely underreported.

A reasonable response time would depend on the situation at hand. Physicians who cover broad rural or congested urban areas should be given reasonable considerations simply due to travel time. CMS demands that each hospital review its own situation as far as response times for its specialists.[72] Each hospital should have a written policy regarding response times in minutes and the medical staff should be educated on what is expected of them with regards to response time. Simply formulating a policy is not enough. The hospital then needs to maintain a close watch on response times to on-call coverage. If any physician demonstrates a pattern of delayed response, the hospital needs to deal with it, imposing discipline if necessary. To do otherwise would risk citations because CMS investigations routinely check to see whether there is a policy and whether it is enforced.

Hospitals will find it problematic to designate a specific response time in minutes. Many states set maximum response times for on-call physicians. For example, the maximum response time for an emergency is 30 minutes in Missouri, New Jersey, and West Virginia.[73] What if an on-call physician responds in 40 minutes, instead of a policy's stated 30-minute requirement, without endangering a patient's medical condition? Is the on-call physician in violation even if there is good patient outcome? Each patient situation is different; therefore, hospitals need to be flexible in the wording of their policies.

---

[69] U.S. Dep't HHS, CMS, State Operations Manual, App. V, Emergency Medical Treatment and Labor Act (EMTALA) Interpretive Guidelines, Part II, Tag A-2404/C-2404 (revised 5/29/2009).

[70] 59 Fed. Reg. 32,090.

[71] U.S. Dep't HHS, CMS, State Operations Manual, App. V, Emergency Medical Treatment and Labor Act (EMTALA) Interpretive Guidelines, Part II, Tag A-2401/C-2401 (revised 5/29/2009).

[72] U.S. Dep't HHS, CMS, State Operations Manual, App. V, Emergency Medical Treatment and Labor Act (EMTALA) Interpretive Guidelines, Part II, Tag A-2404/C-2404 (revised 5/29/2009).

[73] L. Johnson, *The Emergency Department On-call Backup Crisis: Finding Remedies for a Serious Public Health Problem*, 37 Ann. Emerg. Med. 495, 497 (2001).

For example, a vascular surgeon needs to respond much more quickly for a patient with a rupturing abdominal aortic aneurysm than does an orthopedic surgeon responding for an otherwise stable Colles fracture. Hospitals should more reasonably stipulate an expected range of response such as "response within 30 to 45 minutes" instead of a single time span. A layered response time, such as 30 minutes for Stat Response and 60 minutes for routine medical conditions, may also work. The hospital must be diligent in enforcing its response time policies when a staff physician abuses them.

Q 8:17   Simultaneous Call: Can a physician be on call at more than one facility simultaneously?

Yes. Physicians may be on call at more than one hospital simultaneously.

The State Operations Manual states:

> Hospitals are permitted to allow physicians to be on-call simultaneously at two or more facilities. Hospitals are also permitted to adopt a policy that does not allow physicians to take simultaneous call at more than one hospital. If a hospital permits simultaneous call, then it must have written policies and procedures to follow when the on-call physician is not available to respond because he/she has been called to another hospital. All hospitals where the physician is on-call need to be aware of the details of the simultaneous call arrangements for the physician and have back-up plans established.[74]

Cautions: As compared to a formal community call plan (see Q 8:12), this ruling allows physicians to take call at more than one hospital simultaneously. This accommodates areas where there is a shortage of specialists such as neurosurgeons. Invariably, there will be times when a physician may be busy responding to a call at one hospital only to be called to respond to a second hospital. There should be contingency policies to attend to these situations. Hospitals need to be cooperative when physicians are on simultaneous call since CMS requires that all hospitals be "aware" when physicians are on simultaneous call.

Q 8:18   Non-physician Practitioners: May a non-physician practitioner respond to a call from the emergency department?

CMS regulations distinctly require the hospital to provide on-call *physicians*,[75] so non-physicians cannot be listed on the on-call list as taking formal call. However, CMS does allow critical access hospitals to allow physician assistants or nurse practitioners to take emergency call under limited circumstances.[76]

---

[74] U.S. Dep't HHS, CMS, State Operations Manual, App. V, Emergency Medical Treatment and Labor Act (EMTALA) Interpretive Guidelines, Part II, Tag A-2404/C-2404 (revised 5/29/2009).

[75] 42 U.S.C. § 1395cc(a)(1)(I)(iii); 42 C.F.R. § 489.20(r)(2).

[76] 42 C.F.R. § 485.618(d)(1).

Although non-physicians cannot take formal call, CMS states in the *Federal Register*:

> We agree that there may be circumstances in which a physician assistant may be the appropriate practitioner to respond to a call from an emergency department or other hospital department that is providing screening or stabilization mandated by EMTALA. However, any decision as to whether to respond in person or direct the physician assistant to respond should be made by the responsible on-call physician, based on the individual's medical needs and the capabilities of the hospital, and would, of course, be appropriate only if it is consistent with applicable State scope of practice laws and hospital bylaws, rules, and regulations.[77]

Cautions: CMS cautions that the responsibility to allow the physician's assistant to respond must be made by the on-call physician after discussion with the emergency physician. Automatic response by the non-physician practitioner in lieu of the on-call physician is not permitted. The on-call physician must still respond to a page by calling the emergency department and discussing the medical needs of the patient with the emergency physician. After discussing the patient's medical needs, the on-call physician can then make a proper decision about going to the emergency department personally or sending the physician's assistant.

The State Operations Manual states:

> If it is permitted under the hospital's policies, an on-call physician has the option of sending a representative, i.e., directing a licensed non-physician practitioner as his or her representative to appear at the hospital and provide further assessment or stabilizing treatment to an individual. This determination should be based on the individual's medical need and the capabilities of the hospital and the applicable State scope of practice laws, hospital by-laws and rules and regulations. There are some circumstances in which the non-physician practitioner can provide the specialty treatment more expeditiously than the physician on-call. It is important to note, however, that the designated on-call physician is ultimately responsible for providing the necessary services to the individual in the DED, regardless of who makes the in-person appearance. Furthermore, in the event that the treating physician disagrees with the on-call physician, then the on-call physician is required under EMTALA to appear in person. Both the hospital and the on-call physician who fails or refuses to appear in a reasonable period of time may be subject to sanctions for violation of the EMTALA statutory requirements.[78]

The hospital's Board of Directors should establish the scope of care that non-physician practitioners may provide in these settings. It is advisable that the

---

[77] 68 Fed. Reg. 53,250 (2003).

[78] U.S. Dep't HHS, CMS, State Operations Manual, App. V, Emergency Medical Treatment and Labor Act (EMTALA) Interpretive Guidelines, Part II, Tag A-2404/C-2404 (revised 5/29/2009).

Board develops written protocols covering the use of non-physicians who can provide such on-call services and the limitations of services.

The on-site emergency physician holds the ultimate authority on deciding whether the on-call physician must personally respond or come to the hospital. When an EMC can be handled only by the specialist, the emergency physician must be able to contact the specialist directly at any time.

Q 8:19   Nonemergencies: Does EMTALA obligate specialists to respond to nonemergency medical conditions?

No. Once an appropriate MSE shows the absence of an EMC, meaning that the patient is *stable*, EMTALA no longer applies. The treating emergency physician has the responsibility for making this determination.

Often, patients insist on the services of specialists such as plastic surgeons to repair common lacerations. A hospital and its specialists could meet to draft appropriate guidelines covering proper response to emergency calls. For example, a plastic surgery group in Louisiana was burdened by frequent calls from the emergency department to treat lacerations that turned out to be minor in nature. Recognizing their EMTALA obligations, they responded but were exasperated when they had to interrupt their own office practice or hospital work for minor injuries that did not really require a plastic surgeon specialist.

The plastic surgeons met with the hospital administration and set up guidelines for appropriate plastic surgery consultation and wound management. The guidelines stated that plastic surgical consultation would be proper for (1) wounds that require skin grafting or flap development for coverage; (2) repair of complex wounds that require more than layered closure, or areas of involvement of nerves, blood vessels, and/or tendons; (3) full-thickness lacerations of the eyelid including skin, muscle, and conjunctivae; (4) full-thickness lacerations of the lip including skin, vermillion, muscle, and mucosa; and (5) full-thickness lacerations of skin, cartilage, and mucosa involving the nose. The guidelines specified that a request by a patient or family member for a plastic surgeon was not itself a sufficient plastic surgery consultation request.[79]

Q 8:20   Private Patients: Can physicians selectively see private patients for emergency care when not on-call?

Yes. However, the physician should be a willing participant in the hospital's on-call system first. The State Operations Manual has stated in the past:

> Physicians that refuse to be included on a hospital's on-call list but take calls selectively for patients with whom they or a colleague at the hospital have established a doctor-patient relationship while at the same time refusing to see other patients (including those individuals whose

---

[79] E. Clyde Smoot, MD, *EMTALA Laws and the Plastic Surgeon in the Emergency Department,* 109 Plast. Reconstr. Surg. 7, 2603-4 (June 2002).

ability to pay is questionable) may violate EMTALA. If a hospital permits physicians to selectively take call while the hospital's coverage for that particular service is not adequate, the hospital would be in violation of its EMTALA obligation by encouraging disparate treatment.[80]

While CMS has removed this text from the 2009 revision of the manual, they have not indicated a change in ruling on this matter. Until CMS clarifies this issue, it would be judicious for a hospital to allow physicians who refuse to take on-call duties to see selective patients in the emergency department only if they already have sufficient on-call coverage in that specialty area.

CMS states in the *Federal Register*:

> We understand that physicians may sometimes come to a hospital to see their own patients, either as part of regular rounds or in response to requests from the patient or the patient's family, and agree that visits of this type should not necessarily be interpreted as meaning that the physician is on call. On the other hand, some physicians have in the past expressed a desire to refuse to be included on a hospital's on-call list but nevertheless take calls selectively. These physicians might, for example, respond to calls for patients with whom they or a colleague at the hospital have established a doctor-patient relationship, while declining calls from other patients, including those whose ability to pay may be in question. Such a practice would clearly be a violation of EMTALA.[81] On the other hand, the CMS administrator for Region 1 has publicly advised that if a physician takes his or her share of equitable calls and is not on call for a particular day, he or she can come into the emergency department to see his or her own patients or those of a colleague on his or her off days.[82]

Cautions: CMS is saying that if a physician refuses to provide general on-call services, he or she cannot then selectively take call only for private patients unless the hospital already has full on-call coverage in that physician's specialty. Taking call for himself or herself or other physicians on a private basis means that the physician has the ability to take general call. CMS is emphatic on this point. The State Operations Manual maintains: "If a hospital permits physicians to selectively take call while the hospital's coverage for that particular service is not adequate, the hospital would be in violation of its EMTALA obligation by encouraging disparate treatment."[83] This stance by CMS creates tensions with accepted medical practice and state laws. For example, consider a patient who arrives at the emergency department and tells the emergency staff that he has a regular physician and would prefer that

---

[80] U.S. Dep't HHS, CMS, State Operations Manual, App. V, Emergency Medical Treatment and Labor Act (EMTALA) Interpretive Guidelines, Part II, Tag A-2404/C-2404 (revised 5/29/2009).

[81] 68 Fed. Reg. 53,255 (2003).

[82] R. Rockefeller, *The Emergency Medical Treatment and Active Labor Act*, Mass. Health & Hosp. L. Manual, 11(12) (2004).

[83] U.S. Dep't HHS, CMS, State Operations Manual, App. V, Emergency Medical Treatment and Labor Act (EMTALA) Interpretive Guidelines, Part II, Tag A-2404/C-2404 (revised 5/29/2009).

his own physician treat him. If the private physician has refused to take call generally for the emergency department, she cannot come to see her own patient in the emergency department without violating EMTALA. State medical boards would expect a physician to see his or her own patients if asked.

Q 8:21   Transfer to Office: May the on-call specialist transfer the patient to his or her office for treatment?

Generally, no. If the patient has an EMC that is unstable, the State Operations Manual states:

> When a physician is on call for the hospital and seeing patients with scheduled appointments in his private office, it is generally not acceptable to refer emergency cases to his or her office for examination and treatment of an EMC. The physician must come to the hospital to examine the individual if requested by the treating emergency physician. If, however, it is medically appropriate to do so, the treating emergency physician may send an individual needing the services of the on call physician to the physician's office if it is a provider-based part of the hospital (i.e., department of the hospital sharing the same CMS certification number as the hospital), It must be clear that this transport is not done for the convenience of the specialist but that there is a genuine medical reason to move the individual, that all individuals with the same medical condition, regardless of their ability to pay, are similarly moved to the specialist's office, and that the appropriate medical personnel accompany the individual to the office.[84]

Cautions: The key element in this decision-making is the stability of the patient. If, after an appropriate examination and/or stabilizing treatment by the emergency physician, a patient is deemed "stable," then EMTALA's requirements end. The stable patient may be sent to the specialist's office or anywhere else for further care. However, EMTALA still applies if a patient's condition remains unstable. Once a patient is in the emergency department with an unstable EMC, an on-call specialist generally cannot refer an unstable patient to his or her own office for evaluation. CMS is concerned that such a transfer of an unstable condition would jeopardize the patient's condition. However, CMS allows an exception when the physician is on the hospital campus in a hospital-owned practice that is under the Outpatient Prospective Payment System (OPPS) billing system of the hospital.

Emergency departments commonly allow transfer of patients to specialists like orthopedists and ophthalmologists for specific care. If the transfer to the office is for specialty care where, for example, the ophthalmologist has special equipment not available in the emergency department (a medical "benefit" to the transfer), the transfer is permitted, but certification requirements should be completed just as for any transfer to another hospital. A transfer to a specialist's

---

[84] U.S. Dep't HHS, CMS, State Operations Manual, App. V, Emergency Medical Treatment and Labor Act (EMTALA) Interpretive Guidelines, Part II, Tag A-2404/C-2404 (revised 5/29/2009).

office merely for the convenience of the specialist is not allowed, as this may endanger the well-being of the patient. The fact that it may seem more efficient to transfer a patient to the office is irrelevant to compliance. If an on-call specialist happens to be on call at the same time at another hospital, an unstable patient may not be transferred to the other hospital just for the specialist's convenience as this may endanger an unstable patient.

In determining whether a hospital has appropriately moved an individual from the hospital to the on-call physician's office, surveyors may consider whether:

- All persons with the same medical condition are moved in such circumstances, regardless of their ability to pay for treatment;
- There is a bona fide medical reason to move the patient; and
- Appropriate medical personnel accompany the patient.[85]

Q 8:22   Penalties: Do EMTALA penalties apply to on-call physicians?

Yes. The Act states:

> If, after an initial examination, a physician determines that the individual requires the services of a physician listed by the hospital on its list of on-call physicians (required to be maintained under section 1395dd(a)(1)(I) of this title) and notifies the on-call physician and the on-call physician fails or refuses to appear within a reasonable period of time, and the physician orders the transfer of the individual because the physician determines that without the services of the on-call physician the benefits of transfer outweigh the risks of transfer, the physician authorizing the transfer shall not be subject to a penalty under subparagraph (B). However, the previous sentence shall not apply to the hospital or to the on-call physician who failed or refused to appear.[86]

Direct EMTALA penalties for violation include:

- civil monetary penalties (CMPs) up to $50,000 per violation, and
- termination from Medicare and Medicaid for gross and flagrant violations.

Cautions: EMTALA obligates the transferring emergency physician to report the offending on-call physician who neglects to fulfill his or her on-call duties. EMTALA requires that the patient's medical record be sent along with the patient transfer. That medical record must contain "the name and address of any on-call physician . . . who has refused or failed to appear within a reasonable time to provide necessary stabilizing treatment."[87] EMTALA then obligates the receiving hospital to report the offending on-call physician or be in violation of EMTALA and subject to termination from the Medicare program and/or CMPs up to $50,000 per incident.

---

[85] Interpretive Guidelines, § 489.24 (j)(1), at 21.

[86] 42 U.S.C. § 1395dd(d)(1)(C).

[87] 42 U.S.C. § 1395dd(c)(2)(C).

If the on-call physician refuses to provide services in a medical emergency, the emergency physician who then is forced to transfer the patient is relieved of liability, and the on-call physician becomes liable for penalties. EMTALA penalties apply to on-call physicians who fail or refuse to respond in a timely manner to a call from the emergency department. On-call in this sense pertains to those physicians listed as on call to the hospital and does not reach those who are merely on call for their group's patients.

The State Operations Manual states:

> If a physician who is on-call, either directly, or indirectly pursuant to a CCP, refuses or fails to appear at the hospital where he/she is directly on call in a reasonable period of time, then that physician as well as the hospital may be found to be in violation of EMTALA. Likewise, if a physician who is on-call typically directs the individual to be transferred to another hospital instead of making an appearance as requested, then that physician as well as the hospital may be found to be in violation of EMTALA. While CMs' enforcement of the EMTALA section of the Act and regulations and the EMTALA-related provisions of the provider agreement section of the Act and regulations are directed solely against hospitals, it is important to note that Section 1867 of the Act also provides for the Office of the Inspector General (OIG) to levy civil monetary penalties or take other actions against hospitals or physicians for EMTALA violations. CMS refers cases it has investigated to the OIG when CMS finds violations that appear to fall within the OIG's EMTALA jurisdiction. Section 1867(d)(1)(C) of the Act specifically provides for penalties against both a hospital and the physician when a physician who is on-call either fails to appear or refuses to appear within a reasonable period of time. Thus, a hospital would be well-advised to establish in its on-call policies and procedures specific guidelines—e.g., the maximum number of minutes that may elapse between receipt of a request and the physician's appearance for what constitutes a reasonable response time, and to make sure that its on-call physicians and other staff are aware of these time-sensitive requirements.[88]

In addition, although the emergency physician is immune from private lawsuits under EMTALA, on-call physicians may be subject to EMTALA lawsuits. When on call, the physician acts as the agent of the hospital, in the capacity of representing the hospital, not in the capacity of representing his or her own private practice. By accepting the hospital medical staff privileges and responsibilities under the hospital bylaws, physicians can be deemed agents of the hospital when they act under the on-call basis. On-call physicians are generally ignorant of their EMTALA responsibilities and risks. They need to be aware that they face potential double liabilities of governmental fines and penalties, as well as exposure to civil lawsuits.

A hospital should monitor the on-call system and responses of on-call physicians. If there is a physician who is negligent in his or her on-call

---

[88] U.S. Dep't HHS, CMS, State Operations Manual, App. V, Emergency Medical Treatment and Labor Act (EMTALA) Interpretive Guidelines, Part II, Tag A-2404/C-2404 (revised 5/29/2009).

responsibilities, the hospital needs to address the problem immediately before an EMTALA violation occurs. A hospital and/or its medical staff leadership could be sued under corporate negligence theories and be responsible for possible punitive damages for "intentional failure to protect the patient from known hazard," when it has knowledge of chronic negligent on-call physician behavior but does not act to remedy the situation.

Q 8:23 Legal Responsibility: Do on-call physicians owe a legal responsibility to patients they never directly treated?

Yes. On-call physicians may have legal responsibility to patients in the emergency department even when they never directly treated the patients. They are liable if they are negligent in their duty to provide on-call coverage. Physicians whose names appear on the on-call list are responsible for finding coverage if they cannot be available for duty. If changes need to be made for coverage, the original on-call physician has the responsibility of notifying the hospital with the name and pertinent information of his or her replacement physician.

The Missouri Court of Appeals ruled that on-call physicians owe potential patients the legal duty to provide reasonable notice when unavailable and may be sued for the breach of that duty. In *Millard*,[89] Dr. Joseph Corrado was scheduled to be on call at Audrain Medical Center's emergency department on November 5, 1994. Corrado attended a Missouri College of Surgeons meeting 30 miles away and did not notify the hospital of his unavailability.

That day, Marjorie Millard was brought to the emergency department with severe injuries from a motor vehicle accident. The emergency department attempted to call Dr. Corrado but was unsuccessful until almost an hour later. Dr. Corrado discussed the situation with the emergency physician and decided that the patient should be transferred to the University of Missouri Medical Center at Columbia.

Because of bad flying weather, Millard had to be transferred by ground ambulance and was not operated on until four hours after the accident. Millard underwent surgery to remove one kidney, her gallbladder, colon, and part of the small intestine. Millard sued Dr. Corrado, claiming that the delay in surgery aggravated her injuries and necessitated the severe surgical results. Corrado filed a motion for summary judgment, arguing that Millard failed to establish a physician-patient relationship because he never directly saw or treated her.

The Missouri Court of Appeals reversed the trial court's summary judgment for Dr. Corrado. The court declared that public policy and the foreseeability of harm dictated that a physician who places himself on on-call status must be available to treat patients within a reasonable period of time, notify the hospital of his unavailability, or supply a qualified replacement.

---

[89] *Millard,* 14 S.W.3d 42.

A concurring judge stated that in the alternative, the Restatement (Second) of Torts, § 324(A),[90] provided a basis for recovery that did not depend on establishing a physician-patient relationship. That section provides that one who undertakes to render services to another, which he should recognize as necessary for the protection of a third person or his possessions, is subject to liability to that person for physical harm resulting from his failure to exercise reasonable care to protect his undertaking if, among other things, his failure to exercise reasonable care increases the risk of such harm. Also, an on-call physician's failure to notify a hospital of his or her unavailability may be a violation of EMTALA.[91]

The State Operations Manual states:

> If a physician on-call does not fulfill his/her on-call obligation, but the hospital arranges in a timely manner for another of its physicians in that specialty to assess/specialize an individual as requested by the treating physician in the DED, then the hospital would not be in violation of CMs' on-call requirements. However, if a physician on-call does not fulfill his/her on-call obligation and the individual is, as a result, transferred to another hospital, then the hospital may be in violation of CMs' requirements and both the hospital and the on-call physician may be subject to enforcement action by the OIG under the Act.[92]

EMTALA mandates a paradigm shift in how on-call physicians must view their duties to provide care when called on for a medical emergency. Traditionally, staff physicians viewed their on-call duties for the emergency department as a voluntary favor to the hospital in return for the privilege for being a member of the medical staff. The on-call duties were usually flexible in regard to how the care was provided with response time, method of providing care, and location of care. It was generally up to the on-call physician in his or her opinion as the specialist to decide how the care should be provided. Neither the hospital nor the government mandated any specific guidelines on how this care was to be provided. There were no legal risks to being on-call other than malpractice suits arising from direct patient care, as with any other patient. This system worked well in the majority of hospitals for many years. However, EMTALA's mandates as well as court cases such as *Millard* have heightened on-call physicians' responsibilities and duties. Physicians must not take their on-call duties lightly.

Q 8:24   Follow-Up Care: Does EMTALA govern follow-up care for patients discharged from the emergency department?

No. EMTALA does not govern once a patient is discharged from the hospital.

Cautions: The key word applicable here is "stable." EMTALA's mandates are fulfilled and no longer apply once a physician determines that the patient

---

[90] Restatement (Second) of Torts, § 324(A).

[91] *See Physician's Duty to Patient He Never Saw*, 12 Emerg. Dep't L. 1 (Jan. 2000).

[92] U.S. Dep't HHS, CMS, State Operations Manual, App. V, Emergency Medical Treatment and Labor Act (EMTALA) Interpretive Guidelines, Part II, Tag A-2404/C-2404 (revised 5/29/2009).

is stable for transfer or stable for discharge with no EMC. CMS can decide what is considered stable and will look to common practice to determine whether discriminatory activity is involved. For instance, if an orthopedic surgeon routinely comes to the emergency department to treat an angulated fracture for paying patients, he or she cannot direct the emergency physician to simply splint similar fractures for non-paying patients with office follow-up. Once a patient is stable for discharge, follow-up care is determined by policies in the hospital's bylaws.

The State Operations Manual states:

> A patient is considered stable for discharge (vs. for transfer from one facility to a second facility) when, within reasonable clinical confidence, it is determined that the patient has reached the point where his/her continued care, including diagnostic work-up and/or treatment, could be reasonably performed as an outpatient or later as an inpatient, provided the patient is given a plan for appropriate follow-up care with the discharge instructions. The EMC that caused the individual to present to the dedicated ED must be resolved, but the underlying medical condition may persist. Hospitals are expected within reason to assist/provide discharged individuals the necessary information to secure the necessary follow-up care to prevent relapse or worsening of the medical condition upon release from the hospital.[93]

Although EMTALA does not provide definitive governance over follow-up care in a physician's office, the above statement places the responsibility of providing "appropriate follow-up care" on the hospital through the emergency department. This means that the hospital must have reasonable assurances that proper follow-up care will be provided by the follow-up physician before discharge. For instance, an orthopedic surgeon should not direct the emergency physician to splint a fracture and refer the patient to his or her office for follow-up care only to refuse care at the office when he or she finds out that the patient cannot pay. If the emergency staff has reason to believe that a certain specialist will not provide this care, then they have the responsibility to refer the patient to a specialist who will. The hospital should then immediately address such problems with follow-up care by on-call specialists.

Hospital bylaws should specifically define follow-up care responsibilities in the medical staff bylaws so that everyone understands in advance what follow-up care expectations are. It is probably not enough that the specialist see the patient once in the office. The better and less legally risky policy would be to require the physician to attend to the present medical condition until it is reasonably resolved. An orthopedic surgeon would treat a fracture until it is healed. An internist would treat a case of pneumonia until it is resolved. A pediatrician would follow an infant's febrile illness until the child is out of danger. Refusing care short of such resolution would invite patient abandonment issues. After resolution of the present medical condition, the specialist

---

[93] U.S. Dep't HHS, CMS, State Operations Manual, App. V, Emergency Medical Treatment and Labor Act (EMTALA) Interpretive Guidelines, Part II, Tag A-2407/C-2407 (revised 5/29/2009).

would have no further responsibility to follow the patient for other conditions. The orthopedist would not need to follow a patient's chronic back pain. The internist is not required to follow a patient's hypertension. The pediatrician does not need to provide further routine care such as vaccinations.

In the case of *Phillips v. Bristol Regional Medical Center*, [94] the patient had a fractured ankle that would later require surgery. In the emergency department, the patient was splinted and referred to the on-call orthopedic surgeon for follow-up care. The orthopedic surgeon saw the patient in the office but refused to operate because the patient was covered by Medicaid. The court held that the patient was stable or no longer had an EMC at the time of discharge from the emergency department and, as such, EMTALA did not reach the office of the orthopedic surgeon.

Referring a patient with an unstable emergent medical condition to a physician's office is allowed only under very limited situations when there is a definitive benefit to the transfer. An emergency physician referring a patient with an eye emergency to an ophthalmologist's office because he or she has specialized equipment that the emergency department lacks is allowed. CMS reserves the right to decide retrospectively who was truly stable after discharge from the emergency department.

Q 8:25   Physician Groups: Can physician groups be listed on the on-call list?

No. CMS requires that a "physician" must be listed on the on-call list. CMS states:

> Title 42 C.F.R. § 489.20(r)(2) requires a "list of physicians who are on-call for duty after the initial examination . . ."; therefore: physician group names (i.e., The Kaiser Foundation) are not acceptable for identifying the on-call physician. Individual physician names are to be identified on the list.[95]

The State Operations Manual specifically states:

> The list of on-call physicians must be composed of physicians who are current members of the medical staff or who have hospital privileges. If the hospital participates in a community call plan, then the list must also include the names of physicians at other hospitals who are on-call pursuant to the plan. The list must be up-to-date, and accurately reflect the current privileges of the physicians on-call. Physician group names are not acceptable for identifying the on-call physician. Individual

---

[94] 1997 U.S. App. LEXIS 17919 (6th Cir. July 14, 1997).

[95] *On-Call Requirements—EMTALA*, CMS letter to Regional Administrators, Steven A. Pelovitz, Ref: S&C-02-07 (Jan. 28, 2002).

physician names are to be identified on the list with their accurate contact information.[96]

Cautions: CMS probably insists that a physician's name be on the on-call list so that if there is a violation, CMS can more easily identify the specific individual physician who is charged. In actual practice in many hospitals, even though an individual physician's name is on the hospital on-call list, when the hospital calls, it is the answering service for a group (such as an orthopedic group) that answers and whoever is on-call for that group on that day responds regardless of which name is on the hospital on-call list. As long as a physician responds in a responsible manner to address the call for care, there should be no EMTALA violation.

Q 8:26   Telemedicine: Can on-call physicians utilize telemedicine services to respond to the emergency department call for assistance?

Yes. The State Operations Manual specifically allows the use of telemedicine. Individuals are eligible for telemedicine services only when, due to the individual's geographic location, it is not possible for the on-call physician to physically assess the patient.

The State Operations Manual states:

> There is no EMTALA prohibition against the treating physician consulting on a case with another physician, who may or may not be on the hospital's on-call list, by telephone, video conferencing, transmission of test results, or any other means of communication. CMS is aware that it is increasingly common for hospitals/CAHs to use telecommunications to exchange imaging studies, laboratory results, EKG's, real-time audio and video images of patients, and/or other clinical information with a consulting physician not on the hospital/CAH premises. Such practices may contribute to improved patient safety and efficiency of care. In some cases it may be understood by the hospitals and physicians who establish such remote consulting arrangements that the physician consultant is not available for an in-person assessment of the individual at the treating physician's hospital.[97]

Cautions: The State Operations Manual continues to warn:

However, *if* a physician:

- is on a hospital's on-call list; and
- has been requested by the treating physician to appear at the hospital; and

---

[96] U.S. Dep't HHS, CMS, State Operations Manual, App. V, Emergency Medical Treatment and Labor Act (EMTALA) Interpretive Guidelines, Part II, Tag A-2404/C-2404 (revised 5/29/2009).

[97] U.S. Dep't HHS, CMS, State Operations Manual, App. V, Emergency Medical Treatment and Labor Act (EMTALA) Interpretive Guidelines, Part II, Tag A-2404/C-2404 (revised 5/29/2009).

- fails or refuses to appear within a reasonable period of time, then the on-call physician may be subject to sanctions for violation of the EMTALA statutory requirements.

It is only when the treating physician requests an in-person appearance by the on-call physician that a failure by the latter to appear in person may constitute an EMTALA violation.

It is an entirely separate issue, outside the scope of EMTALA enforcement, whether or not insurers or other third party payers, including Medicare, will provide reimbursement to physicians who provide remote consultation services.[98]

CMS sent out a memo regarding EMTALA on-call requirements and telecommunications. CMS emphasizes that using telecommunications does not change the obligation under EMTALA of a physician who is on call to make an in-person appearance in the dedicated emergency department when requested to do so by the emergency physician. The CMS memo states:

The treating physician in a hospital's or critical access hospital's (CAH) dedicated emergency department (DED) who is conducting the Medical Screening Examination and/or providing stabilizing treatment of an individual required by the EMTALA regulations at 42 C.F.R. § 489.24 may, without violating EMTALA, consult on the individual's case with a physician who is not present in the DED by means of any telecommunications medium that the physicians choose to use.

- This does not change the obligation under EMTALA of a physician who is on-call to make an in-person appearance in the DED **when requested to do so by the treating physician.**

- This guidance does not affect policy by any health care third party payer, including Medicare, governing the circumstances under which it will or will not pay for remote consultation services.

- The portions of the interpretative guidelines for 42 C.F.R. § 489.20(r) and § 489.24(j) that discuss telemedicine or telehealth are superseded by this guidance.

It has been brought to the attention of the Centers for Medicare & Medicaid Services (CMS) that the interpretative guidelines for 42 C.F.R. § 489.20(r) and § 489.24(j), concerning hospital/CAH on-call physician requirements under EMTALA, are being interpreted by some parties as prohibiting emergency department physicians from utilizing modern telecommunications to facilitate consultation with specialists who are not present in the hospital/CAH. There is no such prohibition under EMTALA. It is necessary to distinguish among:

- a hospital's/CAH's obligation under EMTALA to maintain an on-call list of physicians on its medical staff in a manner that best meets the needs of its patients;

---

[98] U.S. Dep't HHS, CMS, State Operations Manual, App. V, Emergency Medical Treatment and Labor Act (EMTALA) Interpretive Guidelines, Part II, Tag A-2404/C-2404 (revised 5/29/2009).

- the obligation of an on-call physician to make an in-person appearance when requested to do so by the physician who is treating an individual who has come to the emergency department of the hospital/CAH; and

- remote consultation on the individual's case by the treating physician with another physician, who may or may not be on the hospital's/CAH's on-call list.

The EMTALA statute at Sections 1866 and 1867 of the Social Security Act and EMTALA regulations at 42 C.F.R. § 489.20(r) and § 489.24(j) establish requirements regarding hospital/CAH on-call lists and the obligations of on-call physicians to make in-person appearances. These provisions apply to hospitals/CAHs participating in Medicare Section 1866(a)(1)(I)(iii) and 42 C.F.R. § 489.20(r)(2) require hospitals/CAHs to "maintain a list of physicians who are on call for duty after the initial examination to provide treatment necessary to stabilize an individual with an emergency medical condition." Each hospital/CAH must maintain its on-call list in a manner that best meets the needs of the hospital's patients who receive services required under EMTALA. The resources available to a hospital/CAH, including the availability of on-call physicians, are taken into account when assessing the adequacy of its on-call list.[99]

Q 8:27 Specialty Hospitals: Do on-call physicians for specialty hospitals have to comply with EMTALA?

Yes. CMS has decided that if the specialty hospital is a Medicare-participating hospital, even if it does not have a dedicated emergency department, it still must abide by EMTALA obligations.

Cautions: Contributing to the nation's on-call shortage is an increase in physician specialization. Accompanying this trend has been a corresponding emergence of specialty care centers.[100] These health care delivery systems include specialty hospitals, ambulatory surgical centers, imaging and diagnostic centers, and other specialized facilities or niche providers.[101] If these specialty hospitals accept Medicare and meet the definition of a Medicare-participating hospital, then EMTALA does apply. If the specialty hospital has a treatment area that meets the broad definition of a "dedicated emergency department," then an individual will be found to have "come to the emergency department" when the patient presents to the dedicated emergency department or presents on hospital property and requests examination or treatment for what the individual believes to be an emergency condition. In addition, even if the specialty hospital does not have a dedicated emergency

---

[99] CMS S&C-07-23, Emergency Medical Treatment and Labor Act (EMTALA) On-call Requirements and Remote Consultation Utilizing Telecommunications Media, June 22, 2007.

[100] M. Lando, *The Specialty Care Debate: Is There an Answer?*, 18 Healthcare Executive 1 (Jan. 1, 2003).

[101] *Number of Niche Hospitals Rises, GAO Says*, 12 Health L. Rep. (BNA) 851, 851 (May 29, 2003).

department, it still must accept requests for appropriate transfers from requesting hospitals if capacity is available.[102]

The increasing use of specialty care centers significantly affects the problem of specialists available to be on call at our nation's hospitals. By practicing exclusively at these centers, specialists can avoid being on call for full-service hospital emergency departments. Additionally, specialists practicing at these centers often receive higher reimbursement. For example, Medicare reimbursement rates are often higher for procedures performed at ambulatory surgical centers than for those performed at hospital outpatient facilities.[103] For these reasons, specialists are finding it increasingly attractive to forego hospital staff privileges and simply practice in specialty care centers. However, CMS has decided that on-call physicians for these specialty hospitals cannot avoid EMTALA obligations for accepting appropriate hospital transfers. To specifically address this issue, CMS changed the Code of Federal Regulations on August 18, 2006, to state:

> (f) *Recipient hospital responsibilities.* A participating hospital that has specialized capabilities or facilities (including, but not limited to, facilities such as burn units, shock-trauma units, neonatal intensive care units, or (with respect to rural areas) regional referral centers, which, for purposes of this subpart, means hospitals meeting the requirements of referral centers found a § 412.96 of this chapter) may not refuse to accept from a referring hospital within the boundaries of the United States an appropriate transfer of an individual who requires such specialized capabilities or facilities if the receiving hospital has the capacity to treat the individual. This requirement applies to any participating hospital with specialized capabilities, regardless of whether the hospital has a dedicated emergency department.[104]

Q 8:28 Opting Out of Call: Can a physician refuse to take on-call duties?

Because hospitals have the statutory obligation to provide on-call services, they should not allow physicians to refuse to participate in on-call duties unless there are valid reasons.

Cautions: CMS addressed this issue in the Preamble to the 2003 Guidelines:

> Regarding situations in which physicians may irresponsibly refuse to fulfill the on-call responsibilities they have agreed to accept, we note that current law (section 1867(d)(1)(B) of Act) provides penalties for physicians who negligently violate a requirement of section 1867 of the Act, including on-call physicians who refuse to appear when called. We

---

[102] 42 C.F.R. § 489.24(f).

[103] M. Lando, *The Specialty Care Debate: Is There an Answer?*, 18 Healthcare Executive 1 (Jan. 1, 2003).

[104] 42 C.F.R. § 489.24(f).

further note that physicians who practice in hospitals do so under privileges extended to them by those hospitals, and that hospitals facing a refusal by physicians to assume on-call responsibilities or to carry out the responsibilities they have assumed could suspend, curtail, or revoke the offending physician's practice privileges. Moreover, when an EMTALA violation involving on-call coverage is found to have occurred, surveyors and CMS regional office staff will review all facts of the situation carefully to ensure that hospitals that have acted in good faith to ensure on-call coverage are not unfairly penalized for failure by individual physicians to fulfill their obligations.[105]

CMS wants to see that hospitals enforce their EMTALA obligations. If a physician refuses to take call, the hospital should take appropriate action. The medical staff bylaws should spell out the enforcement policy and procedures to follow through the chain of department chairman, executive committee, and hospital Board. The hospital and medical staff leadership need to be clear and united on this issue of on-call obligations for all physicians on the medical staff. Also note that CMS forbids a physician to take call for his or her own or a colleague's patients if the physician refuses to participate in the general on-call schedule (see Q 8:20).

The courts have long held that hospitals can require physicians to be on call for the emergency department as a condition of the physicians' medical staff appointment and clinical privileges. For example, in *Yeargin v. Hamilton Memorial Hospital,*[106] the Supreme Court of Georgia upheld the revocation of the medical staff appointment of a physician who refused to provide backup coverage of the hospital's emergency room. The fact that physicians may not be compensated for services that they provide in the emergency room does not relieve them of the duty to respond. In *Clair v. Center Community Hospital,*[107] the Pennsylvania Superior Court held that a hospital requirement that OB/GYNs see indigent patients at the hospital, imposed at the behest of the state department of health, did not violate the physician's Fourteenth Amendment substantive due process rights. In *Coker v. Hunt Memorial Hospital,*[108] a federal court in Texas specifically rejected a physician's argument that a hospital policy requiring all medical staff members to treat indigents without compensation constituted "slavery." Therefore, if a hospital so desires, case law would support a decision to require ED call coverage as a condition of medical staff membership. However, even if the decision is not to pay for call, efforts should be made to ease call burdens and address physician concerns.

Another problematic issue occurs with some specialists who narrow their practice to a subspecialty and appropriately refuse to take call for the broader practice area. For example, some orthopedic surgeons have limited their practice to "hand specialist" and treat only hand injuries. After many years of treating only hand injuries, their expertise in other areas of orthopedics, such as

---

[105] 68 Fed. Reg. 53,253 (2003).

[106] 195 S.E. 2d 8 (Ga. Sup. Ct. 1972).

[107] 463 A. 2d 1065 (Pa. Super. Ct. 1983).

[108] CA-3-86-1200-H (N.D. Tex. July 29, 1986).

hip or back injuries, certainly becomes limited. Even if forced to take general orthopedic call, such surgeons cannot operate on a fractured hip, nor do they have the needed expertise to treat a complex spinal injury. Many physicians have limited privileges on their credentialing files so that they are prohibited from performing certain surgeries even if called on to come to the emergency department. Hospitals should notify their local EMS of limitations to their on-call specialist coverage, such as when a neurosurgeon who does not have privileges to perform intracranial surgery is on call, so that EMS can decide to transport specific patients to hospitals with full coverage.

A hospital should have language in its bylaws to address a new limitation of privileges when faced with a physician who requests limited clinical privileges after being on the general call list. The bylaws should lay out the process that will be followed in response to the request. The hospital should consider issues such as the impact to the on-call services to the community, the burden to other specialists on call, and availability of the involved services by other hospitals in the area. The bylaws should make it clear that a request to resign privileges is not effective on submission but rather requires review by the medical executive committee and final action by the board of directors.

CMS says it will consider the following in evaluating hospital compliance with the on-call requirement:

1. Number of physicians on staff (and in each specialty);
2. Frequency with which patients need the specialty services;
3. Other demands on the physicians; and
4. Provisions made when specialists are unavailable.[109]

Most medical staff bylaws require active medical staff members to take call for the emergency department. CMS expects hospitals to enforce the bylaws or amend them to remove the requirement. But the bylaws are an unwieldy tool for addressing the on-call situation. Physician due process rights can make taking disciplinary action a lengthy, complicated process, and remedies under bylaws are either ineffective or go too far. A hospital that revokes the privileges of all physicians who refuse to take call for the emergency department can end up without enough physicians on staff, at least in specialties that are already underrepresented, such as orthopedics or neurosurgery. There is also a major economic loss for the hospital when these specialists take their patient business to other hospitals. Hospitals and medical staffs have responded in other ways to the on-call frustrations, with varying success:

1. Scheduling with gaps in coverage for particular specialties;
2. Providing no coverage in a specialty;
3. Providing only surgery/medicine call without providing coverage by specialists/subspecialists;

---

[109] U.S. Dep't HHS,CMS, State Operations Manual, Appendix V, commentary under Tag A404 regarding 42 C.F.R. §§ 489.20(r)(2) and 489.24(j)(1).

4. Getting outlying hospitals to assist with pay for call coverage;

5. Requiring physicians to contribute to a fund to pay those physicians who are willing to take call;

6. Coordinating call schedules with nearby hospitals to assure the most complete coverage across the area;

7. Using more hospitalists to assist the emergency department with stabilization.[110]

---

[110] Hilary H. Young, *EMTALA: An Update on Call Coverage and Payments for Services to Undocumented Aliens,* ABA Health eSource, Jan. 2006, vol. 2 No. 5.

Chapter 9

EMTALA and Managed Care

Managed healthcare plans cannot deny a hospital permission to examine or treat their enrollees. They may only state what they will and will not pay for, and regardless of whether a hospital is to be reimbursed for the treatment, it is obligated to provide the services specified in EMTALA.

59 Fed. Reg. 32086, 32116

The State Operations Manual states:

> If an individual seeking care is a member of a managed health care plan (e.g., HMO, PPO or CMP), the hospital is obligated to comply with the requirements of § 489.24 regardless of the individual's payor source or financial status. The hospital is obligated to provide the services necessary to determine if an EMC is present and provide stabilizing treatment if indicated. This is true regardless if the individual is enrolled in a managed care plan that restricts its enrollees' choice of health care provider. EMTALA is a requirement imposed on hospitals, and the fact that an individual who comes to the hospital is enrolled in a managed care plan that does not contract with that hospital has no bearing on the obligation of the hospital to conduct a Medical Screening Examination and to at least initiate stabilizing treatment. A managed health care plan may only state the services for which it will pay or decline payment, but that does not excuse the hospital from compliance with EMTALA.[1]

Major conflicts and confusion occur when EMTALA crosses paths with managed care. EMTALA did not address managed care issues because it was passed in 1985 when managed care was in its infancy. Since then, managed care has become the dominant form of health care insurance and delivery. Managed care plans prefer to keep patients who do not require acute emergency care out of the emergency department because it is perceived as a high-cost area. Managed care primary care physicians, therefore, commonly refuse emergency

---

[1] U.S. Dep't HHS, Centers for Medicare & Medicaid Servs. (CMS), State Operations Manual, App. V, Emergency Medical Treatment and Labor Act (EMTALA) Interpretive Guidelines, Part II, Tag A-2407/ C-2407 (revised 5/29/2009).

care authorization for patients whom they believe do not need emergency care. EMTALA's provisions stand as a barrier between financially driven managed care programs and the patient by mandating care and prohibiting financial preauthorization processes.

The EMTALA statute can be misused by managed care organizations to effectively eliminate insurers' responsibility to reimburse providers for services that are rendered in the emergency department. The managed care organization may rule after the fact that the patient's visit to the emergency department was not an actual emergency and thus deny payment for services. Hospitals and physicians assume the risk of nonpayment. This discrepancy has been addressed in two unsuccessful attempts in Congress to pass patient rights legislation. Many states, however, have addressed the issue and mandate payment for "prudent layperson" visits. Prudent layperson laws call for coverage of emergency services by managed care organizations without preauthorization when symptoms are severe enough to lead a prudent layperson, possessing an average knowledge of medicine and health, to believe that his or her health or the health of an unborn child is in immediate jeopardy. The Balanced Budget Act of 1997 banned preauthorization requirements and provided prudent layperson language in Medicare and Medicaid programs.[2]

The State Operations Manual states:

> A hospital that is not a managed care plan network of designated providers cannot refuse to screen and treat (or appropriately transfer, if the medical benefits of the transfer outweigh the risks or if the individual requests the transfer) individuals who are enrolled in the plan who come to the hospital if that hospital participates in the Medicare program.[3]

The U.S. Department of Health and Human Services (HHS) further reinforced this requirement in a special advisory bulletin issued November 10, 1999.[4] The 2003 EMTALA regulations formally codify this special advisory bulletin.[5] The bulletin, issued jointly by the HHS Office of Inspector General (OIG) and the Centers for Medicare & Medicaid Services (CMS), states emphatically:

> Notwithstanding the terms of any managed care agreements between plans and hospitals, the anti-dumping statute continues to govern the obligations of hospitals to screen and provide stabilizing medical treatment to individuals who come to the hospital seeking emergency services regardless of the individual's ability to pay. While managed care plans have a financial interest in controlling the kinds of services for which they will pay, and while they may have a legitimate interest in deterring their enrollees from over-utilizing emergency services, no

---

[2] Sections 4001 and 4702 of Pub. L. No. 105-33 (1997), 42 U.S.C. §§ 1395ww-22 and 1396u-2.

[3] U.S. Dep't HHS, CMS, State Operations Manual, App. V, Emergency Medical Treatment and Labor Act (EMTALA) Interpretive Guidelines, Part II, Tag A-2406/C-2406 (revised 5/29/2009).

[4] OIG/HCFA Special Advisory Bulletin on the Patient Anti-Dumping Statute, 64 Fed. Reg. 61,353 (1999).

[5] Medicare Program; Clarifying the Policies Related to the Responsibilities of Medicare-Participating Hospitals in Treating Individuals with Emergency Medical Conditions, 68 Fed. Reg. 53,224 (2003).

contract between a hospital and a managed care plan can excuse the hospital from its anti-dumping statute obligations. Once a managed care enrollee comes to a hospital that offers emergency services, the hospital must provide the services required under the anti-dumping statute without regard for the patient's insurance status or any prior authorization requirement of such insurance.[6]

However, this statement does not carry the weight of law for managed care organizations because there is no liability for health plans under EMTALA. Health plans are therefore free to deny authorization without EMTALA risks. Although this situation seems unfair, the emergency physician nevertheless needs to understand absolutely that if he or she directs a patient out of the emergency department for managed care reasons before performing an adequate screening examination or stabilizing treatment, he or she risks violation of EMTALA.

Managed care companies that contract for services through Medicare and Medicaid do have obligations to authorize emergency medical care. In 1997, President Clinton signed the Balanced Budget Act,[7] which applied the EMTALA definition of an emergency condition to Medicare and Medicaid patients and managed care companies supplying such services. The act requires the insurance company to pay for emergency medical services if, at the time of the request for such care, the patient's symptoms were sufficiently severe that a "prudent layperson, who possesses an average knowledge of health and medicine, could reasonably expect the absence of immediate medical attention to result in (i) placing the health of the individual . . . in serious jeopardy, (ii) serious impairment to bodily functions, or (iii) serious dysfunction of any bodily organ or part."[8]

Managed care companies that contract with Medicare and Medicaid are required to provide coverage for emergency services needed to stabilize emergency medical conditions (EMCs) as defined by the prudent layperson standard. The Balanced Budget Act also mandates that these managed care companies may not retroactively deny a claim for an emergency department evaluation because the condition, which appeared to be an EMC under the prudent layperson standard, turned out to be nonemergency in nature.[9] In addition, President Clinton issued an executive memorandum directing that all federal employee health plans incorporate the principles outlined in a patient bill of rights, including a provision that requires health plans to cover emergency services in situations in which a prudent layperson could reasonably expect the absence of care to place the individual's health in serious jeopardy.[10]

---

[6] 64 Fed. Reg. 61,356 (1999).

[7] Balanced Budget Act of 1997, Pub. L. No. 105-33, § 4001, 111 Stat. 251 (1997).

[8] H.R. 815 § 9811(a)(2)(A); see S. 356, 105th Cong. § 9811(a)(2)(A) (1997).

[9] State Medicaid Director Letter (Emergency Services), Medicaid Policies under the Balanced Budget Act of 1997 (Feb. 20, 1998).

[10] White House Memorandum, Federal Agency Compliance with the Patient Bill of Rights (Feb. 20, 1998).

Some states have adopted similar standards for identifying the EMCs described in EMTALA for which third-party payers must reimburse providers. In 1995, Maryland enacted a statute designed to curtail the ability of managed care insurers to deny claims for emergency department evaluations and treatment. As in the Balanced Budget Act of 1997, the Maryland statute adopted a prudent layperson definition of an EMC and requires health maintenance organizations (HMOs) to "reimburse a health care provider for services provided to a subscriber or enrollee in a hospital emergency facility."[11]

The prudent hospital and emergency physician should continue to treat all managed care patients in exactly the same way as they would treat any other patient who arrives at the hospital seeking care. Hospitals should be cautious not to sign managed care contracts that call for preauthorization, which may expose the hospital to EMTALA violations. At present, the hospital and emergency physician must either absorb the cost of unauthorized medical care or send bills directly to the patient.

The medical screening examination (MSE) must be the exact same examination that is provided to other patients in both timing and method. If an EMC is found, further stabilizing treatment must never wait for coverage authorization. The patient can never be moved out of the emergency department to a managed care gatekeeper physician's office or transferred to a managed care plan-approved hospital without first fulfilling all EMTALA's stabilizing and appropriate transfer guidelines. To do otherwise would jeopardize the health and safety of patients, as well as risk an EMTALA violation.

Q 9:1   Managed Care Liability: Does a health maintenance organization face liability under EMTALA?

HMOs have not been held liable under EMTALA for consequences of authorization denial. All EMTALA's liabilities, including fines, lawsuits, and termination from Medicare participation, rest solely on the shoulders of hospitals and physicians.

Cautions: EMTALA does not extend liability to HMOs that refuse emergency care authorization. CMS states that a managed health care organization cannot deny a hospital permission to examine or treat its enrollees. The HMO can only deny payment for services. A hospital is still obligated to provide the services specified in EMTALA, regardless of whether the services are authorized by a managed care plan or not.[12] For example, a Florida district court dismissed a case against an HMO that had transferred a patient because of HMO requirements. In *Dearmas v. Av-Med, Inc.*,[13] an employee was allegedly injured as a result of repeated transfers from hospitals, caused by requirements of an HMO. The court held in *Dearmas* that (1) the employee-sponsored group medical plan was an Employee

---

[11] Md. Code Ann., Health-Gen. § 19-701(d) (1996); Ark. Code Ann. § 20-9-309(c)(1).

[12] 59 Fed. Reg. 32,086, 32,116 (1994).

[13] 814 F. Supp. 1103 (S.D. Fla. 1993).

Retirement Income Security Act (ERISA)[14] employee welfare plan, (2) ERISA preempted the employee's Florida law claims against the HMO, and (3) EMTALA did not apply to HMOs.

Because of this relative immunity, HMOs have no incentive to comply with EMTALA; authorization denial leaves the hospital and emergency physician with all of EMTALA's risks. This conflict between the economics of managed care authorization and EMTALA duties poses a major dilemma for hospitals and emergency physicians.

CMS does emphasize that separate and apart from EMTALA, the Social Security Act[15] authorizes the OIG to impose intermediate sanctions against Medicare- and Medicaid-contracting managed care plans that fail to provide medically necessary services, including emergency services, to enrollees where the failure adversely affects (or has a substantial likelihood of adversely affecting) the enrollee. Medicare and Medicaid managed care plans that fail to comply with the preceding provision are subject to civil money penalties (CMPs) of up to $25,000 for each denial of medically necessary services.[16]

Q 9:2   Prior Authorization: May a hospital obtain managed care authorization before the medical screening examination?

CMS clarifies in the 2003 rules that a hospital can seek insurance information during routine admissions procedures as long as no delay in examination or treatment results from those procedures.[17] Authorization is a different matter. A hospital may not seek authorization from a managed care organization until after the required EMTALA screening examination.[18] Once an MSE is completed or in process, a hospital may seek managed care authorization concurrent with the provision of stabilizing treatment, as long as no delay in providing such treatment occurs.[19]

The State Operations Manual states:

> A hospital that is not in a managed care plan's network of designated providers cannot refuse to screen and treat (or appropriately transfer, if the medical benefits of the transfer outweigh the risks or if the individual requests the transfer) individuals who are enrolled in the plan

---

[14] The Employee Retirement Income Security Act of 1974 (ERISA) established uniform national standards for employee benefit plans and broadly preempted state regulation of these plans. The Act states that ERISA supersedes state laws to the extent that they "relate to any employee benefit plan" covered by ERISA. 29 U.S.C. § 81144(a).

[15] Social Security Act, Title 42, §§ 81857(g), 1876(i)(6), 1903(m)(5), 1932(e).

[16] 64 Fed. Reg. 61,356 (1999).

[17] 42 C.F.R. § 489.24(d)(4)(iv).

[18] 42 C.F.R. § 489.24(d)(4)(ii).

[19] 42 C.F.R. § 489.24(d)(4)(ii).

who come to the hospital if that hospital participates in the Medicare program.[20]

In the final rules discussion on prior authorization in the *Federal Register*, CMS states:

> Some managed care plans may seek to pay hospitals for services only if the hospitals obtain approval from the plan for the services before providing the services. Requirements for this approval are frequently referred to as "prior authorization" requirements. However, EMTALA (specifically, sec. 1867(h) of the Act and our existing regulation at Sec. 489.24 (c)(3) explicitly prohibits hospitals from delaying screening or stabilization services in order to inquire about the individual's method of payment or insurance status. Thus, prior authorization requirements are a matter of concern because a hospital's actions in seeking prior authorization from an insurer could result in a delay in the provision of services required by EMTALA. Our existing policy prohibits a participating hospital from seeking authorization from the individual's insurance company for screening services or services required to stabilize an emergency medical condition until after the hospital has provided the appropriate medical screening examination required by EMTALA to the individual and has initiated any further medical examination and treatment that may be required to stabilize the patient's emergency medical condition.[21]

Technically, EMTALA dictates that hospitals may not delay the MSE or stabilizing treatment to inquire about an individual's method of payment or insurance status.[22] HCFA's (now CMS) November 1999 Special Advisory Bulletin states:

> It is not appropriate for a hospital to seek, or direct a patient to seek, authorization to provide screening or stabilizing services to an individual from the individual's health plan or insurance company until after the hospital has provided (1) an appropriate medical screening examination to determine the presence or absence of an emergency medical condition, and (2) any further medical examination and treatment necessary to commence stabilization of an emergency medical condition.[23]

The hospital may seek authorization for payment for all services after providing an MSE and once necessary stabilizing treatment is "initiated." The CMS standard, then, is to provide triage, obtain sufficient initial data to generate a chart, and provide the appropriate MSE. If no emergency medical condition (EMC) is found, EMTALA no longer governs and further activity is free of EMTALA requirements. If an EMC is found, necessary stabilization (which

---

[20] U.S. Dep't HHS, CMS, State Operations Manual, App. V, Emergency Medical Treatment and Labor Act (EMTALA) Interpretive Guidelines, Part II, Tag A-2406/C-2406 (revised 7/16/2010).

[21] 68 Fed. Reg. 53,225 (2003).

[22] 42 C.F.R. § 489.24(d)(4)(i).

[23] 64 Fed. Reg. 61,358 (1999).

might include admission and/or surgery) must be initiated. Once stabilization services have been initiated, the hospital then may provide notification to the insurance carrier or managed care plan. To avoid EMTALA violation, it is absolutely vital that all patients be treated in exactly the same way, depending on presenting signs and symptoms, regardless of type of insurance coverage or form of payment. For instance, managed care patients must never be treated differently from any other patient by having examination or treatment delayed while waiting for insurance authorization. CMS cautions in the *Federal Register*:

> We would like to clarify again that hospitals that choose to seek concurrent authorization while administering stabilizing treatment must not delay such treatment in order to obtain authorization. Even if the approving insurer or physician denies authorization for the stabilizing treatment, the hospital is obligated under EMTALA to provide the necessary stabilizing treatment (if the hospital has such capabilities).[24]

Q 9:3   Qualified Medical Personnel: Who should be qualified to contact the managed care organization?

CMS comments in the *Federal Register*:

> We agree . . . that the prior authorization policies apply equally to hospital services, physician services, and nonphysician practitioner services, and are revising Sec. 489.24(d)(4)(ii) to clarify this point. We also agree that qualified medical personnel other than physicians, such as nonphysician practitioners (physician assistants and nurse practitioners), should be permitted to initiate such contacts, and are revising Sec. 489.24(d)(4)(iii) in this final rule accordingly.[25]

Cautions: Historically, the authorization policies under the proposed rule were limited only to hospital and physician services. Specifically, only emergency treating physicians were recognized as qualified medical personnel (QMP). By contrast, the final rule broadened the prior authorization policies to apply equally to hospital services, physician services, and nonphysician practitioner services and revised Section 489.24(d)(4)(iii) to reflect this change. The final rule also expanded the definition of "qualified medical personnel" permitted to initiate contact with an individual's personal physician for purposes of obtaining information and advice, relevant to the individual's medical history, deemed necessary to treat the individual's EMC. The final rule permits non-physician practitioners (nurse practitioners, physician assistants) to be treated as "qualified medical personnel" and revises Section 489.24(d)(4)(iii) to incorporate this change. Despite the various enhancements to the final rule, CMS did not, however, relinquish the caveat that such initiated contact should not inappropriately delay screening services or stabilizing treatment. Rather, when addressing objections to the caveat, CMS would only go so far as to state that it is not the agency's intent

---

[24] 68 Fed. Reg. 53,226 (2003).
[25] 68 Fed. Reg. 53,226 (2003).

(and further added that the regulations dispel this concern) that a physician in any way be restricted in his or her ability to communicate with an individual's own physician.[26]

It is vital that hospitals that allow non-physicians to contact managed care organizations provide education to these personnel on the requirements of EMTALA. Specifically, these personnel must know when EMTALA is triggered; EMTALA's specific requirements for examination, stabilization, and transfer; and when EMTALA requirements end. Without such knowledge, these personnel can easily violate EMTALA and expose the hospital to penalties.

Q 9:4   Reasonable Registration: When may a hospital obtain insurance information?

A hospital may obtain insurance information at any time as long as such activity does not delay an EMTALA MSE or stabilization care. CMS states in the *Federal Register*:

> We recognize that section 1867(h) of the Act states only that a hospital may not delay an EMTALA screening or stabilization in order to inquire about the individual's method of payment or insurance status, and does not specifically address the issue of when it is appropriate for contact with the individual's insurer to be made. Hospitals have in the past expressed a need for further guidance on the agency's policy in this area and the Special Advisory Bulletin cited earlier was developed to provide guidance on this and other issues. We do not wish to be overly prescriptive on this issue, but do believe that hospitals should have a clear statement of the agency's policy and that the policy should strike a reasonable balance between the need to avoid creating circumstances in which screening or stabilization will be likely to be delayed and the equally important need to protect the individual from avoidable liability for the costs of emergency health care services. We believe the policy in the Special Advisory Bulletin and reiterated in proposed rule strikes that balance.[27]

Cautions: A hospital may obtain insurance information at any time, such as from family members who accompany the patient to the hospital, concurrent registration at the bedside (as long as this does not interfere with screening and stabilization), or once a screening examination reveals no EMC. If a patient is in dire straits and is unable to provide any information, then obtaining insurance information must be delayed appropriately.

The State Operations Manual states:

> It is not impermissible under EMTALA for a hospital to follow normal registration procedures for individuals who come to the emergency

---

[26] Decanda Faulk, *EMTALA: The Real Deal,* 16 No. 2 Health Lawyer 10 (Dec. 2003).

[27] Decanda Faulk, *EMTALA: The Real Deal,* 16 No. 2 Health Lawyer 10 (Dec. 2003).

department. For example, a hospital may ask the individual for an insurance card, so long as doing so does not delay the medical screening examination. In addition, the hospital may seek other information (not payment) from the individual's health plan about the individual such as medical history. And, in the case of an individual with an emergency medical condition, once the hospital has conducted the medical screening examination and has initiated stabilizing treatment, it may seek authorization for all services from the plan, again, as long as doing so does not delay the implementation of the required Medical Screening Examination and stabilizing treatment.[28]

CMS comments in the *Federal Register*:

As noted in the Special Advisory Bulletin cited earlier (64 FR 61355), current Interpretive Guidelines indicate that hospitals may continue to follow reasonable registration processes for individuals presenting with an emergency medical condition. Reasonable registration processes may include asking whether an individual is insured and, if so, what that insurance is, as long as that inquiry does not delay screening or treatment. Reasonable registration processes should not unduly discourage individuals from remaining for further evaluation. As requested by the commenter, in this final rule, we are revising proposed Sec. 489.24(d)(4) by adding a new paragraph (iv) to clarify this policy. To avoid any misunderstanding of the requirement, we have revised the language of the interpretative guidelines to state that reasonable registration processes must not unduly discourage individuals from remaining for further evaluation.[29]

CMS further comments in the *Federal Register*:

Further, we note that many insurers now provide a "window" of at least 24 hours following emergency department treatment during which authorization can be obtained. In addition, many States have enacted revisions to their insurance statutes over the past several years that explicitly contemplate the existence of the Federal EMTALA statute. As a practical matter, we believe this feature of private insurance contracts, as well as State laws governing health insurance contracts, will allow screening and stabilization to go forward without compromising the individual's rights to have care covered under his or her health plan.[30]

---

[28] U.S. Dep't HHS, CMS, State Operations Manual, App. V, Emergency Medical Treatment and Labor Act (EMTALA) Interpretive Guidelines, Part II, Tag A-2406/C-2406 (revised 7/16/2010).

[29] 68 Fed. Reg. 53,227 (2003).

[30] 68 Fed. Reg. 53,226 (2003).

Q 9:5   Physician Communication: When may the emergency physician communicate with the managed care physician to discuss care issues?

The emergency department is free to call the managed care physician for medical consultations at any time. However, the MSE and needed stabilization treatment cannot be delayed for this.

The ban on calling a managed care plan for prior screening authorization or stabilizing treatment authorization does not preclude an emergency physician from contacting the managed care plan for medical advice regarding the patient's medical history or other medical issues when it is in the best interest of the patient. CMS stated in its 1999 special advisory bulletin:

> However, we have amended the prior authorization section of the bulletin slightly to make it absolutely clear that an emergency physician is free to phone a physician in a managed care plan at any time for a medical consultation when it is in the best interest of the patient. Further, we have clarified that once stabilizing treatment is under way, a managed care plan may be contacted for payment authorization.[31]

Although it is perfectly permissible to call a managed care office to attempt to determine whether there is a specialist available to consult on patient care issues, calls for "medical advice" cannot turn into de facto financial preauthorization. Careful documentation must support all such calls. It is foreseeable that contact with a plan physician may result in a "request" to transfer and references to nonpayment. These conversations should be clearly documented, and the treating physician should then proceed in a manner that is EMTALA-compliant and in the best medical interests of the patient.

The case of *Barris v. County of Los Angeles*[32] illustrates the harm that patients can incur when physicians place managed care authorization ahead of proper patient care. On May 6, 1993, at 5:30 P.M., Dawnelle Barris brought her 18-month-old daughter, Mychelle Williams, to the emergency department at Martin Luther King/Drew Medical Center by ambulance. Mychelle had vomiting, diarrhea, and lethargy with difficulty breathing. She had a temperature of 106.6°, tachypnea, and low oxygen saturation. Dr. Trach Dang, the emergency physician, examined Mychelle and felt that her condition was consistent with sepsis. However, Dr. Dang did not order tests or start treatment since he believed that he needed to obtain authorization from Kaiser Foundation Health Plan, the patient's managed care company. Kaiser had developed a program called the Emergency Prospective Review Program to deal with situations where a Kaiser member is brought to a non-Kaiser facility for emergency care. The program's purpose was to facilitate the transfer of such patients to a Kaiser facility. Dr. Dang contacted Dr. Brian Thompson, a Kaiser physician handling transfers that night. Dr. Dang discussed the case with Dr. Thompson and indicated that he thought blood tests were necessary. Dr. Thompson instructed

---

[31] 64 Fed. Reg. 61,354 (1999).

[32] 972 P.2d 966 (Cal. Sup. Ct. 1999).

him not to perform the tests, saying that the blood work would be done at Kaiser. Dr. Dang telephoned Dr. Thompson a second time expressing concern about the delay in treatment. Again, Dr. Thompson instructed Dr. Dang not to perform any tests. At 8 P.M., Mychelle suffered a seizure and became more lethargic. Dr. Dang treated her symptoms of fever, dehydration, dypsnea, and seizure but did not administer antibiotics. Shortly after 9 P.M., Mychelle was transferred by ambulance to Kaiser. At 9:50 P.M., within 15 minutes of her arrival, Mychelle suffered a cardiac arrest and was pronounced dead shortly thereafter.

Barris filed suit alleging an EMTALA violation for failure to provide an appropriate medical screening as well as failure to stabilize the patient's EMC before transferring to Kaiser. A jury found a violation of EMTALA for failing to stabilize Mychelle's EMC before transfer and awarded $1.35 million to Barris against Los Angeles County, Kaiser Foundation Health Plan, and the two physicians.

Q 9:6   Advanced Beneficiary Notices: When may a hospital present advance beneficiary notices to a patient?

The hospital should not discuss advance beneficiary notices (ABNs) with patients until an MSE and needed stabilizing care have been provided. As with insurance information, a hospital may not delay an MSE or necessary stabilizing treatment for a patient with an EMC. CMS reasons that a patient in medical duress is not in the frame of mind to make a reasoned informed consumer decision.

Cautions: Medicare requires ABNs to be provided to beneficiaries if the hospital is to be permitted to bill the beneficiary later for a non-covered service, even for services provided in an emergency context. Thus, if a Medicare managed care patient arrives at the hospital and the emergency department physician is concerned that the plan may not cover the services, the physician must have the patient sign an ABN so that the hospital will not be precluded from billing the patient for the service if the plan does not pay. In the November 1999 special advisory bulletin, CMS explains:

> It continues to be our view that a hospital would violate the patient anti-dumping statute if it delayed a medical screening examination or necessary stabilizing treatment in order to prepare an ABN and obtain a beneficiary signature. The best practice would be for a hospital not to give financial responsibility forms or notices to an individual, or otherwise attempt to obtain the individual's signature until stabilizing treatment is under way. This is because the circumstances surrounding the need for such services, and the individual's limited information about his or her medical condition, may not permit an individual to make a rational, informed consumer decision.[33]

---

[33] 64 Fed. Reg. 61,355 (1999).

CMS further explains:

> It normally is permissible to ask for general registration information prior to performing an appropriate medical screening examination. The hospital may not, however, condition such a screening and further treatment upon the individual's completion of a financial responsibility form or provision of a co-payment for any services. Such a practice could unduly deter the individual from remaining at the hospital to receive care to which he or she is entitled and which the hospital is obligated to provide regardless of ability to pay, and could cause unnecessary delay.[34]

This view is shared by the courts, as illustrated by *Stevison v. Enid Health Systems.*[35] Thirteen-year-old Twina Stevison went to the emergency department of Enid Memorial Hospital with complaints of severe stomach pain. Her mother was asked to fill out registration forms that included insurance information. The mother maintains that when she told the clerk that she only had "welfare," the clerk told her that the girl would not be seen without a $50 deposit. The clerk maintains that she merely told the mother that because welfare did not normally cover emergency department visits, she would be billed for the visit. As a result of the conversation, the Stevisons left the emergency department. The girl later sustained a ruptured appendix and was left unable to have children.

The Tenth Circuit upheld a lower court's finding that the hospital had the burden of showing that the plaintiff withdrew the request for care, as opposed to having been denied access to care.

OIG and CMS look at financial discussions before medical screening in terms of "financial coercion," and hospitals are well advised to avoid any financial discussions or financial forms until after the MSE has been performed. In any case, ABNs do not seem to have application in the emergency setting. CMS states that even after a patient has been stabilized, thus ending EMTALA requirements, an ABN should not be given to a Medicare beneficiary unless the hospital has some genuine reason to expect that Medicare will deny payment for services. Giving routine "blanket" ABNs to beneficiaries is not permitted. There must always be a reason for believing that Medicare will deny payment for the services furnished to an individual patient on a specific occasion, and that reason must appear on the ABN.[36]

The hospital should appeal any denial of claim for emergency services because the circumstances of an emergency department visit present a significantly different situation than for elective services. When a patient presents to the emergency department, even the most benign complaints may turn out to be an emergency, such as a sore throat that turns out to be a tonsillar abscess. Clinical evaluation, intervention, and testing are all initiated without regard for

---

[34] 64 Fed. Reg. 61,355 (1999).

[35] 920 F.2d 710 (10th Cir. 1990).

[36] Interaction of ABNs and EMTALA FAQs, formerly available at http://www.HCFA.gov/medlearn/ faqemtala.htm, 8/30/2001.

such issues as ABNs. If a claim is denied because of reasons such as frequency limitation (e.g., a CBC had been performed just six weeks earlier) or negative testing (e.g., a CT scan for head injury is negative and the Medicare contractor denies the scan as medically unnecessary because it is negative), the appeal should stipulate that the hospital could not reasonably have been expected to know of previous tests, or that the CT scan was a response to acute signs and symptoms. A claim for emergency services should always be defendable because in an emergency situation, the hospital could not reasonably have been expected to know that Medicare would deny payment.

Q 9:7   Prior Authorization for Care: May a hospital assist patients with seeking managed care approval?

Even if a patient requests help in seeking managed care approval, a hospital risks violating EMTALA if the hospital attempts to obtain managed care preauthorization, regardless of whether the hospital believes this delays the implementation of an MSE and stabilizing treatment or not. However, once stabilizing treatment is under way, a managed care plan may be contacted for payment authorization.[37]

Cautions: The exact point at which the patient has progressed adequately in stabilization to allow contact with the insurance company or managed care provider remains unclear. The process of screening and stabilization often overlaps with re-screening and re-stabilization. It seems reasonable, however, that once the plan of care for the patient is in place (i.e., a determination that admission or surgery will be required) and noted in the record, contact with the plan may be initiated for financial approvals. The failure to obtain approval, however, must not result in a change of the plan of care for the patient, or EMTALA liability is all but ensured.

Some hospitals implement measures designed to assist patients in obtaining managed care approval for the emergency department visit, such as inquiring about insurance status during registration, posting signs in the waiting areas alerting patients to the requirements of some managed care plans, providing phones, or assisting the patient in calling for approval. All these measures delay the required MSE and risk EMTALA violation.

In *Correa v. Hospital San Francisco*,[38] Mrs. González arrived at the emergency department of Hospital San Francisco with symptoms of chills, cold sweat, dizziness, and chest pains. She was given a number and instructed to wait while they checked her insurance. In disregard to established hospital policy, González was not afforded a medical record, vital signs were not taken, and no physical examination was provided despite her chest pain. Her insurance plan required that patients be seen at a clinic during daytime hours, and the hospital tried to direct her care to that clinic. After waiting two hours at the hospital

---

[37] 64 Fed. Reg. 61,355 (1999).
[38] 69 F.3d 1184 (1st Cir. 1995).

without medical attention, González was driven to the clinic by her daughter and there she suffered cardiopulmonary arrest and died.

Her son filed suit against the hospital for EMTALA violation. The jury awarded $100,000 to each of the patient's three surviving children, $50,000 to each of her four grandchildren, and $200,000 for pain and suffering experienced by the patient. The appellate court affirmed the decision and awards. Emergency departments must create a chart and provide the screening examination for every single patient who comes to the emergency department, regardless of insurance plans.

Q 9:8   Refusal of Authorization: What if a managed care plan refuses authorization for further care?

The patient must still be offered an appropriate MSE to determine whether an EMC exists. If an EMC is found, the patient must either be treated and stabilized or transferred appropriately if the benefit is deemed greater than the risk, in compliance with EMTALA.

The State Operations Manual states:

> A hospital that is not in a managed care plan's network of designated providers cannot refuse to screen and treat (or appropriately transfer, if the medical benefits of the transfer outweigh the risks or if the individual requests the transfer) individuals who are enrolled in the plan who come to the hospital if that hospital participates in the Medicare program.[39]

In 1996, Harrington Memorial Hospital in Worcester, Massachusetts, was threatened with Medicare provider termination for a managed care issue. The parents of two-and-a-half-year-old Jinely Maldonado brought the child, who had a fever and was vomiting, to Harrington Memorial Hospital's emergency department. The managed care policies of the hospital required the Maldonados to call their primary care physician, Dr. Vincent J. Fuselli, for authorization. Mr. Maldonado called Dr. Fuselli's office but then waited about two hours in the hospital emergency waiting room without getting a response.

The child continued to exhibit illness with a high fever and vomiting, but emergency personnel still refused to register the child for treatment. A second call was placed to Dr. Fuselli's office, and an employee in the office said that Dr. Fuselli would not authorize emergency department treatment. The child was directed to Dr. Rose K. Tharakan, a pediatrician with an office in the adjacent medical arts building. Dr. Tharakan examined the child, prescribed Advil, and sent the child home after blood tests. Jinely died eight hours later from bacterial meningitis.

---

[39] U.S. Dep't HHS, CMS, State Operations Manual, App. V, Emergency Medical Treatment and Labor Act (EMTALA) Interpretive Guidelines, Part II, Tag A-2406/C-2406 (revised 7/16/2010).

In addition to a state malpractice lawsuit, Harrington Memorial Hospital faced Medicare termination sanctions by CMS for EMTALA violation. The CMS state investigation team found an additional 15 patient charts in which patients were referred out of the emergency department without an MSE.[40] Harrington Memorial Hospital also faced a possible $50,000 fine from CMS for each offense.

There is nothing in EMTALA that requires insurance carriers to pay for an enrollee's care. Nor does EMTALA prohibit managed care plans from advising emergency physicians and patients of the anticipated denial of payment. The hospital may not refuse to screen enrollees of a managed care plan because the plan refuses to authorize treatment or to pay for such screening and treatment. Likewise, if a hospital has a contract with a managed care plan, the managed care plan cannot deny screening and treatment or appropriate transfer for individuals who are not enrolled in the plan but who come to a plan hospital that participates in the Medicare program.[41]

If the patient chooses to stay and receive care, this choice must be honored. The patient should be informed that EMTALA obligates a hospital to provide stabilizing care regardless of his or her means or ability to pay. The hospital needs to be careful in advising its patients and in keeping detailed documentation; telling patients that their plan will not pay for treatment and that they will receive a bill may be construed as illegal "financial coercion." As with all patients, once an appropriate MSE reveals no EMC, EMTALA's requirements stop, and the hospital is free to seek prior authorization for treatment or transfer. However, by the time the examination has progressed as required, the patient typically needs only a prescription or discharge instructions and further authorizations are not fruitful. If a patient is referred to a health plan location, there is also an inference that the patient had conditions for which he or she was not adequately evaluated or treated. If the patient requires hospitalization, the patient probably qualifies as having an EMC, unless the requested services are elective in nature.

Q 9:9   Patient Stability: What if the managed care physician insists that the patient is stable for discharge or transfer?

The hospital and the emergency physician treating the patient have sole responsibility for complying with EMTALA, regardless of what a managed care gatekeeper may say.

The State Operations Manual states:

> Once an individual has presented to the hospital seeking emergency care, the determination of whether an EMC exists is made by the

---

[40] Gerard F. Russell, *Mom Says She Feared for Life of Child*, Telegram & Gazette (Worcester, Mass.), Sept. 4, 1996, at A1, A4.

[41] U.S. Dep't HHS, CMS, State Operations Manual, App. V, Emergency Medical Treatment and Labor Act (EMTALA) Interpretive Guidelines, Part II, Tag A-2406/C-2406 (revised 7/16/2010).

examining physician(s) or other qualified medical personnel of the hospital.[42]

Cautions: At times, a managed care physician may insist that the patient be discharged for follow-up care or transferred to another hospital or clinic for further care. Once a patient has arrived at the hospital for emergency care, it is up to the physician or other QMP who actually examines the patient to determine whether an EMC exists. An emergency physician is still responsible for the patient under EMTALA and must not allow the managed care physician to dissuade him or her. The medical judgment of the treating physician always takes precedence over that of an off-site physician and EMTALA makes the transferring physician who has direct knowledge of the patient responsible as a patient advocate for safety.

Dr. Larry Bedard, past president of the American College of Emergency Physicians, relates that the emergency physician must spell out in no uncertain terms EMTALA's requirements for HMO gatekeeper physicians. If the gatekeeper threatens, "Unless you transfer this patient, we won't reimburse you," Dr. Bedard responds, "You are in violation of the law, because you want me to transfer an inappropriate patient. I need your name and address, because the law is very clear on this." Dr. Bedard says that this approach works every time to persuade the gatekeeper physician to allow treatment. Hospitals and HMOs should not wait for confrontations.[43] Hospitals, managed care organizations, and emergency physicians need to meet beforehand to establish what EMTALA's requirements are and how everyone can best comply while providing optimum patient care.

Barris v. County of Los Angeles[44] presents a case in point. In May 1993, Dawnelle Barris brought her 18-month-old daughter, Mychelle Williams, to the emergency department of Martin Luther King/Drew Medical Center of Los Angeles County. Mychelle had vomiting, diarrhea, lethargy, and difficulty breathing. Dr. Dang, the emergency physician, found that Mychelle had a temperature of 106.6°, tachycardia, tachypnea, low oxygen saturation, and bilateral otitis media. Suspecting sepsis, Dr. Dang called Barris' health insurance, Kaiser Foundation Health Plan, for authorization to perform tests and treat.

Dr. Brian Thompson, a Kaiser physician, instructed, Dr. Dang not to perform tests but to transfer Mychelle to Kaiser for testing. Still concerned, Dr. Dang called Dr. Thompson a second time, and again authorization was denied. Mychelle was transferred by ambulance to Kaiser, where she suffered cardiac arrest within 15 minutes of arrival and died. Autopsy confirmed sepsis as the cause of death. A jury found a violation of EMTALA for failing to stabilize

---

[42] U.S. Dep't HHS, CMS, State Operations Manual, App. V, Emergency Medical Treatment and Labor Act (EMTALA) Interpretive Guidelines, Part II, Tag A-2406/C-2406 (revised 7/16/2010).

[43] *See New EMTALA Guidelines Hot Off the Press: Here's What Your ED Needs to Know*, 10 Emerg. Dep't Mgmt. 97-108 (Sept. 1998).

[44] *Barris*, 972 P.2d 966.

Mychelle's EMC before transfer and awarded $1.35 million to Barris against Los Angeles County, Kaiser Foundation Health Plan, and the two physicians.

The lesson in this case is twofold: first, the patient was still in the process of medical screening and required further testing; therefore, the physician improperly sought approval of payment for tests that were mandated under the circumstances; second, the emergency physician allowed his best medical judgment to be subverted by the denial of payment by the managed care plan.

Perhaps less obvious, a third lesson is also present: insurance companies and managed care organizations consider litigation and possible losses a "cost of doing business," whereas to the physician or hospital, it is an issue of devastating administrative penalties and sanctions that are not covered by insurance. The emergency physician and hospital must recognize their exposed position in these cases and act in their patient's best medical interest, which ultimately serves their own best interest.

Q 9:10   Dual Staffing: What if a managed care organization demands that its "hospitalist" see the patient first?

Some managed care companies have physicians (hospitalists) who work solely in the hospital to attend patients under the managed care insurance plan. This practice is commonly referred to as "dual staffing." The managed care plan may dictate that its physician be the only physician to attend to emergency department patients. This practice may create difficulties that could expose the hospital to possible EMTALA violations.

Cautions: A patient who comes to the hospital for emergency care must first be provided with an MSE that cannot be delayed in order to obtain insurance information. This requirement alone causes problems with deciding when to call the hospitalist because the emergency physician, rather than the hospitalist, must provide a screening examination before asking about insurance coverage. In addition, because the hospitalist is usually not stationed in the emergency department, there may be a delay before he or she can be summoned to the department to screen a patient under the plan once the insurance information is obtained. Such a delay in providing the screening examination violates EMTALA's requirements for an immediate screening examination and stabilization.

Conflicts may also arise if the hospitalist and the emergency physician disagree on whether the patient has an actual or even a potential EMC requiring emergency care. Case law has placed the legal responsibility of patient care on the shoulders of the emergency physician for *all* patients who enter the emergency department, not just the patients that he or she sees. Hospitals must not allow hospitalists the authority to override the medical judgment of the emergency physician, who has the primary legal responsibility for all patients who come to the emergency department.

The presence of the "dual staffing" model in a hospital inherently creates a discrimination in treatment among patients with similar conditions by providing a "separate but equal" track. If clear and well-detailed criteria or operational practices are enacted in the department, it may be possible to minimize the discrepancies between the two tracks, but the logic of two parallel and costly systems in the same department is inconsistent with "equal treatment."

The only rationale in which dual staffing could be financially justifiable would rest on the ability of the hospitalist to preempt admissions and divert patients who might otherwise be admitted to plan hospitals and clinics at a significant cost savings to the plan. That rationale implicitly confirms that the standard operations of the hospital would be to admit patients, and that dual staffing standard operations would be to not admit patients of a similar nature. In agreeing to such a system, the hospital would be placed at significant risk of EMTALA violation.

Although the managed care plan may profess to "hold the hospital harmless," the EMTALA citation will be issued to the hospital and not the managed care plan. Fines are assessed against the hospital, and not against the managed care plan; and most state laws prohibit indemnity for violations of law, so the hospital is again the victim. The only circumstances under which the plan might participate in liability is if the hospital is sued under EMTALA and brings a third-party indemnity claim against the managed care plan.

CMS and OIG are obviously skeptical of the dual staffing pattern but choose to let the development of the system proceed with a strong warning against duality of treatment.

This issue was addressed in CMS's special advisory bulletin of November 1999. CMS believes that EMTALA does not prohibit the use of dual staffing, reasoning:

> For the Federal Government to prohibit in advance, on a national level, arrangements, which might increase access to health care services, would require some greater likelihood of risk or harm than we currently foresee. (In this context, we note that States are able to restrict or prohibit dual staffing arrangements within their borders.) It may or may not become evident that dual staffing impedes the goals of EMTALA, or that it advances publicly beneficial goals of managed care and other innovations in health care delivery, such as coordination of services and health promotion. If we were to declare that all dual staffing arrangements violate EMTALA, we might unnecessarily prevent the development of health care delivery practices, which could improve access to health care.

> Thus, we have concluded that while dual staffing raises serious issues, it would not necessarily constitute a per se violation of the anti-dumping statute.[45]

---

[45] 64 Fed. Reg. 61,354 (1999).

Q 9:11 Dual Emergency Services: May a hospital set up dual emergency services for managed care organizations?

Yes. But the hospital must make sure that the two emergency departments are equivalent in services provided.

CMS clarifies its stance on this issue by advising:

> If a hospital constructs two equally good emergency service "tracks" each adequately staffed and each with equally good access to all of the medical capabilities of the hospital, such that both MCO and non-MCO patients receive equal access to screening and stabilizing medical treatment, then such an arrangement would seem to not violate the requirements of the anti-dumping statute.

Absent such equivalency, implementation of dual staffing raises concerns under EMTALA. The following are potential violations:

- Where the emergency department directs a hospital-owned and operated ambulance differently in field care or facility destination depending on which members of a dual staff (that is, either MCO or non-MCO physicians or practitioners) are either on the radio to emergency medical services (EMS) or are expected to see the patient;

- If the emergency department alert status affecting acceptance of EMS cases differs depending on which "side" (MCO or non-MCO) is expected to see the patient;

- If either the MCO or non-MCO track is understaffed or simply overcrowded, and a patient in a particular track is subjected to a delay in screening and stabilizing treatment, even though a physician in the alternative track was available to see the individual. Where there is no emergency department policy or procedure, or custom or practice, which requires cross-over coverage between the dual staffs as required for patient care. (Delays in screening or stabilization of patients on one track but not the other are delays in screening or stabilization based on the insurance status of the individual and thus represent potential violations of EMTALA);

- If the hospital's emergency department quality oversight plan differs between the two "sides" (MCO and non-MCO) of the dually staffed ED; and/or

- Where the protocols for transfer of unstable patients differ other than administratively, for example, (1) if the substance of stability determination criteria between the two staffs are [sic] different, or (2) when patients are unstable and are transferred routinely to different facilities that are not equivalent to each other in level of care or distance, and their destinations depend on their insurance status.

While we recognize that dual staffing will add to a hospital's burden to assure that it is not violating EMTALA, we do not believe the EMTALA statute makes dual staffing illegal per se. We expect that practical experience with dually staffed emergency departments will reveal whether or not they can be maintained without violating EMTALA.[46]

Given the extra expense and these EMTALA restrictions, most hospitals would probably find dual emergency department tracks impractical.

Q 9:12   Location of Screening Examination: May the medical screening examination be performed in the managed care physician's office?

No. Once the patient comes to the dedicated emergency department, the patient may not be referred to another area for the MSE for insurance reasons.

Cautions: Patients may not be referred to other areas of the hospital campus for the MSE except for defined beneficial medical reasons such as obstetrics care. Patients with a defined medical reason can be moved only to a contiguous hospital facility that is "on-campus." All patients with the same defined medical reason must be moved and treated identically. Referring a patient to a managed care physician's office, even if the office is on-campus, violates EMTALA, because the referral is for insurance purposes and not for medical benefit.

After an appropriate MSE by approved personnel in the emergency department shows that there is no EMC, the requirements of EMTALA stop, and the hospital is free to refer the patient anywhere it wants, but referral for current evaluation or acute definitive care will be evidence of a failure to adequately screen and stabilize. Referrals for care that are purely for "status" follow-up would not be a violation.

Q 9:13   Medicaid Managed Care: Are state Medicaid managed care programs exempt from EMTALA?

No. State Medicaid managed care programs may not circumvent EMTALA's requirements.

Cautions: When some states initially implemented Medicaid managed care plans, the plans attempted to set up their own procedures to screen patients from inappropriate emergency department visits. Patients deemed "stable" by a brief triage process were denied access to an emergency physician until authorization for payment was obtained from the managed care organization. CMS concluded that this practice was a violation of EMTALA because appropriate MSEs were delayed due to insurance status. The Medicaid patients were treated differently from other patients who came to the emergency department, thus triggering the basic antidiscrimination mandates of EMTALA. EMTALA is a federal law that preempts all conflicting state

---

[46] 64 Fed. Reg. 61,357 (1999).

laws. CMS cited hospitals in West Virginia, Georgia, and Colorado for violating EMTALA by using this system of patient care.[47]

Many states implemented various Medicaid variations in attempts to bring costs under control and were issued "waivers" from federal Medicaid requirements. Many of these agencies then mistakenly assumed that they were also "waivered" from EMTALA requirements. In fact, they are not, and policies and procedures that violate EMTALA will result in citations, fines, and litigation against hospitals that innocently participate in the illegal processes.

CMS guidance clearly indicates that state plans may not impose prior authorization or notification requirements for payments. Hospitals that comply with these Medicaid plan practices leave themselves open to potential violations if Medicaid patients receive a level of care different from other classes of patients. This applies to mental health plan participants as well as to general medical plan participants.

Q 9:14   Informing Patients: May the hospital tell a patient whether his or her managed care insurance authorizes care?

Before the MSE and commencement of stabilization, telling a patient of authorization may be seen as coercion to deny medical care. Once stabilizing treatment is ongoing, however, CMS does allow the hospital to seek authorization from managed care plans if the process does not delay necessary treatment.[48]

Cautions: Some hospitals assist patients in calling their managed care organizations for authorization before a physician sees the patient. Some believe that it is only right for patients to understand their economic liability before agreeing to further medical services. However, this is a dangerous practice in light of EMTALA. Informing patients whether there is insurance coverage for their visit could be seen as a form of financial coercion to prevent the patient from seeking emergency care. CMS warns that "[h]ospitals should not attempt to coerce individuals into making judgments against their best interest by informing them that they will have to pay for their care if they remain."[49]

In a 1994 study in California, researchers analyzed what happened when HMO patients came to a university hospital emergency department, where calls seeking authorization for treatment were made to their HMOs before the patients were seen by a physician. The study found that of the 545 patients for whom their HMO denied authorization for emergency care, 95 percent left the emergency department without receiving treatment. The authors noted with

---

[47] *See* Robert A. Bitterman, *Dealing with Managed Care Under COBRA*, 7 Emerg. Physician Legal Bull. (1997).

[48] 64 Fed. Reg. 61,354, 61,358 (Nov. 10, 1999).

[49] 59 Fed. Reg. 32,101 (1994). *See* 42 C.F.R. § 489.24(c)(3); CMS, State Operations Manual, Tag No. A408.

concern that "[t]hese patients left [against medical advice] despite the fact that [they] had hands-on evaluations by a trained registered nurse who determined that they needed evaluation for emergency conditions."[50]

The prudent procedure is for the hospital to provide a prompt MSE regardless of insurance authorization. If the MSE reveals no EMC, then the hospital or the patient is free to seek insurance authorization.

The problem occurs when the MSE is inconclusive and reveals only the possibility of an emergency condition. At that point, EMTALA would mandate additional testing and/or specialty consult, which should be secured before contacting the managed care plan. If the plan denies coverage, the treatment plan should proceed as intended.

A competent adult may sign out against medical advice. But what if a responsible adult wants to sign out an incompetent geriatric patient or a minor because of authorization denial, despite the physician's concerns? A physician has ethical and moral duties to protect and treat the patient under his or her care. Depending on state child neglect and elder abuse laws, the physician may be required to take the minor or elderly person into protective custody or to notify enforcement authorities, and the physician should comply with those duties. EMTALA permits refusals of care if properly documented. Although this does not resolve the ethical concerns in a given case, it answers the question of what the law demands of the physician.

Q 9:15   Cost Information: What if a patient insists on knowing the costs of his or her emergency care?

Hospital personnel knowledgeable about EMTALA should provide information to the patient regarding potential financial liability and the hospital's EMTALA obligations.

CMS advises:

> If a patient inquires about his or her obligation to pay for emergency services, such an inquiry should be answered by a staff member who has been well trained to provide information regarding potential financial liability. This staff member also should be knowledgeable about the hospital's anti-dumping statute obligations and should clearly inform the patient that, notwithstanding the patient's ability to pay, the hospital stands ready and willing to provide an MSE and stabilizing treatment, if necessary. Hospital staff should encourage any patient who believes that he or she may have an EMC to remain for the MSE and any necessary stabilizing treatment. Staff should also encourage the patient to defer further discussion of financial responsibility issues, if possible, until after the medical screening has been performed. If the patient chooses to withdraw his or her request for examination or treatment, a

---

[50] Robert W. Derlet & Bridget Hamilton, *The Impact of Health Maintenance Organization Care Authorization Policy on an Emergency Department Before California's New Managed Care Law*, 3 Acad. Emerg. Med. 338, 342 (1996).

staff member with appropriate medical training should discuss the medical issues related to a voluntary withdrawal.[51]

Cautions: This situation can present a bind for hospitals. A patient would certainly be entitled to know the costs for services if he or she requested such information. There would be major customer relation problems if such information were refused and the patient subsequently received a substantial hospital bill for uncovered services. However, CMS does not give the hospital much breathing room on this issue. CMS states in the Special Advisory Bulletin:

> A reasonable argument can be made that patients (other than those arriving in dire condition) should be informed when they request emergency services of their potential financial liability for services. Some would go further and argue that the hospital itself should seek prior approval from the patient's health plan for emergency services to preserve the patient's right to seek coverage for such services. However, our concern is that such an inquiry may improperly or unduly influence patients to leave the hospital without receiving an appropriate medical screening examination. This result would be inconsistent with the goals of the anti-dumping statute and could leave the hospital exposed to liability under the statute.[52]

It is incumbent on the hospital to provide proper education to its emergency department personnel on the requirements of EMTALA. At all times, the hospital must have an individual present (e.g., an emergency department employee, the on-call hospital administrator, a hospital charge nurse) who has proper knowledge of EMTALA so as to properly inform the patient when these situations occur.

Q 9:16 Patient Refusal: What if a patient refuses any examination until his or her managed care organization is called?

A competent adult patient is free to refuse any type of care. The burden is on the hospital to explain its EMTALA obligations and adequately document the refusal if the patient persists in refusal of care.

Cautions: Any competent adult is free to refuse any form of medical care for himself or herself. The burden is on the hospital to prove that (1) the patient understood the hospital's EMTALA obligations, (2) the hospital did not coerce the patient into leaving, and (3) the hospital offered the MSE. Use of an "Against Medical Advice" form here is inappropriate because as yet there is no medical advice. Without an MSE, the hospital cannot know whether further treatment is warranted, so medical advice is impossible. For these situations, the hospital should draft a "Refusal to be Medically Screened" form. The form should specify that the patient understands the hospital's

---

[51] 64 Fed. Reg. 61,359 (1999).

[52] OIG/HCFA [now CMS] Special Advisory Bulletin on the Patient Anti-Dumping Statute, 64 Fed. Reg. 61,353 (1999).

EMTALA obligations and its benefits. If the patient refuses to sign the form, then one or more of the hospital personnel should sign the form, documenting that the MSE was offered but that the patient still refused the examination.

Q 9:17 Voluntarily Leaving Before MSE: What if a patient voluntarily leaves the emergency department before any medical screening examination?

A competent patient may voluntarily choose to leave the hospital without a screening examination. However, the hospital must do all it can to inform the patient of his or her EMTALA rights beforehand.

CMS stated in its November 1999 Special Advisory Bulletin:

> If an individual chooses to withdraw his or her request for examination or treatment at the presenting hospital, and if the hospital is aware that the individual intends to leave prior to the screening examination, a hospital should take the following steps:
>
> 1. Offer the individual further medical examination and treatment within the staff and facilities available at the hospital as may be required to identify and stabilize an emergency medical condition;
>
> 2. Inform the individual of the benefits of such examination and treatment, and of the risks of withdrawal prior to receiving such examination and treatment; and
>
> 3. Take all reasonable steps to secure the individual's written informed consent to refuse such examination and treatment.
>
> The medical record should contain a description of risks discussed and of the examination, treatment, or both, if applicable, that was refused. If an individual leaves without notifying hospital personnel, the hospital should, at a minimum, document the fact that the person had been there, what time the hospital discovered that the patient had left, and should retain all triage notes and additional records, if any. However, the burden rests with the hospital to show that it has taken appropriate steps to discourage an individual from leaving the hospital without evaluation.[53]

CMS's concern is illustrated in *Consumer Health Foundation v. Potomac Hospital*.[54] On May 22, 1993, Gerald Helmann was shopping at a mall in Woodbridge, Virginia, when he began experiencing tightness in his chest and pain in his left arm. Helmann drove to the emergency room at Potomac Hospital, proceeded to the front reception desk, and signed in. After explaining his symptoms to the registrar and a triage nurse, Helmann asked whether the cost of his treatment would be covered by his insurance carrier, Consumer Health Foundation (CHF).

---

[53] OIG/HCFA [now CMS] Special Advisory Bulletin on the Patient Anti-Dumping Statute, 64 Fed. Reg. 61353 (1999).

[54] 172 F.3d 43 (4th Cir. 1999).

The registrar told him that Potomac Hospital would treat him irrespective of his coverage but advised him to contact CHF to ensure that it would pay the cost of his treatment at Potomac. Helmann contacted CHF and was denied coverage at Potomac Hospital but was authorized coverage at CHF's Annandale, Virginia, facility. Helmann voluntarily left Potomac Hospital to go to Annandale. However, he collapsed en route and died three days later. After Helmann's death, his estate settled an action against CHF for $1.2 million. CHF sought contribution from Potomac Hospital, asserting that the hospital had breached its duty to provide Helmann with reasonable care. The Fourth Circuit[55] upheld the federal district court's ruling in favor of Potomac.

Although the court in this case ruled in favor of the hospital, CMS would not necessarily agree with the outcome. Under its guidance, someone knowledgeable in EMTALA and financial issues should be the one to discuss coverage issues. There must be adequate written evidence of refusal of care.

The fact that a plan resists paying at an institution or states that it will not pay "out of plan" is not conclusive of its obligations under the law. Most plans are responsible for out-of-plan visits that qualify as emergencies.

Nurses, clerks, and physicians should not attempt to represent to patients what their plan will or will not cover. The safest answer is "I don't know." It is both truthful and fair, unless the nurse, clerk, or physician is a health insurance law specialist with a thorough knowledge of the exact language of the master insurance policy for a given plan.

Q 9:18 Managed Care Transfers: Can a patient be transferred to a hospital under contract with a patient's managed care plan?

As with any other transfer, EMTALA requirements must first be fulfilled. A patient found to be legally stable after an adequate MSE may be transferred. A patient found to be potentially at risk to deteriorate from or during transfer must receive stabilizing treatment and can be transferred only if EMTALA transfer guidelines are fulfilled.

In *Clark v. Baton Rouge General Medical Center*,[56] Rosemary Roubique had a massive stroke and was rushed to Opelousas General Hospital (OGH) by ambulance. The emergency physician stabilized her and contacted her cardiologist, Dr. James Calvin, who instructed that she be transferred to Baton Rouge General Medical Center (BRG), where he would treat her. [Note: this transfer may be a violation if OGH had the capabilities to treat the patient. If not, the hospital may have been under a duty to obtain acceptance of a neurologist rather than a cardiologist.]

On arrival at BRG, Roubique was seen by a nurse, and her vital signs were recorded. Dr. Kilpatrick, who was now on call for Dr. Calvin, ordered that a

---

[55] The Fourth Circuit covers Maryland, West Virginia, Virginia, North Carolina, and South Carolina, 28 U.S.C. § 41.

[56] 657 So. 2d 741 (La. Ct. App. 1995), *cert. denied*, 661 So. 2d 1347 (La. 1995).

health plan neurologist and a heart specialist be consulted to examine the patient, but Dr. Kilpatrick did not go to the hospital to examine Roubique himself. An emergency department receptionist at BRG advised the family that Roubique's insurance provider, Community Health, had changed primary care provider hospitals from BRG to Our Lady of the Lake Hospital (OLOL), and, therefore, BRG could not treat Roubique.

While waiting in the emergency department, Roubique began to vomit and appeared to become worse. The family became concerned and asked the emergency personnel for help. The family did not want her transferred again and informed the emergency personnel that they would accept financial responsibility for services rendered at BRG if the health plan would not pay. Despite this offer, BRG personnel insisted that they could not treat Roubique because she was a Community Health patient.

Later, a neurologist examined her and determined that she was stable for transfer to OLOL. After being transferred to OLOL, Roubique had a second stroke and died. A jury found that BRG violated EMTALA by failing to provide an appropriate MSE. The jury also concluded that Dr. Calvin and/or Dr.Kilpatrick had breached the standard of care required of physicians. The jury assigned 25 percent liability to BRG and 75 percent liability to Drs. Calvin and Kilpatrick. The jury awarded damages against BRG.

On appeal, BRG asserted that EMTALA did not apply because this was not an emergency care situation, and it denied any failure to perform an appropriate MSE. The court responded, "Regardless of whether BRG initially had a duty to provide an appropriate medical screening, when members of her family sought assistance from ER medical personnel, BRG violated its own emergency department policy by failing to examine her."[57]

The message here is that if a patient needs care, emergency personnel should never be concerned about payment issues. In addition, if a patient's condition changes while waiting for transfer, a new MSE is mandated.

Unfortunately, incidents like these will keep the need for EMTALA in place. *Clark* also brings the strong warning that the system is sometimes subverted and corrupted by the financial pressures of health care management organizations to the point where care may be readily compromised in the name of finances. Although EMTALA was enacted to prevent dumping of nonpaying patients, it has been extended to apply to prohibit disparate emergency department treatment of patients enrolled in managed care plans. EMTALA forbids the movement of patients before an appropriate MSE and stabilizing treatment.

---

[57] *Clark*, 657 So. 2d 741, 746.

Chapter 10

EMTALA and Psychiatry

In the case of psychiatric emergencies, an individual expressing suicidal or homicidal thoughts or gestures, or determined dangerous to self or others, would be considered to have an Emergency Medical Condition.

U.S. Dep't HHS, CMS, State Operations Manual, App. V, Emergency Medical Treatment and Labor Act (EMTALA) Interpretive Guidelines, Part II, Tag A-2407/C-2407 (revised 5/29/2009).

EMTALA definitely covers psychiatric patients. The Centers for Medicare & Medicaid Services (CMS) specifically expanded the definition of "emergency medical condition" to include psychiatric disturbances and symptoms of substance abuse in its interim rules.[1] Like any patient with a medical condition, psychiatric patients must be provided with an adequate medical screening examination (MSE), stabilizing treatment, and appropriate transfer. The MSE must be adequate not only to define the psychiatric problem but also to reveal any other physical illnesses or trauma. Chronically mentally ill, homeless, and intoxicated patients are at increased risk of additional physical illnesses. This is a challenging burden for the physician because physical conditions like stroke, subdural hematomas, drug overdose, medication side effects, and gastrointestinal bleeding are often hidden behind the presenting psychiatric condition.

The application of EMTALA to psychiatric emergencies remains nebulous. CMS's comments are restricted mainly to discussions of suicidal and homicidal tendencies as psychiatric emergencies. Other psychiatric conditions are difficult to apply to EMTALA because mental harm is more difficult to quantify than physical harm. EMTALA defines emergency medical conditions (EMCs) as (1) placing the health of the individual in serious jeopardy, (2) serious impairment to bodily functions, or (3) serious dysfunction of any bodily organ or part.[2] Only when a psychiatric condition can produce one of these physical results does it rise to the level of an EMC. This is why nearly every EMTALA case claiming a psychiatric emergency involves suicide.

---

[1] 42 C.F.R. § 489.24(b)(1).

[2] 42 U.S.C. § 1395dd(e)(1)(A).

Q 10:1   Psychiatric Hospitals: Does EMTALA govern psychiatric hospitals?

Yes. If the hospital accepts Medicare, then psychiatric hospitals are liable for EMTALA violations just as other hospitals are.

CMS stated in its 1998 State Operations Manual:

> If a psychiatric hospital offers services for medical, psychiatric, or substance abuse emergency conditions, it is obligated to comply with all of the anti-dumping requirements of §§ 489.20 and 489.

> Most psychiatric hospitals are accredited by the Joint Commission and have an emergency department which provides reasonable care in determining whether an emergency exists, renders life saving first aid, and makes appropriate referrals to the nearest organizations that are capable of providing needed services. The emergency department must have a mechanism for providing physician coverage at all times.[3]

Most psychiatric hospitals have an emergency department and emergency personnel who can reasonably determine whether an emergency condition exists, render basic lifesaving care, and make appropriate referrals to the nearest organizations that can provide the needed services. Psychiatric hospitals that provide emergency services are obligated under EMTALA to respond within the limits of their capabilities and have a process to provide physician coverage at all times.[4]

Q 10:2   Lack of Psychiatric Capabilities: What if a hospital lacks the capabilities to perform a mental health examination?

Hospitals that operate emergency departments but do not offer psychiatric treatment and have no psychiatrists, psychologists, or any other mental health professionals on staff do not have a duty under EMTALA to provide mental health screening beyond their capabilities.

In the case of *Baker v. Adventist Health, Inc.*,[5] a hospital that operated an emergency department, but that did not offer psychiatric treatment and had no psychiatrists, psychologists, or any other mental health professionals on staff, did not have a duty under EMTALA to provide a mental health screening for an emergency room patient who had reported suicidal ideations, and thus did not violate EMTALA when it called in a crisis worker from a county medical health department, pursuant to its written policy, to screen the patient. The hospital was required under EMTALA only to provide a screening examination that was within its capabilities, which did not include mental health examinations. Henry Baker presented at the emergency department of Redbud Community Hospital.

---

[3] HCFA, State Operations Manual: Provider Certification (HCFA Pub. 7, Transmittal No. 2, June 1, 1998), Tag No. A404, V-16.

[4] HCFA, State Operations Manual: Provider Certification (HCFA Pub. 7, Transmittal No. 2, June 1, 1998), Tag No. A404, V-16.

[5] 260 F.3d 987 (9th Cir. 2001).

He requested psychiatric care for depression. Dr. Wolfgang Schug, the emergency physician, examined Baker and found no acute emergent condition. Redbud Hospital had a written policy requiring the emergency department to request a mental health evaluation from the county health system when a medical screening turned up evidence of a "psychiatric disturbance." Dr. Schug called the Lake County crisis line and requested a mental health evaluation of Baker. Dennis Skinner, a Lake County crisis worker, arrived at the emergency department and evaluated Baker. Skinner found that Baker did not constitute a danger to himself or others. Baker was discharged from the emergency department for follow-up care. However, Baker committed suicide shortly after discharge.

Baker's family filed a lawsuit against the hospital for violation of EMTALA, claiming that EMTALA required the hospital to provide psychiatric examinations with its own personnel. The Ninth Circuit affirmed a ruling for the defense, holding that (1) the hospital, which did not offer psychiatric treatment, and which had no psychiatrists, psychologists, or mental health professionals on staff, did not have a duty under EMTALA or state law to provide mental health screening for Baker; and (2) the hospital did not disparately apply its screening policies.

In *Baker*, the hospital had a solid defense since it indeed did not have any mental health professionals on staff and also had a written policy requiring the emergency physician to call the county crisis mental health worker. A hospital only has to provide MSEs within its capabilities. Hospitals that have psychiatrists or other mental health professionals on staff cannot use the *Baker* defense. The emergency department physician would be prudent to use all the hospital's mental health resources if he or she has reason to believe that the patient may be dangerous to self or others.

Q 10:3   The Psychiatric Medical Screening Examination: What is the medical screening examination requirement for psychiatric patients?

The emergency physician is faced with a dual duty when presented with a psychiatric patient. The MSE must be adequate to reveal not only emergent psychiatric conditions but also any emergent physical medical conditions. EMTALA applies to patients who go to psychiatric intake services, if it meets the definition of a "dedicated emergency department," as well as to the emergency department. The CMS State Operations Manual states, "For individuals with psychiatric symptoms, the medical records should indicate an assessment of suicide or homicide attempt or risk, disorientation, or assaultive behavior that indicates danger to self or others."[6]

---

[6] U.S. Dep't HHS, Centers for Medicare & Medicaid Servs. (CMS), State Operations Manual, App. V, Investigation Procedures for Responsibilities of Medicare Participating Hospitals in Emergency Cases, Part 1, V, Task 3—Record Review.

Cautions: Psychiatric patients pose a significant area of risk for emergency physicians. Psychiatric patients often have occult emergent physical medical conditions, such as cerebral vascular accidents, subdural hematomas, drug overdoses, medication side effects, gastrointestinal bleeding, and infections, which the emergency physician should reasonably attempt to reveal. This added burden requires that before transferring the patient to a psychiatric facility, the emergency physician must extend the screening examination to include appropriate laboratory and/or radiologic tests to ensure (within reason) that the patient is free of an emergent physical medical condition.

In addition to the physical examination, a thorough mental status examination should be performed and be well documented in the patient's record. It would be prudent to include an alcohol level and drug screening in laboratory tests. Any head trauma should prompt a computed tomography (CT) scan of the head. The prudent emergency physician should not be too quick to attribute symptoms entirely to psychiatric causes.

Psychiatric transfers often involve transfer to public psychiatric facilities that are ill-equipped to provide medical care. Transferring a patient who turns out to have an unstabilized EMC to such a facility risks an EMTALA violation for inappropriate medical screening.

Q 10:4 Complete Diagnosis: Does EMTALA require a hospital to detect every possible diagnosis?

No. EMTALA requires that an appropriate medical screening be performed to reasonably rule out medical, toxic, or traumatic causes for the behavior. It does not place on physicians the heavy burden of being perfect in detecting EMCs.

In *Baber v. Hospital Corp. of America,*[7] Brenda Baber convulsed and fell while roaming around the emergency department in a hyperactive and agitated state. After the fall, she exhibited increased agitation and slurred speech. The emergency physician attributed the symptoms to her underlying psychiatric condition and medications. Baber was transferred to a psychiatric facility, where she had another seizure. She was found to have a fractured skull and subdural hematoma. She was transferred back to the original hospital, where she died that same day. The patient's brother sued the hospital, alleging an EMTALA violation for failure to provide an appropriate MSE that would have detected the fractured skull. But the court in *Baber* held that "while EMTALA requires a hospital emergency department to apply its standard screening examination uniformly, it does not guarantee that the emergency personnel will correctly diagnose a patient's condition as a result of this screening."[8]

In *Eberhardt v. City of Los Angeles,*[9] Eberhardt was seen in the emergency department for complications from the use of cocaine and heroin. He was

---

[7] 977 F.2d 872 (4th Cir. 1992).

[8] *Baber,* 977 F.2d 872, 878.

[9] 62 F.3d 1253 (9th Cir. 1995).

released with instructions to follow up at a drug rehabilitation facility. The next day, he committed apparent suicide when, with a machete in hand, he yelled "kill me" and "put me out of my misery" and charged policemen, who then shot and killed him. Eberhardt's father sued the hospital for releasing him in an unstable medical condition in violation of EMTALA. The court in *Eberhardt* rejected the argument that a non-apparent suicidal tendency constituted an EMC under EMTALA. In so holding, the court reasoned that although in hindsight the medical record may have suggested the patient had a "self-destructive disposition," the patient at the time of screening did not manifest any suicidal tendency by acute or severe symptoms and did not present any condition requiring immediate medical attention.

The case of *Jackson v. East Bay Hospital*,[10] decided in April 2001, continued to confirm that as long as an appropriate MSE is performed, the hospital is not liable under EMTALA for any medical condition not discovered. On April 2, 1996, Jackson visited the Lake County Mental Health Department for psychiatric symptoms. The Lake County staff instructed Jackson to go to the Redbud Hospital emergency department for a physical medical clearance. Dr. Schug, the emergency physician, examined Jackson and cleared him for follow up with Lake County. On April 4, Jackson returned to Redbud's emergency department with a sore throat, chest pains, and nausea. Dr. Ollada, another emergency physician, ordered a battery of tests, including an electrocardiogram, urine drug screen, blood tests, and an arterial blood gas. The evaluation did not reveal an EMC so Jackson was released once again for follow-up at Lake County.

On April 5, Jackson again returned to Redbud's emergency department with confusion and agitation. This time a Lake County crisis worker evaluated Jackson and committed him to East Bay Hospital for psychiatric treatment. After admission to East Bay, Jackson suffered a cardiac arrest and died. An autopsy determined that Jackson died from cardiac arrhythmia caused by toxic levels of his prescribed medication, clomipramine (Anafranil). Jackson's survivors sued, arguing that the physicians failed to provide an adequate MSE that would have revealed Jackson's toxic state. The court held that a hospital satisfies EMTALA's medical screening requirement once it provides a patient with an examination comparable to the one offered to any other patient presenting with similar symptoms, unless the examination is so cursory that it is not designed to identify the EMC. There also was no stabilization violation because "a hospital's duty to stabilize the patient does not arise until the hospital first detects an emergency medical condition."[11]

CMS, however, will closely scrutinize the medical screening to determine whether a patient was actually assessed with a purpose of ruling out other conditions or whether the examination was a perfunctory "cleared for psych" that failed to address potential underlying issues. Similarly, CMS will look at the adequacy of the psychiatric assessment to ensure that it addressed all appropriate issues and appropriate disposition of the patient.

---

[10] 246 F.3d 1248 (9th Cir. 2001).

[11] *Jackson*, 246 F.3d 1248, 1257. The court was here citing *Eberhardt*, 62 F.3d 1253, 1259.

To meet the CMS burden, the physician is well advised to document his or her examination and impressions in great detail.

Q 10:5 Psychiatric Stabilization: What is the stabilization requirement for psychiatric patients?

Once a patient is deemed "stable," EMTALA no longer applies, and patients may be transferred even for economic reasons. The operative word for stabilizing psychiatric patients is "protected." A psychiatric patient is considered stable for transfer when, by use of either medication or physical restraints, the patient can be protected from hurting himself or herself or others.

The State Operations Manual states:

> Psychiatric patients are considered stable when they are protected and prevented from injuring or harming him/herself or others. The administration of chemical or physical restraints for purposes of transferring an individual from one facility to another may stabilize a psychiatric patient for a period of time and remove the immediate EMC but the underlying medical condition may persist and if not treated for longevity the patient may experience exacerbation of the EMC. Therefore, practitioners should use great care when determining if the medical condition is in fact stable after administering chemical or physical restraints.[12]

For years, hospitals were confused as to when a psychiatric patient could reasonably be considered "stable" for transfer. An emergency physician cannot cure a psychiatric patient, so a suicidal or psychotic patient cannot be truly "stabilized" psychiatrically while in the emergency department. An emergency physician can subdue a patient temporarily with drugs and/or restraints, but the patient may still be a potential danger to self or to others. A psychotic patient may not truly understand or agree to a transfer. For these reasons, hospitals that possess some capabilities to treat a psychiatric patient face difficulties in transferring a psychiatric patient without risks of an EMTALA violation.

The dilemma was clarified in the interpretive guidelines issued by CMS in June 1998. For purposes of transferring a psychiatric patient from one facility to a second facility, the patient is considered to be stable "when he/she is protected and prevented from injuring himself/herself or others. For purposes of discharging a patient [versus transfer], for psychiatric conditions, the patient is considered to be stable when he/she is no longer considered to be a threat to him/herself or to others."[13] A psychiatric patient may be made "stable" and no longer considered a threat to self or others by medical treatment (e.g., tranquilizers) or physical means (e.g., restraints or adequate physical control by ambulance personnel). A public psychiatric facility without adequate capacity to treat medical emergencies has the right to refuse a transfer if the patient has

---

[12] U.S. Dep't HHS, CMS, State Operations Manual, App. V, Emergency Medical Treatment and Labor Act (EMTALA) Interpretive Guidelines, Part II, Tag A-2407/C-2407 (revised 5/29/2009).

[13] U.S. Dep't HHS, CMS, State Operations Manual, App. V, Emergency Medical Treatment and Labor Act (EMTALA) Interpretive Guidelines, Part II, Tag A-2407/C-2407 (revised 5/29/2009).

additional dangerous medical problems. A patient who is stable in a hospital with a large staff and available technical support may be considered unstable in a psychiatric hospital where close medical monitoring is less available.[14] EMTALA terminology is now the law of the land, and before a psychiatric transfer the prudent emergency physician should always document in the medical chart that "the patient is stable for psychiatric transfer because of either (1) medical evaluation, (2) chemical restraints, or (3) physical restraints."

In 1998, however, CMS issued patient rights requirements that included stiff new restrictions on use of restraints and seclusion. Before a patient can be restrained for transfer, the provider must affirmatively document that no less restrictive measures are feasible (such as retaining the patient at the initial hospital). Strict time limits on use of restraints and requirements for physician evaluation are also in place.

Although the physician may be tempted to believe that the patient is not restrained, placing a patient on a stretcher and strapping him or her down such that he or she cannot release the straps constitutes restraint under this standard.

Likewise, the physician may not appreciate that the placing of the patient in a room or ambulance or squad car, from which he or she is not free to exit, is seclusion and is also strictly limited in usage.

Indeed, strapping a patient to a cot, giving him or her drugs, and sending him or her out in an ambulance amounts to restraint and seclusion and mandates hospital personnel be in constant face-to-face observation of the patient during the transport.

Although the language of the site review guidelines might appear at first reading to allow transfers by simply restraining and transferring the patient, such practices are likely to violate EMTALA and patient rights requirements. Strict adherence to the restraint and seclusion rules should be mandated for all psychiatric transfers.

A patient successfully sued a hospital for an unstabilized psychiatric emergency in *Carlisle v. Frisbie Memorial Hospital*.[15] On May 6, 2000, Heidi Carlisle drove to Frisbie Memorial Hospital because she was depressed and suicidal. In the emergency department, Dr. Jackson, the emergency physician, asked her if she wanted to see a counselor from the Strafford Guidance Center, an organization that treats patients with mental illnesses in the hospital. She declined because she was involved with the organization through her job. She was willing to see other counselors. Dr. Jackson proceeded to call the local police who came to the emergency department, arrested Carlisle for alcohol consumption, and took her to jail in handcuffs. Dr. Jackson gave a note to the police officer claiming that Carlisle was medically cleared to enter protective custody for suicidal intent and alcohol intake. Carlisle was held in jail for 14 hours before

---

[14] *See* Richard L. Elliott, *Patient Dumping, COBRA, and the Public Psychiatric Hospital*, 44 Hosp. & Cmty. Psychiatry 155 (Feb. 1993).

[15] 888 A.2d 405 (N.H. Sup. Ct. 2005).

release. As a result of the events, Carlisle's mental condition deteriorated to the point where she became more suicidal and depressed and drank more alcohol. Carlisle brought three causes of action: (1) for violation of EMTALA against Frisbie Hospital; (2) for professional negligence against Dr. Jackson; and (3) for violation of the Patient Bill of Rights against Frisbie Hospital. The jury found for the plaintiff on all three counts. The New Hampshire Supreme Court upheld this verdict on appeal. Focusing primarily on EMTALA's requirements, the court initially determined that Carlisle had produced sufficient evidence that she presented an "emergency medical condition" when she arrived at the hospital intoxicated and feeling suicidal with a plan to carry out her suicide. The court further determined that she had not been properly "stabilized" before being transferred because a psychiatric patient is considered stable for purposes of discharge under EMTALA only when he or she is no longer considered to be a threat to self or others. The court found that the evidence indicated that neither her suicidal ideation and plan nor her alcohol intoxication had been stabilized when she was transferred to the jail. The court added that for a transfer to be permissible under EMTALA, the transfer must be to another medical facility. The court also ruled that EMTALA trumped a state law that permitted police officers to take into protective custody and place for up to 24 hours in jail a person who is intoxicated in the judgment of an officer. The court reasoned that EMTALA was enacted to prevent hospitals from transferring patients without first assessing or stabilizing their emergency conditions, and allowing a hospital to summon a police officer for the purpose of removing and jailing an intoxicated, unstabilized patient would undercut this goal.[16]

Q 10:6   Psychiatric Discharge: When is a psychiatric patient stable for discharge?

If, after an appropriate MSE, a hospital does not find an EMC as defined by EMTALA and is not aware of any EMC, then the patient is stable for discharge.

In *Pettyjohn v. Mission-St. Joseph's Health System, Inc.,*[17] Steven Pettyjohn went to St. Joseph's Hospital in Asheville, North Carolina, on August 23, 1997, with feelings of isolation and depression. Dr. Ogron examined him and found him to be physically stable. Dr. Counts-Kuzma, the on-call psychiatric social worker, conducted a psychiatric profile and concluded that Pettyjohn was suffering from a mixed-state bipolar disorder but was not in danger. Dr. Ogron offered to admit Pettyjohn, but he refused. Pettyjohn was discharged with instructions to resume taking lithium and to report to a psychiatric center. Six days later, Pettyjohn committed suicide. In a suit, Pettyjohn's parents claimed that his death resulted from the hospital's failure to stabilize his bipolar disorder before discharging him. The trial court granted summary judgment to the hospital. The appeals court noted that there was no evidence that the hospital treated Pettyjohn any differently from any other patient with similar symptoms.

---

[16] *See Developments in Other State Courts*, 25 Dev. Mental Health L. 130 (July 2006).

[17] 21 Fed. Appx. 193 (4th Cir. 2001).

In addition, the hospital was not liable for not stabilizing a suicidal condition that was not apparent after an appropriate examination.

Q 10:7   Psychiatric Inpatient Transfers: Does EMTALA govern transfers from inpatient psychiatric units?

No. The final rules presented by CMS in the *Federal Register* on September 9, 2003, established that EMTALA does not apply to inpatients, whether medical or psychiatric.

Cautions: As stated in the *Federal Register* in final rules for inpatients, CMS will adopt in the Code of Federal Regulations at § 489.24(b) that:

> Comes to the emergency department means, with respect to an individual who is not a patient . . .

CMS further defines "patient" as:

> (1) An individual who has begun to receive outpatient services as part of an encounter, as defined in Sec. 410.2 of this chapter, other than an encounter that the hospital is obligated by this section to provide;
>
> (2) An individual who has been admitted as an inpatient, as defined in this section.

Finally, the definition of "inpatient" is:

> Inpatient means an individual who is admitted to a hospital for bed occupancy for purposes of receiving inpatient hospital services as described in Sec. 409.10(a) of this chapter with the expectation that he or she will remain at least overnight and occupy a bed even though the situation later develops that the individual can be discharged or transferred to another hospital and does not actually use a hospital bed overnight.[18]

For emergency department patients who are admitted to the hospital, CMS amended the Code of Federal Regulations at Section 489.24(d)(2) to state:

> (2) Exception: Application to inpatients. (i) if a hospital has screened an individual under paragraph (a) of this section and found the individual to have an emergency medical condition, and admits that individual as an inpatient in good faith in order to stabilize the emergency medical condition, the hospital has satisfied its special responsibilities under this section with respect to that individual.[19]

There have been few reported cases dealing with alleged violation of EMTALA for psychiatric inpatient transfers. In *Teufel v. United States*,[20] a

---

[18] 68 Fed. Reg. 53,263 (2003).

[19] 68 Fed. Reg. 53,263 (2003).

[20] No. 89-1272-K (D. Kan. June 15, 1992).

chronic psychiatric patient was hospitalized and transferred to another mental health facility, from which he escaped and committed suicide. The court in *Teufel* found that EMTALA sets standards for persons who show "acute symptoms" of an EMC, and, therefore, EMTALA has no application in the event of long-term, nonemergency treatment of patients in mental institutions.

In *Gossling v. Hays Medical Center, Inc.,*[21] Jonathan Gossling was admitted to Hays Medical Center because of a suicide attempt. After five days of evaluation and therapy, Gossling was discharged by Dr. Tan, who believed that Gossling had improved and was no longer suicidal. Gossling committed suicide three days after being discharged. Ronald Gossling and Genae Lamb, as individuals, and Ronald Gossling, as administrator of the estate of Jonathan Gossling, filed suit against the hospital alleging negligence and violation of EMTALA. The court determined that the plaintiffs' assertions were allegations of negligence governed by tort law, not by EMTALA. The plaintiffs' claim against the hospital based on alleged EMTALA violations was dismissed.

Q 10:8   Psychiatric Emergency Conditions: Which psychiatric conditions are covered by EMTALA?

The CMS California Regional Office suggested some psychiatric conditions that may be considered EMCs at a 1995 California Association of Hospitals and Health Systems Seminar. This is not an official list recognized as inclusive or exclusive by the national CMS offices in Washington, D.C.; however, the list may serve as a useful guideline. Patients with psychiatric EMCs should not be transferred unless the benefits outweigh the risks so that the patient would meet criteria for an appropriate unstable transfer allowed by EMTALA. The CMS California regional office gave the following examples of psychiatric EMCs covered by EMTALA:

- History of drug ingestion in a patient with coma or impending coma
- Depression with feelings of suicidal hopelessness
- Delusions, severe insomnia, or helplessness
- History of recent assaultive, self-mutilative, or destructive behavior
- Objective documentation of inability to maintain nutrition in an individual with altered mental status
- Impaired reality testing accompanied by disordered behavior (psychotic)

Cautions: Individuals with impending delirium tremens, detoxification, or seizures (withdrawal or toxic) are included. (Patients who are not in full delirium tremens but are seen with certain clinical signs and symptoms such as rapid heart rate, high blood pressure, and profuse sweating may be deemed to be in "impending" delirium tremens. Such patients are treated prophylactically in an attempt to prevent the progression to the full clinical entity of delirium tremens.)

---

[21] Nos. 92-1488-PFK, 93-1302-PFK, 93-1492-PFK (D. Kan. Apr. 21, 1995).

A patient expressing suicidal or homicidal thoughts or gestures, if determined to be dangerous to self or others, would be considered to have an EMC.[22] Intoxicated individuals may meet the definition of "emergency medical condition" because lack of medical treatment may cause their health to be in jeopardy, their bodily functions to be seriously impaired, or a bodily organ to become seriously dysfunctional. Furthermore, it is not unusual for intoxicated individuals to have unrecognized trauma.[23] If a screening examination shows that a psychiatric patient does not have an EMC, the emergency physician is urged by CMS to be cautious and to keep careful documentation of the reasons why.[24]

Q 10:9   Community Psychiatric Transfers: What if a community or state plan dictates that psychiatric patients be cared for at a specific facility?

EMTALA is a federal law that preempts any conflicting state laws, and thus it renders irrelevant any state programs created for the treatment of psychiatric patients.

The State Operations Manual states:

> If community wide plans exist for specific hospitals to treat certain EMCs (e.g., psychiatric, trauma, physical or sexual abuse), the hospital must meet its EMTALA obligations (screen, stabilize, and or appropriately transfer) prior to transferring the individual to the community plan hospital. An example of a community wide plan would be a trauma system hospital. A trauma system is a comprehensive system providing injury prevention services and timely and appropriate delivery of emergency medical treatment for people with acute illness and traumatic injury. These systems are designed so that patients with catastrophic injuries will have the quickest possible access to an established trauma center or a hospital that has the capabilities to provide comprehensive emergency medical care. These systems ensure that the severely injured patient can be rapidly cared for in the facility that is most appropriately prepared to treat the severity of injury.

> Community plans (not a formal community call plan provided for under § 489.24(j)(iii)) are designed to provide an organized, pre-planned response to patient needs to assure the best patient care and efficient use of limited health care resources. Community plans are designed to augment physician's care if the necessary services are not within the capability of the hospital but does not mandate patient care nor transfer patterns. Patient health status frequently depends on the appropriate use of the community plans. The matching of the appropriate facility

---

[22] U.S. Dep't HHS, CMS, State Operations Manual, App. V, Emergency Medical Treatment and Labor Act (EMTALA) Interpretive Guidelines, Part II, Tag A-2406/C-2406 (revised 7/16/2010).

[23] U.S. Dep't HHS, CMS, State Operations Manual, App. V, Emergency Medical Treatment and Labor Act (EMTALA) Interpretive Guidelines, Part II, Tag A-2406/C-2406 (revised 7/16/2010).

[24] Lowell C. Brown, *The New Federal Patient-Dumping Regulations: Some Commonly Asked Questions and Answers*, 10 Health Care L. Newsl. 16 (Feb. 1995).

with the needs of the patient is the focal point of this plan and assures every patient receives the best care possible. Therefore, a sending hospital's appropriate transfer of an individual in accordance with community wide protocols in instances where it cannot provide stabilizing treatment would be deemed to indicate compliance with § 1867.[25]

Cautions: Prearranged community or state plans may identify certain hospitals that will care for selected psychiatric individuals. Some states may require that patients who are uninsured or on Medicaid be directed to state psychiatric facilities. These plans or statutes do not relieve the original hospital of EMTALA responsibilities. The hospital must still provide an appropriate screening examination and treatment before making an appropriate transfer. The transferring hospital must determine that the patient is "medically clear" from the physical dangers of intoxication or any other medical condition found by examination so that the patient's psychiatric emergency is the only emergency condition needing further care. The transferring hospital must finally ensure that the patient is "stable" for psychiatric transfer by medical assessment and by means of chemical or physical restraints only if that can be justified and properly documented under the patient rights rules on restraint and seclusion.

Q 10:10   Psychiatric Certification: What are the certification requirements for psychiatric transfers?

In addition to EMTALA certification requirements, the transferring hospital must also comply with various civil commitment statutes for committing patients. The transferring physician needs to complete EMTALA certifications and proper civil commitment certificates as required by the state.

Cautions: A hospital has dual certification requirements for psychiatric patients. If a patient is being committed against his or her will, all certification records required by state civil commitment statutes must be completed. The patient must sign any voluntary commitment papers. In conjunction with necessary certificates for psychiatric admissions and commitments, the EMTALA certificate must also be completed prior to transfer.

The U.S. District Court for the Eastern District of Kentucky decided on August 24, 2009, that a hospital did not violate EMTALA's screening and stabilization requirements when physicians transferred a patient from a hospital emergency department, in compliance with a court order, to a facility for treatment of a suspected mental condition.[26]

On July 25, 2007, James Caristo presented himself to the emergency department at the Clark Regional Medical Center (CRMC) for a leg injury incurred in a motor vehicle accident. Caristo was on Klonopine for a mental condition. X-rays revealed a fractured leg. The physician splinted the leg and referred Caristo to an

---

[25] U.S. Dep't HHS, CMS, State Operations Manual, App. V, Emergency Medical Treatment and Labor Act (EMTALA) Interpretive Guidelines, Part II, Tag A-2407/C-2407 (revised 5/29/2009).

[26] Caristo v. Clark Reg'l Med. Ctr., Inc., 5:08-cv-343-JBT (E.D. Ky. Aug. 24 2009).

orthopedic surgeon for follow-up. Caristo failed to follow up with the orthopedist. Five days later, on July 30, police officers delivered Caristo to the emergency department because his mother had called them concerned about his erratic behavior. The physician ordered various tests and diagnostic checks to ascertain the cause of his behavior. A social worker documented that Caristo became "angry," began to remove his IV, and "started demanding to leave." The physician diagnosed Caristo with "psychosis," "hostility," and "substance abuse" and initiated involuntary admission procedures. The district court judge, finding probable cause to believe that Caristo presented a danger or threat of danger to himself and/or others, ordered Caristo be transferred to Comprehensive Care, a community mental health center, for examination by a qualified mental health professional. Caristo was delivered to Comprehensive Care, where a certified social worker eventually filed a certification indicating that she did not regard Caristo to be mentally ill. Based on that certification, the district judge allowed Caristo to be released to his mother's home. On the following day, Caristo presented himself to Saint Joseph East Hospital, where he was hospitalized for five days for treatment of his fractured leg and alcohol withdrawal.

Caristo sued CRMC, alleging that when he presented himself to the emergency department for treatment on July 30, CRMC's employees and agents failed to provide stabilizing care. The court found that defendant CRMC did not violate EMTALA when discharging plaintiff Caristo on July 30, because Caristo was released and transferred to Comprehensive Care in compliance with a court order after he had been screened at CRMC's emergency department, where the medical staff thought he was experiencing some form of mental illness that CRMC did not have the resources to adequately diagnose or treat.

Q 10:11   Refusal of Transfer: What if the patient refuses to be transferred?

A patient who is a danger to self or others can be committed to an inpatient unit against the patient's will for his or her own well-being. Likewise, a committable psychiatric patient may be transferred to a psychiatric facility for admission against his or her wishes if he or she is stabilized.

If a psychiatric patient requires commitment to a psychiatric facility for his or her own good, the patient can be either admitted or transferred against his or her wishes without EMTALA violation. "Commitment" by definition is an involuntary process. Once a patient is stabilized (either by chemical or physical means), the transferring facility needs only to meet the requirements of an appropriate transfer. An appropriate transfer of a stable psychiatric patient does not require patient consent for transfer. If a psychiatrically committable patient continues to refuse consent for transfer, the transfer may be accomplished without the patient's consent if the criteria for civil commitment under state law are met and the transfer is appropriate under EMTALA's transfer requirements. A patient who does not have an acute psychiatric medical emergency condition, and who therefore is not committable, is free to refuse a transfer or admittance and may even sign out of the emergency department against medical advice.

Chapter 11

Role of Quality Improvement Organizations

In considering allegations of violations of the requirements of this section in imposing sanctions under paragraph (1), the Secretary shall request the appropriate utilization and quality control peer review organization (with a contract under part B of subchapter XI of this chapter) to assess whether the individual involved had an emergency medical condition which had not been stabilized, and provide a report on its findings.

42 U.S.C. § 1395dd(d)(3)

Congress amended EMTALA in 1990 to require that a peer review organization (PRO) (now referred to as Quality Improvement Organization, or QIO) must review an EMTALA case before the U.S. Department of Health and Human Services (HHS) imposes any fines.[1] At present, once a regional office (RO) for the Centers for Medicare & Medicaid Services (CMS) issues a preliminary determination of an EMTALA violation, it may request a QIO review if the quality of medical care is at issue and if there is no immediate or serious threat to the patient.[2] If the RO determines that there is an immediate or serious threat to patients, Medicare termination may proceed without QIO review. Most ROs request an expedited "5-day" QIO review of medical issues before issuance of a citation. After a citation, QIO review must occur before the HHS Office of Inspector General (OIG) can impose fines.[3]

A QIO must provide the physician and the hospital with reasonable notice of its review, a reasonable opportunity for discussion, and the opportunity to submit additional information before issuing its report. The QIO must make a tentative finding within 15 days of receiving the case from CMS.[4] Within 60

---

[1] Pub. L. No. 101-508 (1989), § 4008(b)(3)(A)(i), (ii); 42 U.S.C. § 1395dd(d)(3).

[2] 42 C.F.R. § 489.24(h).

[3] 42 U.S.C. § 1395dd(d)(3).

[4] 42 C.F.R. § 489.24(h)(2)(I).

calendar days of receiving the case, the QIO must report its full findings to CMS.[5] CMS will provide a copy of the report to the providers and to the OIG. CMS may also provide a copy to the person who filed the initial complaint.[6]

Q 11:1 Quality Improvement Organizations: What is the role of the QIO review in an EMTALA investigation?

The Act states:

> In considering allegations of violations of the requirements of this section in imposing sanctions under paragraph (1), the Secretary shall request the appropriate utilization and quality control peer review organization (with a contract under part B of subchapter XI of this chapter) to assess whether the individual involved had an emergency medical condition which had not been stabilized, and provide a report on its findings. Except in the case in which a delay would jeopardize the health or safety of individuals, the Secretary shall request such a review before effecting a sanction under paragraph (1) and shall provide a period of at least 60 days for such review.[7]

The Code of Federal Regulations states:

> Except as provided in paragraph (h)(3) of this section, in cases where a medical opinion is necessary to determine a physician's or hospital's liability under section 1867(d)(1) of the Act, CMS requests the appropriate QIO (with a contract under Part B of title XI of the Act) to review the alleged section 1867(d) violation and provide a report on its findings in accordance with paragraph (g)(2)(iv) and (v) of this section. CMS provides to the QIO all information relevant to the case and within its possession or control. CMS, in consultation with the OIG, also provides to the QIO a list of relevant questions to which the QIO must respond in its report.[8]

Cautions: If the initial investigation indicates that a hospital may have violated EMTALA, the RO may request a professional medical review from the respective state's QIO, or a state agency (SA) physician reviewer to assist the RO, or utilize the RO's own consultant physician to determine whether there is an EMTALA violation. While SAs' surveyors may make preliminary findings during the course of the investigation, a physician must usually determine the appropriateness of the medical screening examination (MSE), stabilizing treatment, and transfer. The surveyor may recommend to the RO the need for a medical review.

---

[5] 42 C.F.R. § 489.24(h)(2)(v).

[6] 42 C.F.R. § 489.24(h).

[7] 42 U.S.C. § 1395dd(d)(3).

[8] 42 C.F.R. § 489.24(h).

The CMS State Operations Manual states:

> The purpose of professional medical review (physician review) is to provide peer review using information available to the hospital at the time the alleged violation took place. Physician review is required prior to the imposition of CMPs or the termination of a hospital's provider agreement to determine if:
>
> - The screening examination was appropriate. Under EMTALA, the term "appropriate" does not mean "correct," in the sense that the treating emergency physician is not required to correctly diagnose the individual's medical condition. The fact that a physician may have been negligent in his screening of an individual is not necessarily an EMTALA violation. When used in the context of EMTALA, "appropriate" means that the screening examination was suitable for the symptoms presented and conducted in a non-disparate fashion. Physician review is not necessary when the hospital did not screen the individual;
>
> - The individual had an emergency medical condition. The physician should identify what the condition was and why it was an emergency (e.g., what could have happened to the patient if the treatment was delayed);
>
> - In the case of a pregnant woman, there was inadequate time to effect a safe transfer to another hospital before delivery, or the transfer posed a threat to the health and safety of the woman or the unborn child;
>
> - The stabilizing treatment was appropriate within a hospital's capability (note that the clinical outcome of an individual's medical condition is not the basis for determining whether an appropriate screening was provided or whether the person transferred was stabilized);
>
> - The transfer was effected through qualified personnel and transportation equipment, including the use of medically appropriate life support measures;
>
> - If applicable, the on-call physician's response time was reasonable; and
>
> - The transfer was appropriate for the individual because the individual requested the transfer or because the medical benefits of the transfer outweighed the risk.[9]

If the QIO finds a violation of any of these items, then this constitutes an immediate and serious threat to patient health and safety and CMS implements the 23-day termination process. The QIO examines the medical records in the case and completes a physician review form for each medical record reviewed. The form addresses the items listed above. The QIO is not asked to determine whether an EMTALA violation occurred. Physician review may also be provided

---

[9] U.S. Dep't HHS, Centers for Medicare & Medicaid Servs. (CMS), State Operations Manual, App. V, Investigation Procedures for Responsibilities of Medicare Participating Hospitals in Emergency Cases, Part 1 VIII, Task 6—Professional Medical Review.

by other qualified physicians, such as those who are employees of the state survey agency or RO and those who have contracts with state or local medical societies.[10]

Q 11:2 Consultation Procedures: What are the procedures for the QIO to follow?

The QIO shall provide the physician and the hospital with a reasonable notice of its review, a reasonable opportunity for discussion, and an opportunity for the physician and the hospital to submit additional information before issuing its report.[11] When a QIO receives a request for consultation under Section 489.24(h)(2), the following provisions apply:

    (i) The QIO reviews the case before the 15th calendar day and makes its tentative findings.

    (ii) Within 15 calendar days of receiving the case, the QIO gives written notice, sent by certified mail, return receipt requested, to the physician or the hospital (or both if applicable).

    (iii) The written notice must contain the following information:

        [1] The name of each individual who may have been the subject of the alleged violation.

        [2] The date on which each alleged violation occurred.

        [3] An invitation to meet, either by telephone or in person, to discuss the case with the PRO, and to submit additional information to the QIO within 30 calendar days of receipt of the notice, and a statement that these rights will be waived if the invitation is not accepted. The QIO must receive the information and hold the meeting within the 30-day period.

        [4] A copy of the regulations at 42 C.F.R. § 489.24.9.

    (iv) For purposes of paragraph (g)(2)(iii)(A) of this section, the date of receipt is presumed to be 5 days after the certified mail date on the notice, unless there is a reasonable showing to the contrary.[12]

Q 11:3 Hospital Meeting: May the hospital request a meeting with the QIO?

The Code of Federal Regulations states:

Notice of review and opportunity for discussion and additional information.

---

[10] Report to Congressional Committees, United States General Accounting Office GAO, June 2001 Emergency Care, EMTALA, Implementation and Enforcement Issues, n.12, at 8.

[11] 42 C.F.R. § 489.24(h)(2).

[12] 42 C.F.R. § 489.24(h)(2).

The QIO shall provide the physician and hospital reasonable notice of its review, a reasonable opportunity for discussion, and an opportunity for the physician and hospital to submit additional information before issuing its report.[13]

The physician or hospital (or both where applicable) may request a meeting with the QIO. This meeting is not designed to be a formal adversarial hearing or a mechanism for discovery by the physician or hospital. The meeting is intended to afford the physician and/or the hospital a full and fair opportunity to present the views of the physician and/or hospital regarding the case. The following provisions apply to that meeting:

(A)   The physician and/or hospital has the right to have legal counsel present during that meeting. However, the QIO may control the scope, extent, and manner of any questioning or any other presentation by the attorney. The QIO may also have legal counsel present.

(B)   The QIO makes arrangements so that, if requested by CMS or the OIG, a verbatim transcript of the meeting may be generated. If CMS or OIG requests a transcript, the affected physician and/or the affected hospital may request that CMS provide a copy of the transcript.

(C)   The QIO affords the physician and/or the hospital an opportunity to present, with the assistance of counsel, expert testimony in either oral or written form on the medical issues presented. However, the QIO may reasonably limit the number of witnesses and length of such testimony if such testimony is irrelevant or repetitive. The physician and/or hospital, directly or through counsel, may disclose patient records to potential expert witnesses without violating any non-disclosure requirements set forth in part 476 of this chapter.

(D)   The QIO is not obligated to consider any additional information provided by the physician and/or the hospital after the meeting, unless, before the end of the meeting, the QIO requests that the physician and/or hospital submit additional information to support the claims. The QIO then allows the physician and/or the hospital an additional period of time, not to exceed 5 calendar days from the meeting, to submit the relevant information to the QIO.[14]

Q 11:4   Reporting Requirements: What are the reporting requirements for the QIO?

The Code of Federal Regulations states:

Within 60 calendar days of receiving the case, the QIO must submit to CMS a report on the PRO's findings. CMS provides copies to the OIG and

---

[13] 42 C.F.R. § 489.24(h)(2).

[14] 42 C.F.R. § 489.24(h)(2)(iv).

to the affected physician and/or the affected hospital. The report must contain the name of the physician and/or the hospital, the name of the individual, and the dates and times the individual arrived at and was transferred (or discharged) from the hospital. The report provides expert medical opinion regarding whether the individual involved had an emergency medical condition, whether the individual's emergency medical condition was stabilized, whether the individual was transferred appropriately, and whether there were any medical utilization or quality of care issues involved in the case.[15]

The report should not state an opinion or conclusion as to whether a section of EMTALA has been violated.[16]

Q 11:5   Medicare Termination: May CMS impose Medicare termination before the QIO review?

Yes. If the RO determines that the case poses an obvious immediate and serious threat to patient health, it does not have to wait for a QIO review. The QIO pretermination review is not the same as the QIO processes for review before fine. The hospital can be placed on the 23-day termination track without QIO review.

The Code of Federal Regulations states:

> If a delay would jeopardize the health or safety of individuals or when there was no screening examination, the QIO review described in this section is not required before the OIG may impose civil monetary penalties or an exclusion in accordance with section 1867(d)(1) of the Act and 42 CFR part 1003 of this title.[17]

Cautions: If the initial investigation reveals a possible immediate and serious threat to patient health, CMS has no choice but to start the 23-day termination process. Due to concerns for patient safety, CMS does not want any delay in initiating remedies; therefore there is no need to wait for a full QIO report.

Q 11:6   QIO Findings: What if the QIO finds no violation of EMTALA?

The Code of Federal Regulations states:

> If the QIO determines after a preliminary review that there was an appropriate medical screening examination and the individual did not have an emergency medical condition, as defined by paragraph (b) of this section, then the QIO may, at its discretion, return the case to CMS

---

[15] 42 C.F.R. § 489.24(h)(2)(v).

[16] 42 C.F.R. § 489.24(h)(2)(vi).

[17] 42 C.F.R. § 489.24(h)(3).

and not meet the requirements of paragraph (h) except for those in paragraph (h)(2)(v).[18]

The QIO does not express an opinion on whether EMTALA was violated, but rather on the specific medical issues listed earlier. If, after a preliminary review, the QIO determines that there was an appropriate MSE, that the individual did not have an emergency medical condition, that transport mode and care were appropriate, or other medical issues under review, then the QIO may, at its discretion, return the case to CMS or the OIG without meeting all of the report/meeting requirements.[19]

CMS citations for procedural violations can be issued without QIO input. OIG sanctions may still be pursued by referral of the case for outside review, but the OIG seldom pursues a case that has not been supported by QIO review.

Q 11:7   Report Availability: Are physicians and/or hospitals entitled to review the QIO report?

Yes. On request, CMS may release a QIO assessment to the physician and/or hospital or to the affected individual or his or her representative. The QIO physician's identity is confidential unless he or she consents to its release.[20]

Q 11:8   QIO Physician Qualifications: What qualifications are required of the QIO physician reviewer?

CMS states that the specialty of the reviewing physician should be matched, if possible, to the specialty or specialties of the physician or physicians who treated the patient. Reviewing physicians should be board certified (if the physician being reviewed is board certified) and should be actively practicing in the same medical specialty as the physician treating the patient whose case led to an alleged violation.

---

[18] 42 C.F.R. § 489.24(h)(4).

[19] 42 C.F.R. § 489.24(h)(4).

[20] 42 C.F.R. § 489.24(h)(4)(i).

Chapter 12

EMTALA Preemption

The provisions of this section do not preempt any State or local law requirement, except to the extent that the requirement directly conflicts with a requirement of this section.

42 U.S.C. § 1395dd(f)

Preemption is a legal doctrine adopted by the U.S. Supreme Court "holding that certain matters are of such a national, as opposed to local, character that federal laws preempt or take precedence over state laws. As such, a state may not pass a law inconsistent with the federal law."[1] Traditionally, medical malpractice is an area controlled by state laws. EMTALA preempts any state or local law requirement to the extent that the state or local law directly conflicts with EMTALA requirements. However, under the Eleventh Amendment, federal courts are barred from hearing claims for money damages against the states.[2] As a result of this constitutional protection, state hospitals are immune from EMTALA liability.

A malpractice crisis in Nevada closed the University Medical Center's Trauma Center—Nevada's only Level I trauma center—in Las Vegas for ten days in July 2002. A special session of the Nevada state legislature voted to include on-call specialists for the trauma center under the county hospital's $50,000 cap.[3] The spine surgeons and orthopedic surgeons returned to the hospital as part-time employees, sidestepping their need to get their own liability insurance and keeping them under the hospital's protective umbrella.

Florida is also exploring the idea of approving a cap on liability for on-call physicians in the emergency department. Florida's Access to Care laws are similar to the federal EMTALA mandates in that they stipulate that emergency departments cannot turn anyone away. Some Florida physicians, with the help

---

[1] *Black's Law Dictionary* 1177 (6th ed. 1990).

[2] *See* Lebron v. Ashford Presbyterian Cmty. Hosp., 995 F. Supp. 241 (D.P.R. 1998); Vázquez Morales v. Estado Libre Asociado de P.R., 967 F. Supp. 42 (D.P.R. 1997).

[3] American College of Emergency Physicians, *Sovereign Immunity May Provide Protection from Lawsuits*, ACEP News (Dec. 2002).

of a constitutional lawyer, are exploring the idea that the state law should include litigation immunity.[4]

Q 12:1   Preemption Clause: What is EMTALA's preemption clause?

The Act states that "[t]he provisions of this section do not preempt any State or local law requirement, except to the extent that the requirement directly conflicts with a requirement of this section."[5]

State laws governing this area of medical practice remain in effect. However, if a certain practice is allowed by state statutes but forbidden by EMTALA, EMTALA will prevail. Hospitals and physicians must now toe a fine line, being careful to follow all state statutes on patient care and transfer, as well as all the EMTALA provisions, to avoid violating either one or both.

In *Williams v. County of Cook*,[6] a woman who was pregnant with twins came to Provident Hospital, a public hospital in Chicago operated by Cook County. Without receiving any examination or evaluation, the patient was told to wait in the emergency waiting room while arrangements for transfer were made. After three hours of waiting, the woman began to deliver the first twin in the waiting room. The emergency physician and an obstetrician attempted an emergency breech vaginal delivery, during which the first twin was tragically decapitated. Without telling the mother of the situation, all staff left the treatment room. When the mother got up after a lengthy wait to go to the bathroom, she delivered the head of the baby on the floor. The physicians were not aware of the second twin and admitted the patient to the hospital without further assessment.

While the woman was being induced to deliver the first twin's placenta, the undiagnosed second twin was born and died later that day. The hospital then proceeded with autopsies on the infants and disposed of their remains as medical waste.

The hospital first argued that because it did not transfer the patient, EMTALA was not violated. The district court ruled that the complaint adequately stated a cause of action for failure to provide medical screening and stabilization.

The hospital then unsuccessfully argued that as a public hospital, it was immune from EMTALA liability under the Illinois Tort Immunity Act. The court in *Williams* defeated this argument when it pointed out that EMTALA contains language stating that it preempts state law directly conflicting with its requirements. As a result, the court found that EMTALA preempted the state law and suit could proceed against the hospital.

---

[4] American College of Emergency Physicians, *Sovereign Immunity May Provide Protection from Lawsuits*, ACEP News (Dec. 2002). *See also* American College of Emergency Physicians, *Profiles: EM Doc Fighting for Malpractice Protection in Florida*, ACEP News (Mar.21, 2012).

[5] 42 U.S.C. § 1395dd(f).

[6] No. 97 C 1069 (N.D. Ill. July 24, 1997).

In *Merce v. Greenwood,*[7] because a potential direct conflict exists between Utah's state law prelitigation screening requirements for medical malpractice cases and EMTALA's statute of limitations, EMTALA preempts state law on this point. As a result, Utah state prelitigation screening requirements are not incorporated into EMTALA and do not toll EMTALA's two-year limitations period.

In *Spradlin v. Acadia-St. Landry Medical Foundation,*[8] the court found that a medical review panel requirement of Louisiana's Medical Malpractice Act directly conflicted with the statute of limitations in EMTALA and thus was preempted, as the state tolling provisions could not toll the running of EMTALA's two-year statute of limitations. Even if it were theoretically possible to comply with both the presuit medical review panel requirement and EMTALA's two-year limitation period, engrafting such a procedural requirement onto an EMTALA claim would obstruct accomplishment and execution of Congress's purpose and objectives.

In *Hardy v. New York City Health & Hospital Corp.,*[9] the court found that a New York statute requiring notice of claim as a condition precedent to bringing personal injury actions against municipal corporations was applicable in an action brought against a municipal hospital under EMTALA. Because the statute was consistent with EMTALA's objectives, EMTALA gave express deference to state law, and EMTALA served the role of "gap-filler" for state malpractice law.

Q 12:2   State Sovereign Immunity: Can EMTALA abrogate a state's sovereign immunity?

No. EMTALA does not abrogate a state's sovereign immunity from civil suits. State hospitals do remain liable for CMS citations and Office of Inspector General (OIG) fines.

Cautions: The Eleventh Amendment bars the federal courts from entertaining claims for monetary damages against the states, including the Commonwealth of Puerto Rico.[10] Federal courts cannot proceed in lawsuits for money damages against states or state agencies. The Supreme Court has ruled that Congress may abrogate the Eleventh Amendment only by expressing its intention unequivocally: "Congress may abrogate the states' constitutionally secured immunity from suit in federal court only by making its intention unmistakably clear in the language of the statute."[11] The language of EMTALA does not show unmistakably clear intent to abrogate the Eleventh Amendment immunity of the states. In addition, Congress may abrogate the states' Eleventh Amendment immunity when exercising its powers under the Fourteenth Amendment. Congress does not have this power when acting

---

[7] 348 F. Supp. 2d 1271 (D. Utah 2004).

[8] 758 So. 2d 116 (La. Sup. Ct. 2000).

[9] 164 F.3d 789 (2d Cir. 1999).

[10] U.S. Const. Amend. XI.

[11] Atascadero State Hosp. v. Scanlon, 473 U.S. 234, 242 (1985).

under Article I of the Constitution. The Social Security Act (of which Medicare, including EMTALA, forms a part) is an exercise of Congress's powers under Article I of the United States Constitution to tax and to regulate interstate commerce. Therefore, even if it had so intended, Congress could not have abrogated the states' Eleventh Amendment immunity by enactment of EMTALA.

In *Vázquez Morales v. Estado Libre Asociado de Puerto Rico*,[12] José Luís Vázquez Morales was injured in an automobile accident in Guanica and taken by ambulance to the emergency department of Yauco Area Hospital. The provisional medical diagnosis was thoracic trauma, bilateral pneumothorax with multiple rib fractures. Dr. Ramón, the emergency physician, ordered a transfer to the Ponce District Hospital. The ambulance encountered mechanical difficulties, and the transfer was delayed. Vázquez Morales arrived at Ponce District Hospital in cardiopulmonary arrest.

He was resuscitated and subsequently underwent splenectomy and nephrectomy. Vázquez Morales lost his remaining kidney one year later from antibiotic nephrotoxicity after surgery at another hospital, when a gauze sponge was left in his hip area, causing severe infection. Vázquez Morales sued the University of Puerto Rico, owner of the Yauco Area Hospital, for an EMTALA violation, alleging failure to implement an appropriate medical screening examination (MSE) and failure to stabilize him before transfer.

The University of Puerto Rico claimed that the Eleventh Amendment shielded it from liability. The U.S. District Court in Puerto Rico agreed and held that Eleventh Amendment immunity indeed prohibited any EMTALA claim against Puerto Rico. The motion to dismiss the suit was granted.

That provision, however, does not prohibit CMS from issuing citations and potentially terminating a state hospital. OIG may impose fines on state facilities as well.

In *Johnson v. The University of Virginia Medical Center*,[13] the plaintiff presented to the University of Virginia Medical Center's emergency department with neurologic symptoms of weakness, dizziness, and tremors. The plaintiff alleges that due to the defendant's failure to provide him with an adequate MSE, he suffered permanent neurologic deficits including "loss of ability to swallow, sit up without assistance, serious cognitive impairment and incontinence, and total renal failure."

The federal district court for the Western District of Virginia granted the hospital's motions to dismiss and held that a patient's EMTALA claim against a university hospital operating as an arm of the state could not survive because

---

[12] 967 F. Supp. 42. *See also* Drew v. University of Tenn. Reg'l Med. Ctr. Hosp., 211 F.3d 1268 (6th Cir. 2000) "EMTALA . . . contains no clear expression of intent to abrogate the states' immunity." However, in Root v. New Liberty Hosp. Dist., 209 F.3d 1068 (8th Cir. 2000), the Eighth Circuit Court of Appeals ruled that the state's sovereign immunity statute was in direct conflict with EMTALA and was thus preempted by EMTALA pursuant to the supremacy clause.

[13] No. 3:06cv00061 (W.D. Va. May 24, 2007).

the state had not waived its sovereign immunity, nor had Congress abrogated the state's sovereign immunity.

The court held that the Eleventh Amendment provides a bar to the EMTALA lawsuit brought by the patient unless Congress unequivocally expressed its intent to abrogate the state's immunity from suit under EMTALA or the state consented to the suit under EMTALA. In determining that Congress did not abrogate the state's immunity, the court pointed out that Congress did not unequivocally express its intent to abrogate the immunity, nor could it abrogate the immunity, because it was acting pursuant to its Article 1 power when it enacted EMTALA.

Q 12:3   Municipal Sovereign Immunity: Are counties and municipalities protected from EMTALA suits?

The Eleventh Amendment may protect state hospitals from EMTALA, but this immunity does not extend to municipal corporations or other political subdivisions.[14] EMTALA can preempt a defense claim of sovereign immunity by a county or municipal hospital.

In *Etter v. Board of Trustees of North Kansas City Memorial Hospital*,[15] Gerald Etter severed his thumb while working at home and sought emergency care at North Kansas City Memorial Hospital. Hospital personnel admitted Etter, started an intravenous line, and gave him a tetanus shot. Etter was then transferred to another hospital. Etter filed a complaint against North Kansas City Memorial Hospital and its staff under EMTALA, contending that they had transferred him when they learned about his insurance carrier, before his condition had been stabilized. The hospital moved to dismiss the suit on the ground of sovereign immunity. The court in *Etter* denied the hospital's motion, concluding that a total rejection of damage suits would conflict directly with the expressed Congressional intent of EMTALA.

EMTALA's preemption clause also barred the operation of a Virginia law limiting liability of certain charitable hospitals for negligence or other torts in *Power v. Arlington Hospital Association*.[16] The court in *Power* ruled that Virginia's statute conflicted directly with the intent, scope, and application of EMTALA.[17]

On appeal, however, the Fourth Circuit reinstated the Virginia cap on damages and articulated a state-by-state analysis of the scope and application of

---

[14] *See* Paul A. Craig, *Favorable EMTALA Court Decisions in 1997*, Emerg. Dep't Legal Letter, at 13 (Feb. 1998).

[15] 1995 WL 634472 (W.D. Mo. 1995); *see also* Helton v. Phelps County Reg'l Med. Ctr., 817 F. Supp. 789 (E.D. Mo. 1993) (direct conflict existed between Missouri's doctrine of sovereign immunity and EMTALA to extend a public hospital's claim of immunity to cover patient dumping claims, and, therefore, EMTALA preempted the doctrine of sovereign immunity).

[16] 42 F.3d 851 (4th Cir. 1994).

[17] *Power*, 42 F.3d 851, 864.

similar caps to determine whether the cap actually applies to EMTALA actions and whether the cap would be preempted if it were applicable.

Q 12:4   State Malpractice Caps: Does a state's cap on medical malpractice awards apply in EMTALA verdicts?

Since the enactment of EMTALA and the emergence of medical malpractice reform as a primary issue on legislative agendas, courts have struggled to draw a clear distinction between EMTALA liability and traditional medical malpractice liability. This is due, in part, to the similarities in the nature of the conduct often at issue in both EMTALA and state medical malpractice claims. In an EMTALA case, there is frequently an underlying issue of possible medical negligence or substandard care; however, EMTALA does not create a cause of action on the basis of that type of conduct or theory. In addition, while courts generally agree that EMTALA does not create a federal cause of action for medical malpractice, courts still disagree as to whether federal EMTALA claims are subject to caps on damages provided for in state medical malpractice statutes. This disagreement stems from the issue of what constitutes "damages available for personal injury" provided for in EMTALA's damages provision,[18] as well as the varying ways in which states define "malpractice." When an EMTALA claim seems to implicate medical malpractice issues, the issue of the applicability of state medical malpractice damage caps to EMTALA damages becomes an important concern.[19]

Substantive state laws,[20] such as those applying to caps on noneconomic damages, may remain in effect and not be preempted by EMTALA, depending on the wording of the individual state laws. The majority view among courts is that state malpractice award caps do apply in EMTALA claims.

The Fourth Circuit[21] ruled that Virginia's $1 million cap on medical malpractice awards covers verdicts under EMTALA. In *Power*,[22] the Fourth Circuit set aside the $5 million awarded by a jury to Susan Power, ruling that an EMTALA claim would be deemed a malpractice action under Virginia law "because EMTALA is a tort action and Ms. Power's action is against a claimed tax-exempt hospital."[23] The court applied Virginia's medical malpractice damage cap to EMTALA because (1) EMTALA specifically provides for recovery of "those damages available for personal injury under the law of the state where the hospital is located," and (2) Virginia would characterize a claim of patient

---

[18] 42 U.S.C. § 1395dd(d)(2)(A).

[19] *See* Lauren Grattenthaler, *Policy, Plain Language, and Legislative Purpose: Applying State Medical Malpractice Caps on Damages to Federal EMTALA Claims,* 4 Ind. Health L. Rev. 85, (2007).

[20] "Substantive" law means "[t]hat part of law which creates, defines, and regulates rights and duties of parties, as opposed to 'adjective, procedural, or remedial law,' which prescribes method of enforcing the rights or obtaining redress for their invasion." *Black's Law Dictionary* 1429 (6th ed. 1990).

[21] The Fourth Circuit covers Maryland, West Virginia, Virginia, North Carolina, and South Carolina. 28 U.S.C.A. § 41.

[22] *Power,* 42 F.3d 851, 865.

[23] *Power,* 42 F.3d 851, 865.

dumping as one for "malpractice" within the meaning of the state damage cap statute. In addition, a patient is barred from recovering additional damages for injuries if the patient already won the $1 million award under EMTALA. Power contended that she was entitled to two separate million-dollar caps—one for her EMTALA claim and one for her state law malpractice claim—because the two claims involved different defendants, different causes of action, and different wrongful acts. But the court held that Virginia's medical malpractice cap bars recovery for malpractice injuries for which the plaintiff already has recovered the cap limit in an EMTALA suit against the hospital.[24] If state malpractice caps did not apply, then plaintiff lawyers would certainly double their efforts to file EMTALA claims, because there would be no ceiling to monetary awards.

The California Supreme Court has also ruled that noneconomic damages awarded for EMTALA claims based on "professional negligence" are subject to the same state law limit of $250,000 that is applied in medical malpractice cases. In *Barris v. County of Los Angeles*,[25] Barris sued Los Angeles County, Kaiser Foundation Health Plan, and two doctors for failing to stabilize his 18-month-old daughter before transfer, resulting in her death. A jury returned a verdict for an EMTALA violation in favor of Barris for $1.35 million in noneconomic damages and $3,000 for funeral expenses, but the trial court reduced the noneconomic damages award to $250,000 pursuant to the California Medical Injury Compensation Reform Act (MICRA), which limits the award of noneconomic damages to $250,000 in any action against a health care provider on the basis of professional negligence.

The California Supreme Court noted that although the EMTALA claim is not identical to a state medical malpractice claim, similar conduct must be shown. The court explained that an EMTALA plaintiff alleging failure to stabilize must prove that the hospital did not provide treatment to ensure, within reasonable medical probability, that no deterioration of the condition would occur. "Reasonable medical probability" is an objective standard "inextricably interwoven" with the professional standard for rendering care, the court said.[26] The court's opinion is limited to EMTALA claims for failure to stabilize. The court expressed no opinion on whether state damages caps were applicable to claims for inadequate medical screening.

Federal courts in California, however, have ruled that the state cap did not apply to EMTALA actions, leaving the exact status of the MICRA cap in question.

In the case of *Smith v. Botsford General Hospital*,[27] the Sixth Circuit ruled that Michigan's cap on medical malpractice damages does not violate the rights to a jury trial or equal protection. In this case, Andrea Smith sued Botsford General

---

[24] *Power*, 42 F.3d 851, 865; *see also* Reid v. Indianapolis Osteopathic Med. Hosp., 709 F. Supp. 853 (S.D. Ind. 1989) (federal statute authorizing private cause of action against a hospital for improperly transferring a patient incorporated Indiana's substantive limitation on maximum amount recoverable for personal injury from a health care provider).

[25] 972 P.2d 966 (Cal. Sup. Ct. 1999).

[26] *Barris*, 972 P.2d 966, 974.

[27] 419 F.3d 513 (6th Cir. 2005).

Hospital for violating EMTALA by failing to stabilize her husband's condition before transporting him to another hospital. He had an open femur fracture when he arrived, and Botsford decided to transfer him due to its limited capacity to care for someone of his size (about 600 pounds). He died of blood loss while en route. A district court jury awarded Smith economic and noneconomic damages, but Botsford Hospital appealed, saying the noneconomic damages should be reduced in accordance with Michigan's $359,000 cap on noneconomic damages in medical malpractice cases. A three-judge panel of the Sixth Circuit agreed with Botsford Hospital.

Q 12:5 State Prelitigation Procedures: Can a state's statutes requiring prelitigation procedures apply to EMTALA?

Procedural state laws,[28] such as notice requirements, review panels, expert witness rules, restraints of the discovery process, statutes of limitation, sovereign immunity, and charitable immunity, are all preempted by EMTALA. The scope of the state statute, however, may determine whether the EMTALA claim falls within the actions for which prelitigation procedures are required.

A Louisiana appellate court ruled that a state medical malpractice reform statute requiring prelitigation review of medical malpractice claims does not apply to EMTALA. In *Spradlin*,[29] a patient came to the emergency department with vomiting, upper back pain, and flu-like symptoms. The patient was diagnosed with pneumonia and transferred to a charitable hospital, where she died the following day. A lawsuit was filed, alleging violation of EMTALA. The hospital sought dismissal on the basis that the plaintiff had failed to comply with a Louisiana statute that requires prelitigation review of medical malpractice claims before a court action may be filed. The court denied the dismissal, reasoning that the prelitigation review statute specifically applies to actions for "malpractice," which is defined as "any *unintentional* tort or any breach of contract based on health care or professional services rendered, or which should have been rendered, by a health care provider."[30]

The court strictly construed this definition, because the prelitigation review statute limits the common-law rights of tort plaintiffs. In the court's view, the allegations of abandonment for financial reasons were based on economics, and did not arise from negligent medical treatment.

Statutes that require prelitigation procedures solely for medical malpractice claims will not govern claims under EMTALA. This is beneficial to plaintiff lawyers, who avoid the prelitigation procedures such as required arbitration, which poses a barrier to the suit. In *Holcomb v. Monahan*,[31] the court held that the state statute requiring enhanced specificity in complaints claiming medical

---

[28] "Procedural laws" are "those which merely prescribe the manner in which such [civil] rights and responsibilities may be exercised and enforced in a court." *Black's Law Dictionary* 1203 (6th ed. 1990).

[29] *Spradlin,* 758 So. 2d 116.

[30] *Spradlin,* 758 So. 2d 116, 120.

[31] 807 F. Supp. 1526 (M.D. Ala. 1992).

malpractice does not apply to EMTALA. The hospital argued that the suit should be dismissed because the plaintiff had not complied with the Alabama state malpractice codes.

The court denied the motion, stating:

> [EMTALA] is based upon liability for violation of statutory requirements. The federal cause of action is independent of and wholly separate from any state cause of action for breach of a standard of care. The pleading necessary for a state medical malpractice action, a state procedural requirement, is totally different from and irrelevant to a cause of action based upon violation of a federal statute.[32]

In *Reid v. Indianapolis Osteopathic Medical Hospital*,[33] the court ruled that Indiana law, which required a review panel in malpractice cases, directly conflicted with EMTALA, which has no such procedural barriers. The court concluded that EMTALA creates a federal cause of action that is subject to state substantive limitations but not to state procedural limitations.

In *Brooks v. Maryland General Hospital, Inc.*,[34] the court ruled that although the scope of the Maryland Malpractice Act's language, which requires arbitration, broadly covers all claims against health care providers for medical injuries, it applies only to traditional malpractice claims. The court held that "the Maryland Malpractice Act does not apply to cover the conduct alleged as the basis for Brooks' EMTALA claim."[35]

However, a statute with a broad enough scope may apply. In *Draper v. Chiapuzio*,[36] the court held that Oregon's one-year notice requirement for wrongful death claims against public bodies was not preempted in an action filed against the county, as operator of the county hospital, for violating EMTALA even though EMTALA has a two-year statute of limitations. A plaintiff may comply with both federal and state law by giving notice required under the state statute within one year and filing a lawsuit under EMTALA within two years. The plaintiff's action under EMTALA was time-barred for failure to notify the state of a wrongful death claim against a public facility within one year of the injury, as required by state statute. The court in *Draper* held that Oregon's statute did not "directly conflict" with EMTALA and was therefore not preempted.

Finally, the Second Circuit ruled in *Hardy v. New York City Health and Hospitals Corp.*[37] that a state law governing notice of claims against public entities applied to a patient's EMTALA claim. Winifred Hardy came to Queens Hospital on January 27, 1991, with hypertension, nausea, vomiting, and

---

[32] *Holcomb*, 807 F. Supp. 1526, 1530.

[33] 709 F. Supp. 853.

[34] 996 F.2d 708 (4th Cir. 1993).

[35] *Brooks*, 996 F.2d 708, 713.

[36] 9 F.3d 1391 (9th Cir. 1993).

[37] 164 F.3d 789.

dizziness. The emergency physician at Queens Hospital administered medications and observed her for seven hours. She was discharged with instructions to follow up with her private physician. The next day, Hardy had a cerebral hemorrhage, leaving her partially paralyzed. Hardy sued New York City's Health and Hospitals Corporation, which operates Queens Hospital. Hardy claimed that the hospital violated EMTALA by failing to give her an appropriate medical screening when she first arrived and then discharged her without having stabilized her medical condition. The hospital moved to dismiss the complaint on the ground Hardy had not filed a notice of claim against it within 90 days of the occurrence, as required by New York State law. The trial court granted the motion.

The court in *Hardy* said that in its opinion, although a respectable argument can be made that Congress intended the EMTALA damages provision to be read narrowly as referring only to the specific type and amount of damages available under state law, as the Fourth Circuit did in *Power*,[38] a broader reading of the statute was required. It concluded that New York's notice-of-claim requirement is part of the "applicable law of the state"[39] that must be applied under EMTALA.

EMTALA declares it does not preempt any state or local law requirement except to the extent the requirement directly conflicts with a requirement of the federal law. New York's notice-of-claim law does not thwart EMTALA's purpose. Rather, it simply addresses areas that the federal law does not cover, such as the historical concern of governmental bodies that they be given reasonably prompt notice of personal injury claims against them. Because the state law does not directly conflict with any requirement of EMTALA, it is not preempted, the court said.[40]

Q 12:6 Federal Immunity: Is the federal government immune from EMTALA lawsuits?

Yes. The federal government is immune from EMTALA suits.

A federal district court in New Mexico held that the federal government is immune from suits under EMTALA. In *Cheromiah v. United States*,[41] a patient was treated several times in the emergency department of a hospital operated by the Indian Health Service. The patient died of an undiagnosed bacterial infection. The estate filed suit against the United States government for inadequate MSEs in violation of EMTALA. The government moved for dismissal of the EMTALA claim on the basis of sovereign immunity.

The court in *Cheromiah* granted the motion for dismissal. The court explained that the federal government is protected by sovereign immunity unless that immunity had been expressly waived by statute. EMTALA contains no such

---

[38] *Power*, 42 F.3d 851.

[39] *Power*, 42 F.3d 851, 864.

[40] *See* 11 Emerg. Dep't L. (Burness Publishers, Inc. Feb. 1999).

[41] No. CIV 97-1418 MV/RLP (D.N.M. June 29, 1999).

reference to waiver. The lack of an express statutory waiver of immunity precluded consideration of the plaintiff's arguments that EMTALA claims against the government were supported by (1) EMTALA's authorization of suits against "any" hospital, (2) EMTALA's legislative history, and (3) public policy.

CMS, however, has enforced EMTALA requirements against Indian Health Service facilities with the citation process.

Appendix A

The Emergency Medical Treatment and Active Labor Act (EMTALA)

42 U.S.C. § 1395dd

Examination and treatment for emergency medical conditions and women in labor.

(a) MEDICAL SCREENING REQUIREMENT.—In the case of a hospital that has a hospital emergency department, if any individual (whether or not eligible for benefits under this subchapter) comes to the emergency department and a request is made on the individual's behalf for examination or treatment for a medical condition, the hospital must provide for an appropriate medical screening examination within the capability of the hospital's emergency department, including ancillary services routinely available to the emergency department, to determine whether or not an emergency medical condition (within the meaning of subsection (e)(1) of this section) exists.

(b) NECESSARY STABILIZING TREATMENT FOR EMERGENCY MEDICAL CONDITIONS AND LABOR.

(1) In general. If any individual (whether or not eligible for benefits under this subchapter) comes to a hospital and the hospital determines that the individual has an emergency medical condition, the hospital must provide either—

(A) within the staff and facilities available at the hospital, for such further medical examination and such treatment as may be required to stabilize the medical condition, or

(B) for transfer of the individual to another medical facility in accordance with subsection (c) of this section.

(2) Refusal to consent to treatment. A hospital is deemed to meet the requirement of paragraph (1)(A) with respect to an individual if the hospital

offers the individual the further medical examination and treatment described in that paragraph and informs the individual (or a person acting on the individual's behalf) of the risks and benefits to the individual of such examination and treatment, but the individual (or a person acting on the individual's behalf) refuses to consent to the examination and treatment. The hospital shall take all reasonable steps to secure the individual's (or person's) written informed consent to refuse such examination and treatment.

(3) Refusal to consent to transfer. A hospital is deemed to meet the requirement of paragraph (1) with respect to an individual if the hospital offers to transfer the individual to another medical facility in accordance with subsection (c) of this section and informs the individual (or a person acting on the individual's behalf) of the risks and benefits to the individual of such transfer, but the individual (or a person acting on the individual's behalf) refuses to consent to the transfer. The hospital shall take all reasonable steps to secure the individual's (or person's) written informed consent to refuse such transfer.

(c) RESTRICTING TRANSFERS UNTIL INDIVIDUAL STABILIZED.

(1) RULE. If an individual at a hospital has an emergency medical condition which has not been stabilized (within the meaning of subsection (e)(3)(B) of this section), the hospital may not transfer the individual unless—

(A)(i) the individual (or a legally responsible person acting on the individual's behalf) after being informed of the hospital's obligations under this section and of the risk of transfer, in writing requests transfer to another medical facility,

(ii) a physician (within the meaning of section 1395x(r)(1) of this title) has signed a certification that based upon the information available at the time of transfer, the medical benefits reasonably expected from the provision of appropriate medical treatment at another medical facility outweigh the increased risks to the individual and, in the case of labor, to the unborn child from effecting the transfer, or

(iii) if a physician is not physically present in the emergency department at the time an individual is transferred, a qualified medical person (as defined by the Secretary in regulations) has signed a certification described in clause (ii) after a physician (as defined in section 1395x(r)(1) of this title), in consultation with the person, has made the determination described in such clause, and subsequently countersigns the certification; and

(B) the transfer is an appropriate transfer (within the meaning of paragraph (2)) to that facility. A certification described in clause (ii) or (iii) of subparagraph (A) shall include a summary of the risks and benefits upon which the certification is based.

(2) APPROPRIATE TRANSFER.—An appropriate transfer to a medical facility is a transfer—

(A) in which the transferring hospital provides the medical treatment within its capacity which minimizes the risks to the individual's health and, in the case of a woman in labor, the health of the unborn child;

(B) in which the receiving facility—

(i) has available space and qualified personnel for the treatment of the individual, and

(ii) has agreed to accept transfer of the individual and to provide appropriate medical treatment;

(C) in which the transferring hospital sends to the receiving facility all medical records (or copies thereof), related to the emergency condition for which the individual has presented, available at the time of the transfer, including records related to the individual's emergency medical condition, observations of signs or symptoms, preliminary diagnosis, treatment provided, results of any tests and the informed written consent or certification (or copy thereof) provided under paragraph (1)(A), and the name and address of any on-call physician (described in subsection (d)(1)(C) of this section) who has refused or failed to appear within a reasonable time to provide necessary stabilizing treatment;

(D) in which the transfer is effected through qualified personnel and transportation equipment, as required including the use of necessary and medically appropriate life support measures during the transfer; and

(E) which meets such other requirements as the Secretary may find necessary in the interest of the health and safety of individuals transferred.

(d) ENFORCEMENT.

(1) Civil money penalties.

(A) A participating hospital that negligently violates a requirement of this section is subject to a civil money penalty of not more than $50,000 (or not more than $25,000 in the case of a hospital with less than 100 beds) for each such violation. The provisions of section 1320a-7a of this title (other than subsections (a) and (b)) shall apply to a civil money penalty under this subparagraph in the same manner as such provisions apply with respect to a penalty or proceeding under section 1320a-7a(a) of this title.

(B) Subject to subparagraph (C), any physician who is responsible for the examination, treatment, or transfer of an individual in a participating hospital, including a physician on-call for the care of such an individual, and who negligently violates a requirement of this section, including a physician who—

(i) signs a certification under subsection (c)(1)(A) of this section that the medical benefits reasonably to be expected from a transfer to another facility outweigh the risks associated with the transfer, if the physician knew or should have known that the benefits did not outweigh the risks, or

(ii) misrepresents an individual's condition or other information, including a hospital's obligations under this section, is subject to a civil money penalty of not more than $50,000 for each such violation and, if the violation is gross and flagrant or is repeated, to exclusion from participation in this subchapter and State health care programs. The provisions of section 1320a-7a of this title (other than the first and second sentences of subsection (a) and subsection (b)) shall apply to a civil money penalty and exclusion under this subparagraph in the same manner as such provisions apply with respect to a penalty, exclusion, or proceeding under section 1320a-7a(a) of this title.

(C) If, after an initial examination, a physician determines that the individual requires the services of a physician listed by the hospital on its list of on-call physicians (required to be maintained under section 1395cc(a)(1)(I) of this title) and notifies the on-call physician and the oncall physician fails or refuses to appear within a reasonable period of time, and the physician orders the transfer of the individual because the physician determines that without the services of the on-call physician the benefits of transfer outweigh the risks of transfer, the physician authorizing the transfer shall not be subject to a penalty under subparagraph (B). However, the previous sentence shall not apply to the hospital or to the on-call physician who failed or refused to appear.

(2) CIVIL ENFORCEMENT.

(A) Personal harm. Any individual who suffers personal harm as a direct result of a participating hospital's violation of a requirement of this section may, in a civil action against the participating hospital, obtain those damages available for personal injury under the law of the State in which the hospital is located, and such equitable relief as is appropriate.

(B) Financial loss to other medical facility. Any medical facility that suffers a financial loss as a direct result of a participating hospital's violation of a requirement of this section may, in a civil action against the participating hospital, obtain those damages available for financial loss, under the law of the State in which the hospital is located, and such equitable relief as is appropriate.

(C) Limitations on actions. No action may be brought under this paragraph more than two years after the date of the violation with respect to which the action is brought.

(3) CONSULTATION WITH PEER REVIEW ORGANIZATIONS.—In considering allegations of violations of the requirements of this section in imposing sanctions under paragraph (1) or in terminating a hospital's participation

under this title,—the Secretary shall request the appropriate utilization and quality control peer review organization (with a contract under part B of subchapter XI of this chapter) to assess whether the individual involved had an emergency medical condition which had not been stabilized, and provide a report on its findings. Except in the case in which a delay would jeopardize the health or safety of individuals, the Secretary shall request such a review before effecting a sanction under paragraph (1) and shall provide a period of at least 60 days for such review. Except in the case in which a delay would jeopardize the health or safety of individuals, the Secretary shall also request such a review before making a compliance determination as part of the process of terminating a hospital's participation under this title for violations related to the appropriateness of a medical screening examination, stabilizing treatment, or an appropriate transfer as required by this section, and shall provide a period of 5 days for such review. The Secretary shall provide a copy of the organization's report to the hospital or physician consistent with confidentiality requirements imposed on the organization under such part B.

(4) NOTICE UPON CLOSING AN INVESTIGATION—The secretary shall establish a procedure to notify hospitals and physicians when an investigation under this section is closed.

(e) DEFINITIONS.—In this section:

(1) The term "emergency medical condition" means—

(A) a medical condition manifesting itself by acute symptoms of sufficient severity (including severe pain) such that the absence of immediate medical attention could reasonably be expected to result in—

(i) placing the health of the individual (or, with respect to a pregnant woman, the health of the woman or her unborn child) in serious jeopardy,

(ii) serious impairment to bodily functions, or

(iii) serious dysfunction of any bodily organ or part; or

(B) with respect to a pregnant woman who is having contractions—

(i) that there is inadequate time to effect a safe transfer to another hospital before delivery, or

(ii) that transfer may pose a threat to the health or safety of the woman or the unborn child.

(2) The term "participating hospital" means a hospital that has entered into a provider agreement under section 1866 of this title.

(3)(A) The term "to stabilize" means, with respect to an emergency medical condition described in paragraph (1)(A), to provide such medical treatment of the condition as may be necessary to assure, within reasonable medical probability, that no material deterioration of the condition is likely to result from or occur during the transfer of the individual from a facility, or, with respect to an emergency medical condition described in paragraph (1)(B), to deliver (including the placenta).

(B) The term "stabilized" means, with respect to an emergency medical condition described in paragraph (1)(A), that no material deterioration of the condition is likely, within reasonable medical probability, to result from or occur during the transfer of the individual from a facility, or, with respect to an emergency medical condition described in paragraph (1)(B), that the woman has delivered (including the placenta).

(4) The term "transfer" means the movement (including the discharge) of an individual outside a hospital's facilities at the direction of any person employed by (or affiliated or associated, directly or indirectly, with) the hospital, but does not include such a movement of an individual who (A) has been declared dead, or (B) leaves the facility without the permission of any such person.

(5) The term "hospital" includes a rural primary care hospital (as defined in section 1861(mm)(1) of this title).

(f) PREEMPTION.—The provisions of this section do not preempt any State or local law requirement, except to the extent that the requirement directly conflicts with a requirement of this section.

(g) NONDISCRIMINATION.—A participating hospital that has specialized capabilities or facilities (such as burn units, shock-trauma units, neonatal intensive care units, or (with respect to rural areas) regional referral centers as identified by the Secretary in regulation) shall not refuse to accept an appropriate transfer of an individual who requires such specialized capabilities or facilities if the hospital has the capacity to treat the individual.

(h) NO DELAY IN EXAMINATION OR TREATMENT.—A participating hospital may not delay provision of an appropriate medical screening examination required under subsection (a) of this section or further medical examination and treatment required under subsection (b) of this section in order to inquire about the individual's method of payment or insurance status.

(i) WHISTLEBLOWER PROTECTIONS.—A participating hospital may not penalize or take adverse action against a qualified medical person described in subsection (c)(1)(A)(iii) of this section or a physician because the person or physician refuses to authorize the transfer of an individual with an emergency medical condition that has not been stabilized or against any hospital employee because the employee reports a violation of a requirement of this section.

Appendix B

EMTALA Regulations

42 C.F.R. 489.24
§ 489.24 Special responsibilities of Medicare hospitals in emergency cases.

(a) *Applicability of provisions of this section.* (1) In the case of a hospital that has an emergency department, if an individual (whether or not eligible for Medicare benefits and regardless of ability to pay) "comes to the emergency department", as defined in paragraph (b) of this section, the hospital must—

(i) Provide an appropriate medical screening examination within the capability of the hospital's emergency department, including ancillary services routinely available to the emergency department, to determine whether or not an emergency medical condition exists. The examination must be conducted by an individual(s) who is determined qualified by hospital bylaws or rules and regulations and who meets the requirements of § 482.55 of this chapter concerning emergency services personnel and direction; and

(ii) If an emergency medical condition is determined to exist, provide any necessary stabilizing treatment, as defined in paragraph (d) of this section, or an appropriate transfer as defined in paragraph (e) of this section. If the hospital admits the individual as an inpatient for further treatment, the hospital's obligation under this section ends, as specified in paragraph (d)(2) of this section.

(2) (i) When a waiver has been issued in accordance with section 1135 of the Act that includes a waiver under section 1135(b)(3) of the Act, sanctions under this section for an inappropriate transfer or for the direction or relocation of an individual to receive medical screening at an alternate location do not apply to a hospital with a dedicated emergency department if the following conditions are met:

(A) The transfer is necessitated by the circumstances of the declared emergency in the emergency area during the emergency period.

(B) The direction or relocation of an individual to receive medical screening at an alternate location is pursuant to an appropriate State emergency preparedness plan or, in the case of a public health emergency that involves a pandemic infectious disease, pursuant to a State pandemic preparedness plan.

(C) The hospital does not discriminate on the basis of an individual's source of payment or ability to pay.

(D) The hospital is located in an emergency area during an emergency period, as those terms are defined in section 1135(g)(1) of the Act.

(E) There has been a determination that a waiver of sanctions is necessary.

(ii) A waiver of these sanctions is limited to a 72-hour period beginning upon the implementation of a hospital disaster protocol, except that, if a public health emergency involves a pandemic infectious disease (such as pandemic influenza), the waiver will continue in effect until the termination of the applicable declaration of a public health emergency, as provided under section 1135(e)(1)(B) of the Act.

(b) *Definitions.* As used in this subpart—

Capacity means the ability of the hospital to accommodate the individual requesting examination or treatment of the transferred individual. Capacity encompasses such things as numbers and availability of qualified staff, beds and equipment and the hospital's past practices of accommodating additional patients in excess of its occupancy limits.

Comes to the emergency department means, with respect to an individual who is not a patient (as defined in this section), the individual—

(1) Has presented at a hospital's dedicated emergency department, as defined in this section, and requests examination or treatment for a medical condition, or has such a request made on his or her behalf. In the absence of such a request by or on behalf of the individual, a request on behalf of the individual will be considered to exist if a prudent layperson observer would believe, based on the individual's appearance or behavior, that the individual needs examination or treatment for a medical condition;

(2) Has presented on hospital property, as defined in this section, other than the dedicated emergency department, and requests examination or treatment for what may be an emergency medical condition, or has such a request made on his or her behalf. In the absence of such a request by or on behalf of the individual, a request on behalf of the individual will be considered to exist if a prudent layperson observer would believe, based on the individual's appearance or behavior, that the individual needs emergency examination or treatment;

(3) Is in a ground or air ambulance owned and operated by the hospital for purposes of examination and treatment for a medical condition at a hospital's dedicated emergency department, even if the ambulance is not on hospital grounds. However, an individual in an ambulance owned and operated by the hospital is not considered to have "come to the hospital's emergency department" if—

(i) The ambulance is operated under communitywide emergency medical service (EMS) protocols that direct it to transport the individual to a hospital other than the hospital that owns the ambulance; for example, to the closest appropriate facility. In this case, the individual is considered to have come to the emergency department of the hospital to which the individual is transported, at the time the individual is brought onto hospital property;

(ii) The ambulance is operated at the direction of a physician who is not employed or otherwise affiliated with the hospital that owns the ambulance; or

(4) Is in a ground or air nonhospital-owned ambulance on hospital property for presentation for examination and treatment for a medical condition at a hospital's dedicated emergency department. However, an individual in a nonhospital-owned ambulance off hospital property is not considered to have come to the hospital's emergency department, even if a member of the ambulance staff contacts the hospital by telephone or telemetry communications and informs the hospital that they want to transport the individual to the hospital for examination and treatment. The hospital may direct the ambulance to another facility if it is in "diversionary status," that is, it does not have the staff or facilities to accept any additional emergency patients. If, however, the ambulance staff disregards the hospital's diversion instructions and transports the individual onto hospital property, the individual is considered to have come to the emergency department.

Dedicated emergency department means any department or facility of the hospital, regardless of whether it is located on or off the main hospital campus, that meets at least one of the following requirements:

(1) It is licensed by the State in which it is located under applicable State law as an emergency room or emergency department;

(2) It is held out to the public (by name, posted signs, advertising, or other means) as a place that provides care for emergency medical conditions on an urgent basis without requiring a previously scheduled appointment; or

(3) During the calendar year immediately preceding the calendar year in which a determination under this section is being made, based on a representative sample of patient visits that occurred during that calendar year, it provides at least one-third of all of its outpatient visits for the treatment of emergency medical conditions on an urgent basis without requiring a previously scheduled appointment.

Emergency medical condition means—

(1) A medical condition manifesting itself by acute symptoms of sufficient severity (including severe pain, psychiatric disturbances and/or symptoms of substance abuse) such that the absence of immediate medical attention could reasonably be expected to result in—

(i) Placing the health of the individual (or, with respect to a pregnant woman, the health of the woman or her unborn child) in serious jeopardy;

(ii) Serious impairment to bodily functions; or

(iii) Serious dysfunction of any bodily organ or part; or

(2) With respect to a pregnant woman who is having contractions—

(i) That there is inadequate time to effect a safe transfer to another hospital before delivery; or

(ii) That transfer may pose a threat to the health or safety of the woman or the unborn child.

Hospital includes a critical access hospital as defined in section 1861(mm)(1) of the Act.

Hospital property means the entire main hospital campus as defined in § 413.65(b) of this chapter, including the parking lot, sidewalk, and driveway, but excluding other areas or structures of the hospital's main building that are not part of the hospital, such as physician offices, rural health centers, skilled nursing facilities, or other entities that participate separately under Medicare, or restaurants, shops, or other nonmedical facilities.

Hospital with an emergency department means a hospital with a dedicated emergency department as defined in this paragraph (b).

Inpatient means an individual who is admitted to a hospital for bed occupancy for purposes of receiving inpatient hospital services as described in § 409.10(a) of this chapter with the expectation that he or she will remain at least overnight and occupy a bed even though the situation later develops that the individual can be discharged or transferred to another hospital and does not actually use a hospital bed overnight.

Labor means the process of childbirth beginning with the latent or early phase of labor and continuing through the delivery of the placenta. A woman experiencing contractions is in true labor unless a physician, certified nurse-midwife, or other qualified medical person acting within his or her scope of practice as defined in hospital medical staff bylaws and State law, certifies that, after a reasonable time of observation, the woman is in false labor.

Participating hospital means (1) a hospital or (2) a critical access hospital as defined in section 1861(mm)(1) of the Act that has entered into a Medicare provider agreement under section 1866 of the Act.

Patient means—

(1) An individual who has begun to receive outpatient services as part of an encounter, as defined in § 410.2 of this chapter, other than an encounter that the hospital is obligated by this section to provide;

(2) An individual who has been admitted as an inpatient, as defined in this section.

Stabilized means, with respect to an "emergency medical condition" as defined in this section under paragraph (1) of that definition, that no material deterioration of the condition is likely, within reasonable medical probability, to result from or occur during the transfer of the individual from a facility or, with respect to an "emergency medical condition" as defined in this section under paragraph (2) of that definition, that the woman has delivered the child and the placenta.

To stabilize means, with respect to an "emergency medical condition" as defined in this section under paragraph (1) of that definition, to provide such medical treatment of the condition necessary to assure, within reasonable medical probability, that no material deterioration of the condition is likely to result from or occur during the transfer of the individual from a facility or that, with respect to an "emergency medical condition" as defined in this section under paragraph (2) of that definition, the woman has delivered the child and the placenta.

Transfer means the movement (including the discharge) of an individual outside a hospital's facilities at the direction of any person employed by (or affiliated or associated, directly or indirectly, with) the hospital, but does not include such a movement of an individual who (i) has been declared dead, or (ii) leaves the facility without the permission of any such person.

(c) *Use of dedicated emergency department for nonemergency services.* If an individual comes to a hospital's dedicated emergency department and a request is made on his or her behalf for examination or treatment for a medical condition, but the nature of the request makes it clear that the medical condition is not of an emergency nature, the hospital is required only to perform such screening as would be appropriate for any individual presenting in that manner, to determine that the individual does not have an emergency medical condition.

(d) *Necessary stabilizing treatment for emergency medical conditions.*— (1) *General.* Subject to the provisions of paragraph (d)(2) of this section, if any individual (whether or not eligible for Medicare benefits) comes to a hospital and the hospital determines that the individual has an emergency medical condition, the hospital must provide either—

(i) Within the capabilities of the staff and facilities available at the hospital, for further medical examination and treatment as required to stabilize the medical condition.

(ii) For transfer of the individual to another medical facility in accordance with paragraph (e) of this section.

(2) *Exception: Application to inpatients.* (i) If a hospital has screened an individual under paragraph (a) of this section and found the individual to have an emergency medical condition, and admits that individual as an inpatient in good faith in order to stabilize the emergency medical condition, the hospital has satisfied its special responsibilities under this section with respect to that individual.

(ii) This section is not applicable to an inpatient who was admitted for elective (nonemergency) diagnosis or treatment.

(iii) A hospital is required by the conditions of participation for hospitals under Part 482 of this chapter to provide care to its inpatients in accordance with those conditions of participation.

(3) *Refusal to consent to treatment.* A hospital meets the requirements of paragraph (d)(1)(i) of this section with respect to an individual if the hospital offers the individual the further medical examination and treatment described in that paragraph and informs the individual (or a person acting on the individual's behalf) of the risks and benefits to the individual of the examination and treatment, but the individual (or a person acting on the individual's behalf) does not consent to the examination or treatment. The medical record must contain a description of the examination, treatment, or both if applicable, that was refused by or on behalf of the individual. The hospital must take all reasonable steps to secure the individual's written informed refusal (or that of the person acting on his or her behalf). The written document should indicate that the person has been informed of the risks and benefits of the examination or treatment, or both.

(4) *Delay in examination or treatment.* (i) A participating hospital may not delay providing an appropriate medical screening examination required under paragraph (a) of this section or further medical examination and treatment required under paragraph (d)(1) of this section in order to inquire about the individual's method of payment or insurance status.

(ii) A participating hospital may not seek, or direct an individual to seek, authorization from the individual's insurance company for screening or stabilization services to be furnished by a hospital, physician, or nonphysician practitioner to an individual until after the hospital has provided the appropriate medical screening examination required under paragraph (a) of this section, and initiated any further medical examination and treatment that may be required to stabilize the emergency medical condition under paragraph (d)(1) of this section.

(iii) An emergency physician or nonphysician practitioner is not precluded from contacting the individual's physician at any time to seek advice regarding the individual's medical history and needs that may be relevant to the medical treatment and screening of the patient, as long as this consultation does not inappropriately delay services required under paragraph (a) or paragraphs (d)(1) and (d)(2) of this section.

(iv) Hospitals may follow reasonable registration processes for individuals for whom examination or treatment is required by this section, including asking whether an individual is insured and, if so, what that insurance is, as long as that inquiry does not delay screening or treatment. Reasonable registration processes may not unduly discourage individuals from remaining for further evaluation.

(5) *Refusal to consent to transfer.* A hospital meets the requirements of paragraph (d)(1)(ii) of this section with respect to an individual if the hospital offers to transfer the individual to another medical facility in accordance with paragraph (e) of this section and informs the individual (or a person acting on his or her behalf) of the risks and benefits to the individual of the transfer, but the individual (or a person acting on the individual's behalf) does not consent to the transfer. The hospital must take all reasonable steps to secure the individual's written informed refusal (or that of a person acting on his or her behalf). The written document must indicate the person has been informed of the risks and benefits of the transfer and state the reasons for the individual's refusal. The medical record must contain a description of the proposed transfer that was refused by or on behalf of the individual.

(e) *Restricting transfer until the individual is stabilized*—(1) *General.* If an individual at a hospital has an emergency medical condition that has not been stabilized (as defined in paragraph (b) of this section), the hospital may not transfer the individual unless—

(i) The transfer is an appropriate transfer (within the meaning of paragraph (e)(2) of this section); and

(ii)(A) The individual (or a legally responsible person acting on the individual's behalf) requests the transfer, after being informed of the hospital's obligations under this section and of the risk of transfer. The request must be in writing and indicate the reasons for the request as well as indicate that he or she is aware of the risks and benefits of the transfer;

(B) A physician (within the meaning of section 1861(r)(1) of the Act) has signed a certification that, based upon the information available at the time of transfer, the medical benefits reasonably expected from the provision of appropriate medical treatment at another medical facility outweigh the increased risks to the individual or, in the case of a woman in labor, to the woman or the unborn child, from being transferred. The certification must contain a summary of the risks and benefits upon which it is based; or

(C) If a physician is not physically present in the emergency department at the time an individual is transferred, a qualified medical person (as determined by the hospital in its by-laws or rules and regulations) has signed a certification described in paragraph (e)(1)(ii)(B) of this section after a physician (as defined in section 1861(r)(1) of the Act) in consultation with the qualified medical person, agrees with the certification and subsequently countersigns the certification. The certification must contain a summary of the risks and benefits upon which it is based.

(2) A transfer to another medical facility will be appropriate only in those cases in which—

(i) The transferring hospital provides medical treatment within its capacity that minimizes the risks to the individual's health and, in the case of a woman in labor, the health of the unborn child;

(ii) The receiving facility—

(A) Has available space and qualified personnel for the treatment of the individual; and

(B) Has agreed to accept transfer of the individual and to provide appropriate medical treatment;

(iii) The transferring hospital sends to the receiving facility all medical records (or copies thereof) related to the emergency condition which the individual has presented that are available at the time of the transfer, including available history, records related to the individual's emergency medical condition, observations of signs or symptoms, preliminary diagnosis, results of diagnostic studies or telephone reports of the studies, treatment provided, results of any tests and the informed written consent or certification (or copy thereof) required under paragraph (e)(1)(ii) of this section, and the name and address of any on-call physician (described in paragraph (g) of this section) who has refused or failed to appear within a reasonable time to provide necessary stabilizing treatment. Other records (e.g., test results not yet available or historical records not readily available from the hospital's files) must be sent as soon as practicable after transfer; and

(iv) The transfer is effected through qualified personnel and transportation equipment, as required, including the use of necessary and medically appropriate life support measures during the transfer.

(3) A participating hospital may not penalize or take adverse action against a physician or a qualified medical person described in paragraph (e)(1)(ii)(C) of this section because the physician or qualified medical person refuses to authorize the transfer of an individual with an emergency medical condition that has not been stabilized, or against any hospital employee because the employee reports a violation of a requirement of this section.

(f) *Recipient hospital responsibilities.* A participating hospital that has specialized capabilities or facilities (including, but not limited to, facilities such as burn units, shock-trauma units, neonatal intensive case units, or, with respect to rural areas, regional referral centers (which, for purposes of this subpart, mean hospitals meeting the requirements of referral centers found at § 412.96 of this chapter)) may not refuse to accept from a referring hospital within the boundaries of the United States an appropriate transfer of an individual who requires such specialized capabilities or facilities if the receiving hospital has the capacity to treat the individual.

(1) The provisions of this paragraph (f) apply to any participating hospital with specialized capabilities, regardless of whether the hospital has a dedicated emergency department.

(2) The provisions of this paragraph (f) do not apply to an individual who has been admitted to a referring hospital under the provisions of paragraph (d)(2)(i) of this section.

(g) *Termination of provider agreement.* If a hospital fails to meet the requirements of paragraph (a) through (f) of this section, CMS may terminate the provider agreement in accordance with § 489.53.

(h) *Consultation with Quality Improvement Organizations (QIOs)*—(1) *General.* Except as provided in paragraph (h)(3) of this section, in cases where a medical opinion is necessary to determine a physician's or hospital's liability under section 1867(d)(1) of the Act, CMS requests the appropriate QIO (with a contract under Part B of title XI of the Act) to review the alleged section 1867(d) violation and provide a report on its findings in accordance with paragraph (h)(2)(iv) and (v) of this section. CMS provides to the QIO all information relevant to the case and within its possession or control. CMS, in consultation with the OIG, also provides to the QIO a list of relevant questions to which the QIO must respond in its report.

(2) *Notice of review and opportunity for discussion and additional information.* The QIO shall provide the physician and hospital reasonable notice of its review, a reasonable opportunity for discussion, and an opportunity for the physician and hospital to submit additional information before issuing its report. When a QIO receives a request for consultation under paragraph (h)(1) of this section, the following provisions apply—

(i) The QIO reviews the case before the 15th calendar day and makes its tentative findings.

(ii) Within 15 calendar days of receiving the case, the QIO gives written notice, sent by certified mail, return receipt requested, to the physician or the hospital (or both if applicable).

(iii)(A) The written notice must contain the following information:

(1) The name of each individual who may have been the subject of the alleged violation.

(2) The date on which each alleged violation occurred.

(3) An invitation to meet, either by telephone or in person, to discuss the case with the QIO, and to submit additional information to the QIO within 30 calendar days of receipt of the notice, and a statement that these rights will be waived if the invitation is not accepted. The QIO must receive the information and hold the meeting within the 30-day period.

(4) A copy of the regulations at 42 CFR 489.24.

(B) For purposes of paragraph (h)(2)(iii)(A) of this section, the date of receipt is presumed to be 5 days after the certified mail date on the notice, unless there is a reasonable showing to the contrary.

(iv) The physician or hospital (or both where applicable) may request a meeting with the QIO. This meeting is not designed to be a formal adversarial hearing or a mechanism for discovery by the physician or hospital. The meeting is intended to afford the physician and/or the hospital a full and fair opportunity to present the views of the physician and/or hospital regarding the case. The following provisions apply to that meeting:

(A) The physician and/or hospital has the right to have legal counsel present during that meeting. However, the QIO may control the scope, extent, and manner of any questioning or any other presentation by the attorney. The QIO may also have legal counsel present.

(B) The QIO makes arrangements so that, if requested by CMS or the OIG, a verbatim transcript of the meeting may be generated. If CMS or OIG requests a transcript, the affected physician and/or the affected hospital may request that CMS provide a copy of the transcript.

(C) The QIO affords the physician and/or the hospital an opportunity to present, with the assistance of counsel, expert testimony in either oral or written form on the medical issues presented. However, the QIO may reasonably limit the number of witnesses and length of such testimony if such testimony is irrelevant or repetitive. The physician and/or hospital, directly or through counsel, may disclose patient records to potential expert witnesses without violating any non-disclosure requirements set forth in part 476 of this chapter.

(D) The QIO is not obligated to consider any additional information provided by the physician and/or the hospital after the meeting, unless, before the end of the meeting, the QIO requests that the physician and/or hospital submit additional information to support the claims. The QIO then allows the physician and/or the hospital an additional period of time, not to exceed 5 calendar days from the meeting, to submit the relevant information to the QIO.

(v) Within 60 calendar days of receiving the case, the QIO must submit to CMS a report on the QIO's findings. CMS provides copies to the OIG and to the affected physician and/or the affected hospital. The report must contain the name of the physician and/or the hospital, the name of the individual, and the dates and times the individual arrived at and was transferred (or discharged) from the hospital. The report provides expert medical opinion regarding whether the individual involved had an emergency medical condition, whether the individual's emergency medical condition was stabilized, whether the individual was transferred appropriately, and whether there were any medical utilization or quality of care issues involved in the case.

(vi) The report required under paragraph (h)(2)(v) of this section should not state an opinion or conclusion as to whether section 1867 of the Act or § 489.24 has been violated.

(3) If a delay would jeopardize the health or safety of individuals or when there was no screening examination, the QIO review described in this section is not required before the OIG may impose civil monetary penalties or an exclusion in accordance with section 1867(d)(1) of the Act and 42 CFR part 1003 of this title.

(4) If the QIO determines after a preliminary review that there was an appropriate medical screening examination and the individual did not have an emergency medical condition, as defined by paragraph (b) of this section, then the QIO may, at its discretion, return the case to CMS and not meet the requirements of paragraph (h) except for those in paragraph (h)(2)(v).

(i) *Release of QIO assessments.* Upon request, CMS may release a QIO assessment to the physician and/or hospital, or the affected individual, or his or her representative. The QIO physician's identity is confidential unless he or she consents to its release. (See §§ 476.132 and 476.133 of this chapter.)

(j) *Availability of on-call physicians.* In accordance with the on-call list requirements specified in § 489.20(r)(2), a hospital must have written policies and procedures in place—

(1) To respond to situations in which a particular specialty is not available or the on-call physician cannot respond because of circumstances beyond the physician's control; and

(2) To provide that emergency services are available to meet the needs of individuals with emergency medical conditions if a hospital elects to—

(i) Permit on-call physicians to schedule elective surgery during the time that they are on call;

(ii) Permit on-call physicians to have simultaneous on-call duties; and

(iii) Participate in a formal community call plan. Notwithstanding participation in a community call plan, hospitals are still required to perform medical screening examinations on individuals who present seeking treatment and to conduct appropriate transfers. The formal community plan must include the following elements:

(A) A clear delineation of on-call coverage responsibilities; that is, when each hospital participating in the plan is responsible for on-call coverage.

(B) A description of the specific geographic area to which the plan applies.

(C) A signature by an appropriate representative of each hospital participating in the plan.

(D) Assurances that any local and regional EMS system protocol formally includes information on community on-call arrangements.

(E) A statement specifying that even if an individual arrives at a hospital that is not designated as the on-call hospital, that hospital still has an obligation under § 489.24 to provide a medical screening examination and stabilizing treatment within its capability, and that hospitals participating in the community call plan must abide by the regulations under § 489.24 governing appropriate transfers.

(F) An annual assessment of the community call plan by the participating hospitals.

[59 FR 32120, June 22, 1994, as amended at 62 FR 46037, Aug. 29, 1997; 65 FR 18548, Apr. 7, 2000; 65 FR 59748, Oct. 6, 2000; 66 FR 1599, Jan. 9, 2001; 66 FR 59923, Nov. 30, 2001; 68 FR 53262, Sept. 9, 2003; 71 FR 48143, Aug. 18, 2006; 72 FR 47413, Aug. 22, 2007; 73 FR 48758, Aug. 19, 2008; 74 FR 44001, Aug. 27, 2009]

Effective Date Note: At 59 FR 32120, June 22, 1994, § 489.24 was added. Paragraphs (d) and (g) contain information collection and recordkeeping requirements and will not become effective until approval has been given by the Office of Management and Budget.

Appendix C

State Operations Manual: Provider Certification

Appendix V—Interpretive Guidelines—Responsibilities of Medicare Participating Hospitals in Emergency Cases (Rev. 60, 07-16-10)

Part I—Investigative Procedures

I. General Information
II. Principal Focus of Investigation
III. Task 1—Entrance Conference
IV. Task 2—Case Selection Methodology
V. Task 3—Record Review
VI. Task 4—Interviews
VII. Task 5—Exit Conference
VIII. Task 6—Professional Medical Review
IX. Task 7—Assessment of Compliance and Completion of the Deficiency Report
X. Additional Survey Report Documentation

Part II—Interpretive Guidelines—Responsibilities of Medicare Participating Hospitals in Emergency Cases

§ 489.20 Basic Section 1866 Commitments Relevant to Section 1867 Responsibilities

§ 489.20(l)

§ 489.20(m)

§ 489.20(q)

§ 489.20(r)

§ 489.24(j) Availability of On-Call physicians

§ 489.24 Special Responsibilities of Medicare Hospitals in Emergency Cases

§ 489.24(a) Applicability of Provisions of this Section

§ 489.24(c) Use of Dedicated Emergency Department for Nonemergency Services

§ 489.24(d) Necessary Stabilizing Treatment for Emergency Medical Conditions

§ 489.24(e) Restricting Transfer Until the Individual Is Stabilized

§ 489.24(f) Recipient Hospital Responsibilities

Part I—Investigative Procedures

I. General Information

Medicare participating hospitals must meet the Emergency Medical Treatment and Labor Act (EMTALA) statute codified at § 1867 of the Social Security Act, (the Act) the accompanying regulations in 42 CFR § 489.24 and the related requirements at 42 CFR 489.20(l), (m), (q), and (r). EMTALA requires hospitals with emergency departments to provide a medical screening examination to any individual who comes to the emergency department and requests such an examination, and prohibits hospitals with emergency departments from refusing to examine or treat individuals with an emergency medical condition (EMC). The term "hospital" includes critical access hospitals. The provisions of EMTALA apply to all individuals (not just Medicare beneficiaries) who attempt to gain access to a hospital for emergency care. The regulations define "hospital with an emergency department" to mean a hospital with a dedicated emergency department (ED). In turn, the regulation defines "dedicated emergency department" as any department or facility of the hospital that either (1) is licensed by the state as an emergency department; (2) held out to the public as providing treatment for emergency medical conditions; or (3) on one-third of the visits to the department in the preceding calendar year actually provided treatment for emergency medical conditions on an urgent basis. These three requirements are discussed in greater detail at Tag A406.

The enforcement of EMTALA is a complaint driven process. The investigation of a hospital's policies/procedures and processes and any subsequent sanctions are initiated by a complaint. If the results of a complaint investigation indicate that a hospital violated one or more of the anti-dumping provisions of § 1866 or 1867 (EMTALA), a hospital may be subject to termination of its provider agreement and/or the imposition of civil monetary penalties (CMPs). CMPs may be imposed against hospitals or individual physicians for EMTALA violations.

The RO evaluates and authorizes all complaints and refers cases to the SA that warrant investigation. The first step in determining if the hospital has an EMTALA obligation is for the surveyor verify whether the hospital in fact has a dedicated emergency department (ED). To do so, the surveyor must check whether the hospital meets one of the criteria that define whether the hospital has a dedicated emergency department.

As discussed above, a dedicated emergency department is defined as meeting one of the following criteria regardless of whether it is located on or off the main hospital campus: The entity: (1) is licensed by the State in which it is located under applicable State law as an emergency room or emergency department; or (2) is held out to the public (by name, posted signs, advertising, or other means) as a place that provides care for emergency medical conditions (EMC) on an urgent basis without requiring a previously scheduled appointment; or (3) during the preceding calendar year, (i.e., the year immediately preceding the calendar year in which a determination under this section is being made), based on a representative sample of patient visits that occurred during the calendar year, it provides at least one-third of all of its visits for the treatment of EMCs on an urgent basis without requiring a previously scheduled appointment. This includes individuals who may present as unscheduled ambulatory patients to units (such as labor and delivery or psychiatric units of hospitals) where patients are routinely evaluated and treated for emergency medical conditions.

Hospitals with dedicated emergency departments are required to take the following measures:

- Adopt and enforce policies and procedures to comply with the requirements of 42 CFR § 489.24;
- Post signs in the dedicated ED specifying the rights of individuals with emergency medical conditions and women in labor who come to the dedicated ED for health care services, and indicate on the signs whether the hospital participates in the Medicaid program;
- Maintain medical and other records related to individuals transferred to and from the hospital for a period of five years from the date of the transfer;
- Maintain a list of physicians who are on-call to provide further evaluation and or treatment necessary to stabilize an individual with an emergency medical condition;
- Maintain a central log of individual's who come to the dedicated ED seeking treatment and indicate whether these individuals:
  - Refused treatment,
  - Were denied treatment,
  - Were treated, admitted, stabilized, and/or transferred or were discharged;
- Provide for an appropriate medical screening examination;
- Provide necessary stabilizing treatment for emergency medical conditions and labor within the hospital's capability and capacity;
- Provide an appropriate transfer of an unstabilized individual to another medical facility if:
  - The individual (or person acting on his or her behalf) after being informed of the risks and the hospital's obligations requests a transfer,
  - A physician has signed the certification that the benefits of the transfer of the patient to another facility outweigh the risks or

- A qualified medical person (as determined by the hospital in its by-laws or rules and regulations) has signed the certification after a physician, in consultation with that qualified medical person, has made the determination that the benefits of the transfer outweigh the risks and the physician countersigns in a timely manner the certification. (This last criterion applies if the responsible physician is not physically present in the emergency department at the time the individual is transferred.
- Provide treatment to minimize the risks of transfer;
- Send all pertinent records to the receiving hospital;
- Obtain the consent of the receiving hospital to accept the transfer,
- Ensure that the transfer of an unstabilized individual is effected through qualified personnel and transportation equipment, including the use of medically appropriate life support measures;

- Medical screening examination and/or stabilizing treatment is not to be delayed in order to inquire about payment status;

- Accept appropriate transfer of individuals with an emergency medical condition if the hospital has specialized capabilities or facilities and has the capacity to treat those individuals; and

- Not penalize or take adverse action against a physician or a qualified medical person because the physician or qualified medical person refuses to authorize the transfer of an individual with an emergency medical condition that has not been stabilized or against any hospital employee who reports a violation of these requirements.

If the hospital does not have a dedicated emergency department as defined in 42 CFR § 489.24(b), apply 42 CFR § 482.12(f) which requires the hospital's governing body to assure that the medical staff has written policies and procedures for appraisal of emergencies and the provision of initial treatment and referral (Form CMS-1537, "Medicare/Medicaid Hospital Survey Report").

Hospitals that violate the provisions in 42 CFR § 489.24 or the related requirements in 42 CFR § 489.20(l), (m), (q), and (r) are subject to civil monetary penalties or termination.

A hospital is required to report to CMS or the State survey agency promptly when it suspects it may have received an improperly transferred individual. Notification should occur within 72 hours of the occurrence. Failure to report improper transfers may subject the receiving hospital to termination of its provider agreement.

To assure that CMS is aware of all instances of improper transfer or potential violations of the other anti-dumping requirements, the State survey agencies must promptly report to the RO all complaints related to violations of 42 CFR § 489.24 and the related requirements at 42 CFR § 489.20(l), (m), (q), and (r). The RO will decide whether a complaint alleges a violation of these requirements and warrants an investigation.

Quality of care review performed either by the SA or other physicians must not delay processing of a substantiated EMTALA violation. If during the course of the investigation, you identify possible quality of care issues other than those related to the provisions of this regulation, obtain a copy of the patient's medical record and send the case to the RO for referral to the appropriate Quality Improvement Organization (QIO). Contact the RO if the hospital refuses to provide a copy of the medical record.

If you suspect emergency services are being denied based on diagnosis (e.g., AIDS), financial status, race, color, national origin, or handicap, refer the cases to the RO. The RO will forward the cases to the Office of Civil Rights (OCR) for investigation of discrimination.

A hospital must formally determine who is qualified to perform the initial medical screening examinations, i.e., qualified medical person. While it is permissible for a hospital to designate a non-physician practitioner as the qualified medical person, the designated non-physician practitioners must be set forth in a document that is approved by the governing body of the hospital. Those health practitioners designated to perform medical screening examinations are to be identified in the hospital by-laws or in the rules and regulations governing the medical staff following governing body approval. It is not acceptable for the hospital to allow the medical director of the emergency department to make what may be informal personnel appointments that could frequently change.

If it appears that a hospital with an dedicated ED does not have adequate staff and equipment to meet the needs of patients, consult the RO to determine whether or not to expand the survey for compliance with the requirements of 42 CFR § 482.55 ("Condition of Participation: Emergency Services").

Look for evidence that the procedures and policies for emergency medical services (including triage of patients) are established, evaluated, and updated on an ongoing basis.

The hospital should have procedures, which assure integration with other hospital services (e.g., including laboratory, radiology, ICU, and operating room services) to ensue continuity of care.

II. Principal Focus of Investigation

Investigate for compliance with the regulations in 42 CFR § 489.24 and the related requirements in 42 CFR § 489.20(l), (m), (q), and (r). All investigations are to be unannounced. The investigation is based on an allegation of noncompliance. The purpose of the investigation is to ascertain whether a violation took place, to determine whether the violation constitutes an immediate and serious threat to patient health and safety, to identify any patterns of violations at the facility, and to assess whether the facility has policies and procedures to address the provisions of the EMTALA law. The investigation must be completed within 5 working days of the RO authorization.

The focus of the investigation is on the initial allegation of violation and the discovery of additional violations. If the allegation is not confirmed, the surveyors must still be assured that the hospital's policies and procedures, physician certifications of transfers, etc., are in compliance with the requirements of 42 CFR § 489.24 and the related requirements at 42 CFR § 489.20(l), (m), (q), and (r). If the allegation(s) is confirmed, the investigation would continue, but with an emphasis on the hospital's compliance within the last 6 months.

Ensure that the case(s), if substantiated, is (are) fully documented on Form CMS-2567, Statement of Deficiencies and Plan of Correction. The investigation paperwork should be completed within ten working days following completion of the onsite survey if it appears there may be a violation of §§ 1866 and 1867 of the Act (**the paperwork is to be in the RO possession by the 20th working day or less following completion of the onsite survey. This includes the 5 days allowed to complete the onsite investigation**). If there appears not to be a violation, and the responsibilities of Medicare participating hospitals in emergency cases appear to be met, the time frame to complete the paperwork and return to the RO may be extended to 15 working days (**the paperwork is to be in the RO possession by the 25th working day or less following completion of the onsite survey. This includes the 5 days allowed to complete the onsite investigation**).

Once the investigation is complete the RO is strongly encouraged to share as much information with the hospital as possible in accordance with the Privacy Act and the Health Insurance Portability and Accountability Act (HIPAA) regarding the complaint and investigation. The RO may also include any facts about the violation, a copy of any medical reviews (the identity of the reviewer must be deleted), and the identity of the patient involved (not the identity of the complainant or source of the complaint). CMS will determine if the violation constitutes immediate jeopardy to patient health and safety.

The hospital has the opportunity to present evidence to CMS that it believes demonstrates its compliance and the opportunity to comment on evidence CMS believes demonstrates the hospital's noncompliance. CMS' regional offices retain delegated enforcement authority and final enforcement decisions are made there.

III. Task 1—Entrance Conference

A brief entrance conference must be held with the CEO/president of the hospital (or his or her designee) and any other staff the CEO considers appropriate to explain the nature of the allegation, the purpose of the investigation, and the requirements against which the complaint will be investigated. The identity of the complainant and patient must always be kept confidential unless written consent is obtained. Ask the CEO to have the staff provide you with the following information (as appropriate):

- Dedicated ED logs for the past 6-12 months;
- The dedicated ED policy/procedures manual (review triage and assessment of patients presenting to the ED with emergency medical conditions, assessment of labor, transfers of individuals with emergency medical conditions, etc.);
- Consent forms for transfers of unstable individuals;
- Dedicated ED committee meeting minutes for the past 12 months;

- Dedicated ED staffing schedule (physicians for the past 3 months and nurses for the last 4 weeks) or as appropriate;
- Bylaws/rules and regulations of the medical staff;
- Minutes from medical staff meetings for the past 6-12 months;
- Current medical staff roster;
- Physician on-call lists for the past 6 months;
- Credential files (to be selected by you) include the director of the emergency department and emergency department physicians. Review of credentials files is optional. However, if there has been a turnover in significant personnel (e.g., the ED director) or an unusual turnover of ED physicians, or a problem is identified during record review of a particular physician's screening or treatment in the ER, credentials files should be obtained and reviewed;
- Quality Assessment and Performance Improvement (QAPI) Plan (formally known as Quality Assurance);
- QAPI minutes (request the portion of the quality improvement minutes and plan, which specifically relates to EMTALA regulations. If a problem is identified that would require a more thorough review, additional portions of the quality improvement plan and minutes may be requested for review);
- List of contracted services (request this list if a potential violation of § 1866 and 1867 of the Act is noted during the investigation and the use of contracted services is questioned);
- Dedicated ED personnel records (optional);
- In-service training program records, schedules, reports, etc. (optional review if questions arise through interview and record review regarding the staff's knowledge of 42 CFR § 489.24);
- Ambulance trip reports and memoranda of transfer, if available (to be selected by you if the cases you are reviewing concern transfers); and
- Ambulance ownership information and applicable State/regional/community EMS protocols.

In addition, if the case you are investigating occurred prior to the time frames mentioned, examine the above records for a three-month period surrounding the date of the alleged violation.

Inform the CEO that you will be selecting a sample of cases (medical records) for review from the ED log and that you will require those records in a timely fashion.

IV. Task 2—Case Selection Methodology

Even though a single occurrence is considered a violation a sample is done to identify additional violations and/or patterns of violations.

A. Sample Size. Select 20-50 records to review in depth, using the selection criteria described below. The sample is not intended to be a statistically valid sample and the sample selection should be focused on potential problem areas. The sample size should be expanded as necessary in order to adequately investigate possible violations or patterns of violations.

B. Sample Selection. The type of records sampled will vary based on the nature of the complaint and the types of patients requesting emergency services. Do not allow the facility staff to select the sample. Use the emergency department log and other appropriate information, such as patient charts, to identify:

- Individuals transferred to other facilities;
- Gaps, return cases, or nonsequential entries in the log;
- Refusals of examination, treatment, or transfer;
- Patients leaving against medical advice or left without being seen (LWBS); and
- Patients returning to the emergency department within 48 hours.

Sample selection requires that:

1. You identify the number of emergency cases seen per month for each of the 6 months preceding the survey. Place this information on Form CMS-1541B, "Responsibilities of Medicare Participating Hospitals in Emergency Cases Investigation Report," (Exhibit 137).

2. You identify the number of transfers of emergency patients to other acute care hospitals per month for each of the preceding 6 months. Review in-depth, transfers of patients where it appears that the transferring hospital could have provided continuing medical care. Place this information on Form CMS-1541B.

3. You include the complaint case (s) in the sample, regardless of how long ago it occurred. Select other cases at the time of the complaint in order to identify patterns of hospital behavior and to help protect the identity of the patient.

4. If the complaint case did not involve an inappropriate transfer (e.g., the complaint was for failure to provide an adequate screening examination, or a hospital with specialized capabilities refused an appropriate transfer), identify similar cases and review them.

5. If you identify additional violations, determine, if possible, whether there is a pattern related to:
   - Diagnosis (e.g., labor, AIDS, psych);
   - Race;
   - Color;
   - Type of health insurance (Medicaid, uninsured, under-insured, or managed care);
   - Nationality; or
   - Disability.

Representative Sample Size for the dedicated emergency department if applicable:

The SA surveyor should consult with the RO prior to conducting the representative sample of patient visits for a hospital department to determine whether the department meets the criteria of being a dedicated emergency department.

To determine if a hospital department is a dedicated emergency department because it meets the "one-third requirement" described above (i.e., the hospital, in the preceding year, had at least one-third of all of its visits for the treatment of EMCs on an urgent basis without requiring a previously scheduled appointment) the surveyor is to select a representative sample of patient visits that occurred the previous calendar year in the area of the hospital to be evaluated for status as a dedicated emergency department. This includes individuals who may present as unscheduled ambulatory patients to units (such as labor and delivery or psychiatric units of hospitals) where patients are routinely admitted for evaluation and treatment. The surveyors will review the facility log, appointment roster and other appropriate information to identify patients seen in the area or facility in question. Surveyors are to review 20 - 50 records of patients with diagnoses or presenting complaints, which may be associated with an emergency medical condition (e.g., cardiac, respiratory, pediatric patients (high fever, lethargic), loss of consciousness, etc.). Surveyors have the discretion (in consultation with the regional office) to expand the sample size as necessary in order to adequately investigate possible violations or patterns of violations. Do not allow the facility staff to select the sample. Review the selected cases to determine if patients had an emergency medical condition and received stabilizing treatment. If at least one-third of the sample cases reviewed were for the treatment of EMCs on an urgent basis without requiring a previously scheduled appointment, the area being evaluated is a dedicated emergency department, and therefore, the hospital has an EMTALA obligation. Hospitals that may meet this one-third criterion may be specialty hospitals (such as psychiatric hospitals), hospitals without "traditional" emergency departments, and urgent care centers. In addition, it is not relevant if the entity that meets the definition of a dedicated ED is not located on the campus of the main hospital.

Guidelines to determine if a department of a hospital meets the one-third criteria of being a dedicated emergency department:

For each case, the surveyors should answer three questions.

1. Was the individual an outpatient?

Y N If not, what was his or her status (e.g., inpatient, visitor or other)?

2. Was the individual a walk-in (unscheduled appointment)?

Y N

3. Did the individual have an EMC, and received stabilizing treatment?

Y N

(**NOTE**—an affirmative yes must be present for both parts of this question for the case to be counted toward the one-third criterion to be met. If **no** is answered for any part of this question, the criterion was **not met**, and select no for the overall answer).

All questions must have an answer of yes to confirm that the case is included as part of the percentage (one-third) to determine if the hospital has a dedicated emergency department. If one-third of the total cases being reviewed receive answers of "yes" to the three questions above, then the hospital has an EMTALA obligation.

Document information concerning your sample selection on a blank sheet of paper or SA worksheet and label it "Summary Listing of Sampled Cases." Include the dates the individuals requested services, any identifier codes used to protect the individual's confidentiality, and the reasons for your decision to include these individuals in your sample.

V. Task 3—Record Review

While surveyors may make preliminary findings during the course of the investigation, a physician must usually determine the appropriateness of the MSE, stabilizing treatment, and transfer. Because expert medical review is usually necessary, obtain copies of the medical and other record(s) of the alleged violation case (both hospitals if an individual sought care at two hospitals or were transferred) and any other violation cases identified in the course of the investigation.

Also, review documents pertaining to QAPI activities in the emergency department and remedial actions taken in response to a violation of these regulations. Document hospital corrective actions taken prior to the survey and take such corrective action into account when developing your recommendation to the RO.

In an accredited hospital, if it appears that CoPs are not met, contact the RO for authorization to extend the investigation. If you are conducting the investigation in a non-accredited hospital, you may expand the investigation to include other conditions without contacting the RO first. When there is insufficient information documented on the emergency record regarding a request for emergency care, it may be helpful to interview hospital staff, physicians, witnesses, ambulance personnel, the individual, or the individual's family. Ask for RO guidance if you are still unable to obtain a consistent and reliable account of what happened.

Any time delivery of a baby occurs during transfer, obtain a copy of all available records and refer the case for review to the QIO physician reviewer.

If you are unsure whether qualified personnel and or transportation equipment were used to effectuate a transfer, review the hospital's transfer policies, and obtain a copy of the medical record and transfer records.

In cases where treatment is rendered to stabilize an EMC, the medical records should reflect the medically indicated treatment necessary to stabilize it, the medications, treatments, surgeries and services rendered, and the effect of treatment on the individual's emergency condition or on the woman's labor and the unborn child.

The medical records should contain documentation such as: medically indicated screenings, tests, mental status evaluation, impressions, and diagnoses (supported by a history and physical examination, laboratory, and other test results) as appropriate.

For pregnant women, the medical records should show evidence that the screening examination included ongoing evaluation of fetal heart tones, regularity and duration of uterine contractions, fetal position and station, cervical dilation, and status of the membranes, i.e., ruptured, leaking, intact.

For individuals with psychiatric symptoms, the medical records should indicate an assessment of suicide or homicide attempt or risk, orientation, or assaultive behavior that indicates danger to self or others.

In cases where an individual (or person acting in the individual's behalf) withdrew the initial request for a medical screening examination (MSE) and/or treatment for an EMC and demanded his or her transfer, or demanded to leave the hospital, look for a signed informed refusal of examination and treatment form by either the individual or a person acting on the individual's behalf. Hospital personnel must inform the individual (or person acting on his or her behalf) of the risks and benefits associated with the transfer or the patient's refusal to seek further care. If the individual (or person acting in the individual's behalf) refused to sign the consent form, look for documentation by the hospital personnel that states that the individual refused to sign the form. The fact that an individual has not signed the form is not, however, automatically a violation of the screening requirement. Hospitals must, under the regulations, use their best efforts to obtain a signature from an individual refusing further care.

Examine the ambulance trip reports in questionable transfer cases (if available). These records can answer questions concerning the appropriateness of a transfer and the stability of the individual during the transfer.

Appropriate record review should also be conducted at the receiving (or recipient) hospital if the alleged case and any other suspicious transfer cases involve the transfer or movement of the individual to another hospital.

Document all significant record review findings in the complaint investigation narrative.

VI. Task 4—Interviews

To obtain a clear picture of the circumstances surrounding a suspected violation of the special responsibilities of Medicare hospitals in emergency cases, it is necessary to interview facility staff. For example, you may be able to gather a great deal of information from the admitting clerk in the emergency department, the nurses on shift at the time the individual sought treatment, and the Director of Quality Improvement in the hospital to name a few. You may also need to interview witnesses, the patient, and/or the patient's family. The physician(s) involved in the incident should be interviewed. Document each interview you conduct on a blank sheet of paper or SA worksheet and label it "Summary of Interviews." Include the following information, as appropriate, in your notes for each interview:

- The individual's job title and assignment at the time of the incident;
- Relationship to the patient and/or reason for the interview; and
- Summary of the information obtained.

Appropriate interviews should also be conducted at the receiving hospital in cases of transfer or movement of the individual to another hospital.

VII. Task 5—Exit Conference

The purpose of the exit conference is to inform the hospital of the scope of the investigation, including the nature of the complaint, investigation tasks, and requirements investigated, and any hospital CoPs surveyed. Explain to the hospital staff the consequences of a violation of the requirements in 42 CFR § 489.24 or the related requirements in 42 CFR § 489.20(l), (m), (q), and (r) and the time frames that will be followed if a violation is found. Do not tell the hospital whether or not a violation was identified since it is the responsibility of the RO to make that determination. Inform the CEO (or his or her designee) that the RO will make the determination of compliance based on the information collected during this investigation and any additional information acquired from physician review of the case. Do not leave a draft of the deficiencies of Form CMS-2567 with the hospital. Inform the hospital that the RO will send that information to the hospital once it is complete.

VIII. Task 6—Professional Medical Review

The purpose of a professional medical review (physician review) is to provide peer review using information available to the hospital at the time the alleged violation took place. Physician review is required prior to the imposition of CMPs or the termination of a hospital's provider agreement to determine if:

- The screening examination was appropriate. Under EMTALA, the term "appropriate" does not mean "correct", in the sense that the treating emergency physician is not required to correctly diagnose the individual's medical condition. The fact that a physician may have been negligent in his screening of an individual is not necessarily an EMTALA violation. When used in the context of EMTALA, "appropriate" means that the screening examination was suitable for the symptoms presented and conducted in a non-disparate fashion. Physician review is not necessary when the hospital did not screen the individual;
- The individual had an emergency medical condition. The physician should identify what the condition was and why it was an emergency (e.g., what could have happened to the patient if the treatment was delayed);

- In the case of a pregnant woman, there was inadequate time to affect a safe transfer to another hospital before delivery, or the transfer posed a threat to the health and safety of the woman or the unborn child;

- The stabilizing treatment was appropriate within a hospital's capability (**NOTE** that the clinical outcome of an individual's medical condition is not the basis for determining whether an appropriate screening was provided or whether the person transferred was stabilized);

- The transfer was effected through qualified personnel and transportation equipment, including the use of medically appropriate life support measures;

- If applicable, the on-call physician's response time was reasonable; and

- The transfer was appropriate for the individual because the individual; requested the transfer or because the medical benefits of the transfer outweighed the risk.

If you recommend a medical review of the case, indicate on Form CMS-1541B that you recommend such a review.

IX. Task 7—Assessment of Compliance and Completion of the Deficiency Report

A. Analysis. Analyze your findings relative to each provision of the regulations for the frequency of occurrence, dates of occurrence, and patterns in terms of race, color, diagnosis, nationality, handicap, and financial status. A single occurrence constitutes a violation and is sufficient for an adverse recommendation. Older cases where the hospital implemented corrective actions with no repeat violations may require consultation with the RO concerning appropriate recommendations.

If a team conducted the investigation, the team should meet to discuss the findings. Consider information provided by the hospital. Ask the hospital for additional information or clarification about particular findings, if necessary.

Review each regulation tag number sequentially in this Appendix, and come to a consensus as to whether or not the hospital complies with each stated requirement. The following outline may be helpful in this review. For each requirement recommended as not met, record all salient findings on the Form CMS-2567.

Outline of Data Tags Used for Citing Violations of Responsibilities of Medicare Participating Hospitals in Emergency Cases

Deficiency Tags	Requirements
A400	(§ 489.20) Policies and Procedures Which Address Anti-Dumping Provisions

Deficiency Tags	Requirements
A401	(§ 489.20(m)) Receiving Hospitals Must Report Suspected Incidences of Individuals With An Emergency Medical Condition Transferred in Violation of § 489.24(e)
A402	(§ 489.20(q)) Sign Posting
A403	(§ 489.24(r)) Maintain Transfer Records for Five Years
A404	(§ 489.20(r)(2); § 489.24(j)) On-Call Physicians
A405	(§ 489.20(r)(3)) Logs
A406	(§ 489.24(a); § 489.24(c)) Appropriate Medical Screening Examination
A407	(§ 489.24(d)(3)) Stabilizing Treatment (§ 489.24(d)(4))
A408	(§ 489.24(d)(4) and (5)) No Delay in Examination or Treatment in Order to Inquire About Payment Status
A409	(§ 489.24(e)(1) and (2)) Appropriate Transfer
A410	(§ 489.24(e)(3)) Whistleblower Protections
A411	(§ 489.24(f)) Recipient Hospital Responsibilities (Nondiscrimination)

B. Composing the Statement of Deficiencies (Form CMS-2567). Support all deficiency citations by documenting evidence obtained from your interviews and record reviews on Form CMS-2567, "Statement of Deficiencies and Plan of Correction." Deficiencies related to the Conditions of Participation should also be documented on Form CMS-2567. Indicate whether your findings show that the deficiency constitutes an immediate jeopardy to patient health and safety (e.g., a situation that prevents individuals from getting medical screening examinations and/or a lack of treatment reflecting both the capacity and capability of the hospital's full resources, as guaranteed under § 1867 of the Act). Some examples include stabilizing treatment not provided when required; failure of an on-call physician to respond appropriately, improper transfer; or evidence that there was a denial of medical screening examinations and/or treatment to persons with emergency medical conditions as a direct result of requesting payment information before assessment of the individual's medical condition. Examples of noncompliance, which usually does not pose an immediate jeopardy, include the following scenarios:

1. A transfer which was appropriate, but the physician certification was not signed or dated by the physician;

2. An appropriate, functioning central log that on one particular day in not fully completed; and

3. A written hospital policy that is missing, but nonetheless being implemented.

Do not make a medical judgment, but focus on the processes of the facility "beyond the paper." Identify whether single incidents of patient dumping, which do not represent a hospital's customary practice, are nonetheless serious and capable of being repeated.

Immediate jeopardy violations require a 23-day termination track. Non-immediate jeopardy violations require a 90-day termination track.

Write the deficiency statement in terms specific enough to allow a reasonably knowledgeable person to understand the aspect(s) of the requirement(s) that is (are) not met. **Do not prescribe an acceptable remedy**. Indicate the data prefix tag and regulatory citation, followed by a summary of the deficiency and supporting findings. When it is necessary to use specific examples, use individual identifier codes, not individual names.

The emergency services condition, or any other condition, is not automatically found out of compliance based on a violation of 42 CFR § 489.20 and/or 42 CFR § 489.24. A determination of noncompliance must be based on the regulatory requirements for the individual condition.

X. Additional Survey Report Documentation

Upon completion of each investigation, the team leader assures that the following additional documentation has been prepared for submission, along with Forms CMS-1541B, CMS-562, CMS-2567, and a copy of the medical record(s) to the RO:

A. Summary Listing of Sample Cases and Description of Sample Selection (See Task 2). At a minimum, identify:

- The name of each individual chosen to be a part of the sample and the date of their request for emergency services;
- Any individual identifier codes used as a reference to protect the individual's confidentiality;
- The reason for including the individual in the sample (e.g., unstabilized transfer, lack of screening, lack of treatment, failure to stabilize, diagnosis, race, color, financial status, handicap, nationality); and
- Include a copy of the medical record(s) for all individuals where the hospital violated the provisions in 42 CFR § 489.24.

Also identify:

- How the sample was selected;
- The number of individuals in the sample; and
- Any overall characteristics of the individuals in the sample, such as race, color, nationality, handicap, financial status, and diagnosis.

B. Summary of Interviews (See Task 4). Document interviews conducted with patients, families, staff, physicians, administrators, managers, and others. At a minimum, include the individual's job title and/or assignment at the time of the incident, the relationship to the patient and/or reason for the interview, and a summary of the information obtained in each interview.

C. Complaint Investigation Narrative (See Task 3). Summarize significant findings in the medical records, meeting minutes, hospital policies and procedures, staffing schedules, quality assurance plans, hospital by-laws, rules and regulations, training programs, credential files, personnel files, and contracted services reviewed in the course of the investigation. Briefly summarize your findings in the investigation and the rationale used for the course of action recommended to the RO.

Part II—Interpretive Guidelines—Responsibilities of Medicare Participating Hospitals in Emergency Cases

The Interpretive Guidelines is a tool for surveyors where the regulation is broken into regulatory citations (tag numbers), followed by the regulation language and provides detailed interpretation of the regulation(s) to surveyors.

Basic Section 1866 Commitments Relevant to Section 1867 Responsibilities—Tags A-2400/C2400—A2405/C2405 (Rev. 46, Issued: 05-29-09, Effective/Implementation: 05-29-09)

Tag A-2400/C-2400

(Rev. 46, Issued: 05-29-09, Effective/Implementation: 05-29-09)

§ 489.20(l)

[The provider agrees to the following:]

(l) In the case of a hospital as defined in § 489.24(b) to comply with § 489.24.

Interpretive Guidelines: § 489.20(l)

The term "hospital" is defined in § 489.24(b) as including critical access hospitals as defined in § 1861(mm)(1) of the Act. Therefore, a critical access hospital that operates a dedicated emergency department (as that term is defined below) is subject to the requirements of EMTALA.

Section 42 CFR 489.20(l) of the provider's agreement requires that hospitals comply with 42 CFR 489.24, special responsibilities of Medicare hospitals in emergency cases. Under the provisions of § 489.24, hospitals with an emergency department that participate in Medicare are required under EMTALA to do the following:

- Provide an appropriate MSE to any individual who comes to the emergency department;
- Provide necessary stabilizing treatment to an individual with an EMC or an individual in labor;

- Provide for an appropriate transfer of the individual if either the individual requests the transfer or the hospital does not have the capability or capacity to provide the treatment necessary to stabilize the EMC (or the capability or capacity to admit the individual);

- Not delay examination and/or treatment in order to inquire about the individual's insurance or payment status;

- Obtain or attempt to obtain written and informed refusal of examination, treatment or an appropriate transfer in the case of an individual who refuses examination, treatment or transfer; and

- Not take adverse action against a physician or qualified medical personnel who refuses to transfer an individual with an emergency medical condition, or against an employee who reports a violation of these requirements.

Further, any participating Medicare hospital is required to accept appropriate transfers of individuals with emergency medical conditions if the hospital has the specialized capabilities not available at the transferring hospital, and has the capacity to treat those individuals.

Hospitals are required to adopt and enforce a policy to ensure compliance with the requirements of § 489.24. Noncompliance with EMTALA requirements will lead CMS to initiate procedures for termination from the Medicare program. Noncompliance may also trigger the imposition of civil monetary penalties by the Office of the Inspector General.

Surveyors review the following documents to help determine if the hospital is in compliance with the requirement(s):

- Review the bylaws, rules, and regulations of the medical staff to determine if they reflect the requirements of § 489.24 and the related requirements at § 489.20.

- Review the emergency department policies and procedure manuals for procedures related to the requirements of § 489.24 and the related requirements at § 489.20.

If a hospital violates § 489.24, surveyors are to cite a corresponding violation of § 489.20(l), Tag A-2400/C-2400.

Tag A-2401/C-2401

(Rev. 46, Issued: 05-29-09, Effective/Implementation: 05-29-09) § 489.20(m)

[The provider agrees to the following:]

In the case of a hospital as defined in § 489.24(b), to report to CMS or the State survey agency any time it has reason to believe it may have received an individual who has been transferred in an unstable emergency medical condition from another hospital in violation of the requirements of § 489.24(e).

Interpretive Guidelines: § 489.20(m)

A hospital (recipient) that suspects it may have received an improperly transferred (transfer of an unstable individual with an emergency medical condition who was not provided an appropriate transfer according to § 489.24(e)(2)), individual is required to promptly report the incident to CMS or the State Agency (SA) within 72 hours of the occurrence. If a recipient hospital fails to report an improper transfer, the hospital may be subject to termination of it's provider agreement according to 42 CFR 489.53(a).

Surveyors are to look for evidence that the recipient hospital knew, or suspected the individual had been to a hospital prior to the recipient hospital, and had not been transferred in accordance with § 489.24(e). Evidence may be obtained in the medical record or through interviews with the individual, family members or staff.

Review the emergency department log and medical records of patients received as transfers. Look for evidence that:

- The hospital had agreed in advance to accept the transfers;
- The hospital had received appropriate medical records;
- All transfers had been effected through qualified personnel, transportation equipment and medically appropriate life support measures; and
- The hospital had available space and qualified personnel to treat the patients.

Tag A-2402/C-2402

(Rev. 46, Issued: 05-29-09, Effective/Implementation: 05-29-09)

§ 489.20(q)

[The provider agrees to the following:]

In the case of a hospital as defined in § 489.24(b)—

(1) **To post conspicuously in any emergency department or in a place or places likely to be noticed by all individuals entering the emergency department, as well as those individuals waiting for examination and treatment in areas other than traditional emergency department (that is, entrance, admitting area, waiting room, treatment area) a sign (in a form specified by the Secretary) specifying the rights of individuals under section 1867 of the Act with respect to examination and treatment of emergency medical conditions and women in labor; and**

(2) **To post conspicuously (in a form specified by the Secretary) information indicating whether or not the hospital or rural primary care hospital (e.g., critical access hospital) participates in the Medicaid program under a State plan approved under Title XIX;**

Interpretive Guidelines: § 489.20(q)(1) and (2)

Section 1866(a)(1)(N)(iii) of the Act requires the posting of signs which specify the rights of individuals with EMCs and women in labor.

To comply with the requirements hospital signage must at a minimum:

- Specify the rights of individuals with EMCs and women in labor who come to the emergency department for health care services;
- Indicate whether the facility participates in the Medicaid program;
- The wording of the sign(s) must be clear and in simple terms and language(s) that are understandable by the population served by the hospital; and
- The sign(s) must be posted in a place or places likely to be noticed by all individuals entering the emergency department, as well as those individuals waiting for examination and treatment (e.g., entrance, admitting area, waiting room, treatment area).

Tag A-2403/C-2403

(Rev. 46, Issued: 05-29-09, Effective/Implementation: 05-29-09)

§ 489.20(r)

[The provider agrees to the following:]

In the case of a hospital as defined in § 489.24(b) (including both the transferring and receiving hospitals), to maintain—

(1) Medical and other records related to individuals transferred to or from the hospital for a period of 5 years from the date of transfer;

Interpretive Guidelines: § 489.20(r)(1)

The medical records of individuals transferred to or from the hospital must be retained in their original or legally reproduced form in hard copy, microfilm, microfiche, optical disks, computer disks, or computer memory for a period of 5 years from the date of transfer.

Tag A-2404/C-2404

(Rev. 46, Issued: 05-29-09, Effective/Implementation: 05-29-09)

§ 489.20(r)(2)

[The provider agrees to the following:

In the case of a hospital as defined in § 489.24(b) (including both the transferring and receiving hospitals), to maintain—]

(2) An on-call list of physicians who are on the hospital's medical staff or who have privileges at the hospital, or who are on staff or have privileges at another hospital participating in a formal community call plan, in accordance with § 489.24(j)(2)(iii), available to provide treatment necessary after the initial examination to stabilize individuals with emergency medical conditions who are receiving services under § 489.24 in accordance with the resources available to the hospital;

§ 489.24(j)—Availability of On-call Physicians

In accordance with the on-call requirements specified in § 489.20(r)(2), a hospital must have written policies and procedures in place—

(1) To respond to situations in which a particular specialty is not available or the on-call physician cannot respond because of circumstances beyond the physician's control;

(2) To provide that emergency services are available to meet the needs of individuals with emergency medical conditions if a hospital elects to—

(i) Permit on-call physicians to schedule elective surgery during the time they are on call

(ii) Permit on-call physicians to have simultaneous on-call duties;

(iii) Participate in a formal community call plan. Notwithstanding participation in a community call plan, hospitals are still required to perform medical screening examinations on individuals who present seeking treatment and to conduct appropriate transfers. The formal community call plan must include the following elements:

(A) A clear delineation of on-call coverage responsibilities; that is, when each hospital participating in the plan is responsible for on-call coverage.

(B) A description of the specific geographic area to which the plan applies.

(C) A signature by an appropriate representative of each hospital participating in the plan.

(D) Assurances that any local and regional EMS system protocol formally includes information on community-call arrangements.

(E) A statement specifying that even if an individual arrives at a hospital that is not designated as the on-call hospital, that hospital still has an obligation under § 489.24 to provide a medical screening examination and stabilizing treatment within its capability, and that hospitals participating in the community call plan must abide by the regulations under § 489.24 governing appropriate transfers.

(F) An annual assessment of the community call plan by the participating hospitals.

Interpretive Guidelines § 489.20(r)(2) and § 489.24(j)

On-Call List Requirements and Options

Section 1866(a)(1)(I)(iii)of the Act states, as a requirement for participation in the Medicare program, that hospitals must maintain a list of physicians who are on-call for duty after the initial examination to provide treatment necessary to stabilize an individual with an emergency medical condition. This on-call list requirement is a general provider agreement requirement for all hospitals and is thus technically an "EMTALA-related" requirement rather than a specific requirement of the EMTALA portion of the Act. When determining compliance with the on-call list requirement as part of an EMTALA survey it must be remembered that the on-call list requirement applies not only to hospitals with dedicated emergency departments, but also to hospitals subject to EMTALA requirements to accept appropriate transfers. (See discussion of § 489.24(f).) The on-call list clearly identifies and ensures that the hospital's personnel is prospectively aware of which physicians, including specialists and sub-specialists, are available to provide stabilizing treatment for individuals with emergency medical conditions.

The list of on-call physicians must be composed of physicians who are current members of the medical staff or who have hospital privileges. If the hospital participates in a community call plan then the list must also include the names of physicians at other hospitals who are on-call pursuant to the plan. The list must be up-to-date, and accurately reflect the current privileges of the physicians on-call. Physician group names are not acceptable for identifying the on-call physician. Individual physician names are to be identified on the list with their accurate contact information.

Hospital administrators and the physicians who provide the on-call services have flexibility regarding how to configure an on-call coverage system. Several options to enhance this flexibility are permitted under the regulations. It is crucial, however, that hospitals are aware of their responsibility to ensure that they are providing sufficient on-call services to the meet the needs of their community in accordance with the resources they have available. CMS expects a hospital to strive to provide adequate specialty on-call coverage consistent with the services provided at the hospital and the resources the hospital has available. (73 FR 48662).

Permitted On-Call Options

Community Call Plan

CMS permits hospitals to satisfy their on-call obligations through participation in a community call plan (CCP). It is strictly voluntary. Under such a community on-call plan, a hospital may augment its on-call list by adding to it physicians at another hospital. There are different ways a CCP could be organized. For example, if there are two hospitals that choose to participate in community call, Hospital A could be designated as the on-call facility for the first 15 days of the month and Hospital B could be designated as the on-call facility for the remaining days of the month. Alternatively, Hospital A could be designated as on-call for cases requiring specialized interventional cardiac care, while Hospital B could be designated as on-call for neurosurgical cases. Ideally, a CCP could allow various physicians in a certain specialty in the aggregate to be on continuous call (24 hours a day, 7 days a week) without putting a continuous call obligation at the participating hospitals on any one physician. Even if this ideal cannot be achieved, given the resources of the participating hospitals, at a minimum, hospitals choosing to participate in a CCP should to be able to provide more on-call specialty coverage than they would on their own.

The plan must clearly articulate which on-call services will be provided on which dates/times by each hospital participating in the plan. Furthermore, the

DED in each hospital must have specific information based on the allocation of on-call responsibilities in the plan readily available as part of the on-call list, so that personnel who are providing required services to individuals protected under EMTALA know which specialists based in which hospital(s) are available on-call to provide the necessary specialist services.

Participation in a community call plan does not mean that on-call physicians must travel from the hospital where they practice to the hospital needing their on-call services. Instead, this arrangement facilitates appropriate transfers to the hospital providing the specialty on-call services pursuant to the plan. The hospital where the individual initially presents still has an EMTALA obligation to conduct a medical screening examination, and, for individuals found to have an emergency medical condition, to provide stabilizing treatment within its capability and capacity. However, when the individual is appropriately transferred pursuant to a CCP for further stabilizing treatment, it can generally be assumed that the transferring hospital has provided treatment within its capability and capacity and that its on-call list is adequate for that specialty. For example, if an individual requires the services of a neurologist on a date when the neurologist on-call pursuant to the CCP is based at hospital B, and that neurologist is part of hospital A's on-call list, then a transfer to hospital B to obtain the services of the neurologist on-call would be in order, assuming all other transfer requirements have been met.

In those cases where, for example, hospitals A and B participate in a CCP and a physician who is a member of the medical staff or has privileges at both hospitals is on-call directly at hospital B, but only indirectly through the CCP to hospital A, there is no regulatory prohibition against the on-call physician going to hospital A to provide the stabilizing treatment, rather than transferring the individual to hospital B. The treating and on-call physician might consider which approach is in the best interests of the patient and also maintains the availability of the on-call specialist pursuant to the CCP.

The regulations establish a number of specific requirements for community call plans:

- The plan must include the geographic parameters of the on-call coverage, indicating what patient origin areas the plan expects to service (e.g., certain communities, counties, regions, municipalities). CMS does not stipulate geographic criteria that a community call plan must meet, since the intent of the plan is to promote flexibility amongst the participating hospitals in developing a call plan that best meets the needs of their communities and utilizes the resources within the region. Similarly, there is no requirement that all hospitals within a defined geographic area must participate in the community call plan.

  Regardless of the geographic specifications of the community call plan, the existence of a CCP in a specific area does not eliminate the EMTALA obligations of hospitals with respect to making appropriate transfers. Among other things this means that:

— hospitals participating in the community call plan are not relieved of their recipient hospital obligations to accept appropriate transfers from hospitals not participating in the plan.

— non-participating hospitals must accept appropriate transfers, regardless of whether the transferring hospital participates in a CCP with the recipient hospital or any other hospital.

— non-participating hospitals must provide stabilizing treatment within their capability and capacity before seeking to transfer an individual to another hospital, regardless of whether the recipient hospital is providing on-call services to other hospitals pursuant to a CCP.

In other words, all Medicare-participating hospitals must fulfill their transfer responsibilities under EMTALA, notwithstanding the presence or absence of a transfer agreement and regardless of whether the transferring or recipient hospital is participating in a formal community call plan (73 FR 48667).

- The community call plan for each participating hospital must show evidence that the duly authorized representative of each hospital has officially signed the plan. The regulations do not require that the plan be signed by an appropriate representative as part of the annual assessment but it is expected that updated signatures would be included in any subsequent revision of the CCP.

- The delivery of pre-hospital medical services is quite varied throughout the country and there are no specific EMTALA requirements that pertain to the development of EMS protocols. However, if there are EMS protocols in effect in part or all of the areas served by the CCP, then there must be an attestation by the CCP-participating hospitals that the CCP arrangement information has been communicated to the EMS providers and will be updated as needed so that EMS providers have the opportunity to consider this information when developing protocols. In addition, hospitals which are in the process of developing and refining their own CCPs may want to consider including input from the EMS providers that serve their DEDs so as to facilitate the efficient implementation of the CCP. For communities that do not have formalized EMS protocols, hospitals participating in a CCP would still be well-advised to inform individual EMS providers of the CCP arrangements amongst the hospitals in the geographic area specified in the plan.

- The formal language of the CCP must contain a statement that each hospital participating in the CCP will continue to follow the regulations requiring the provision of MSEs, and stabilizing treatment for individuals determined to have EMCs.

- Hospitals must conduct an annual reassessment of their CCP, including an analysis of the specialty on-call needs of the communities for which the CCP is effective (73 FR 48665). It is expected that the CCP would expand specialty coverage to the communities served by the plan and improve, within the hospitals' capabilities and capacities, the adequacy of the on-call list for the hospitals participating in the plan. CMS expects the annual assessment to support a Quality Assurance/Performance Improvement approach to the functioning of the CCP, and that hospitals would, as necessary and feasible, adjust the CCP based on the annual reassessment. Hospitals participating in the CCP have flexibility to determine how to design and implement the assessment.

Simultaneous Call

Hospitals are permitted to allow physicians to be on-call simultaneously at two or more facilities. Hospitals are also permitted to adopt a policy that does not allow physicians to take simultaneous call at more than one hospital. If a hospital permits simultaneous call, then it must have written policies and procedures to follow when the on-call physician is not available to respond because he/she has been called to another hospital. All hospitals where the physician is on-call need to be aware of the details of the simultaneous call arrangements for the physician and have back-up plans established.

Scheduled Elective Surgery

Hospitals are permitted to allow physicians to perform elective surgery or other procedures while they are on-call. Hospitals are also permitted to adopt a policy that does not allow physicians to perform elective surgery or other procedures while they are on-call. (Critical Access Hospitals (CAHs) should be aware that if they reimburse physicians for being on-call, there are Medicare payment policy regulations, outside the scope of EMTALA requirements, that the CAH might want to consider before making a decision to permit on-call physicians to schedule elective procedures.)

When a physician has agreed to be on-call at a particular hospital during a particular period of time, but also has scheduled elective surgery or an elective diagnostic or therapeutic procedure during that time as permitted by hospital policy, that physician and the hospital must have planned back-up in the event the physician is called while performing elective surgery and is unable to respond to an on-call request in a reasonable time.

Medical Staff Exemptions

There is no EMTALA or Medicare provider agreement requirement for all physicians on the medical staff and/or having hospital privileges to take call. A hospital policy allowing exemptions to medical staff members (e.g., senior physicians) would not in of itself violate EMTALA-related Medicare provider agreement requirements. However, if a hospital permits physicians to selectively take call only for their own established patients who present to the ED for evaluation, then the hospital must be careful to assure that it maintains adequate on-call services, and that the selective call policy is not a substitute for the on-call services required by the Medicare provider agreement.

Other On-call List Regulatory Requirements

A hospital must have written on-call policies and procedures and must clearly define the responsibilities of the on-call physician to respond, examine and treat patients with an EMC. Among other things, the policies and procedures must address the steps to be taken if a particular specialty is not available or the on-call physician cannot respond due to circumstances beyond his/her control (e.g., transportation failures, personal illness, etc.). The policies and procedures must also ensure that the hospital provides emergency services that meet the needs of an individual with an EMC if the hospital chooses to employ any of the on-call options permitted under the regulations, i.e., community call, simultaneous call, or elective procedures while on-call. In other words, there must be a back-up plan to these optional arrangements. For instance, some hospitals may employ the use of "jeopardy" or back-up call schedules to be used only under extreme circumstances. The hospital must be able to demonstrate that hospital staff is aware of and able to execute the back-up procedures.

Assessment of On-call List Adequacy by Surveyors

CMS expects that a hospital should strive to provide adequate on-call coverage consistent with the services provided at the hospital and the resources the hospital has available, including the availability of specialists. (42 FR 48662). CMS does not have specified requirements regarding how frequently on-call physicians are expected to be available to provide on-call coverage. However, CMS recognizes that in order to supply safe and effective care it would not be prudent for a hospital to expect one physician to be on-call every day of the week, every week of the year. There is also no pre-determined ratio CMS uses to identify how many days a hospital must provide medical staff on-call coverage for a particular specialty based on the number of physicians on staff for that particular specialty. In particular, CMS has no rule stating that whenever there are at least three physicians in a specialty, the hospital must provide 24-hour/7-day coverage in that specialty.

If a hospital participates in a community call plan, its on-call list must reflect this. The plan does not have to be pre-approved or require formal authorization by CMS or any local, State or Federal agency, in order to be instituted. However, during a complaint investigation, the design and implementation of the CCP will come under review.

Generally, in determining a hospital's on-call list compliance, CMS will consider all relevant factors in a case-specific manner, including the number of physicians on the medical staff/holding hospital privileges, other demands on these physicians, the frequency with which individuals with EMCs typically require the stabilizing services of the hospital's on-call physicians, and the provisions the hospital has made for situations in which a physician on-call is not available or is unable to respond due to circumstances beyond his/her control.

For instance, if the hospital under investigation performs a significant amount of interventional cardiac catheterizations and holds itself out to the public through various advertising methods as a center of excellence in providing this specialized procedure to the community, it would be reasonable to expect that there would be adequate on-call coverage by a physician who is able to perform an emergent interventional cardiac procedure on individuals who present to that hospital's DED in need of such an intervention or who are appropriately transferred to that hospital for such an intervention. On the other hand, it may not be reasonable to expect a CAH to have an interventional radiologist on call if that service is not routinely provided at the CAH or in the local vicinity of the CAH, unless the CAH participates in a community call plan that provides for this service.

On-call Physician Appearance Requirements

Although the on-call list requirement is found in Section 1866, which is the provider agreement section of the Act, Section 1867, the EMTALA section of the Act, provides for enforcement actions against both a physician and a hospital when a physician who is on the hospital's on-call list fails or refuses to appear within a reasonable period of time after being notified to appear. Hospitals would be well-advised to make physicians who are on-call aware of the hospital's on-call policies and the physician's EMTALA obligations when on call.

If a physician is listed as on-call and requested to make an in-person appearance to evaluate and treat an individual, that physician must respond in person in a reasonable amount of time. If an individual presents to Hospital A with an EMC that requires the specialty services provided by Hospital B pursuant to the CCP, then the physician who is based at Hospital B is required to report to Hospital B to provide the stabilizing treatment for the individual who presented to Hospital A and was subsequently transferred to Hospital B.

When a physician is on-call for the hospital and seeing patients with scheduled appointments in his/her private office, it is generally not acceptable to refer emergency cases to his or her office for examination and treatment of an EMC. The physician must come to the hospital to examine the individual if requested to do so by the treating physician. If, however, it is medically indicated, the treating physician may send an individual needing the specialized services of the on-call physician to the physician's office if it is a provider-based part of the hospital (i.e., department of the hospital sharing the same CMS certification number as the hospital) It must be clear that this transport is not done for the convenience of the specialist but that there is a genuine medical reason to move the individual, that all individuals with the same medical condition, regardless of their ability to pay, are similarly moved to the specialist's office, and that the appropriate medical personnel accompany the individual to the office.

If it is permitted under the hospital's policies, an on-call physician has the option of sending a representative, i.e., directing a licensed non-physician practitioner as his or her representative to appear at the hospital and provide further assessment or stabilizing treatment to an individual. This determination should be based on the individual's medical need and the capabilities of the hospital and the applicable State scope of practice laws, hospital by-laws and rules and regulations. There are some circumstances in which the non-physician practitioner can provide the specialty treatment more expeditiously than the physician on-call. It is important to note, however, that the designated on-call physician is ultimately responsible for providing the necessary services to the individual in the DED, regardless of who makes the in-person appearance. Furthermore, in the event that the treating physician disagrees with the on-call physician's decision to send a representative and requests the actual appearance of the on-call physician, then the on-call physician is required under EMTALA to appear in person. Both the hospital and the on-call physician who fails or refuses to appear in a reasonable period of time may be subject to sanctions for violation of the EMTALA statutory requirements.

There is no EMTALA prohibition against the treating physician consulting on a case with another physician, who may or may not be on the hospital's on-call list, by telephone, video conferencing, transmission of test results, or any other means of communication. CMS is aware that it is increasingly common for hospitals to use telecommunications to exchange imaging studies, laboratory results, EKGs, real-time audio and video images of patients and/or other clinical information with a consulting physician not on the hospital's premises. Such practices may contribute to improved patient safety and efficiency of care. In some cases it may be understood by the hospitals and physicians who establish such remote consulting arrangements that the physician consultant is not available for an in-person assessment of the individual at the treating physician's hospital. However, if a physician:

- is on a hospital's on-call list;
- has been requested by the treating physician to appear at the hospital; and
- fails or refuses to appear within a reasonable period of time;

then the hospital and the on-call physician may be subject to sanctions for violation of the EMTALA statutory requirements.

It is an entirely separate issue, outside the scope of EMTALA enforcement, whether or not insurers or other third party payers, including Medicare, will provide reimbursement to physicians who provide remote consultation services. Hospitals and/or physicians interested in Medicare reimbursement policy for telemedicine or telehealth services should consult Medicare Benefit Policy Manual, Pub. 100-02, Chapter 18, § 270.

If a physician who is on-call, either directly, or indirectly pursuant to a CCP, refuses or fails to appear at the hospital where he/she is directly on call in a reasonable period of time, then that physician as well as the hospital may be found to be in violation of EMTALA. Likewise, if a physician who is on-call typically directs the individual to be transferred to another hospital instead of making an appearance as requested, then that physician as well as the hospital may be found to be in violation of EMTALA. While CMS' enforcement of the EMTALA section of the Act and regulations and the EMTALA-related provisions of the provider agreement section of the Act and regulations are directed solely against hospitals, it is important to note that Section 1867 of the Act also provides for the Office of the Inspector General (OIG) to levy civil monetary penalties or take other actions against hospitals or physicians for EMTALA violations. CMS refers cases it has investigated to the OIG when CMS finds violations that appear to fall within the OIG's EMTALA jurisdiction. Section 1867(d)(1)(C) of the Act specifically provides for penalties against both a hospital and the physician when a physician who is on-call either fails to appear or refuses to appear within a reasonable period of time. Thus, a hospital would be well-advised to establish in its on-call policies and procedures specific guidelines—e.g., the maximum number of minutes that may elapse between receipt of a request and the physician's appearance for what constitutes a reasonable response time, and to make sure that its on-call physicians and other staff are aware of these time-sensitive requirements.

If a physician on-call does not fulfill his/her on-call obligation, but the hospital arranges in a timely manner for another of its physicians in that specialty to assess/stabilize an individual as requested by the treating physician in the DED, then the hospital would not be in violation of CMS' on-call requirements. However, if a physician on-call does not fulfill his/her on-call obligation and the individual is, as a result, transferred to another hospital, then the hospital may be in violation of CMS's requirements and both the hospital and the on-call physician may be subject to enforcement action by the OIG under the Act.

Tag A-2405/C-2405

(Rev. 46, Issued: 05-29-09, Effective/Implementation: 05-29-09)

Section 489.20(r)(3)—A central log on each individual who—comes to the emergency department, as defined in § 489.24(b), seeking assistance and whether he or she refused treatment, was refused treatment, or whether he or she was transferred, admitted and treated, stabilized and transferred, or discharged.

Interpretive Guidelines: § 489.20(r)(3)

The purpose of the central log is to track the care provided to each individual who comes to the hospital seeking care for an emergency medical condition.

Each hospital has the discretion to maintain the log in a form that best meets the needs of the hospital. The central log includes, directly or by reference, patient logs from other areas of the hospital that may be considered dedicated emergency departments, such as pediatrics and labor and delivery where a patient might present for emergency services or receive a medical screening examination instead of in the "traditional" emergency department. These additional logs must be available in a timely manner for surveyor review. The hospital may also keep its central log in an electronic format.

Review the emergency department log covering at least a 6-month period that contains information on all individuals coming to the emergency department and check for completeness, gaps in entries or missing information.

Section 489.24—Special Responsibilities of Medicare Hospitals in Emergency Cases (Section 1867 EMTALA Requirements—Tags A2406/C2406—A2411/C2411)

Tag A-2406/C-2406

(Rev. 60, Issued: 07-16-10, Effective: 07-16-10, Implementation: 07-16-10)

§ 489.24(a)—Applicability of Provisions of this Section

(1) In the case of a hospital that has an emergency department, if an individual (whether or not eligible for Medicare benefits and regardless of ability to pay)—comes to the emergency department, as defined in paragraph (b) of this section, the hospital must—

　(i) Provide an appropriate medical screening examination within the capability of the hospital's emergency department, including ancillary services routinely available to the emergency department, to determine whether or not an emergency medical condition exists. The examination must be conducted by an individual(s) who is determined qualified by hospital bylaws or rules and regulations and who meets the requirements of § 482.55 of this chapter concerning emergency services personnel and direction; and

Interpretive Guidelines § 489.24(a)(1)(i)

A "hospital with an emergency department" is defined in § 489.24(b) as a hospital with a dedicated emergency department. An EMTALA obligation is triggered for such a hospital when an individual comes by him or herself, with another person, to a hospital's **dedicated emergency department** (as that term is defined above) and a request is made by the individual or on the individual's behalf, or a prudent layperson observer would conclude from the individual's appearance or behavior a need, for examination or treatment of a **medical condition.** In such a case, the hospital has incurred an obligation to provide an appropriate medical screening examination (MSE) for the individual and stabilizing treatment or an appropriate transfer. The purpose of the MSE is to determine whether or not an emergency medical condition exits.

If an individual who is not a hospital patient comes elsewhere on **hospital property** (that is, the individual comes to the hospital but not to the dedicated emergency department), an EMTALA obligation on the part of the hospital may be triggered if either the individual requests examination or treatment for an **emergency** medical condition or if a prudent layperson observer would believe that the individual is suffering from an **emergency** medical condition. The term "hospital property" means the entire main hospital campus as defined in § 413.65(a), including the parking lot, sidewalk and driveway or hospital departments, including any building owned by the hospital that are within 250 yards of the hospital).

If an individual is registered as an outpatient of the hospital and they present on hospital property but not to a dedicated emergency department, the hospital does not incur an obligation to provide a medical screening examination for that individual if they have begun to receive a scheduled course of outpatient care. Such an individual is protected by the hospital Conditions of Participation (CoPs) that protect patient's health and safety and to ensure that quality care is furnished to all patients in Medicare-participating hospital. If such an individual experiences an EMC while receiving outpatient care, the hospital does not have an obligation to conduct an MSE for that patient. As discussed in greater detail below, such a patient has adequate protections under the Medicare CoPs and state law.

If an individual is initially screened in a department or facility on-campus outside of the ED, the individual could be moved to another hospital department or facility on-campus to receive further screening or stabilizing treatment without such movement being regarded as a transfer, as long as: (1) all persons with the same medical condition are moved in such circumstances, regardless of their ability to pay for treatment; (2) there is bona fide medical reason to move the individual; and (3) appropriate medical personnel accompany the individual. The same is also true for an individual who presents to the dedicated emergency department (e.g., patient with an eye injury in need of stationary ophthalmology equipment located in the eye clinic) and must be moved to another hospital-owned facility or department on-campus for further screening or stabilizing treatment. The movement of the individual between hospital departments is not considered an EMTALA transfer under this section, since the individual is simply being moved from one department of a hospital to another department or facility of the same hospital.

Hospitals should not move individuals to off-campus facilities or departments (such as an urgent care center or satellite clinic) for a MSE. If an individual comes to a hospital-owned facility or department, which is off-campus and operates under the hospital's Medicare provider number, § 1867 (42 CFR 489.24) will not apply to that facility and/or department unless it meets the definition of a dedicated emergency department.

If, however, such a facility does not meet the definition of a dedicated ED, it must screen and stabilize the patient to the best of its ability or execute an appropriate transfer if necessary to another hospital or to the hospital on whose Medicare provider number it is operated. Hospital resources and staff available at the main campus are likewise available to individuals seeking care at the off campus facilities or departments within the capability of the hospital. Movement of the individual to the main campus of the hospital is not considered a transfer since the individual is simply being moved from one department of a hospital to another department or facility of the same hospital. In addition, a transfer from such an entity (i.e., an off-campus facility that meets the definition of a dedicated ED) to a nonaffiliated hospital (i.e., a hospital that does not own the off-campus facility) is allowed where the facility at which the individual presented cannot stabilize the individual and the benefits of transfer exceed the risks of transfer. In other words, there is no requirement under EMTALA that the individual be always transferred back to the hospital that owns and operates the off-campus dedicated ED. Rather, the requirement of EMTALA is that the individual be transferred to an appropriate facility for treatment.

If a request were made for emergency care in a hospital department **off** the hospital's main campus that does not meet the definition of a dedicated emergency department, EMTALA would not apply. However, such an off-campus facility must have policies and procedures in place as how to handle patients in need of immediate care. For example, the off-campus facility policy may direct the staff to contact the emergency medical services/911 (EMS) to take the patient to an emergency department (not necessarily the emergency department of the hospital that operates the off-campus department, but rather the closest emergency department) or provide the necessary care if it is within the hospital's capability. Therefore, a hospital off-campus facility that does not meet the definition of a dedicated emergency department does not have an EMTALA obligation and not required to be staffed to handle potential EMC.

Medicare **hospitals** that do not provide emergency services must meet the standard of § 482.12(f), which requires hospitals to have written policies and procedures for the appraisal of emergencies, initial treatment within its capability and capacity, and makes an appropriate referral to a hospital that is capable of providing the necessary emergency services.

If a hospital has an EMTALA obligation, it must screen individuals to determine if an EMC exists. It is not appropriate to merely "log in" an individual and not provide a MSE. An MSE is the process required to reach, with reasonable clinical confidence, the point at which it can be determined whether the individual has an EMC or not. An MSE is not an isolated event. It is an ongoing process that begins, but typically does not end, with triage.

Triage entails the clinical assessment of the individual's presenting signs and symptoms at the time of arrival at the hospital, in order to prioritize when the individual will be seen by a physician or other qualified medical personnel (QMP).

Individuals coming to the emergency department must be provided an MSE appropriate to the individuals' presenting signs and symptoms, as well as the capability and capacity of the hospital. Depending on the individual's presenting signs and symptoms, an appropriate MSE can involve a wide spectrum of actions, ranging from a simple process involving only a brief history and physical examination to a complex process that also involves performing ancillary studies and procedures, such as (but not limited to) lumbar punctures, clinical laboratory tests, CT scans, and/or other diagnostic tests and procedures. The medical record must reflect continued monitoring according to the individual's needs until it is determined whether or not the individual has an EMC and, if he/she does, until he/she is stabilized or appropriately transferred. There should be evidence of this ongoing monitoring prior to discharge or transfer.

The MSE must be the same MSE that the hospital would perform on any individual coming to the hospital's dedicated emergency department with those signs and symptoms, regardless of the individual's ability to pay for medical care. If a hospital applies in a nondiscriminatory manner (i.e., a different level of care must not exist based on payment status, race, national origin, etc.) a screening process that is reasonably calculated to determine whether an EMC exists, it has met its obligations under EMTALA. If the MSE is appropriate and does not reveal an EMC, the hospital has no further obligation under 42 CFR 489.24.

Regardless of a positive or negative individual outcome, a hospital would be in violation of the anti-dumping statute if it fails to meet any of the medical screening requirements under 42 CFR 489.24. The clinical outcome of an individual's condition is not a proper basis for determining whether an appropriate screening was provided or whether a person transferred was stable. However, the outcome may be a "red flag" indicating that a more thorough investigation is needed. Do not make decisions base on clinical information that was not available at the time of stabilizing or transfer. If an individual was misdiagnosed, but the hospital utilized all of its resources, a violation of the screening requirement did not occur.

It is not impermissible under EMTALA for a hospital to follow normal registration procedures for individuals who come to the emergency department. For example, a hospital may ask the individual for an insurance card, so long as doing so does not delay the medical screening examination. In addition, the hospital may seek other information (not payment) from the individual's health plan about the individual such as medical history. And, in the case of an individual with an emergency medical condition, once the hospital has conducted the medical screening examination and has initiated stabilizing treatment, it may seek authorization for all services from the plan, again, as long as doing so does not delay the implementation of the required MSE and stabilizing treatment.

A hospital that is not a managed care plan's network of designated providers cannot refuse to screen and treat (or appropriately transfer, if the medical benefits of the transfer outweigh the risks or if the individual requests the transfer) individuals who are enrolled in the plan who come to the hospital if that hospital participates in the Medicare program.

Once an individual has presented to the hospital seeking emergency care, the determination of whether an EMC exists is made by the examining physician(s) or other qualified medical personnel of the hospital.

Medicare participating hospitals that provide emergency services must provide a medical screening examination to any individual regardless of diagnosis (e.g., labor, AIDS), financial status (e.g., uninsured, Medicaid), race, and color, national origin (e.g. Hispanic or Native American surnames), and/or disability, etc.

A hospital, regardless of size or patient mix, must provide screening and stabilizing treatment within the scope of its abilities, as needed, to the individuals with emergency medical conditions who come to the hospital for examination and treatment.

"Labor" is defined to mean the process of childbirth beginning with the latent or early phase of labor and continuing through the delivery of the placenta. A woman experiencing contractions is in true labor, unless a physician, certified nurse-midwife, or other qualified medical person acting within his or her scope of practice as defined in hospital medical staff bylaws and State law, certifies that, after a reasonable time of observation, the woman is in false labor.

An infant that is born alive is a "person" and an "individual" under 1 U.S.C. 8(a) and the screening requirement of EMTALA applies to "any individual" who comes to the emergency department. If an infant was born alive in a dedicated emergency department, and a request was made on that infant's behalf for screening for a medical condition (or if a prudent layperson would conclude, based on the infant's appearance or behavior, that the infant needed examination or treatment for a medical condition), the hospital and physician could be liable for violating EMTALA for failure to provide such a medical screening examination.

If an infant is born alive elsewhere on the hospital's campus (i.e., not in the hospital's dedicated emergency department) and a prudent layperson observer would conclude, based on the born-alive infant's appearance or behavior, that the infant was suffering from an emergency medical condition, the hospital and its medical staff are required to perform a medical screening examination on the infant to determine whether or not an emergency medical condition exists. Whether in the DED or elsewhere on the hospital's campus, if the physician or other authorized qualified medical personnel performing the medical screening examination determines that the infant is suffering from an emergency medical condition, the hospital has an obligation under EMTALA to provide stabilizing treatment or an appropriate transfer. If the hospital admits the infant, its obligation under EMTALA ends.

A minor (child) can request an examination or treatment for an EMC. The hospital is required by law to conduct the examination if requested by an individual or on the individual's behalf to determine if an EMC exists. Hospital personnel should not delay the MSE by waiting for parental consent. If after screening the minor, it is determined than no EMC is present, the staff can wait for parental consent before proceeding with further examination and treatment.

On-campus provider-based entities (such as rural health clinics or physician offices) are not subject to EMTALA, therefore it would be inappropriate to move individuals to these facilities for a MSE or stabilizing treatment under this Act.

If an individual is not on hospital property (which includes a hospital owned and operated ambulance), this regulation is not applicable. Hospital property includes ambulances owned and operated by the hospital, even if the ambulance is not on the hospital campus. An individual in a non-hospital owned ambulance, which is on hospital property is considered to have come to the hospital's emergency department. An individual in a non- hospital owned ambulance not on the hospital's property is not considered to have come to the hospital's emergency department when the ambulance personnel contact "Hospital A" by telephone or telemetry communications. If an individual is in an ambulance, regardless of whether the ambulance is owned by the hospital, a hospital may divert individuals when it is in "diversionary" status because it does not have the staff or facilities to accept any additional emergency patients at that time. However, if the ambulance is owned by the hospital, the diversion of the ambulance is only appropriate if the hospital is being diverted pursuant to community-wide EMS protocols. Moreover, if any ambulance (regardless of whether or not owned by the hospital) disregards the hospital's instructions and brings the individual on to hospital campus, the individual has come to the hospital and the hospital has incurred an obligation to conduct a medical screening examination for the individual.

Hospitals that deliberately delay moving an individual from an EMS stretcher to an emergency department bed do not thereby delay the point in time at which their EMTALA obligation begins. Furthermore, such a practice of "parking" patients arriving via EMS, refusing to release EMS equipment or personnel, jeopardizes patient health and adversely impacts the ability of the EMS personnel to provide emergency response services to the rest of the community. Hospitals that "park" patients may also find themselves in violation of 42 CFR 482.55, the Hospital Condition of Participation for Emergency Services, which requires that hospitals meet the emergency needs of patients in accordance with acceptable standards of practice.

On the other hand, this does not mean that a hospital will necessarily have violated EMTALA and/or the hospital CoPs if it does not, in every instance, immediately assume from the EMS provider all responsibility for the individual, regardless of any other circumstances in the ED. For example, there may be situations when a hospital does not have the capacity or capability at the time of the individual's presentation to provide an immediate medical screening examination (MSE) and, if needed, stabilizing treatment or an appropriate transfer. So, if the EMS provider brought an individual to the dedicated ED at a time when ED staff was occupied dealing with multiple major trauma cases, it could under those circumstances be reasonable for the hospital to ask the EMS provider to stay with the individual until such time as there were ED staff available to provide care to that individual. However, even if a hospital cannot immediately complete an appropriate MSE, it must still assess the individual's condition upon arrival to ensure that the individual is appropriately prioritized, based on his/her presenting signs and symptoms, to be seen by a physician or other QMP for completion of the MSE. The hospital should also assess whether the EMS provider can appropriately monitor the individual's condition.

Should a hospital, which is not in diversionary status, fail to accept a telephone or radio request for transfer or admission, the refusal could represent a violation of other Federal or State requirements (e.g., Hill-Burton). If you suspect a violation of related laws, refer the case to the responsible agency for investigation.

The following two circumstances will not trigger EMTALA:

- The use of a hospital's helipad by local ambulance services or other hospitals for the transport of individuals to tertiary hospitals located throughout the State does not trigger an EMTALA obligation for the hospital that has the helipad on its property when the helipad is being used for the purpose of transit as long as the sending hospital conducted the MSE prior to transporting the individual to the helipad for medical helicopter transport to a designated recipient hospital. The sending hospital is responsible for conducting the MSE prior to transfer to determine if an EMC exists and implementing stabilizing treatment or conducting an appropriate transfer. Therefore, if the helipad serves simply as a point of transit for individuals who have received a MSE performed prior to transfer to the helipad, the hospital with the helipad is not obligated to perform another MSE prior to the individual's continued travel to the recipient hospital. If, however, while at the helipad, the individual's condition deteriorates, the hospital at which the helipad is located must provide another MSE and stabilizing treatment within its capacity **if requested** by medical personnel accompanying the individual.

- If as part of the EMS protocol, EMS activates helicopter evacuation of an individual with a potential EMC, the hospital that has the helipad does not have an EMTALA obligation if they are not the recipient hospital, **unless a request** is made by EMS personnel, the individual or a legally responsible person acting on the individual's behalf for the examination or treatment of an EMC.

Hospitals are not relieved of their EMTALA obligation to screen, provide stabilizing treatment and/or an appropriate transfer to individuals because of pre-arranged community or State plans that have designated specific hospitals to care for selected individuals (e.g., Medicaid patients, psychiatric patients, pregnant women). Hospitals located in those States which have State/local laws that require particular individuals, such as psychiatric or indigent individuals, to be evaluated and treated at designated facilities/hospitals may violate EMTALA if the hospital disregards the EMTALA requirements and does not conduct an MSE and provide stabilizing treatment or conduct an appropriate transfer prior to referring the individual to the State/local facility. If, after conducting the MSE and ruling out an EMC (or after stabilizing the EMC) the sending hospital needs to transfer an individual to another hospital for treatment, it may elect to transfer the individual to the hospital so designated by these State or local laws. Hospitals are also prohibited from discharging individuals who have not been screened or who have an emergency medical condition to non-hospital facilities for purposes of compliance with State law. The existence of a State law requiring transfer of certain individuals to certain facilities is not a defense to an EMTALA violation for failure to provide an MSE or failure to stabilize an EMC therefore hospitals must meet the federal EMTALA requirements or risk violating EMTALA.

If a screening examination reveals an EMC and the individual is told to wait for treatment, but the individual leaves the hospital, the hospital did not "dump" the individual unless:

- The individual left the emergency department based on a "suggestion" by the hospital;
- The individual's condition was an emergency, but the hospital was operating beyond its capacity and did not attempt to transfer the individual to another facility, or
- If an individual leaves a hospital Against Medical Advice (AMA) or LWBS, on his or her own free will (no coercion or suggestion) the hospital is not in violation of EMTALA.

Hospital resources and staff available to inpatients at the hospital for emergency services must likewise be available to individuals coming to the hospital for examination and treatment of an EMC because these resources are within the capability of the hospital. For example, a woman in labor who presents at a hospital providing obstetrical services must be treated with the resources available whether or not the hospital normally provides unassigned emergency obstetrical services.

The MSE must be conducted by an individual(s) who is determined qualified by hospital by-laws or rules and regulations and who meets the requirements of § 482.55 concerning emergency services personnel and direction. The designation of the qualified medical personnel (QMP) should be set forth in a document approved by the governing body of the hospital. If the rules and regulations of the hospital are approved by the board of trustees or other governing body, those personnel qualified to perform the medical screening examinations may be set forth in the rules and regulations, or the hospital by-laws. It is not acceptable for the hospital to allow informal personnel appointments that could frequently change.

> **(ii)** **If an emergency medical condition is determined to exist, provide any necessary stabilizing treatment, as defined in paragraph (d) of this section, or an appropriate transfer as defined in paragraph (e) of this section. If the hospital admits the individual as an inpatient for further treatment, the hospital's obligation under this section ends, as specified in paragraph (d)(2) of this section.**

Interpretive Guidelines § 489.24(a)(1)(ii)

Refer to Tag A-2407/C-2407 for stabilizing treatment and inpatients, and Tag A-2409/C-2409 for an appropriate transfer for EMTALA.

EMTALA does not apply to hospital inpatients. The existing hospital CoPs protect individuals who are already patients of a hospital and who experience an EMC. Hospitals that fail to provide treatment to these patients may be subject to further enforcement actions.

If the surveyor discovers during the investigation that a hospital did not admit an individual in good faith with the intention of providing treatment (i.e., the hospital used the inpatient admission as a means to avoid EMTALA requirements), then the hospital is considered liable under EMTALA and actions may be pursued.

§ 489.24(a)(2)

> *(i)* *When a waiver has been issued in accordance with Section 1135 of the Act that includes a waiver under Section 1135(b)(3) of the Act, sanctions under this section for an inappropriate transfer or for the direction or relocation of an individual to receive medical screening at an alternate location, do not apply to a hospital with a dedicated emergency department if the following conditions are met:*
>
> *(A)* *The transfer is necessitated by the circumstances of the declared emergency in the emergency area during the emergency period.*

(B) *The direction or relocation of an individual to receive medical screening at an alternate location is pursuant to an appropriate State emergency preparedness plan or, in the case of a public health emergency that involves a pandemic infectious disease, pursuant to a State pandemic preparedness plan.*

(C) *The hospital does not discriminate on the basis of an individual's source of payment or ability to pay.*

(D) *The hospital is located in an emergency area during an emergency period, as those terms are defined in Section 1135(g)(1) of the Act.*

(E) *There has been a determination that a waiver of sanctions is necessary.*

(ii) *A waiver of these sanctions is limited to a 72-hour period beginning upon the implementation of a hospital disaster protocol, except that, if a public health emergency involves a pandemic infectious disease (such as pandemic influenza), the waiver will continue in effect until the termination of the applicable declaration of a public health emergency, as provided under Section 1135(e)(1)(B) of the Act.*

Interpretive Guidelines: § 489.24(a)(2)

What can be Waived Under Section 1135?

In accordance with Section 1135(b)(3) of the Act, hospitals and CAHs operating under an EMTALA waiver will not be sanctioned for:

- *Redirecting an individual who "comes to the emergency department," as that term is defined at §489.24(b), to an alternate location for an MSE, pursuant to a State emergency preparedness plan or, as applicable, a State pandemic preparedness plan. Even when a waiver is in effect there is still the expectation that everyone who comes to the ED will receive an appropriate MSE, if not in the ED, then at the alternate care site to which they are redirected or relocated.*

- *Inappropriately transferring an individual protected under EMTALA, when the transfer is necessitated by the circumstances of the declared emergencies. Transfers may be inappropriate under EMTALA for a number of reasons.*

However, even if a hospital/CAH is operating under an EMTALA waiver, the hospital/CAH would not be exempt from sanctions if it discriminates among individuals based on their ability to pay for services, or the source of their payment for services when redirecting or relocating them for the MSE or when making inappropriate transfers.

All other EMTALA-related requirements at 42 CFR 489.20 and EMTALA requirements at 42 CFR 489.24 continue to apply, even when a hospital is operating under an EMTALA waiver. For example, the statute does not provide for a waiver of a recipient hospital's obligation to accept an appropriate transfer of an individual protected under EMTALA. (As a reminder, even without a waiver, a hospital is obligated to accept an appropriate EMTALA transfer only when that recipient hospital has specialized capabilities required by the individual and the requisite capacity at the time of the transfer request.)

Waiver of EMTALA requirements in accordance with a Section 1135 waiver does not affect a hospital's or CAH's obligation to comply with State law or regulation that may separately impose requirements similar to those under EMTALA law and regulations. Facilities are encouraged to communicate with their State licensure authorities as to the availability of waivers under State law.

When Can a Waiver Be Issued?

In accordance with Section 1135 of the Act, an EMTALA waiver may be issued only when:

- The President has declared an emergency or disaster pursuant to the National Emergencies Act or the Robert T. Stafford Disaster Relief and Emergency Assistance Act; and
- The Secretary has declared a public health emergency (PHE) pursuant to Section 319 of the Public Health Service Act; and
- The Secretary has exercised his/her waiver authority pursuant to Section 1135 of the Act and notified Congress at least 48 hours in advance of exercising his/her waiver authority.

In exercising his/her waiver authority, the Secretary may choose to delegate to the Centers for Medicare & Medicaid Services (CMS) the decision as to which Medicare, Medicaid, or CHIP requirements specified in Section 1135 should be temporarily waived or modified, and for which health care providers or groups of providers such waivers are necessary. Specifically, the Secretary may delegate to CMS decision-making about whether and for which hospitals/CAHs to waive EMTALA sanctions as specified in Section 1135(b)(3).

In addition, in order for an EMTALA waiver to apply to a specific hospital or CAH:

- The hospital or CAH must activate its disaster protocol; and
- The State must have activated an emergency preparedness plan or pandemic preparedness plan in the emergency area, and any redirection of individuals for an MSE must be consistent with such plan. It is not necessary for the State to activate its plan statewide, so long as it is activated in the area where the hospital is located. It is also not necessary for the State plan to identify the specific location of the alternate screening sites to which individuals will be directed, although some may do so.

How Long Does an EMTALA Waiver Last?

Except in the case of waivers related to pandemic infectious disease, an EMTALA waiver is limited in duration to 72 hours beginning upon activation of the hospital's/CAH's disaster protocol. In the case of a public health emergency (PHE) involving pandemic infectious disease, the general EMTALA waiver authority will continue in effect until the termination of the declaration of the

PHE. However, application of this general authority to a specific hospital/CAH or groups of hospitals and CAHs may limit the waiver's application to a date prior to the termination of the PHE declaration, since case-specific applications of the waiver authority are issued only to the extent they are necessary, as determined by CMS.

Furthermore, if a State emergency/pandemic preparedness plan is deactivated in the area where the hospital or CAH is located prior to the termination of the public health emergency, the hospital or CAH no longer meets the conditions for an EMTALA waiver and that hospital/CAH waiver would cease to be in effect as of the deactivation date. Likewise, if a hospital or CAH deactivates its disaster protocol prior to the termination of the public health emergency, the hospital or CAH no longer meets the conditions for an EMTALA waiver and that hospital/CAH waiver would cease to be in effect as of the deactivation date.

What is the Process for Seeking an EMTALA Waiver?

Section 1135 provides for waivers of certain Medicare, Medicaid, or CHIP requirements, including waivers of EMTALA sanctions, but only to the extent necessary, to ensure sufficient health care items and services are available to meet the needs of Medicare, Medicaid, and CHIP beneficiaries. The waivers also ensure that health care providers who provide such services in good faith but are unable to comply with one or more of the specified requirements may be reimbursed for such items and services and exempted from sanctions for noncompliance, absent any fraud or abuse.

When the Secretary has exercised his/her waiver authority and delegated to CMS decision-making about specific EMTALA waivers, CMS policy in exercising its authority for granting EMTALA waivers is as follows:

Localized Emergency Area: In the case of localized disasters, such as those related to floods or hurricanes, CMS may exercise its discretion to advise hospitals/CAHs in the affected areas that they are covered by the EMTALA waiver, **without requiring individual applications for each waiver.** However, hospitals or CAHs that activate their disaster protocol and expect to take advantage of the area-wide waiver must notify their State Survey Agency (SA) at the time they activate their disaster protocol.

Nationwide Emergency Area: In the case of a nationwide emergency area, CMS may also exercise its discretion to advise hospitals/CAHs in a specific geographical area(s) that they are covered by the EMTALA waiver **for a time-limited period.** CMS expects to do this only if the State has activated its emergency or pandemic preparedness plan in the affected area(s), and if there is other evidence of need for the waiver for a broad group of hospitals or CAHs. CMS will rely upon SAs to advise their CMS Regional Office (RO) whether and where a State's preparedness plan has been activated, as well as when the plan has been deactivated.

In the absence of CMS notification of area-wide applications of the waiver, hospitals/CAHs must contact CMS and request that the waiver provisions be *applied to their facility. In all cases, the Act envisions that individuals protected under EMTALA will still receive appropriate MSEs somewhere (even if the MSE is not conducted not at the hospital or CAH where they present), and that individuals who are transferred for stabilization of their emergency medical condition will be sent to a facility capable of providing stabilizing services, regardless of whether a waiver is in effect.*

Unless CMS advises otherwise, in cases of a public health emergency involving pandemic infectious disease, hospitals/CAHs in areas covered by time-limited, area-wide applications of the EMTALA waiver that seek to extend the waiver's application to a later date within the waiver period (that is, within the period of the PHE declaration) must submit individual requests for extension. The requests must demonstrate their need for continued application of the waiver. Such requests must be received at least three calendar days prior to expiration of the time-limited waiver. Extensions of an EMTALA waiver in emergencies that do not involve pandemic infectious disease are not available.

Waiver Request Process

Hospitals or CAHs seeking an EMTALA waiver must demonstrate to CMS that application of the waiver to their facility is necessary, and that they have activated their disaster protocol. CMS will confirm with the SA whether the State's preparedness plan has been activated in the area where the hospital or CAH is located. CMS will also seek to confirm when the hospital activated its disaster protocol, whether other measures may address the situation in a manner that does not require a waiver, and other factors important to the ability of the hospital to demonstrate that a waiver is needed.

What will CMS do in response to EMTALA complaints concerning events occurring during the waiver period?

EMTALA enforcement is a complaint-driven process. CMS will assess any complaints/allegations related to alleged EMTALA violations concerning the MSE or transfer during the waiver period to determine whether the hospital or CAH in question was operating under an EMTALA waiver at the time of the complaint, and, if so, whether the nature of the complaint involves actions or requirements not covered by the EMTALA waiver and warrants further on-site investigation by the SA.

§ 489.24(c) Use of Dedicated Emergency Department for Non-emergency Services

If an individual comes to a hospital's dedicated emergency department and a request is made on his or her behalf for examination or treatment for a medical condition, but the nature of the request makes it clear that the medical condition is not of an emergency nature, the hospital is required only to perform such screening as would be appropriate for any individual presenting in that manner, to determine that the individual does not have an emergency medical condition.

Interpretive Guidelines § 489.24(c)

Any individual with a medical condition that presents to a hospital's ED must receive an MSE that is appropriate for their medical condition. The objective of the MSE is to determine whether or not an emergency medical condition exists. This does not mean that all EMTALA screenings must be equally extensive. If the nature of the individual's request makes clear that the medical condition is not of an emergency nature, the MSE is reflective of the individual presenting complaints or symptoms. A hospital may, if it chooses, have protocols that permit a QMP (e.g., registered nurse) to conduct specific MSE(s) if the nature of the individual's request for examination and treatment is within the scope of practice of the QMP (e.g., a request for a blood pressure check and that check reveals that the patient's blood pressure is within normal range). Once the individual is screened and it is determined the individual has only presented to the ED for a nonemergency purpose, the hospital's EMTALA obligation ends for that individual at the completion of the MSE. Hospitals are not obligated under EMTALA to provide screening services beyond those needed to determine that there is no EMC.

For a hospital to be exempted from its EMTALA obligations to screen individuals presenting at its emergency department for nonemergency tests (e.g., individual has consulted with physician by telephone and the physician refers the individual to a hospital emergency department for a nonemergency test) the hospital must be able to document that it is only being asked to collect evidence, not analyze the test results, or to otherwise examine or treat the individual. Furthermore, a hospital may be exempted from its EMTALA obligations to screen individuals presenting to its dedicated emergency department if the individual had a previously scheduled appointment.

If an individual presents to an ED and requests pharmaceutical services (medication) for a medical condition, the hospital generally would have an EMTALA obligation. Surveyors are encouraged to ask probing questions of the hospital staff to determine if the hospital in fact had an EMTALA obligation in this situation (e.g., did the individual present to the ED with an EMC and informed staff they had not taken their medication? Was it obvious from the nature of the medication requested that it was likely that the patient had an EMC?). The circumstances surrounding why the request is being made would confirm if the hospital in fact has an EMTALA obligation. If the individual requires the medication to resolve or provide stabilizing treatment of an EMC, then the hospital has an EMTALA obligation. Hospitals are not required by EMTALA to provide medication to individuals who do not have an EMC simply because the individual is unable to pay or does not wish to purchase the medication from a retail pharmacy or did not plan appropriately to secure prescription refills.

If an individual presents to a dedicated emergency department and requests services that are not for a medical condition, such as preventive care services (immunizations, allergy shots, flu shots) or the gathering of evidence for criminal law cases (e.g., sexual assault, blood alcohol test), the hospital is not obligated to provide a MSE under EMTALA to this individual.

Attention to detail concerning blood alcohol testing (BAT) in the ED is instrumental when determining if a MSE is to be conducted. If an individual is brought to the ED and law enforcement personnel request that emergency department personnel draw blood for a **BAT only** and does not request examination or treatment for a medical condition, such as intoxication and a prudent lay person observer would not believe that the individual needed such examination or treatment, then the EMTALA's screening requirement is not applicable to this situation because the only request made on behalf of the individual was for evidence. However, if for example, the individual in police custody was involved in a motor vehicle accident or may have sustained injury to him or herself and presents to the ED a MSE would be warranted to determine if an EMC exists.

When law enforcement officials request hospital emergency personnel to provide clearance for incarceration, the hospital has an EMTALA obligation to provide a MSE to determine if an EMC exists. If no EMC is present, the hospital has met its EMTALA obligation and no further actions are necessary for EMTALA compliance.

Surveyors will evaluate each case on its own merit when determining a hospital's EMTALA obligation when law enforcement officials request screening or BAT for use as evidence in criminal proceedings. This principle also applies to sexual assault cases.

Tag A-2407/C-2407

(Rev. 46, Issued: 05-29-09, Effective/Implementation: 05-29-09)

§ 489.24(d) Necessary Stabilizing Treatment for Emergency Medical Conditions

(1)   **General. Subject to the provisions of paragraph (d)(2) of this section, if any individual (whether or not eligible for Medicare benefits) comes to a hospital and the hospital determines that the individual has an emergency medical condition, the hospital must provide either—**

(i)   **Within the capabilities of the staff and facilities available at the hospital, for further medical examination and treatment as required to stabilize the medical condition.**

Interpretive Guidelines § 489.24(d)(1)(i)

A hospital is obligated to provide the services specified in the statute and this regulation regardless of whether a hospital will be paid. After the medical screening has been implemented and the hospital has determined that an emergency medical condition exists, the hospital must provide stabilizing treatment within its capability and capacity.

Capabilities of a medical facility mean that there is physical space, equipment, supplies, and specialized services that the hospital provides (e.g., surgery, psychiatry, obstetrics, intensive care, pediatrics, trauma care).

Capabilities of the staff of a facility means the level of care that the personnel of the hospital can provide within the training and scope of their professional licenses. This includes coverage available through the hospitals on-call roster.

The capacity to render care is not reflected simply by the number of persons occupying a specialized unit, the number of staff on duty, or the amount of equipment on the hospital's premises. Capacity includes whatever a hospital customarily does to accommodate patients in excess of its occupancy limits § 489.24(b). If a hospital has customarily accommodated patients in excess of its occupancy limits by whatever mean (e.g., moving patients to other units, calling in additional staff, borrowing equipment from other facilities) it has, in fact, demonstrated the ability to provide services to patients in excess of its occupancy limits.

A hospital may appropriately transfer (see Tag A-2409/C-2409) an individual before the sending hospital has used and exhausted all of its resources available if the individual requests the transfer to another hospital for his or her treatment and refuses treatment at the sending hospital.

To comply with the MSE and stabilization requirements of § 1867 all individuals with similar medical conditions are to be treated consistently. Compliance with local, State, or regionally approved EMS transport of individuals with an emergency is usually deemed to indicate compliance with § 1867; however a copy of the protocol should be obtained and reviewed at the time of the survey.

If community wide plans exist for specific hospitals to treat certain EMCs (e.g., psychiatric, trauma, physical or sexual abuse), the hospital must meet its EMTALA obligations (screen, stabilize, and or appropriately transfer) prior to transferring the individual to the community plan hospital. An example of a community wide plan would be a trauma system hospital. A trauma system is a comprehensive system providing injury prevention services and timely and appropriate delivery of emergency medical treatment for people with acute illness and traumatic injury. These systems are designed so that patients with catastrophic injuries will have the quickest possible access to an established trauma center or a hospital that has the capabilities to provide comprehensive emergency medical care. These systems ensure that the severely injured patient can be rapidly cared for in the facility that is most appropriately prepared to treat the severity of injury.

Community plans (not a formal community call plan provided for under § 489.24(j)(iii)) are designed to provide an organized, pre-planned response to patient needs to assure the best patient care and efficient use of limited health care resources. Community plans are designed to augment physician's care if the necessary services are not within the capability of the hospital but does not mandate patient care nor transfer patterns. Patient health status frequently depends on the appropriate use of the community plans. The matching of the appropriate facility with the needs of the patient is the focal point of this plan and assures every patient receives the best care possible. Therefore, a sending hospital's appropriate transfer of an individual in accordance with community wide protocols in instances where it cannot provide stabilizing treatment would be deemed to indicate compliance with § 1867.

If an individual seeking care is a member of a managed health care plan (e.g., HMO, PPO or CMP), the hospital is obligated to comply with the requirements of § 489.24 regardless of the individual's payor source or financial status. The hospitals is obligated to provide the services necessary to determine if an EMC is present and provide stabilizing treatment if indicated. This is true regardless if the individual is enrolled in a managed care plan that restricts its enrollees' choice of health care provider. EMTALA is a requirement imposed on hospitals, and the fact that an individual who comes to the hospital is enrolled in a managed care plan that does not contract with that hospital has no bearing on the obligation of the hospital to conduct an MSE and to at lease initiate stabilizing treatment. A managed health care plan may only state the services for which it will pay or decline payment, but that does not excuse the hospital from compliance with EMTALA.

Section 42 CFR 489.24(b) defines **stabilized** to mean:

> ". . . that no material deterioration of the condition is likely, within reasonable medical probability, to result from or occur during the transfer of the individual from a facility, or with respect to an "emergency medical condition" as defined in this section under paragraph (2) of that definition, that a woman has delivered the child and the placenta."

The regulation sets the standard determining when a patient is stabilized.

If a hospital is unable to stabilize an individual within its capability, an appropriate transfer should be implemented. To be considered stable the emergency medical condition that caused the individual to seek care in the dedicated ED must be resolved, although the underlying medical condition may persist. For example, an individual presents to a hospital complaining of chest tightness, wheezing, and shortness of breath and has a medical history of asthma. The physician completes a medical screening examination and diagnoses the individual as having an asthma attack that is an emergency medical condition. Stabilizing treatment is provided (medication and oxygen) to alleviate the acute respiratory symptoms. In this scenario the EMC was resolved and the hospital's EMTALA obligation is therefore ended, but the underlying medical condition of asthma still exists. After stabilizing the individual, the hospital no longer has an EMTALA obligation. The physician may discharge the individual home, admit him/her to the hospital, or transfer (the "appropriate transfer" requirement under EMTALA does not apply to this situation since the individual has been stabilized) the individual to another hospital depending on his/her needs. The preceding example does not reflect a change in policy, rather it is a clarification as to when an appropriate transfer is to be implemented to decrease hospitals risk of being in violation of EMTALA due to inappropriate transfers.

An individual will be deemed stabilized if the treating physician or QMP attending to the individual in the emergency department/hospital has determined, within reasonable clinical confidence, that the emergency medical condition has been resolved.

For those individuals whose EMCs have been resolved the physician or QMP has several options:

- **Discharge home with follow-up instructions.** An individual is considered stable and ready for discharge when, within reasonable clinical confidence, it is determined that the individual has reached the point where his/her continued care, including diagnostic work-up and/or treatment, could be reasonably performed as an outpatient or later as an inpatient, provided the individual is given a plan for appropriate follow-up care as part of the discharge instructions. The EMC that caused the individual to present to the dedicated ED must be resolved, but the underlying medical condition may persist. Hospitals are expected within reason to assist/ provide discharged individuals the necessary information to secure the necessary follow-up care to prevent relapse or worsening of the medical condition upon release from the hospital; or

- **Inpatient admission for continued care.**

Hospitals are responsible for treating and stabilizing, within their capacity and capability, any individual who presents him/herself to a hospital with an EMC. The hospital must provide care until the condition ceases to be an emergency or until the individual is properly transferred to another facility. An inappropriate transfer or discharge of an individual with an EMC would be a violation of EMTALA.

If a hospital is alleged to have violated EMTALA by transferring an unstable individual without implementing an appropriate transfer according to § 489.24(e), and the hospital believes that the individual was stable (EMC resolved) the burden of proof is the responsibility of the transferring hospital. When interpreting the facts the surveyor should assess whether or not the individual was stable. Was it reasonable to believe that the transferring hospital should have been knowledgeable of the potential complications during transport? To determine whether the individual was stable and treated appropriately surveyors will request that the QIO physician review the case. If the treating physician is in doubt that an individual's EMC is stabilized the physician should implement an appropriate transfer (see Tag A-2409/C-2409) to prevent a potential violation of EMTALA, if his/her hospital cannot provide further stabilizing treatment.

If a physician is not physically present at the time of transfer, then the qualified medical personnel (as determined by hospital bylaws or other board-approved documents) must consult with a physician to determine if an individual with an EMC is to be transferred to another facility for further stabilizing treatment.

The failure of a receiving facility to provide the care it maintained it could provide to the individual when the transfer was arranged should not be construed to mean that the individual's condition worsened as a result of the transfer.

In the case of psychiatric emergencies, if an individual expressing suicidal or homicidal thoughts or gestures, if determined dangerous to self or others, would be considered to have an EMC.

Psychiatric patients are considered stable when they are protected and prevented from injuring or harming him/herself or others. The administration of chemical or physical restraints for purposes of transferring an individual from one facility to another may stabilize a psychiatric patient for a period of time and remove the immediate EMC but the underlying medical condition may persist and if not treated for longevity the patient may experience exacerbation of the EMC. Therefore, practitioners should use great care when determining if the medical condition is in fact stable after administering chemical or physical restraints.

A hospital's EMTALA obligation ends when a physician or qualified medical person has made a decision:

- That no emergency medical condition exists (even though the underlying medical condition may persist);
- That an emergency medical condition exists and the individual is appropriately transferred to another facility; or
- That an emergency medical condition exists and the individual is admitted to the hospital for further stabilizing treatment.

(ii) For transfer of the individual to another medical facility in accordance with paragraph (e) of this section.

Interpretive Guidelines: § 489.24(d)(1)(ii)

When a hospital has exhausted all of its capabilities in attempting to resolve the EMC, it must effect an appropriate transfer of the individual (see Tag A-2409/C-2409). Section 42 CFR 489.24(b) defines **transfer** to mean:

> ". . . the movement (including the discharge) of an individual outside a hospital's facilities at the direction of any person employed by (or affiliated or associated, directly or indirectly, with) the hospital, but does not include such a movement of an individual who (i) has been declared dead, or (ii) leaves the facility without the permission of any such person."

If an individual is admitted as an inpatient, EMCs must be stabilized either by the hospital to which an individual presents or the hospital to which the individual is transferred. If a woman is in labor, the hospital must deliver the baby and the placenta or transfer appropriately. She may not be transferred unless she, or a legally responsible person acting on her behalf, requests a transfer and a physician or other qualified medical personnel, in consultation with a physician, certifies that the benefits to the woman and/or the unborn child outweigh the risks associated with the transfer.

If the individual's condition requires immediate medical stabilizing treatment and the hospital is not able to attend to that individual because the emergency department is operating beyond its capacity, then the hospital should transfer the individual to a hospital that has the capability and capacity to treat the individual's EMC.

(2) Exception: Application to Inpatients.

(i) If a hospital has screened an individual under paragraph (a) of this section and found the individual to have an emergency medical condition, and admits that individual as an inpatient in good faith in order to stabilize the emergency medical condition, the hospital has satisfied its special responsibilities under this section with respect to that individual

Interpretive Guidelines: § 489.24(d)(2)(i)

A hospital's EMTALA obligation ends when the individual has been admitted in good faith for inpatient hospital services whether or not the individual has been stabilized. An individual is considered to be "admitted" when the decision is made to admit the individual to receive inpatient hospital services with the expectation that the patient will remain in the hospital at least overnight. Typically, we would expect that this would be documented in the patient's chart and medical record at the time that a physician signed and dated the admission order. Hospital policies should clearly delineate, which practitioners are responsible for writing admission orders.

A hospital continues to have a responsibility to meet the patient emergency needs in accordance with hospital CoPs at 42 CFR Part 482. The hospital CoPs protect individuals who are admitted, and they do not permit the hospital to inappropriately discharge or transfer any patient to another facility. The hospital CoPs that are most relevant in this case are as follows: emergency services, governing body, discharge planning, quality assurance and medical staff.

Hospitals are responsible for assuring that inpatients receive acceptable medical care upon admission. Hospital services for inpatients should include diagnostic services and therapeutic services for medical diagnosis, treatment, and care of the injured, disabled or sick persons with the intention of treating patients.

If during an EMTALA investigation there is a question as to whether an individual was admitted so that a hospital could avoid its EMTALA obligation, the SA surveyor is to consult with RO personnel to determine if the survey should be expanded to a survey of the hospital CoPs. After completion of the survey, the case is to be forwarded to the RO for violation determination. If it is determined that the hospital admitted the individual solely for the purpose of avoiding its EMTALA obligation, then the hospital is liable under EMTALA and may be subject to further enforcement action.

    (ii) **This section is not applicable to an inpatient who was admitted for elective (non-emergency) diagnosis or treatment.**

Interpretive Guidelines: § 489.24(d)(2)(ii)

Individuals admitted to the hospital for elective medical services are not protected by EMTALA. The hospital CoPs protect all classifications of inpatients, elective and emergent.

    (iii) **A hospital is required by the conditions of participation for hospitals under Part 482 of this chapter to provide care to its inpatients in accordance with those conditions of participation.**

Interpretive Guidelines: § 489.24(d)(2)(iii)

If an inpatient develops an EMC, the hospital is required to meet the patient's emergency needs in accordance with acceptable standards of practice. The hospital CoPs protects patients who are admitted, and the hospital may not discharge or transfer any patient to another facility inappropriately. The protective CoPs are found at 42 CFR Part 482. The five CoPs that are most relevant in affording patients protection in cases when patients with an EMC is admitted are as follows:

- Emergency services (§ 482.55)
- Governing body (§ 482.12)
- Discharge planning (§ 482.43)
- Quality assessment and performance improvement (§ 482.21)
- Medical staff (§ 482.22)

If a hospital is noncompliant with any of the above COPs, the hospital will be subject to enforcement action.

(3) Refusal to consent to treatment.

A hospital meets the requirements of paragraph (d)(1)(i) of this section with respect to an individual if the hospital offers the individual the further medical examination and treatment described in that paragraph and informs the individual (or a person acting on the individual's behalf) of the risks and benefits to the individual of the examination and treatment, but the individual (or a person acting on the individual's behalf) does not consent to the examination or treatment. The medical record must contain a description of the examination, treatment, or both if applicable, that was refused by or on behalf of the individual. The hospital must take all reasonable steps to secure the individual's written informed refusal (or that of the person acting on his or her behalf). The written document should indicate that the person has been informed of the risks and benefits of the examination or treatment, or both.

Interpretive Guidelines: § 489.24(d)(3)

The medical record should reflect that screening, further examination, and or treatment were offered by the hospital prior to the individual's refusal.

In the event an individual refuses to consent to further examination or treatment, the hospital must indicate in writing the risks/benefits of the examination and/or treatment; the reasons for refusal; a description of the examination or treatment that was refused; and the steps taken to try to secure the written, informed refusal if it was not secured.

Hospitals may not attempt to coerce individuals into making judgments against their interest by informing them that they will have to pay for their care if they remain but that their care will be free or at a lower cost if they transfer to another hospital.

An individual may only refuse examination, treatment, or transfer on behalf of a patient if the patient is incapable of making an informed choice for him/herself.

Tag A-2408/C-2408

(Rev. 46, Issued: 05-29-09, Effective/Implementation: 05-29-09)

§ 489.24(d)(4) and (5)

(4) Delay in Examination or Treatment.

(i) **A participating hospital may not delay providing an appropriate medical screening examination required under paragraph (a) of this section or further medical examination and treatment required under paragraph (d)(1) of this section in order to inquire about the individual's method of payment or insurance status.**

(ii) **A participating hospital may not seek, or direct an individual to seek, authorization from the individual's insurance company for screening or stabilization services to be furnished by a hospital, physician, or non-physician practitioner to an individual until after the hospital has provided the appropriate medical screening examination required under paragraph (a) of this section, and initiated any further medical examination and treatment that may be required to stabilize the emergency medical condition under paragraph (d)(1) of this section.**

(iii) **An emergency physician or non-physician practitioner is not precluded from contacting the individual's physician at any time to seek advice regarding the individual's medical history and needs that may be relevant to the medical treatment and screening of the patient, as long as this consultation does not inappropriately delay services required under paragraph (a) or paragraphs (d)(1) and (d)(2) of this section.**

(iv) **Hospitals may follow reasonable registration processes for individuals for whom examination or treatment is required by this section, including asking whether an individual is insured and, if so, what that insurance is, as long as that inquiry does not delay screening or treatment. Reasonable registration processes** may not unduly discourage individuals from remaining for further evaluation.

Interpretive Guidelines § 489.24(d)(4)(i), (ii), (iii) and (iv)

Hospitals should not delay providing a medical screening examination or necessary stabilizing treatment by inquiring about an individual's ability to pay for care. All individuals who present to a hospital and request an MSE for a medical condition (or have a request for an MSE made on their behalf) must receive that screening examination, regardless of the answers the individual may give to the insurance questions asked during the registration process. In addition, a hospital may not delay screening or treatment to any individual while it verifies the information provided.

Hospitals may follow reasonable registration processes for individuals presenting with an EMC. Reasonable registration processes may include asking whether an individual is insured and, if so, what the insurance is, as long as this inquiry do not delay screening, treatment or unduly discourage individuals from remaining for further evaluation. The registration process permitted in the dedicated ED typically consists of collecting demographic information, insurance information, whom to contact in an emergency and other relevant information.

If a managed care member comes to a hospital that offers emergency services, the hospital must provide the services required under the EMTALA statute without regard for the individual's insurance status or any prior authorization requirement of such insurance.

This requirement applies equally to both the referring and the receiving (recipient) hospital. Therefore, it may be a violation if the receiving hospital delays acceptance of the transfer of an individual with an unstabilized EMC pending receipt or verification of financial information. It would not be a violation if the receiving hospital delayed acceptance of the transfer of an individual with a stabilized EMC pending receipt or verification of financial information because EMTALA protections no longer apply once a patient is stabilized.

If a delay in screening was due to an unusual internal crisis whereby it was simply not within the capability of the hospital to provide an appropriate screening examination at the time the individual came to the hospital (e.g., mass casualty occupying all the hospital's resources for a time period), surveyors are to interview hospital staff members to elicit the facts surrounding the circumstances to help determine if there was a violation of EMTALA.

(5) Refusal to Consent to Transfer.

A hospital meets the requirements of paragraph (d)(1)(ii) of this section with respect to an individual if the hospital offers to transfer the individual to another medical facility in accordance with paragraph (e) of this section and informs the individual (or a person acting on his or her behalf) of the risks and benefits to the individual of the transfer, but the individual (or a person acting on the individual's behalf) does not consent to the transfer. The hospital must take all reasonable steps to secure the individual's written informed refusal (or that of a person acting on his or her behalf). The written document must indicate the person has been informed of the risks and benefits of the transfer and state the reasons for the individual's refusal. The medical record must contain a description of the proposed transfer that was refused by or on behalf of the individual.

Interpretive Guidelines: § 489.24(d)(5)

For individuals who refuse to consent to a transfer, the hospital staff must inform the individual of the risks and benefits and document the refusal and, if possible, place a signed informed consent to refusal of the transfer in the individual's medical record.

If an individual or the individual's representative refuses to be transferred and also refuses to sign a statement to that effect, the hospital may document such refusals as they see fit.

Tag A-2409/C-2409

(Rev. 46, Issued: 05-29-09, Effective/Implementation: 05-29-09) § 489.24(e) Restricting Transfer Until the Individual Is Stabilized

(1) General. If an individual at a hospital has an emergency medical condition that has not been stabilized (as defined in paragraph (b) of this section), the hospital may not transfer the individual unless—

(i) The transfer is an appropriate transfer (within the meaning of paragraph (e)(2) of this section); and

(ii)

(A) The individual (or a legally responsible person acting on the individual's behalf) requests the transfer, after being informed of the hospital's obligations under this section and of the risk of transfer. The request must be in writing and indicate the reasons for the request as well as indicate that he or she is aware of the risks and benefits of the transfer;

(B) A physician (within the meaning of Section 1861(r)(1) of the Act) has signed a certification that, based upon the information available at the time of transfer, the medical benefits reasonably expected from the provision of appropriate medical treatment at another medical facility outweigh the increased risks to the individual or, in the case of a woman in labor, to the woman or the unborn child, from being transferred. The certification must contain a summary of the risks and benefits upon which it is based; or

(C) If a physician is not physically present in the emergency department at the time an individual is transferred, a qualified medical person (as determined by the hospital in its bylaws or rules and regulations) has signed a certification described in paragraph (e)(1)(ii)(B) of this section after a physician (as defined in Section 1861(r)(1) of the Act) in consultation with the qualified medical person, agrees with the certification and subsequently countersigns the certification. The certification must contain a summary of the risks and benefits upon which it is based.

(2) A transfer to another medical facility will be appropriate only in those cases in which—

(i) The transferring hospital provides medical treatment within its capacity that minimizes the risks to the individual's health and, in the case of a woman in labor, the health of the unborn child;

(ii) The receiving facility –

(A) Has available space and qualified personnel for the treatment of the individual; and

(B) Has agreed to accept transfer of the individual and to provide appropriate medical treatment;

(iii) The transferring hospital sends to the receiving facility all medical records (or copies thereof) related to the emergency condition which the individual has presented that are available at the time of the transfer, including available history, records related to the individual's emergency medical condition, observations of signs or symptoms, preliminary diagnosis, results of diagnostic studies or telephone reports of the studies, treatment provided, results of any tests and the informed written consent or certification (or copy thereof) required under paragraph (e)(1)(ii) of this section, and the name and address of any on-call physician (described in paragraph (g) of this section) who has refused or failed to appear within a reasonable time to provide necessary stabilizing treatment. Other records (e.g., test results not yet available or historical records not readily available from the hospital's files) must be sent as soon as practicable after transfer; and

(iv) The transfer is effected through qualified personnel and transportation equipment, as required, including the use of necessary and medically appropriate life support measures during the transfer.

Interpretive Guidelines: § 489.24(e)

The EMTALA regulations at 42 CFR 489.24(b) define—"transfer" as ". . . the movement (including the discharge) of an individual outside a hospital's facilities at the direction of any person employed by (or affiliated or associated, directly or indirectly, with) the hospital, but does not include such a movement of an individual who (i) has been declared dead, or (ii) leaves the facility without the permission of any such person."

The requirements in 42 CFR 489.24(e) apply to transfers to another hospital.

Transfer of Individuals with Unstabilized EMCs

In the case of individuals found to have an EMC a hospital is required under EMTALA rules at 42 CFR 489.24(d) to provide stabilizing treatment within the capabilities of the staff and facilities available in the hospital, or to provide a transfer to another hospital as required by 42 CFR 489.24(e). Transfer of the individual to another hospital may be reasonable and permissible, but the regulations establish a number of requirements that each transfer must meet in order to comply with EMTALA. If an individual's EMC has not been stabilized, prior to transferring the individual to another hospital, the sending hospital is required under EMTALA to pursue a transfer **because either:**

- the individual requests the transfer; **or**
- the expected benefits of the transfer outweigh the increased risks of the transfer.

In either case, the transfer must also always meet the four requirements of an "appropriate" transfer.

If an individual is moved to a diagnostic facility located at another hospital for diagnostic procedures not available at the transferring hospital, and the hospitals arrange to return the individual to the transferring hospital, the transfer requirements must still be met by the sending hospital. The recipient hospital is not obligated to meet the EMTALA transfer requirements when implementing an appropriate transfer back to the transferring hospital. However, it is reasonable to expect the recipient hospital with the diagnostic capability to communicate (e.g., telephonic report or documentation within the medical record) with the transferring hospital its findings of the medical condition and a status report of the individual during and after the procedure.

The transfer requirements apply only to individuals who have been determined to have an EMC that has not been stabilized. The hospital has no further EMTALA obligation to an individual who has been determined not to have an EMC or whose EMC has been stabilized, or who has been admitted as an inpatient (See discussion related to the requirements of 42 CFR 489.24(d), concerning stabilizing treatment.) However, the hospital has other obligations to the individual under the Hospital Conditions of Participation.

These transfer requirements do not apply to an individual who is moved to another part of the hospital, because technically the patient has not been transferred. This is also the case when an individual who presents to an off-campus dedicated emergency department is found to have an EMC and is moved to the hospital's main campus for stabilizing treatment that cannot be provided at the off-campus site.

Transfer at the Request of the Individual

A transfer may be made at the request of the individual with an EMC or of a person legally responsible for that individual. The hospital must assure that the individual or legally responsible person is first informed of the hospital's obligations under EMTALA, e.g., its obligation to provide stabilizing treatment within its capability and capacity, regardless of the individual's ability to pay. The hospital must also assure that the individual has been advised of the medical risks associated with transfer. After the hospital has communicated this information, the individual's request for a transfer must be in writing. The request must include the reason(s) why the transfer is being requested and a statement that the individual is aware of the risks and benefits associated with the transfer. The individual or individual's representative must sign the written request.

Transfer with a Physician Certification

Alternatively, a transfer may be made when a physician certifies that the expected benefits of the transfer outweigh the risks. Specifically, a physician must certify that the medical benefits to the individual with the EMC that could reasonably be expected from provision of appropriate treatment at another hospital outweigh the increased risks that result from being transferred. In the case of a pregnant woman in labor, the physician must certify that the expected benefits outweigh the risk to both the pregnant woman and the unborn child. Under certain circumstances qualified medical personnel other than a physician may sign the certification. A qualified medical person (QMP) may sign the certification of benefits versus risks of a transfer only after consultation with a physician who agrees with the transfer. The physician must subsequently countersign the certification. The physician's countersignature must be obtained within the established timeframe according to hospital policies and procedures. Hospital by-laws or rules or regulations must specify the criteria and process for granting medical staff privileges to QMPs, and, in accordance with the hospital or CAH Conditions of Participation, each individual QMP must be appropriately privileged.

The date and time of the physician (or the QMP) certification should closely match the date and time of the transfer.

Section 1861(r)(i) of the Act defines **physicians** as:

A doctor of medicine or osteopathy legally authorized to practice medicine and surgery by the State in which he performs such function or action. (This provision is not to be construed to limit the authority of a doctor or medicine or osteopathy to delegate tasks to other qualified health care personnel to the extent recognized under State law or a State's regulatory mechanism).

The regulation at § 489.24(e)(1) requires an express written certification. Physician certification cannot simply be implied from the findings in the medical record and the fact that the patient was transferred.

The certification must state the reason(s) for transfer. The narrative rationale need not be a lengthy discussion of the individual's medical condition reiterating facts already contained in the medical record, but it should give a complete picture of the benefits to be expected from appropriate care at the receiving (recipient) facility and the risks associated with the transfer, including the time away from an acute care setting necessary to effect the transfer. The risks and benefits certification should be specific to the condition of the patient upon transfer.

This rationale may be included on the certification form or in the medical record. In cases where the individual's medical record does not include a certification, the hospital may be given the opportunity to retrieve the certification. Certifications may not be backdated.

Women in Labor

- Regardless of practices within a State, a woman in labor may be transferred only if she or her representative requests the transfer or if a physician or other qualified medical personnel signs a certification that the benefits outweigh the risks. If the hospital does not provide obstetrical services, the benefits of a transfer may outweigh the risks. A hospital cannot cite State law or practice as the basis for transfer.

- Hospitals that are not capable of handling high-risk deliveries or high-risk infants often have written transfer agreements with facilities capable of handling high-risk cases. The hospital must still meet the screening, treatment, and transfer requirements.

Four Requirements for an Appropriate Transfer

1. **§ 489.24(e)(2)(i)—The transferring hospital provides medical treatment within its capacity that minimizes the risks to the individual's health and, in the case of a woman in labor, the health of the unborn child;**

   Before implementing a transfer of an individual with an unstablized EMC, a hospital is required to provide stabilizing treatment within its capability and capacity. See discussion of stabilizing treatment, 42 CFR 489.24(d). This includes treatment to minimize the transfer risk to the health of the individual and, in the case of a pregnant woman in labor, the health of the unborn child.

   If Hospital A participates in a community call plan with Hospital B and an individual with an EMC requires the services of an on-call specialist who, pursuant to the community call plan, is on-call at Hospital B to respond to the specialty needs of individuals at Hospital A, then generally a transfer of the individual to Hospital B is warranted. However, Hospital A is still required to provide treatment within its on-site capability and capacity to minimize the risks of transfer, and all other transfer requirements must also be met, notwithstanding the participation in the community call plan.

2. **§ 489.24(e)(2)(ii)—The receiving facility—**

   (A) **Has available space and qualified personnel for the treatment of the individual; and**

   (B) **Has agreed to accept transfer of the individual and to provide appropriate medical treatment;**

   The transferring hospital must obtain permission from the receiving (recipient) hospital to transfer an individual. The transferring hospital should document its communication with the receiving (recipient) hospital, including the date and time of the transfer request and the name and title of the person accepting the transfer.

3. § 489.24(e)(2)(iii)—The transferring hospital sends to the receiving facility all medical records (or copies thereof) related to the emergency condition which the individual has presented that are available at the time of the transfer, including available history, records related to the individual's emergency medical condition, observations of signs or symptoms, preliminary diagnosis, results of diagnostic studies or telephone reports of the studies, treatment provided, results of any tests and the informed written consent or certification (or copy thereof) required under paragraph (e)(1)(ii) of this section, and the name and address of any on-call physician (described in paragraph (g) of this section) who has refused or failed to appear within a reasonable time to provide necessary stabilizing treatment. Other records (e.g., test results not yet available or historical records not readily available from the hospital's files) must be sent as soon as practicable after transfer;

Necessary medical records must accompany individuals being transferred to another hospital. If a transfer is in an individual's best interest, it should not be delayed until records are retrieved or test results come back from the laboratory. Whatever medical records are available at the time the individual is transferred should be sent to the receiving (recipient) hospital with the patient. Test results that become available after the individual is transferred should be telephoned to the receiving (recipient) hospital, and then mailed or sent via electronic transmission consistent with HIPAA provisions on the transmission of electronic data.

4. § 489.24(e)(2)(iv)—The transfer is effected through qualified personnel and transportation equipment, as required, including the use of necessary and medically appropriate life support measures during the transfer.

Emergency medical technicians may not always be "qualified personnel" for purposes of transferring an individual under these regulations. Depending on the individual's condition, there may be situations in which a physician's presence or some other specialist's presence might be necessary. The physician at the sending hospital (not at the receiving hospital) has the responsibility to determine the appropriate mode, equipment, and attendants for transfer.

While the sending hospital is ultimately responsible for ensuring that the transfer is affected appropriately, the hospital may meet its obligations as it sees fit. These regulations do not require that a hospital operate an emergency medical transportation service.

Tag A-2410/C-2410

(Rev. 46, Issued: 05-29-09, Effective/Implementation: 05-29-09) § 489.24(e)(3)

(3) A participating hospital may not penalize or take adverse action against a physician or a qualified medical person described in paragraph (e)(1)(ii)(C) of this section because the physician or qualified medical

person refuses to authorize the transfer of an individual with an emergency medical condition that has not been stabilized, or against any hospital employee because the employee reports a violation of a requirement of this section.

Interpretive Guidelines: § 489.24(e)(3)

A "participating hospital" means a hospital that has entered into a provider agreement under § 1866 of the Act.

Hospital employees reporting alleged EMTALA violations are also protected by this regulation.

Tag A-2411/C-2411

(Rev. 46, Issued: 05-29-09, Effective/Implementation: 05-29-09) § 489.24(f)

Recipient Hospital Responsibilities

A participating hospital that has specialized capabilities or facilities (including, but not limited to, facilities such as burn units, shock-trauma units, neonatal intensive care units, or, with respect to rural areas, regional referral centers (which, for purposes of this subpart, mean hospitals meeting the requirements of referral centers found at § 412.96 of this chapter)) may not refuse to accept from a referring hospital within the boundaries of the United States an appropriate transfer of an individual who requires such specialized capabilities or facilities if the receiving hospital has the capacity to treat the individual.

(1) The provisions of this paragraph (f) apply to any participating hospital with specialized capabilities, regardless of whether the hospital has a dedicated emergency department.

(2) The provisions of this paragraph (f) do not apply to an individual who has been admitted to a referring hospital under the provisions of paragraph (d)(2)(i) of this section.

Interpretive Guidelines: § 489.24(f)

A Medicare-participating hospital that has specialized capabilities or facilities may not refuse to accept an appropriate transfer from another hospital of an individual with an unstabilized emergency medical condition who is protected under EMTALA and requires such specialized capabilities or facilities. This assumes that, in addition to its specialized capabilities, the recipient hospital has the capacity to treat the individual, and that the transferring, i.e. referring, hospital lacks that capability or capacity. Hospitals with specialized capabilities or facilities may include, but are not limited to, hospitals with burn units, shock trauma units, neonatal intensive care units or hospitals that are regional referral centers that serve rural areas as defined by the requirements at 42 CFR 412.96.

This requirement to accept an appropriate transfer applies to any Medicare-participating hospital with specialized capabilities, regardless of whether the hospital has a dedicated emergency department. In other words, while some obligations under EMTALA apply only to hospitals that have a dedicated emergency department, e.g., requirements related to providing a medical screening examination, the EMTALA recipient hospital obligation can also apply to hospitals that do not have a dedicated emergency department. For example, if an individual is found to have an emergency medical condition that requires specialized psychiatric capabilities, a psychiatric hospital that participates in Medicare and has capacity is obligated to accept an appropriate transfer of that individual. It does not matter if the psychiatric hospital does not have a dedicated emergency department.

The regulation states that a recipient hospital's EMTALA obligations do not extend to individuals who are inpatients of another hospital. Thus, a hospital may not be cited for violating EMTALA if it refuses to accept the transfer of an inpatient from the referring hospital.

Section 489.24(b) defines inpatient: "Inpatient means an individual who is admitted to a hospital for bed occupancy for purposes of receiving inpatient hospital services as described in § 409.10(a) of this chapter with the expectation that he or she will remain at least overnight and occupy a bed even though the situation later develops that the individual can be discharged or transferred to another hospital and does not actually use a hospital bed overnight."

Individuals who are placed in observation status are not inpatients, even if they occupy a bed overnight. Therefore, placement in an observation status of an individual who came to the hospital's DED does not terminate the EMTALA obligations of that hospital or a recipient hospital toward the individual.

There is no EMTALA obligation for a Medicare-participating hospital with specialized capabilities to accept transfers from hospitals located outside the boundaries of the United States. In accordance with Section 210(i) of the Social Security Act, the term "United States," when used in a geographical sense, means the States, the District of Columbia, the Commonwealth of Puerto Rico, the Virgin Islands, Guam, and American Samoa. Hospitals that request transfers must recognize that the appropriate transfer of individuals with unstabilized emergency medical conditions that require specialized services should not routinely be made over great distances, bypassing closer hospitals with the needed capability and capacity.

A hospital with specialized capabilities or facilities that has the necessary capacity to treat an individual with an emergency medical condition may not condition or attempt to condition its acceptance of an appropriate transfer of an individual protected under EMTALA on the use of a particular mode of transport or transport service. It is the treating physician at the transferring hospital who decides how the individual is transported to the recipient hospital and what transport service will be used, since this physician has assessed the individual personally. The transferring hospital is required to arrange transport that minimizes the risk to the individual who is being transferred, in accordance with the requirements of § 489.24(e)(2)(B)(iv).

A hospital with specialized capabilities that delays the treatment of an individual with an emergency medical condition who arrives as a transfer from another facility could be in violation of EMTALA, depending on the circumstances of that delay. For instance, if there is evidence that the recipient hospital unreasonably delayed the treatment of certain individuals and expedited the treatment of other individuals, based on their ability to pay for the services or some other form of discrimination, then the recipient hospital may be in violation of EMTALA. Hospitals that deliberately delay moving an individual from an EMS stretcher do not thereby delay the point in time at which their EMTALA obligation begins. Furthermore, such a practice of "parking" individuals arriving via EMS, refusing to release EMS personnel or equipment, can potentially jeopardize the health and safety of the transferred individual and other individuals in the community who may need EMS services at that time. On the other hand, this does not mean that a hospital will necessarily have violated EMTALA and/or the hospital CoPs if it does not, in every instance, immediately assume from the EMS provider all responsibility for the individual, regardless of any other circumstances in the hospital.

Lateral transfers, that is, transfers between facilities of comparable resources and capabilities, are not required by § 489.24(f), because the benefits of such a transfer would not be likely to outweigh the risks of the transfer, except when the transferring hospital has a serious capacity problem, a mechanical failure of equipment, or similar situations, such as loss of power or significant flooding.

Assessment of whether the transferring hospital with the requisite capabilities lacked the capacity to provide stabilizing treatment, or of whether the recipient hospital lacked the capacity to accept an appropriate transfer requires a review of the hospital's general practices in adjusting its capacity. If a hospital generally has a record of accommodating additional patients by various means, such as moving patients from one unit to another, calling in additional staff, and temporarily borrowing additional equipment from other facilities, then that hospital would be expected under EMTALA to take reasonable steps to respond to the treatment needs of an individual requiring stabilizing treatment for an emergency medical condition. The determination of a hospital's capacity would depend on the case-specific circumstances and the hospital's previous implementation of capacity management actions.

The criteria for classifying hospitals as rural regional referral centers are defined in 42 CFR 412.96. A designated rural regional referral center is obligated to accept appropriate transfers of individuals who require the hospital's specialized capabilities if the hospital has the capacity to treat the individual.

Transmittals Issued for this Appendix

Rev #	Issue Date	Subject	Impl Date	CR#
R60SOM	07/16/2010	Revisions to Appendix V,—Interpretive Guidelines-Responsibilities of Medicare Participating Hospitals in Emergency Cases	07/16/2010	N/A

Rev #	Issue Date	Subject	Impl Date	CR#
R46SOM	05/29/2009	Revisions to Appendix V, "Emergency Medical Treatment and Labor Act (EMTALA) Interpretive Guidelines"	05/29/2009	N/A
R01SOM	05/21/2004	Initial Release of Pub 100-07	N/A	N/A

Appendix D

Glossary

ABN. Advanced Beneficiary Notice.

Amicus Curiae. "Literally, friend of the court. A person with strong interest in or views on the subject matter of a lawsuit, but not a party to the suit, may petition the court for permission to file a brief, ostensibly on behalf of a party but actually to suggest a rationale consistent with its own views." *Black's Law Dictionary* 82 (6th ed. 1990).

Apparent Agent. "A person who, whether or not authorized, reasonably appears to [a] third person, because of manifestations of another, to be authorized to act as an agent for such other." *Black's Law Dictionary* 63-64 (6th ed. 1990). In healthcare, for instance, if a hospital's advertising and policies lead a patient to believe that a physician is an agent (employee) of the hospital, even when the physician is an independent contractor, then apparent agency may apply in a lawsuit.

Circuit. "Judicial divisions of the United States (e.g., thirteen judicial circuits wherein U.S. Courts of Appeal sit) or a state, originally so called because the judges traveled from place to place within the circuit, holding court in various locations." *Black's Law Dictionary* 242 (6th ed. 1990). *See also* United States Courts of Appeals, *below*.

Circuit Courts of Appeals. "Former name for federal intermediate appellate courts, changed in 1948 to present designation of United States Courts of Appeals." *Black's Law Dictionary* 242 (6th ed. 1990).

CMS. Centers for Medicare and Medicaid Services (formally HCFA).

COBRA. Consolidated Omnibus Budget Reconciliation Act.

Code of Federal Regulations (C.F.R.). "[T]he annual cumulation of executive agency regulations published in the daily Federal Register, combined with regulations issued previously that are still in effect. Divided into 50 titles, each representing a broad subject area, individual volumes of the Code of Federal

Regulations are revised at least once each calendar year and issued on a staggered quarterly basis. The CFR contains the general body of regulatory laws governing practice and procedure before federal administrative agencies." *Black's Law Dictionary* 257 (6th ed. 1990).

Comprehensive Omnibus Budget Reconciliation Act of 1986 (COBRA). The budget act, Pub. L. No. 99-272, § 9121, 100 Stat. 82 (1986), passed pursuant to a concurrent resolution, S. Con. Res. 32, 99th Cong. (1985), mandating major budget reductions for fiscal years 1986 through 1988. S. Rep. No. 99-146, at 3 (1985), *reprinted in* 1986 U.S.C.C.A.N. 42, 43. The reconciliation procedure allows Congress to consider broad-based budgetary changes within a single bill, reserving to individual committees the power to determine what changes will be made in laws within their respective jurisdiction.

Contribution. The principle under which "[a] tort-feasor [*see below*] against whom a judgment is rendered is entitled to recover proportional shares of judgment from other joint tort-feasors whose negligence contributed to the injury and who were also liable to the plaintiff." *Black's Law Dictionary* 328 (6th ed. 1990).

Declaratory Judgment. "Statutory remedy for the determination of a justifiable controversy where the plaintiff is in doubt as to his legal rights. A binding adjudication of the rights and status of litigants even though no consequential relief is awarded. . . . Such judgment is conclusive in a subsequent action between the parties as to the matters declared and, in accordance with the usual rules of issue preclusion, as to any issues actually litigated and determined." *Black's Law Dictionary* 409 (6th ed. 1990).

DRG. Diagnosis Related Group.

ED. Emergency Department.

Eleventh Amendment. Amendment number eleven, added to the United States Constitution in 1798 (the first new amendment after the Bill of Rights), which provides that "[t]he judicial power of the United States shall not be construed to extend to any suit in law or equity, commenced or prosecuted against one of the United States by citizens of another State, or by citizens or subjects of any foreign state." U.S. Const. amend. XI.

EMC. Emergency Medical Condition.

Emergency Medical Treatment and Active Labor Act. The Emergency Medical Treatment and Active Labor Act (EMTALA), Pub. L. No. 99-272, Title IX, § 9121(b), 100 Stat. (codified as amended at 42 U.S.C. § 1395dd [1995]).

Employee Retirement Income Security Act (ERISA). The Employee Retirement Income Security Act of 1974, 29 U.S.C. § 1144, which established uniform national standards for employee benefit plans and broadly preempted state regulation of these plans. Section 1144(a) states that ERISA supersedes state laws to the extent that they "relate to any employee benefit plan" covered by ERISA.

EMS. Emergency Medical System.

EMTALA. The Emergency Medical Treatment and Active Labor Act.

Federal District Court. One of the United States trial courts for federal cases. "Each state is comprised of one or more federal judicial districts, and in each district there is a district court. 28 U.S.C.A. § 81 *et seq.* The United States district courts are the trial courts with general federal jurisdiction over cases involving federal laws or offenses and actions between citizens of different states. Each state has at least one district court, though many have several judicial districts (e.g., northern, southern, middle districts) or divisions." *Black's Law Dictionary* 476 (6th ed. 1990) (under "District courts"). There are 95 federal district courts, including one for the District of Columbia and one for the Commonwealth of Puerto Rico. Decisions of the federal district courts may be appealed to a United States Court of Appeals (*see below*).

Federal Intermediate Appellate Court. One of the United States Courts of Appeals, which comprise 13 circuits covering specific geographic areas and the federal government. Individual circuits do not have to follow the judgments and rulings of other circuits. This results in different interpretations of the same statute, like EMTALA, between the different circuits. *See* United States Courts of Appeals, *below.*

Federal Register (Fed. Reg.). "[The daily] medium for making available to the public Federal agency regulations and other legal documents of the executive branch. These documents cover a wide range of Government activities. An important function of the Federal Register is that it includes proposed changes (rules, regulations, standards, etc.) of governmental agencies. Each proposed change published carries an invitation for any citizen or group to participate in the consideration of the proposed regulation through the submission of written data, views, or arguments, and sometimes by oral presentations. Such regulations and rules as finally approved appear thereafter in the Code of Federal Regulations." *Black's Law Dictionary* 612 (6th ed. 1990).

Fourteenth Amendment. Amendment number fourteen, added to the United States Constitution in 1868, which provides that "[n]o State shall make or enforce any law which shall abridge privileges or immunities of citizens of the United States; nor shall any State deprive any person of life, liberty, or property, without due process of law, nor deny to any person within its jurisdiction the equal protection of the laws." U.S. Const. amend. XIV § 1.

Guardian ad litem. "A special guardian appointed by the court in which a particular litigation is pending to represent an infant, ward or unborn person in that particular litigation, and the status of guardian ad litem exists only in that specific litigation in which the appointment occurs." *Black's Law Dictionary* 706 (6th ed. 1990).

HCFA. Health Care Financing Administration.

Health Care Financing Administration (HCFA). Part of the Department of Health and Human Services (HHS), to which is delegated responsibility for administering Medicare and the federal portion of Medicaid. HCFA is given the authority to terminate a hospital from Medicare participation for EMTALA violations. HCFA is now the centers for Medicare & Medicaid Services.

Health Maintenance Organization (HMO). A kind of prepaid medical insurance plan in which the HMO assumes a contractual obligation to ensure delivery of health services to enrollees who pay a fixed premium. An HMO generally provides, offers, or arranges for coverage of designated health services needed by plan members for a fixed, prepaid premium. There are four basic models of HMOs: group model, individual practice association, network model, and staff model.

HHS. Department of Health and Human Services.

Hill-Burton Act. The Hospital Survey and Construction Act, Pub. L. No. 79-725, ch. 958, 60 Stat. 1040 (1946) (42 U.S.C. §§ 290 *et seq.*). The Hill-Burton Act was actually public works legislation designed to provide hospitals with new construction and improvement funds in light of a perceived shortage and to create construction jobs for the military personnel who were returning from World War II. Interestingly, as with EMTALA within COBRA, in the main body of the act was a small section that required hospitals that receive Hill-Burton funds to provide a "reasonable volume of services" to "persons unable to pay therefore" and also services to "all persons residing in the territorial area of the [hospital]."

HMO. Health Maintenance Organization.

ICU. Intensive Care Unit.

Indemnity. "Reimbursement. A contractual or equitable right under which the entire loss is shifted from a tortfeasor [*sic*] who is only technically or passively at fault to another who is primarily or actively responsible." *Black's Law Dictionary* 769 (6th ed. 1990).

Knowingly. "With knowledge; consciously; intelligently; willfully; intentionally. An individual acts 'knowingly' when he acts with awareness of the nature of his conduct. . . . [An a]ct is done 'knowingly' or 'purposely' if it is willed, is [the] product of conscious design, intent or plan that it be done, and is done with awareness of probable consequences." *Black's Law Dictionary* 872 (6th ed. 1990). Initially, hospitals could violate EMTALA by "knowingly" violating the statute. This was changed in 1991 to "negligently" (*see below*).

Managed Care. A range of health care delivery and financing arrangements that seek to control costs through a variety of mechanisms. Common strategies include use of primary care "gatekeeper" physicians, prior authorization for specialized care, and stringent utilization review procedures. Many insurers that pay for health care on a traditional fee-for-service basis have also adopted some managed care techniques, often by paying a substantially greater portion of the bill for services furnished by a "preferred provider" under contract to the insurer.

Managed Care Organization (MCO). A generic term that includes all forms of organizations that provide managed health care services (e.g., HMOs, PPOs, etc.).

Medicaid. "A form of public assistance sponsored jointly by the federal and state governments providing medical aid for people whose income falls below a certain level." *Black's Law Dictionary* 981 (6th ed. 1990). Created in 1965 when President Lyndon Johnson signed Public Law No. 89-97, Medicaid is a joint federal-state program to furnish medical care to those unable to afford it. Federal law authorizes Medicaid, but the states operate the program. The federal government makes grants to the states to assist them in furnishing medical assistance to families with dependent children and to the aged, blind, or disabled who have insufficient financial resources to pay for necessary health services.

Medicare. "Federal Act (Health Insurance for the Aged Act) to provide hospital and medical insurance for aged persons under Social Security Act. 42 U.S.C.A. § 1395 *et seq.*" *Black's Law Dictionary* 982 (6th ed. 1990). Established by 1965 under Title XVIII amendments to the Social Security Act, Medicare provides health insurance for the elderly and disabled. Generally, persons are permitted to participate in Part A, the hospital insurance program, if they are 65 years or older and are receiving retirement benefits under Title II of the Social Security Act or the Railroad Retirement Act. Part A is financed by a tax on employers, employees, and the self-employed. Medicare applies to all qualified persons regardless of need. Part B is designed to cover physicians' services, but also covers a variety of other goods and services including outpatient hospital services, physical and occupational therapy, prosthetic devices, durable medical equipment, and ambulance services.

MSE. Medical Screening Examination.

Negligence. "The omission to do something which a reasonable man, guided by those ordinary considerations which ordinarily regulate human affairs, would do, or the doing of something which a reasonable and prudent man would not do. . . . Conduct which falls below the standard established by law for the protection of others against unreasonable risk of harm; it is a departure from the conduct expectable of a reasonably prudent person under like circumstances." *Black's Law Dictionary* 1034 (6th ed. 1990).

Negligently. Behaving in a negligent manner; involving "a gross deviation from the standard of care that a reasonable person would observe in the actor's situation." *Black's Law Dictionary* 1034 (6th ed. 1990). In 1991, Congress changed the word describing the way for hospitals to violate EMTALA from "knowingly" to "negligently" so that hospitals cannot plead innocence due to ignorance of EMTALA's requirements.

Office of the Inspector General (OIG). The enforcement arm of the Department of Health and Human Services, which imposes civil monetary penalties for EMTALA violations. "Various agencies of the federal government have an office of Inspector General whose primary function is to conduct and supervise audits and investigations relating to programs and operations of the particular agency." *Black's Law Dictionary* 769 (6th ed. 1990) (under "Inspector general").

OIG. Office of Inspector General.

OPPS. Outpatient Prospective Payment System.

Patient Dumping. The practice of denying emergency medical care to patients who come to a hospital with inadequate or no insurance, or who are on Medicaid, and who therefore get "dumped" back on the street or transferred to a public charity hospital.

Peer Review Organization (PRO). Physicians group of which a request may be made by HCFA to review medical services in a hospital under investigation. Medicare was created without controls on regulating the medical necessity, appropriateness, and quality of services provided to Medicare beneficiaries. The Professional Standards Review Organization (PSRO), which used regional non-profit physicians groups to review independently the use of medical services by beneficiaries of federal medical assistance programs, including Medicare, was set up to deal with the deficiency, but the PSRO program was a failure. In 1982, the Tax Equity and Fiscal Responsibility Act (TEFRA) abolished the PSRO program and created in its stead the PRO program. Unlike PSROs, PROs can be for profit entities. The PROs were given enhanced authority over sanctions and payment denial to enforce their power.

Per curiam. "A phrase used to distinguish an opinion of the whole court from an opinion written by any one judge. Sometimes it denotes an opinion written by the chief justice or presiding judge, or to a brief announcement of the disposition of a case by court not accompanied by a written opinion." *Black's Law Dictionary* 1136 (6th ed. 1990).

PPO. Preferred Provider Organization.

PRO. Peer Review Organization.

Preferred Provider Organization (PPO). A party to a contractual arrangement, generally between healthcare providers and an employer or insurance company, to provide fee-for-service health care, usually at a discount. The major distinction between HMOs and PPOs is that the former are organizations that provide service on a prepaid basis; whereas the latter involve contractual relationships that arrange for coverage on a fee-for-service basis.

Privacy Act. The federal law (5 U.S.C.A. § 552a) that "provides for making known to the public the existence and characteristics of all personal information systems kept by every Federal agency. The Act permits an individual to have access to records containing personal information on that individual and allows the individual to control the transfer of that information to other Federal agencies for nonroutine uses. . . . The Act further provides for civil remedies for the individual whose records are kept or used in contravention of the requirements of the Act." *Black's Law Dictionary* 1195 (6th ed. 1990) (under "Privacy laws").

Procedural Law. "That which prescribes method of enforcing rights or obtaining redress for their invasion. . . . As a general rule, laws which fix duties, establish rights and responsibilities among and for persons, natural or otherwise, are 'substantive laws' in character, while those which merely prescribe the manner in which such rights and responsibilities may be exercised and enforced in a court are 'procedural laws.'" *Black's Law Dictionary* 1203 (6th ed. 1990).

QMP. Qualified Medical Person.

Regional Office (RO). For HCFA administration, the United States is divided into ten regions. Each region is administered by a regional office, which investigates complaints of EMTALA violation and may prescribe sanctions.

Right of action. "The right to bring suit; a legal right to maintain an action, growing out of a given transaction or state of facts and based thereon. Right of injured one to secure redress for violation of his rights." *Black's Law Dictionary* 1325 (6th ed. 1990).

RO. Regional Office.

Sovereign immunity. "A judicial doctrine which precludes bringing suit against the government without its consent . . . it bars holding the government or its political subdivisions liable for the torts of its officers or agents unless such immunity is expressly waived by statute or by necessary inference from legislative enactment." *Black's Law Dictionary* 1396 (6th ed. 1990).

Standard of care. "In law of negligence, that degree of care which a reasonably prudent person should exercise in same or similar circumstances. If a person's conduct falls below such standard, he may be liable in damages for injuries or damages resulting from his conduct. . . . In medical . . . malpractice cases a standard of care is applied to measure the competence of the professional. The traditional standard for doctors is that he exercise the 'average degree of skill, care, and diligence exercised by members of the same profession, practicing in the same or a similar locality in light of the present state of medical and surgical science'. . . . With increased specialization, however, certain courts have disregarded geographical considerations holding that in the practice of a board-certified medical or surgical specialty, the standard should be that of a reasonable specialist practicing medicine or surgery in the same special field." *Black's Law Dictionary* 1404–05 (6th ed. 1990).

Substantive law. "That part of law which creates, defines, and regulates rights and duties of parties, as opposed to 'adjective, procedural, or remedial law,' which prescribes method of enforcing the rights or obtaining redress for their invasion. . . . The basic law of rights and duties (contract law, criminal law, tort law, etc.) as opposed to procedural law (law of pleading, law of evidence, law of jurisdiction, etc.)." *Black's Law Dictionary* 1429 (6th ed. 1990).

Summary judgment. "Procedural device available for prompt and expeditious disposition of controversy without trial when there is no dispute as to either material fact or inferences to be drawn from undisputed facts, or if only question of law is involved." *Black's Law Dictionary* 1435 (6th ed. 1990).

Toll. "To suspend or stop temporarily as the statute of limitations is tolled during the defendant's absence from the jurisdiction and during the plaintiff's minority." *Black's Law Dictionary* 1488 (6th ed. 1990).

Tort. "A private or civil wrong or injury, including action for bad faith breach of contract, for which the court will provide a remedy in the form of an action for damages. . . . A legal wrong committed upon the person or property independent of contract. It may be either (1) a direct invasion of some legal right of the individual; (2) the infraction of some public duty by which special damage accrues to the individual; [or] (3) the violation of some private obligation by which like damage accrues to the individual." *Black's Law Dictionary* 1489 (6th ed. 1990).

Tort-Feasor. "A wrong-doer; an individual or business that commits or is guilty of a tort." *Black's Law Dictionary* 1489 (6th ed. 1990).

United States Code (U.S.C.). The main publication of federal laws. "Prior to 1926, the positive law for federal legislation was contained in the one volume of the Revised Statutes of 1875 and then in each subsequent volume of the Statutes at Large. In 1925, Congress authorized the preparation of the United States Code. This was prepared by a Revisor of Statutes appointed by Congress, who extracted all sections of the Revised Statutes of 1875 that had not been repealed and then all of the public and general laws from the Statutes at Large since 1873 that were still in force. These were then rearranged into fifty titles and published as the United States Code, 1926 ed., in four volumes. Each year thereafter a cumulative supplement containing the laws passed since 1926 was published. In 1932 a new edition was issued which incorporated the cumulated supplements to the 1926 edition, and this became the United States Code, 1932 ed. Every six years a new edition of the U.S. Code is published with cumulative supplement volumes being issued during the intervening years." *Black's Law Dictionary* 1533-34 (6th ed. 1990).

United States Code Annotated (U.S.C.A.). Multivolume publication including "the complete text of the United States Code, together with case notes of state and federal decisions which construe and apply specific Code sections, cross references to related sections, historical notes, and library references. U.S.C.A. is further supplemented with United States Code Congressional and Administrative News [U.S.C.C.A.N.] and periodic pamphlet supplements containing laws as passed by Congress during the current session." *Black's Law Dictionary* 1534 (6th ed. 1990).

United States Courts of Appeals. Courts of appeals having "appellate jurisdiction over most cases decided by the United States District Courts and review and enforce orders of many federal administrative bodies. The decisions of the courts of appeals are final except as they are subject to discretionary review on appeal by the Supreme Court. *See* 28 U.S.C.A. §§ 41, 43, 1291." *Black's Law Dictionary* 361-62 (6th ed. 1990) (under "Courts of Appeals, U.S.").

Appendix E

Office of Inspector General—EMTALA

The Enforcement
Process

Department of Health and Human Services

OFFICE OF
INSPECTOR GENERAL

THE EMERGENCY MEDICAL
TREATMENT AND LABOR ACT

The Enforcement Process

JANUARY 2001
OEI-09-98-00221

OFFICE OF INSPECTOR GENERAL

The mission of the Office of Inspector General (OIG), as mandated by Public Law 95-452, is to protect the integrity of the Department of Health and Human Services programs as well as the health and welfare of beneficiaries served by them. This statutory mission is carried out through a nationwide program of audits, investigations, inspections, sanctions, and fraud alerts. The Inspector General informs the Secretary of program and management problems and recommends legislative, regulatory, and operational approaches to correct them.

Office of Evaluation and Inspections

The Office of Evaluation and Inspections (OEI) is one of several components of the Office of Inspector General. It conducts short-term management and program evaluations (called inspections) that focus on issues of concern to the Department, the Congress, and the public. The inspection reports provide findings and recommendations on the efficiency, vulnerability, and effectiveness of departmental programs.

OEI's San Francisco regional office prepared this report under the direction of Paul A. Gottlober, Regional Inspector General. Principal OEI staff included:

REGION

Cindy Lemesh, *Project Leader*
Jay Davidson, *Lead Analyst*
Scott Hutchison, *Program Analyst*

HEADQUARTERS

Bambi Straw, *Program Specialist*

To obtain copies of this report, please call the San Francisco Regional Office at 415-437-7900. The Report is available on the World Wide Web at

http://oig.hhs.gov/oei/reports/oei-09-98-00221.pdf

EXECUTIVE SUMMARY

PURPOSE

The purpose of this inspection was to evaluate the enforcement process for the Emergency Medical Treatment and Labor Act (EMTALA).

BACKGROUND

Congress passed EMTALA, part of the Consolidated Omnibus Reconciliation Act (COBRA) of 1985, in April 1986 to address the problem of "patient dumping." The term "patient dumping" refers to certain situations where hospitals fail to screen, treat, or appropriately transfer patients. According to Section 9121 of COBRA, Medicare-participating hospitals must provide a medical screening exam to any individual who comes to the emergency department and requests examination or treatment for a medical condition. If a hospital determines that an individual has a medical emergency, it must then stabilize the condition or provide for an appropriate transfer. The hospital is obligated to provide these services regardless of the individual's ability to pay and without delay to inquire about the individual's method of payment or insurance status.

Congress created a bifurcated enforcement mechanism for EMTALA within the Department of Health and Human Services. The Health Care Financing Administration (HCFA) authorizes investigations of dumping complaints by State survey agencies, determines if a violation occurred, and, if appropriate, terminates a hospital's provider agreement. The Office of Inspector General (OIG) assesses civil monetary penalties against hospitals and physicians and may exclude physicians from the Medicare program for repeated or gross and flagrant behavior. The HCFA *may* seek the input of the local peer review organization (PRO) after the State's investigation to help determine whether the hospital adequately screened, examined, and treated a patient but *must* seek PRO input in most circumstances before forwarding a case to the OIG if the alleged violation involves a question of medical judgment.

We interviewed staff at HCFA regional offices, State survey agencies, the PROs, and the OIG between June and December 1999. We also reviewed relevant HCFA manuals and guidelines as well as law journals. We obtained logs from HCFA that contain information about EMTALA complaints and the outcomes of investigations between Fiscal Years 1986 and 1998.

FINDINGS

The EMTALA enforcement process is compromised by long delays and inadequate feedback. Timely processing of EMTALA cases is a longstanding problem. Delays have worsened in recent years, despite a decline in dumping cases. In addition, HCFA regional offices often fail to communicate their decisions to State survey agencies and the PROs.

The number of EMTALA investigations and their ultimate disposition vary widely by HCFA region and year. Regional offices vary greatly in the number of EMTALA investigations that they conduct and the outcomes of those investigations. For example, one region found violations in 22 percent of its investigations while another region found violations in 68 percent of its investigations.

Poor tracking of EMTALA cases impedes oversight. The HCFA's investigation logs contain numerous errors and omit key information about dumping complaints and EMTALA investigations. Although HCFA's central office chose a particular software application for tracking EMTALA cases, some regional offices continue to use their own methods for data collection.

Peer review is not always obtained before HCFA considers terminating a hospital for medical reasons. The HCFA instructs States to obtain professional medical review during an EMTALA investigation, but this does not always occur. The HCFA has the option of requesting peer review, but this is discretionary even if the State did not obtain peer review. In most cases, the OIG must seek PRO input and may drop a case if the PRO finds that medical care was adequate.

RECOMMENDATIONS

We recommend that HCFA:

▶   increase its oversight of regional offices,

▶   improve collection and access to EMTALA data,

▶   ensure that peer review occurs for cases involving medical judgment, and

▶   establish an EMTALA technical advisory group.

AGENCY COMMENTS

We received written comments from HCFA on the draft report, which are included in the appendix. The HCFA concurred with our recommendations. The comments describe a dedicated HCFA effort to reduce backlogs, improve data collection, and increase coordination among the regions. The HCFA also offered several technical comments, which we have incorporated where appropriate.

TABLE OF CONTENTS

INTRODUCTION

PURPOSE

The purpose of this inspection was to evaluate the enforcement process for the Emergency Medical Treatment and Labor Act (EMTALA).

BACKGROUND

Requirements of the Emergency Medical Treatment and Labor Act

Congress passed EMTALA, part of the Consolidated Omnibus Reconciliation Act (COBRA) of 1985, in April 1986[1] to address the problem of "patient dumping." The term "patient dumping" refers to certain situations where hospitals fail to screen, treat, or appropriately transfer patients. According to Section 9121 of COBRA, Medicare-participating hospitals must provide a medical screening exam to any individual who comes to the emergency department and requests examination or treatment for a medical condition. If a hospital determines that an individual has an emergency medical condition,[2] it must then stabilize the condition or provide for an appropriate transfer. The hospital is obligated to provide these services regardless of the individual's ability to pay and without delay to inquire about the individual's method of payment or insurance status. Hospitals may transfer unstable patients only if a physician determines that the benefits of the transfer outweigh the risks or if requested by a patient who has been informed of both the hospital's EMTALA obligations and the risks of transfer. Hospitals with specialized care facilities, such as burn units, must, within their capacity, accept requests for appropriate transfers of patients who require such specialized care. The following diagram illustrates the basic EMTALA requirements:

---

[1] EMTALA became effective on August 1, 1986.

[2] Emergency medical condition is defined by law as "a medical condition manifesting itself by acute symptoms of sufficient severity (including severe pain) such that the absence of immediate medical attention could reasonably be expected to result in (i) placing the health of the individual (or, with respect to a pregnant woman, the health of the woman or her unborn child) in serious jeopardy; (ii) serious impairment to bodily functions; or (iii) serious dysfunction of any bodily organ or part . . ."

EMTALA — Enforcement   5   OEI-09-98-00221

Figure 1: Basic EMTALA Requirements

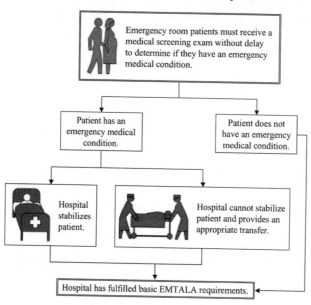

The specific requirements of EMTALA are incorporated in each hospital's Medicare provider agreement. The Health Care Financing Administration (HCFA) requires that in addition to providing a medical screening examination and necessary stabilizing treatment and appropriate transfers (i.e., the statutory requirements), hospitals must post signs, maintain a central log, an on-call roster and patient transfer records, and report EMTALA violations to HCFA or the State survey agency. All such obligations are considered equal, and failure to meet any of them constitutes a breach of the Medicare provider agreement and possible basis for termination. Hospitals also may be subject to civil monetary penalties of up to $50,000 per violation ($25,000 for hospitals with fewer than 100 beds) and civil action. Physicians who negligently violate EMTALA also are subject to civil monetary penalties and, for repeated or gross and flagrant violations, exclusion from Medicare.

Enforcement Mechanisms and Trends

The HCFA and the Office of Inspector General (OIG) are responsible for enforcing EMTALA (see Figure 2 for more information on the EMTALA enforcement process). The HCFA authorizes investigations of dumping complaints by State survey agencies, determines if a violation occurred, and, if appropriate, terminates a hospital's provider

Figure 2: EMTALA Enforcement Process

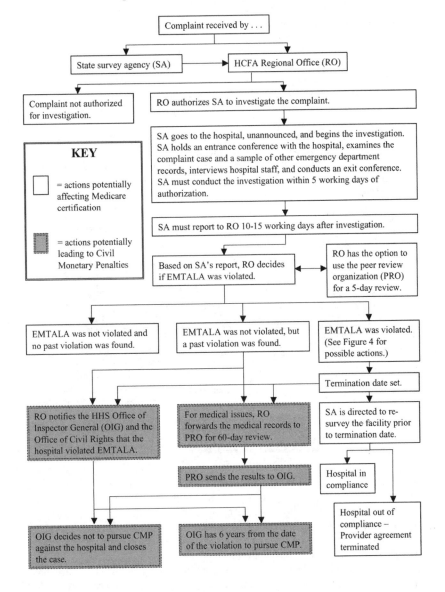

agreement. Within the OIG, the Office of Counsel to the Inspector General assesses civil monetary penalties against hospitals and physicians and may exclude physicians from the Medicare program. The HCFA may seek the input of the local peer review organization

(PRO) after the investigation, when HCFA must decide whether a violation occurred. However, by law HCFA must seek PRO input before it forwards a case to OIG which requires a medical judgement of a hospital's or physician's liability.[3]

State survey agencies perform unannounced, on-site investigations of hospitals and forward the results to the regional office. The purpose of these investigations is to determine whether a violation occurred, to assess whether the violation endangers patient health and safety, to identify any patterns of violations at the facility, and to assess whether the hospital has policies and procedures that implement EMTALA's provisions.

The number of EMTALA investigations, averaging 400 a year between Fiscal Years 1994 and 1998, is very small compared to the number of emergency department visits in the United States, which totaled approximately 97 million in 1999. In general, less than 50 percent of investigations confirm a dumping violation (see Figure 3).

Figure 3

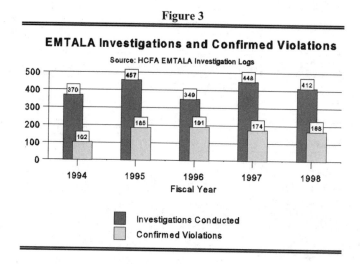

EMTALA Investigations and Confirmed Violations

Source: HCFA EMTALA Investigation Logs

Investigations Conducted
Confirmed Violations

Hospitals cited for dumping violations rarely lose their provider agreements. Since 1986, HCFA has terminated 13 hospitals from Medicare due to EMTALA violations. Only one of these terminations occurred after 1993, and it was voluntary. In practice, HCFA does not terminate a hospital's provider agreement if the hospital takes corrective action to prevent future violations.

Civil monetary penalties are relatively uncommon. The OIG closes more than half of the cases it reviews. To date, the OIG has processed 677 dumping cases; it has declined

---

[3]The OIG can impose a civil monetary penalty without PRO review "[i]f a delay would jeopardize the health or safety of individuals or when there was no screening examination. . ." 42 C.F.R. § 489.24 (g)(3)

353 cases and settled 226 (decisions in the remaining cases are pending). The number of civil monetary penalties assessed by OIG has increased dramatically in recent years, from a total of 79 settlements in Fiscal Years 1987 to 1997 to 61 settlements and judgments in 1999 alone. The increased activity reflects additional OIG staffing that resulted in the elimination of a backlog of cases rather than a surge in dumping complaints and confirmed violations (the statute of limitations for assessing civil monetary penalties is 6 years from the date of violation).

Recent Policy Developments

Implementation of EMTALA has evolved over the years due in part to a lengthy delay before final regulations were issued and growing concerns about the impact of managed care on access to emergency department services. In addition, issues continue to arise over the application of EMTALA to different hospital departments and operations.

In 1996, HCFA convened a work group composed of representatives of professional organizations and regulatory agencies to address enforcement issues as well as the definition of key terms in the law and the impact of managed care. The work group's objective "was to produce consensus recommendations for clarifications or changes to the statute, regulation, or HCFA's interpretive guidelines (enforcement procedures), with emphasis on changes that could be implemented quickly without legislative action or a formal rulemaking process."[4] The work group formed subgroups to address definitions, the enforcement process, and the relationship between EMTALA and managed care. The group submitted its recommendations in January 1997. The HCFA adopted some of these changes when it developed new guidelines for HCFA regional offices and State surveyors. These guidelines became effective in July 1998.

In 1998, HCFA also issued new instructions to State surveyors about the types of violations that warranted a 23-day rather than a 90-day termination process. Before 1998, HCFA treated almost all EMTALA violations as potential threats to patient health and safety that warranted a 23-day termination process. The new guidelines distinguished between violations that pose an immediate threat to patient health and safety that would trigger 23-day termination and those violations that do not affect health and safety and would justify a 90-day termination schedule (see Figure 4 on the following page). For example, violations involving a failure to complete required paperwork do not pose a threat to health and safety and therefore warrant a 90-day process.

In November 1999, HCFA and OIG published a Special Advisory Bulletin that recommended a number of "best practices" designed to help hospitals comply with EMTALA in a managed care environment where health plans may require hospitals to obtain prior authorization for emergency services. The Bulletin recommended that hospitals not seek such authorization but acknowledged that HCFA and OIG have no

---

[4]Joan M. Stieber and Linda J. Spar, "EMTALA in the '90s — Enforcement Challenges," *Health Matrix: Journal of Law-Medicine*, Volume 8, Number 1, Winter 1998, pp. 65-66.

authority to require health plans to pay for the screening and stabilizing treatment that hospitals are obligated to provide under EMTALA.

Figure 4: EMTALA Determination and HCFA Actions

Regional Office Determination	Regional Office Action	Hospital Action
Hospital is in compliance— No past violation	No action	No action
Hospital is in compliance— Past violation	Past violation is referred to OIG for consideration of possible civil monetary penalties	No action
Hospital is not in compliance— Violation does not pose an immediate and serious threat to patient health and safety	RO begins termination procedures and refers the case to OIG for consideration of possible civil monetary penalties	Hospital has 90 days to develop and implement a corrective action plan to cease termination procedures[5]
Hospital is not in compliance— Violation poses an immediate and serious threat to patient health and safety	RO begins termination procedures and refers the case to OIG for consideration of possible civil monetary penalties and to the Office for Civil Rights for possible action under Hill-Burton	Hospital has 23 days to develop and implement a corrective action plan to cease termination procedures[4]

Previous Office of Inspector General Studies on EMTALA

In 1988, shortly after Congress enacted EMTALA, the OIG issued two reports on the new law. The first report assessed whether hospital records provided enough information to determine the incidence of patient dumping. The study concluded that reviewing these records alone was inconclusive. The second report assessed the complaint and investigation process for dumping cases and found that the process was still evolving, coordination among different components needed improvement, and resolution of dumping complaints was time-consuming. In 1995, the Office of Inspector General issued a third report on enforcement of EMTALA and focused on HCFA. Although the report concluded that the investigation process was generally effective, it highlighted inconsistency among the regional offices with respect to their procedures and compliance with HCFA guidelines.

---

[5] If the hospital does not implement a corrective action plan within 21 days (in the case of a 23-day termination) or 75 days (in the case of a 90-day termination), the regional office notifies the public of the hospital's pending termination through "the most expeditious means available" (e.g., newspaper, television, or radio).

METHODOLOGY

We interviewed staff at four HCFA regional offices, eight State survey agencies, five PROs, and the OIG between June and December 1999. We visited HCFA regional offices in San Francisco, Dallas, New York, and Atlanta. We chose these regions because they have jurisdiction over half the nation's hospitals, and they have historically processed a large number of EMTALA cases.[6] We also reviewed some actual EMTALA cases. In each region, we visited two State survey agencies and interviewed surveyors and managers. We also interviewed staff from the PROs in the four HCFA regions. We used standardized discussion guides for all interviews.

In addition to interviews with Federal and State staff, we interviewed emergency department nurses and physicians as well as health care attorneys. We conducted a mail survey of emergency department staff and telephone interviews with more than 100 emergency department managers nationwide for a separate study on awareness and impact of EMTALA. During the telephone interviews, we asked managers about the impact of EMTALA and their experiences with EMTALA investigations. The companion report entitled *The Emergency Medical Treatment and Labor Act: A Survey of Emergency Department Staff (OEI-09-98-00220)*, discusses the results of our mail survey and interviews with emergency department staff.

We reviewed relevant HCFA manuals and guidelines as well as law journals. We also obtained logs from HCFA that contain information about EMTALA complaints and the outcomes of investigations between Fiscal Years 1986 and 1998.

---

[6]These four regions accounted for 65 percent of all EMTALA investigations between Fiscal Years 1994 and 1998 (1,330 out of 2,036).

FINDINGS

The EMTALA enforcement process is compromised by long delays and inadequate feedback

The HCFA requires State survey agencies to complete investigations within 5 working days of authorization and submit their reports 10 to 15 working days after the investigation is complete. These investigations are labor-intensive and require surveyors to review a large volume of documents, including a log of emergency department cases for the past 6 to 12 months, policy manuals, minutes from medical staff meetings for the past 6 to 12 months, credential files, and quality assurance minutes. In addition, State staff must review 20 to 50 medical records for emergency department patients. We found that State agencies generally meet the mandatory time frames.

Long delays. Although strict time frames apply to State survey agencies that investigate complaints of patient dumping, HCFA itself is not subject to any. Hospitals may wait a long time to find out the outcome of an investigation and could be subject to a fast-track termination for an incident that occurred months or years before. Long delays in reviewing and deciding cases defeat the purpose of the 23-day termination process, which is to address immediate threats to patient health and safety.

The logs that we obtained from HCFA central office confirm that timely processing of cases is a longstanding problem (see Figure 5). Between 1994 and 1998, the period reflected in the logs, regional offices took an average of 65 days after the State's investigation to determine if a violation occurred. Seven of the 10 HCFA regional offices sometimes took as long as a year or more to decide whether a hospital violated EMTALA. Many cases in the logs were marked as "pending," despite the fact that the original complaint often was received years before. For example, the 1998 logs show 20 cases dating from 1996 as "decision pending."

Three State survey agencies that we visited expressed concern about long processing times in HCFA regional offices. Staff in one State told us that in some cases 2 years or more elapse before the hospital finds out its status. We heard similar concerns from emergency department administrators. Three administrators whom we interviewed told us that their hospitals had been investigated a year or more earlier, but they were still unsure of the outcomes. In one case, the hospital was not cited until 4 years after the investigation had occurred. "[The investigation] loses punch if it takes too long," said one emergency department director, "[because] the staff in question leave." Staff in HCFA regional offices acknowledged that they have a backlog of cases.

Figure 5

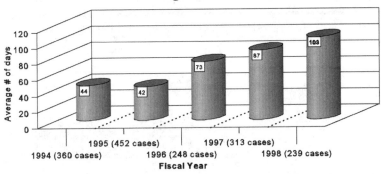

Time between Investigation and Determination

Inadequate feedback. State survey agencies, PROs, and hospitals repeatedly complained about lack of feedback from HCFA about the outcome of EMTALA cases. State agencies and the PROs, which review material related to alleged dumping violations, rarely learn the outcome of the cases they review. The survey agencies are particularly interested in the outcome, because they also license hospitals for the State.

The number of EMTALA investigations and their ultimate disposition vary widely by HCFA region and year

The volume of investigations within regions occasionally shifts sharply by year, and we identified no reason for these swings. In 1994, for example, one of the largest HCFA regions handled 119 EMTALA cases, the second highest total nationally. The workload has since dropped precipitously, and in 1998 the same region handled only three EMTALA cases. Another region logged 42 cases in 1996 and only 7 in 1998. Conversely, 7 of the 10 regional offices have seen a rise in their EMTALA caseloads since 1994. One region's caseload climbed from 18 cases in 1994 to 74 cases in 1998. Another region's caseload jumped from 13 cases in 1994 to 48 in 1998.

This inconsistency may mean that hospitals have a higher or lower chance of being investigated, depending in large part on their location (see Figure 6). Nationally, we identified 1 investigation for every 15 hospitals between Fiscal Years 1994 and 1998. In one region, however, there was one EMTALA investigation for every eight hospitals in the region during the same period. At the other extreme, the average was 1 investigation for every 40 hospitals in another region. These variations may, in part, be explained by staffing differences, regional priorities, or the fact that some regional offices are more aggressive about screening complaints before they authorize State survey agencies to conduct investigations.

Figure 6

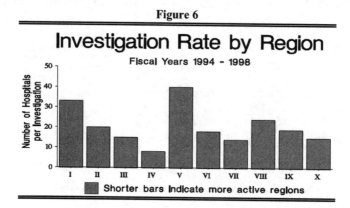

Investigation Rate by Region
Fiscal Years 1994 - 1998

Shorter bars indicate more active regions

The percentage of investigations that confirm a dumping violation varies greatly by region (see Figure 7). Nationally, 40 percent of investigations substantiated a violation between Fiscal Years 1994 and 1998. One region, however, found violations in 22 percent of its investigations while another region found violations in 68 percent of its investigations.

Figure 7

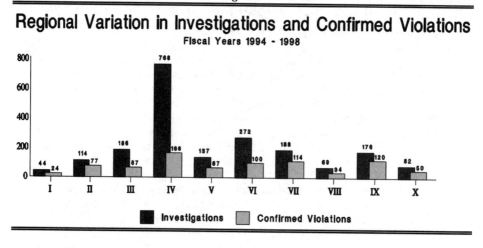

Regional Variation in Investigations and Confirmed Violations
Fiscal Years 1994 - 1998

Investigations   Confirmed Violations

In 1997, the Enforcement Process and Procedures Subgroup of the EMTALA Work Group noted "that there was substantial inconsistencies from state agency to state agency and from region to region, in both understanding of the guidelines and in the application of the guidelines and law at the respective levels." To address these inconsistencies, the subgroup recommended that HCFA consolidate all rules, regulations, and guidelines for State survey agencies and HCFA regional offices in a single manual.

Poor tracking of EMTALA cases impedes oversight

Data collection for EMTALA cases has historically been inconsistent and incomplete. We requested investigation logs from HCFA central office in November 1998 and received an incomplete set in June 1999. The documents contained numerous errors and omissions; each page was stamped "draft," even though the logs reflected activity between 1994 and 1998. Key information was absent. Details were missing concerning the complaints that did not result in an investigation, the dates investigations were authorized, and the nature of the violations, which can range from technical violations involving a failure to complete necessary paperwork to more serious infractions such as failure to perform a medical screening exam. Common errors in the 1998 logs include illogical dates (e.g., dates of investigation precede dates of complaint) and incorrect provider numbers.

Inconsistencies in data collection formats between regions and central office may explain the serious and ongoing problems with the logs. The HCFA central office decided to track EMTALA cases in 1995 and requires regions to submit monthly logs, but regional offices continue to use their own methods for data collection. One region uses a different software application to track cases and previously tracked cases manually (staff reported that they have lost EMTALA files). Another region developed its own spreadsheet, and staff there told us that they had received no guidance from central office about tracking cases. At the time of our interview with this region in June 1999, staff had not submitted logs for Fiscal Year 1998. Another region maintains both electronic and manual logs.

The historical absence of an accurate, complete central database limits HCFA's ability to oversee regional offices. Specifically, central office cannot track regional workloads and address longstanding problems. Such problems include lengthy delays before regional offices determine whether violations occurred, unacceptable backlogs of cases that are several years old, and insufficient screening of complaints to assess their legitimacy.

Peer review is not always obtained before HCFA considers terminating a hospital for medical reasons

Although HCFA instructs State survey agencies to conduct professional medical review (physician review) during their investigations of alleged dumping violations and provides explicit guidelines about what this review should entail, this does not always occur. In 1998, HCFA specified that "review physicians should be board-certified (if the physician being reviewed is board-certified) and should be actively practicing in the same medical specialty as the physician treating the patient whose case led to an alleged violation." Three State survey agencies out of the eight that we contacted had problems obtaining appropriate physician review. One agency does not employ or contract with any physicians, and the remaining two had longstanding problems finding physicians to work for the State.

After the State's investigation, regional offices may ask their local PRO to perform a 5-day review to obtain additional medical expertise. This review is discretionary, even if the State did not obtain professional medical review during its investigation. Four out of the five PROs that we contacted either conduct few or no 5-day reviews.

In contrast, PRO review is, in nearly all circumstances, mandatory before OIG assesses civil monetary penalties, and in many instances the PRO's assessment leads OIG to drop a case. In 1990, Congress added a provision to section 1867 of the Social Security Act that requires PRO review under certain circumstances before imposition of civil monetary penalties. By statute, the PRO has 60 days to complete this review. The PRO assesses whether a patient had an emergency medical condition that was not stabilized, in addition to other medical issues. According to HCFA guidelines, "the PRO must offer to discuss the case with the involved physician(s) and hospital(s) and provide them with an opportunity to submit additional information." In 1997, the OIG noted that in some regions the PROs disputed HCFA's decision about a case as much as 33 percent of the time.[7]

---

[7]Recommendations, The Enforcement Process and Procedures Subgroup, p. 4.

RECOMMENDATIONS

The HCFA central office should increase its oversight of regional offices

The EMTALA enforcement process is marked by considerable inconsistency; this is the result of the decentralized nature of the process and the sheer number of agencies involved.

We recommend that HCFA central office:
- ▶ monitor regions' conduct of investigations more closely;
- ▶ consolidate all rules, regulations, and guidelines in a single manual; and
- ▶ establish time frames for regional decisions and intervene if regional offices fail to meet them.

The HCFA should continue to improve collection and access to EMTALA data

To facilitate oversight of the regional offices and State survey agencies that play critical roles in EMTALA enforcement, HCFA central office should continue to improve data collection. Without aggregate data on complaints and the nature of dumping violations, it is impossible to assess the prevalence of patient dumping or whether the violations threaten patient health and safety. Also, PROs and State survey agencies should have access to data on EMTALA cases so that they can learn the outcomes.

The HCFA should ensure that peer review occurs before initiating termination actions in cases involving medical judgment

The HCFA expects States to obtain professional medical review when they investigate hospitals but does not seek peer review if State agencies fail to follow HCFA's instructions. As a result, hospitals may be subject to termination without the benefit of peer review of a physician's actions. The HCFA should ensure that peer review occurs before it seeks termination of a hospital's provider agreement on medical grounds. According to HCFA guidelines, "appropriate physician review may be performed by qualified SA [State agency] physicians or under agreements or contracts with the State PRO, the State or local medical association, or other physician groups or individuals."

The HCFA should establish an EMTALA technical advisory group

The HCFA disbanded the EMTALA Work Group after it submitted its recommendations in January 1997. Questions about EMTALA continue to arise, however, and the health care landscape continues to change. Given the enormous complexity and impact of EMTALA on hospitals and physicians, HCFA should consider establishing a technical advisory group comprised of representatives from organizations such as the American College of Emergency Physicians, American Hospital Association, and the American Association of Health Plans as well as State surveyors, patient advocacy groups, and staff from the PROs. Like the original Work Group, the new group could help the agency resolve any emerging issues related to implementation of the law. Current issues include specialists who refuse to serve on call panels and inconsistencies between State and Federal law governing emergency medical services.

AGENCY COMMENTS

We received written comments from HCFA on the draft report, which are included in the appendix. The HCFA concurred with our recommendations. The comments describe a dedicated HCFA effort to reduce backlogs, improve data collection, and increase coordination among the regions. The HCFA also offered several technical comments, which we have incorporated where appropriate.

APPENDIX

Agency Comments

DEPARTMENT OF HEALTH & HUMAN SERVICES

Health Care Financing Administration

Deputy Administrator
Washington, D.C. 20201

DATE: JAN 1 6 2001

TO: June Gibbs Brown
Inspector General

FROM: Robert A. Berenson, M.D. *Robert A. Berenson M.D.*
Acting Deputy Administrator

SUBJECT: Office of Inspector General (OIG) Draft Reports: "The Emergency Treatment and Labor Act: Survey of Hospital Emergency Departments," (OEI-09-98-00220) and "The Emergency Treatment and Labor Act: The Enforcement Process," (OEI-09-98-00221)

Thank you for the opportunity to comment on the above draft reports. The Health Care Financing Administration (HCFA) is absolutely committed to vigorously implementing the Emergency Medical Treatment and Labor Act (EMTALA). Our efforts are two-pronged: by providing clear guidance to hospitals about EMTALA requirements through effective outreach and education we try to prevent violations, while taking fair and timely action when EMTALA violations occur.

Enacted in 1986 in response to concerns that patients were being denied emergency care for financial reasons, EMTALA has played a critical role in ensuring that individuals with emergency medical conditions receive a medical screening and stabilization, or an appropriate transfer to another facility. Between 1986 and 1994, the number of complaints of EMTALA violations rose steadily from 3 (of which 2 were confirmed) to 1,851 (465 confirmed). In 1994, we published an interim final rule, clarifying the obligations of hospitals under EMTALA. Since then, the number of complaints has hovered between 300 and 500, with confirmed violations ranging between 180 and 210 per year.

While no violation is acceptable, we think the dramatic decline in number of complaints is a testimony to EMTALA's success in ensuring patient access to emergency care. At the same time, we are taking a number of steps to bolster our EMTALA efforts.

Between fiscal years 1996 and 2000, we received over 2,000 EMTALA complaints across the country. Of those, more than one-third were attributable to one HCFA region, which, as a result, developed a backlog of unresolved cases. We have been addressing this problem by increasing the number of staff devoted to processing backlogs and redistributing a portion of the complaints to other ROs for reviews. In the past 6 weeks, for example, we have processed 127 cases in this region, reducing the backlog by 29 percent. Based on this experience, we expect to eliminate the backlog of complaints within 4 to 6 months.

Page 2- June Gibbs Brown

Similarly, we have found a disproportionate number of complaints in one state. We are working in that state, through focused intervention such as outreach and training to hospitals, to avert future EMTALA violations.

For the longer term, we are stepping up communication and coordination of our prevention and enforcement activities. We are revising our State Operations Manual and our Interpretative Guidelines to provide clearer guidance to our Regional Offices and the State Agencies on investigating EMTALA complaints. We are also developing standardized forms and procedures for handling EMTALA complaints, and maintaining regular contact via conference call with our regions, so we can intervene more promptly when problems arise.

We also plan to issue a Notice of Proposed Rulemaking in the near future that will further clarify EMTALA requirements as they apply to a changing healthcare delivery system.

It is in this context that we view the OIG reports. We welcome the OIG's recommendations and look forward to working together to ensure that the statute is effectively and appropriately enforced.

We find the observations in the first report, *Survey of Hospital Emergency Departments*, to be largely consistent with our own assessments of EMTALA compliance issues based on our own interviews with hospital emergency departments. We agree with the conclusions of this report, and have submitted only the attached technical comments.

We also agree with the conclusions of the second report, *The Enforcement Process*, regarding needed changes in how HCFA responds to complaints of EMTALA violations. We are pleased to report that we have already made significant inroads in strengthening our processes for complaint investigation and resolution. We have reduced complaint backlogs, developed resource redeployment strategies to address the geographic variation in complaints received, and improved data reporting.

We appreciate the opportunity to comment on the issues raised. Detailed information on concrete steps we have taken or planned are contained in our responses to each recommendation below.

OIG Recommendation
The HCFA central office (CO) should increase its oversight of ROs.

HCFA Response
HCFA concurs that there should be greater communication and coordination between the CO and the regions, and has already taken steps to achieve this. For example, in May 1999, CO staff implemented an improved log reporting process to assist RO staff in reporting complaints to CO and changed the reporting cycle from quarterly to monthly. In addition, monthly conference

APPENDIX

Page 3- June Gibbs Brown

calls have been initiated to discuss EMTALA issues and clarify policies to promote consistent EMTALA enforcement across the regions.

Currently the State Operations Manual (SOM), rules, regulations, and interpretative guidelines are located on the HCFA website. The Center for Medicaid and State Operations is in the process of redesigning the website to establish clear and precise links to these documents. In addition, HCFA will review and examine the SOM policies and procedures concerning EMTALA enforcement and make revisions as appropriate.

In April 2000, a HCFA work group convened in Baltimore to begin revising the Interpretative Guidelines-Responsibilities of Medicare Participating Hospitals in Emergency Cases (Appendix V). The goal of this revision is to clarify national policies and to include in the SOM timeframes for HCFA to review State agencies' investigative findings. HCFA will monitor the status of these investigations and review activities and work closely with its regions to ensure that complaints are promptly and appropriately resolved.

OIG Recommendation
The HCFA should continue to improve collection and access to EMTALA data.

HCFA Response
EMTALA is a complaint-driven process requiring precise documentation to evaluate enforcement activity and assess the complaint investigation process. In 1999, HCFA took numerous steps to improve the timeliness and accuracy of reports of EMTALA allegations and investigations. Specifically, HCFA is now compiling reports monthly, rather than quarterly. The agency has also developed log instructions and a standardized log format to promote consistency of reporting among the regions. Although some advances in reporting have been made, HCFA will continue to work to identify other mechanisms to improve the reporting of EMTALA complaints.

We also expect that enhancements in a new survey and certification data system (Quality Improvement and Evaluation System or QIES) will address EMTALA enforcement issues, including more timely access and public disclosure of EMTALA findings.

OIG Recommendation
The HCFA should ensure that peer review occurs before initiating termination actions in cases involving medical judgment.

HCFA Response
HCFA generally agrees that prior to initiating termination actions in cases involving medical judgment, peer review of a physician's action should be performed by a physician (State agency consultant or Peer Review Organization (PRO)). HCFA is currently reviewing its hospital complaint investigation procedures, including handling of EMTALA complaints and will revise these policies as needed.

APPENDIX

Page 4- June Gibbs Brown

The group reviewing these procedures is also coordinating its efforts with HCFA's Office of Clinical Standards and Quality, which is reexamining the PROs role in responding to complaints.

OIG Recommendation
The HCFA should establish an EMTALA technical advisory group.

HCFA Response
In 1996-1997, HCFA met with a group of interested stakeholders from professional organizations and consumer advocate groups. The group discussed possible clarifications or changes to the statute, regulation, and interpretive guidelines for EMTALA, and HCFA has developed and implemented some of the recommendations raised by the various stakeholders.

HCFA agrees that continued consultation with stakeholders is necessary and that a more formal approach may be effective. We will work closely with the OIG and the Office of the General Counsel to determine the best strategy to ensure meaningful consultation.

Attachment

Appendix F

EMTALA Compliance Checklist

Initials/Date

1.0	Does the organization maintain on-campus and off-campus outpatient care areas that qualify as hospital departments under the outpatient PPS rule? *(If the answer is no, skip the entire Section G.)* (NOTE: EMTALA does not apply to doctors' offices, public health centers, day-surgery clinics, or any other facilities that are not on hospital property unless they regularly provide emergency services.)	Y	N	
2.0	Does the organization have policies, procedures and protocols that meet the requirements of the amended Emergency Medical Treatment and Active Labor Act (EMTALA)?	Y	N	
3.0	Screening requirements (on-campus and off-campus)			
	3.1 Does the organization provide an appropriate medical screening examination (MSE) to determine if an emergency medical condition exists or if the patient is in active labor?	Y	N	
	3.2 Are the screenings within the hospital's physical capabilities (all sophisticated imaging techniques as well as out-of-hospital specialists)?	Y	N	
	3.3 Are the screenings within the hospital's personnel capabilities (number and availability of qualified staff, open beds, and available equipment)?	Y	N	
	3.4 Do the policies and procedures ensure that qualified medical personnel perform MSEs?	Y	N	
	3.5 Do the screening policies and procedures include communication between outpatient departments and the main hospital?	Y	N	

_____

_____

_____

_____

Initials/Date

3.6		Are the results of the MSE recorded on a screening examination form that becomes a part of the patient's permanent medical record?	Y	N	
		Does the MSE include the following elements?			
	a.	Assessment of chief symptom?	Y	N	
	b.	Vital signs?	Y	N	
	c.	Mental state?	Y	N	
	d.	General appearance?	Y	N	
	e.	Degree of pain?	Y	N	
	f.	Skin?	Y	N	
	g.	Focused physical examination results?	Y	N	
	h.	Ability to walk?	Y	N	
	i.	Pregnancy/near term?	Y	N	
3.7		Is the MSE performed uniformly on all patients who come to the emergency department requesting medical care?	Y	N	
3.8		Are staff members instructed not to ask patients to complete a financial responsibility form or advanced beneficiary notification form before screening?	Y	N	
3.9		Are staff members instructed on criteria for seeking payment authorization, including who may do so and when?	Y	N	

_____

_____

_____

_____

Initials/Date

	3.10	Are patients clearly informed that, notwithstanding their ability to pay, the hospital is willing to provide a medical screening examination and stabilizing treatment?	Y	N	
	3.11	Does the facility utilize a "Refusal to be Medically Screened" form rather than an "Against Medical Advice" form for patients who refuse the MSE?	Y	N	
	3.12	Are the MSEs performed by "qualified" individuals (as identified by hospital bylaws or rules and regulations)?	Y	N	
	3.13	Do the screening policies include MSE requirements for psychiatric patients?	Y	N	
4.0	Stabilization				
	4.1	Do the policies and procedures require that patients be provided such medical treatment to assure that no material deterioration of the condition is likely to result from or occur during transfer?	Y	N	
	4.2	Do the policies and procedures require that a woman in labor be considered stable only if contractions stop, the baby and placenta are delivered, or a physician certifies that the labor is false?	Y	N	
	4.3	Do the policies and procedures require that a psychiatric patient be considered stable when he or she is protected and prevented from injuring himself or herself or others?	Y	N	
	4.4	Do the policies and procedures require documentation of the means used to stabilize a psychiatric patient (medical treatment, physical means)?	Y	N	
5.0	Discharge				
	5.1	Do the policies and procedures require a proper plan for reevaluation at a later time for patients who are "stable for discharge"?	Y	N	

						Initials/Date
	5.2	Do the policies and procedures require that psychiatric patients be considered stable for discharge if they are no longer a threat to themselves or to others?		Y	N	
6.0	Transfer					
	6.1	Do the policies and procedures include requirements for any movement of the patient to leave the hospital system (ambulance, discharge, referral, or leaving on his or her own)?		Y	N	
	6.2	Do the policies and procedures include conditions for transferring a patient who is not stable?		Y	N	
		Do the conditions include:				
		a.	Written request by the individual for transfer to another facility?	Y	N	
		b.	Physician certification that the medical benefits at another medical facility outweigh the increased risks of transfer?	Y	N	
		c.	Certification by a qualified medical person after consultation with a physician (who subsequently countersigns the certification)?	Y	N	
		d.	Provision of medical treatment to minimize the risk to the individual or unborn child?	Y	N	
		e.	Available space and qualified personnel at the receiving facility?	Y	N	
		f.	Transfer of all medical records to the receiving facility?	Y	N	
		g.	Qualified transportation equipment and personnel?	Y	N	

Initials/Date

	6.3	Does the facility maintain transfer certificates for all unstabilized transfers?		Y	N	
		Does the transfer certificate include the following components?				
		a.	Patient condition?	Y	N	
		b.	Benefits of transfer?	Y	N	
		c.	Risks of transfer?	Y	N	
		d.	Receiving hospital?	Y	N	
		e.	Mode of transportation?	Y	N	
		f.	Patient consent?	Y	N	
		g.	Transferring physician certification?	Y	N	
	6.4	Has the facility established policies and procedures for transfer agreements with outside facilities?		Y	N	
7.0	Recordkeeping					
	7.1	Do the policies and procedures include the EMTALA recordkeeping requirements?		Y	N	
		Do the recordkeeping requirements include:				
		a.	Maintenance of a list of on-call physicians? *(NOTE: Physicians whose names appear on the on-call list are responsible for finding a suitable replacement if they cannot be available for duty and for updating the on-call list with the replacement physician's name and other appropriate information.)*	Y	N	
		b.	Posting signs informing the public of the hospital's EMTALA obligations?	Y	N	

Initials/Date

	c.	Maintenance of records of persons transferred to or from the hospital?	Y	N	
	d.	Maintenance of records related to individuals transferred for a period of five years?	Y	N	
	e.	Maintenance of a central log on each and every individual who comes to the hospital seeking assistance?	Y	N	
7.2		Are medical records maintained on every patient seeking care for a potential emergency condition?	Y	N	
		Do the records include the following, where applicable?			
	a.	Record of the medical screening examination?	Y	N	
	b.	Notation that the patient was stable for discharge or transfer, if applicable?	Y	N	
	c.	Record of any communications with the main hospital, other outpatient departments, or other facilities?	Y	N	
	d.	Record of the discussion of risks and benefits of transfer?	Y	N	
	e.	Record of refusal of treatment with documentation of explanatory details?	Y	N	
	f.	Record of the transfer consent or certification, including a notation of physician consultation (where not certified by a physician)?	Y	N	
	g.	Copy of records accompanying a transfer and details of all records to be sent to the receiving hospital?	Y	N	
	h.	Record documenting the failure of on-call physicians to provide medical care?	Y	N	

Initials/Date

8.0	Has the organization posted a conspicuous sign that specifies the rights of individuals under EMTALA?	Y	N	
	8.1 Does the sign include the following elements?			
	a. Specifies the rights of the individuals with emergency conditions and women in labor?	Y	N	
	b. Indicates whether the facility participates in the Medicaid program?	Y	N	
	c. Is clear and expressed in simple terms and language understandable by the population served by the hospital?	Y	N	
	d. Is posted in a place or places likely to be noticed by all individuals entering the emergency department, as well as those individuals waiting for examination and treatment?	Y	N	

_____

_____

_____

_____

_____

_____

_____

_____

Signature of Auditor	Initials/Date	Signature of Auditor	Initials/Date
Signature of Auditor	Initials/Date	Signature of Auditor	Initials/Date

Appendix G

Applicability of EMTALA to Hospital Inpatients and Hospitals with Specialized Capabilities (77 Fed. Reg. 5213-5217 (Feb. 2, 2012))

DEPARTMENT OF HEALTH AND HUMAN SERVICES

Centers for Medicare & Medicaid

Services

42 CFR Part 489

[CMS–1350–NC]

RIN 0938–AQ51

Medicare Program; Emergency Medical Treatment and Labor Act (EMTALA):

Applicability to Hospital Inpatients and Hospitals With Specialized Capabilities AGENCY: Centers for Medicare & Medicaid Services (CMS), HHS.

ACTION: Request for comments.

SUMMARY: This request for comments addresses the applicability of the Emergency Medical Treatment and Labor Act (EMTALA) to hospital inpatients.

DATES: *Comment Date:* To be assured consideration, comments on the Applicability of EMTALA to Hospitals with Specialized Capabilities (section II.B. of this document) must be received at one of the addresses provided below,no later than 5 p.m. EST on April 2, 2012.

ADDRESSES: In commenting, please refer to file code CMS–1350–NC. Because of staff and resource limitations, we cannot accept comments by facsimile (FAX) transmission.

You may submit comments in one of four ways (please choose only one of the ways listed):

1. *Electronically.* You may submit electronic comments on this regulation to *http://www.regulations.gov.* Follow the "Submit a comment" instructions.

2. *By regular mail.* You may mail written comments to the following address ONLY: Centers for Medicare & Medicaid Services, Department of Health and Human Services, Attention:

   CMS–1350–NC, P.O. Box 8013, Baltimore, MD 21244–8013.

   Please allow sufficient time for mailed comments to be received before the close of the comment period.

3. *By express or overnight mail.* You may send written comments to the following address ONLY: Centers for Medicare & Medicaid Services, Department of Health and Human Services, Attention: CMS–1350–NC, Mail Stop C4–26–05, 7500 Security Boulevard, Baltimore, MD 21244–1850.

4. *By hand or courier.* If you prefer, you may deliver (by hand or courier) your written comments before the close of the comment period to either of the following addresses:

   a. For delivery in Washington, DC—Centers for Medicare & Medicaid Services, Department of Health and Human Services, Room 445–G, Hubert H. Humphrey Building, 200 Independence Avenue SW., Washington, DC 20201 (Because access to the interior of the Hubert H. Humphrey Building is not readily available to persons without Federal government identification, commenters are encouraged to leave their comments in the CMS drop slots located in the main lobby of the building. A stamp-in clock is available for persons wishing to retain a proof of filing by stamping in and retaining an extra copy of the comments being filed.)

   b. For delivery in Baltimore, MD—Centers for Medicare & Medicaid Services, Department of Health and Human Services, 7500 Security Boulevard, Baltimore, MD 21244–1850. If you intend to deliver your comments to the Baltimore address, please call telephone number (410) 786–1066 in advance to schedule your arrival with one of our staff members. Comments mailed to the addresses indicated as appropriate for hand or courier delivery may be delayed and received after the comment period. For information on viewing public comments, see the beginning of the **SUPPLEMENTARY INFORMATION** section. **FOR FURTHER INFORMATION CONTACT:** Renate Dombrowski, (410) 786–4645, Ankit Patel, (410) 786–4537.

SUPPLEMENTARY INFORMATION:

Inspection of Public Comments: All comments received before the close of the comment period are available for viewing by the public, including any personally identifiable or confidential business information that is included in a comment. We post all comments received before the close of the comment period on the following Web site as soon as possible after they have been received: *http://www.regulations.gov.* Follow the search instructions on that Web site to view public comments. Comments received timely will also be available for public inspection as they are received, generally beginning approximately 3 weeks after publication of a document, at the headquarters of the Centers for Medicare & Medicaid Services, 7500 Security Boulevard, Baltimore, Maryland 21244, Monday through Friday of each week from 8:30 a.m. to 4 p.m. To schedule an appointment to view public comments, phone 1–800–743–3951.

I. Background

Sections 1866(a)(1)(I), 1866(a)(1)(N), and 1867 of the Social Security Act (the Act) were enacted as parts of the Emergency Medical Treatment and Labor Act (EMTALA). These statutory provisions impose specific obligations on certain Medicare-participating hospitals and critical access hospitals (CAHs). (Throughout this document, when we reference the obligation of a "hospital" under these sections of the Act and in our regulations, we mean to include CAHs as well.) These obligations concern individuals who come to a hospital's "dedicated emergency department" (as defined at 42 CFR 489.24(b)) and request examination or treatment for a medical condition and apply to all of these individuals regardless of whether they are beneficiaries of any program under the Act.

EMTALA, also known as the patient antidumping statute, was passed in 1986 as part of the Consolidated Omnibus Budget Reconciliation Act of 1985 (COBRA), Public Law 99–272. Congress incorporated these antidumping provisions within the Social Security Act to ensure that any individual with an emergency medical condition (EMC), regardless of the individual's insurance coverage, is not denied essential lifesaving services. Under section 1866(a)(1)(I)(i) of the Act, a hospital that fails to fulfill its EMTALA obligations under these provisions may be subject to termination of its Medicare provider agreement which would result in the loss of Medicare and Medicaid payments. In addition, section 1867(d) of the Act provides for the imposition of civil monetary penalties on a hospital or physician who negligently violates a requirement of EMTALA under section 1867 of the Act. Section 1867 of the Act sets forth requirements for medical screening examinations for individuals who come to the emergency department of a hospital and request examination or treatment for a medical condition. The statute further provides that, if a hospital finds that such an individual has an EMC, it is obligated to provide that individual with either necessary stabilizing treatment or an appropriate transfer to another medical facility where stabilization can occur. The EMTALA statute also separately outlines the obligation of hospitals to receive appropriate transfers from other hospitals.

Section 1867(g) of the Act states that "A participating hospital that has specialized capabilities or facilities (such as burn units, shock-trauma units, neonatal intensive care units, or (with respect to rural areas) regional referral centers as identified by the Secretary in regulation) shall not refuse to accept an appropriate transfer of an individual who requires such specialized capabilities or facilities if the hospital has the capacity to treat the individual." The regulations implementing section 1867 of the Act are found at 42 CFR 489.24. The regulations at 42 CFR 489.20(l), (m), (q), and (r) also refer to certain EMTALA requirements outlined in section 1866 of the Act. The Interpretive Guidelines concerning EMTALA are found at Appendix V of the CMS State Operations Manual: *http://www.cms.gov/manuals/ Downloads/som107ap_v_emerg.pdf.*

A. Applicability of EMTALA to Hospital Inpatients

The focus of EMTALA routinely involves the treatment of individuals who "come to the emergency department," as we have defined that term at 42 CFR 489.24(b); that is, the individual is in a hospital-owned and operated ambulance or "has presented at a hospital's dedicated emergency department * * * and requests examination or treatment for a medical condition, or has such a request made on his or her behalf [or] [h]as presented on hospital property * * * other than the dedicated emergency department, and requests examination or treatment for what may be an emergency medical condition, or has such a request made on his or her behalf."

However, concerns have also arisen about the continuing applicability of EMTALA to hospital inpatients. We have previously discussed the applicability of EMTALA to hospital inpatients in the May 9, 2002 (67 FR 31475) Hospital Inpatient Prospective Payment System (IPPS) proposed rule entitled "Medicare Program; Changes to the Hospital Inpatient Prospective Payment Systems and Fiscal Year 2003 Rates" (hereinafter referred to as the FY 2003 IPPS proposed rule) and the September 9, 2003 (68 FR 53243) standalone final rule on EMTALA entitled "Medicare Program; Clarifying Policies Related to the Responsibilities of Medicare-Participating Hospitals in Treating Individuals With Emergency Medical Conditions" (hereinafter referred to as the 2003 EMTALA final rule). As we noted in these prior proposed and final rules, in 1999, the United States Supreme Court considered a case (*Roberts* v. *Galen of Virginia,* 525 U.S. 249 (1999)) that involved, in part, the question of whether EMTALA applies to hospital inpatients. In the context of that case, the United States Solicitor General advised the Court that HHS would develop a regulation clarifying its position on this issue. In the FY 2003 IPPS proposed rule, we proposed that EMTALA continues to apply to admitted individuals who are not stabilized (who presented under EMTALA), but that it would not otherwise apply to inpatients. We indicated that individuals whose conditions go in and out of apparent stability rapidly and frequently would not be considered "stabilized" and the hospital would continue to have an obligation to such individuals even after they are admitted. However, for all other inpatients we stated that EMTALA was intended to provide protection to individuals coming to a hospital to seek care for an EMC. Therefore, we stated that we believe the EMTALA requirements do not extend to stabilized inpatients even if they subsequently become unstable because those inpatients are protected by a number of Medicare conditions of participation (CoPs) as well as the hospital's other legal, licensing, and professional obligations with respect to the continued proper care and treatment of its patients.

In the 2003 EMTALA final rule, we refined this position to state that a hospital's obligation under EMTALA ends either when the individual is stabilized or when that hospital, in good faith, admits an individual with an EMC as an inpatient in order to provide stabilizing treatment. That is, we stated that EMTALA does not apply to any inpatient, even one who was admitted through the dedicated emergency department and for whom the hospital had initially incurred an EMTALA obligation to stabilize an EMC, and who remained unstabilized after admission as an inpatient. We noted that other patient safeguards protect all inpatients, including the hospital CoPs as well as State malpractice law. In addition, we noted that judicial interpretation of the matter and comments we received on the proposed rule helped shape the policy articulated in the final rule. However, we also stated in the rule that a hospital could not escape liability under EMTALA by admitting an individual with no intention of treating the individual and then inappropriately transferring or discharging that individual without having met the stabilization requirement.

B. EMTALA Technical Advisory Group Recommendation Regarding Responsibilities of Hospitals With Specialized Capabilities

Section 945 of the Medicare Prescription Drug, Improvement, and Modernization Act of 2003 (MMA), Public Law 108–173, required the Secretary to establish a Technical Advisory Group (TAG) to advise the Secretary on issues related to the regulations and implementation of EMTALA. The EMTALA TAG's functions, as identified in the charter for the EMTALA TAG, were as follows:

- Review EMTALA regulations.
- Provide advice and recommendations to the Secretary concerning these regulations and their application to hospitals and physicians.
- Solicit comments and recommendations from hospitals, physicians, and the public regarding the implementation of such regulations.
- Disseminate information concerning the application of these regulations to hospitals, physicians, and the public.

The TAG met 7 times during its 30- month term, which ended on September 30, 2007. At its meetings, the TAG heard testimony from representatives of physician groups, hospital associations, and others regarding EMTALA issues and concerns. During each meeting, recommendations developed by subcommittees established by the TAG were discussed and voted on by members of the TAG.

One of these recommendations, presented by the TAG to CMS during its September 2007 meeting, called for CMS to revise its regulations to address the situation of an individual who: (1) Presents to a hospital that has a dedicated emergency department and is determined to have an EMC; (2) is admitted to the hospital as an inpatient for purposes of stabilizing the EMC; and (3) subsequently needs a transfer to a hospital with specialized capabilities to receive stabilizing treatment that cannot be provided by the referring hospital that originally admitted the individual. This recommendation can be found at the following Web site: *http:// www.cms.gov/EMTALA/Downloads/ EMTALA_Final_Report_Summary.pdf.*

C. Applicability of EMTALA to Hospital Inpatients and Responsibilities of Hospitals With Specialized Capabilities

To further clarify our position on the applicability of EMTALA and the responsibilities of hospitals with specialized capabilities to accept appropriate transfers, the agency included as part of the April 30, 2008 Hospital IPPS proposed rule (73 FR 23669) entitled, "Medicare Program; Proposed Changes to the Hospital Inpatient Prospective Payment Systems and Fiscal Year 2009 Rates; Proposed Changes to Disclosure of Physician Ownership in Hospitals and Physician Self-Referral Rules; Proposed Collection of Information Regarding Financial Relationships Between Hospitals and Physicians" (hereinafter referred to as the FY 2009 IPPS proposed rule), two proposals that addressed the issue of hospital inpatients. First, we stated that we believe that the obligation of EMTALA does not end for all hospitals once an individual is admitted as an inpatient to the hospital where the individual first presented with a medical condition that was determined to be an EMC. Rather, once the individual is admitted, the admission only affects the EMTALA obligation of the hospital where the individual first presented (the admitting hospital). In the FY 2009 IPPS proposed rule (73 FR 23670), we stated that section 1867(g) of the Act (which refers to responsibilities of hospitals with specialized capabilities) * * * requires a receiving hospital with specialized capabilities to accept a request to transfer an individual with an unstable emergency medical condition as long as the hospital has the capacity to treat that individual, regardless of whether the individual had been an inpatient at the admitting hospital.

We stated that we believe that permitting inpatient admission at the admitting hospital to end EMTALA obligations for another hospital would seemingly contradict the intent of section 1867(g) of the Act to ensure that hospitals with specialized capabilities provide medical treatment to individuals with EMCs in order to stabilize those conditions. We further noted that while a hospital inpatient is protected under Medicare CoPs and may also have additional protections under State law, the obligations of another hospital under the CoPs apply only to that hospital's patients, and there is no CoP that requires a hospital to accept the transfer of a patient from another facility. We proposed to interpret section 1867(g) of the Act as creating an obligation on hospitals with specialized capabilities to accept appropriate transfers of individuals for whom the admitting hospital originally had an EMTALA obligation under section 1867 of the Act, if the hospital with specialized capabilities has the capacity to treat the individuals. Thus, in the FY 2009 IPPS proposed rule (73 FR 23670), we proposed to amend the regulations * * * to add a provision to state that when an individual covered by EMTALA was admitted as an inpatient and remains unstabilized with an emergency medical condition, a receiving hospital with specialized capabilities has an EMTALA obligation to accept that individual, assuming that the transfer of the individual is an appropriate transfer and the participating hospital with specialized capabilities has the capacity to treat the individual.

We received many comments opposing the proposal concerning hospitals with specialized capabilities included in the FY 2009 IPPS proposed rule. The commenters stated that the proposed rule would effectively "reopen" EMTALA for the admitting hospital by extending EMTALA's requirements for an "appropriate transfer" despite the fact that the admitting hospital's general EMTALA obligations ended, under regulation, when it admitted an individual as an inpatient. The commenters also stated that, because the original admitting hospital may claim that it lacks the capability to stabilize the individual's EMC, finalizing the proposed policy would result in an increase in patient dumping and inappropriate transfers, especially to teaching hospitals, tertiary care centers, and urban safety net hospitals. Commenters further asserted that finalizing CMS' policy as proposed would exacerbate confusion surrounding the determination of whether an individual is considered stable. That is, the hospital would be required to continuously monitor the individual to determine if at any point in the emergency department or even as an inpatient, the individual experienced a period of stability since such stability would end EMTALA obligations for all hospitals that might otherwise have obligations under the law. Under this scenario, the commenters asserted that the hospital with specialized capabilities would be forced to accept the transfer of an individual, potentially increasing the number of inappropriate or unnecessary transfers, because that hospital would be unable, with complete certainty, to determine whether the individual being transferred had ever experienced a period of stability.

As a result, in the August 19, 2008 IPPS final rule (73 FR 48659) entitled, "Medicare Program; Changes to the Hospital Inpatient Prospective Payment Systems and Fiscal Year 2009 Rates; Payments for Graduate Medical Education in Certain Emergency Situations; Changes to Disclosure of Physician Ownership in Hospitals and Physician Self-Referral Rules; Updates to the Long-Term Care Prospective Payment System; Updates to Certain IPPS-Excluded Hospitals; and Collection of Information Regarding Financial Relationships Between Hospitals" (hereinafter referred to as the FY 2009 IPPS final rule) we stated that,

> Due to the many concerns that the commenters raised which are noted above, we believe it is appropriate to finalize a policy to state that if an individual with an unstable emergency medical condition is admitted, the EMTALA obligation has ended for the admitting hospital and even if the individual's emergency medical condition remains unstabilized and the individual requires special services only available at another hospital, the hospital with specialized capabilities does not have an EMTALA obligation to accept an appropriate transfer of that individual.

Put another way, we finalized a policy that a hospital with specialized capabilities does not have an EMTALA obligation to accept an appropriate transfer of an individual who has been admitted in good faith as an inpatient at the first hospital. In the FY 2009 IPPS final rule (73 FR 48659), we stated that we believe that,

> * * * finalizing the policy as proposed may negatively impact patient care, due to an increase in inappropriate transfers which could be detrimental to the physical and psychological health and well-being of patients [and we were] concerned that finalizing our proposed rule could further burden the emergency services system and may force hospitals providing emergency care to limit their services or close, reducing access to emergency care.

In addition, we stated that we were concerned about the possible disparate treatment of inpatients under the proposed policy because an individual who presented to a hospital under EMTALA might have different transfer rights than an inpatient who was admitted for an elective procedure. In the FY 2009 IPPS final rule (73 FR 48659) we stated—

> [W]e believe that, in the case where an individual is admitted and later found to be in need of specialized care not available at the admitting hospital, hospitals with specialized capabilities generally do accept the transfer, even in the absence of a legal requirement to do so.

Finally, while we adopted a final rule that limits the EMTALA responsibilities of a hospital with specialized capabilities (73 FR 48661), we

> * * * encourage[d] the public to make CMS aware if this interpretation of section 1867(g) of the Act should result in harmful refusals by hospitals with specialized capabilities to accept the transfer of inpatients whose emergency medical condition remains unstabilized, or any other unintended consequences.

D. Litigation Related to the Applicability of EMTALA to Hospital Inpatients

We are aware that there continues to be a range of opinions, even at the Federal circuit court level, on the topic of EMTALA's application to inpatients. For example, in *Thornton* v. *Southwest Detroit Hospital*, 895 F.2d 1131, 1134 (6th Cir. 1990), the Sixth Circuit stated that, "once a patient is found to suffer from an [EMC] in the emergency room, she cannot be discharged until the condition is stabilized * * *." However, other courts have concluded that a hospital's obligations under EMTALA end at the time that a hospital admits an individual to the facility as an inpatient. (See *Bryan* v. *Rectors and Visitors of the University of Virginia*, 95 F.3d 349 (4th Cir. 1996) and *Bryant* v. *Adventist Health System/ West*, 289 F.3d 1162 (9th Cir. 2002)). More recently, in *Moses* v. *Providence Hospital and Medical Centers Inc.*, 561 F.3d 573 (6th Cir. 2009), the Sixth noted that the policy articulated in the 2003 EMTALA final rule that a hospital's obligation under EMTALA would end when that hospital, in good faith, admits an individual with an EMC as an inpatient was contrary to the plain language of the

EMTALA statute. Rather, the court stated that a hospital's EMTALA obligations to an individual continue until that individual's EMC is stabilized regardless of the individual's status as an inpatient or outpatient.

E. Advance Notice of Proposed Rulemaking: Applicability of EMTALA to Hospital Inpatients and Hospitals With Specialized Capabilities

In 2010, United States Solicitor General advised the Supreme Court that HHS had committed to initiating a rulemaking process to reconsider the policy articulated in its current regulations, which state that a hospital's EMTALA obligations end upon the good faith admission as an inpatient of an individual with an EMC. In the December 23, 2010 **Federal Register** (75 FR 80762), we published an advance notice of proposed rulemaking (ANPRM) entitled "Medicare Program; Emergency Medical Treatment and Labor Act: Applicability to Hospital and Critical Access Hospital Inpatients and Hospitals With Specialized Capabilities" to solicit comments regarding whether we should revisit the policies established in the 2003 EMTALA final rule and the FY 2009 IPPS final rule. In addition, we sought real world examples that would inform our understanding of the current policy's impact on patients' access to care for an EMC. We noted that we would find it particularly helpful whether commenters could submit specific real-world examples that demonstrate if it would be beneficial to revisit these policies. We stated (75 FR 80765) that we—

> * * * are interested in hearing whether commenters are aware of situations where an individual who presented under EMTALA with an unstable EMC was admitted to the hospital where he or she first presented and was then transferred to another facility, even though the admitting hospital had the capacity and capability to treat that individual's EMC.

We further stated (75 FR 80765) that we were "* * * interested in receiving information regarding the accuracy of our statement in the August 19, 2008 IPPS final rule that a hospital with specialized capabilities would accept the transfer of an inpatient with an unstabilized EMC absent an EMTALA obligation." Lastly, we stated (75 FR 80765) that we were interested in learning whether commenters were "* * * aware of situations where an individual with an unstabilized EMC was admitted as an inpatient and continued to have an unstabilized EMC requiring the services of a hospital with specialized capabilities that refused to accept the transfer of the individual because current policy does not obligate hospitals with specialized capabilities to do so."

II. Provisions of the Request for Comments

A. Applicability of EMTALA to Hospital Inpatients

In the 2003 EMTALA final rule, we took the position that a hospital's obligation under EMTALA ends when that hospital, in good faith, admits an individual with an unstable emergency medical condition as an inpatient to that hospital. In that rule, we noted that other patient safeguards including the CoPs as well as State malpractice law protect inpatients. In response to our request for comments in the ANPRM as to whether we should revisit the policies that were established in the 2003 EMTALA final rule, very few commenters took the position that the admitting hospital should continue to have an EMTALA obligation after the individual is admitted as an inpatient. While some commenters advocated extending EMTALA to inpatients who do not experience a period of stability, the commenters did not provide any evidence that the existing policy has resulted in patients being admitted and then subsequently discharged before they were stable, adversely affecting the clinical outcome of those patients. Most commenters expressed support for the current policy that EMTALA does not apply to any inpatient of a hospital, even a patient who was admitted through that hospital's dedicated emergency department and continues to be unstable. These commenters referred to our 2003 EMTALA final rule and concurred with our assessment that, under our existing policy, the numerous hospital CoPs that protect inpatients as well as inpatients' rights under State law afford individuals admitted to a hospital with sufficient protection. Moreover, commenters appreciated the clarity and predictability of a bright line policy. Commenters also noted that our current policy regarding inpatients is achieving Congress' intent by ensuring that every individual, regardless of their ability to pay for emergency services, should have access to hospital services provided in hospitals with emergency departments.

Therefore, in light of the comments we received regarding the extension of the EMTALA obligations for hospitals admitting an individual through their dedicated emergency departments, we are not proposing to change the current EMTALA requirements for these hospitals. That is, we are maintaining our current policy that, if an individual "comes to the [hospital's] emergency department," as we have defined that term in regulation, and the hospital provides an appropriate medical screening examination and determines that an EMC exists, and then admits the individual in good faith in order to stabilize the EMC, that hospital has satisfied its EMTALA obligation towards that patient. We continue to believe that this policy is a reasonable interpretation of the EMTALA statute and is supported by several Federal courts that have held that an individual's EMTALA protections end upon admission as a hospital inpatient. For further explanation, we refer readers to the 2003 EMTALA final rule (68 FR 53244), in which we finalized the policy that a hospital's EMTALA obligations end upon admission.

B. Applicability of EMTALA to Hospitals With Specialized Capabilities

The second issue upon which the ANPRM solicited comment was, whether EMTALA should apply to situations where a hospital seeks to transfer an individual, who was admitted by that hospital as an inpatient after coming to the hospital's dedicated emergency department with an EMC, to a hospital with specialized capabilities because the admitted inpatient continues to have an unstabilized EMC that requires specialized treatment not available at the admitting hospital. Under current regulations, if an individual comes to the hospital's dedicated emergency department, is determined to have an EMC, is admitted as an inpatient, and continues to have an unstabilized EMC which requires the specialized capabilities of another hospital, the EMTALA obligation for the admitting hospital has ended and a hospital with specialized capabilities also does not have an EMTALA obligation towards that individual.

Although we received some comments that supported amending the current regulations to require hospitals with specialized capabilities to accept the appropriate transfer of an inpatient who had presented to the admitting hospital under EMTALA and requires specialized capabilities to stabilize his or her EMC not available at the admitting hospital, most comments supported making no change to the current policies regarding the applicability of EMTALA to hospitals with specialized capabilities.

Therefore, at this time, we are making no proposals with respect to our policies regarding the applicability of EMTALA to hospitals with specialized capabilities. However, we will continue to monitor whether it may be appropriate in the future to reconsider this issue. Thus, we are providing a 60- day comment period to allow the public to submit data or real world examples that are relevant to this issue.

III. Response to Comments

Because of the large number of public comments we normally receive on **Federal Register** documents, we are not able to acknowledge or respond to them individually. We will consider all comments we receive by the date and time specified in the **DATES** section of this preamble. If we proceed to issue a subsequent document on the issues raised therein, we will respond to those comments in the preamble to that document.

(Catalog of Federal Domestic Assistance Program No. 93.773, Medicare— Hospital Insurance; and Program No. 93.774)

Dated: January 9, 2012.

Marilyn Tavenner,

Acting Administrator, Centers for Medicare & Medicaid Services.

Approved: January 26, 2012.

Kathleen Sebelius,

Secretary, Department of Health and Human Services.

[FR Doc. 2012–2287 Filed 1–31–12; 4:15 pm]

Appendix H

The Legislative History of EMTALA

Eugene Barnes's tragic death in California's emergency medical system triggered a series of events that ultimately led to the congressional passage of the Emergency Medical Treatment and Active Labor Act (EMTALA).

On January 28, 1985, Eugene "Red" Barnes sustained a gaping stab wound to the side of his head during an altercation. An ambulance rushed Barnes to Brookside Hospital in San Pablo, California. The emergency physician at Brookside obtained a CT scan, which showed an intracranial injury that required immediate emergency surgical intervention by a neurosurgeon. However, the neurosurgeon who was on call for Brookside refused to come to the hospital. A second Brookside staff neurosurgeon refused to assume care because he was not on call. Brookside's emergency physician desperately tried to transfer Barnes to an area hospital that would provide the critical surgery. Attempts to transfer Barnes to Contra Costa County Hospital in Martinez as well as Alameda County's Highland General Hospital were unsuccessful. San Francisco General Hospital finally agreed to accept Barnes in transfer. Barnes had spent four hours in Brookside's emergency department before being transferred to San Francisco General. Despite immediate surgery, Barnes died three days later.[1]

The United States mass media communicated the tragic story of Barnes's death to the country. First, local television and radio stations broadcast the story with critical editorial comments. Local newspapers such as the *San Francisco Chronicle, Contra Costa Times,* and the *Oakland Tribune* continued to provide extensive coverage. The story reached national attention when Dan Rather reported on the case on the "CBS Nightly News."[2] Other cases came to light as the national press dug up more incidents. The *Los Angeles Times* reported that a man who had alcoholism, anemia, and pneumonia died during transfer in an ambulance after being declared "stable" by the transferring hospital.[3] The *New*

---

[1] *See* Robert A. Bitterman, *Providing Emergency Care Under Federal Law: EMTALA,* Am. College of Emergency Physicians (2000), 7.

[2] Robert A. Bitterman, *Providing Emergency Care Under Federal Law: EMTALA,* Am. College of Emergency Physicians (2000), 7.

[3] *Hospital Dumping of Poor, Lawmakers Seek Cure,* Los Angeles Times, Apr. 7, 1986, at 3.

York Times reported that a woman arrived unannounced at Cook County Hospital clutching a note written by a doctor stating: "Please assume medical care of Mrs. Smith. She is no longer eligible for medical assistance and cannot afford to see me."[4] The *Washington Post* related the story of a man with third-degree grease burns who was turned away from three hospitals because he was unable to pay deposits. Finally arriving at a public hospital seven hours later, he was carrying an IV bottle that had been attached as a precaution at one of the private hospitals.[5] The CBS news magazine "60 Minutes" ran a segment showing the treatment of three "dumped" patients at Parkland Memorial Hospital in Dallas.

Congress responded to the resulting public outcry by initiating brief hearings on this practice that came to be termed "dumping." Dumping refers to transferring patients from one hospital to another before they are stabilized, refusing to treat patients, or delaying care to patients because the patients are indigent or do not possess insurance coverage.[6] Such patients are "dumped" back onto the streets or transferred in an unstable and dangerous medical condition to a public charity hospital.[7] A House of Representatives subcommittee investigating patient dumping reported further incidents of it:

> Sharon Ford went to the Brookside Hospital's emergency department in active labor. She was transferred to Samuel Merritt Hospital in Oakland because she was a member of a Medicaid HMO that had a contract with Merritt rather than Brookside. However, the HMO was late in adding Ford's name to the eligibility list. Because of this, Merritt Hospital transferred Ford to Highland General Hospital, Oakland's county hospital. Shortly after arrival at Highland, Ford delivered a stillborn baby. This case was the reason EMTALA specifically covers "active labor" as an emergency medical condition. William Jenness was taken to a private hospital after a car accident in Stanislaus County. The hospital asked for a $1,000 deposit in advance because he was uninsured. Because Jenness couldn't pay, he was transferred to the county hospital, where it took four hours before he reached the operating room. Six hours after the accident, Jenness died. In labor and uninsured, Anna Grant went to a private hospital, where she was kept in a wheelchair in the lobby for two hours and 15 minutes. She was checked only once, and no tests were done, although tests would have shown that her fetus was in profound distress. She was told to "get herself" to the county hospital. The transferring hospital misrepresented her condition to the county hospital by phone. The baby was later stillborn at the county hospital. David Rios was critically wounded with two gunshot wounds and was brought to a private hospital in Ventura County. Because he was uninsured, he was transferred to the county hospital, arriving one hour and 15 minutes

---

[4] *Private Hospital's Dumping of Patients*, N.Y. Times, Oct. 28, 1985, at A19.

[5] *Ailing Uninsured and Turned Away Americans without Health Coverage Finding Hospitals Doors Closed*, Wash. Post, June 30, 1985, at A1.

[6] H.R. Rep. No. 100-531, 2d Sess. 2-3 (1988).

[7] *See* H.R. Rep. No. 99-241, pt. 2, at 27 (1986).

later in a medically unstable condition and in shock. He died later that night.[8]

Significantly, even medicine's own publications published studies on the problem of patient dumping. Drs. Robert L. Schiff and David A. Ansell reported in the *Journal of the American Medical Association* that one Chicago hospital placed a yellow sticker on the front of charts of patients not covered by private insurance or Medicaid as a reminder to avoid admitting them.[9] Drs. Schiff and Ansell also reported in the *New England Journal of Medicine* that of 430 patients transferred to Cook County Hospital, 46 percent had no insurance, 46 percent received aid from the Illinois Department of Public Aid, 3 percent had Medicare coverage, and only 4 percent had private insurance.

Dr. Ansell described the condition of some of the patients transferred to Cook County Hospital during the fourth three-day period of the study. They included a 36-year-old man who had had a stroke and had severe hypertension; a shooting victim with a neck wound that was bleeding profusely from a major artery; a 41-year-old man with gunshot wounds to his head, chest, and abdomen who was in a coma and on a respirator; an unconscious woman with a suspected drug overdose; a patient who had fallen from a third-floor window; a 40-year-old woman with meningitis; and a woman with heart failure who was experiencing shortness of breath and severe hypertension.[10]

Congress responded by initiating the process of passing legislation in order to address this perceived crisis in patient care. Representative Fortney "Pete" Stark (D-Ca.), the U.S. Representative from Oakland and chairman of the Subcommittee on Health of the House Ways and Means Committee, introduced the original bill in the House of Representatives. Senator Edward M. Kennedy (D-Mass.) introduced a companion bill in the Senate. Discussions in Congress clearly show that EMTALA was created as antidiscrimination legislation to protect people who could not afford emergency care services. Representative Michael Bilirakis (R-Fla.) stated in the House of Representatives:

> I introduced legislation, which expresses the sense of the Congress that no person should be denied emergency health care or hospital admittance because of a lack of money or insurance. I firmly believe the American people should continue to expect that when they see an emergency sign on a hospital or free-standing clinic, they can expect access to emergency care. Unfortunately, there are countless examples where this isn't the case. I am pleased that in the bill before us the thrust of my legislation has been included. The quality of American health care is unparalleled throughout the world and it should be the national policy

---

[8] H.R. Rep. No. 100-531, at 6-7 (1988). *See* Andrew Jay McClurg, *Your Money or Your Life: Interpreting the Federal Act Against Patient Dumping*, 24 Wake Forest L. Rev. 173, 181 (1989).

[9] Robert L. Schiff & David A. Ansell, *Patient Dumping: Status, Implications, and Policy Recommendations*, 257 JAMA 1500 (1987).

[10] Robert L. Schiff & David A. Ansell, *Transfers to a Public Hospital: A Prospective Study of 467 Patients*, 314 New Eng. J. Med. 552 (1986).

for hospitals and free-standing emergency centers to provide high-quality emergency care to all patients without discriminating on the grounds of economic status, color, race, religion, sex, or national origin. Judging by the numbers of cosponsors of my legislation, this is a view shared by the majority of this body.[11]

In addition, Senator David Durenberger (R-Minn.) addressed the Senate, saying:

> The practice of rejecting indigent patients in life threatening situations for economic reasons alone is unconscionable. All Americans, rich or poor, deserve access to quality health care. At the same time while we in the Congress and the State legislatures are groping for areas to get quality health care to the uninsured Americans, we cannot stand idly by and watch those Americans who lack the resources be shunted away from immediate and appropriate emergency care whenever and wherever it is needed. The purpose of this amendment is to send a clear signal to the hospital community, public and private alike, that all Americans, regardless of wealth or status, should know that a hospital will provide what services it can when they are truly in distress. Whatever additional steps GAO recommends, whether further Medicare action or refinements in Medicaid, the aim of Congress should be to encourage states to take definite action to guard against "dumping" at the local level.[12]

Both of these statements illustrate that the broad, encompassing purpose of EMTALA was to ensure access to health care.

Senator Orrin G. Hatch (R-Utah) was aware of the broad scope of EMTALA and foresaw possible dangerous implications of Congress addressing the problem legislatively:

> Therefore, I do not support the provisions of S. 1615 [EMTALA] included in this bill. I believe they are premature, over-regulatory, and unnecessarily punitive.[13]

A Senate Judiciary Committee Report exposed the fact that EMTALA was written with "no hearings in either the House or the Senate on this issue or on the language recommended by the Ways and Means Committee." The Judiciary Committee was also concerned that there was no information available to it regarding the potential impact of these enforcement provisions on "the current medical malpractice crisis."[14] Without complete Congressional hearings, the exact scope of the problem of dumping could not have been well defined. Congress in essence legislated EMTALA on the basis of anecdotal reports. In fact, Senator Dave Durenberger (R-Minn.) stated on the Senate floor: "Frankly, we do

---

[11] 131 Cong. Rec. H9503 (Oct. 31, 1985) (statement of Representative Bilirakis).

[12] 131 Cong. Rec. S13903 (Oct. 23, 1985) (statement of Senator Durenberger).

[13] S. Rep. No. 99-146, 99th Cong., 2d Sess., reprinted in 1986 U.S.C.C.A.N. 419.

[14] H.R. Rep. No. 99-241, 99th Cong., 2d Sess., pt. 3, at 6, 7 (1986), reprinted in 1986 U.S.C.C.A.N. 726, 728.

not know how pervasive this practice of dumping the sick and the indigent from emergency rooms actually is. The evidence I have seen so far is primarily anecdotal."[15] In addition, there was very limited opportunity for public comment since less than two months passed from the time the bill came out of the House Ways and Means Committee on July 31, 1985, until final amendments were made after the Judiciary Committee's report of September 11, 1985. The only recorded public comments came from letters by Bruce D. Janiak, M.D., president of the American College of Emergency Physicians, and Paul M. Bunge of the Miami law firm Kenny Nachwalter & Seymour.[16] They both expressed strong concerns on the severe criminal sanctions and new federal civil cause of action issues reflected in the Judiciary Committee's final recommendations.

On April 7, 1986, President Reagan signed into law the Consolidated Omnibus Budget Reconciliation Act of 1985 (COBRA).[17] This massive budget bill of over 2,000 pages legislated expenditures for a wide range of federal spending, from agriculture programs to the postal service. Inconspicuously tucked into Title IX, the Medicare and Medicaid amendment section of COBRA, was the small section that came to be known as the Emergency Medical Transfer and Labor Act (EMTALA). Initially, the medical profession referred to this legislation as the "COBRA" law, using the first letters of its mother legislation package. However, the term "COBRA" has also been applied to other sections from the same budget legislation that deal with the extension of health insurance after leaving one's job. The term "Anti-Dumping Act" came into temporary vogue but this term was confused with a law governing the disposal of toxic waste. All medical and legal literature now uses the term EMTALA.

---

[15] *See* H.R. Rep. No. 99-241, 99th Cong., 2d Sess., pt. 3, at 8 (1986), reprinted in 1986 U.S.C.C.A.N. 726, 728.

[16] H.R. Rep. No. 99-241, 99th Cong., 2d Sess., pt. 3, at 15-37.

[17] The Consolidated Omnibus Budget Reconciliation Act of 1985, Pub. L. No. 99-272, § 9121, 100 Stat. 82 (1986).

Appendix I

Implementation of Emergency and Disaster-Related Policies and Procedures Relating to EMTALA: With and Without a Section 1135 Waiver

June 13, 2012

Medicare Fee-For-Service

Emergency and Disaster-Related Policies and Procedures
That May Be Implemented <u>Only With a § 1135 Waiver</u>

NOTE: The following Q&As address matters that, in the event of a disaster or emergency, could potentially be the subject of or be affected by a waiver or modification of certain requirements of the Social Security Act (the Act). Section 1135 of the Act authorizes the Secretary of the Department of Health and Human Services to waive or modify certain Medicare, Medicaid, CHIP, and HIPAA requirements. However, two prerequisites must be met before the Secretary may invoke the § 1135 waiver authority. First, the President must have declared an emergency or disaster under either the Stafford Act or the National Emergencies Act. Second, the Secretary must have declared a Public Health Emergency under Section 319 of the Public Health Service Act. Then, with respect to the geographic area(s) and time periods provided for in those declarations, the Secretary may elect to authorize waivers/modifications of one or more of the requirements described in Section 1135(b). The implementation of such waivers or modifications is typically delegated to the Administrator of CMS who, in turn, determines whether and the extent to which sufficient grounds exist for waiving such requirements with respect to a particular provider, or to a group or class of providers, or to a geographic area.

In the following Q&As, CMS identifies policies and procedures that may be available when the section 1135 waiver authority is invoked. However, the decisions to grant specific waivers or modifications will be made during or after each emergency or disaster (if a specific waiver or modification is granted after the emergency or disaster, it may be retroactive to the beginning of the emergency or disaster). Moreover, as noted previously, implementation of such waivers or modifications may apply to a particular provider, or a group or class of providers, or to a geographic area and may require additional fact-finding to ensure that sufficient grounds exist for waiving or modifying requirements in a particular circumstance. See the Q&As in *Section B – Waiver of Certain Medicare Requirements* for information concerning making requests for waivers or modifications under the Section 1135 authority.

Current/Recent Emergencies
> Section 1 – 2009/2010 H1N1 Influenza Pandemic (10-23-09 – 6-23-10)
> Section 2 – 2010 North Dakota: Floods (2-26-10 – 6-15-10)
> Section 3 – 2011 North Dakota: Floods (4-5-11 – 8-24-11)
> Section 4 – 2011 Missouri: Severe Storms and Tornadoes (5-22-11 – 5-14-12)
> Section 5 – 2011 New York: Tropical Storm *Lee* (9-24-11 – 3-12-12)

All Emergencies

Section A - Flexibilities Available in the Event of an Emergency or Disaster
Section B - Waiver of Certain Medicare Requirements
Section C - General Payment Policies

Section D - General Billing Procedures
Section E - Physician Services
Section F - Ambulance Services
Section G - Laboratory & Other Diagnostic Services
Section H - Drugs & Vaccines Payable Under Part B
Section I - Durable Medical Equipment, Prosthetics, Orthotics, and Supplies
Section J - End Stage Renal Disease (ESRD) Facility Services
Section K - Home Health Services
Section L - Hospice Services
Section M - Hospital Services – General
Section N - Hospital Services – EMTALA
Section O - Hospital Services – Acute Care
Section P - Hospital Services – Critical Access Hospitals (CAH)
Section Q - Hospital Services – Inpatient Rehabilitation Facilities (IRF)
Section R - Hospital Services – Long Term Care Hospitals (LTCH)
Section S - Hospital Services – Mobile Emergency Hospitals
Section T - Skilled Nursing Facility (SNF) Services
Section U - Mental Health Counseling
Section V - Rural Health Clinics / Federally Qualified Health Clinics
Section W - Fee-for-Service Administration
Section X - Financial Management Policies

***

N	Hospital Services – Emergency Medical Treatment and Labor Act (EMTALA)
1135N-1	**Question:** What is HHS's process for approving and issuing Emergency Medical Treatment and Labor Act (EMTALA) waivers in response to an emergency (aside from both a public health emergency (PHE) being declared by the HHS Secretary and an emergency/disaster being declared by the President)? **Answer:** There are 5 prerequisites to a waiver of EMTALA sanctions under § 1135 of the Social Security Act. They are: (1) The President declares an emergency or disaster under the Stafford Act or the National Emergencies Act, (2) The Secretary of HHS declares a Public Health Emergency (PHE) under § 319 of the Public Health Service Act, (3) The Secretary of HHS authorizes waivers under § 1135 of the Social Security Act and has delegated to CMS the specific authority to waive sanctions for certain EMTALA violations that arise as a result of the circumstances of the emergency, (4) The hospital in the affected area has implemented its hospital disaster protocol, and (5) CMS has determined that sufficient grounds exist for waiving EMTALA sanctions with respect to a particular hospital or geographic area.
1135N-2	**Question:** What is the time frame for the EMTALA waiver of sanctions? **Answer:** Waivers of sanctions under the Emergency Medical Treatment and Labor Act (EMTALA) in the emergency area end 72 hours after implementation of the hospital's disaster plan. (If a public health emergency involves pandemic infectious disease, the waiver of sanctions under EMTALA is extended until the termination of the applicable declaration of a public health emergency.)
1135N-3	**Question:** Can the 72-hour waiver time frame be extended if the disaster plan is still in effect? **Answer:** No. Waivers for EMTALA (for public health emergencies that do not involve a pandemic disease) and HIPAA requirements are limited to a 72-hour period beginning upon implementation of a hospital disaster protocol. Waiver of EMTALA requirements for emergencies that involve a pandemic disease last until the termination of the pandemic-related public health emergency.
1135N-4	**Question:** Are hospitals required to comply with all of the requirements of EMTALA during the public health emergency period in the emergency area? **Answer:** Generally, yes. However, under the Section 1135 waiver authority, the Secretary has the authority to waive sanctions if a hospital in the emergency area during the emergency period directs or relocates an individual to receive medical screening in an alternate location pursuant to either a state emergency preparedness plan or a state pandemic preparedness plan or transfers an individual who has not been stabilized if the transfer is necessitated by the circumstances of the declared emergency. These waivers are limited to a 72-hour period beginning upon implementation of a hospital's emergency or disaster protocol (unless the emergency involves a pandemic infectious disease) and are not effective with respect to any action taken that discriminates among individuals on the basis of their source of payment or their ability to pay.

1135N-5	**Question:** Would it be possible for the HHS Secretary to waive all of EMTALA's provisions, or only some of them? **Answer:** There are only two EMTALA provisions for which the sanctions can be waived under a § 1135 waiver. Under the §1135 authority, CMS can be authorized to waive the following sanctions: (1) For an inappropriate transfer (if the transfer is necessitated by the circumstances of the declared emergency in the emergency area during the emergency period), and (2) For the relocation or direction of an individual to receive medical screening in an alternate location pursuant to an appropriate State emergency preparedness plan or State pandemic preparedness plan. However, the Secretary must first invoke the section 1135 waiver authority to authorize the waiver of these sanctions, and then each hospital must implement its disaster protocol in order for either of the waivers to apply to that hospital. Moreover, the statute provides that the waiver is applicable only if the hospital's actions do not discriminate among individuals based on their source of payment or ability to pay.
1135N-6	**Question:** It was my understanding that only the HHS Secretary had the authority to issue § 1135 waivers but a 12/7/07 CMS memo (Waiver of Emergency Medical Treatment and Labor Act (EMTALA) Sanctions in Hospitals Located in Areas Covered by a Public Health Emergency Declaration) indicates that the Regional Office (RO) "may issue an advisory notice that hospitals with dedicated emergency departments in the emergency area will not, during the emergency period, be subject to" certain EMTALA sanctions, if both the President and Secretary declare emergencies. Does the issuance of an advisory notice by the RO carry the same weight as a § 1135 waiver? **Answer:** No. The December 7, 2007 CMS memorandum referenced in the question is part of the standard operating procedure describing how CMS will implement the EMTALA provisions of a § 1135 waiver issued by the Secretary. The RO's issuance of an "advisory notice" occurs only <u>after</u> the Secretary has invoked his or her § 1135 waiver authority to authorize the waiver of EMTALA sanctions and CMS has determined that the waiver of certain EMTALA sanctions is necessary for the hospital(s) in the emergency area (or portion of the emergency area) with dedicated emergency departments that have implemented their hospital disaster protocol. Furthermore, in a refinement to the process described in the cited memorandum, hospitals in the emergency area (or portion of the emergency area) are required to notify the appropriate State Survey Agency when they implement a hospital disaster protocol.
1135N-7	**Question:** Would it be considered an EMTALA violation if the hospital did not have any medical records available because of the disaster? **Answer:** The waiver of EMTALA sanctions in § 1135 pertains to sanctions for either a transfer of an individual who has not been stabilized if the transfer is necessitated by the circumstances of the declared emergency or the direction or relocation of an individual to receive medical screening at an alternate location pursuant to an appropriate state emergency or pandemic preparedness plan. Section 1135 does not authorize a waiver of the EMTALA requirement on hospitals to maintain medical and other records of individuals transferred from the hospital. While we would still expect hospitals to make every effort to transfer essential information with individuals so that the receiving hospital could treat them safely, when the Secretary has invoked her waiver authority under section 1135 of the Social Security Act, the Secretary may waive any sanctions applicable under EMTALA for a transfer of an individual who has not been stabilized, including the failure to send available medical records to the receiving hospital.
1135N-8	**Question:** If a hospital remains open during a disaster, and is operating at or in excess of its normal operating capacity and cannot get sufficient staff, may the hospital shut down its emergency department (ED) without violating EMTALA? **Answer:** Hospitals are not required under the Medicare Conditions of Participation to operate emergency departments, and thus always have the option of closing this service, so long as there is no State law requirement for the hospital to maintain an ED, and so long as the hospital employs an orderly closure process. Once the hospital no longer has a dedicated emergency department, it no longer has an EMTALA obligation to provide screening and stabilization to individuals who come to the hospital. However, if the question is about whether an ED may temporarily refuse to see all new patients, due to capacity problems, such refusal may not be permitted under EMTALA in certain circumstances. The EMTALA regulations do permit hospitals to place themselves on "diversionary" status when they lack the staff or facilities to accept additional emergency patients, i.e., they may, by phone or other electronic communications system, advise non-hospital-owned ambulances to go to another hospital. Again, while they are permitted to do this under EMTALA, their actions must also be consistent with State or local requirements governing ambulances and hospital diversionary status. However, even in this circumstance, if the ambulance nevertheless brings an individual onto the property of the hospital on diversion, then the hospital has an EMTALA obligation to provide an appropriate medical screening examination and, if the individual has
	an emergency medical condition, to provide stabilizing treatment. Furthermore, if a hospital with a dedicated emergency department is operating under a section 1135 waiver, which includes a waiver under section 1135(b)(3) of the Act, sanctions for the direction or relocation of an individual to receive medical screening at an alternate location do not apply so long as the direction or relocation is pursuant to an appropriate State emergency preparedness plan or State pandemic preparedness plan and the hospital does not discriminate on the individual's source of payment or ability to pay.

June 13, 2012

Medicare Fee-For-Service

Emergency-Related Policies and Procedures
That May Be Implemented Without § 1135 Waivers

Current/Recent Emergencies
    Section 1 – 2009/2010 H1N1 Influenza Pandemic (10-23-09 – 6-23-10)
    Section 2 – 2010 North Dakota Floods (2-26-10 – 6-15-10)
    Section 3 – 2011 North Dakota Floods (4-5-11 – 8-24-11)
    Section 4 – 2011 Missouri Severe Storms and Tornadoes (5-22-11 – 5-14-12)
    Section 5 – 2011 New York Remnants of Tropical Storm *Lee* (9-24-11 – 3-12-12)

All Emergencies

Section A – Flexibilities Available in the Event of an Emergency or Disaster
Section B – Waiver of Certain Medicare Requirements
Section C – General Payment Policies
Section D – General Billing Procedures
Section E – Physician Services
Section F – Ambulance Services
Section G – Laboratory & Other Diagnostic Services
Section H – Drugs & Vaccines Payable Under Part B
Section I – Durable Medical Equipment, Prosthetics, Orthotics, and Supplies
Section J – End Stage Renal Disease (ESRD) Facility Services
Section K – Home Health Services
Section L – Hospice Services
Section M – Hospital Services – General
Section N – Hospital Services – EMTALA
Section O – Hospital Services – Acute Care
Section P – Hospital Services – Critical Access Hospitals (CAH)
Section Q – Hospital Services – Inpatient Rehabilitation Facilities (IRF)
Section R – Hospital Services – Long Term Care Hospitals (LTCH)
Section S – Hospital Services – Mobile Emergency Hospitals
Section T – Skilled Nursing Facility (SNF) Services
Section U – Mental Health Counseling
Section V – Rural Health Clinics / Federally Qualified Health Clinics
Section W – Fee-for-Service Administration
Section X – Financial Management Policies

* * *

N	Hospital Services – Emergency Medical Treatment and Labor Act (EMTALA)
N-1	**Question:** Evacuees from States affected by the public health emergency may arrive at hospital emergency departments merely to obtain refills of prescriptions that they lost when they evacuated during a disaster or public health emergency. Must these individuals be given an EMTALA medical screening examination when they come to the emergency department? **Answer:** Even under non-emergency circumstances, the Emergency Medical Treatment and Labor Act (EMTALA) regulations make it clear that individuals seeking examination or treatment for a medical condition (e.g. prescription refills) need not be given a complete medical screening examination, but rather, one that is appropriate for the request that they make in order to determine that an EMD does not exist. Hospitals may wish to develop specific protocols that include a streamlined screening examination for individuals seeking prescription refills, consistent with the EMTALA regulations at 42 CFR § 489.24.
N-2	**Question:** Is it permissible for a hospital to triage individuals with suspected cases of an infectious disease (including particularly an H1N1 flu virus infection) to an alternative site for evaluation under EMTALA? If so, how do we bill for these services?
	Answer: Under current Emergency Medical Treatment and Labor Act (EMTALA) law and regulations, hospitals are permitted to move individuals out of their dedicated emergency departments to another part of the hospital (on the hospital's same campus) in order to provide the required medical screening examination (MSE) and then, if an emergency medical condition is found to exist, to provide stabilizing treatment or arrange for an appropriate transfer. Sometimes hospitals refer to these as "fast-track clinics" and use them either all year round or during surge in demand for emergency department services during the seasonal cold and flu season. The medical screening examination provided in the "clinic" must be performed consistent with the requirements of the EMTALA provision, by qualified medical personnel who can perform an MSE that is appropriate to the individual's presenting signs and symptoms. If, prior to directing the individual elsewhere in the hospital, qualified medical personnel in the emergency department completed an appropriate MSE and determined that the individual does not have an emergency medical condition, then the hospital has no further EMTALA obligation to that individual and the issue of moving the individual to an alternate site, either on or off the hospital's campus, would be moot from an EMTALA perspective. For services rendered to Medicare fee-for-service (FFS) beneficiaries, standard Medicare FFS billing rules apply. Hospitals should work with their other payers to determine if special billing rules may apply.
N-3	**Question:** What is CMS's procedure for addressing requests to waive EMTALA? **Answer:** Because each emergency or disaster presents a unique set of circumstances, especially as they relate to the demand for emergency treatment, CMS calibrates its response to EMTALA-related issues to coincide with the nature of each emergency. But, in general, CMS handles these matters on a case-by-case basis. In an emergency or disaster, CMS, both centrally and through its Regional Offices, will open communications with affected State governments (especially the State Survey Agencies) and with providers, trade groups, and other stakeholders to learn about local conditions. In addition, the State survey agencies are responsible for reporting the status of health care providers affected by the emergency to their CMS Regional Office and CMS relies upon that information to make recommendations to the Secretary regarding the need for EMTALA waivers.
N-4	**Question:** Has HHS issued any § 1135 waivers in the past that specifically address EMTALA? **Answer:** Since § 143 of the Public Health Security and Bioterrorism Preparedness and Response Act of 2002 amended § 1135 of the Social Security Act to add the waiver authority, § 1135 waivers have been issued for Hurricanes Katrina, Rita, Gustav and Ike, for the flooding in Iowa and Indiana during CY 2008, and for the flooding in North Dakota and Minnesota in CY 2009. In each emergency event, sanctions for certain types of EMTALA violations were waived for 72 hours after implementation of an affected hospital's disaster protocol. However, if a public health emergency were to involve a pandemic infectious disease, the Secretary could invoke his or her waiver authority under § 1135 to waive certain EMTALA sanctions and such an EMTALA waiver would continue in effect until the termination of the applicable public health emergency declaration (in accordance with § 1135(e)(1)(B) of the Act).
N-5	**Question:** If a hospital remains open during a disaster, and is operating at or in excess of its normal operating capacity and cannot get sufficient staff, may the hospital shut down its emergency department (ED) without violating EMTALA? **Answer:** Hospitals are not required under the Medicare Conditions of Participation to operate emergency departments, and thus always have the option of closing this service, so long as there is no State law requirement for the hospital to maintain an ED, and so long as the hospital employs an orderly closure process. Once the hospital no longer has a dedicated emergency department, it no longer has an EMTALA obligation to provide screening and stabilization to individuals who come to the hospital. However, if the question is about whether an ED may temporarily refuse to see all new patients, due to capacity problems, such refusal may not be permitted under EMTALA in certain circumstances. The EMTALA regulations do permit hospitals to place themselves on "diversionary" status when they lack the staff or facilities to accept additional emergency patients, i.e., they may, by phone or other electronic communications system, advise non-hospital-owned ambulances to go to another hospital. Again, while they are permitted to do this under EMTALA, their actions must also be consistent with State or local requirements governing ambulances and hospital diversionary status. However, even in this circumstance, if the ambulance nevertheless brings an individual onto the property of the hospital on diversion, then the hospital has an EMTALA obligation to provide an appropriate medical screening examination and, if the individual has an emergency medical condition, to provide stabilizing treatment. Furthermore, if a hospital with a dedicated emergency department is operating under a section 1135 waiver, which includes a waiver under section 1135(b)(3) of the Act, sanctions for the direction or relocation of an individual to receive medical screening at an alternate location do not apply so long as the direction or relocation is pursuant to an appropriate State emergency preparedness plan or State pandemic preparedness plan and the hospital does not discriminate on the individual's source of payment or ability to pay.

N-6	**Question:** Emergency Flu Response--We are planning to use an outpatient area of the hospital as an Emergency Department (ED) extension to see overflow patients from the ED. Can we still bill the ED Levels for the facility charges (99281 - 99285)? If the physician seeing these patients is not board certified in Emergency Medicine but is board certified in Family Practice, can the facility bill the ED levels? This question is only in regard to the OPPS facility-side, not professional billing.
	Answer: The hospital may bill CPT codes 99281 through 99285 for emergency visit services furnished in the outpatient area where this separately identifiable area meets the definition of a Type A emergency department (ED) (and complies with all other applicable requirements). If the separately identifiable area operates less than 24 hours per day, 7 days per week for emergency services, and it meets the definition of a Type B ED (dedicated emergency department that incurred EMTALA obligations, but did not meet the CPT definition of an ED) (and meets all other applicable requirements), then it may bill emergency visit services using HCPCS codes G0380 through G0384 as appropriate. The specialty of the physician ordering the emergency services for hospital outpatients (emergency physician, family medicine, or other) in the area of the hospital where emergency services are furnished does not affect whether the facility is considered a Type A or B ED for purposes of billing under the OPPS.
N-7	**Question:** Given that EMTALA requires Medicare participating hospitals with emergency departments to provide certain health care services regardless of individuals' legal status when they present with emergency medical conditions, and given that the MMA provided monies under section 1011 of the Act to reimburse hospitals for services related to EMTALA, would these provisions (EMTALA and section 1011) cover prophylaxis of contacts (treatment for an individual who has been exposed to a contagious disease) or vaccination?
	Answer: The answer depends on the specific medical circumstances involved. EMTALA requires that if an individual presents to a hospital with a dedicated emergency department, and requests treatment for a medical condition, the hospital is required to provide an appropriate medical screening to determine if an emergency medical condition exists. If an emergency medical condition does exist, the hospital is required to provide necessary stabilizing treatment or provide for an appropriate transfer to another facility. Section 1011 provides reimbursement to eligible providers for services required by or related to EMTALA when furnished to certain undocumented aliens. Therefore, if an individual who is an undocumented alien (or otherwise eligible under section 1011) presents to a hospital with a medical condition and requires treatment to stabilize an emergency medical condition, that treatment would be considered to be an EMTALA-related service and may be eligible for reimbursement under section 1011. Not all individuals who have been exposed to a contagious disease or are seeking a vaccination may have an emergency medical condition as that term is defined under EMTALA. For instance, if treatment is provided that is solely for preventative purposes, that treatment could not be considered an EMTALA-related service.

Table of Cases

[References are to question, chapter, or appendix number.]

Index

[References are to question, chapter, or appendix number.]

N

O

Q

R